Lecture Notes in Computer Science   9186

Commenced Publication in 1973
Founding and Former Series Editors:
Gerhard Goos, Juris Hartmanis, and Jan van Leeuwen

More information about this series at http://www.springer.com/series/7409

Aaron Marcus (Ed.)

Design, User Experience, and Usability

Design Discourse

4th International Conference, DUXU 2015
Held as Part of HCI International 2015
Los Angeles, CA, USA, August 2–7, 2015
Proceedings, Part I

 Springer

Editor
Aaron Marcus
Aaron Marcus and Associates
Berkeley, CA
USA

ISSN 0302-9743 ISSN 1611-3349 (electronic)
Lecture Notes in Computer Science
ISBN 978-3-319-20885-5 ISBN 978-3-319-20886-2 (eBook)
DOI 10.1007/978-3-319-20886-2

Library of Congress Control Number: 2015942614

LNCS Sublibrary: SL3 – Information Systems and Applications, incl. Internet/Web, and HCI

Springer Cham Heidelberg New York Dordrecht London

Printed on acid-free paper

Springer International Publishing AG Switzerland is part of Springer Science+Business Media
(www.springer.com)

Foreword

The 17th International Conference on Human-Computer Interaction, HCI International 2015, was held in Los Angeles, CA, USA, during 2–7 August 2015. The event incorporated the 15 conferences/thematic areas listed on the following page.

A total of 4843 individuals from academia, research institutes, industry, and governmental agencies from 73 countries submitted contributions, and 1462 papers and 246 posters have been included in the proceedings. These papers address the latest research and development efforts and highlight the human aspects of design and use of computing systems. The papers thoroughly cover the entire field of Human-Computer Interaction, addressing major advances in knowledge and effective use of computers in a variety of application areas. The volumes constituting the full 28-volume set of the conference proceedings are listed on pages VII and VIII.

I would like to thank the Program Board Chairs and the members of the Program Boards of all thematic areas and affiliated conferences for their contribution to the highest scientific quality and the overall success of the HCI International 2015 conference.

This conference could not have been possible without the continuous and unwavering support and advice of the founder, Conference General Chair Emeritus and Conference Scientific Advisor, Prof. Gavriel Salvendy. For their outstanding efforts, I would like to express my appreciation to the Communications Chair and Editor of HCI International News, Dr. Abbas Moallem, and the Student Volunteer Chair, Prof. Kim-Phuong L. Vu. Finally, for their dedicated contribution towards the smooth organization of HCI International 2015, I would like to express my gratitude to Maria Pitsoulaki and George Paparoulis, General Chair Assistants.

May 2015

Constantine Stephanidis
General Chair, HCI International 2015

HCI International 2015 Thematic Areas
and Affiliated Conferences

Thematic areas:

- Human-Computer Interaction (HCI 2015)
- Human Interface and the Management of Information (HIMI 2015)

Affiliated conferences:

- 12th International Conference on Engineering Psychology and Cognitive Ergonomics (EPCE 2015)
- 9th International Conference on Universal Access in Human-Computer Interaction (UAHCI 2015)
- 7th International Conference on Virtual, Augmented and Mixed Reality (VAMR 2015)
- 7th International Conference on Cross-Cultural Design (CCD 2015)
- 7th International Conference on Social Computing and Social Media (SCSM 2015)
- 9th International Conference on Augmented Cognition (AC 2015)
- 6th International Conference on Digital Human Modeling and Applications in Health, Safety, Ergonomics and Risk Management (DHM 2015)
- 4th International Conference on Design, User Experience and Usability (DUXU 2015)
- 3rd International Conference on Distributed, Ambient and Pervasive Interactions (DAPI 2015)
- 3rd International Conference on Human Aspects of Information Security, Privacy and Trust (HAS 2015)
- 2nd International Conference on HCI in Business (HCIB 2015)
- 2nd International Conference on Learning and Collaboration Technologies (LCT 2015)
- 1st International Conference on Human Aspects of IT for the Aged Population (ITAP 2015)

Conference Proceedings Volumes Full List

1. LNCS 9169, Human-Computer Interaction: Design and Evaluation (Part I), edited by Masaaki Kurosu
2. LNCS 9170, Human-Computer Interaction: Interaction Technologies (Part II), edited by Masaaki Kurosu
3. LNCS 9171, Human-Computer Interaction: Users and Contexts (Part III), edited by Masaaki Kurosu
4. LNCS 9172, Human Interface and the Management of Information: Information and Knowledge Design (Part I), edited by Sakae Yamamoto
5. LNCS 9173, Human Interface and the Management of Information: Information and Knowledge in Context (Part II), edited by Sakae Yamamoto
6. LNAI 9174, Engineering Psychology and Cognitive Ergonomics, edited by Don Harris
7. LNCS 9175, Universal Access in Human-Computer Interaction: Access to Today's Technologies (Part I), edited by Margherita Antona and Constantine Stephanidis
8. LNCS 9176, Universal Access in Human-Computer Interaction: Access to Interaction (Part II), edited by Margherita Antona and Constantine Stephanidis
9. LNCS 9177, Universal Access in Human-Computer Interaction: Access to Learning, Health and Well-Being (Part III), edited by Margherita Antona and Constantine Stephanidis
10. LNCS 9178, Universal Access in Human-Computer Interaction: Access to the Human Environment and Culture (Part IV), edited by Margherita Antona and Constantine Stephanidis
11. LNCS 9179, Virtual, Augmented and Mixed Reality, edited by Randall Shumaker and Stephanie Lackey
12. LNCS 9180, Cross-Cultural Design: Methods, Practice and Impact (Part I), edited by P.L. Patrick Rau
13. LNCS 9181, Cross-Cultural Design: Applications in Mobile Interaction, Education, Health, Transport and Cultural Heritage (Part II), edited by P.L. Patrick Rau
14. LNCS 9182, Social Computing and Social Media, edited by Gabriele Meiselwitz
15. LNAI 9183, Foundations of Augmented Cognition, edited by Dylan D. Schmorrow and Cali M. Fidopiastis
16. LNCS 9184, Digital Human Modeling and Applications in Health, Safety, Ergonomics and Risk Management: Human Modeling (Part I), edited by Vincent G. Duffy
17. LNCS 9185, Digital Human Modeling and Applications in Health, Safety, Ergonomics and Risk Management: Ergonomics and Health (Part II), edited by Vincent G. Duffy
18. LNCS 9186, Design, User Experience, and Usability: Design Discourse (Part I), edited by Aaron Marcus
19. LNCS 9187, Design, User Experience, and Usability: Users and Interactions (Part II), edited by Aaron Marcus
20. LNCS 9188, Design, User Experience, and Usability: Interactive Experience Design (Part III), edited by Aaron Marcus

Design, User Experience and Usability

Program Board Chair: Aaron Marcus, USA

- Sisira Adikari, Australia
- Claire Ancient, UK
- Randolph G. Bias, USA
- Jamie Blustein, Canada
- Jan Brejcha, Czech Republic
- Marc Fabri, UK
- Patricia Flanagan, Hong Kong
- Emilie Gould, USA
- Luciane Maria Fadel, Brazil

- Brigitte Herrmann, Germany
- Steffen Hess, Germany
- Nouf Khashman, Canada
- Francisco Rebelo, Portugal
- Kerem Rızvanoğlu, Turkey
- Javed Anjum Sheikh, Pakistan
- Marcelo Soares, Brazil
- Carla G. Spinillo, Brazil
- Katia Canepa Vega, Brazil

The full list with the Program Board Chairs and the members of the Program Boards of all thematic areas and affiliated conferences is available online at:

http://www.hci.international/2015/

HCI International 2016

The 18th International Conference on Human-Computer Interaction, HCI International 2016, will be held jointly with the affiliated conferences in Toronto, Canada, at the Westin Harbour Castle Hotel, 17–22 July 2016. It will cover a broad spectrum of themes related to Human-Computer Interaction, including theoretical issues, methods, tools, processes, and case studies in HCI design, as well as novel interaction techniques, interfaces, and applications. The proceedings will be published by Springer. More information will be available on the conference website: http://2016.hci.international/.

General Chair
Prof. Constantine Stephanidis
University of Crete and ICS-FORTH
Heraklion, Crete, Greece
Email: general_chair@hcii2016.org

http://2016.hci.international/

Contents – Part I

DUXU Management and Practice

Emotional and Persuasion Design

Storytelling, Narrative and Fiction in DUXU5

Contents – Part II

Women in DUXU

Information Design

Touch and Gesture DUXU

Mobile DUXU

Wearable DUXU

Contents – Part III

Designing the Learning Experience

Designing the Playing Experience

Designing the Urban Experience

Designing the Driving Experience

Designing the Healthcare Patient's Experience

Designing for the Healthcare Professional's Experience

Design Thinking

The Cold Desert of Software Reality

Jiří Bystřický[1] and Jan Brejcha[2(✉)]

[1] Catholic Theological Faculty, Charles University, Prague, Czech Republic
jiribystricky@seznam.cz
[2] Frame Institute, Prague, Czech Republic
jan@brejcha.name

Abstract. The current state of knowledge of our lived world is in constant confrontation of two environments that does not yet fully converge. On the one hand stands a person with his or her own cultural traditions and historical development, and on the other hand stands the technology per se, in its relatively rapid development phase. These two parts constantly roam without bringing us a significant breakthrough in knowledge, which is the needed human cognitive reference point when interacting with computers. Our aim is to find out certain nodes of understanding between these two worlds, and propose a hypothesis for their possible approximation.

Keywords: Cognition · Cultural techniques · De-abstraction · De-reality · Interface hermeneutics · Knowledge · Human-computer interaction · Processive subject · Post-media · Proto-medium · Reflexive interface · Simulacra · Software reality · Visual thinking

1 Introduction

"Thought can be raised up from its powerlessness only through something that exceeds the order of thought. [...] it is certain that every thought emits a dice-throw, but it is just as certain that it will be unable to ultimately think the chance that has thus engendered it." (Badiou, 2003) [2][pages 84–85].

The current state of knowledge of our lived world is in constant confrontation of two environments that does not yet fully converge. On the one hand stands a person with his or her own cultural traditions and historical development, and now an intense user of technology, and on the other hand stands the technology per se, in its relatively rapid development phase (super technology, computational systems, complex physics algorithms of elementary particles, etc.). These two parts constantly roam without bringing us a significant breakthrough in knowledge, which is the needed human cognitive reference point when interacting with computers. Our aim is to find out certain nodes of understanding between these two worlds, and propose a hypothesis for their possible approximation. We proceed from the point of view suggested by Vilém Flusser:

"Design [same as *in-formare* on the side of *techné*] means, among others, faith. The fact of posing questions is a collective attempt at laying hold of faith, and to give it a form." [9].

© Springer International Publishing Switzerland 2015
A. Marcus (Ed.): DUXU 2015, Part I, LNCS 9186, pp. 3–11, 2015.
DOI: 10.1007/978-3-319-20886-2_1

To arrive at a certain contact area, we must begin to use terms referring as closely as possible to the state of technological progress.

Therefore, we introduce in the hypothesis of the project the following concepts: *proto-medium, processive subject, reflexive hermeneutics,* art as a form of realization of *visual thinking* ("Visual perception is visual thinking" [1][page 16]), the term *post-media,* and ultimately *de-abstraction.* With this we want to point out the necessity of new differentiation procedures, giving rise to forms of thinking in their own territory.

Only in such in its own territory can we construct new social and cultural realities, which will no longer be rather primitively distinguished between the virtual and the real [7], but will use them for new integrations.

This is especially true for the concept of a *processive subject,* which of course is based on a traditional framework: "Logic is beneficial for the subject in that the subject acquires certain education for other purposes. The education supplied to the subject by logic is based in the training of thought, because this science is a thought about thought, and lets the subject have in his head thoughts regarded as thoughts." [10].

Analogously, we can talk about art and aesthetitcs in a new context, i.e. searching the original media for lines, shapes, colors and light, which can be translated above all in a reflexive process: "[...] aesthetic phrase is the phrase par excellence of the faculty of presentation, but that it has no concept for which to present its sensible or imaginative intuition, it cannot therefore determine a realm, but only a field. Moreover, the field is only determined to a second degree, reflectively, so to speak: not by the commensurability between the capacity for presenting and the capacity for conceptualizing. This commensurability is itself an Idea, its object is not directly presentable." [11][page 168].

2   Baudrillard/Virilio

"The simulacrum is never that which conceals the truth—it is the truth which conceals that there is none. The simulacrum is true." (Ecclesiastes in Baudrillard, 1988). [5].

A pair of inspirational authors of the so called French theory, Jean Baudrillard and Paul Virilio, each presented in numerous studies a fairly serious view of the gradual transformation of the concept of social reality.

Certainly, it is not a classic approach to a sociological topic, but rather a particular social philosophical construct, which points to an apparent inconsistency between the traditional concept of a contemporary, especially post-structuralist and late systems theory.

For both the authors is problematic the very principle of construction of a social fact, since the advent of new technologies is gradually easing the presumed *original* link between the constructed subject and its *target* object.

This *game* is now entering a new mediation logistics, which strongly obscures the principle and definition of the boundaries of the real.

Let's say a limit, at which each theory begins as from its original line of demarcation, and which exhibits a foothold interpretation or concept and which, if it is to remain the default, fixed point, can no longer be *mediated.*

If we would have expected a next possible mediation of this limit, it would become just a sort of transitional phase of mediation, and not the necessary, constitutive element of a new theoretical foundation.

Now, if we leave aside the question of what exactly is the output of the actual social construction, because the issue involves an interdisciplinary rather than narrowly socio-logical, we can look at how the two protagonists of the French theory approach the topic.

Baudrillard's thinking leads to understanding the difference between the assumption of a solid foundation of theory, which is situated at an exact location, and a somewhat vague territory, on which to draw the border. Touted at this point is the question of whether Baudrillard was willing to build such a differing line, i.e. the difference of a *reflective interface*: the internal and external interface, where simulation procedures and simulacra may take place in a so called real.

Strictly speaking, Baudrillard is concerned here about a mis-match and instability of both *spaces*, because the localization of theory in the place of the real is clearly hypothetical, and the very border of the real location is only analogous. We can talk about the unclear boundary lines, on which then arises every conception of reality that wants to define the realm of reality. To simplify, we can say that even if the boundary lines within the theory were most precise, nothing can change the fact that they are plotted in just an approximate and unstable space, and what is most important, the plot-ting is limited to the practice of using tools for marking transport lines. It does not give us anything accurate about how eventually the lines *fit* in the construction of reality.

This means that during the construction of theories we cannot be based on the assumption that we have a certain map beforehand that allows us to follow the right path in terrain of the real.

The very concept of abstraction faces the problem of the initial definition when decribing a reality: Namely that we start from a certain map (i.e. from a pre-bounded territory) of what we will after refer to as reality. From this view it is obvious that the construction of the social fact somewhat brings the real model in advance together with the way how a given fact will appear.

The design of theory more or less pre-characterize the space, into which will the social reality be placed.

And from here, there is only a short journey to the discovery that given models in principle start only from possibilities how forms (maps) are created. According to these maps it is possible to construct a specific version of the real.

"Today abstraction is no longer that of the map, the double, the mirror, or the concept. Simulation is no longer that of a territory, a referential being, or a substance. I tis the generation by models of a real without origin or reality: a hyperreal. The territory no longer precedes the map, nor does it survive it. In is nevertheless the map that precedes the territory–*precession of simulacra*–that engenders the territory, and if one must return to the fable, today i tis the territory whose shreds slowly rot across the extent of the map. I tis the real, and not the map, whose vestiges persist here and there in the desert that are no longer those of the Empire, but ours. *The desert of the real itself.*" [4][page 1].

In a sense, we are talking about the need of **de-abstraction**, and thinking about the concept of **de-reality**.

In essence, we get into a situation where one can quite justifiably speak of various **synthetic versions of the real**, in which different versions of social reality are true, if they are firstly defined, how they should be displayed.

With a little exaggeration, we could use Baudrillard's example: "Go and simulate a theft in a large department store: how do you convince the security guards that it is a simulated theft? There is no 'objective' difference: the same gestures and the same signs exist as for a real theft; in fact the signs mclme neither to one side nor the other. As far as the established order is conccrned, they are always of the order of the real." [6][page 181].

For Paul Virilio is the very own design or version of reality limited by the acceleration potential of each mediation, which means that we are talking about the use of speed in the mode of display, show or transmission of data to establish the *real*, which is more or less dependent on the cultural limitations of speed:

The development proces of civilization history according to Virilio corresponds rather to certain systems of braking, a strenuous reduction of excessive acceleration, so that the format of the reality was available within the normal, everyday activities and thus stable in the *slow* logic of perception.

The starting fact is then the traditional reality in the context of an appropriate *constraint*, say to a certain extent a slowing, or at present vice versa, a gradual acceleration, which, however, shall not exceed the limits of ordinary human perception.

The reality of contemporary reality is, however, that most data streams takes place at speeds considerably in excess of that normally lived in everyday life.

The logic of perception gradually begins to be expanded and supplemented by increasingly rapid movement of intermediating data and it is at the expense of the *slow*, but long maintained traditional version of the social construction of reality. The very problem of construction of the real is now starting to be closely associated with the concept of vision.

"With photography, seeing the world becomes not only a matter of spatial distance but also of the *time-distance* to be eliminated: a matter of speed, of acceleration or deceleration." [13][page 21].

With the advent and use of modern technologies will therefore come to the stage *units of information,* for which we do not sufficiently have a matching empirical coverage, thus we are replacing the slower perception logic with binary simulation models.

"[…] what is given is exactly the information but not the sensation; it is *apatheia*, this scientific impassibility which makes it so that the more informed man is the more the desert of the world expands around him, the more the repetition of information (already known) upsets the stimuli of observation, overtaking them automatically, not only in memory (interior light) but first of all in the look, to the point that from now on it's the speed of light itself which limits the reading of information and the important thing in electronic-information is no longer the storage but the display. As the rational universe goes, so goes the effect of the real." [12][pages 46–47].

Under these circumstances the system of construction of social reality is effectively altered, especially in terms of the intervention of gradually accelerating forms of mediation, which we cannot then adequately rewrite into the construction of the lived reality, but only through a binary analog model. Thus, with considerable limitations.

The constructed reality it is still socially encoded, but its range of visible parameters begins to exceed the dimensions of the lived everyday life. It is quite adequate to note the constantly generated differences in the system of expansion, and in some respects even the acceleration of *reality*: Mainly because the generated differences can become in the long run a new and very effective element of the procedure of stratification.

3 The Software Reality

It is necessary to remember: In sociology we still have to work with a certain minimal concept of reality, which, however, currently holds two risks:

- The first risk is a low level of intermediation of the so called *software reality* of modern technology. We are talking mostly about the secondary slowing, when the response rate of human perception on intermediation of data and on new forms of display is not only slow, but also inadequate. For example, the analysis of the social situation in film or television productions disregards in majority of the cases the fact that firstly a cinematographic model of reality is supplied (i.e. cinematic reality), and only then some forms of social action are depicted.
- The second risk is the new *traffic light optics*. Fast data streams are usually getting high priority, which is supporting the accelerating optics, and not the slowing. Which of course means that the construction of social reality is a whole series of co-creation of the acceleration phase of cultural techniques and forms of mediation, which gradually displace the original format of human perception.

However, the actual risk would be neglecting or ignoring warnings that the new optics indicator above suggests. Social reality is going to be steadily ahead of us rather than behind us. And here lies the first problem, according to the authors.

We should now ask, what theory of the real we talking about, when is the *position* (the borderline of the real, say the definition line) in motion, which ultimately dictate the *field* or placing of the unstable social reality and subject to incompleteness (see the work of Gödel).

"Yes, we must now get used to the fact that there are alternative spaces and times. Because of the technology that allows us to project the scenes that we can at least compare to the concreteness of the scenes that we perceive with our senses, we are forced to philosophize as an alternative as well. [...] Because there is no non-virtual reality, because reality is only a borderline concept that we are approaching and that we can never achieve, that is why I can talk about alternative ways of achieving reality. Achieve it can be done technically and theoretically. We can say that a number of theoretical considerations discusses the alternative realities". [8][pages 11–12]

At this point shows up the question of interpretation of complexity, or different versions of the oscillation between alternate realities. And we ask mainly because the current concept of social contribution to the construction of reality (i.e. the space of real) is certainly not completely emptied, but partly relegated to the background in favor of alternative concepts of the real.

This procedure leads to subsequent findings: Let's say that the concept of Berger and Luckmann [6] is based on certain, unspecified assumption of elementary continuity of the social, the seen and the mediated. Because the latter is more problematic, it is necessary to try to sort out the disparity of the said parts. Such disparity results from the fact that the chosen form of social structure of the reality does not specify those three elements and puts them in one row or to the same level.

Baudrillard's concept of the real can serve us as a certain approximate guide. Let us first look at the impact of modern technology, which almost fundamentally changes the relationship of mediation and *reality*. Mainly for the simple reason that it is actually a cultural technique of the access to what is known as reality.

Devices and technological tools for the creation of the visible world of our PC terminals, digital satellite communications and high definition television data formats offer new techniques of imaging procedures, as well as more sophisticated *norms* of software design of reality. Basically, these are discreetly, but steadily, changing paradigm of *social reality* before our eyes.

The current accelerated and especially *data neutral* production of the world of displaying points to one remarkable turnaround. The world is currently using advanced and sophisticated techniques while displaying is not becoming closer, but just the opposite: it is increasingly distant, removed, and mediated. For example, in the case of photos we've seen a shift in vision logistics: All the details of pictures are essentially equally important, are on the same level of relevance, and even though a part is removed, the whole remains essentially the same.

The situation is different in case of the mental and display maps of humans: Exposure is set to produce the differences, in agreement with Freud that cultural movement or development is happening possibility of creating differences rather than sameness. In other words: Culture is about setting differences, controlling the events probability by means of differentiation. The synthetic production of reality actually eliminates the differences by their static fixation.

Technological gadgetry of media create in advance each event by capturing partial segment and by its formatting in alternative environments of the software reality. Differentiation in this case is falling victim to the unification of communication.

While photographs, for example, highlight the sameness of details, the concept of human vision is different. Photographs work with depth of context, mutual differences between the features, but also with a considerable motivation for remembering. The whole of the seen is never the same, as in the case of the just mentioned photographs, but rather structured, profiled and particularly differentiated in its parts. Technologically profiled reality introduces another concept of displaying and showing than that, with which humans *ordinarily* work. Its principle is a certain sameness of distributing individual points for display.

Our daily experienced reality, however, does not accept such a sameness of deployment, not only because it works from a certain principle of *anesthesis*: Thus, the fact that something in perception must be suppressed in order to see something; but also and especially because we use profiling of a system of the seen into a system **ordering data linearly**, not in parallel, as in the case of display technology.

In our daily process of social construction of reality we create procedures that put in the logic of viewing the necessary contexts, which replace (and thus make us perceive) the parallel ordering of data.

The technology of *display* does not produce contextual links as a replacement for putting the data in parallel, but on the contrary, the technology is the very principle of connecting one-direction data. This creates a different *reality*, say a *software reality*, which is different from the original idea of the social construction of reality.

This of course brings us into a situation that highlights the problem of *social construction of reality* as a type of model, say modeling reality according to different logic of perception: The social construction of reality always depends on the parameters of available vision techniques. And vision techniques have currently very significantly changed since stable versions prevailed of a so called social construction of reality.

Current technologies offer the processing of data in a form that requires complicated theoretical modes of mediation, and its output no longer corresponds to the *normal* state of vision of the real in its everyday, stable form.

4 Conclusion

We do not need to go too far to recall that the *stable form* of reality is still in place: Of course it is not possible to say that e.g. buildings, streets, cars and parks were something other than they seem, but the thing is somewhat more complicated. Although the original reality is still in *its place*, it seems to have, to put it mildly, somewhat shifted to the background, just as our machines for thinking and seeing begin to read the *reality* of the virtual as something more open.

The actual boundaries of the original reality are not easy to tell, but are constantly reinforced by tradition and the lived experience, so they remain in the normal contours of a relatively stable arrangement, which one cannot say about the world of the virtual. This ambiguity, however, was fully realized e.g. by Vilém Flusser:

"I do not know whether we are in the world. We are in the field of options from which arises the world. And do not like the term that we are situated in the world neither. Rather, we should say that we realize ourselves in the world." [8][pages 11–12].

It is the reliance of the virtual field on the multiple mediation of devices and advanced imaging techniques that highlights the gradual separation between the relatively stable boundaries of the real world and the slightly but steadily shifting borders of the virtual world.

The critical point of separation, the line that still holds together both of the worlds as credibly as possible, is inexorably approaching closer, forcing a new paradigm to describe what we call social reality.

Because it will be the human, who takes that description and with its help will need to cope with a changed situation. This human cannot get enough reassurance that some things still remain within their borders.

The human boundary will have most likely to be attacked again, perhaps even exceeded, at least in the sense how it will answer the questions provided by the virtual world.

Baudrillard's description of this new state of affairs is very close to finding that the spectacularity of the new imaging techniques flips the so far fixed points of bounded reality towards a software designed reality.

And what's more, the problem of truth as a correspondence between a description and an account of a fact gets another form.

This theory is necessarily based on a certain assumption about the possibility of establishing a harmony, say some consistency between what is being described, and what should be matched by the description. The theory is thus a systemic procedure in the sense in which both sides of the movement thought certain data can be fixed into a conventional or validable framework.

However, in a software designed reality there comes a change: The technology of the virtual production occupies a space for coupling data so that they can form a certain proportion or logic of arrangement, which could be further simulated.

These are generated entities that have no necessary connection to the empirical coverage in the mode of everyday life, or to the previous move in a tradition of thought, but may be assembled purely according to the rules of connecting data sequences. This means that it is possible to perform e.g. a continual upgrade of objects or their duplication without having the underlying software platform to capture their configuration as the ideal state of order, which would be the target of efforts to understand the truth of such a state.

But then the space to determine the state of affairs is therefore already occupied, because the state of affairs (say the facts) is already part of the actual production of that software reality. If we are to search for truth in such a regime, then we must admit that this regime is a space that cannot be filled, because it is already set to self-relatedness of each such a whole so established. But then it is true, what Baudrillard says:

"The secret of theory is that truth does not exist. [...] Truth establishes a space that cannot be filled." [3].

As long as the cultural differentiation technique works, it is not possible to statically fix a single space of truth. If we claimed truth as a border of a certain area of reality, then such an area can no longer be occupied, and it cannot be therefore productively differentiated.

In principle, such an area falls out of the cultural production techniques, because the possibility of laying differences is deprecated. To construct reality in the social régime will be a little more difficult in the given state of affairs, because a theory that would allow such construction will gradually involve a far greater proportion of probability than the current notion of reality *is able to hold*.

We assume that this is a time to explore the *hermeneutics of the interface*. Mainly for the reason that the dyadics of the current thinking is still lingering on the level of the intellectual dimension, whereas it is necessary to take into account the spiritual dimension as well.

References

1. Arnheim, R.: Visual Thinking. University of California Press, Berkeley (1971)
2. Badiou, A.: Saint Paul: The Foundation of Universalism. Stanford University Press, Redwood City (2003)

3. Baudrillard, J.: Fragments: Cool Memories III, 1990–1995. Verso (2006)
4. Baudrillard, J.: Simulacra and Simulation. University of Michigan (1994)
5. Baudrillard, J., Poster, M. (eds.): Selected Writings. Polity, Cambridge (1988)
6. Berger, P., Luckmann, T.: The Social Construction of Reality: A treatise in the sociology of knowledge. Anchor Books (1966)
7. Bystřický, J.: Virtuální a reálné. Praha, Sofis (2002)
8. Flusser, V.: Absolute V. Flusser. Orange-press: Freiburg (2003a)
9. Flusser, V.: Filosofia del Design. Bruno Mondadori (2003b)
10. Hegel, G.W.F.: Encyclopedia of the Philosophical Sciences in Basic Outline. In: Brinkmann, K., Dahlstrom, D.O. (eds.) Part I: Science of Logic. Cambridge University Press, Cambridge (2010)
11. Lyotard, J-F.: The Differend: Phrases in Dispute. University of Minnesota Press (1988)
12. Virilio, P.: The Aesthetics of Dissapearance. Semiotext(e), New York (1991)
13. Virilio, P.: The Vision Machine. British Film Institute (1994)

Design Thinking Methods and Tools for Innovation

Dimitra Chasanidou[1](✉), Andrea Alessandro Gasparini[2], and Eunji Lee[1]

[1] SINTEF ICT, Blindern, P.O. Box 124 0373 Oslo, Norway
{dimitra.chasanidou,eunji.lee}@sintef.no
[2] University of Oslo Library, Blindern, P.O. Box 1085 0373 Oslo, Norway
a.a.gasparini@ub.uio.no

Abstract. Design thinking (DT) is regarded as a system of three overlapping spaces—viability, desirability, and feasibility—where innovation increases when all three perspectives are addressed. Understanding how innovation within teams can be supported by DT methods and tools captivates the interest of business communities. This paper aims to examine how DT methods and tools foster innovation in teams. A case study approach, based on two workshops, examined three DT methods with a software tool. The findings support the use of DT methods and tools as a way of incubating ideas and creating innovative solutions within teams when team collaboration and software limitations are balanced. The paper proposes guidelines for utilizing DT methods and tools in innovation projects.

Keywords: Design thinking · Design thinking methods · Design thinking tools · Innovation · Personas · Stakeholder map · Customer journey map

1 Introduction

Design Thinking (DT) has attracted the interest of both scholarly and practitioner literature because of the applicability of design methods for promoting innovation and the applicability of DT across many areas, such as in business [25]. The DT is regarded as a system of three overlapping spaces, in which *viability* refers to the business perspective of DT, *desirability* reflects the user's perspective, and *feasibility* encompasses the technology perspective. Innovation increases when all three perspectives are addressed. The DT's ability to solve more complex problems, so-called wicked problems [6], has designated it in the business milieu as a promising approach for innovation. A large number of design methods and tools facilitate the DT process and support fostering innovations in teams, consisting of both designers and non-designers. From a designer's or a human–computer interaction designer's perspective, this methodology incorporates ideation and creative process attributes, such as empathy for the user, and methods including rapid prototyping and abductive reasoning [19]. From a business perspective, the establishment of a deep understanding within a team of targeted users is one of the important components of DT methodology [22].

Businesses recognize innovativeness as a driving factor for business growth to maintain a competitive advantage in the market and as more likely to offer unique

© Springer International Publishing Switzerland 2015
A. Marcus (Ed.): DUXU 2015, Part I, LNCS 9186, pp. 12–23, 2015.
DOI: 10.1007/978-3-319-20886-2_2

benefits to customers [26]. Understanding how innovation within teams can be supported by DT methods and tools captivates the interest of business communities. However, there are few relevant studies [1, 2, 13] and a lack of specific design guidelines on how to foster innovations with DT methods and tools that could be used by teams of non-designers, such as in a business community. For this purpose, a case-based qualitative approach was employed in this study, extending a previous work on DT methods and tools [7]. The research design includes data collection across two workshops, in order to provide rich insights. The findings support the use of DT methods and tools as a way of incubating ideas and creating innovative solutions within teams when team collaboration and software limitations are balanced. In conclusion, the paper proposes guidelines for utilizing DT methods and tools in innovation projects.

The paper is organized as follows: Sect. 2 provides a review of relevant studies; Sect. 3 analyzes a list of DT methods and tools that could be used to foster innovations. Section 4 describes two workshops conducted with different setups, while Sect. 5 discusses the results and make suggestions for DT methods and tools. The study's limitations are presented as well in the Sect. 5, followed by the conclusions.

2 Design Thinking as an Innovation Approach

Companies and organizations need to innovate in response to the competition and rapidly changing market demands. For this reason, DT is considered a supportive approach for a range of business challenges that should be pursued by both designers and non-designers [25]. Especially for the first phases of innovation, DT has been argued as a successful method for generating ideas [24]. Several connections between DT and innovation, as well as factors affecting the growth of innovation, can be found in the literature [e.g. 4, 14, 25]. According to Harhoff, Henkel, and Von Hippel [17], "innovation is often a process to which several actors with complementary capabilities contribute." Similarly, Baregheh et al. [3] defined innovation as a "multi-stage process whereby organizations transform ideas into new/improved products, service[s] or processes," focusing also on the multidisciplinary aspect of innovation.

On the other hand, DT can also be viewed as "the application of design methods by multidisciplinary teams to a broad range of innovation challenges" [25]. Seidel and Fixson [25] studied the adoption of DT by novice multidisciplinary teams. "If design thinking is to be widely adopted, less-experienced users will employ these methods together, but we know little about their effect when newly adopted" [25]. Their study's [25] implications are that novice multidisciplinary teams will more likely succeed in applying DT when they can be guided to combine methods, are aware of the limits of brainstorming, and can transition from more- to less-reflexive practices. Moreover, companies adopt multidisciplinary teams during DT processes as a strategy to increase team performance [30]. The process of innovation and how it is managed constitute a key strategic issue for companies that rely on multidisciplinary teams. In turn, the adoption of multiple design perspectives is expected to increase performance in terms of the quality of decision making or the innovativeness of problem solving [30]. West et al. [30] examined the relationships among team processes, leadership clarity, and innovation in a healthcare context. In the innovation process, models of brainstorming imply that group creativity can benefit from multidisciplinarity, as brainstorming groups often generate creative and novel ideas, and the group setting is believed to elicit a higher level of cognitive stimulation [12]. Moreover, higher degrees of multidisciplinarity are associated with a broader range of knowledge, skills, and abilities available to a team [30].

A relevant effect of the DT process that may have on team collaboration is the divergent and convergent thinking [5]. During an innovation process supported by DT, a team needs first to broaden their thinking, making it divergent, allowing multiple inputs for their problem area. This creative part of the innovation process usually results in a correct definition of the real problem [5, 15]. In the phase of divergent thinking, searching relevant information and creating new about the task will give a better insight and will also balance the lack of entrepreneurial experience a team may have [15]. As stated by Gurteen's [15] "creativity and innovation concern the process of creating and applying new knowledge," supporting divergent thinking as a relevant attribute for innovation. The composition of a team is also affecting the process at this stage. As it was mentioned earlier, the multidisciplinarity is a relevant aspect to take into account when fostering and stimulating creative inputs [12] in divergent thinking. The last phase of the innovation process entails putting ideas into action, adopting a more convergent thinking [5, 15] and employ an innovative solution.

Garcia et al. [13] described a study whose workshops used service design tools as frameworks to generate, develop, prototype, and assess business ideas that could potentially become business opportunities. They argued that both a "designerly mindset" and the above-mentioned service design toolset might be transferred from design to entrepreneurship to support the development of new entrepreneurial ventures. Finally, Beckman and Barry [4] discussed strategies for encouraging innovation through education and design of organizations and work spaces, suggesting that design constitutes of two phases of design: (1) an analytical phase of finding and discovery and (2) a synthetic phase of invention and creation. They [4] proposed a combination of these theories that would lead to innovation through observational or ethnographic research, creating frameworks for understanding data, analyzing new customer needs, and developing solutions or new products to meet these needs.

Consequently, DT addressed by DT methods and tools is considered supportive for generating innovation and a number of factors could affect the development of innovativeness. Although DT methods have been connected with generation of innovations, how DT tools foster innovations has received little attention in existing research and captivates the interest of business communities.

3   Design-Thinking Methods and Tools

A large number of design methods and tools facilitate the DT innovation process. Alves and Nunes [1] surveyed various sources from both industry and academia and collected more than 164 methods and tools related to service design (SD). The suggested taxonomy of the selected 25 SD tools and methods [1] provides guidance to novice participants and enforces team coherence, while it can be supportive for practitioners.

Using a four-quadrant chart, Alves and Nunes [1] clustered the most relevant methods according to various dimensions, such as the motivation to use it, the audience, the representations used, and activities in the design process. The majority of these methods are used to understand the problem [1], and thus selecting the right methods is important especially in first phases of the DT process.

The DT process consists of five stages: empathizing, defining, ideating, prototyping, and testing [5]. Empathizing relates to direct interaction with users, on whom the definition is based. Ideation phase includes brainstorming and generating solutions, while the prototype phase implies rapidly making numerous prototypes. Finally, the test phase can also include the final implementation. From a design perspective, it is possible to address DT as the creation of meaning [20] and making sense of things [9]. Selecting the right tools is undoubtedly important for effective decision making and communication in a multidisciplinary team. The tools can be physical, such as a pen, paper, and whiteboard, or software tools with rich graphics that support the DT process. The tools can also be used to help a team adopt a new perspective on design tasks, to visualize the system's complexity and depending on the design stage reflect a convergent or divergent view of design.

The rest of this section presents six selected DT methods, with a corresponding, web-based software tool that can be used to implement each method. The criteria for choosing these methods lie in their visualization techniques and ability to enhance communication within multidisciplinary teams, but also in their simplicity in use by non-experts.

3.1 Personas

The persona method can help identify the user's needs and desires. A persona is "a user representation intending to simplify communication and project decision making by selecting project rules that suit the real propositions" [18]. Personas represent a "character" with which client and design teams can engage and use efficiently in the design process. The method is used for the development of marketing products, for communication and SD purposes, to reflect the human perspective of DT [28]. Personas can be used during the empathizing or defining phases of DT. An example of a software tool for creating personas is Smaply,[1] a web service that hosts and presents personas and other methods, such as stakeholder maps and customer journey maps. Smaply provides several options for describing personas, including ready-made avatars, quotes, options for collaboration, and engaging visualizations.

3.2 Stakeholder Map

A stakeholder map is a visual or physical representation of the various groups involved in a particular product or service, such as customers, users, partners, organizations, companies, and other stakeholders [28]. A stakeholder approach reflects the human and business perspective of DT. The interplay and connections among these various stakeholders can be charted and analyzed for various purposes. Curedale [11] argued for the

---

[1] Website: www.smaply.com.

importance of identifying key stakeholders and their relationships as part of the defining process in DT. An example of a software tool for creating stakeholder maps is Stakeholder Circle.[2] It was designed to put stakeholders on the management radar, facilitating regular updating of the assessment as the stakeholder community changes to reflect the dynamic nature of the project and its relationships.

3.3 Customer Journey Map

A customer journey map (CJM), which originated from the technique of service blueprinting [27], describes a collection of touchpoints from the beginning to the end of the service delivery, as seen from the customer's point of view. A touchpoint is defined as "an instance or a potential point of communication or interaction between a customer and a service provider" [16]. The CJM helps the identification of chances for service innovation and problem areas for service improvement [20]. It is a common perspective shared by design/consultancy firms and experiential service providers [21, 29], categorizing the method in the human and technical sides of DT. It can be used during the empathy phase. Visualization of a service user's experience can be presented by Touchpoint Dashboard,[3] a web-based system for creating CJM. It uses common visual notations to unite a team and converts the information into an intuitive, data-rich map of a customer journey.

3.4 Service Blueprint

Introduced by Shostack [27], the service blueprint is a template that shows the steps and flows of service delivery that are related to stakeholders' roles and the process. Service blueprints show the actions between customers and service providers during a service delivery. It is a process-oriented method for the business and technical perspectives of DT and shows all actions, including technical activities. Such a blueprint may benefit designers in the early innovation process, such as defining a phase, by showing the series of actions of both in-front tasks—actions that can be seen by the customer—and back tasks—actions that cannot be seen by customers, such as those among employees in the back office. A web-based tool for blueprint diagrams is Creately[4] that is based on the early version of the service blueprint made by Shostack.

3.5 Business Model Innovation

The business model (BM) innovation is about exploring market opportunities; the challenge is to define what the BM actually entails. The Business Model Canvas (BMC) [23] is a visual way of handling a BM and related economic, operational, and managerial decisions. Generally, a BMC describes the business logic of an idea, product, or service

---

[2] Website: www.stakeholder-management.com/.
[3] Website: www.touchpointdashboard.com.
[4] Website: http://www.creately.com/.

in a simple and visual representation. The BMC mostly reflects the business perspective of DT and can be effectively used in the ideation phase. An example of BM innovation web-based tool is Strategyzer.[5] It includes the nine building blocks of a BMC with simple Post-it notes that can be placed on the blocks. It also supports economic analysis, conversations among users, and an engaging interface.

3.6 Rapid Prototyping

The rapid prototype (RP) is a quick formation of visual and experiential manifestations of concepts [22]. It can assist in determining which solutions are technologically possible. Prototypes can be created and quickly tested using the RP method. It can thus support communication in multidisciplinary teams in collaborative settings, such as workshops, by facilitating conversations and feedback regarding solutions for a particular product or service. The RP reflects more than the technical perspective of DT and supports the DT prototype phase, which should be robust and fast. An example of an RP software tool is Axure RP,[6] which provides wireframing, prototyping, and the specification tools needed. It has a graphical user interface for creating mockups of websites and applications. Axure RP can help users generate quick ideas to immediately improve the design and obtain direct feedback.

4 Case Study

We conducted workshops with users to investigate how the DT methods and tools support innovation and collaboration within teams. To gain rich insights into the associations between innovation and collaboration, we selected two different setups in terms of the participants' backgrounds and motivations for using DT methods through the tools. The selection of DT tools for the workshops had the prerequisite of providing both convergent and divergent thinking in a task [14, 15] and simplicity in usage. Therefore, we selected a web-based tool that incorporates three DT methods, personas, stakeholder map and CJM. The Smaply tool was found to meet our requirements, with an intuitive user interface and attractive visualizations.

4.1 Workshop 1

The first workshop took place in January 2015 and was hosted by an academic library in a Scandinavian country. Six participants took part in a 2-hour workshop. Due to some organizational issues, four library staff members were present, together with two PhD candidates and the three authors of this paper. All the participants had previously joined different seminars and workshops [10], where the main method used pen, paper, and SD cards [8]; they were also familiar with one DT method (CJM). None of the participants had used Smaply before, and they had very good computer skills. The objective here

---

[5] Website: www.strategyzer.com.
[6] Website: www.axure.com/.

was to use the Smaply tool to transfer a service from a previous workshop, and the second task was to develop a new service. In their previous workshop some days ago, the participants used DT method, the CJM for a working project, using SD cards, post-it notes, and paper. The CJM envisioned how a university researcher could gain access to, borrow, and download e-books by using a library website.

Divided into three groups, all participants were informed about the process and were active during the workshop. Each one of the authors joined one group, with an assistive participant role during the process, mainly to facilitate and observe the flow of activities. The groups worked with one laptop each and in the same room, allowing communication and collaboration with one another. Field notes were taken during the process and screen-shots of the generated material from Smaply were used as data collection methods. After a short introduction to Smaply, the participants worked consecutively on the three tasks, personas, stakeholder maps (Fig. 1) and CJM, with a small break among tasks. At the end, they joined a short discussion with the facilitators to share their personal reflections.

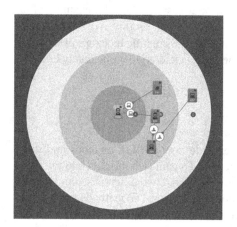 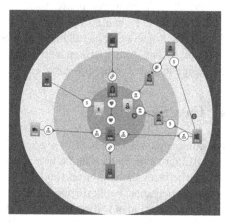

Fig. 1. Artifacts from Workshop 1 (left) and Workshop 2 (right)

4.2 Workshop 2

The second workshop took place in February 2015 and was hosted by university facilities. Seven participants, both MSc and PhD students, took part in a 2-hour workshop. The participants had no prior experience with workshops, but they had previously utilized other DT methods and tools (business modeling). None of the participants had experience with Smaply, but they had very good computer skills. The objective of this workshop was to use the Smaply tool as a part of their semester project, where they would utilize SD for a new application (app) service.

The participants were divided into three groups, with both students and one of the authors of this paper having the same role as in the previous workshop. All participants were informed about the process. The three groups worked with their laptops in the same room, allowing communication and collaboration with one another. Field notes taken during the process and screenshots from the generated material were used as data collection methods. After a short introduction to the Smaply tool, the participants worked on the three tasks, with a small break among tasks. Finally, they joined a short discussion with the facilitators to share their personal reflections.

4.3   Results

Overall, the workshops had positive outcomes; the participants were actively involved and worked during the 2 h of the sessions. Once the participants became familiar with the tool and the process, it was easier for the authors of this paper to observe the process. Table 1 summarizes the results from both workshops, with the corresponding objectives, DT methods, and three related characteristics: type of thinking that DT reflects, collaboration, and multidisciplinarity of the groups.

Table 1. Summarized findings

Objective	DT method (with Smaply)	Type of thinking	Collaboration	Multidisciplinarity
Workshop 1				
Redesign a service, design a service	a. Personas	Convergent	Method-driven	Yes
	b. Stakeholder map	Divergent	Method-driven	Yes
	c. Customer journey map	Convergent/ Divergent	Tool-driven	Yes
Workshop 2				
Redesign part of a service, design a service	a. Personas	Convergent	Method-driven	Yes
	b. Stakeholder map	Divergent	Method-driven	Yes
	c. Customer journey map	Convergent/ Divergent	Method-driven	Yes

The first main observation for the first workshop is related to the technical constraints of the tool. The objective to replicate a task from a previous workshop gave the participants training time to familiarize themselves with the user interface of Smaply. Creating personas seemed easier than the other two tasks, and one group enjoyed the simplicity of the interface. The other two tasks (stakeholder map and customer journey) were more complex for the participants, where they followed an iterative process to improve the first task (personas). Some participants mentioned encountering technical issues when performing the customer journey task in Smaply, which was the most important task for them (tool-driven collaboration). One group created three customer journeys, reporting "the lack of richness of Smaply" and other technical issues regarding icons, labels of buttons, space limitations, and difficulty in using option personas in customer journeys.

Another observation topic for the first workshop was how they will overcome the constraints of the tool. Generally, all the groups worked intensively, but they shifted the focus away from the real task. One group ended up with a new solution, apart from redesigning the service. For the other groups, the final results didn't provide new services and innovations, but the compromise between discussion and accomplishment of the task gave fruitful reflections on Smaply. One group followed a more cooperative pattern throughout the workshop, sharing ideas and supporting each other to accomplish the tasks. The other groups interacted more on problem solving for the Smaply interface.

The second workshop demonstrated different results. The first main observation was the extensive cooperation during the session. Before working on the tasks, the groups engaged in long discussions about different aspects of the tasks and tried to frame and conceptualize the tasks in relation to their previous experiences in DT methods (method-driven collaboration). Generally, the participants defined their roles in group work, where one participant was interacting with the software and the rest of the group members were discussing about how to proceed with the task. Especially after the first task (personas) the discussions opened up to the overall picture of the project and became more animated concerning project-related problems, such as how to solve dependencies among stakeholders. The groups also faced some technical issues with Smaply, but they were secondary in general, for example one group couldn't delete a stakeholder from the stakeholder map after the user created it. The discussions regarding Smaply were at the concept level, such as about the meaning of a concept such as "persona," but not at the technical level, for example, how to create a persona. The groups ended up with new solutions and fresh perspectives on the project.

5 Discussion

The use of DT methods and tools is a way of incubating ideas and creating innovative solutions within teams. Several connections between DT and innovation exist, as mentioned in Sect. 2. Our case study raised the issues of type of thinking, collaboration and multidisciplinary in teams as more significant for the growth of innovation.

The DT methods and tools should be handled by both designers and non-designers. Multidisciplinary teams, consisting of people with diverse competencies and backgrounds, are more likely to succeed in applying DT when they can be guided to combine methods and can transition from more- to less-reflexive practices [25]. Our participants had different backgrounds, and generated fruitful discussions during workshops. Our suggestion is to *engage different people with various backgrounds (business, technical, etc.) in order to establish a DT perspective.*

Additionally, thinking like a designer may improve the way companies and organizations develop their products and services. All three perspectives of DT are essential for innovation. Using human- and business-oriented methods, such as stakeholder maps, thus leaving out the feasibility of the technology, can spark innovation. On the other hand, relying exclusively on business and technical tools does not help project effective decisions, especially as the user may prefer another path. Including the user's perspective and combining convergent and divergent DT methods and tools are therefore critical.

Moreover, DT tools (Table 1) can be used in the first phases of the DT process and reflect both types of thinking. Our suggestion is to *keep both convergent and divergent types of thinking in DT methods or tools for an innovation project.*

The use of software tools that support DT methods is also an insightful way of working with teams. For example, using Smaply to visualize a stakeholder map might be fun and inspiring, enhancing the work with a visual exercise and an analytical tool. Engaging interfaces and visualizations help different people adopt new perspectives on projects that they might have lacked earlier, unless they deal with technical difficulties. Our suggestion is to *provide the participants with a training session in the DT method or tool.*

The value of using DT tools in companies is related to the adoption of a broader view on projects and an effective communication tool for multidisciplinary teams. The value for teams lies in their shared basis for communication, as they can embody their own ideas in real time, in collaboration with other partners. This procedure can lead to making better decisions and visualizing complex system problems and their potential solutions. Some limitations in our study prevent an unambiguous interpretation of the findings. We have to note that the generalizability of our results is limited, and further studies in the field are needed to strengthen the case. However, we think that our results suggest considering three characteristics when including DT methods and tools for innovation projects: multidisciplinarity of participants, embedding two types of thinking, and a training session in the DT method or tool.

6 Conclusion

Understanding how DT tools foster innovations is an area of increasing importance that has received little attention in existing research. To answer this, we suggest including three characteristics in our current understanding of utilizing DT tools, as it was mentioned above: collaboration, multidisciplinarity and twofold type of thinking. In view of the fact that organizations are encouraged to adopt DT in the teams where people may not have prior experience with such methods [25], more collaborative strategies and engaging tools are required. The results of the study suggest the adoption of a method-driven approach to collaboration while utilizing DT tools. The latter should be characterized by simplicity and ease of use in order to help the users' focus on the method. The need for DT methods and tools to cover both convergent and divergent type of thinking is in line with the holistic nature of DT. The list of methods and tools that we discussed here is only a starting point for additional work in this field. Further research might focus on how multidisciplinary teams use design methods and tools for innovation in each design phase and what the most suitable ones are. Another future research topic could be the functional diversity of a team that could maximize innovativeness by using these methods and tools. Case studies, field studies, or similar ones from businesses would be enlightening for this research area.

Acknowledgments. We thank our participants of the two workshops and everyone involved in the case study.

References

1. Alves, R., Jardim Nunes, N.: Towards a taxonomy of service design methods and tools. In: Falcão e Cunha, J., Snene, M., Nóvoa, H. (eds.) IESS 2013. LNBIP, vol. 143, pp. 215–229. Springer, Heidelberg (2013)
2. Bae, K.M., Lee, K.S., Kim, Y.S.: Relationship between service design tools and service innovation - focused on Korean healthcare cases. Asia Pac. J. Multimedia Serv. Convergent Art Humanit. Sociol. **4**(2), 63–70 (2014)
3. Baregheh, A., Rowley, J., Sambrook, S.: Towards a multidisciplinary definition of innovation. Manage. Decis. **47**(8), 1323–1339 (2009)
4. Beckman, S.L., Barry, M.: Innovation as a learning process: embedding design thinking. Calif. Manage. Rev. **50**(1), 25–56 (2007)
5. Brown, T.: Change by Design: How Design Thinking Transforms Organizations and Inspires Innovation. Harper Business, New York (2009)
6. Buchanan, R.: Wicked problems in design thinking. Des. Issues **8**(2), 5–21 (1992)
7. Chasanidou, D., Gasparini, A.A., Lee, E.: Design Thinking Methods and Tools for Innovation in Multidisciplinary Teams. IN: Innovation in HCI: What Can We Learn from Design Thinking?, pp. 27–30 (2014). ISBN 978-82-7368-407-3
8. Clatworthy, S.D.: Service Innovation Through Touch-points: Development of an Innovation Toolkit for the First Stages of New Service Development. Int. J. Des. **5**(2), 15–28 (2011)
9. Cross, N.: From a design science to a design discipline: understanding designerly ways of knowing and thinking. In: Design Research Now, pp. 41–54 (2007)
10. Culén, A., Gasparini, A.A.: Find a book! unpacking customer journeys at academic library. In: ACHI 2014 the Seventh International Conference on Advances in Computer-Human Interactions, p. 7 (2014)
11. Curedale, R.: Design Thinking: Process and Methods Manual. Design Community College Incorporated, Topanga (2013)
12. Fay, D., Borrill, C., Amir, Z., Haward, R., West, M.A.: Getting the most out of multidisciplinary teams: a multi-sample study of team innovation in health care. J. Occup. Organ. Psychol. **79**, 553–567 (2006)
13. Garcia Mata, L., Deserti, A., Teixeira, C.: Service design tools as frameworks in the generation of business ideas an action research case study. In: 2013 IEEE Tsinghua International Design Management Symposium (TIDMS), pp. 338–344 (2013)
14. Gielnik, M.M., Krämer, A.C., Kappel, B., Frese, M.: Antecedents of business opportunity identification and innovation: investigating the interplay of information processing and information acquisition. Appl. Psychol. **63**(2), 344–381 (2014)
15. Gurteen, D.: Knowledge, Creativity and Innovation. J. Knowl. Manage. **2**(1), 5–13 (1998)
16. Halvorsrud, R., Lee, E., Haugstveit, I.M., Følstad, A.: Components of a visual language for service design. In: Proceedings of ServDes 2014, pp. 291–300 (2014)
17. Harhoff, D., Henkel, J., Von Hippel, E.: Profiting from voluntary information spillovers: how users benefit by freely revealing their innovations. Res. Policy **32**(10), 1753–1769 (2003)
18. Junior, P.T.A., Filgueiras, L.V.L.: User modeling with personas. In: Proceedings of CLIHC 2005 Latin American Conference on Human Computer Interaction, pp. 277–282 (2005)
19. Kolko, J.: Wicked Problems: Problems Worth Solving: A Handbook And Call To Action. Ac4d, Austin Center for Design, Austin (2012)
20. Krippendorff, K.: The Semantic Turn: A New Foundation for Design. Taylor and Francis, Boca Raton, FL, USA (2006)

21. Lee, E., Karahasanović, A.: Can business management benefit from service journey modeling language? In: Proceedings of ICSEA 2013 Eighth International Conference on Software Engineering Advances, pp. 579–582 (2013)
22. Liedtka, J., Ogilvie, T.: Designing for Growth: A Design Thinking Tool kit for Managers. Columbia University Press, NY (2011)
23. Osterwalder, A., Pigneur, Y.: Business Model Generation. Wiley, Hoboken (2010)
24. Plattner, H., Meinel, C., Leifer, L.: Design Thinking Research: Studying Co-creation in Practice. Springer, Berlin (2012)
25. Seidel, V.P., Fixson, S.K.: Adopting design thinking in novice multidisciplinary teams: the application and limits of design methods and reflexive practices. J. Prod. Innov. Manage **30**(1), 19–33 (2013)
26. Shepherd, D.A., DeTienne, D.R.: Prior knowledge, potential financial reward, and opportunity identification. Entrepreneurship Theor. Pract. **29**, 91–112 (2005)
27. Shostack, G.L.: Designing services that deliver. Harvard Bus. Rev. **62**(1), 133–139 (1984)
28. Stickdorn, M., Schneider, J.: This is Service Design Thinking; Basics, Tools, Cases. BIS Publishers, Amsterdam (2010)
29. Voss, C.: Innovation in experiential services: an empirical view. Dissertation London Business School (2007)
30. West, M.A., Borrill, C.S., Dawson, J.F., Brodbeck, F., Shapiro, D.A., Haward, B.: Leadership clarity and team innovation in health care. Leadersh. Q. **14**(4–5), 393–410 (2003)

Semantic Research of Military Icons Based on Behavioral Experiments and Eye-Tracking Experiments

Xiao Jiao Chen, Chengqi Xue[✉], Yafeng Niu, Haiyan Wang,
Jing Zhang, and Jiang Shao

School of Mechanical Engineering, Southeast University, Nanjing 211189, China
ipd_xcq@seu.edu.cn

Abstract. As a type of symbol, there are four dimensions in icons' symbolic interpretation, namely semantic, syntactic, contextual and pragmatic dimension. Among those dimensions, semantic dimension is the most important one in user's cognitive analysis. Based on the representation of semantics, icons can be classified into four types, namely function-metaphor, operation-metaphor, object-metaphor and meaning-metaphor icon. Here we conducted behavioral experiment and eye-tracking experiment to evaluate those four types of icons selected from military aeronautical system. The behavioral experiment showed that subjects have lowest reaction time to function-metaphor icons and highest accuracy to identify object-metaphor icons. The eye-tracking system showed that subjects have the most fixations when searching for object-metaphor icons and the least fixations when searching for function-metaphor icons. Our research is the first endeavor into the investigation of human's response to different types of icons in the military systems and thus provided novel and valuable guidance to the design of icons in those systems.

Keywords: Aeronautical system · Icons · Semantics · Behavioral experiment · Eye-tracking experiment

1 Introduction

In computer science and software technology, icons are a main part of human computer interfaces, which bridge users and digital interface. As a type of symbol, there are four dimensions in an icon's symbolic interpretation: semantic, syntactic, contextual and pragmatic dimension, among which semantic dimension is the most important one in human's cognitive analysis [1]. Previous psychological study showed that icon's cognition is related to human's cognitive habits, capability of abstract thinking, domain knowledge and cultural background. Generally speaking, icons need be easy to recognize and interpret so that users with no special training can understand the meaning of them. Therefore, the semantic dimension of icons is the most important one. Based on the representation of semantics, icons can be classified into four types, namely function-metaphor, operation-metaphor, object-metaphor and meaning-metaphor icon [1].

A well-designed icon can facilitate the delivery of information and reduce the complexity of a digital interface, thus plays a critical role in digital interface. Based on

© Springer International Publishing Switzerland 2015
A. Marcus (Ed.): DUXU 2015, Part I, LNCS 9186, pp. 24–31, 2015.
DOI: 10.1007/978-3-319-20886-2_3

the applications, icons can be classified as civil application icons and military application icons, where civil application icons are usually widely used in commercial products and interact with a large population in a daily basis while military application icons are used in military systems, such as geographic information system, operational chain of command system and battle-field situations real-time display system [2]. Comparing to commercial products, military systems have a higher demand in terms of digital interfaces and thus icons, as those systems are critical to assist military persons to accomplish special missions under sophisticated situations. For example, when fighters are carrying out urgent tasks in the air, with the situation changing rapidly, it can easily lead to fighter fleeting. Pilot's decision is directly related to personal life and national security, and that all channels of information acquisition host on the digital interfaces. Therefore icons in those digital interfaces should be designed to enhance pilot's ability to acquire information and reduce pilot's cognitive load in order to assist pilots to make critical decisions and accomplish military tasks. In this paper, we evaluated four types of icons selected from military aeronautical system and based on behavioral experiment and eye-tracking experiment. We provided a framework to compare different types of icons the results provided a novel and valuable guidance to the design of icons in military systems.

The metrics we used to evaluate different icons are accuracy rate, reaction time, fixation point diagram and heat map. Accuracy rate is defined as the ratio of successful operation times to the total operation times. Reaction time is response time, timing from the appearance of stimulus to testers' reacting. Fixation point diagram consists of fixation location switching within the area of interest, which is described by scanning path and used for investigating visual search path and strategy of testers. Heat map reflects the spatial distribution of fixations, with the depth of color indicating the length of time watching this area [3–5].

2 Methodology

2.1 Materials

The experimental materials are icons selected from real military aeronautical systems. As is shown in Fig. 1, icons are selected and redesigned based on expert score and Likert scale. Each row represents one type of icons. Each type of icon is used to represent two words and for each word, we designed two similar but distinct icons. From top to bottom are function-metaphor icons (A), operation-metaphor icon (B), object-metaphor icon (B) and meaning-metaphor icons (D). In the rest of the paper, we will use A, B, C and D to represent those four types of icons separately.

The size of each image is 1024 * 768px, where the size of text is 36pt and the size of icon image is 96 * 96px. And the perspective is controlled in 0.7 degrees, which is equivalent to reading an icon with the size of 0.5 cm * 0.5 cm at a distance of 40 cm [6].

2.2 Subjects

Twenty students, with thirteen males and seven females, whose ages are all between 20–35 years old, 14 males and 6 females, are chosen as subjects. Among those, 15 are with related background knowledge and 5 are without. They all satisfy the following

Fig. 1. Icons from military aeronautical systems

conditions: physical and mental health, normal or rectified vision, and with many years' experience in using graphics device. Subjects are trained to be familiar with task flow and operation requirements before the formal experiment. During the experiment, subjects are asked to keep their eyes 550–600 mm away from the screen and both horizontal and vertical perspective is controlled in 2.3 degrees [7] (Fig. 2).

2.3 Experimental Equipment and Experimental Procedures

Behavioral data includes the accuracy rate and reaction time, which were acquired by Eprime. The eye movement data includes fixation point diagram and heat map, which were

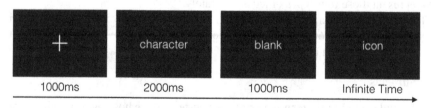

Fig. 2. Process of behavioral experiment

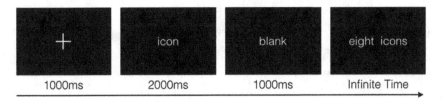

Time

Fig. 3. Process of eye-tracking experiment

acquired by Tobii X2-30 Eye-tracking Device. Behavioral experiment and eye-tracking experiment were conducted separately, and specific information was as follows [8].

Behavioral experimental procedure is as follows. Each experiment covers all icons in A, B, C and D which accounts for 16 trials. In each trial, there are four phases: Phase I: a white cross appeared in the center of the screen with the background to be black, and continuously lasted for 1000 ms then disappeared; Phase II: text appeared in the center of the screen, and continuously lasted for 2000 ms then disappeared. In this phase, subjects are asked to remember and understand the text; Phase III: blank appeared and continuously lasted for 1000 ms then disappeared. This phase is to eliminate visual persistence; Phase IV: an icon picture appeared in the center of the screen and the subject is asked to decide whether the semantics of the icon matches that of the text in Phase II. Then the subject is asked to press key 'A' to indicate a correct match and press key 'L' to indicate an incorrect match. After pressing the key, subject enters the next trial. During the experiment, each icon will show up twice, once with the matched text and once with a mismatched text in random sequence.

Next we used Tobii X2-30 to conduct eye-tracking experiment. The process is as follows: Phase I: a white cross appeared in the center of the screen with the background to be black, and continuously lasted for 1000 ms then disappeared; Phase II: an icon appeared in the center of the screen, and continuously lasted for 2000 ms then disappeared. In this phase, subjects are asked to remember and understand the icon; Phase III: blank appeared and continuously lasted for 1000 ms then disappeared. This phase is to eliminate visual persistence; Phase IV: eight icons appeared in the screen at the same time which is consist of 2 icons from A, 2 icons from B, 2 icons from C and 2 icons from D. Subjects are asked to conduct visual search task, which is to find the icon that is the same as the one presented in Phase II. After that the subject is asked to press any key to proceed into next trial. During the experiment, fixation time, the fixation number, scan path and heat map are recorded for data analysis [9]. The experiment process is shown in Fig. 3.

3   Analysis and Results

3.1 Behavioral Data Analysis

Behavioral data includes the accuracy rate and reaction time. As is shown in Fig. 4, the average reaction time over all subjects for 4 different types of icons are: operation-metaphor icon (B) 1446.725 ms > meaning-metaphor icon (D) 1328.406 ms > function-metaphor icon

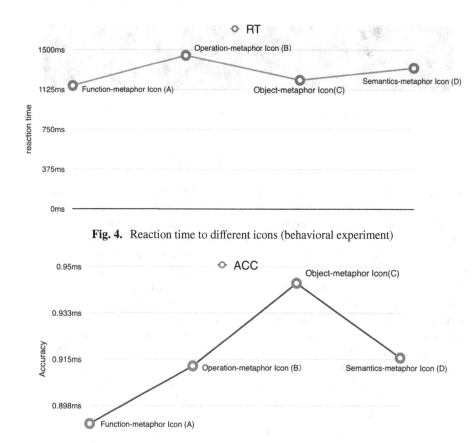

Fig. 4. Reaction time to different icons (behavioral experiment)

Fig. 5. Accuracy rate of icon recognition (behavioral experiment)

(A) 1213.522 ms > object-metaphor icon (C) 1159.947 ms. The results showed that object-metaphor icons require shortest reaction time while operation-metaphor icons require longest reaction time.

As is shown in Fig. 5, the accuracy rate of identifying icons are: object-metaphor icon (C) 0.944 > meaning-metaphor icon (D) 0.916 > operation-metaphor icon (B) 0.913 > function-metaphor icon (A) 0.891. The results showed that subjects have highest accuracy rate identifying object-metaphor icons.

3.2   Eye-Tracking Experiment Data Analysis

As is shown in Fig. 6, the results of fixation number is as follows: Object-metaphor icon (c) 5.368 > Operation-metaphor icon (B) 5.200 > meaning-metaphor icon (D) 4.950 > function-metaphor icon (A) 4.450. The result suggested that subjects tend to have lower fixation numbers when searching for function-metaphor icons which suggested that function-metaphor icons are easier to be detected by human beings.

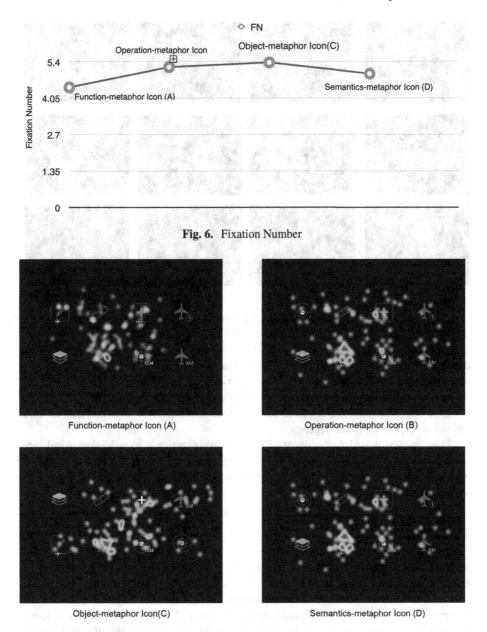

Fig. 6. Fixation Number

Function-metaphor Icon (A)

Operation-metaphor Icon (B)

Object-metaphor Icon(C)

Semantics-metaphor Icon (D)

Fig. 7. Heat map

As is shown in Fig. 7, all subjects completed the assigned task, which is to search for icons at the second position of second row. It is also shown in Fig. 7 that heat map of function-metaphor icons are more concentrated comparing to other three types of icons. This suggested that function-metaphor icons easier easy to be identified.

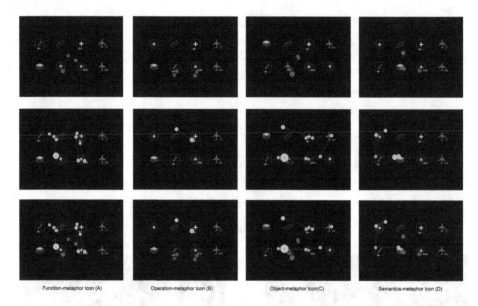

Function-metaphor Icon (A)   Operation-metaphor Icon (B)   Object-metaphor Icon(C)   Semantics-metaphor Icon (D)

Fig. 8. Fixation point diagram

As is shown in Fig. 8, red dots in the first row represent fixation numbers and scan path of subjects with experience of icon designs while yellow dots represent fixation numbers and scan path of subjects without experience of icon designs. And we combined the results of first row and second row for direct comparison in the third row. The results in Fig. 8 suggested that experienced subjects tend to have small fixation numbers and cleaner scan path with less zigzags.

This conclusion is also consistent with the general practice of icon designs in military systems where function-metaphor icons are preferred. The icons used in this paper also provided a good example of function-metaphor icons in terms of simplicity, recognizability and mnemonically.

4 Conclusions

In this paper, we used Eprime and eye-tracking device to evaluate the icons used in military aeronautical systems. The results showed that function-metaphor icon is better than others in terms of easy to recognize and easy to memorize. Our investigation is the first endeavor into the statistical study of the recognizability and memorability of icons in the military aeronautical systems. The results would provide valuable guidance to further studies and future design of icons in military systems.

Acknowledgement. This paper is supported by National Natural Science Foundation of China (No. 71271053, 71471037), Aeronautical Science Foundation of China (No. 20135169016) and Scientific Innovation Research of College Graduates in Jiangsu Province (No. CXLX13_082).

References

1. Zhou, Y.X., Luo, S.J., Chen, G.C.: Design semiotics based icon design. J. Comput. Aided Des. Comput. Graph. **24**, 1319–1328 (2012)
2. Wang, H.Y., Bian, T., Xue, C.Q.: Experimental evaluation of fighter's interface layout based on eye tracking. Electro – Mech. Eng. **27**, 50–53 (2011)
3. Farzan, R., Brusilovsky, P.: Social navigation support for information seeking: if you build it, will they come? In: Houben, G.-J., McCalla, G., Pianesi, F., Zancanaro, M. (eds.) UMAP 2009. LNCS, vol. 5535, pp. 66–77. Springer, Heidelberg (2009)
4. Kaminerer, Y., Gerjets, P.: How the Interface design influences users'spontaneous trustworthinessevaluations of web search results:comparing a list and a grid interface. In: Proceedings of the 2010 Symposium on Eye-Tracking Research d-Applications, pp. 299–306. ACM (2010)
5. Fang, X., Holsapple, C.W.: Toward a knowledge acquisition framework for web site design. In: Proceedings of the Americas Conference on Information Systems, Long Beach, pp. 10–13 (2000)
6. Lindberg, T., Risto, N.: The effect of icon spacing and size on the speed of icon processing in the human visual system. Displays **24**, 111–120 (2003)
7. Huang, K.C.: Effects of computer icons and figure/background area ratios and color combinations on visual search performance on an LCD monitor. Display **29**, 237–242 (2008)
8. Gong, Y., Yang, Y., Zhang, S.Y., Qian, X.F.: Event-related potential study on concretness effects to icon comprehension. J. Zhejiang Univ. (Eng. Sci.) **47**, 1000–1005 (2013)
9. Luo, S.J., Zhu, S.S., Sun, S.Q.: Case study of product conceptual design based on integrated knowledge. J. Comput. Aided Des. Comput. Graph. **16**, 261–266 (2004)

Thinking with a New Purpose: Lessons Learned from Teaching Design Thinking Skills to Creative Technology Students

Marc Fabri[✉]

Faculty of Art, Environment and Technology,
Leeds Beckett University, Leeds, UK
m.fabri@leedsbeckett.ac.uk

Abstract. This paper reports on the insights gained from introducing Design Thinking into the final year of a UK university course where students created positive behavior change interventions. The rationale for course design and teaching process is outlined, with a discussion of design as an engineering process versus an innovation process. The students followed Stanford University's d.school 5-step approach of Empathize-Define-Ideate-Prototype-Test, and their journey is described in detail. We observed that initially students found the Design Thinking approach counter-intuitive and confusing, yet on further progress they recognized the strengths and opportunities it offers. On the whole, students reflected positively on their learning and the re-evaluation of their role as a designer of digital artefacts. Lessons learned from a teaching point of view are outlined, the most poignant being the realization that it was required to 'un-teach' certain design practices students had come to adopt, in particular the view of design as a self-inspired process where users are consulted for feedback but not as a source for innovation.

Keywords: Design education · Situated learning · Design thinking · Service design · Human-Centered design · Behavior change · Persuasive design

1 Introduction

This paper presents insights from introducing a new semester-long teaching course called "Design Thinking" to final year undergraduate students on a Creative Technology degree in the UK. During the course, students conceive and design a behavior change product. Prior to taking this course, students were taught traditional design skills in the key areas of graphic design, visual communication and interaction design, supported by training in industry-standard software. Previous teaching put an emphasis on design as a profession, with a core set of practical skills that can be taught [20]. Looking at design through this lens, tutors encouraged their students to create artefacts with a focus on aesthetic design principles, technical skills, personal preferences, assumed end-user needs, predictions of usability, and within the contained environment of higher education. The rationale behind introducing Design Thinking was to mature the students'

© Springer International Publishing Switzerland 2015
A. Marcus (Ed.): DUXU 2015, Part I, LNCS 9186, pp. 32–43, 2015.
DOI: 10.1007/978-3-319-20886-2_4

abilities for conceptualizing and approaching creative challenges, and in the process engage with potential end users in order to create artefacts that closely meet those people's needs and desires – rather than those of the student. It was hoped that at the end of the course, students would have broadened their understanding of what design is, and their role in the design process of interactive experiences.

In this paper we evaluate the impact of the new curriculum introduction on the students' learning experience, their design practice, their achievements and reflections as well as the wider lessons that can be learned from a pedagogical perspective.

2 Design Thinking

Design Thinking is a human-centered methodology that uses co-design and intuitive problem-solving techniques to match people's needs with what is technologically feasible and organizationally viable [1]. It is typically applied to deal with difficult, multi-dimensional problems that lack recognizable requirements and solutions – traditionally referred to as "wicked problems" [19]. Based on the premise that by combining empathy, creativity and analytical processes, true innovation can emerge in the process of solving such problems. This process utilizes our ability to be intuitive, to discover patterns, and to construct ideas that are both meaningful and functional [2]. Unlike scientific thinking where the focus is on analyzing patterns and facts to identify solutions, Design Thinking promotes the invention of new patterns to realize new possibilities – aptly coined as "the reverse of scientific thinking" [5].

There has been an increased uptake of Design Thinking in design, business and more recently sustainability, health and social innovation [24]. Much of the rise can be attributed to a few key organizations such as design consultancy IDEO, Stanford's d.school group, Toronto's Rotman School of Management, and the UK Design Council. A number of frameworks are available that help with the execution of a Design Thinking approach, the most popular ones being IDEO's educator's toolkit [9] with 5-steps Discovery-Interpretation-Ideation-Experimentation-Evolution; IDEO's HCD toolkit [10] with the 3-phase process of Hear-Create-Deliver; UK Design Council's double-diamond [4] stages Discover-Define-Develop-Deliver; Stanford University's d.school [3] 5-step approach of Empathize-Define-Ideate-Prototype-Test which is closely aligned with IDEO's educator's toolkit. It should be noted that the terminology used to describe the concepts and steps in Design Thinking is not universal, e.g. in Northern Europe the term "Service Design" is preferred – which to some encompasses more than Design Thinking [18]. However, the underlying ethos and many of the methods are markedly similar.

3 Behavior Change Context

Services, as opposed to goods or products, are typically characterized by intangible resources, by relationships, and by the co-creation of value [22]. Arguably, any behavior change intervention, whether facilitated face-to-face or through digital technology, is a service rather than a delivered good. The Design Thinking approach works particularly well with the design of service experiences where the outcome is not particularly tangible, e.g. "This app helped me adopt a healthier lifestyle", rather than the tangible benefit of "owning" a product or of having "completed a task". The success of such a service may instead derive from lived experiences, habits adopted, views changed, or encounters with digital interfaces and with humans.

Outcomes like these can be difficult to design for, particularly for students who lack the professional experience as well as the insight and knowledge about end users' circumstances. A Design Thinking approach can help here as design-thinkers are "encouraged to think broadly about problems, develop a deep understanding of users and recognize the value in the contributions of others" [5, p512]. Another strong correlator between the challenge of creating a behavior change intervention and the ethos of the design thinking approach is the inherently personal nature of human behavior. We are all individuals, and any attempt at influencing or helping with maintaining a newly adopted behavior is likely to work better if the intervention is based on a good understanding of people's mindset and the different facets of self [23].

Creating the course around a behavior change service challenge was therefore considered appropriate, offering sufficient practical and intellectual complexity whilst at the same time providing students with a set of tools to tackle an unfamiliar challenge. We worked closely with the Behaviour Change Research group at Leeds Beckett University (www.leedsbehaviourlab.org), which is primarily concerned with the role of digital technology in behavior change interventions. The research group provided the theoretical background as well as the design challenges for students to work on.

After careful consideration of the available Design Thinking frameworks, we chose Stanford's d.school 5-step model [3] as it contains and further granulizes other frameworks well. This is in line with Lugmayr et al.'s approach to teaching media students at a Finnish university [14]. Figure 1 illustrates the 5 key steps:

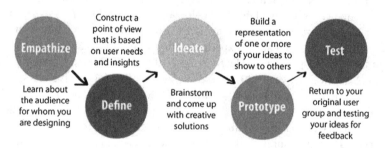

Fig. 1. The 5-step design thinking process (adapted from [3])

Each step is supported by a set of Method Cards that provide detailed guidance on techniques and artefacts designers can use in their practice. For example, for the Empathize stage there is guidance on interviewing, observing, or dealing with extreme users. For the Ideate stage, method cards cover brainstorming, translating problem statements into idea prompts, documenting and selecting ideas, and more.

4 Pedagogical Context

There are several learning and teaching theories underpinning the approach chosen for the Design Thinking course, outlined in [20, 24] and briefly below. Firstly, Constructivism emphasizes student-centered learning where students construct their own understanding through experiencing things and then reflecting on their experience in a 'learning by doing' approach [17]. Experiential Learning - building on constructivism - values learning through 'reflection on doing'. Students learn through their own reflection and that of their peers, which is important for students' metacognitive development. The approach considers a cyclic model with four stages of learning: concrete experience, reflection, abstract conceptualization and active experimentation [12].

These experiences and reflections are closely correlated to the principles of Design Thinking with its focus on empathy, making sense of observed phenomena through reflection and conceptualization, collaboration between learners as well as with users, creativity and imagination, and solution refinement through iterative prototyping.

Situated Learning [13] is learning that takes place in the same context in which it is applied, typically in a community of practice where a group of people work towards a common goal. In this way, learning is seen as the process of becoming a member of this community through collaborating with individuals with greater experience [21]. Hung [8] argues that this provides authentic social experiences and when students are in these real-life situations, they are more compelled to take part and to learn.

The introduction of Design Thinking into the curriculum, both as a process and a philosophy, clearly offers an opportunity for situated learning to take place: students collaborate in order to find creative solutions to a given problem, under the guidance of an experienced tutor, through engagement with potential end-users and in an authentic environment outside of the classroom.

5 Course Structure

The 13-week 'Design Thinking' course (Table 1) was offered to final year Creative Media students during the 2013/14 academic year. This was the first time it ran. Students could choose from a number of different courses, of which Design Thinking was one. The high level learning outcomes for this course were: (1) Investigate and think creatively about design problems and opportunities; (2) Demonstrate a critical awareness of how design thinking can be applied in a variety of contexts; and finally (3) Work effectively in a creative team. Students had 2 h of scheduled contact time per week with their tutor and were expected to spend another 6 h per week on course related activities, as independent learners. Timetabled sessions took place in a computer lab with projector, two large white-boards, break out space for group work and ample wall space for post-it notes and posters.

During weeks 1 and 2 students were expected to do background reading and were given resources covering design thinking ([1, 3] Chapter 1 of [21]) as well as behavior change theory [6, 7, 11] Chapter 1 of [23]).

Table 1. Course lesson plan

Week	Timetabled 2-hour session	Additional Activities
1	Course introduction and discussion	Background reading
2	5-step Design Thinking practice run	Background reading
3	Introduction to design challenges	Conduct research into challenges
4	Process steps 'Empathize' & 'Define'	Form groups and start process
5	Formal presentation: Proposal	Act on tutor feedback
6	Process step 'Ideate'	Further Ideation in spare time
7	Process steps 'Prototype' and 'Test'	Start of prototyping and testing
8-12	Opportunity to discuss progress and gain feedback from tutor	Further prototyping, documenting, final presentation preparation
13	Formal presentation: Final Service	n/a

The assignment was a design challenge that drew from real-life problems, provided by organizations with an actual need for a behavior change intervention. Representatives of these organizations presented their challenge to the students during a tutorial in week 3. There were two challenges to choose from:

1. Create a virtual writing coach that helps aspiring and active writers develop their practice and keep their projects on track.
2. Create a mobile companion app to a weight management program that is currently based on facilitator-run face-to-face group meetings.

Students worked in groups of 3–5 and were assessed twice: in week 5 when results from preliminary user research were presented (20 % of grade), and in week 13 when the full service proposal was delivered (80 %). It should be pointed out that students were not expected to create working versions of these products. Instead, the course required the design of a concept and test of a prototype. The final deliverable was a written proposal accompanied by a promotional video that illustrated both the rationale for the design choices and the key features of the product. All students already had advanced skills in graphic design, video production and motion graphics.

15 students out of 45 in that year group, students chose the Design Thinking course. Students formed four groups, three of which chose the weight management challenge whilst one group chose the writing coach challenge. Attendance throughout the course duration was high (75 % on average), which is significantly higher than on other courses that ran simultaneously (ranging between 48 % and 57 %).

5.1 Practice Run

In week 2, students were introduced to the d.school 5-step Design Thinking process during a short lecture. They then did a test-run through the 5-steps within a compressed 2 h period, in a learning-by-doing fashion. The task was to re-imagine university library services. Students went into the library to spend some time observing and talking to people (the Empathize stage). Students were initially reluctant to talk to strangers.

However, all returned with some useful information on library user behavior, likes and dislikes. These were collated and potential design problems were articulated as 'How Might We…?' statements (the Define stage, cf. [3]).

During the Ideate stage, some surprising and innovative proposals emerged, e.g. having books with wings that fly to the waiting customer, or the idea that students who have been fined for not returning books in time could work off these fines by delivering books to other students' houses. The 'book with wings' idea in particular sparked lively discussions, stemming from students' unwillingness to walk along long book shelves to locate individual items. The idea eventually led to the design concept of an interactive order system that allows students to request books, which are then delivered automatically to their study desk by a flying drone, with attached camera that documents the delivery via live feed to the student's mobile device. During the Prototype stage students developed concepts of the accompanying app, seeking feedback on their prototypes from their peers.

What started out as an 'absurd' idea (book with wings) was rapidly transformed into an innovative, disruptive and arguably feasible solution to a problem – somewhat supporting the claim that Design Thinking can lead to dramatic new solutions [1].

6   Observations on the 5-Step Process

A key purpose of this paper was to examine how students responded to using a hitherto unfamiliar design approach – Design Thinking – when creating a Behavior Change intervention app, and how their perception of the role of a designer may be affected. Since there was no control group, the prime instruments to assess this were tutor observations of the students, material produced by the students, and a short reflective report each student wrote at the end of the course.

In the following sections we will look at the student journey in detail by considering one of the student groups that consisted of 4 members and selected the first challenge: *Create a virtual writing coach that helps aspiring and active writers develop their practice and keep their projects on track.* The group was chosen as a case study because it took particular care in documenting the design activities and learning progress throughout the weeks. Outcomes by other groups were comparable. The Design Thinking process is illustrated alongside examples of work from this particular group. Student quotes were drawn from the written reflections of all course attendants.

Empathize. During the Empathize stage the group members interviewed a small number of writers from different disciplines: a professional journalist working for a national newspaper, a part-time novelist, a poet and a professional music blogger. Taking the initiative to contact and observe these writers proved difficult initially. This was not because people were not available – in fact the teaching team provided students with contact details of potential users. The main reason was that students felt uncomfortable approaching these people. It was something they were not used to and several students suggested creating a draft design concept first, before talking to potential end users so that they had something to show them. Method cards for interviewing were highly valued by the students as they provided a framework for approaching, learning from and empathizing with the writers. Students also created 'A day in the life of...' maps which track daily activities and habits, in order to identify existing habits, technology touchpoints and ultimately to spot opportunities for new coaching support. Gradually students understood the purpose of this step. In the words of one of the students: *"I began to see how engaging with people can open your eyes to the way they think about the subject, rather than one's own preconceptions"*.

Define. The Define phase prompted students to consider users and their needs, and then develop insights based on these needs. Some examples (Table 2):

Table 2. Users, needs and insights

User	Need	Insight
Journalist	To write creatively as well as for the job/money	There is little time and energy for creative writing at the moment because it is seen as being completely separate from the paid work.
Novelist	To get more feedback on one's writing	Friends are willing to give feedback but it's difficult to know when to send them a draft and then it takes a long time to get feedback.
Music Blogger	To have the time to write more	There is a lot of brief free time during a typical day which could be filled with short bursts of writing.

These insights eventually led to the articulation of several 'How Might We...' topics, designed to focus on different aspects of an overall challenge. These topics provide the seeds for the Ideate step when the group can churn out a large quantity of compelling ideas [3]. Examples of the many topics students covered are:

- *How might we...* make him/her feel good about writing?
- *How might we...* give rewards for small progress?
- *How might we...* nurture creativity?
- *How might we...* make writing playful?
- *How might we...* encourage constructive feedback?
- *How might we...* allow the user to quickly dip in and out?
- *How might we...* encourage regular breaks?

Student found this phase exciting as they realized how the Design Thinking process can foster the emergence of new and unexpected viewpoints, as illustrated in this quote from a student's final reflections: *"I found the 'How Might We...' topics particularly effective for generating ideas because it prevents you from coming up with direct solutions, which could potentially risk losing other, sometimes better solutions that were not as apparent at first."*

Ideate. The Ideate step is characterized by 'going wide' with ideas, concepts and possible outcomes. During a timetabled tutorial session and starting with the "How Might We..." topics, students enjoyed generating plenty of ideas on post-it notes whilst deferring judgment on their suitability or feasibility until later (see Fig. 2). Students were then encouraged to continue with generating ideas in their spare time during the week, before the next timetabled session.

Fig. 2. Ideation: sorting and selecting ideas written on post-it notes

In that session, a structured idea filtering process was introduced where each student had three votes, selecting the ideas that were (a) most likely to delight end users; (b) the most rational and feasible given today's technology; and (c) the most unexpected. Ideas that received the most votes were carried forward into prototyping. Some examples:

1. Set challenges for the user to complete
2. Make it easy to share writing with trusted friends, and receive feedback quickly
3. Keep a timeline of writing activity
4. Remind the user when they have free time
5. Give personalized inspirations at opportune moments
6. Provide opportunities for discussion and mutual support
7. Remind the user to take breaks
8. Introduce brain activities during rest periods
9. Disable other apps during work hours
10. Help organize work into manageable chunks

6.1 Prototype and Test

These two steps are best considered together as they represent a cyclic process of prototyping, testing, reflecting, and refining before another cycle of testing commences. It has its roots in the iterative design methodology commonly used in engineering, product design and software development [15]. Pedagogically, iterative design relates well to the cyclic concept of experiential learning [12]. Often, quite some effort goes into a first prototype before it is tested. Following the Design Thinking philosophy, however, students were encouraged to take a different approach (based on [3]) (Fig. 3):

- **Start building quickly and early**, even if it is not quite clear yet what the prototype may end up as. This promotes experimentation.

- **Keep fidelity low** and do not spend too much time on any one prototype. This avoids emotional attachment to concepts that turn out to be unpromising.
- **Identify what is being tested with each prototype** – ideally it answers just one particular question. This avoids getting lost in complexity.
- **Build with the user in mind** and be clear about which user behavior is expected and being tested. This helps focusing on receiving meaningful feedback.

Fig. 3. Examples of prototypes and user testing

Deciding when a prototype was ready for testing and when to stop adding details was not always easy, as this student reflection confirms:

"I found the 'Prototype' stage quite difficult initially because I imagined that they needed to be functioning things to be able to test them properly. When I tested them on X she was surprisingly open to the concept of what I was testing and her feedback was useful because it contradicted some of the ideas I had had to solve the problem."

Most Students, however, were already familiar with the general concept of prototyping and keen to try out their ideas. Working together towards a common goal appeared to further motivate them, each having developed their own ideas to start with and then collaboratively improving these ideas:

"Working in a group was an advantage because we got to see what other people's thoughts are on how they would alter things for the public, what they would improve and what they did with my ideas, how they added things and made them better."

6.2   Final Product

Many of the initial ideas did not make it into and through prototyping. This is a normal aspect of Design Thinking and students accepted that. For the design of the final product (see Fig. 4), students focused on six key features of the virtual writing coach app, which they named 'WriteTime'. Students also produced a promotional video (available at http://leedsbehaviourlab.org/news/teaching-design-thinking/):

1. **Challenges** – get daily challenges that provide a sense of continuous improvement;
2. **Quickshare** – share writing effortlessly and receive feedback quickly;
3. **Calendar** – identify free time that can be used for writing to keep the momentum;
4. **Timeline** – set goals, see progress and get reminders for milestones along the way;
5. **Writing Tool** – simple editor to write often and in quick bursts;
6. **Rest Time** – get regular breaks from writing and fill them with nurturing activities.

We would like to reiterate that the app was not actually developed. Testing was based on designs and user experience only, therefore no data about the efficacy of the behavior change intervention is available. This is not considered a weakness of the research, as the focus was on students' engagement with the Design Thinking process.

Fig. 4. Selection of app interface designs – see video for full UX

7 Discussion

A key purpose of this paper was to examine how students responded to using the Design Thinking approach when creating a Behavior Change intervention app, and how perception of the role of a creative technology designer may be affected. Observing the students throughout the 13 weeks revealed a number of things:

Students were reluctant to engage with end users before they themselves had engaged with the given challenge in their role as designers. They wanted to create an artefact first and then get feedback, rather than explore with users what that artefact may be. This is in line with the lens of design as a profession, almost an engineering discipline, with a set of practical skills and rules to obey that can be applied to a given problem [7, 20]. Through this lens, design seeks to find specific solutions rather than develop ideas further or empathize with end users, and students were indeed well trained to follow this 'introvert' approach. The same became evident during the Ideation phase when many students had to be repeatedly reminded that it is not about finding solutions just yet – a problem also observed by Lugmayr et al. [14]. At the end of the course, the view of the role of designer appeared to have shifted however, as evidenced by several self-reflection reports and the quote already shown above.

Attendance was consistently high throughout the course duration when compared to other courses. This may have been due to the intense group-work nature of the course which may motivate students and may also provide some degree of peer pressure to attend. None of the students reported negative impacts of group work, however, and we would tentatively argue that the course program did indeed foster Situated Learning which according to Hung [8] can compel students to take part and ultimately learn more. Some lessons can be learnt regarding curriculum development for creative technology design courses:

Firstly, we believe that Design Thinking – or human-centered design in general – should be an integral part of the higher education curriculum for any design-oriented degree right from the start. Our perception was that by introducing this in the final year of study, we had to 'un-teach' some of the practices that students had come to take for granted, in particular the view of design as a linear process driven by the desire to manage it carefully, or what Howard et al. [7] call 'engineering design'. As soon as end users join the design process as co-creators, more uncertainty is introduced and a robust process such as the d.school 5-step approach used here is required to maintain manageability, for novices and experienced designers alike.

Secondly, students need to feel empowered and supported to go outside of the higher education environment to talk to potential end users. Providing a good set of method cards helps, as does a practice-run in order to refine interview skills and raise awareness of why observing and talking to end users is critical to the design process.

Thirdly, it is important to create a relaxed, non-judgmental atmosphere for all idea generating activities so that new and unusual ideas can emerge. This is not a new insight [16] but it is worth reminding of in an education system that is more often than not focused on analytical thinking, solution finding and rigid processes and schedules.

We conclude with the final reflections of a student on the Design Thinking course which encapsulates many of the aspects discussed above:

> *"My initial thoughts about the design thinking process were that it was perhaps a little bit over the top and unrealistic in the field of multimedia design. Having completed the course and witnessed my own journey through the process I began to look at it in a different light. ... I began to see how engaging with people can open your eyes to the way they think about the subject, rather than one's own preconceptions. ... It wasn't until we developed the 'How might we' topics at the 'Ideate' stage when I really began to see the value in the previous stages. It allowed us to identify specific problems and break up the challenge into manageable chunks. ... It would be interesting to see what outcome I would have arrived at had I not employed the design thinking process."*

References

1. Brown, T.: Design thinking. Harvard Bus. Rev. **86**(6), 84–95 (2008)
2. Brown, T., Wyatt, J.: Design thinking for social innovation. Stanford Soc. Innov. Rev. **8**(1), 29–35 (2010)

3. d.school: Design Thinking Bootcamp Bootleg (2013). http://dschool.stanford.edu/wp-content/uploads/2013/10/METHODCARDS-v3-slim.pdf
4. Design Council UK: Design Methods for developing services (2014). https://connect.innovateuk.org/web/3338201/service-design-methods
5. Dunne, D., Martin, R.: Design thinking and how it will change management education: an interview and discussion. Acad. Manage. Learn. Educ. **5**(4), 512–523 (2006)
6. Fogg, B.J.: A behavior model for persuasive design. In: Proceedings of the 4th International Conference on Persuasive Technology. ACM, Claremont (2009)
7. Howard, T., Culley, S., Dekoninck, E.: Describing the creative design process by the integration of engineering design and cognitive psychology literature. Des. Stud. **29**, 160–180 (2008)
8. Hung, D.: Situated cognition and problem-based learning: implications for learning and instruction with technology. J. Interact. Learn. Res. **13**(4), 393–415 (2002)
9. IDEO: Design Thinking for Educators, v2. (2013). http://www.designthinking foreducators.com/toolkit/
10. IDEO: Human-Centered Design Toolkit, 2nd edn. (2014). http://www.designkit.org/resou rces/1
11. Jean, J., Marcus, A.: The green machine. User Experience **8**(4), 20–29 (2009)
12. Kolb, D.A.: Experiential Learning: Experience as the Source of Learning and Development. Prentice Hall, Englewood Cliffs (1984)
13. Lave, J., Wenger, E.: Situated Learning. Cambridge University Press, Cambridge (1990)
14. Lugmayr, A., Jalonen, M., Zou, Y., Libin, L., Anzenhofer, S.: Design thinking in media management education - a practical hands-on approach. In: Proceedings of 4th Semantic Ambient Media Experience (SAME) Workshop in Conjunction with the 5th International Convergence on Communities and Technologies, Brisbane, Australia (2011)
15. Nielsen, J.: Iterative user interface design. IEEE Comput. **26**(11), 32–41 (1993)
16. Osborn, A.F.: Applied Imagination: Principles and Procedures of Creative Thinking. Scribner, New York (1953)
17. Piaget, J.: The Origins of Intelligence in Children. International Universities Press, New York (1952)
18. Polaine, A., Løvlie, L., Reason, B.: Service Design – From Insight to Implementation. Rosenfeld Media, Brooklyn New York (2013)
19. Rittel, H., Webber, M.: Dilemmas in a general theory of planning. Policy Sci. **4**, 155–179 (1973)
20. Sas, C.: Learning approaches for teaching interaction design, inventivity: teaching theory, design and innovation in HCI. In: Hvannberg, E.T. et al. (eds.) Proceedings of HCIEd 2006, Limerick, Ireland, pp. 53–59 (2006)
21. Stickdorn, M., Schneider, J.: This is Service Design Thinking. BIS, Amsterdam (2014)
22. Vargo, S.L., Lusch, R.F.: From goods to service(s): divergences and convergences of logics. Ind. Mark. Manage. **37**(3), 254–259 (2008)
23. Wendel, S.: Designing for Behavior Change. O'Reilly, Sebastopol (2013)
24. Withell, A., Heigh, N.: Developing design thinking expertise in higher education. In: 2nd International Conference for Design Education Researchers, Oslo, pp. 14–17, May 2013

HCI and the Community of Non-users

Michael Heidt[1]([✉]), Kalja Kanellopoulos[1], Linda Pfeiffer[2], and Paul Rosenthal[2]

[1] Research Training Group crossWorlds, Chemnitz University of Technology,
Reichenhainer Straße 70A, 09126 Chemnitz, Germany
michael.heidt@informatik.tu-chemnitz.de,
kalja.kanellopoulos@phil.tu-chemnitz.de
[2] Visual Computing Group, Chemnitz University of Technology,
Straße der Nationen 62, 09111 Chemnitz, Germany
{linda.pfeiffer,paul.rosenthal}@informatik.tu-chemnitz.de

Abstract. HCI's success as a discipline is based on its ability of dealing with the problems, desires, and requirements of technology users. Through its turn to user experience, the community was able to create products whose use is pleasant and exciting. There are, however, design contexts where the corresponding focus on fostering use might be in need of a complementing perspective.

During the last couple of years, the topic of technology *non-use* has appeared within the scope of HCI. Within this text, we will explore how these recent conceptualisations and analyses can be employed in order to turn non-use into a design resource. We do so by discussing them in the context of a concrete development project aimed at creating interactive technology for exhibition contexts.

Keywords: Non-use · HCI · Prototyping · Interdisciplinarity · Cultural informatics · Critical technical practice

1 Introduction

Recently, phenomena of non-use have received an increasing amount of attention from the HCI community [1–3]. These approaches typically focus on analysing, describing and problematising phenomena involving technology eschewal. Non-use is seen as a novel concept within the intellectual landscape of HCI, traditionally preoccupied with describing and designing for contexts of use. Consequently, existing approaches try to elucidate the complexity of reasons and behavioural dynamics underlying observed or anticipated patterns of non-use [4].

1.1 Designing for Non-use

Building on and extending these frameworks, we provide a discussion of how to employ non-use as a *design resource*. Our approach wants to build on the realisation that the implicit focus on technology use is not adequate in every design context. As an example, when creating an interactive museum guide, apart

A. Marcus (Ed.): DUXU 2015, Part I, LNCS 9186, pp. 44–52, 2015.
DOI: 10.1007/978-3-319-20886-2_5

from creating a pleasant user experience, it also is of paramount importance to create a device that users are willing to put away when engaging with actual exhibits. Otherwise, the rich experiential structure of the museum environment is eclipsed by attention consuming technological elements.

Our discussion bases itself on material semiotics as formulated by Bruno Latour. As explicated by Fuchsberger et al. [3], Latour's Actor-Network theory can be employed in order to provide concise descriptions of phenomena of non-use.

2 Conceptual Apparatus

2.1 Programs and Antiprograms

Latour's theory provides an elegant mode of description through the concept of an *antiprogram* [5]. The notion of programs and antiprograms as discussed by Fuchsberger et al. [3] provides the key element for conceptualising non-use as design goal. The framework is applied in order to pursue the following goal: Creating an ensemble of programs and antiprograms that engender use when desired and non-use otherwise. The strategy of individual technological elements is that of ultimately replacing itself with a non-technological node. This entails presence of adequate antiprograms targeted at prolonged technology use.

It has to be stressed how the simple juxtaposition of program and antiprogram provides for a relatively simple instance of translation. The 'fight' between two programs marks the simplest conceivable form of translation in the presence of multiple programs. In the future experiments with 'higher dimensional' program translation diagrams are planned.

3 (Non-)Use and HCI

Within the discussed conceptual frame, dynamic interplay between programs and antiprograms constitutes a consistent phenomenon. An analysis of a familiar scenario using the concepts outlined might thus serve to elucidate the approach.

3.1 Smartphones/Laptops

Smartphones accompany most of their users every day, intermittently being used and put away. Within the conceptual frame outlined, this dynamic has to be framed within the language of programs and antiprograms. The question thus becomes: How do smartphones do it? How do they allow us to put them away? The environment supplies the antiprograms. An antiprogram might be supplied by a leather case, designed to accommodate the phone.

We thus are left with two conflicting programs, the touchscreen's program of binding fingers as well as the case's program of containing the phone breaking the connection between touchscreen and skin. Both cannot be active at the same time.

An analogous case is that of a laptop computer and an accompanying bag.

The resulting dynamic is depicted in Fig. 1. Following Fuchsberger et al.'s approach, Latour's original mode of visual presentation [5] is adapted. The

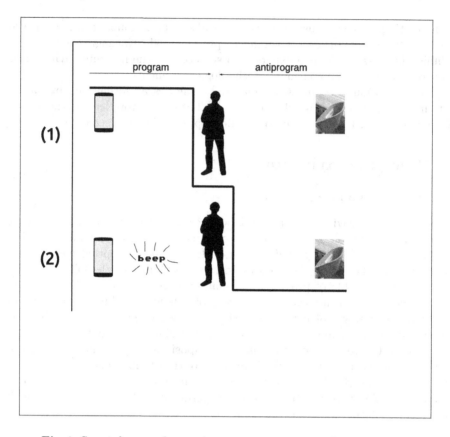

Fig. 1. Smartphone and smarphone-case - programs and antiprograms

analysis deals with a single user and the possible patterns of use and non use. In situation (1) the smartphone remains within its case, the antiprogram being more successful than the program. Adding an auditive signal to the smartphone's statement strengthens the program in a manner prompting the power dynamics within the controversy to shift (2). The dividing line consequently crosses the human body, turning the previous non-user into user.

In practice, this set of programs is rendered meaningful in the context of another program such as writing an article, sending a message to a physically distant person, reading the news.

Hence, what demands analysis is the interplay of programs and antiprograms within concrete situations of (non-)use. Within the examples provided, designed artefacts purposefully provided this dynamic, thus forming a system of artefact-bound programs.

3.2 Systematicity

The problem of systematicity is by no means new to the design discourse [6,7]. Integrative design, modularity [8,9] all point towards the importance of systemic approaches.

Foldable colanders, scabbards, collapsible batons all attest to the necessity of non-use. Within the realm of digital artefacts however, the discussion appears to remain in a nascent stage. Here the problem poses itself differently - achieving a problem that draws the attention from users through the space, causing them to disengage from digital devices.

3.3   Interactive Installation

Following discussion of introductory scenarios, a more complex example is analysed. The interactive installation PRMD was developed in order to explore the relationship between interactive narrative, user-generated content and biographical content [10]. It was developed using a blend of design and social research methodologies [11,12], gradually becoming part of a system of interactive objects aimed at exhibition spaces [13]. The wider project context provides inspiration in the form of artefact designs [14] as well as design knowledge [15,16].

The installation consists of a projection screen, situated next to an interactive zone tracked via motion sensors. The interaction area is marked by red carpets, thereby directing users' movements. Interaction dynamics proved to be based on the interplay between active users of the artefact and what was perceived as an audience, watching users perform on the stage. Hence, in order to sustain its mode of operation, the artefact has to produce performers as well as bystanders. An analysis of the artefact is outlined in (Fig. 2).

The analysis demonstrates a crucial aspect: Design of interactive artefacts is not solely about strengthening their programs. While shiny, 'irresistible' artefacts will unquestionably bind people's attention, they might fail at fitting into the envisaged situational assembly.

Of course a mere analysis according to Latour's AND dimension will proof to be inadequate. It is not a mere linear sequence of symbols that substantiates the program. Their relative position also matters, that what might be called grammar.

More importantly, program and antiprogram have to relate in a specific way in order to produce the desired effects. The artefact has to partition the set of human bodies within the exhibition space into a pair of users, an audience, and a set of non-users. Failing to do so causes the artefact's interaction logic to fail.

Additionally, non-use does not constitute a uniform phenomenon. While selective strengthening of antiprograms is also an important design goal, this must not occur indiscriminately. For the artefact to act like a stage, it has to produce an audience.

In any case, Latour's original analysis followed a specific strategic-epistemological goal. Thus, in various respects our analysis has left the frame of the original analysis. This might indeed be congruent with the basic tenets of Latour's position: Energy has to be spent while translating the theory into a new context of application. This translation remains only partially faithful to the theory, losing some aspects, while adding others.

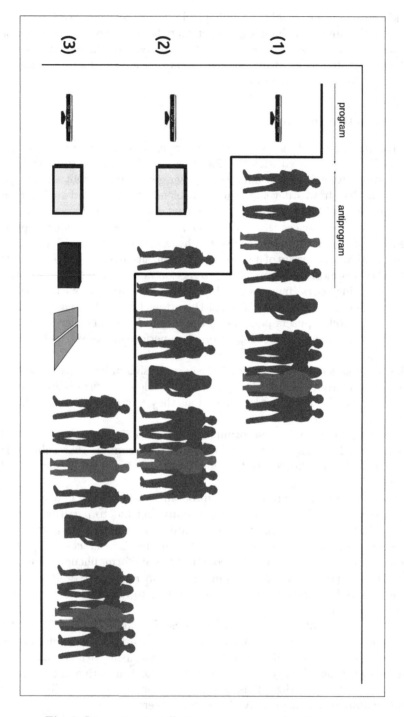

Fig. 2. Interactive installation - programs and antiprograms

4 Epistemological Relations

Latour's theory has undergone quite a few epistemological shifts during its development [17,18]. Within Fuchsberger et al.'s text, these are juxtaposed, possibly implying that they remain inconsequential to discussion within HCI. However, Latour's shifts might not be limited to a mere substitution of terminology. In any case, when employing his theories as a communicative device within interdisciplinary contexts, discussion of epistemological and theoretical foundations seems inevitable. The proposed method of appropriation is a reflective one. While it might be most productive to allow for gracious glossing over [16] of captious terminological distinctions, scholars should remain aware of underlying epistemological contradictions.

Within the cases discussed the project context demanded a certain amount of reflexivity. As social researchers were well versed in Latour's theories, the ingenuous modes of theorising employed by computer professionals had to be amended. Especially valuable for the discussion process were the perspectives of Mayring and Metcalfe.

Metcalfe argues for the possibility of what he calls the 'Ironist View' [19]. The belief that conflicting perspectives can be valid at the same time.

Mayring on the other hand, argues for the need of establishing syntheses [20].

Within both positions, acknowledging the respective implications and limitations of knowledge claims is key.

In effect, a more reflective claim might be more appropriate. Possibly the positions outlined constitute a 'productive misreading' or a disloyal appropriation of Latour's positions. This need not lead to fatal problems as long as researchers remain aware of the phenomenon. Consequently, future claims might be framed in a way designating them as theory-methods packages inspired by (among others) Latour's theories.

In a similar vein, the notion of the *boundary object* might be employed [21]. However, the scope of the concept of boundary objects might itself have its limits [22]. Any negotiation of the status of boundary objects has to decide if it wants to extend or limit the concept of boundary object in relation to the phenomena at hand.

5 Related Work

A large quantity of non-use discourse deals with the topic of social media. Exemplary analyses explore the reasons for not using platforms such as Facebook [23,24]. The disappearance of technology has been a central topic within the project of 'Ubiquitous Computing' [25,26]. Here the focus is not on non-use as such, instead the degree of attention consumed by technology is lowered. Technology eventually becomes an invisible, tacit aspect of human life.

6 Discussion

Scenario Writing. The implicit focus on use translates itself into everyday design activities such as scenario writing. Usually, stories focus on use of a specific artefact. The aspect how individuals start their non-use of a designed thing receives a far more modest amount of attention.

When dealing with culturally complex design projects this focus might prove to be thoroughly unhelpful. If only a fraction of people actually use a specific product, telling the story from the perspective of the community of non-users becomes essential.

Conflicts of interest certainly can arise. Putting non-users at a disadvantage can further adoption of a particular product or service. In a case like that the non-users perspective gains even more importance: Developers try to render it as miserable as possible.

Design for Non-use in Complex Environments. Within the museum a multitude of artefacts is present at once, providing for a countless array of programs and antiprograms. Few dedicated 'sheaths' are available, non-use of one artefact blends in with use of another.

Usually, a designer does only control a small fraction of the environment. Consequently, she must be careful to take existing programs into account when designing those parts she *has* control over. In effect, a system of artefacts acts as facilitator and filter, increasing the likelihood of certain patterns, lowering that of others.

The janiform role of complexity in interaction has been acknowledged in the design community [27]. As is so often the case with design problems, their nature prohibits specification of ready-made solutions or uniform methodologies.

Limitations. The perspective remains inherently artefact centric. Derthik [28] points to this problematic in her analysis of facebook non-users. The text discusses how their analysis as non-users prohibits an adequate description of their motivations.

Implications for User-Experience. User Experience also extends into the realm of non-use. This has long been acknowledged on the level of design, by creating artefacts that continue to provide value while not being used. E.g. a notebook that looks beautiful while sitting in a shelf.

Following Fuchsberger et al., one could refer to the *Non-User-Experience* as essential design concern. In a similar vein, the programme of slow-technology [29] is geared towards unobtrusive artefacts. Drawing on these positions one can envision an environment where artefacts do not compete for potential user's attention, instead lending themselves to programmes such as aesthetic education.

After providing the analysis of non-use as a design resource, we proceed by discussing some of the wider implications of the phenomenon of non-use.

Interdisciplinarity. The perspective of non-use carries implications for the development context of digital artefacts as well. Colleagues from other disciplines can be construed as non-users of disciplinary artefacts: The social scientist as IDE non-user, the programmer as ethnography non-user. The dimension of non-use at work in these cases are more likely to be categorised as deliberate long term non-use.

Responsibility/Conclusion. Whatever we are designing, the concerns of non-users will almost always outweigh those of users. This is especially true in the context of sustainability. When creating genetically modified plants, the implications for non-users might be much more complex and much more severe than for product developers and users. As Fuchsberger et al. point out [3], the phenomenon of involuntary non-use deserves attention in its own right.

Against this backdrop, the question of transforming non-use into a positive design resource gains a new level of importance. The described practice of program/antiprogram diagramming might provide a first step into this direction. It thus seeks to align itself with future efforts of makers and scholars seeking to tap into the long neglected resources of non-use.

References

1. Baumer, E.P., Adams, P., Khovanskaya, V.D., Liao, T.C., Smith, M.E., Schwanda Sosik, V., Williams, K.: Limiting, leaving, and (re)lapsing: an exploration of facebook non-use practices and experiences. In: Proceedings of the SIGCHI Conference on Human Factors in Computing Systems, CHI 2013, pp. 3257–3266. ACM, New York (2013)
2. Baumer, E.P., Ames, M.G., Brubaker, J.R., Burrell, J., Dourish, P.: Refusing, limiting, departing: why we should study technology non-use. In: CHI 2014 Extended Abstracts on Human Factors in Computing Systems, CHI EA 2014, pp. 65–68. ACM, New York (2014)
3. Fuchsberger, V., Murer, M., Tscheligi, M.: Human-computer non-interaction: the activity of non-use. In: Proceedings of the 2014 Companion Publication on Designing Interactive Systems, DIS Companion 2014, pp. 57–60. ACM, New York (2014)
4. Satchell, C., Dourish, P.: Beyond the user: use and non-use in HCI. In: Proceedings of the 21st Annual Conference of the Australian Computer-Human Interaction Special Interest Group: Design: Open 24/7, OZCHI 2009, pp. 9–16. ACM, New York (2009)
5. Latour, B.: Technology is society made durable. Sociol. Rev. **38**(S1), 103–131 (1990)
6. Alexander, C.: Notes on the Synthesis of Form. Harvard University Press, Cambridge (1964)
7. Alexander, C., Ishikawa, S., Silverstein, M.: A Pattern Language: Towns, Buildings, Construction (Center for Environmental Structure Series). Oxford University Press, New York (1978)
8. Sosa, M.E., Eppinger, S.D., Rowles, C.M.: Designing modular and integrative systems. In: ASME Design Engineering Technical Conference Proceedings, DETC00/DTM, vol. 14571 (2000)
9. Sosa, M.E., Eppinger, S.D., Rowles, C.M.: Identifying modular and integrative systems and their impact on design team interactions. J. Mech. Design **125**(2), 240–252 (2003)
10. Heidt, M., Pfeiffer, L., Berger, A., Rosenthal, P.: PRMD. In: Mensch and Computer 2014 - Workshopband, pp. 45–48. De Gruyter Oldenbourg (2014)
11. Heidt, M.: Examining interdisciplinary prototyping in the context of cultural communication. In: Marcus, A. (ed.) DUXU 2013, Part II. LNCS, vol. 8013, pp. 54–61. Springer, Heidelberg (2013)

12. Heidt, M., Kanellopoulos, K., Pfeiffer, L., Rosenthal, P.: Diverse ecologies – interdisciplinary development for cultural education. In: Kotzé, P., Marsden, G., Lindgaard, G., Wesson, J., Winckler, M. (eds.) INTERACT 2013, Part IV. LNCS, vol. 8120, pp. 539–546. Springer, Heidelberg (2013)

13. Wuttke, M., Heidt, M.: Beyond presentation - employing proactive intelligent agents as social catalysts. In: Kurosu, M. (ed.) HCI 2014, Part II. LNCS, vol. 8511, pp. 182–190. Springer, Heidelberg (2014)

14. Storz, M., Kanellopoulos, K., Fraas, C., Eibl, M.: ComforTable: a tabletop for relaxed and playful interactions in museums. In: Proceedings of the Ninth ACM International Conference on Interactive Tabletops and Surfaces, ITS 2014, pp. 447–450. ACM, New York (2014)

15. Berger, A., Heidt, M., Eibl, M.: Towards a vocabulary of prototypes in interaction design – a criticism of current practice. In: Marcus, A. (ed.) DUXU 2014, Part I. LNCS, vol. 8517, pp. 25–32. Springer, Heidelberg (2014)

16. Berger, A., Heidt, M., Eibl, M.: Conduplicated symmetries: renegotiating the material basis of prototype research. In: Chakrabarti, A. (ed.) ICoRD 2015 Research into Design Across Boundaries. Number 34 in Smart Innovation, Systems and Technologies, vol. 1, pp. 71–78. Springer, India (2015)

17. Latour, B.: Coming out as a philosopher. Soc. Stud. Sci. **40**(4), 599–608 (2010)

18. Latour, B.: On recalling ANT. In: Law, J., Hassard, J. (eds.) Actor Network Theory and After, pp. 15–25. Blackwell, Oxford (1999)

19. Metcalfe, M.: Generalisation: learning across epistemologies. Forum Qual. Sozialforschung/Forum Qual. Soc. Res. **6**(1), 27 (2005)

20. Mayring, P.: On generalization in qualitatively oriented research. Forum Qual. Sozialforschung/Forum: Qual. Soc. Res. **8**(3), 1–8 (2007)

21. Star, S.L., Griesemer, J.R.: Institutional ecology, 'Translations' and boundary objects: amateurs and professionals in Berkeley's museum of vertebrate Zoology, 1907–39. Soc. Stud. Sci. **19**(3), 387–420 (1989)

22. Star, S.L.: This is not a boundary object: reflections on the origin of a concept. Sci. Technol. Hum. Values **35**(5), 601–617 (2010)

23. Wyatt, S.: Non-users also matter: the construction of users and non-users of the internet. In: Oudshoorn, N., Pinch, T.J. (eds.) How Users Matter: The Co-construction of Users and Technologies, Inside Technology, pp. 67–79. MIT Press, Cambridge (2003)

24. Selwyn, N.: Apart from technology: understanding people's non-use of information and communication technologies in everyday life. Technol. Soc. **25**(1), 99–116 (2003)

25. Weiser, M.: Some computer science issues in ubiquitous computing. Commun. ACM **36**(7), 75–84 (1993)

26. Weiser, M.: The computer for the 21st century. SIGMOBILE Mob. Comput. Commun. Rev. **3**(3), 3–11 (1999)

27. Janlert, L.E., Stolterman, E.: Complex interaction. ACM Trans. Comput.-Hum. Interact. **17**(2), 8:1–8:32 (2008)

28. Derthick, K.: Exploring meditation and technology to problematize the use-or-non-use binary. In: Refusing, Limiting, Departing - Workshop @CHI 2014 (2014)

29. Hallnäs, L., Redström, J.: Slow technology - designing for reflection. Pers. Ubiquit. Comput. **5**(3), 201–212 (2001)

The Conflict Resolution in Product Experience Design Based on Evaporating Cloud of the Theory of Constraints

Lu Jin[✉]

JD.COM, Interaction Designer, Shanghai China
beforux@126.com

Abstract. In design practice, we will meet with various target conflict and challenges. On most of the times, compromising is usually used to solve the conflict. However, in this paper we are trying to solve it by making win-win design solution other than making compromise. This can help satisfy different needs and still target to have outstanding user experience. In order to make no compromise design solution, a new thinking process will be introduced—the evaporating cloud of the theory of constraint to resolve the conflict during the design practice. The results obtained in this paper include a new approach to thinking method in design practice. The impacts of our obtained results are reducing the prejudice towards compromise in design practice and make people believe win-win solution existing on the complicated design practice. This thinking method can also be permeated into a wide range of detail design practice.

Keywords: Design thinking · Evaporating cloud · Conflict resolution · Product experience design

1 Introduction

In design field, since design is a problem solving activity, so conflict cannot be avoided during the design practice. Compromise is usually used to solve it. In real design practice, these compromise during the design process leads to unsatisfactory design results which is not consistence with what designers plan at the starting point. The user experience of products will be reduced during the continuous compromise.

In Juhani's law, the compromise will always be more expensive than either of the suggestions it is compromising. And from the literature review, few studies have be made on how to solve conflict in product experience design.

Thus, in this paper we are trying to solve it by making win-win design solution other than making compromise. This can help satisfy different needs and still target to have outstanding user experience.

In this paper, an analysis of this situation will be stated and in order to resolve it, our design process and a new thinking method will be introduced. It is the evaporating cloud of the theory of constraint (TOC)—a thinking method that commonly used in business management that will be employed to resolve the conflict during the design practice.

© Springer International Publishing Switzerland 2015
A. Marcus (Ed.): DUXU 2015, Part I, LNCS 9186, pp. 53–62, 2015.
DOI: 10.1007/978-3-319-20886-2_6

The structure of the paper is as below:

First, an analysis of conflict situation in design field will be made and we will have a discussion on why the compromise will reduce the product user experience.

Then we will conduct a survey on different elements of the measurement of user experience. In the discussion, it's needed to differentiate the various measurement elements based on various products. In this paper, the sample for new thinking method of real project will be based on web-based product, so here we focus on clarifying the elements of the measurement of experience on web-based product. We will make analysis towards different metrics of user experience and find the one most suitable for web-based product.

After that, there will be a brief introduction of the theory of constraint (TOC) will be made and especially one of its thinking process—the evaporating cloud used in this paper to solve design conflict. The Evaporating Cloud (EC) is a logical diagram representing a problem that has no obvious satisfactory solution.

Finally, we will combine the evaporating cloud with the user experience metrics [11, 17] and set a real project to see to what extent it can solve the design conflict [1, 2, 7, 8, 13, 16]. A real project is a statement of this design process and conflict solution.

2 Background

2.1 Conflict Exists in Design Practice

According to definition in dictionary, conflict means an open clash between things, which can be two opposing groups (or individuals); a state of opposition between persons or ideas or interests; an incompatibility of dates or events; a disagreement or argument about something important. Conflict exists on everywhere. There has been a large amount of research concerning the resolution of conflict that occur between individuals or groups of individuals in contexts such as business, jurisprudence, international relations, and so on.

Since design is a problem solving activity, we cannot avoid conflict during the design practice. The complication and diversity of problem will definitely lead to conflict. Also, design activity is usually a cooperation one [9] with different kinds of people, the participants have different background which leads to different perspectives (e.g. different goals, different ways of achieving similar goals, etc), they will occasionally come into conflict concerning some aspect of the design.

2.2 The Compromise is not a Wise Way to Solve Design Conflict

Compromise means a middle way between two extremes in dictionary. It is a doctrine of the mean which means it never meet each side's needs. To some extent, design process has been restricted considering the money and time cost during some real product development process. These limitation will cause designers choose compromise resolution towards conflict. Sometimes, it is ones who do not figure out a good conflict solution and believe that compromise is a wise way to solve the conflict problem. Sometimes, the decision made during the conflict mainly depends on current situation. When we are in the progress, we rarely think from an integrated point of view, resulting in shallow decision or sometimes consensus by sacrificing user experience, thus causing the final product not in accordance with our previous expectation. Thus, for many situation, the results of product will never meet each side's expectation with unfriendly user experience.

2.3 Win-Win Solution

Conflict resolution plays a central role in making a satisfactory design and making win-win solution [10] is more better than consensus used for working out an agreement during design conflict resolution. Some authors have made a research on how to solve conflict in design practice like Mark Klein [3, 4, 6] - a research on describes the conflict resolution model and provides examples of its operation from an implemented cooperative design system. From the literature review, few studies have be made on how to solve conflict in product experience design. In this paper, design practice on making win-win solution towards conflict will be introduced.

3   Theoretical Background

3.1 The Evaporating Cloud of the Theory of Constraints

Literature Review on the Theory of Constraints and Its Thinking Processes. The theory of constraints (TOC) [5, 15] has been widely known as a management philosophy coined by Goldratt (1990) that aims to initiate and implement breakthrough improvement through focusing on a constraint that prevents a system from achieving a higher level of performance. Goldratt and Cox (1992) define a constraint as any element or factor that limits the system from doing more of what it was designed to accomplish.

According to Goldratt [14] (1990), in order to deal with constraints, three generic decisions need to be made. (1) Decide what to change; (2) Decide what to change to; (3) Decide how to cause the change. These three provide the framework for what's called the TOC Thinking Processes, a suite of logic trees that provide a roadmap for change. They guide the user through the decision making process of problem structuring, problem identification, solution building, identification of barriers to be overcome, and implementation of the solution.

The Thinking Processes comprise a suite of five logic diagrams (four trees and a "cloud") and a set of logic rules. The five logic tools are: current reality tree (CRT), The Evaporating Cloud (EC), future reality tree (FRT), prerequisite tree (PRT), and transition tree (TT). The development of the TOC and accounts of its application have been existed for many years. Rahman (1998) reviews the TOC approach on manufacturing firms. Siha (1999) applies the TOC approach to addressing problems in different types of service organizations. Beyond business firms, Klein and Debruine (1995) and Dettmer (1998) used the TOC thinking processes to identify core problems in public policies. Womack and Flowers (1999) applied the TOC approach to the healthcare system to improve its performance [19].

The Evaporating Cloud. The Evaporating Cloud (EC) [18] - also referred to in the literature as "the cloud", or as a "conflict resolution diagram" - is a logical diagram representing a problem that has no obvious satisfactory solution. The EC was designed to address conflict or dilemma situations (trade-off situations where there is no acceptable compromise) by diagramming the logic behind the conflict and methodically examining the assumptions behind the logic.

The EC has a set format with five boxes, labelled A, B, C, D, D', that are usually laid out as follows:

The boxes represent two opposing wants that represent the conflict (D, D'), the needs that each want is trying to satisfy (B, C), and a common goal (A) that both needs are trying to fulfill. The lines or arrows connecting the nodes represent the rationale or causal assumptions that are used to link the nodes. Underlying each of the arrows in the EC [20] is one or more assumptions explaining the conditions under which the relationship between two entities in the cloud is valid. Assumptions underlying arrow C–D' in Fig. 1 explain why D' is a necessary condition in order for the need C to be met. In the event that a necessary assumption under arrow C–D' can be rendered invalid, D' will no longer be a necessary condition for achieving need C. By removing D' as a necessary condition for C, the conflict between D and D' is eliminated.

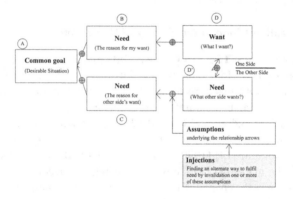

Fig. 1. The generic structure of an evaporating cloud diagram

In the EC, assumptions are statements about reality that are accepted as true even if the statement is untested. One way to invalidate an assumption is thus to provide evidence that the assumption is not valid, that is, that the entity at the base of the arrow is not actually necessary in order to have the entity at the head of the arrow. When the assumption is valid, another approach is to come up with an action or change in conditions (referred to as an injection) that will make the assumption invalid. When the relation between A–B or A–C is broken, D or D' is no longer a reasonable action.

The general process for applying an EC to problem solving is described by Cohen (2010) as follows:

(a) Identify the type of problem (there are variations in the way the diagrams are constructed for different types of problems.)
(b) Write a storyline of this problem in a factual, objective way, even if the problem causes an emotional upset.
(c) Build the Cloud.

(d) Check the logical statements of the Cloud and make necessary corrections and upgrades.
(e) Surface the assumptions behind the logical connections to find the one that is supporting the conflict.
(f) Construct your solution and check it for win-win.

Communicate the solution to the people involved in dealing with the problem.

Goldratt claims that each of the logical connections in the EC represent an (often hidden) assumption. One of the most basic fundamentals of logic is that behind any logical connection there is an assumption. The way to break conflict is to break these assumption existing on the logical connections. The end result of this process of analyzing the cloud should be at least one feasible injection that invalidates an assumption and breaks an arrow between any two entities in the cloud (Goldratt 1990).

Some scholars have demonstrated the EC application. Gupta et al. (2011) demonstrated that the evaporating cloud incorporates well-accepted principles of achieving win–win solutions, such as separating the people from the problem, focusing on needs but not on positions, and helping identify the assumptions blocking win–win solutions (Fisher and Ury 1982).

3.2   The Experience Design Target of Web-Based Product

Design nowadays is not only about designing the product itself, but also about dealing with the relationship between user and product. Designers need to demystify and classify the specific design goals of product experience. These measurement on experience can help design better user experience during the process and make wise decision towards conflict. Product experience goals should be set on the first step towards product development, thus leading product progress [12] in the right ways and driving product decisions.

In this paper, the real project we employed is based on web-based product, so here we will focus on clarifying the measurement elements of experience on web-based product. Owing to the rapid development of internet, there will be more products being deployed on the web which boardens the vision for measurement of experience on a large scale.

Literature Review. Researchers have proposed many different dimensions towards experience measurement. Gehrke and Turban (1999) identified five major categories of factors that ought to be considered while designing web sites for business: page loading, content, navigation efficiency, security, and a consumer/marketing focus [21]. These factors only focus on website for business. The most commonly used large-scale metrics are focused on business or technical aspects of a product, and they (or similar variations) are widely used by many organizations to track overall product health. We call these PULSE metrics: Page views, Uptime, Latency, Seven-day active users (i.e. the number of unique users who used the product at least once in the last week), and Earnings. The PULSE has its limitation for use. For the page views measurement, it is suitable for business website but not applicant to backend system .The Microsoft Usability Guidelines (MUG) are providing a comprehensive basis for the heuristic evaluation of Web sites, the Microsoft Usability Guidelines are organized around five major categories:

content, ease of use, promotion, made-for-the-medium, and emotion. These categories are expected to cover the range of usability-related aspects of a Web site. The MUG provide a comprehensive range of categories and subcategory, it is a standard web analytics metrics may be too generic to apply to a particular product goal or research question. For some small system, we do not need to make such more measurement. Instead, some key measurement and reduce the experience goals to some specific and clear target could be made and thus leads to swift product development.

The Google HEART METRICS. Google has introduced practical process of HEART framework for user-centered metrics, as well as a process for mapping product goals to metrics. It can help product teams make decisions.

HEART METRICS is created by Google Research based on the shortcomings in PULSE, the framework of HEART is: Happiness, Engagement, Adoption, Retention, and Task success.

Happiness. We use the term "Happiness" to describe metrics that are attitudinal in nature. These relate to subjective aspects of user experience, like satisfaction, visual appeal, likelihood to recommend, and perceived ease of use. Engagement is the user's level of involvement with a product; in the metrics context, the term is normally used to refer to behavioral proxies such as the frequency, intensity, or depth of interaction over some time period. "Adoption and Retention" metrics can be used to provide stronger insight into counts of the number of unique users in a given time period (e.g. seven-day active users), addressing the problem of distinguishing new users from existing users. "Task Success" category encompasses several traditional behavioral metrics of user experience, such as efficiency (e.g. time to complete a task), effectiveness (e.g. percent of tasks completed), and error rate. The HEART METRICS,simple and clear, has achieved well progress during the google product development. But as the author said in the paper, It is not always appropriate to employ metrics from every category, but referring to the framework helps to make an explicit decision about including or excluding a particular category.

3.3 Our Design Process

- **Research.** We will make research on the project background, such as project goals, user need, project resource. After that, competitive analysis will be employed to explore our vision towards this new project.
- **Define Experience goals.** When all of the research is completed, the experience goals will come to our design aspect. Our experience goals only focus on two or three goals since it is impossible to focus on too many things at one time based on some research findings.
- **Collect User Needs and Discuss Information Architecture.** In this process, we will meet some conflict during the decision-making. So we employed the new thinking method towards this decision-making process- The evaporating cloud from TOC which is used to clarify the conflict and resolve it on the company management.
- **Make Detail Page Design.** The design process mainly complies with the experience goals we made before.

From the four steps above, we can finish a project as we expected. Below we employ a real project to discuss how we activate our development progress and apply the evaporating cloud thinking method.

4   Application Evaporating Cloud to Conflict Resolution in Design Process

This real project is a web-based software that aims at making communication with App user, the APP operator can send messages to their end App user through this software.

The real design process is stated as below:

4.1   Research

We will make research on the project background, such as project goals, user need, and project resource. After we collect enough information and make competitive analysis, design target will be made on what problem this software aims to solve.

4.2   Define Product Experience Goals

Combing the research and Google HEART METRICS, we set two objective as targets of this product experience: Happiness and Task Success and each one has its further detail targets as below:

Happiness

- Simple: this product focus on user action, so we want make the user interface simple to highlight the content.

Task Success

- Efficiency: user can make switch between business operations effectively and swiftly.
- Clear: clear scenario enables user to clearly know where he is and where to go.

4.3   Collect User Needs and Discuss Information Architecture

During this process, we use the new method of evaporating cloud to solve our conflict. In order to clarify the application of new method, I only capture part of design process. Let us see the progress below.

On this stage, we need to build the information architecture with the information we collected before and experience target we defined before.

We can see here (Fig. 2 show example), in order to satisfy the target of efficiency, we make design solution—swiftly operation between the interfaces. In order to satisfy the target of clearity, we make design solution—clearly classified navigation structure. There is a conflict between to the two wants—swiftly operation between interface and clearly classified navigation structure. We cannot satisfy both because the first wants mainly means it needs a flat navigation structure which has a conflict with the clearly classified navigation structure. So we can use the EC cloud logic to solve this conflict.

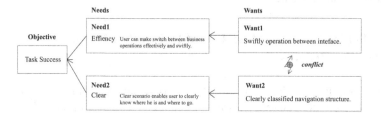

Fig. 2. The logic of real design thinking

For clearly statement, I use number to mark them. They will be Objective, Need1, Need 2, Want 1, Want 2. (Fig. 3 show example).

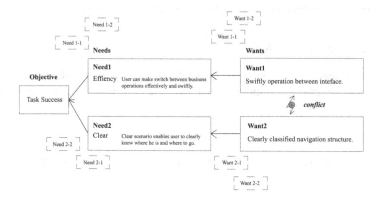

Fig. 3. The logic of real design thinking

- Think the logic between want 1 and need 1, is there any other interpretation of wants for need1, has it got want1–1, want 1–2.
- Likewise, Think the logic between want 2 and need 2, is there any other interpretation of wants for need 2, has it got other wants based on need 2, we can call it—want 2–1, want 2–2.
- After we check the two, we also need to check the logic between Need1 to Objective and Need 2 to Objective. Does it anything else that can satisfy the objective, we can called it —Need1–1, Need1–2, Need 2–1, Need 2–2, etc.
- After we check all, we can make a win-win solution to remove conflict between want1 and want 2. In this case, we find that efficiency can also means the flow that conform with user operation and it does not conflict with clearly classified navigation structure. It will be a navigation design that conform to user operation flow as well as classified navigation structure. Thus, it perfectly solved the conflict.

- Then we will use the three targets and its action wants to direct information architecture design.

From the real example, the core thinking method of evaporating cloud is to break the logic of interpretation between two things and question the link logic in order to find the third way to remove the conflict. That is how we use the evaporating cloud to solve the conflict and make win-win solution. This thinking method teaches us not to think from one-way facet. You need to question the logic between the two reasonable links and make design solution towards core target.

5 Conclusion and Future Direction

The findings obtained in this paper include a new approach thinking method and process in design practice. Also in the project development, many unexpected conflicts cannot be avoided during the progress. We rarely think from an integrated point of view and question the logic of our interpretation, resulting in shallow decision or sometimes consensus by sacrificing user experience. This thinking method which always keep the core target builds a broadly new vision towards our previous thinking one. An expectable product results can be made under such vision.

The impacts of our obtained results are reducing the prejudice towards compromise in design practice other than win-win solution existing on the complicated design practice. The thinking method of evaporating cloud which question the logic of interpretation and make a try to break it in order to remove the conflict and make win-win solution can be used into a wide range of detail design.

References

1. Simatupang, T.M., Wright, A.C., Sridharan, R.: Applying the theory of constraints to supply chain collaboration. Supply Chain Manage. Int. J. **9**(1), 57–70 (2004)
2. Rand, G.K.: Critical chain: the theory of constraints applied to project management. Int. J. Proj. Manage. **18**(3), 173–177 (2000)
3. Klein, M., Lu, S.C.Y.: Conflict resolution in cooperative design. Artif. Intell. Eng. **4**(4), 168–180 (1989)
4. Klein, M.: Supporting conflict resolution in cooperative design systems. IEEE Trans. Syst. Man Cybern. **21**(6), 1379–1390 (1991)
5. Burton-Houle, T.: The theory of constraints and its thinking processes (2001). https://www.goldratt.com
6. Klein, M.: Supporting conflict resolution in cooperative design systems. IEEE Trans. Syst. Man Cybern. **21**(6), 1379–1390 (1991)
7. Lin, Z.: Using TOC thinking process tools to improve safety performance software engineering, 2009. In: WRI World Congress on WCSE 2009, vol. 3, pp. 13–17. IEEE (2009)
8. Andersen, S., Gupta, M., Gupta, A.: A managerial decision-making web app: Goldratt's evaporating cloud. Int. J. Prod. Res. **51**(8), 2505–2517 (2013)
9. Lu, S.C.Y., Cai, J., Burkett, W., et al.: A methodology for collaborative design process and conflict analysis. CIRP Ann. Manufact. Technol. **49**(1), 69–73 (2000)

10. Dettmer, H.W.: The conflict resolution diagram: creating win-win solutions: with this tool, there are no losers. Qual. Prog. **32**(3), 41–47 (1999)
11. Rodden, K., Hutchinson, H., Fu, X.: Measuring the user experience on a large scale: user-centered metrics for web applications. In: Proceedings of the SIGCHI Conference on Human Factors in Computing Systems, pp. 2395–2398. ACM (2010)
12. Vredenburg, K., Mao, J.Y., Smith, P.W., et al.: A survey of user-centered design practice. In: Proceedings of the SIGCHI Conference on Human Factors in Computing Systems, pp. 471–478. ACM (2002)
13. Simatupang, T.M., Wright, A.C., Sridharan, R.: Applying the theory of constraints to supply chain collaboration. Supply Chain Manage. Int. J. **9**(1), 57–70 (2004)
14. Goldratt, E.M.: Theory of constraints. North River, Croton-on-Hudson (1990)
15. Burton-Houle, T.: The theory of constraints and its thinking processes (2001). https://www.goldratt.com
16. Simatupang, T.M., Wright, A.C., Sridharan, R.: Applying the theory of constraints to supply chain collaboration. Supply Chain Manage. Int. J. **9**(1), 57–70 (2004)
17. Agarwal, R., Venkatesh, V.: Assessing a firm's web presence: a heuristic evaluation procedure for the measurement of usability. Inf. Syst. Res. **13**(2), 168–186 (2002)
18. Wiki Information. http://en.wikipedia.org/wiki/Evaporating_Cloud
19. Simatupang, T.M., Wright, A.C., Sridharan, R.: Applying the theory of constraints to supply chain collaboration. Supply Chain Manage. Int. J. **9**(1), 57–70 (2004)
20. Andersen, S., Gupta, M., Gupta, A.: A managerial decision-making web app: Goldratt's evaporating cloud. Int. J. Prod. Res. **51**(8), 2505–2517 (2013)
21. Agarwal, R., Venkatesh, V.: Assessing a firm's web presence: a heuristic evaluation procedure for the measurement of usability. Inf. Syst. Res. **13**(2), 168–186 (2002)

How to Design an User Interface Based on Gestures?

Anna C.S. Medeiros[1]([⊠]), Tatiana A. Tavares[2],
and Iguatemi E. da Fonseca[1]

[1] Centro de Informática, Universidade Federal da Paraíba, João Pessoa, Brazil
linnamedeiros@gmail.com, iguatemi@ci.ufpb.br
[2] Laboratório de Aplicações de Vídeo Digital (LAVID), Centro de Informática,
Universidade Federal da Paraíba, João Pessoa, Brazil
tatiana@lavid.ufpb.br

Abstract. The use of our body language to communicate with computer systems is an increasingly possible and applicable feature in the real world. This fact is intensified by the evolution of gesture recognition based commercial solutions. A gesture interface complements or replaces navigation in a conventional interface, it is up to each developer to choose the most appropriate option for their application. When opting for gesture usage, the gestures will be responsible to activate the systems functions. This work presents a gesture development process that can be used to aid the construction of gesture interfaces. The process here described, should help interface designers to incorporate gesture-based natural interaction into their applications in a more systematic way. To illustrate the Process, gestures for the actions "Select", "Rotate", "Translate", "Scale" and "Stop" were developed.

Keywords: Gestures · Process · Gesture interface · Natural interaction

1 Introduction

During the study and research on ways of interaction between humans and electronic devices, using their body as a means, focus of Natural Interaction (NI) study, it was found that there are several possibilities of interaction: through voice commands, haptic devices, olfaction, locomotion, gestures or detection and identification of human body parts such as face, hand, thumb, eye retina [1].

Human-Computer interaction (HCI) studies the communication between people e computational systems, it is situated in the intersection between Behavioral Sciences, Social Sciences and Computational and Information Sciences, involving all aspects related to the interaction between users and systems [2]. The research on HCI stimulated to investigate how to use NI as an alternative to the conventional keyboard and mouse complex, with the intention to make the interaction more simple and intuitive.

Technology is used daily by almost everyone, software solutions are used to perform lots of tasks, therefore simplicity becomes necessary to ease interaction with systems and leads to an easier and more sustainable relationship with the media and technology [3].

© Springer International Publishing Switzerland 2015
A. Marcus (Ed.): DUXU 2015, Part I, LNCS 9186, pp. 63–74, 2015.
DOI: 10.1007/978-3-319-20886-2_7

With the crescent research in NI equipment, such as Kinect (launched in 2010) and Leap Motion (launched in 2013), accuracy in movement detection is improving, thus providing more possibilities in the use of such hardwares. Older NI equipment such as Kinect, have very affordable prices now, which can create another range of possibilities, for example, its use in public schools.

There are studies that focus on perceptual technology and software development, disregarding elements relative to the determination of gestures, for example: [4], which despite being of great importance to the area, does not seek to understand gestures in search of the most appropriate choice for the interfaces created, which can lead to using tiresome, unintuitive or non-functional gestures and can harm the performance of the application.

The process of associating a gesture to a particular action or function of the system is not trivial, because it must take into account a number of factors such as ergonomics, intuitiveness and objectivity [5, 6], which highlights the importance of a Gesture Development Process (GDP). The Process below described aims to help the development of gestures for user interfaces.

2 Describing the Gesture Development Process

The present research shows the construction of a Process that can assist in deciding which gesture would better represent a certain function (action) of a system. The main references used in developing this process can be seen in [7, 8]. This GDP produces artifacts during its execution, the final product of this Process is a Template depicting the finalist and best gestures for the given functions.

The GDP here described has three stages (Fig. 1). In the first stage, "Define Functions", the problem domain is analyzed and the functions of the application to be developed are determined. This stage is not concerned with any kind of gesture, only with determining the functions to which you want to assign gestures.

To better the objective of the first stage, understand observe Fig. 2, this image was taken from the game Fruit Ninja [9], in this game players should "slice" fruits as they jump into the screen, on XBOX360 platform, the Kinect device captures user's gestures in order to make the interaction with the game possible. In this context, the main function of the game is "slice", but in the game's menu other functions such as "select" and "cancel" can be observed. So as to exemplify, in the first stage the developer should define which of these functions it would be desired to be triggered by gestures.

The second stage consists of three steps. The first step, "Apply Test Scenarios", needs volunteers in order to perform tests to generate prototype-gestures for the functions determined in the previous stage. One or more test scenarios, that abstract technical thinking and at the same time contextualize the functions to stimulate the volunteers to execute them, are created. All the interactions at this stage are recorded, the number of participants should be directly proportional to the diversity of the gestures obtained for each function, in other words, as the tests are applied, the more diverse are the gestures for each function, the more volunteers are necessary.

During the second step, "Analyze and Register Recordings", an artifact is created containing the analysis and registers of the identified gestures in the recordings. In this

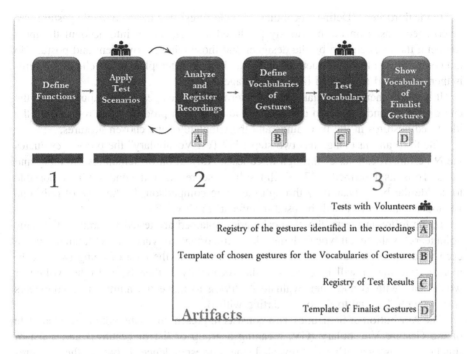

Fig. 1. Illustration of the process here presented

Fig. 2. Fruit Ninja

step a decision must be taken: if the results are not considered sufficiently favorable, it is necessary to go back to the previous step, but now with prototypes-gestures as final suggestions for volunteers, in order to refine the gestures development process. Otherwise, go forward to the third step.

In the third step, "Define Vocabularies of Gestures", the most favorable gestures are determined, based on the previously produced artifact, taking into account the most frequent, the ones chosen by the designer and those whose movement and posture do not compromise physical structures and articulations. A template of the chosen gestures is then generated to be used in the next stages.

It is worth mentioning that one can determine various gesture-vocabularies. At the end of this second stage two artifacts should have been produced: the registers of the identified gestures in the recordings and the template of the chosen gestures.

The third and last stage has two steps, In "Test Vocabulary" the process evaluates the N gesture vocabularies through three tests: Attribution of Semantics, Memory and Stress Tests, as described in [7]. Each test has a score and at the end it will be possible to decide the best vocabulary through the score comparison. In the case of only one vocabulary the score it will be used to infer its quality.

In the following tests, the N vocabularies obtained are tested separately, the same volunteers evaluate all vocabularies, it is important to vary the vocabulary witch each volunteer will start evaluating, in other words, in the case of being two vocabularies, a volunteer will first evaluate the vocabulary A then B, and other volunteer would start with B and later evaluate A, trying to make the numbers of volunteers starting with A equal to the ones starting with B.

The Attribution of Semantics Test consists in presenting to the volunteer a template of the Gesture Vocabulary (GV, meaning a group or list of gestures) and a list of functions, however it's not revealed the correspondence between the gestures and functions. It is then asked for the volunteer indicate which gesture corresponds to each function. The score is the sum of wrong guesses, divided by the number of gestures.

The Memory Test measures the familiarity of the user with the gesture. Only after the user is acquainted with the gestures is that he will able to maintain the focus in the task at hand rather than to how operate the interface. First it is shown a GV to each volunteer, later, a slideshow with all the functions, staying 2 s in each function. The volunteer is then asked to do the correspondent gesture of that function, until being able to get all functions right, when mistaken the presentation is restarted and the vocabulary is revised. The score of the memory test is calculated by the number of restarts necessary, resulting in a measurement of the difficulty for a new user to become familiar with the gesture vocabulary.

The Stress Test shows the volunteers a sequential list of gestures. Each volunteer should repeat the sequence a determined number of times, enough so that the he can infer any possible discomfort. At the end of the test, each volunteer is questioned about how stressing is each gesture, giving a general classification for them: "no problem", "slightly tiresome", "annoying", "painful" or "impossible".

At the end of all tests, in "Show Vocabulary of Finalist Gestures", the vocabularies can be compared through their scores and classifications, then it would be drawn a final template for the gestures of the chosen vocabulary, so as to aid the implementation of these gestures to their respective functions on the application.

3   Applying the Gesture Development Process

To demonstrate the application of the GDP described above, the idea was to develop gestures for common functions in 3D environments, the chosen functions were "Rotate", "Scale" and "Translate", as these are the main two-dimensional and three-dimensional geometric transformations [10], and "Select" and "Stop", because they are related to the beginning and end of interactions in general.

The first stage is to select which function will receive gestures as triggers. In this case; "Rotate", "Scale", "Translate", "Select" and "Stop".

In the "Apply Test Scenarios" step of the second stage, a case scenario application was created to stimulate the volunteers in the production of gestures for the functions mentioned before (Fig. 3). The Cube application featured a colorful cube that could be selected, rotated, translated, scaled and stopped (when stopped, no interactions could be performed with the cube), all through the mouse and keyboard input. The idea was that the volunteers could observe this interactions, then they were asked to perform gestures that, in their minds, would seem intuitive to trigger the before functions. This test was first carried out with 12 volunteers, all students from Computer Science bachelor, all tests were recorded.

Fig. 3. Cube application

With the recordings from the first round of tests, it was time to proceed to the second step, "Analyze and Register Recordings". Here the recordings were analyzed and the gestures captured were registered as shown in the Tables 1 and 2. The most popular gestures were S1, R3, T2, E1 and P2. The decision here was made in favor of another round of tests, in order to see if there would be many more new gestures or if 12 volunteers were enough.

Table 1. "Select", "Rotate", "Translate"

Select	Rotate	Translate
"Click" on the object S1	Move hand around R1	Move hand around T1
"Click" on the object S2	R2	T2
"Capture" the object S3	R3	Point to the object and then point to where it should be moved T3
	R4	With hand facing the floor, move hand around freely T4
	With hand facing the floor, move hand around in X and Z R5	

The first step was then repeated with another 12 volunteers, also students from Computer Science, only now the tests would provide the gestures in Tables 1 and 2 as options at the end of each test, so that the volunteer could change its choice if he preferred one of the gestures presented.

Table 2. "Scale", "Stop"

Scale	Stop
Join fingers to close in and open hand to close out Move arm as well E1	"Click" away from the object P1
Only moves arm to indicate close in and close out E2	P2
E3	P3
Join fingers to close in and open hand to close out Do not move arm E4	P4
E5	"Click" on the Object P5
	Put hand down P6

Going forward to step 2, the registry showed one new gesture for "Select", two new gestures for "Rotate" and "Translate", and three new gestures for "Scale" and "Stop". The most popular gestures now were still S1, R3, T2, E1 and P2. This was a good indicator that the first 12 volunteers produced a good variety of gestures, yet it was decided to do a last round of tests with students from different areas, to see if the results would be alike.

Back in to the first step another 12 volunteers repeated the last test, but now with more gesture options at the end of each test. The volunteers from this third round of tests were students from several majors including: Electrical Engineering, Law, Public Administration and Medicine. Going forward to step 2, the registry showed two new gestures for "Select", "Rotate" and "Scale", four new gestures for "Translate", and no new gestures for "Stop". The most popular gestures with this last group of volunteers were S1, R3, T2, E4 and P2. But in the total 36 volunteers the most popular gestures were still S1, R3, T2, E1 and P2. Seeing as that from 12 to 36 volunteers only one gesture changed (E1 to E4) the results were satisfactory and it was decided to proceed to the next step "Define Vocabularies of Gestures".

It was selected two gestures vocabularies; one containing: S1, R3, T2, E1 and P2, the most popular choice between the 36 volunteers, and another containing: S3, R7 (Table 3), T1, E4 and P8 (Table 3), less popular choices but considered good to be compared to the first vocabulary, in the next stage. The template produced in this third step can be seen in Tables 4 and 5.

In the third stage, Attribution of Semantics, Memory and Stress tests were performed with Gesture Vocabularies 1 (Table 4) and 2 (Table 5). This stage counted with 19 volunteers, students from several majors: Civil Engineering, Medicine, Computer Science, Electric Engineering, Law, among others.

Table 3. Gestures R7 and P8

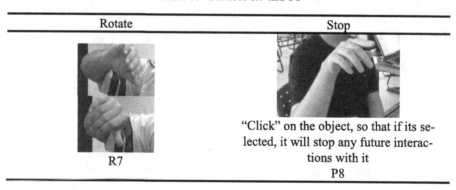

Rotate	Stop
R7	"Click" on the object, so that if its selected, it will stop any future interactions with it P8

In the Attribution of Semantics test the templates (Tables 4 and 5) and a list with the functions before commented were presented to each volunteer. It was then asked for the volunteers to indicate which gesture corresponds to each function. The results for each GV can be seen in Table 6. Bear in mind that the score is the sum of wrong guesses divided by the number of gestures, so a perfect score would be zero.

Table 4. Gesture Vocabulary 1

Table 5. Gesture Vocabulary 2

Table 6. Results from attribution of semantics test

	GV 1	GV 2
Average score	1,4	1,8
	In 19 volunteers there were a total of 7 wrong guesses of the 5 functions	In 19 volunteers there were a total of 9 wrong guesses of the 5 functions

The Memory test showed to each volunteer the GVs 1 and 2 and a slideshow with one slide for the name of each function ("Select", "Rotate", "Translate", "Scale" and "Stop".), the slideshow would linger 2 s on each slide. When reading the name of the function in a slide, the volunteers were asked to do the correspondent gesture of that function, if they did a wrong gesture the presentation was restarted.

The score of the memory test was calculated by the number of restarts necessary until the volunteer got all gestures correct. This was carried out twice for each volunteer since there was two GVs. The results can be seen in Table 7. The best result would be zero.

Table 7. Results from memory test

	GV 1	GV 2
Average score	1	2
	1 restarts out of 19 volunteers	2 restarts out of 19 volunteers

The Stress Test showed the volunteers a sequential list of the gestures from each GV. Each volunteer was then asked to repeat the sequence 50 times, for each gesture in each GV. At the end of the test, each volunteer was questioned about how stressing was each gesture, giving a general classification for each of the gestures in both GVs: "no problem", "slightly tiresome", "annoying", "painful" or "impossible". The result can be seen in Tables 8 and 9.

Table 8. Results from stress test - GV 1

	Select	Rotate	Translate	Scale	Stop
"no problem"	19	15	19	10	19
"slightly tiresome"		4		8	
"annoying"				1	
"painful"					
"impossible"					

Table 9. Results from stress test - GV 2

	Select	Rotate	Translate	Scale	Stop
"no problem"	15	10	18	16	19
"slightly tirsome"	4	5	1	3	
"annoying"		4			
"painful"					
"impossible"					

In the end the Gesture Vocabulary 1 was slightly better them the GV 2. As this work is still in progress the next step will be to implement these gestures in the Cube application (Fig. 3), using the Leap Motion device and with aid of the final template (Table 4).

4 Final Considerations

The interaction style supported by Natural Interaction devices, such as Leap Motion and Kinect, has a wide variety of potential applications, well beyond those described in this paper. When the interaction style is based on gestures, gesture design and development is among the issues to be addressed.

This paper presented a strategy to guide designers throughout the user interfaces based on gestures process. Nowadays, gestures are a realistic solution for user interfaces. Devices like Leap Motion and Kinect make it easier to develop this kind of user interfaces. The challenge is how to design them. This is the main goal of this paper.

In order to do that, the GDP depicted here presented a guide with all the steps to identify and specify gestures. Also, verification techniques are presented. A conceptual proof of the proposed strategy was verified using the Cube application. Also, a prototype using the Leap Motion device was implemented.

So, we turn back to our initial question: How to Design an User Interface Based on Gestures?

We are still thinking of ourselves as working stations, primarily based on computers devices. But things are changing and the physical world's functionalities are devices to access computer's functionalities. This paper approached our first big step in this direction: the gestures design. So, we emphasize the point of view of Pierre Wellner: "Instead of making us work in the computer's world, let us make it work in our world." [11].

References

1. FUTURELAB. Interação Natural (2014). http://www.futurelab.com.br/site/interacao-natural/
2. SBC. Sociedade Brasileira de Computação (2014). http://www.sbc.org.br/index.php?option=com_content&view=category&layout=blog&id=45&Itemid=66
3. Valli, A.: The Design of Natural Interaction (2006)
4. Almeida, F.B.: Sistema Interativo Baseado em Gestos para Utilização de Comandos no Computador. UFPE (2013)
5. Bacim, F., Nabiyouni, M., Bowman, D.A.: Slice-n-Swipe: A Free-Hand Gesture User Interface for 3D Point Cloud Annotation. Virginia Tech, Minnesota (2014)
6. Jeong, S., Jin, J., Song, T., Kwon, K., Jeon, J.W.: Single-Camera Dedicated Television Control System using Gesture Drawing. Sungkyunkwan University, Suwon, South Korea (2012)
7. Nielsen, M., Störring, M., Moeslund, T.B., Granum, E.: A procedure for developingintuitive and ergonomic gesture interfaces for HCI. Aalborg University, Aalborg (2004)

8. Choi, E., Kwon, S., Lee, D., Lee, H., Chung, M.K.: Towards successful user interaction with systems: Focusing on user-derived gestures for smart home systems. Pohang University of Science & Technology (2014)

9. HALBRICK STUDIOS. The Greatest Fruit-Slicing Game in the World! (2010). http://fruitninja.com/. Accessed 2014

10. Foley, D., van Dam, A., Feiner, S., Hughes, J.: Computer Graphics Principles and Practise. Addison-Wesley Publishing Company, Reading (1997)

11. Wellner, P.: Interacting with paper on the DigitalDesk. Commun. ACM Special Issue Comput. Augmented Environ. Back Real World **36**(7), 87–96 (1993)

User Interfaces for Cyber-Physical Systems: Challenges and Possible Approaches

Volker Paelke[1] and Carsten Röcker[2(✉)]

[1] Fraunhofer Application Center Industrial Automation (IOSB-INA), Langenbruch 6, 32657 Lemgo, Germany
volker.paelke@iosb-ina.fraunhofer.de
[2] Ostwestfalen-Lippe UAS & Fraunhofer IOSB-INA, Langenbruch 6, 32657 Lemgo, Germany
carsten.roecker@hs-owl.de

Abstract. Catchwords such as "Cyber-Physical-Systems" and "Industry 4.0" describe the current development of systems with embedded intelligence. These systems can be characterized by an increasing technical complexity that must be addressed in the user interface. In this paper we analyze the specific requirements posed by the interaction with cyber-physical-systems, present a coordinated approach to these requirements and illustrate our approach with a practical example of an assistance system for assembly workers in an industrial production environment.

Keywords: Industrial IT · User-Centered design · Usability · User interfaces · Cyber-Physical-Systems · Industry 4.0 · Augmented reality · Development processes and methods

1 Introduction and Motivation

The term *Cyber-Physical-System* (CPS) was coined by the National Science Foundation [11] and denotes a composition of physical elements (e.g., mechanical, electrical or electronic elements) and software elements (e.g., simulation, analysis, and control) that are connected through a communication infrastructure (e.g., industrial internet). Creating a network of embedded systems and connecting them to sensors and actuators results in complex distributed systems. These cyber-physical-systems exhibit the high degrees of freedom of software systems, but are also subject to the constraints of physical systems. The development and application of cyber-physical-systems raises many challenging research questions [10], which are currently being addressed in a number of international research projects. A key application area is the use of such cyber-physical-systems in industrial production, where they are referred to as *Cyber-Physical-Production-Systems*.

Industry 4.0 can be interpreted as a special form of a cyber-physical-production-system [3, 8]. The term was established by the high-tech strategy of the German federal government and characterizes the development of cyber-physical-production-systems as the fourth industrial revolution, in which "intelligence" is embedded in the elements of a production process [9]. Central technical topics associated with industry 4.0 include

© Springer International Publishing Switzerland 2015
A. Marcus (Ed.): DUXU 2015, Part I, LNCS 9186, pp. 75–85, 2015.
DOI: 10.1007/978-3-319-20886-2_8

networking (internet of things), the use of decentralized "intelligence" that allows the components to adapt to their context, high flexibility and versatility of systems based on modular units, and customized production down to a batch size of 1. Human-machine-interaction faces special challenges in such an environment, firstly because the user must be able to work effectively in such an environment, and secondly because a good user experience will be decisive for the acceptance of such systems in the workplace.

In the BMBF (German ministry of education and research) excellence cluster *Intelligent Technical Systems OstWestfalenLippe* 174 partners from industry and science conduct research and development to address the challenges that arise in making cyber-physical-production-systems a reality [17]. A key component in this research is the *SmartFactoryOWL*, a demonstrator factory that will cover 2000 square-meters in its final installment, and which integrates key research fields such as highly flexible and versatile production, plug-and-produce, and human-machine-interaction in a realistic production environment. The practical experiments for this paper were carried out at workplaces in the *SmartFactoryOWL*.

2   Specific Requirements for the Interaction with "Cyber-Physical Systems"

Interaction with industrial production systems is nowadays largely effected through (complex) graphical user interface. In recent years, many developments from desktop, mobile and web interfaces, as well as new interaction modalities such as multi-touch have been integrated. Current developments pose additional challenges for the designers of user interfaces in this domain [16, 19]:

- Users and customers change their attitude and expect a degree of user-friendliness that is similar to web and mobile apps.
- A growing number of manufacturers regard the quality of their user interfaces and the "user experience" offered by their products as a key differentiator in the market.
- At the same time user diversity increases [14] and customers expect future user interface to effectively assist a wider range of users, e.g., to address some of the needs of an aging workforce [6, 15].

These challenges are exacerbated by the introduction of cyber-physical systems. On one hand, the use of "smart" components leads to more flexible and adaptable systems, on the other hand this leads to increased technological complexity. A key challenge for the developers of user interfaces in this environment is therefore to reduce the perceived system complexity from the user perspective [20].

User-friendly design of human-machine-interaction is important in many domains, e.g., desktop or web applications. In addition to usability, that focuses on functional aspects such as usefulness, efficiency, effectiveness and the learning curve of the user interface, the more expansive concept of user experience, that also considers the emotional response of the user to the interaction with the product, receives increasing attention. Several design processes and design techniques have been developed and adopted in the web and desktop domain to ensure that user interfaces provide a suitable design and an attractive user experience. In theory these are also applicable to the design of user interfaces in industrial environments and for cyber-physical-systems. In practice, however, several important peculiarities prevent a direct application and must be addressed:

- **Interaction Hardware:** An important difference is the lack of standardization of interaction hardware. For desktop applications and web design the interaction hardware can be largely expected as standardized components, e.g., keyboard and mouse. New interaction devices can be added and are often largely compatible with established devices (e.g., mouse > touch-pad > touch-screen). In the context of cyber-physical-systems, such simple expandability is often not possible and the selection of appropriate interaction devices is more limited. This is especially true in industrial environments, where additional requirements such as robustness or dust and explosion protection must be considered.
- **Toolkits:** In the domain of desktop and web development well-established toolkits of interaction and presentation elements (widgets or controls) are available. Because their appearance and function was optimized over years, developers can focus on the composition of user interfaces from these elements. The direct use of these interaction elements in applications for cyber-physical-systems or industrial production systems can be problematic, because the metaphors that were used in their development are based on an office environment and may not fit well into an industrial environment. Also interaction techniques for important tasks (e.g., emergency stop) may be missing.
- **Development Processes:** The established user-centered development processes can in principle be applied to the development of cyber-physical-systems. Differences arise primarily for individual development activities within these processes. An important aspect is the consideration of the real ("physical") environment, on which the developers have very limited influence. Users interacting with classic desktop and web applications operate in a graphical virtual environments (GUI, website) that is entirely under the control of the program and can therefore be designed freely by the developers. When interacting with cyber-physical-systems existing physical system components need to be taken into account [5], on which only limited data is available and that can only be influenced in a limited way through special physical controls. Furthermore, the selection of interaction hardware must be included in the development process due to the problems outlined above.
- **Tools:** In the desktop and web domain rapid prototyping tools are used that allow to quickly create a user interface designs. In addition special test tools are available that support the evaluation of user interfaces in user tests. These tools are difficult to apply in the development of user interfaces for cyber-physical-systems in industrial applications, because they are limited to the standardized interaction elements and the essential integration between virtual elements that are under complete control of the developers, and real "physical" elements that are subject to additional constraints, is not taken into account.

To support the desired rapid iterations with prototypes in early design phases, additional tool components are required, that integrate "physical" components and can possibly simulate them in early design phases.

3   Adjusted Design Approach

To address these challenges, we propose a combination of a user-centered-design process and a toolkit of components, which also includes novel interaction and visualization technologies. Central to user-centered development is a systematic design process. Iterative design processes have been established as "best practice" in user interface design and divide the development into several phases that are iterated taking into account the results of user tests. Our approach is based on the ISO standard DIN EN ISO 9241-210 [7] in which the activities *analysis of the context of use, specification of requirements, design and implementation,* and *evaluation* are iterated.

- **Analysis of the Context of Use:** the analysis and documentation of the context of use forms the basis for the subsequent development. In this activity the user groups, the tasks to be supported, and the usage environment are analyzed and documented. For industrial applications it is important that the technical environment is also analyzed to identify the available sensors and input modalities.
- **Specification of Requirements:** This design activity specifies requirements for the system, taking the context of use into account. In addition to the requirements of the customer and the end user additional requirements, such as usability, regulations concerning occupational safety, etc. need to be considered.
- **Design and Implementation:** The following activity is used to create designs. In the development of user interfaces in industrial environments, rapid prototyping strategies should be applied. The goal is to investigate a wide range of design alternatives at a reasonable cost. Especially with new user interface concepts like augmented reality, such an approach is central, because less experience and knowledge on similar systems is available.
- **Evaluation:** In this activity, the designs and the implemented solutions are tested with real users. Based on the results the other design activities are then iterated to improve the design.

An iterative design process as described in the ISO 9241-210 standard, is the established "best practice" for the development of desktop software, websites and mobile apps. The biggest challenge here is to integrate the user-centered activities into established software engineering processes [12]. In the industrial production environment, there are long-standing efforts to make workplaces ergonomic and user-friendly. While the basic phases of ISO 9241-210 can be applied to an industrial work environment, modified techniques and tools are required for their concrete implementation.

Developers of desktop, web and mobile applications are effectively supported by prototyping tools like Axure, that allow rapid implementation of graphical prototypes, which can then be tested with real users. The development of user interfaces for cyber-physical-systems requires taking physical-components into account, which are also subject to much longer cycles of change. One possible approach is the temporary use of virtual proxies (simulated placeholder) for these physical elements, which are then successively replaced by their real world counter-parts in later design phases. A possible approach is to use the MR-in-the-loop methodology, which includes the Model-View-Controller Environment (MVCE) design patterns to address the incorporation of physical elements in a systematic way [18].

4   Interaction and Visualization Techniques, Tools

Developers can be best supported through a suitable design methodology and appropriate tools that provide interaction and visualization techniques optimized for cyber-physical systems.

In addition to traditional graphical user interfaces and their evolution such as multi-touch interaction techniques, user interfaces based on the paradigms of Mixed and Augmented Reality (MR/AR) have great potential for the interaction with cyber-physical system. Mixed and augmented reality systems enhance a real, physical environment with virtual, computer-generated elements (visualization techniques) and can interpret physical actions of the user (such as gestures or the manipulation of real objects) as interactions with the system (interaction techniques) [2]. Because cyber-physical systems are characterized by the combination of physical elements with computerized "smart" control mechanisms, MR/AR user interfaces form a natural match, since they also use a combination of physical and virtual elements for interaction.

Numerous demonstrators for new interaction technologies (e.g., [1, 20]) indicate the potential for improvement, especially in the industrial environment. However, designers of productivity applications often limit themselves to the functionality of established UI toolkits. Central reasons for this are the lacking maturity of the base technologies (e.g., displays, tracking) and interaction techniques that are often only developed to demonstrator status, lack of familiarity with the new technologies and their advantages and disadvantages, and the higher development effort caused by the absence of effective tools. The central goal of our work is to make new interaction and visualization technologies available to developers and designers. Therefore, we develop a set of interaction and visualization techniques for central interaction tasks in the industrial environment. The goal is it to develop a set of robust techniques that can be used by designers and developers similar to the widgets/control components in established GUI toolkits in close coordination with industrial customers. The central interaction tasks to be supported include:

- Spatial navigation to a place of interest.
- Visual highlighting of an object of interest in the field of view of the user.
- Visual guidance to an object of interest outside of the user's field of view.
- Alerting the user.
- Context-sensitive information presentation fixed to a object.
- Contextual information display on a mobile object.
- Process-oriented information representation.

First examples and results are presented in the following sections.

5   Example: Assistance System in Industrial Production

In the following, we illustrate our approach using the development of an AR-based assistance system for manual assembly tasks as an example [13].

The system guides users with picking and assembly instructions during their assembly tasks, in which it blends relevant information directly in the user's field of view. The current system was developed in a user-centered design process and with a focus on the procedures described above.

The results of this process are summarized below.

5.1   Analysis of the Context of Use

The AR-based assistance system for manual assembly tasks is part of the *SmartFactoryOWL*, a modular factory system addressing many aspects of an in-industry 4.0 environment. The factory uses a modular transport system with workpiece carriers, which combines a number of production cells (e.g., laser cells, robotic cells) as well as workplaces for manual assembly. The control of the system is decentralized and implemented using RFID chips that are embedded in the products or the workpiece carriers and support and act as a digital product memory.

Following the "plug-and-produce" concept, all cells and conveyor belts of *SmartFactoryOWL* are flexible and can be rearranged or removed. Thus, the production of a product could start with a complete manual assembly of a small series. When the production volume increases, robot cells can gradually be integrated into the production in order to reduce the workload for assembly workers.

In such a usage context, special requirements arise for an assistance system, since the system must be able to work with changing configurations of cells and conveyor belts and support dynamic changes in the production tasks controlled by the individual products (Fig. 1).

5.2   Specification of Requirements

As part of the *SmartFactoryOWL* we study the ergonomics and usability of user interfaces relating to various users during the operation of a smart factory (e.g., assembly workers, maintenance staff, plant engineers, etc.). A key component in this context is the support of manual assembly tasks. In order to do this, the assistance system should provide workers with information and instructions related to the product and assembly step the worker is currently performing. Since each product can be configured individually, a high diversity of variants has to be expected and workers need to be supported accordingly. In the *SmartFactoryOWL*, each product or workpiece carrier stores the necessary assembly steps on the integrated RFID chip and each module knows the production steps it can execute. For example, if a robot is present, it assembles parts of the product and registers the assembly steps performed on the RFID chip. In the following step, the assistance system of the manual workplace analyzes the remaining steps and provides the appropriate assembly instructions to the worker.

With respect to the user interface, the workers should be supported in the selection of the next component to be assembled ("picking") and then corresponding assembly instructions ("assembly"). The presented information should not only be easy to understand, but also presented in a way so that the worker is not distracted from his current task. A key requirement is that the hands remain free for the actual assembly tasks and the assembly process does not have to be interrupted for the interaction with the assistance system.

5.3 Design and Implementation

In order to be able to develop the assistance system independently of the rest of the "physical" components, a simple simulation of the system as well as a virtual 3D model of the manual assembly job was implemented in an early phase of the design process. Later, the developed prototypes were integrated in the real assembly context. After having assessed different approaches, the decision was reached to develop a user interface based on augmented reality technology in order to visualize assembly information within the user's field of vision. This is particularly important for "picking" instructions, which can now be located directly adjacent to the corresponding real-world objects and thus enable a hands-free usage of the system.

A key issue in the design process was the selection of suitable display hardware. Design choices included separate displays on the workstation (e.g., tablets or mounted displays), projections, smart glasses (e.g., *Google Glass*) and AR glasses. As a spatial superposition within the user's central filed of vision was required, separate displays and *Google Glass* were discarded. The choice between a projection and using AR glasses was made in favor of the glasses as this allows for a stereoscopic display. At the moment, we are using *Vuzix STAR 1200* data glasses, which operate in the optical-see-through mode and can display stereoscopic 3D graphics. The glasses feature a built-in HD camera as the basis for an optical tracking system.

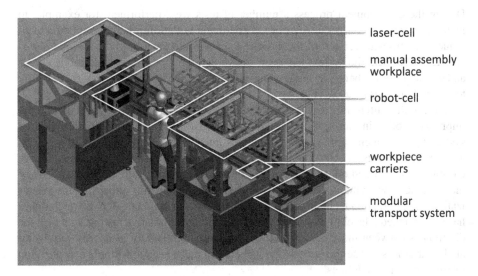

laser-cell

manual assembly workplace

robot-cell

workpiece carriers

modular transport system

Fig. 1. Modular structure of the *SmartFactory OWL*

Another important design decision was the selection and development of appropriate imaging techniques (see Fig. 2). Both for the picking as well as for the assembly instructions various techniques have been examined in order to support efficient communication with minimal distractions.

Fig. 2. Different visualization concepts for picking instructions

The studies showed that the choice of an appropriate representation is highly dependent on the user. Generally, novice users regarded a realistic representation that simplifies visual recognition and the matching of virtual and real-world objects as helpful, and therefore preferred an animated representation of the assembly instructions. In contrast, experienced users preferred an abstract and static representation, especially as such a form of information visualization requires less attention. The development and evaluation of such visualization techniques is an open research field and provides the basis for the subsequent development of a "toolbox", which could comprise different visualization techniques that can be individually combined to suit the personal needs of each user. The strong effects of personal user factors, expertise and duration of usage on the preferred visualization style, makes techniques for dynamically adapting the representation method to the active user and his current task an interesting design approach (Fig. 3).

5.4   Evaluation

During the development process a number of tests were performed, for example, to identify appropriate output devices or to experiment with different representation techniques. A complete version of the system was then integrated into the *Smart FactoryOWL*. Since then, the system has been shown at a number of fairs and public events and was used for further experiments. During this time, the system has been successfully tested by hundreds of users (Fig. 4).

During the initial user tests we were able to identify several aspects that could be improved. Following an iterative design process, we are continuously improving the system by implementing the required features into the system. Especially longer tests with experienced users showed critical limitations. In particular the AR glasses we are currently using turned out to be too heavy and uncomfortable for extended use. While the initial tests were mainly of formative nature and intended for improving the visualization and interaction techniques, the implementation of augmented reality techniques has now reached a level of maturity that allows formal summative testing, in which the differences between individual techniques can be quantitatively measured and evaluated. Our aim is to use the knowledge gathered in these tests to formulate application instructions and guidelines.

Fig. 3. Picking support based on the augmented reality technology: the object of interest is visually highlighted in the user's field of view

6 Experience and Outlook

Our initial results show that the benefits of new interaction technologies are primarily related to specific tasks. For the development of future user interfaces for cyber-physical systems in industrial environments, this means that new interaction concepts, such as augmented reality, should not be seen as a replacement for conventional techniques, but rather as an extension of the design space, which enables designers to better adapted user interfaces to the interaction task. The efficient usage of these new possibilities requires special "toolkits" to make the various interaction technologies easy to use, as well as knowledge about the advantages and disadvantages of the different technologies in specific usage contexts. So far, the focus of our research was mainly on the use of augmented reality techniques in assistance systems for manual assembly tasks. In our current and future work, we extend the scope of our activities to cover additional interaction and technology components for assistance systems in general. The long-term goal is to create a collection of established interaction and visualization components for user interfaces that support interaction designers in the development of industrial applications.

Fig. 4. Manual workstation for the evaluation of interaction and visualization techniques

References

1. Alt, T., Edelmann, M.: Augmented reality for industrial applications: a new approach to increase productivity. In: Proceedings of the International Conference on Work with Display Units, pp. 380–381 (2002)
2. Azuma, R.: A survey of augmented reality. Presence: Teleoperators Virtual Environ. **6**(4), 355–385 (1997)
3. Bauernhansl, T., ten Hompel, M., Vogel-Heuser, B. (eds.): Industrie 4.0 in Produktion, Automatisierung und Logistik. Springer, Heidelberg (2014)
4. Fründ, J., Geiger, C., Grafe, M., Kleinjohann, B.: The augmented reality personal digital assistant. In: Proceedings of the International Symposium on Mixed Reality (ISAR 2001) (2001)
5. Heidrich, F., Ziefle, M., Röcker, C., Borchers, J.: A multi-dimensional analysis of input technologies for augmented environments. In: Proceedings of the ACM Augmented Human Conference (AH 2011), Tokyo, Japan, CD-ROM, 12 – 14 March
6. Holzinger, A., Ziefle, M., Röcker, C.: Human-computer interaction and usability engineering for elderly (HCI4AGING): introduction to the special thematic session. In: Miesenberger, K., Klaus, J., Zagler, W., Karshmer, A. (eds.) ICCHP 2010, Part II. LNCS, vol. 6180, pp. 556–559. Springer, Heidelberg (2010)
7. International Organization for Standardization: ISO 9241-210: Ergonomics of Human-System Interaction—Part 210: Human-Centred design for Interactive Systems (2010)
8. Jasperneite, J.: Was hinter Begriffen wie Industrie 4.0 steckt. In: Computer & Automation (2012)

9. Kagermann, H., Wahlster, W., Helbig, J.: Umsetzungsempfehlungen für das Zukunftsprojekt Industrie 4.0, Abschlussbericht des Arbeitskreises Industrie 4.0 (2014). http://www.bmbf.de/ pubRD/Umsetzungsempfehlungen_Industrie4_0.pdf. Accessed 28 Nov 2014

10. Lee, E.A.: Cyber Physical Systems: Design Challenges, University of California at Berkeley, Technical Report No. UCB/EECS-2008-8 (2014). http://www.eecs.berkeley.edu/Pubs/ TechRpts/2008/EECS-2008-8.html. Accessed 28 Nov 2014

11. National Science Foundation: Workshop on Cyber-Physical Systems, Austin, USA, 2006 (2014). http://varma.ece.cmu.edu/cps/. Accessed 28 Nov 2014

12. Nebe, K., Paelke, V.: Usability-engineering-requirements as a basis for the integration with software engineering. In: Jacko, J.A. (ed.) HCI International 2009, Part I. LNCS, vol. 5610, pp. 652–659. Springer, Heidelberg (2009)

13. Paelke, V.: Augmented reality in the smart factory - supporting workers in an industry 4.0. environment. In: Proceedings of the International Conference of Emerging Technologies & Factory Automation (ETFA 2014), Barcelona, Spain (2014)

14. Röcker, C.: User-centered design of intelligent environments: requirements for designing successful ambient assisted living systems. In: Proceedings of the Central European Conference of Information and Intelligent Systems (CECIIS 2013), 18–20 September, Varazdin, Croatia, pp. 4–11 (2013)

15. Röcker, C., Ziefle, M., Holzinger, A.: From computer innovation to human integration: current trends and challenges for pervasive health technologies. In: Holzinger, A., Ziefle, M., Röcker, C. (eds.) Pervasive Health - State-of-the-Art and Beyond, pp. 1–17. Springer, London (2014)

16. Spath, D., Ganschar, O., Gerlach, S., Hämmerle, M., Krause, T., Schlund, S. (eds.): Produktionsarbeit der Zukunft – Industrie 4.0. Fraunhofer, Germany (2013)

17. Spitzencluster: Intelligente Technische Systeme OstWestfalenLippe - it's OWL (2014). http://www.its-owl.de/home/. Accessed 28 Nov 2014

18. Stöcklein, J., Geiger, C., Paelke, V.: Mixed reality in the loop - design process for interactive mechatronical system. In: Proceedings of the IEEE Virtual Reality Conference (VR 2010), Waltham, MA, USA (2010)

19. van Dam, A.: Post-wimp user interfaces. Commun. ACM **40**(2), 63–67 (1997)

20. Ziefle, M., Röcker, C. (eds.): Human-Centered Design of E-Health Technologies: Concepts, Methods and Applications. IGI Publishing, Niagara Falls (2011)

21. Ziegler, J., Pfeffer, J., Urbas, L.: A mobile system for industrial maintenance support based on embodied interaction. In: Proceedings of the International Conference on Tangible, Embedded, and Embodied Interaction (TEI 2011), Funchal, Portugal (2011)

The Theoretical Landscape of Service Design

Piia Rytilahti[✉], Satu Miettinen, and Hanna-Riina Vuontisjärvi

Faculty of Art and Design, University of Lapland, Rovaniemi, Finland
{piia.rytilahti, satu.miettinen,
hanna-riina.vuontisjarvi}@ulapland.fi

Abstract. This conference paper discusses the theoretical landscape of service design. It will illustrate how service design is situated in a discourse on design research and outline the theoretical background of this multidisciplinary approach from a constructive and generative research perspective. In this paper, the foundation for the conceptual service design framework is based on current debates in the field. Identification of the conceptual framework is based on an analysis of co-creating service design cases that were implemented at the Service Innovation Corner (SINCO) laboratory at the Faculty of Art and Design, University of Lapland. The conceptual framework presents five themes that are closely connected with service design: (1) design research, (2) value co-creation, (3) user experience, (4) learning, and (5) citizen engagement. Using the perspective of service design, this paper attempts to elucidate the effects of service design on development and innovation processes in private and public sectors.

Keywords: Service design · Design research · Value proposition

1 Introduction

This conference paper is a case study based on four business cases run at the Service Innovation Corner (SINCO) laboratory of the Faculty of Art and Design at the University of Lapland [31, 32, 41]. The above-mentioned business cases are analyzed from the value proposition point of view, according to the constructive approach in which service design problem solving is accomplished through the construction of qualitative service management and managerial tools [21].

The data for the research projects were collected, documented, and analyzed using four service development cases from five organizations: Lapin Kansa (a newspaper company in northern Finland), Ranua Zoo (a wildlife park in northern Finland), KL-Kopio (a digital printing company), and LAPPSET Group (a Finnish global playground equipment manufacturer). The service development cases were conducted between 2009 and 2011. The data were collected from multiple sources (video documentations of simulation work in the SINCO laboratory, fieldwork diary notes of participatory observations, self-documented materials of the research participants) and analyzed through descriptive content analysis [34].

In this paper the foundation for the conceptual framework for service design is based on the current debates in the field. Identification of the conceptual framework is based

© Springer International Publishing Switzerland 2015
A. Marcus (Ed.): DUXU 2015, Part I, LNCS 9186, pp. 86–97, 2015.
DOI: 10.1007/978-3-319-20886-2_9

Fig. 1. The theoretical landscape of service design

on an analysis of the case studies presented in research articles. The conceptual framework presents five themes that are closely connected with service design: (1) design research, (2) value co-creation (3) user experience, (4) learning, and (5) citizen engagement (Fig. 1).

Recent research refers to service design as a catalyst for societal change. However, the ways in which service design has developed as a successful research program from the value co-creation point of view has not been fully examined in the literature.

Case study and action research approaches are widely used in the field of design research. In this research, the four company cases serve as iterations in the action research approach. Our research process followed the typical cyclical action research process: identifying the problem, gathering data, designing, performing the actions, analyzing the results, capturing the knowledge, and planning the next steps [9].

As a theoretical concept, constructive design research has strong connotations that are attached to design practice. The aim of constructive design research defies the classical scientific comprehension of the research that is yielding new knowledge. Rather it seeks to concretize the new knowledge into a form, model, or construction that can be put to use [24]. This research introduces some insights for a theoretical framework connected with the service design debate. These impacts or the new general features that are perceived are then set as a hypothesis in forthcoming research where the aim is to concretize service design value in the visualization of even more complex systems, such as systems of digital and software intensive technologies, and the public sector.

Service design addresses services from the perspective of clients. It aims to ensure that service interfaces are useful, usable and desirable from the client's point of view and effective, efficient and distinctive from the supplier's point of view. In service design solutions to problems that do not necessarily exist today are visualized and formulated into possible future services. [27] This process applies explorative, generative, and evaluative design approaches [10].

2 Design Research

Hanington [13] presented a nomenclature of research methods for human-centered design in which he introduced innovative methods used by designers where user information is collected by creative means. Sanders [42] proposed a landscape of human-centered design research where one can distinguish design-led research. Furthermore, Sanders and Stappers [43] defined co-creation as a form of creativity that is shared by two or more people. They define co-design as a specific incident of co-creation where designers and people not trained in design collaborate creatively in the design development process. Co-design work is carried out on a regular basis, and new innovative methods are developed to allow inclusion, creativity, and engagement.

Koskinen, Zimmerman, Binder, Redström and Wensveen [24] have found a constructive design research paradigm that has taken a foothold in the modern age, where design is in its third generation. They highlight the need to revisit the notion of the research programs that are in dialog with society. Raising a debate on economic competitiveness and value creation in the era of major social changes, urbanization, ageing generations, not to mention climate change are to be dealt with a concrete solution exceeding the aims of the modern era of knowledge transfer. Thus, from the commercial product development and global business point of view, the design researchers now face "wicked" problems that can hardly be solved. From the management point of view in the field of constructive design research, there are solutions of value and value propositions that are not found in rational problem-solving methods but rather by way of the methodical work of imagination and design thinking [24].

Yet, the history of service design is brief, originating within interaction design and cognitive psychology. The connection with the interaction design discipline was left in the background when programmatic research on empathic design, co-design, and action research in Scandinavia; service design and design for sustainability in Milan; and research on user experience at Carnegie Mellon began to catch the attention of design researchers. Recently, the original connection with the design "interaction" has strengthened, extending beyond cognitive psychology and toward wider areas of interest, such as identity, emotion, and embodiment. Constructive design research also has its roots in interaction and industrial design. [24]

In business and among actual companies working within the SINCO laboratory environment, the questions related directly to the management and managerial development of small and medium-sized companies have grown into the core of service design expertise. In the collaboration with the Faculty of Art and Design, service design knowledge is desired by the small and medium enterprises (SMEs) in addition to the more traditional industrial and graphic design case studies.

3 Value Co-creation

Service design relates to many theoretical frameworks, such as the debate on value co-creation [12, 48–50]. It is clear that service design plays a strategic role in the co-creation of value. This is realized by applying a wider approach that integrates service thinking and understands the user in connection with service rationales as well as the user's relationship with and construction of service propositions.

Sangiorgi [44] proposed that design researchers can work at two parallel levels. At one level, they introduce Design for Services methods with a focus on improving service experiences and offerings that are designed around customer needs. On another level, they introduce a new way of thinking about value co-creation and innovation (Service Thinking) that could transform the way organizations perceive their role, offerings, and innovation processes. Wetter-Edman [52] discussed the service design discourse in which the relationships among users, designers, and design objects are important per se. In service management, however, underlying rationales are present. There is an increasing interest in the methods and tools that are needed in order to understand the users within their context and in how to transfer that understanding into successful service propositions and profit. There is a need to see and understand the rationales as well as the relationships.

Value co-creation is understood in the context of human action. The context ties down values. The aim of the service design process is to concretize these context-laden values. From the human-centered point of view, values are bound in multiple systems of meanings that are constructed by the groups, communities, and other forms of human assemblies acting in their living contexts. These meanings can be interpreted and researched theoretically in ethnography, but from the service design and "design ethnography" perspectives, the first-hand experience of context is important in building rapid and concrete prototypes during fieldwork and to start a progressive dialog with the people engaged in the co-creation process [24].

The service design process follows much of the end-user oriented design process formula, where the first phase focuses on end-user understanding (i.e., usability and user experience), the second stage focuses on the concept creation based on user understanding, and third stage focuses on the concretization of the implemented ideas. This is how design processes are seen to move ahead.

In addition, value co-creation is bound within the context of human action, which ties down values. The aim of the service design process is to concretize these context-laden values. From the human-centered point of view, values are bound in multiple systems of meanings that are constructed by the groups, communities, and other forms of human assemblies acting within their living contexts. These meanings can be theoretically interpreted and researched in ethnography; however, from the service design and "design ethnography" perspectives, the first hands-on experiences of contexts are important in building rapid and concrete prototypes during fieldwork and to start a progressive dialog with the people in the co-creation process [24].

In the business cases run at the SINCO prototyping laboratory, the value co-creation is attached to the core of the business of the enterprise in question. Service prototyping, for one, is the core area of the SINCO activities, including prototyping of the service concepts and the customer journeys for the company involved. In addition, the companies' value co-creation process still calls for the testing and evaluation of the service design concept that is constructed. From the (positivist) scientific point of view, this would be the phase of research, whether that phase is done at the beginning of the design process for the present set of service products or in a final stage in order to create reliability and validity for the service concept that was constructed during the service prototyping process.

In the project for the LAPPSET Group (a Finnish global playground equipment manufacturer) [41], a student group conceptualized virtual trainer content for public outdoor spaces. The aim of that project was to create a digital service concept for physical products in order to give the company a competitive advantage in the fitness equipment market. The initial design brief included generating ideas that encouraged users to exercise utilizing touchscreens connected to gym devices. The design process followed the cyclical model, repeating working phases based on continuous hands-on prototyping. Different devices and Internet resources were utilized to concretize, understand, and develop various ideas. A remote-guided training program was prototyped with a camera and a screen. The experience of prototyping helped to develop an understanding of the socio-emotional aspects that could not be tested with paper prototypes or mere role-playing. [41]

In a student project for Lapin Kansa (a newspaper company in northern Finland) [32, 41], the aim was to develop the idea of selling newspaper subscriptions as a concrete package in a grocery store. Experience prototyping with service-scape simulation was used throughout the process, including understanding the context, composing new ideas, testing the final concepts, and communicating them to the company representative. In the concept-testing sessions, the think-aloud method was used to capture the intuitive reactions, attitudes, goals, and needs of the test users. This case study concretized the meaning of empathizing with someone else's role. [32, 41]

In service design the phases of prototyping and evaluation are used for value proposition purposes. Concretizing value is still out of the realm of business and managerial perspectives in that sense, but it is to be part of the value of service design. Even if service design is not able to provide a commercial method for a service design system as a construction, it is able to construct a model of future visioning and for re-imagining better futures that a company, such as Alessi, has already done for decades [24].

4   User Experience

The service design process has characteristics from both iterative design process goals [11] and human-centered design [16]. Service design is a process that entails an iterative cycle of design, testing, measuring, and redesign. The human-centered design process model can be applied to problem framing, information gathering and interpretation, solution ideation, development, and evaluation in developing an existing service or in designing a new service solution. Human-centered design thinking captures unexpected insights and produces innovative solutions that more precisely reflect what consumers want [6].

In the old days, products were first designed for enterprises and then marketed and sold to consumers. Today, most products are still not designed and produced in the backyard of the true customer and end user. In addition, social media are changing the definitions of communities, friends, family members, and colleagues. Still, in the field of product and service development, the common practice is to rely on usability testing and skip the earlier co-design and development phases, such as rough prototyping based on the assumptions of the users' needs and indescribable aspirations. As a totally subjective and a psychologically researchable phenomenon, the user experience was ignored until the humanistic paradigm change in design research [7].

Jordan [19] stated at the turn of the 21st century that we are moving from one economic era into another. His main statement is that the consumer demands associated with the previous layer or economy will not disappear during the change. For example, in the case of digital services such as cloud services, this is a question of the trust and confidence in not only the digital transfer of knowledge but also in the emotionally and socially significant contents of human life.

When experience is the key element in understanding customer behaviour, it is in this paper evaluated and compared in relation to the definitions of user experience and value, user-centered design, and user interaction widely used in the disciplines of service design, design research, and human-computer interaction [1, 5, 33, 42]. There are more and more design practices where the role of the user is proactive and the role of the designers inactive. This refers to situations where users take the initiative in adjusting their environment and applying do-it-yourself design tools that are available to them. According to von Hippel [51], reflective design conversation based on interpreting user data and projecting design ideas against it is likely to happen when the most advanced users within specific practices start improving their equipment. Still, there exist challenges on the method of development of human-centred design practices: the development of interaction operations models that are able to structure, focus, and standardize collaborative procedures in a way that still accommodates the relevant aspects of design [22].

According to Sangiorgi [44], value is no longer conceived as embedded in tangible goods created on an assembly line but as value of social, cultural, or semantic use. The end users, customers, and individuals are social creatures. They do not live in a void, but neither are they steady members of certain consumer segments for the rest of their lives. Acting socially is valuable for humans, but social value captured in the design process requires knowledge of more institutionalized traditions or regulations inside various user communities. The other possibility is to concentrate on how people are committed to acting together, as groups and communities [33].

5 Learning

The aim of the SINCO environment is to support experiential learning. In Kolb's [23] experiential learning model, learning is seen as a set of circumferential cycles; the learning event is constantly evolving and deepening the process. This coincides with the iterative service design process through four phases: concrete experience (feeling), reflective observation (watching), abstract conceptualization (thinking), and active experimentation (doing) [23].

The service design approach can be used to redesign pedagogical and mediation processes in cooperation with researchers and participants in various settings [29]. This research gap between simulation pedagogy and service design research was recognized at the University of Lapland, and cooperation between the Faculty of Education and the

Faculty of Art and Design started in 2012 with the MediPro project, a simulation-based pedagogy in education and services for first aid. This research project investigated technology-supported service processes and developed a pedagogical model to support teaching, studying, and learning processes and technology at the simulation-based learning environment. Service design helped in the recognition, understanding, and development of the immaterial processes and resources related to learning and producing know-how. [27].

In recent decades, participatory and collaborative design approaches have gained increasing support and interest in many areas and fields. Different methods of co-development can be used to convert tacit knowledge to explicit knowledge and, in that way, they can foster creative learning [37]. The goal is to form a common space where information is shared and a new understanding of the participants is created based on their experiences and knowledge [40].

In the service design process, prototyping most clearly represents an activity stemming from industrial design. The starting point of the development of SINCO was the analogy of a product mock-up crafting and workshop culture in industrial design. Emphasis put on the aspect for students or other user of the laboratory to feel that the SINCO laboratory, with all its technological tools and equipment, was made for the use of all. As an environment, SINCO also needed to support the experiential learning of design thinking principles and service design methods through doing.

In service design, simulations are often called service prototypes. The goal of a prototype is not to complete the design but to learn about the strengths and weaknesses of the idea and to identify new directions [6]. Service designers find service prototyping central to their work because it is collaborative, makes services visible, and helps communicate the service concept suggestions [2]. Prototypes represent product and technological and social interactions [25]. Service design methods also allow designers and users to enact or perform service experiences before they have been established in an organization [14]. According to Coughlan, Fulton and Canales [8], prototyping is a powerful means to facilitate organizational development and change.

Prototyping enables collaborative work with stakeholders when designing product service systems and multi-channel services. Already at the concept design phase, stakeholders' participation helps facilitate realization of the ideas. The service design process is constructed in a way that the values of the experimental, and in some cases "funny," learning experiences are turned into concretized features of managerial value—in short, how company representatives see some service design constructions used in their everyday practices [21].

6   Citizen Engagement

Service design provides tools for user engagement in public services [38]. User-led design, engagement of users, and co-design are emphasized when designing for new social innovation [36]. As Murray, Caulier-Grice, and Mulgan [36] noted in their study, "Open Book for Social Innovation", designers and design agencies like John Thackara, whose Doors of Perception network tries to cross-pollinate ideas, share emerging practices to stimulate creativity and, thus, create new innovation just in the area of design but also in other fields, casting a wider net. The book also mentions IDEO, Thinkpublic, and Participle and LivelWork that re-design services with users and producers. The innovative design methods used in service design enable user participation in service development [46]. This is one of the reasons why service design increasingly plays a larger role in the public sector.

Policies and reports recognize the role of design and design research methods when designing user-driven public services [35] and when furthering the role of service design in public service development [45]. The co-production of services [4, 15], where users participate in service production, is an increasingly important subject. Service design provides tools for citizen engagement and new radical service innovations. Jäppinen [17] presented service design as a means to include citizens in service development. Blyth and Kimbell [3] tied together design thinking and big society, proposing that a designer's methods can influence the resolution of social problems and can have an effect on policymaking.

Pestoff [39] recognized both economic and political reasons for European governments to include citizens in governance and the development of public services. Aging populations, growing democracy at regional, national, and European levels, and the recent global economic crisis have all affected public finances. The response to these phenomena has resulted in some general trends: the promotion of greater volunteering, the growth of new and different ways to involve users of social services as co-producers of their own and others' services, and the spread of new techniques for the co-management and co-governance of social services. In the last instance, the third sector plays a more prominent role in the development of user councils or other forms of functional representation at the local level to engage users in a dialogue about public services. These actions represent a major social innovation in the provision of public services.

The themes that are closely connected with service design, such as design research, value co-creation, user experience, learning, and citizen engagement, open up novel possibilities and challenges. The fifth theme of citizen engagement especially inspires service designers in the public sector to co-innovate with users. They help to develop novel and fresh service design tools that systematically contribute to discovery phases [26, 28].

However, in the public sector, there are open questions as to who is responsible for implementing the ideation and how it may be done: how does one accomplish co-production? [18] According to Juninger [20], there are also unsolved questions related to social issues, such as questions concerning social inclusion in public management. In the public sector, "services remain first and foremost instruments for policy-implementation", claims Juninger [20].

In conclusion, based on our case study, we propose a contextual framework for service design that might also be applied as a practical tool in social engagement: a compound of human-centered design and its research, value-co-creation, user experience, learning, and citizen engagement. In response to Juniger's concern, overcoming the distrust of social inclusion and social justice in the public sector is possible. In the fields of public service and digital business, there are similarities in their large-scale focus and dispersed stakeholder networks, not to mention problems in identifying services' end-users. The practical and constructive research conducted in design research, value co-creation, user experience, and learning allows them to confidently enter the field of citizen engagement.

7   Conclusion

The theoretical landscape of service design is multi-level and multidisciplinary. According to constructive design research and service design thinking, it is also programmatic. In today's turbulent society, one essential role of service design is to bridge the gap between societal change and business. In service design, the fundamental question is how the scalability of service design tools fit, on a conceptual and theoretical level, with service design thinking in 'minor' constructions, such as SMEs' development in Finland, and major global constructions, such as population aging.

The earlier research conducted on design, co-creation, user experience, and learning now bears witness to a joint service design core that is human-centered and has a social scope of objects in service design. Whether the objects of design are focused toward public safety or digital services, the social nature of human activity remains of central importance [1, 30, 47]. However, thinking about our global society or the omnipresent digital world does not mean that social systems can ever be totally global. Distinct historical and cultural backgrounds are evidence of the diversity of social and systems that have been present throughout history. This diversity is not going to disappear, even in the digital age. On the contrary, service design has the potential to engage its attention toward human-centered perspectives in all the fields that it enters.

This research paper provides some insight into the theoretical frameworks that are connected to service design debates. This is a meta-level model of how service design is situated in design research discourses. It also outlines the theoretical background for this multidisciplinary approach from a constructive and generative research point of view. In forthcoming research, the aim will be to concretize the service design value and proceed with a visualization of more complex systems like digital and information technologies. The focus will be on building innovative programs that boost service design thinking within public organizations and business corporations.

References

1. Battarbee, K.: Co-experience: understanding user experiences in social interaction. Ph.D., University of Art and Design, Helsinki (2004)
2. Blomkvist, J.: Conceptualising prototypes in service design. Ph.D. Linköpings Universitet (2011)
3. Blyth, S., Kimbell, L.: Design Thinking and the Big Society: from Solving Personal Troubles to Designing Social Problems. Actant and Taylor Haig, London (2011). http://www.taylorhaig.co.uk/assets/taylorhaig_designthinkingandthebigsociety.pdf. Accessed 3 Mar 2015
4. Boyle, D., Harris, M.: The challenge of co-production. NESTA, UK (2009). http://www.nesta.org.uk/publications/challenge-co-production. Accessed 3 Mar 2015

5. Boztepe, S.: Competing theories and models. Int. J. Des. **1**(2), 57–65 (2007)
6. Brown, T.: Design thinking. Harward Bus. Rev. **86**(6), 84–92 (2008)
7. Bürdek, B.E.: Design: History. Theory and Practice of Product Design. Birkhäuser, Basel (2005)
8. Coughlan, P., Fulton, S.J., Canales, K.: Prototypes as (design) tools for behavioral and organizational change: a design-based approach to help organizations change work behaviors. J. Appl. Behav. Sci. **43**(1), 1–13 (2007)
9. Ferrance, E.: Themes in Education: Action Research. Brown University, US (2000). http://www.alliance.brown.edu/pubs/themes_ed/act_research.pdf. Accessed 3 Mar 2015
10. Fulton, S.: Informing our intuition: design research for radical innovation. Rotman Magazine, (Winter), 53–55 (2008)
11. Gould, J.D., Lewis, C.: Designing for usability: key principles and what designers think. Commun. ACM **28**(3), 300–311 (1985)
12. Grönroos, C.: Service logic revisited: Who creates value? And who co-creates? Eur. Bus. Rev. **20**(4), 298–314 (2008)
13. Hanington, B.: Methods in the making: a perspective on the state of human research in design. Des. Issues **19**, 9–18 (2003). (4, Autumn 2003)
14. Holmlid, S., Evenson, S.: Bringing service design to service sciences, management and engineering. In: Hefley, B., Murphy, W. (eds.) Service Sciences, Management and Engineering: Education for the 21st Century, pp. 341–345. Springer Science + Business Media, LLC, New York (2008)
15. Horne, M., Shirley, T.: Coproduction in Public Services: A New Partnership with Citizens. Cabinet Office, Strategy Unit, UK (2009)
16. International Standards Office (ISO9241-210) International Standard: Ergonomics of human-system Interaction – Part 210: Human-centred design for interactive systems. First Version 2010-03-15. ISO 9241-210:2010 (E). ISO, Geneva (2010)
17. Jäppinen, T.: Kunta ja käyttäjälähtöinen innovaatiotoiminta. Kunnan ja kuntalaisen vuorovaikutus palveluja koskevassa päätöksenteossa ja niiden uudistamisessa. Helsinki: Suomen Kuntaliitto (2011)
18. Jäppinen, T., Miettinen, S.: Service designing Finland – From policy to action. Touchpoint 7(1), (Forthcoming, 2015)
19. Jordan, P.W.: Designing Pleasurable Products. An Introduction to the New Human Factors. Taylor & Francis, London (2000)
20. Juninger, S.: Public foundations of service design. In: Miettinen, S., Valtonen, A. (eds.) 2012 Service Design with Theory. Discussions on Change, Value and Methods, pp. 18–24. Lapland University Press (LUC), Rovaniemi (2012)
21. Kasanen, E., Lukka, K., Siitonen, A.: Konstruktiivinen tutkimusote: luonne, prosessi ja arviointi. In: Rolin, K., Kakkuri-Knuuttila, M., Henttonen, E. (eds.) Soveltava yhteiskuntatiede ja filosofia, pp. 111–133. Gaudeamus, Helsinki (1993)
22. Keinonen, T.: Design contribution square. Adv. Eng. Inform. **23**, 142–148 (2009)
23. Kolb, D.A.: Experiential Larning: Experience as the Source of Learning and Development. Prentice Hall with Englewood Cliffs, New Jersey (1984)
24. Koskinen, I., Zimmerman, J., Binder, T., Redström, J., Wensveen, S.: Design Research Through Practice. From the Lab Field and Showroom. Morgan Kaufmann, Amsterdam (2011)
25. Kurvinen, E.: Prototyping Social Action. PdD. University of Art and Design, Helsinki (2007)
26. Kuure, E., Miettinen, S.: Considerations of common good in the co-design with publics - workshops as a tool for individual empowerment. In: Nordes 2015, Design Ecologies, vol. 6 (Forthcoming, 2015)

27. Kuure, E., Miettinen, S.: Learning through action: introducing the innovative simulation and learning environment Service Innovation Corner (SINCO). In: E-Learn (World Conference on E-Learning 2013), 21–24 October, Las Vegas, Nevada, USA (2013)

28. Kuure, E., Lindström, A.: The voices of the users - How technology can help in co-innovation. In: Farias, L.P., Calvera, A., da Costa, B.M., Schincariol, Z. (eds.) Design Frontiers: Territories, Concepts and Technologies, Proceedings of the ICDHS 2012, 3–6 September, Sao Paulo, Brazil, pp. 391–395. Edgard Blücher Ltda (2012)

29. Kuzmina, K., Bhamra, T., Triminghan, R.: Service design and its role in changing education. In: Miettinen, S., Valtonen, A. (eds.) 2012, Service Design with Theory. Discussions on Change, Value and Methods, pp. 27–36. Lapland University Press, Rovaniemi (2012)

30. Mead, G.H.: Essays in Social Psychology. Transaction Publishers, New Brunswick (2001)

31. Miettinen, S., Kuure, E.: Designing a multi-channel service experience. Design Management Review. The Changing Nature of Service & Experience Design 24(3), 30–37 (2013)

32. Miettinen, S., Rontti, S., Kuure, E., Lindström, A.: Realizing design thinking through a service design process and an innovative prototyping laboratory – Introducing Service Innovation Corner (SINCO). In: Israsena, P., Tangsantikul, J., Durling, D. (eds.) 2012. Design Research Society 2012, Conference Proceedings, Bangkok, vol.3, pp. 1202–1214 (2012)

33. Miettinen, S., Rytilahti, P., Vuontisjärvi, H., Kuure, E., Rontti, S.: Experience design in digital services. REBCE (Research in Economics and Business: Central and Eastern Europe) 6(1), 29–50 (2014)

34. Miles, M.B., Huberman, M.: Qualitative Data Analysis: An Expanded Sourcebook. SAGE, Thousand Oaks (1994)

35. Ministry of Employment and the Economy, Finland.: Demand and user-driven innovation policy Helsinki, Finland. [e-report] Publications of the MEE: Innovation 48/2010 (2010). https://www.tem.fi/files/27547/Framework_and_Action_Plan.pdf. Accessed 3 Mar 2015

36. Murray, R., Caulier-Grice, J., Mulgan, G.: The open book of social innovation [e-book] NESTA with The Young Foundation (2010). http://www.nesta.org.uk/sites/default/files/the_open_book_of_social_innovation.pdf. Accessed 3 Mar 2015

37. Nonaka, I., Takeuchi, H.: The Knowledge-creating company: How Japanese companies create the dynamics of innovation. Oxford University Press, New York (1995)

38. Parker, S., Heapy, J.: The journey to the interface: How public service design can connect users to reform. [e-book] Demos, London (2006). http://www.demos.co.uk/files/journeytotheinterface.pdf?1240939425. Accessed 3 Mar 2015

39. Pestoff, V.: Innovations in public services: co-production and new public governance in europe. In: Botero, A., Paterson, A.G., Saad-Sulonen, J. (eds.) 2012. Towards Peer Production in Public Services: Cases From Finland, pp. 13–33. Aalto University School of Arts, Design and Architecture. Department of Media, Helsinki (2012)

40. Pöyry-Lassila, P., Teräväinen, H.: Yhteiskehittämisen yleisiä ja yhteisiä periaatteita. In: Smeds, R., Krokfors, L., Ruokamo, H., Staffans, A. (eds.) InnoSchool - Välittävä koulu. Oppimisen verkostot, ympäristöt ja pedagogiikka. SimLab Report Series 31, pp. 17–21. The Aalto University School of Science and Technology, Helsinki (2010)

41. Rontti, S., Miettinen, S., Kuure, E., Lindström, A.: A laboratory concept for service prototyping – service Innovation Corner (SINCO). In: ServDes2012 (Service Design and Innovation Conference), 8–10 February, Helsinki, Finland (2012)

42. Sanders, E.B.: Design research in 2006. Des. Res. Q. 1(1), 1–8 (2006)

43. Sanders, E.B., Stappers, P.J.: Co-creation and new landscapes of design. CoDesign 4(1), 5–18 (2008)

44. Sangiorgi, D.: Value co-creation in design for services. In: Miettinen, S., Valtonen, A. (eds.) Service Design with Theory. Discussions on Change, Value and Methods, pp. 95–104. Lapland University Press (LUC), Rovaniemi (2012)
45. The House of Commons, UK.: User involvement in public services. UK. [e-report] The House of Commons: Public Administration Select Committee (2008). http://www.parliament.uk/pasc. Accessed 3 July 2012
46. Thomas, E.: Innovation by Design in the Public Services. Solace Foundation, London (2008)
47. Tuomela, R.: The Philosophy of Social Practices: A Collective Acceptance View. Cambridge University Press, Cambridge (2002)
48. Vargo, S.L., Lusch, R.F.: Why "service"? J. Acad. Mark. Sci. **36**, 25–38 (2007)
49. Vargo, S.L., Lusch, R.F.: Service-dominant logic: what it is, what it is not, what it might be. In: Vargo, S.L., Lusch, R.F. (eds.) The Service-Dominant Logic of Marketing: Dialog, Debate and Directions, pp. 43–56. Routledge, New York (2006). First published by M.E. Sharpe Inc.
50. Vargo, S.L., Lusch, R.F.: The four services marketing myths: Remnants from a manufacturing model. J. Serv. Res. **6**, 324–335 (2004)
51. von Hippel, E.: Democratizing innovation. MIT Press, Cambridge (2005)
52. Wetter-Edman, K.: Relations and rationales of user's involvement in service design and service management. In: Miettinen, S., Valtonen, A. (eds.) Service Design with Theory. Discussions on Change, Value and Methods, pp. 105–114. Lapland University Press (LUC), Rovaniemi (2012)

User Experience Design and Usability
Methods and Tools

Maareech: Usability Testing Tool for Voice Response System Using XML Based User Models

Siddhartha Asthana[✉] and Pushpendra Singh

Indraprastha Institue of Information Technology, Delhi, India
{siddharthaa,psingh}@iiitd.ac.in

Abstract. Interactive Voice Response Systems (IVRS) are popular voice-based systems to access information over the telephone. In developing regions, HCI researchers have shown keen interest in IVRS due to high affordability and reach among rural, poor, and illiterate users. However, IVRS are also notorious for their usability issues. This makes researchers thrive for more usable IVRS. The lack of automated usability testing tools for voice-based systems makes researchers depend on human subjects for testing their proposed IVR systems that are both costly and time-consuming. To address this research gap, we present Maareech, a usability testing tool for voice response systems using XML-based user models. Maareech has a flexible architecture to accommodate different user models that can be used to perform usability tests. In this paper, we discuss Maareech's architecture and its ability to mimic IVR user behavior based on different user models.

Keywords: User-models · Usability testing

1 Introduction

It is quite common that a telephone call gets attended by an automated Interactive Voice Response (IVR) system while accessing information about an organization [8,13,14]. The humble human operator has now been replaced by IVR systems [6]. In developing regions, IVR systems have emerged as a mean to disseminate information across all the sections of the society [11,16]. HCI researchers have shown the impact of IVR system in several contexts in rural areas including the vital areas of agriculture [9], and healthcare [10,12]. An IVR system provides information in natural language that transcends literacy and can be accessed through low-end phones thus reaching out to sections that cannot access information through other media like Internet or print media.

Due to widespread deployment of IVR systems, it has become imperative to test IVR systems before their deployment. A software developer can test the system functionality, but not the interaction issues faced by its users. The solution to this problem could be to conduct a usability test with few participants through the lab studies, but these lab studies are time-consuming, costly and

© Springer International Publishing Switzerland 2015
A. Marcus (Ed.): DUXU 2015, Part I, LNCS 9186, pp. 101–112, 2015.
DOI: 10.1007/978-3-319-20886-2_10

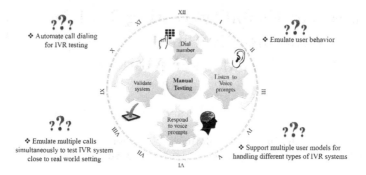

Fig. 1. Steps of IVR testing that are automated by Maareech in call emulation

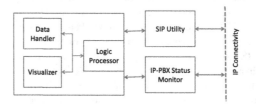

Fig. 2. Maareech's architecture

cannot be done at a large scale. In this paper, we present Maareech[1], a tool that can mimic user behavior to simulate large-scale user testing of a system. Maareech is a complete and robust testing tool to test IVR systems. We had discussed the preliminary design of Maareech in [5], in this paper, we present the complete working system. Maareech has the ability to dial a phone number, listen to a voice prompt, enter the required DTMF[2] or recorded speech input for testing different types of IVR applications (see Fig. 1). Maareech can also use data generated from real world calls for call emulation. Mimicking user behavior provides the ability to optimize and evaluate the performance of IVR applications. Maareech is built to help HCI researcher conducting usability tests. It has the capability to incorporate new user models based on which an HCI researcher can test different system user interactions.

2   Architecture

Maareech has a modular architecture with five basic modules as shown in Fig. 2. It is written in JAVA and designed using the MVC (i.e. Model, View, Controller) pattern. This makes Maareech highly customizable and extendable to different scenarios. In this section, we describe the architectural components of Maareech.

---

[1] Maareech is a daemon in Hindu Epic Ramayana who could assume any form.

[2] Dual-tone multi-frequency signaling (DTMF) is used for telecommunication signaling over analog telephone lines.

Logic Processor: This module is responsible for making all the decisions for the emulation process, e.g., call initiation, event regeneration, etc. It coordinates with other modules to perform call emulations. The Logic processor interprets the underlying user modules. New user models can be created under the Logic Processor to emulate user behavior for different scenarios. It can schedule events and maintain call queues[3].

Visualizer: This module provides the user interface of Maareech. It is responsible for taking inputs from the user for different emulations and showing the output to the user (see Fig. 2). The Visualizer component is responsible for showing calls loaded in the call list, events in each call, and the current operation performed by Maareech in the test.

SIP Utility: This module is responsible for performing all SIP (Session Initiation Protocol) based communication with the IP-PBX software hosting the IVR application. It provides an API for initiating and releasing calls, generates a DTMF key-press, and sends the audio file as a speech utterance. In the current implementation, the SIP Utility of Maareech uses the API of PJsua[4] for all SIP-based communications. PJsua can be replaced with another Java based SIP stacks such as MjSip[5] for developers requiring more control.

Status Monitor: This module gathers information about the present state of IVR by directly communicating with the IP-PBX software. Any IP-PBX with a *command line interface (CLI)* can interact with Maareech by changing the connection configuration in the Status Monitor. This communication enables Maareech to know about the current configuration of the voice menu played by the IVR application hosted on IP-PBX software such as FreeSWITCH or Asterisk. In the current implementation, we have used fs_cli that is a CLI utility for connecting to FreeSWITCH (IP-PBX software).

Data Handler: This module is responsible for reading input data files (in XML format) created from logs of the IVR application and IP-PBX (FreeSWITCH), and converting it into a Java based object and vice-versa. All XML-based communication is done through JAXB[6]. The schema of XML documents defines the underlying user models used in Maareech. Maareech has been designed with rich data models to capture complex call scenarios. The data file contains logs about user responses and their corresponding contextual information that are generated by logging facilities of IP-PBX software. The read data is supplied to the Logic Processor module to emulate desired user behavior. The Data Handler module is also responsible for creating new objects for telephonic queues and call objects in each queue.

---

[3] By call queue, we refer to multiple calls scheduled to be initiated by Maareech one after the other.

[4] pjsua is an open source command line SIP user agent (softphone) system http://www.pjsip.org/pjsua.htm.

[5] MjSip is a complete Java-based implementation of a SIP stack. http://www.mjsip.org/.

[6] Java Architecture for XML Binding http://www.oracle.com/technetwork/articles/javase/index-140168.html.

3   User Models in Maareech

We categorize currently available IVR applications, e.g. [2–4], into two categories: Static menu based IVR and Dynamic menu based IVR. Considering that, we have designed two user models to mimic user behavior.

Simple User Model: Figure 3(a) represents a simple user model that has two composite attributes: meta-data and events. The meta-data attribute has four sub-attributes used for storing the meta-data of the call.

– UniqueId: A unique identifier for the call.
– From: Telephone number of the caller.
– TimeStamp: The time at which this call was made.
– System: The system specific identifier where the IVR system has multiple IVR applications running on it.

User responses are captured in an event attribute that has three sub-attributes: InputType, Data, and Time.

– InputType: It categorizes user responses into key-presses or audio.
– Data: It describes the series of DTMF key-presses or names of audio files, depending upon the corresponding InputType.
– Time: It captures the time in seconds at which the input was generated.

This simple user model is sophisticated enough to replay any call emulating user behavior for testing IVR applications that have static menu configuration. However, to test IVR applications where menu configuration may change dynamically, we need a richer user model.

Intricate User Model: Some IVR applications change their menu configuration based on the time of the day, user preferences etc. Thus, the IVR menu configuration may be based upon information provided by the users, their history, and other factors like time, etc. Faithful emulation of the user behavior of earlier calls in the changed menu configuration requires prediction about user behavior in a new configuration. Correspondingly, it requires that the data used for emulation should have all the intricacies of user behavior required for a new configuration well represented in it. To handle such IVRs, a more intricate XML schema is required as shown in Fig. 3(b).

The Intricate user model contains a tuple of 4 elements (i.e., InputType, Data, ContextInfo, Time) to describe the user response and the context in which the response was created. The InputType and Data attribute in the tuple are same as in the simple user model. This model has an additional attribute, ContextInfo. It is a composite attribute made up of 4 sub-attributes (i.e., Loop, ElementAt, ElementRequested, and UserCategory).

– Loop: It defines the number of times the menu was listened before selecting an option.
– ElementAt: It captures the announcement at the time the users made their selection.

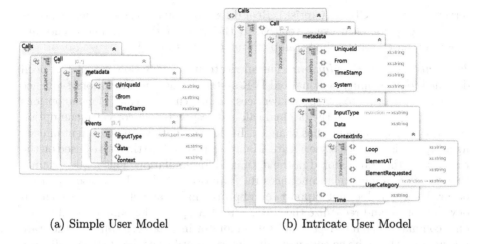

(a) Simple User Model   (b) Intricate User Model

Fig. 3. Maarech Load: The figure on left side (a) shows CPU usage of Maareech in terms of static, running and total load. The figure on right side (b) shows memory usage of Maareech in terms of static, running and total load.

- ElementRequested: This captures the option selected by a user.
- UserCategory: Each user is categorized in one of the two categories: expert or naive. An expert user is the one who selects an option ahead of the full completion of the announcement or just after the announcement was made. The user who waits for the announcement of several menu options before selecting a particular option is categorized as naive.

The intricate user model effectively captures the exact menu options (in case of advanced adaptive IVR systems) at the time of selection. This data is helpful in predicting user behavior in the new context where menu options are reconfigured. The events are regenerated when the contextual information stored in the XML document matches the context in the call.

4   Features

In Maareech, calls are emulated using two modes: user emulation using the previous call records, and testing using random DTMF generation.

User Emulation Using Previous Call Records: In this mode, Maareech reads call logs stored in XML files that are obtained from a real world deployment. Maareech supports two formats that capture user models:

Simple User Emulation: This user emulation works for currently available static IVR systems. In this format, Maareech replicates call events like key-press and speech recording, as they happened in an actual call. In this mode, Maareech does not assume any assistance from IVR applications hosted on the telephony server (FreeSWITCH or Asterisk). Real data stored for this emulation contains a time-stamp for each event relative to the start of the call. The events are generated based on the time-stamp captured in this model.

Intricate User Emulation: The intricate user emulation model has been designed for upcoming personalized IVR systems, where menu options sequence may change in order to give better services. Maareech keeps track of menu options as they were accessed in the original call and responds to a correct menu option even if the menu sequence has changed. In this mode, the announcement of each menu option is assumed to be a state. Maareech responds to this state based on the response to the states stored in the data used for emulation. This mode assumes that the IVR application announces its state over the IP-PBX console as they occur. Maareech does not support sound processing or any other similar technology to capture and recognize the state. The IVR application announces its state on a command line interface. The status monitor in Maareech captures the state information through the command line interface utility of the IP-PBX software. In the current implementation, the application assumes this command line interface to be the FreeSWITCH console. Maareech connects to this console using the fs_cli utility that comes with preinstalled FreeSWITCH binaries.

We have incorporated some more features in Maareech that are helpful in analyzing IVRs for different usages. Maareech provides two basic features in this mode. The trial run of each feature was tested on a machine (HP Probook 4520s) running Ubuntu 12.04 with an Intel Core i5 processor and 2 GB RAM.

Call Reordering: This feature allows to change the original sequence of call arrivals on the IVRS. It is suitable for analyzing upcoming IVR applications that have dynamic menu configuration. It helps to study the dynamic IVR system that will behave differently for the same calls presented in the different order. In a trial run of Maareech, 1120 calls collected from real world usage, were shuffled in less than 3 s.

Number of Telephone Lines: This feature allows developer to check problems which may arise due to shared access to system resources (e.g., accessing the same audio file for reading or log file for writing) when multiple instances of the IVR application handles more than one simultaneous call. By default, Maareech assumes a single line connection with the telephony server and only one call at a time is simulated as per the current call sequence. With this feature, the number of telephone line connections can be increased to view the behavior of the IVR application in handling multiple connections. In a trial run, Maareech was able to open eight lines with linphone[7] (a free SIP VoIP Client) as the SIP utility.

Testing Using Random DTMF Generation: In this mode, Maareech does not read any data file or log to perform tests. These tests are independent of user models and can be used to evaluate the IVR application's system parameters. It generates events like key presses or speech recording based on parameters specified by the user. It supports four types of IVR tests, as shown in Fig. 4:

---

[7] www.linphone.org.

Call Load Test: This test helps in measuring the number of simultaneous calls an IVR application can process. Maareech can test an IVR application hosted at a remote location also, which enhances its utility. On starting this test, the system increases number of calls made to IVR till it fails to handle any more calls. This test reports the integer value at which the IVR application crashes. In our test, we found that FreeSWITCH was able to process 123 simultaneous calls for our sample IVR application under test. The IVR application hosted on FreeSWITCH failed on 124th call because of too many connections open to the MySQL database operating at backend. We would like to mention that this is not a limitation of Maareech, but of the FreeSWITCH module that connects to database. Maareech helped in identifying it and did not report any failure as FreeSWITCH (call receiving module) was running properly even though IVR application was not accepting additional calls.

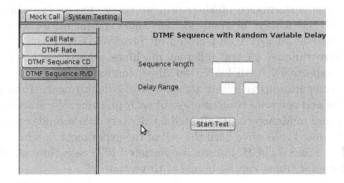

Fig. 4. The tabs on the left showing four type of IVRS tests.

DTMF Rate: This tests helps to detect the rate at which an IVR application can accept input. Maareech starts this test by sending 1 DTMF per second to IVR application under test and keeps on increasing number of DTMF per second. This test reports the integer value beyond which IVR do not accept more DTMF per second.

Sequence Test: This test helps to detect the DTMF input sequence at which an IVR application may fail. The Maareech generates random DTMF key sequences, each with a constant time delay, in seconds, as defined by the IVR developers. An IVR developer needs to specify the desired sequence length to be generated by Maareech. At the end of the test, Maareech reports the sequence test cases if any, at which the IVR application fails to respond. In our test, Maareech was able to check 100 sequences, of sequence length 5 and delay of 5 s within each option, in 2,504 s. In this, 2500 s were taken due to the conditions specified in the test and 4 s in setting up the call.

Sequence Test with Random Delay: This test detects erroneous DTMF inputs in a more complex manner. The constant delay is not helpful when the length of voice prompts played by the IVR application varies for the announcement of menu options. If voice prompts of menu options are of different lengths, then to test such IVR applications, different delays must be put between each DTMF input generated by Maareech. Random delays help create more test cases than just random DTMF sequences. In this test, Maareech generates random DTMF key sequences each with random time delays ranging from t_1 to t_2 s, where t_1 and t_2 are defined by the user in seconds. Ideally, t_1 should correspond to the length of the minimum voice prompt and t_2 be the length of the maximum voice prompt in IVR. This test is more rigorous than the previous sequence test. At the end of the test, Maareech reports the sequence test case at which the IVR application ends the call. In our test, Maareech can check 100 sequences, of sequence length 5 and delay range 5 to 7 s, in 3094 s.

5   Performance Evaluation

To evaluate the performance of Maareech, we conducted an experiment using the *Call Load Test* feature in Maareech. For this experiment, we setup an IVR application written in JAVA and hosted on FreeSWITCH. FreeSWITCH and Maareech were running on two different machines referred as Machine-I and Machine-II respectively, with LAN, 100 Mbps, connectivity between them. We chose this configuration to reflect the real world deployment. Table 1, shows the hardware and software configuration of each machine. We started the *Call load* test feature of Maareech. It initiated a call every two seconds while keeping previously initiated calls alive until the end of the experiment or when they were terminated by FreeSWITCH. In total, we initiated 1024 calls through Maareech. A call in this experiment can be in one of three states:

Table 1. Hardware and Software configuration of machines used for experiment

	Machine-I	Machine-II
OS	Ubuntu 10.04	Ubuntu 12.04
Processor	Intel Core 2 Duo	Intel Core i5
Memory	3 GB DDR2	2 GB DDR3
Model	HP Compaq dx7400	HP Probook 4520s

- Active State: A call that is connected to FreeSWITCH and is not being terminated from either side (Maareech or FreeSWITCH).
- Dropped State: A call that was connected to but later terminated by FreeSWITCH.
- Time-out: A call whose resources were released by Maareech as it was not able to connect to FreeSWITCH.

Figure 5 shows time-series of call states from our test. Initially, the FreeSWITCH was able to accept the calls as the load on Machine-I was low. Due to this, there were no dropped calls observed till the 233rd call. After this, FreeSWITCH started dropping calls at a higher rate that reduced the count of active calls. The number of Active calls stabilizes around 145 calls, beyond this all new calls

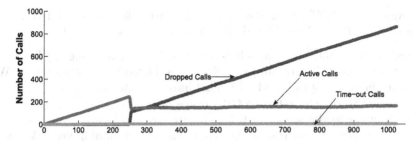

Fig. 5. X-axis represents the calls initiated by Maareech. The four lines representing calls in active,dropped and timed-out states.

are dropped. Our results for the number of active calls (i.e. concurrent calls) for FreeSWITCH running on Machine-I are in-line with the results obtained by other developers as available on FreeSWITCH website[8]. The CPU and memory load were also measured on both the machines during the tests.

FreeSwitch Load: We measure the CPU usage and memory consumption through Linux utilities (e.g. ps) on Machine-I. Figure 6(a) shows the CPU consumption of FreeSWITCH on Machine-I. CPU load saturated around 233rd Call. After this, the rate at which calls were dropped become nearly equal to rate at which new calls were accepted. We also found that three calls timed-out at 110th call because of high network congestion between the two machines.

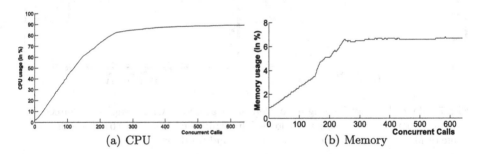

(a) CPU   (b) Memory

Fig. 6. FreeSWITCH Load: On the left side figure shows CPU usage of FreeSWITCH. The Y-axis represents the CPU usage of one core and X-Axis represents the total number (alive + dropped) of calls connected to FreeSWITCH. Figure on the right side shows memory usage of FreeSWITCH. The Y-axis shows the percentage of memory used by FreeSWITCH and X-axis represents the total number of calls connected to FreeSWITCH.

Figure 6(b) shows memory usage of FreeSWITCH in percentage of total memory on Machine-I. Similar to CPU usage, memory usage also saturated around 233rd Call. This shows that memory requirement of FreeSWITCH did

---

[8] Real-world performance data around the FreeSWITCH community. http://wiki. freeswitch.org/wiki/Real-world_results.

not increase after 233rd call as the number of active calls were saturated due to the equal rate of calls dropped and calls accepted by FreeSWITCH.

Maareech Load: Maareech creates logs of various parameters (e.g. CPU usage, memory usage and call data rate) to collect data related to its performance. We categorize the memory load and CPU load into two categories: static load and running load. Static load refers to CPU usage in creating and holding the call objects. Running load refers to CPU load incurred due to handling of underlying SIP communication. Total load is the sum of static and running load. We measured static and running load separately as the respected operation is handled by two different processes.

Figure 7(a), shows CPU usage distribution of Maareech in terms of static load, running load and total load. We can observe that the CPU usage was maximum at 113th call and decreases and stabilizes after 233rd call. We did further investigation and believe that CPU usage increased because of network congestion as the three calls were also timed-out around maximum CPU usage because of network congestion. We also measured the static, running and total load on memory usage. Figure 3(b), shows memory load of Maareech. We find that static load gradually increases from 8.1 % to 9.1 % (i.e. 1 % increase)for emulating 1024 calls. Similarly running load varied from 17.9 % to 18.5 %. Thus, it shows initiating each call in Maareech has memory load of 20 KB (calculated as 1 % of 2 GB system memory divided by 1024 calls).

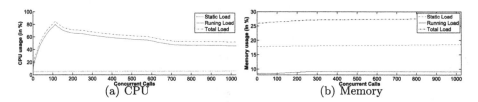

Fig. 7. Maarech Load: The figure on left side (a) shows CPU usage of Maareech in terms of static, running and total load. The figure on right side (b) shows memory usage of Maareech in terms of static, running and total load.

6   Related Work

Simulators have been used in various computer science domain like network simulators [15], and analog and digital circuit simulators. Simulators in the IVR domain are primarily used to simulate call-centers[9]. Various industrial tools provide pre-deployment testing of IVR applications. It mainly includes testing of VoIP infrastructure [1]. *Empirix Hamper*[10] provides an extensive tool-set for IVR

---

[9] http://www.call-center-tech.com/.
[10] http://www.empirix.com.

testing, monitoring and analyzing end-to-end IVR deployment. Nexus8610[11] is a traffic generator that simulates user behavior of various communication technologies including 3G/2G Mobile, VoIP, and PSTN. Cyara Solutions[12] is one of the industrial players that provides IVR testing as a service. Tools like Call center simulators[13] help estimate the resource requirements for optimal performance of IVR.

Although, the industry has a variety of tools for testing IVR at the infrastructure level, developers are still doing manual testing or writing customized test scripts for each IVR application. Hence, an emulation tool like Maareech, which is capable of mimicking user behavior is required to automate testing of IVR applications.

7 Conclusion and Future Work

Measuring the performance of any interactive system involving human is a challenging task. In this paper, we have presented Maareech - a call emulator for user behavior. This enables a developer to test the IVR application from user experience perspective. We presented two user models for testing and measuring the performance of different IVR applications. User model based testing provides characteristic to model different users easily [7] and reduces human effort. Current implementation of Maareech has certain limitations that we would like to address. Currently, Maareech does not have any speech or voice processing capabilities to understand the voice prompts played by IVR application under test. As a result, Maareech can not be used for verification of voice and sound quality. Maareech also lacks any automated data analysis of collected logs, and all analysis need to be manually done on the collected log. Also, the current implementation of Maareech has support only for FreeSWITCH. In future, we intend to overcome some of these challenges.

With increasing use of IVRS, it is imperative to have a robust testing tool for IVR applications. We have built Maareech for the same purpose. Over the time, Maareech has evolved to be very robust and has been used in testing of IVR applications that are deployed in the field.

References

1. Agam, O.: Voice over IP Testing-A Practical Guide. RADCOM White Paper, Bitpipe Inc (2001)
2. Asthana, S., Singh, P.: Mvoice: a mobile based generic ICT tool. In: Proceedings of the Sixth International Conference on Information and Communications Technologies and Development: Notes-Volume 2, pp. 5–8. ACM (2013)

---

[11] http://www.nexustelecom.com/products/nexus8610/.

[12] http://www.cyarasolutions.com/.

[13] http://www.xjtek.com/anylogic/demo_models/4/.

3. Asthana, S., Singh, P., Kumaraguru, P., Singh, A., Naik, V.: Tring! tring!-an exploration and analysis of interactive voice response systems. In:4th International Conference on Human Computer Interaction (2012)
4. Asthana, S., Singh, P., Singh, A.: Exploring the usability of interactive voice response system's design. In: Proceedings of the 3rd ACM Symposium on Computing for Development, p. 36. ACM (2013)
5. Asthana, S., Singh, P., Singh, A.: Mocktell: exploring challenges of user emulation in interactive voice response testing. In: Proceedings of the ACM/SPEC International Conference on International Conference on Performance Engineering (Poster), pp. 427–428. ACM (2013)
6. Chakraborty, D., Medhi, I., Cutrell, E., Thies, W.: Man versus machine: evaluating IVR versus a live operator for phone surveys in india. In: Proceedings of the 3rd ACM Symposium on Computing for Development, p. 7. ACM (2013)
7. Eckert, W., Levin, E., Pieraccini, R.: User modeling for spoken dialogue system evaluation. In: Proceedings of IEEE ASR Workshop, pp. 80–87 (1997)
8. Gupta, A., Thapar, J., Singh, A., Singh, P., Srinivasan, V., Vardhan, V.: Simplifying and improving mobile based data collection. In: Proceedings of the Sixth International Conference on Information and Communications Technologies and Development: Notes-Volume 2, pp. 45–48. ACM (2013)
9. Patel, N., Chittamuru, D., Jain, A., Dave, P., Parikh, T.S.: Avaaj otalo: a field study of an interactive voice forum for small farmers in rural india. In: Proceedings of the 28th International Conference on Human Factors in Computing Systems, CHI 2010, pp. 733–742. ACM, New York (2010)
10. Sherwani, J., Ali, N., Mirza, S., Fatma, A., Memon, Y., Karim, M., Tongia, R., Rosenfeld, R.: Healthline: speech-based access to health information by low-literate users. In: International Conference on Information and Communication Technologies and Development, ICTD 2007, December 2007, pp. 1–9. IEEE (2007)
11. Singh, A., Naik, V., Lal, S., Sengupta, R., Saxena, D., Singh, P., Puri, A.: Improving the efficiency of healthcare delivery system in underdeveloped rural areas. In: 2011 Third International Conference on Communication Systems and Networks (COMSNETS), pp. 1–6. IEEE (2011)
12. Singh, P., Singh, A., Naik, V., Lal, S.: CVDmagic: a mobile based study for CVD risk detection in rural india. In: Proceedings of the Fifth International Conference on Information and Communication Technologies and Development, pp. 359–366. ACM (2012)
13. Srinivasan, V., Vardhan, V., Kar, S., Asthana, S., Narayanan, R., Singh, P., Chakraborty, D., Singh, A., Seth, A.: Airavat: an automated system to increase transparency and accountability in social welfare schemes in india. In: Proceedings of the Sixth International Conference on Information and Communications Technologies and Development: Notes-Volume 2, pp. 151–154. ACM (2013)
14. Vashistha, A., Thies, W.: IVR junction: building scalable and distributed voice forums in the developing world. In: 6th USENIX/ACM Workshop on Networked Systems for Developing Regions (2012)
15. wiki: Network simulator-2. Article, January 2012. http://nsnam.isi.edu/nsnam/index.php/Main_Page
16. Yadav, K., Naik, V., Singh, A., Singh, P., Kumaraguru, P., Chandra, U.: Challenges and novelties while using mobile phones as ICT devices for indian masses: short paper. In: Proceedings of the 4th ACM Workshop on Networked Systems for Developing Regions, p. 10. ACM (2010)

Cultural Effects on Metaphor Design

Muhammad Waqas Azeem[1(✉)], Arslan Tariq[2], Farzan Javed Sheikh[2],
Muhammad Aadil Butt[2], Iqra Tariq[2], and Hafiza Maimoona Shahid[2]

[1] University of Gujrat, Gujrat, Pakistan
waqaskashi87@gmail.com
[2] University of Lahore, Gujrat, Pakistan
{arslan.tariq,muhammad.adil,iqra.tariq,
maimoona.shahid}@cs.uol.edu.pk, farzanjavedsheikh@gmail.com

Abstract. The World Wide Web has shortened the distances between people but it is still hard to find a general user interface for all the users. Because people living in different areas of the world have different cultures, religions, and traditions. Designing a user interface according to the culture of the user is important. Different minds have different views about cultural effects in user interface. This paper presents a detailed review on the recent work and research in cultural effects on metaphor design. This paper also explores the problems and issues regarding localizing metaphors in different cultures.

1 Introduction

The developers usually develop a system design according to their own culture neglecting other cultures. That confines the usability of the system only to the local users. Now days the companies have to compete in international market. For this purpose they have to create product for international users.

Metaphor varies from culture to culture. For example people living in China relate the red color with joy and happiness but in USA it has taken as sign of danger. Metaphors are designed in such a way that they help the users of target culture. People even use language metaphors in their daily life. With the help of metaphor the user can easily understand the complex systems. With the help of metaphors, users use their knowledge about real world items to understand software objects [4,70].

2 Theoretical Background

There are lots of issues regarding cultural based design due to cultural differences of users [57, 64, 65]. Researchers are trying to find a way for improving the usability for users. Designers and researchers have worked on different methods for global interface design [5]. Few problems are discussed here. Byrne explains a process in [58] cited by [5] which named by GILT framework.

© Springer International Publishing Switzerland 2015
A. Marcus (Ed.): DUXU 2015, Part I, LNCS 9186, pp. 113–121, 2015.
DOI: 10.1007/978-3-319-20886-2_11

2.1   GILT Framework

GILT framework consists of Globalization, Internalization, Localization and Translation.

Globalization usually refers as production and consumption of products in all over the world. Globalization comprises issues at intercultural and local level. Globalization affects user-interface design, because for globally used products the designers have to develop interface for global users [59, 67].

Internationalization issues are about language, traditions, and political issues of different countries [59]. Internationalization does not require redesigning the user interface. It provides common way to understand user interface globally without redesigning it for each culture [60, 61] cited by [5].

Localization deals with the issues of small group of people, with same language and culture, and usually group of people which is smaller than a country. The websites are localized due to the difference in cultures of users [59]. Localizing a website according to the culture of target user is very appropriate [5]. The designers have to understand the language, traditions, beliefs and currency of target user in order to design localized website. There are few non- textual elements like images, navigation and metaphor which should be according to the target culture in localized interface.

Translation means transferring text from one language to another. Although language is considered main factor in localized websites but there are few more elements which are part of a culture. But there is lot of research which is about language translation [62, 63] cited by [5].

2.2   Metaphor

The word metaphor means "transport". It is a Greek Word. It transfers a concept from a conceptual area to another area [42]. Metaphors are being used in different fields since very beginning [43]. Metaphor is not only about language, it is way of thinking [44]. Metaphors are unusual they needed to be defining in normal language usage [45]. They are related to the real world objects. Metaphor helps novice user to understand any system. Users can easily understand the metaphor using their real world knowledge and experiences. For example the recycle bin icon represents the image of trash bin and folder icon represents the image of cabinet or folder.

The use of metaphor in interaction design has not been valued [2]. Metaphors are not useful but they are harmful [20] in design. Metaphors are poorly designed because the designers are not aware of the concept that what metaphor is and how to use a metaphor [1]. Those metaphors that are not properly well designed and don't provide any help to the users are useless. However the well designed metaphors and proper metaphor at proper place can help users. Folders although do not exist physically as they are shown on icon image but they provide an easy way to understand their function by their icon.

There are many people opposing user-interface metaphors, giving different point of view on their problems. There are different types of metaphors which have been criticized like desktop metaphor [30, 31], the litter bin metaphor [29], the document metaphor [32], and metaphors for the websites [33, 68, 69].

Metaphors have different types there are verbal metaphors, virtual metaphors, and complex metaphors. The metaphors are also categorized as universal metaphors and local metaphors. Most of the metaphors are cultural based. Websites are designed with the combination of Colors, fonts, icons and metaphors, language and animations. These things if well designed according the culture of target user can attract user. On the other hand the website can not provide the required results if all these things are designed without keeping in mind the culture of target user.

People of different cultures associate their feelings with different colors. The following color's chart represents the meaning of colors in different cultures (Fig. 1) [1, 21]. Colors have influence on user's prospect about navigation, links, and content, as well as overall satisfaction. If a company is designing a website for French users they may not use the green color, because French people relate the green color with criminality. On the other hand, if they are designing website to attract the Egyptian and Middle Eastern users, they may use green color as green has a positive association for them.

Color	China	Japan	Egypt	France	United States
Red	Happiness	Anger Danger	Death	Aristocracy	Danger Stop
Blue	Heavens Clouds	Villainy	Virtue Faith Truth	Freedom Peace	Masculine
Green	Ming Dynasty Heavens	Future Youth Energy	Fertility Strength	Criminality	Safety Go
Yellow	Birth Wealth Power	Grace Nobility	Happiness Prosperity	Temporary	Cowardice Temporary
White	Death Purity	Death	Joy	Neutrality	Purity

Fig. 1. Color-culture chart

2.3 Metaphor and Culture

All the interfaces of computer represent metaphors [22] cited by [3]. Gannon argued that only dimensional approach is not enough. A more content-rich or stranded approach should be added in it, like cultural metaphors [23, 70]. Cultural metaphor is some exclusive or distinctive trend or action that expresses a nation's values.

Normally the people from other culture have difficulty to understand localized metaphor of a specific culture. A member of community can express more emotions about its local metaphor [24]. In Chinese culture the language metaphors are very prominent. Because Chinese culture has great impact on its language [25]. The work done in [27] direct designers to consider user as tourist. According to Lakoff and Johnson "metaphor is a way of conceiving of one thing in terms of another, and its primary function is understanding" [26].

C. Stephanidis and D. Akoumianakis argued in [28] that multiple metaphor environments are required from the variety of users, the changing of background of use and the changing in interaction platforms, all these things make essential changes in the design.

Metaphors reflect thinking of people their language and their culture. Therefore they can be use to explore their thoughts and language [34]. H. Alverson argued in [35] that TIME IS SPACE metaphor can be seen in different languages like English, Mandarin Chinese. Many other researchers also argued that this metaphor issued in many other languages.

2.4   Cultural Impacts on User Interface

The impact of culture in user interface is [12] controversial. Those that are in favor of using culture in user interface are not clear about which type of culture should be used. The other point of view which is not in favor of using culture cited by G. Ford and P. Kotzé, In which they argue that an interface design which accommodate Hofsted's dimensions would provide a more usable interface than the interface which does not accommodate these dimensions.

2.5   Cultural Markers

The work by [6] cited by [5] describes cultural markers as cultural attractors. Cultural markers [8] cited by [10] are combination of fonts, colors, icons, navigation, images, language and metaphors. Cultural markers reflect the signs of local culture in website. The work done by [46] cited in [5] proved with by using two mock websites and found the cultural markers have very helpful effects on user's performance.

Culture has great impact when designing metaphors. The most apparent [7] aspect in which metaphor is changed is the cross-cultural aspect. Different "cultural markers" are identified in [36] after exploring many websites of different regions and cultures. They suggested that using cultural markers can develop the usability.

2.6   Culturability

The term "culturability" was used by [8] cited by [10] which is combination of "culture" and "usability". They used cultural markers to assist the user. Sun interviewed people to examine how cultural markers [11] effect usability of websites. She concluded that people prefer cultural markers in their own culture.

2.7 Semiotics

Semiotics, are signs and symbols. The studies by [9, 37–39] cited by [5] found that the designers design icons, menus, symbols, colors, language according to their own culture to represent cultural specific things. People from different cultures prefer their cultural specific signs or symbols [40].

The researchers chose the AVIS website in [4] to examine the cultural differences in website, they chose it because it was an international application. They find that AVIS is leading car rental brand that is operating in more than 2,100 locations. AVIS has a USA-based Global website and 50 localized versions for countries around the world (Fig. 2).

Fig. 2. Localized website

2.8 Cultural Models

There are several cultural models they provide more detailed aspects of culture. These models [14] cited by [12] identify cultural dimensions. J. Anjum mentioned four cultural models [19], which were developed by Victor, Hall, Trompenaars and Hofstede following [13, 16–18] tables shows these cultural models [19] (Fig. 3).

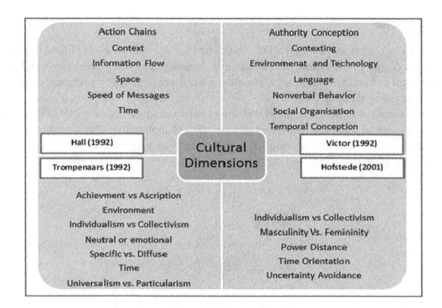

Fig. 3. Cultural dimensions

All these models have their cultural dimensions. Hofstede cultural model has five dimensions. All these dimensions are about subjective culture. It is very popular model in cultural dimensions. Hofstede used 116,000 questionnaires from over 60,000 respondents in his work [13, 47, 48] cited by [49]. He designed five dimensions, collectivism vs. individualism, femininity vs. masculinity, long vs. short-term orientation, power distance and uncertainty avoidance. These dimensions are used in comparison of cultures, to help in study of culture and as a cultural framework [50]. Hofstede used a work oriented approach and use his framework to groups of workers, it is being used largely in business studies [51–56].

3   Conclusion

All the work which has mentioned above shows that culture has great impact on user interface. Although there are few thoughts which are against the accommodation of culture in user interface. Culture has also great impact on metaphor. User prefers metaphor, semiotics and cultural markers in their own culture. The work done by different researchers show that metaphors are really helpful for user. However the designers are still not successful in designing a general user interface for all cultures. The designers design user interface according to their own culture without keeping in mind the target culture. There is more work needed to find such user interface that works for different cultures.

References

1. Badre, A.N.: The Effects of Cross Cultural Interface Design Orientation on World Wide Web User Performance, August 2000
2. Saffer, D.: The Role of Metaphor in Interaction Design, May 2005
3. Evers, V.: Cross-cultural Understanding of Metaphors Ininterface Design (1998)
4. de C. Salgado, L.C., de Souza, C.S., Leitão, C.F.: Using Metaphors to Explore Cultural Perspectives in Cross-Cultural Design, Orlando (Florida), USA, July 2011
5. Duncker, E., Sheikh, J.A., Fields, B.: From Global Terminology to Local Terminology: A Review on Cross-Cultural Interface Design Solutions (2013)
6. Smith, A., et al.: A process model for developing usable cross-cultural websites. In: Interacting with Computers (2004)
7. Kövecses, Z.: Metaphor and Culture. Philologica (2010)
8. Barber, W., Bardre, A.: Culturability: The Merging of Culture and Usability. In: Proceedings of the 4th Conference on Human Factors and Usability (1998)
9. Callahan, E.: Cultural differences in the design of human computer interfaces: A multinational study of university websites. Published thesis, Indiana University (2007)
10. Hsieh, H.C.L., Chen, C., Hong, S.D.: Incorporating Culture in Website Design: A Comparison of Taiwanese and Australian Website Characteristics (2013)
11. Sun, H.: Building a culturally-competent corporate web site: an exploratory study of cultural markers in multilingual web design. In: Proceedings of the 19th Annual International Conference on Computer Documentation, pp. 95–102 (2001)
12. Ford, G., Kotzé, P.: Designing Usable Interfaces with Cultural Dimensions
13. Hofstede, G. (ed.): Culture's Consequences, 2nd edn. Sage Publications, Thousand Oaks (2001)
14. Evers, V.: Cultural Aspects of User Interface Understanding: An Empirical Evaluation of an E-Learning Website by International User Groups, University of Amsterdam (2001)
15. Hoft, N.: Developing a cultural model. In: Del Galdo, E., Nielson, J. (eds.) International User Interfaces. Wiley, New York (1996)
16. Victor, D.: International Business Communications. Harper Collins, New York (1992)
17. Hall, E.: The Silent Language. Doubleday, New York (1959)
18. Trompenaars, F.: Riding the Waves of Culture. Nicholas Brealey Publishing, London (1993)
19. Sheikh, J.A., Duncker, E., Fields, B.: The Power of Cultural Classification: A Process Model for Multi-Cultural User Interface Design. Middlesex University, UK (2012)
20. Alan, C.: The Myth of Metaphor. Visual Basic Programmer's Journal, July 1995
21. Russo, P., Boor, S.: How fluent is your interface? Designing for international users. In: Human Factors in Computing System. In: Proceedings of INTERCHI 1993. ACM, Amsterdam (1993)
22. Lovgren, J.: How to choose good metaphors. IEEE Softw. **11**(3), 86–88 (1994)
23. Gannon, M., Audia, P.: The cultural metaphor: a grounded method for analyzing national cultures. In: Earley, C., Singh, H. (eds.) Work Behavior Across Cultures and Nations. Sage, Thousand Oaks (2000)
24. Gannon, M.J.: Cultural Metaphors: Applications and Exercises. College Park, Maryland, January 2000
25. Lichang, S.: Cultural Effects As Seen in Chinese Metaphors. Intercultural Communication Studies XIII, 3 (2004)
26. Lakoff, G., Johnson, M. (eds.): Metaphors We Live By. University of Chicago Press, Chicago (1980)

27. Salgado, L.C.C., de Souza, C.S., Leitão, C.F.: Conceptual Metaphors for Designing Multi-Cultural Applications. In: Proceedings of the 4th Latin American Conference on Human-Computer Interaction. IEEE Publications, Piscataway (2009)
28. Stephanidis, C., Akoumianakis, D.: Multiple Metaphor Environments: Issues for Effective Interaction Design, Greece
29. Tognazzini, B.: Tog on Interface. Addison Wesley, Reading (1992)
30. Tristram, C.: The next computer interface. Technology Review, 52–59, December 2001
31. Laurel, B.: Computers as Theatre. Addison-Wesley Publishing Company, Inc., Reading (1993)
32. Carroll, J.M., Mack, R.L. (eds.): Learning to Use a Word Processor: By Doing, by Thinking, and by Knowing. Morgan Kaufmann Publishers, Inc, San Francisco (1995)
33. Johnson, S.: Interface Culture: How New Technology Transforms the Way We Create and Communicate. Harper, San Francisco (1997)
34. Su, L.I.: What Can Metaphors Tell Us About Culture?. Language and Linguistics 3(3), 589–613 (2002) (National Taiwan University)
35. Hoyt, A.: Semantics and Experience: Universal Metaphors of Time in English, Mandarin, Hindi, and Sesotho. Johns Hopkins University Press, Baltimore (1994)
36. Barber, W., Badre, A.: Culturability: The merging of culture and usability. In: Proceedings of the Fourth Conference on Human Factors and the Web, AT and T Labs, Basking Ridge (1998)
37. Vatrapu, R.: Culture and International Usability Testing: The Effects of Culture in Interviews. Virginia Polytechnic Institute and State University (2000)
38. French, T., Smith, A.: Semiotically enhanced Web InterfacesforShared Meanings: CanSemiotics Help Us Meet the Challenge of Cross-Cultural HCI Design? IWIPS, Baltimore, US (2000)
39. Frenchand, T., Conrad, M.: Culture and e-Culture through a Semiotic Lens: E-Banking Localization(i-Society) (2012)
40. Fitzgerald, W.: Models for Cross-Cultural Communications for Cross-Cultural Website Design. National Research Council Canada (2004)
41. Lundell, J., Anderson, S.: Designing a front panel for Unix: The evolution of a metaphor. In: Proceedings of CHI 1995, pp. 130–137. ACM, Denver (1995)
42. Thornborrow, J., Wareing, S.: Meaning. In: Patterns in Language: AnIntroduction to Language and Literary Style (1998)
43. Fernandez, J.W. (ed.): Beyond Metaphor. The Theory of Tropes in Anthropology. Stanford University Press, Stanford (1991)
44. Lakoff, G. (ed.): The Contemporary Theory of Metaphor, 2nd edn. Cambridge University Press, Cambridge (1993)
45. Ortony, A. (ed.): Metaphor and Thought, 2nd edn. Cambridge University Press, Cambridge (1993)
46. Sheppard, C., Scholtz, J.: The effects of cultural markers on web site use. In: Fifth Conference on Human Factors and the Web, Gaithersburg, Maryland (1999)
47. Hofstedc, G. (ed.): Culture's Consequences: International Differences in Work-Related Values. Sage Publications, Newbury Park (1984) (Abridged edition)
48. Hofstede, G. (ed.): Cultures and Organizations — Software of the Mind. McGraw Hill, New York (1991)
49. Soares, A.M., Farhangmehr, M., Shoham, A.: Hofstede's dimensions of culture in international marketing studies. J. Bus. Res. 60(3), 277–284 (2007)
50. Lu, L.-C., Rose, G.M., Blodgett, J.G.: The effects of cultural dimensions on ethical decision making in marketing an exploratory study. J. Bus. Ethics, 18(1), 91–105 (1999)

51. Milner, L.M., Fodness, D., Speece, M.W.: Hofstede's research on cross-cultural work-related values implications for consumer behavior. Eur. Adv. Consum. Res. **1**, 70–76 (1993)
52. Sondergaard, M.: Research note: Hofstede's consequences: a study of reviews, citations and replications. Organ Stud. (1994)
53. Engel, J., Blackwell, R., Miniard, P.: Consumer behavior. The Dryden Press, Forth Worth (1995)
54. Dawar, N., Parker, P., Price, L.J., Dawar, N.: A cross-cultural study of interpersonal information exchange. J. Int. Bus. Stud. (1996)
55. Sivakumar, K., Nakata, C.: The stampede toward Hofstede's framework: avoiding the sample design pit in cross-cultural research. J. Int. Bus. Stud. 555–574 (2001)
56. Ford, J., LaTour, M., Shamkarmahesh, M.: Cultural dimensions of switching behavior in importer exporter relationships. Acad. Mark. Sci. Rev. 3 (2003)
57. Smith, A., French, T.: The role of cultural theories within international usability. In: Rauterberg, M., Menozzi, M., Wesson, J. (ed.) 'INTERACT'. IOS Press (2003)
58. Byrne, J.: Localisation: When Language, Culture & Technology Join Forces. Language at Work No. 5 (2000)
59. Marcus, A., Armitage, J., Frank, V.: Globalization of User-Interface Design for the Web. Aaron Marcus and Associates, Inc., Emeryville
60. Nielsen, J.: Why you only need to test with 5 users. Alertbox (2000)
61. Marcus, A.G.: Global/Intercultural user interface design. In: Sears, A., Jacko, J.A. (eds.) The Human-Computer Interaction Handbook: Fundamentals, Evolving Technologies and Emerging Applications, 2nd edn. Lawrence Erlbaum Associates, Hillsdale (2008)
62. Russo, P., Boor, S.: How fluent is your interface?: designing for international users. In: Proceedings of the INTERACT 1993 and CHI 1993 Conference on Human Factors in Computing Systems, pp. 342–347. ACM, New York (1993)
63. Angeli, A.D., et al.: Introducing ATMs in India: a contextual inquiry. Interact. Comput. **16**(1), 29–44 (2004)
64. Duncker, E., Sheikh, J.A., Fields, B.: From global terminology to local terminology: a review on cross-cultural interface design solutions. In: Rau, P. (ed.) HCII 2013 and CCD 2013, Part I. LNCS, vol. 8023, pp. 197–207. Springer, Heidelberg (2013)
65. Sheikh, J.A., Fields, B., Duncker, E.: The cultural integration of knowledge management into interactive design. In: Smith, M.J., Salvendy, G. (eds.) HCII 2011, Part I. LNCS, vol. 6771, pp. 48–57. Springer, Heidelberg (2011)
66. Sheikh, J.A., Fields, B., Duncker, E.: Cultural representation by card sorting. ergonomics for all: celebrating PPCOE's 20 years of excellence. Selected Papers of the Pan-Pacific Conference on Ergonomics, 7–10 November 2010, Kaohsiung, Taiwan, pp. 215 –220. CRC Press (2011)
67. Sheikh, J.A., Fields, B., Duncker, E.: Multi-Culture Interaction Design. In: Advances in Cross-Cultural Decision Making. CRC Press, pp. 406 –415 (2010)
68. Sheikh, J.A., Fields, B., Duncker, E.: Cultural based e-Health information system. Presentation at the Health Libraries Group Conference 2010, 19–20 July. CILIP, Salford Quays (2010)
69. Sheikh, J.A., Fields, B., Duncker, E.: Cultural representation for interactive information system. In: Proceedings of the 2009 International Conference on the Current Trends in Information Technology, Dubai (2009)
70. Sheikh, J.A., Fields, B., Duncker, E.: Cultural representation for multi-culture interaction design. In: Aykin, N. (ed.) IDGD 2009. LNCS, vol. 5623, pp. 99–107. Springer, Heidelberg (2009)

Chinese UI Design Guidelines 2.0

Jan Brejcha[1]([✉]), Hui Li[2], Qing Xu[2], Huitian Miao[2], Menghan Xu[2], Li Wang[2], and Zhengjie Liu[2]

[1] Frame Institute, Prague, Czech Republic
jan@brejcha.name
[2] Sino-European Usability Center (SEUC), Dalian Maritime University, Dalian 116026, People's Republic of China
{lihui082899000,18763600051,tianlidemiao,w18765906978}@163.com,
mh3512@hotmail.com, liuzhj@dlmu.edu.cn

Abstract. This paper presents the preferences of selected UI components of Chinese users. The areas of study were chosen using from a semiotic perspective, which lead us to focus on the cultural context, as well as the linguistic structure of user interaction. This quantitative study based on 50 respondents was targeted at validating the data gathered in a qualitative pilot study. The results are presented as UI design guidelines to simplify their adoption by both HCI researchers, and UX practitioners.

Keywords: Cross-cultural research · Cultural markers · Methodology · Design · Guidelines · User-interface · HCI · Semiotics

1 Introduction

When designing for global users, we are faced with a need to design UIs that are usable and well accepted in a targeted culture. In order to match the user's cultural expectations as closely as possible, designers need to combine usability knowledge with cultural insights. In the field of cross-cultural comparison, we can build upon a body of previous research [6–8]. For an initial analysis of the Chinese user experience we can refer to Marcus and Baradit [5]. In our view, however, only limited work has been done in creating usable guidelines for Chinese UI design.

We worked from a semiotic perspective, which lead us to focus on the cultural context, as well as the linguistic structure of user interaction. From our perspective, the UI is an example of complex language.

Semiotics works with a basic unit of analysis, which is a sign. The sign can be anything in the UI/UX that has a meaning for somebody. The meaning is supported by context and relationships between signs. Semiotic analysis can find implicit assumptions and hidden relations in culture, therefore is very suitable for cross-cultural analysis. The semiotic perspective in this study lead us to focus on specific areas, such as the meaning of composition (UI layout), of color, of icons, and the overall look and feel. The linguistic perspective focused in more detail on the composition (grammar) of icons, wording and structure of menu items (e.g., object + command).

© Springer International Publishing Switzerland 2015
A. Marcus (Ed.): DUXU 2015, Part I, LNCS 9186, pp. 122–129, 2015.
DOI: 10.1007/978-3-319-20886-2_12

Consequently, in our research we focused on different components of the UI language such as: discrete elements, interaction sentences, narration, rhetorical tropes, and patterns [2]. Discrete elements are the smallest elements to have a meaning. The interaction sentence is a meaningful unit describing a task in the user's interaction. The narrative in UI is made both by the designer's meta-communication and the temporal and/or sequential aspects of perceiving UI elements. Rhetorical tropes are devices of persuasion and emphasis, such as metaphors. Patterns are typical configurations of UI language components in different settings. Focusing on these UI language components allowed us to focus the scope of our research.

2 Research Methods

This paper revisits the results gathered during a pilot study in Mainland China in September 2011. The pilot study targeted the UI components' preferences of Chinese users. To continue on the previous study we defined research questions, updated and improved the questions to include more contexts for the given task. We also updated the hypotheses about the Chinese users forming the background of the questions. Then we built a questionnaire of ~40 questions for user interviews using an online reporting tool [9], and recruited participants according to a screener (using the snowball method: friends of friends). One session took about 15 min. After the interviews all the data was checked and translated, when appropriate.

In order to find the prevalent and preferred UI components or cultural markers [1], we focused our study on the five following areas: personal information (demographics, exposure to other cultures and technologies), layout (discrete elements, patterns, interaction sentences and narration), color (discrete elements, rhetorical tropes), symbol (rhetorical tropes) and look and feel (interaction sentences, narration, patterns, and rhetorical tropes).

The previous qualitative pilot study was based on one-to-one interviews supported by note taking and filling in questionnaires. The same method was adopted also for this quantitative study.

To limit the respondent's adaptation to a foreign culture, we worked with students who were enrolled at a local university (Dalian Maritime University in China) and were born and lived in the target cultures of our study. Also, the moderator of the interviews was a native speaker [8]. We worked with a sample consisting of 50 respondents, evenly split between females and males. The respondents had an average age of 22 years.

For evaluating the data we are using a margin of error [3] of 13,9 % (7 respondents) for the whole group of 50 respondents, and 19,6 % for in-group comparison (5 people in a sample of 25 respondents, e.g. male/female, urban/rural).

3 Results

Our findings show there is a strong influence of globalization on the cultural markers, mainly through the use of common software platforms. In spite of that, we found still many important culture-specific differences in both groups which are related to: spatial organization of information [4], shapes, direction of reading, motion, color, color combinations, semantic organization of content, use of icons and metaphors, user's preferences for different types of media, preference for culture-specific content and for cartoon imagery, trustworthiness of the content, navigation tools, visible and interaction grammar of menus and commands. In the following sub-sections, we provide a summary of the hypotheses that were supported by the data, those that were not, as well as other interesting insights and comments. The summary is divided by the main themes of our research:

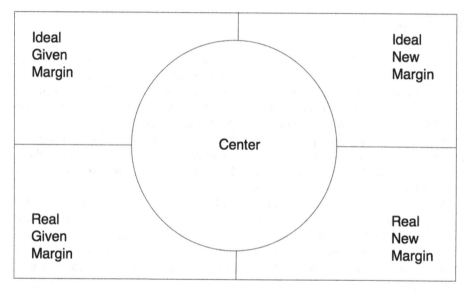

Fig. 1. Semiotics of space used to elicit hypotheses, and to evaluate study results (according to Kress and van Leeuwen).

3.1 Layout

For testing the UI composition we used a matrix with 3 rows and 3 columns. The hypotheses that were supported in relation to the spatial organization of the UI (Fig. 1), shapes, direction of reading and motion are:

- The center would hold important information, the margin the least important information.
- The given information would be on the left of the screen, the new on the right.
- The ideal information would be on the upper part of the screen, the real in the bottom.
- The sequence of comic panels follows the reading direction of text.

3.2   Color

For testing colors we used a 5-color palette (Fig. 2). The supported hypotheses regarding colors and color combinations were:

- Users would prefer lighter shades, combination of pastel colors.

Fig. 2.   Color palette used in the study

3.3   Symbol

For testing symbols we used various examples of existing computer icons, or we created the examples by ourselves (Fig. 3). The supported hypotheses regarding user's preferences for the UI grammar were:

- During Chinese language acquisition in children, verbs are learned first, followed by nouns later.
- Icons with situations would be preferred, because they present a wider context, and focus on actions (verbs).
- There is a close similarity between sequential information structure in language and in visual composition. **Verb (downloading) and adverb (speed of download) would mimic their position in sentence.** The file is in this case the noun.
- There is a close similarity between sequential information structure in language and in visual composition. **Noun (folder) and adjective (star attribute) would mimic their position in sentence** (adjective + noun).
- The sequence of input in **faceted search** would follow the sequence of natural language.

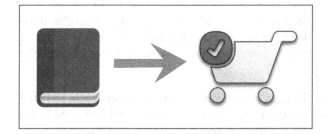

Fig. 3.   Variants of icon sets used in the study. Book icon author: Paomedia, License: creative commons (attribution 3.0 unported); shopping cart icon author: www.inmotionhosting.com, License: creative commons attribution 3.0 unported (CC BY 3.0).

3.4 Look and Feel

For testing the look and feel we used various examples found in different applications, or we created the examples by ourselves (Fig. 4). The supported hypotheses in this section regarding user's preference for cartoon imagery, navigation tools, visible and interaction grammar of menus and commands were:

- Menus starting with a verb are considered more natural than those starting with nouns.
- Menus progressively disclosing a narrative are considered more natural.
- Cartoon imagery (little animals) plays an important role in communication.

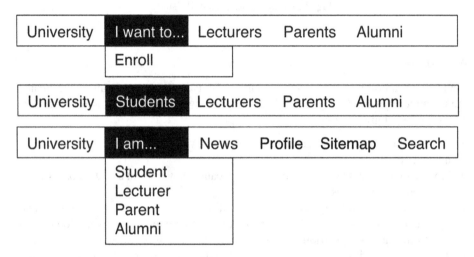

Fig. 4. Three different compositions of menus used in the study. On top a verb-driven menu, in the middle a noun-only menu, on the bottom a role-driven (narrative) menu.

4 Revisited Guidelines for Chinese UI Design

To help cross-cultural UI designers utilize our findings, we present our results in the form of guidelines that could also be used to enhance the user's acceptance of the UI in the Chinese culture. Some of the findings support universal usability tenets, while others are culture-specific:

Layout: Center vs. Margin. The most important message to the user should be in the upper-left and middle part of the screen. The least important should be placed in the bottom-right corner. These results confirm the outcome from the pilot study.

Layout: Given vs. New Information. Given information should be placed in the upper-left and left part of the screen, the new information to the right or below from it.

Layout: Ideal vs. Real Information. The ideal information should be place in the upper part of the screen, the real information in the center of the screen. These results also support the pilot study outcome.

Layout: Focus of Attention. Carefully choose the images: they start the visual narration on the screen, followed by titles.

Layout: Expected Sequence Direction. In a progressively disclosing UI, follow the prevalent reading direction. Expand the options to the right or underneath.

Layout: Originality. For a personal website use a somewhat novel style of design, for a commercial website use rather a somewhat well known style.

Color: Emotions and Preference. Adjust the UI color scheme not only for the target culture, but also to the target group of users. The results underlined the importance of the red color in Chinese culture no matter what segmentation we used.

Color: Combinations Preference. Background/content (white/blue or black), color pairs for a personal website (blue and yellow), color pairs for a commercial website (black and white, black and blue, blue and white).

Color: Image Brightness Preference. Use well-adjusted, or somewhat lighter images in the UI. This is one of the question we presented using a different methodology. In contrast with the previous study we let the respondents choose from visible options.

Symbol: Implicit Interaction. Build UIs on implicit relationships between commands and objects. In the Chinese context users tend to group items according to relations (verbs), rather than categories (nouns).

Symbol: Icon Style Preference. The icons should be as clear as possible, and when representing an action (command), they should present also **the object of the action**. The situations depicted in the icons favored mostly female respondents, while males preferred only a textual description of the action.

Symbol: Verbs and Adverbs. The icons presenting the current system status should be below or on the right of the object, as these placements are most natural for the users.

Symbol: Nouns and Adjectives. The icons presenting object attributes should be on the left of the object; as such a placement seems most natural for the users.

Symbol: Length of Web Pages. When appropriate, use shorter, rather than longer pages on screen. While bandwidth limitations favored longer pages (because of a lower number of requests to a server) during our pilot study in 2011, the quickly improving infrastructure allows the designers to focus more on users' requirements.

Symbol: Trust. Design for the **senses** when building trust. The UX design should account for the preferences of the target group of users, in order **to build trust, and to**

persuade. Although the senses might have a different importance in terms of trustworthiness in different environment, the leading is sight, followed by touch, and taste. In the media, **television still plays a major role** in trust. We see trust as a first step towards persuasion.

Symbol: Learning Online. When designing an online course, **focus on video-recorded lectures**, but add also a choice to **download the slides**, and a possibility to directly **engage with the lecturer** through videoconference. Differences were found between the sexes; we can assume, that females prefer more direct social interaction (video conference), while males prefer quickly skim and scan the texts.

Symbol: Word Order in Faceted Search. The sequence of input in a faceted search follows the sequence of natural language. The Subject comes first (relating to the user's gender, or size), followed by an implied Verb and adverb (purpose), and finally the Object (price, color, rating etc.). The results were the same in the pilot study for the first 3 items.

Look and Feel: Unfolding a Narrative. Construct menus with noun only, as these are clear to the users, and allow for a verb (command) submenu.

Look and Feel: User Roles. Construct menus that are based on the roles of users. In the case of a university website the students find it much more natural to find the information for them, and to **start their interaction** with the site from there.

Look and feel: Cartoons in the UI. Present cartoons in the UI while waiting for system processes to finish, which might take some time.

5   Discussion

The current study validated some of the results from the pilot. However, some of the hypotheses were not fully supported because of a different approach adopted. This was most evident, where the questions were asked differently or in a different sequence in relation to the pilot study. Another reason might be the choice of example images. Although we strived to gather a comparable population as in the previous study, there was a generation change: We worked with students having a different life experience, who were exposed to different social and technological conditions.

As a result, we obtained some new results (also because we introduced exploratory questions), and some trends that we would like to investigate further in a future study. As was the case with the pilot study, we plan to run a comparison study with a Western (Czech) population.

We hope our results and proposed design guidelines will help the international HCI design community and they will contribute to a discussion on how to improve cross-cultural research.

Acknowledgements. The authors wish to thank for the assistance of the Sino-European Usability Center.

References

1. Barber, W., Badre, A.: Culturability: the merging of culture and usability. In: Proceedings of the 4th Conference on Human Factors and the Web (1998)
2. Brejcha, J.: Cross-Cultural Human-Computer Interaction and User Experience Design. CRC Press, Boca Raton (2015)
3. Creative Research Systems. Sample size calculator (2012). http://www.surveysystem.com/sscalc.htm. Accessed Jan 06 2015
4. Kress, G., Van Leeuwen, T.: Reading Images: The Grammar of Visual Design. Routledge, London and New York (2006)
5. Marcus, A., Baradit, S.: Chinese User-Experience Design: An Initial Analysis. In: HCII in Los Angeles. Springer (2015)
6. Marcus, A., Gould, E.W.: Crosscurrents: cultural dimensions and global web user-interface design. Interactions **7**(4), 32–46 (2000)
7. Sheridan, E.F.: Cross-cultural website design. MultiLingual Comput. Technol. **12**(7), 1–5 (2001)
8. Smith, et al.: A process model for developing usable cross-cultural websites. Interacting. Comput. **16**(1), 63–91 (2004)
9. Survey Gizmo. Widgix, LLC dba SurveyGizmo, ©2005–2013. http://www.surveygizmo.com. Online survey software

Combining Principles of Experience, Traditional Heuristics and Industry Guidelines to Evaluate Multimodal Digital Artifacts

Fábio Campos[✉], Rui Belfort, Walkir Fernandes,
Edvar Neto, and Walter Correia

Federal University of Pernambuco, Recife, Pernambuco, Brazil
{fabiocampos,ruibelfort,edvar.vilar}@gmail.com,
fernandeswalquir@hotmail.com, design10@terra.com.br

Abstract. This paper presents how combining principles of user experience, traditional usability and industry design and development guidelines can impact the user knowledge elicitation process. The main objective is to provide an alternative for practitioners and researchers who seek up to date frameworks to evaluate contemporary digital artifacts. These advances generated better results on that matter and elevated an opportunity of a new usability testing, much more adequate in the established context.

Keywords: Principles of experience · Usability testing · Design and development guidelines

1 Introduction

Usability has become one main discipline on the design and development of digital multimodal artifacts. Regardless of this, in the last 10 years new interaction paradigms emerged and became status quo, representing a great challenge for both design practitioners and researchers in regarding of that matter.

Following on this, several studies [1–3] were conducted to verify if traditional usability evaluation is able to produce satisfactory results in the above-mentioned new context of multimodal digital interactions; those that bring to the table, besides others, touching and speaking interactions.

In [1], a framework based on the principles of experience (subjectivity, temporality and situatedness) was build to elicit real-time, real-context and direct user feedback. Through an experiment with casual gamers, it was possible to validate hypothesis on how, when and where those should be assessed.

It becomes clear that users should be elicited directly, in real-time and real-context of use. In order to do that, measurement scales were presented, remotely, during the actual use of a casual web game. Results elevated new parameters for those who work with multimodal digital artifact evaluation of any kind.

Reference [2] adds a critical analysis of traditional usability heuristics. The work presents a comparison of them and compiles a new set, specifically for digital multimodal

© Springer International Publishing Switzerland 2015
A. Marcus (Ed.): DUXU 2015, Part I, LNCS 9186, pp. 130–137, 2015.
DOI: 10.1007/978-3-319-20886-2_13

artifacts. More specifically, experiments were conducted in the context of medical devices with digital composition.

In this study, the collection of heuristics that was build as result of the previously mentioned analysis also achieved better results, considering the number of violations identified, and the severity rating, in comparison with Nielsen's [4]. Both inexperienced and specialist evaluators were able to conduct evaluation.

Last but not least, [3] shows a different perspective on the same issue. It presents newer paradigms that are being employed in the industry, to see what fits the best in the usability testing of contemporary artifacts. Positive results, comparing to traditional usability, were achieved in two experiments, with individuals using mobile devices and digital platforms.

Both procedures suggests that the group working with the collection of multimodal heuristics build in the process of research and in comparison with traditional ones, achieved a better performance in the evaluations. They were able to identify a considerably larger number of problems, with higher severity ratings, and pointed out more enhancement opportunities.

This paper aims to present, analyze and correlate results of these three studies, pointing out common issues, relevant advances and future research and pragmatical opportunities. The aim resides mostly in the need of contribution to update, academically and pragmatically, usability testing discipline and heuristic evaluation frameworks.

It is believed that combining the how, when and where principles, with collection of traditional heuristics remodeled to attend digital multimodal artifacts and the compendium of contemporary ones, based on industry guidelines, improvements can lead to more accurate evaluations.

2   Principles of Experience in the Evaluation of Digital Artifacts

In the design process, evaluating is a phase of major impact on the pursuit of delivering an effective and efficient product. Is well established that it is not possible to accurately evaluate it without consider users' perception. But to capture it is difficult; many concerns have to be addressed in order to make valid user assessment.

When dealing with people, the importance of approaching right, without manipulating (conscious or not) feedback, to extract accurate data on their experience, is consensual; presenting potential responses can enable assess their state of mind even in very quick interactions. So dealing with this correctly is really important.

However, there is a lot more to the data collection. A whole branch of scientific thinking named knowledge elicitation deals with the subtleness of extracting reliable data from the users, as well as the reliability of the data collected, the questions to be asked, the way to ask and the resources used throughout the assessment.

A lot has to be acknowledged about the best way to assess subjective data, such as personal experiences, in a way that it maintains its validity. This is the issue research aims to address. Evidences [1] were achieved that if principles of experience can help achieve that, no matter the assessment model, method, technique or tool that are being employed.

Basically, user experience has three main principles [5–8].

- Every experience is subjective. Observers (researchers) can interpret it from their backgrounds. The best way of assessing it, then, is from the user himself;
- Every experience is temporary. That means when it is over, it cannot be replicated. Each occurrence is different from the other. It is not good to rely on users' memory;
- Every experience is situated. In other words, is not possible to experience it outside (in a lab, for example) the natural context of use.

A framework called TR^2UE (tracking real-time, real context, user experience) were, then, designed in order to incorporate this during the process of elicitation.

To test it, users were challenged to play a game and during the experience, when they became inactive, a pop up with the sentence "How do you feel?" and a Likert 5-Point or Pictorial Scale (A/B testing [9]) appeared with a sequence of numbers or drawings representing potential subjective states. They give feedback choosing one it (Figs. 1 and 2).

Fig. 1. Screenshots of the web game running against time.

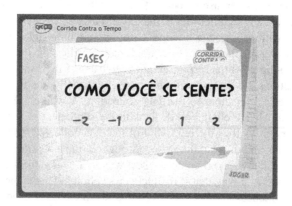

Fig. 2. Courtesy of Joy Street and Jynx playware.

213 users participated in the experiment. Their opinion was accessed directly, in real-time and in natural context of use, while they were playing. That interfered less on the experience, as results pointed out, and generated very rich and not manipulated feedbacks, compared with previous lab and specialist assessments.

Literature already recognizes the subjectivity factor in eliciting users, but *"situatedness and temporality as two other aspect of the user experience are mostly neglected"* [10]. It become clear that any theoretical or methodological construction that seeks to assess users' should consider principles of experience in order to enhance quality of data collection.

3 Traditional Heuristics Compilation for Medical Devices with Digital Composition

As supra-mentioned, in [2] are presented evidences of heuristics that can generate better results in finding and, of course, helping solve, issues related to the use of medical devices with digital composition (and also other digital multimodal artifacts). The failure of this kind of equipment can lead to loss of human life. Because of that, they becoming more and more state of art in terms of digital components.

According to International Eletrotechnical Commision (IEC), a medical device can be described as any instrument, machine, application, software, calibrator and similars, that is fabricated, once or many times, separately or in combination, to one or more of the following medical purposes, but not limited to it:

- Diagnoses, prevention, monitoring, treatment or relief of deceases;
- Diagnoses, prevention, monitoring, treatment, relief or compensation of a damage;
- Investigation, replacement, modification or support for anatomy or physiologic processes;
- Information provision to by examination of derivated parts of human body for medical purposes;
- Support and maintenance of life;
- Birth control.

A great part of them have digital complex components. They became part of daily activities throughout the world. You can find it in Intensive Care Units (ICUs), helping take care of patients 24/7, for example, but also in a home, administrating medicine in the right amount and giving statistics in case of severe deceases.

Considering that the use of complex digital components is a reality when it comes to welfare of patients, possibilities of use are almost infinite; but also, of course, the demand of specialization and work for those who operate it increases a lot [11]. In general, it is evenly proportional the amount of new possibilities and errors [12].

It is already common sense that one of the main reasons of problems during medical procedures is human failure. According to Leape [13], 69 % of injuries to health happen for that cause. As [14], we believe that a poor design can make it even worse for operators and more suitable to accidents.

That kind of human-computer interaction and the cognitive distress associated to the use of medical devices with digital composition can definitely be evaluated through heuristic usability. So we wanted to know if a combination of contemporary heuristics would generate better results, in comparison with Nielsen's.

To make that happen, Principles of Interactive Design [15], 8 Rules of Gold to Design Interfaces [16], Design Principles [17] and Nielsen's were analyzed and, as result, a set of 10 heuristics were combined, in order to better evaluate medical devices with digital composition. The results are heuristics listed below.

- Software-user system-software;
- Learning ability;
- Facilitating the cognition;
- User control and system flexibility;
- The system and the real world;
- Graphic design;
- Navigation and output;
- Consistency and standards;
- Error Management;
- Help and Documentation.

Heuristic evaluation were conducted and results suggests that the combined heuristics were much more effective in identifying problems, pointing out 64 issues to be addressed, with severity rating of 1,75. Compared to Nielsen's, which enabled evaluators identify 36 problems with severity rating of 1,47.

As a conclusion, the combined heuristics represent a starting point to digital artifact evaluation. Besides the fact they presented better results, combination is flexible and can be worked on infinitely, by specialists. The next step must be evaluating different kinds of artifact, in different contexts of use.

4   Industry Design and Development Guidelines; a New Set of Heuristics for Digital Multimodal Artifacts

Nielsen's heuristics gained notoriety over the past decades and have become one of the main tool for the evaluation of digital artifacts. These heuristics were formulated in the early 1990s, as a result of his research on websites and systems for desktop computers. And as we know, a lot has changed since then.

The main issue is that the interaction paradigm of desktop computers, known as WIMP (Windows, Icons, Menus and Pointers), has very different characteristics, when compared with the new emerging computing paradigms, such as multimodal interactions, based on multi-touch and speech, made popular by mobile devices and, more specifically, tablets.

In that sense, the multimodal interactions are a major challenge for traditional usability methods, which may not be able to consider their differences and particularities in evaluation. This problem becomes highly relevant as such emerging paradigms are becoming increasingly part of our daily activities. Usability can present itself fragile before that context.

As much as there are efforts to apply traditional usability literature to emerging devices, which does not mean that the conventions are appropriate to what is presented. It is more likely that designers apply ad hoc methods or sets of empirical techniques based on human factors, which often show as inefficient and outdated [18].

Our research [3] aimed to verify if a traditional usability inspection method show adequate results when faced with digital multimodal artifacts. We also wish to contribute to a new usability, by compiling guidelines of design and development, established in industry, to be use as alternative in the evaluation of these kind of devices, as seen below.

- Visibility and feedback;
- Compatibility;
- Control and freedom;
- Consistency;
- Error prevention;
- Minimum actions;
- Flexibility of use;
- Organized content;
- Error management;
- Direct manipulation;
- Change orientation;
- Human reach.

Two experiments were conducted with two groups, separately. The first, made up of professional designers with greater experience and familiarity with concepts of usability. In the second, they were all science computer professionals with more shallow knowledge of usability and little or no experience in evaluations.

The procedure consisted of presentation of the different heuristics set to their groups, followed by the presentation of scenarios of use. Thereafter, each expert made his evaluation individually. They classified each problem according to the heuristic and then attributed the degree of severity based on the frequency, duration and impact of problem.

Both experiments suggest that the group working with the compilation of multimodal heuristics were able to perform better in heuristic evaluation. The use of heuristics better suited to multimodal interactive paradigm obtained a better performance in to the number of pointed problems and the degree of severity assigned.

The evaluations using multimodal heuristics were able to identify 92 issues with severity rating of 2,55, in comparison with 45 issues and severity rating of 1,53 in the Nielsen's based ones. In the second experiment, with less familiarized evaluators, 39 issues with severity rating of 2,44 pointed out, in caparison with 26 issues and severity rating of 2,29.

5   Conclusions

As we presented throughout the whole paper, eliciting user information has became a major concern in the evaluation of digital multimodal artifacts. It is not difficult to understand why; established paradigms of evaluation, and mainly usability testing, have acknowledged that a lot has changed in regard of human-computer interaction; new paradigms are established.

Three studies explored possibilities on how would it be possible to deal with contemporary interactions without losing advances achieved in the past [1–3]. The major correlation of them lies on doing this in a way that make sense not only for designers, but also for researchers and, of course, and more importantly, users.

Reference [1] elevates the importance of considering subjectivity, temporality and situatedness, the three principles of user experience, while eliciting knowledge. Results shown that the less you affect the actual use of a multimodal digital artifact, the less users will rationalize assessment, and as result more accurate data will be collected.

In parallel, [2] presents a compilation of traditional heuristics; from widely spread used ones, both in industry, and validated results. The effort is to clarify what rules are, and what are not, adequate in the context of contemporary, multimodal interactions, without losing all the advances registered until now.

Also, industry are always moving forward and bringing new techniques, methods, methodologies and models to the table. Reference [3] have put together those updated paradigms, 100 % aligned to what's state of art, creating a new set of heuristics based on the published documentation of leading organizations and recognized researchers.

After all, the opportunity of advancing resides, mostly, in combining those three constructs, as a framework to assess user feedback. That will enhance quality of data collection, maintain rigor of traditional usability testing and put another layer of contemporary validation. Results on 3-step usability testing will be shared as soon as new experiments come to end.

References

1. Belfort, R.: Investigações Teórico-Metodológicas sobre Experiência de Usuário no Âmbito do Design. UFPE, Recife (2011)
2. Fernandes, W.: Verificação da conformidade das atuais Heurísticas de usabilidade quando aplicado aos equipamentos médicos de diagnostico por imagem. UFPE, Recife (2014)
3. Neto, E.: A contribuição para uma nova usabilidade através da compilação de heurísticas para dispositivos com interação multimodal. UFPE, Recife (2013)
4. Nielsen, J.: Usability Engineering. Morgan Kaufmann, San Francisco (1993)
5. Isomorsu, M.: User experience evaluation with experimental pilots. In: CHI 2008 Proceedings, Florence (2008)
6. Law, E., et al.: Towards a UX manifesto. In: HCI 2007 Proceedings, Lancaster (2007)
7. Roto, V., et al.: User experience evaluation methods in academic and industrial contexts. In: Interact 2009 Proceedings, Uppsala (2009)
8. Smith, T.: UX 2.0: Any User, Any Time, Any Channel. TechSmith Corporation, Okemos (2006)
9. Eisenberg, B.: Always Be Testing: The Complete Guide to Google Website Optimizer. Wiley Publishing, Indianapolis (2008)
10. Mahlke, S.: User experience: usability, aesthetics and emotions in human-technology interaction. In: Law, E., et al. (ed.) Towards a UX Manifesto, HCI 2007 Proceedings, Lancaster, p. 29 (2007)

11. Liljegren, E.: Usability in a medical technology context assessment of methods for usability evaluation of medical equipment. Int. J. Ind. Ergon. **36**, 345–352 (2006). Göteborg
12. Reason, J.: Human Error. Cambridge University Press, New York (1990)
13. Leape, L.: Error in medicine. J. Am. Med. Assoc. **272**, 1851–1857 (1994). Boston
14. Hyman, W.: Errors in the use of medical equipment. In: Bogner, M.S. (ed.) Human Error in Medicine. Lawrence Erlbaum Associates Inc., Hillsdale (1994)
15. Tognazzini, B.: First principles of interaction design. http://asktog.com/atc/principles-of-interaction-design. Assessed 6 March 2015
16. Shneiderman, B., et al.: Designing the User Interface. Pearson, Maryland (2005)
17. Tufte, E.: Envisioning Informtion. Graphics Press, Cheshire (1990)
18. Thomas, P., et al.: Introduction to the new usability. ACM Trans. Comput. Hum. Interact. **9**(2), 69–72 (2002)

Usability Heuristics for Heuristic Evaluation of Gestural Interaction in HCI

Ngip Khean Chuan[1(✉)], Ashok Sivaji[2],
and Wan Fatimah Wan Ahmad[3]

[1] MIMOS Berhad, Technology Park Malaysia, Kuala Lumpur, Malaysia
nk.chuan@mimos.my
[2] MIMOS Berhad, Technology Park Malaysia, 57000 Kuala Lumpur, Malaysia
ashok.sivaji@mimos.my
[3] Department of Computer and Information Sciences, Universiti Teknologi
PETRONAS, Perak, Malaysia
fatimhd@petronas.com.my

Abstract. Heuristic evaluation, also known as discounted usability engineering method, is a quick and very effective form of usability testing performed typically by usability experts or domain experts. However, in the field of gestural interaction testing, general-purpose usability heuristic framework may not be sufficient to evaluate the usability validity of gestures used. Gestural interaction could be found in products from mainstream touchscreen devices to emerging technologies such as motion tracking, augmented virtual reality, and holograms. Usability testing by experts during the early stages of product development that utilizes emerging technologies of gestural interaction is desirable. Therefore, this study has the objective to create a set of gesture heuristics that can be used in conjunction and with minimal conflict with existing general-purpose usability heuristics for the purpose of designing and testing new gestural interaction. In order to do so, this study reviews literature of gestural interaction and usability testing to find and evaluate previous gesture heuristics. The result is a condensed set of four gesture-specific heuristics comprising Learnability, Cognitive Workload, Adaptability and Ergonomics. Paired sample t-test analysis revealed that significantly more defects were discovered when gesture heuristics knowledge were used for evaluation of gestural interaction.

Keywords: Gestural interaction · Usability testing · User experience · Heuristic evaluation · Interaction styles

1 Introduction

Heuristic evaluation is a low-cost but effective evaluation method of usability testing [1]. According to the Usability Professional Association (UXPA) Salary Survey 2010, heuristic evaluation is the second highest used testing method by organizations worldwide. In heuristic evaluation, usability practitioners are gathered to review and evaluate interface design [2] based on their expertise and usability heuristics. Compared to usability testing methods such as user acceptance test, and focus group, where

© Springer International Publishing Switzerland 2015
A. Marcus (Ed.): DUXU 2015, Part I, LNCS 9186, pp. 138–148, 2015.
DOI: 10.1007/978-3-319-20886-2_14

a number of users have to be recruited and moderated, less time and resources is used in heuristic evaluation.

A set of usability heuristics had been proposed by Nielsen [3] that could serve as framework for generic usability testing. Sivaji et al. [4] later enhanced the set of heuristics (as shown in Table 1) with study results showing desirable outcome when generic heuristics were integrated with domain-specific heuristics.

Table 1. General-purpose heuristic for usabaility testing

Heuristics	Descriptions
Accessibility	The system should be able to be used by people with the widest range of characteristics and capabilities to achieve a specified goal in a specified context of use.
Compatibility	The way the system looks and works should be compatible with user conventions and expectations.
Consistency & Standards	The way the system looks and works should be consistent at all times.
Error Prevention & Correction	The system should be designed to minimize the possibility of user error, with built-in facilities for detecting and handling errors. Users should be able to check their inputs and correct errors or potential errorroneuous situations before inputs are processed.
Explicitness	The way the system works, and is structured, should be clear to the user.
Flexibility & Control	The interface should be sufficiently flexible in structure, in the way information is presented and in terms of what the user can do, to suit the needs and requirements of all users, and to allow them to feel in control of the system.
Informative Feedback	The system should always keep user informed about what is going on through appropriate feedback within reasonable time.
Language & Content	The information conveyed should be understandable to the targeted users of the application.
Navigation	The system navigation should be structured in a way that allows users to access support for a specific goal as quickly as possible.
Privacy	The system should help the user to protect personal or private information belonging to the user or their clients.
User Guidance & Support	Informative, easy-to-use, and relevant guidance and support should be provided to help user understands and use the system.
Visual Clarity	Information displayed on the screen should be clear, well-organized, unambiguous and easy to read.

The heuristics in [4] originated from software usability expertise where the main form of interaction was done via mouse and keyboard, before the proliferation of mobile touchscreen devices such as smartphones [5] and tablets [6]. Touchscreen mobile devices primary utilize finger gestures [7–9] as main input. The type of gestures used in touchscreen may consists of simple gestures such as tap, swipe, and pinch, or more complex gestures such edge swipe, multiple fingers swipe, tilting, and shaking. The typical technology of touchscreen allows for multiple concurrent fingers and as a result, infinite amount of gestures can be programmed as inputs.

Norman and Nielsen [10] was critical of the gestural interactions of the time (i.e., those in Apple iOS, and Google Android). The interactions are filled with usability issues due to the refusal of developers to follow established fundamental interaction design principles. Further, when touch-oriented Microsoft Windows 8 operating system was launched, its gesture-based interface was also found to provide poor user experience by having hard-to-discover and error-prone gestures [11]. Thus, it is desirable to minimize the usability problems that arise from designing and developing gestures vocabulary for current touchscreen devices and for devices of emerging technologies such as motion tracking [12], augmented virtual reality, and hologram.

2   Problem Statement

Organizations with dedicated usability testing team usually have established usability testing methods and its corresponding usability heuristic framework (e.g., example in Table 1). The existing methods and usability frameworks are designed to for general-purpose usability testing. If the new gesture-specific heuristics are not created, it is hypothesized that fewer problem would be found by heuristics evaluators [10]. The gesture-specific domain knowledge would result in new gesture usability heuristics. These new heuristics need to be created with minimal overlapping with the existing general-purpose heuristics.

In addition, it is harder to find usability problems during early and middle part of the product development life cycle [13] without gesture-specific heuristics. This problem is more severe for complex gestures [14]. When usability problem is found at the late stage of the product development, it may be costly or impossible to fix.

Further, designing gestures is a time-consuming and delicate process [14]. By having gesture-specific heuristics, interaction designer could shorten the gesture design process [15] and also avoid spending time benchmarking on impractical gestures.

3   Literature Review

A systematic literature review is carried out to study previous works. The objective is to adopt a suitable gesture definition and framework. The definition and framework are needed to identify, differentiate, and filter gesture-specific heuristics from subsequent literature review.

3.1   Definition and Framework

The study refers to works done by Karam [16] on gesture framework due to its extensiveness. Here, the term "gestures" refers to an expensive range of interactions enabled through a variety of gesture styles, enabling technologies, system response, and application domain (see Fig. 1). In addition, types of gesture styles (the physical movement of gesture) are reviewed and emphasized. Gesture styles can be grouped into five categories: deictic, gesticulation, manipulation, semaphores, and sign languages.

Deictic gestures involve pointing in order to establish spatial location or identity of the object. This is very similar to director manipulation input of a mouse. Deictic gestures are one of the simplest gestures to implement.

Manipulation gestures are gestures that have tight relationship between actual movements of the gesturing fingers, hand, or arm with the entity being manipulation [17]. Manipulations could include two-dimensional movements or three-dimensional movements, depending on the user interface. Manipulations could also involve the use of tangible objects as a medium of input (e.g., a model of object being controlled). The object being controlled could be an on-screen digital object, or a physical mechanical object such as robots.

Gesticulation gestures evolved from non-verbal communication gesture by human that accompany or substitute speech. The gestures rely on computation analysis of body, hand, or arm movements in the context of speech. When used in conjunction with speech command, the gestures add clarity to the speech. Gesticulation gestures can also be used in lieu of speech such as iconic and pantomime gestures.

Semaphores style can be found in any gesturing system that employs a stylized dictionary of static or dynamic hand or arm gestures. Semaphore gestures are widely applied in literature because of its practicability of not being tied to factors that defines

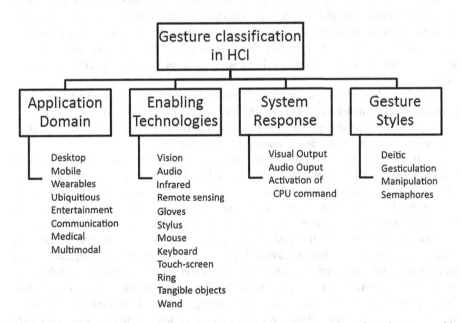

Fig. 1. Classification of gesture with highlight on the gesture styles of study scope with omission of sign language from list of gesture styles.

other type of gesture styles. In addition, the combination of dynamic and static poses offer infinite amount gestures choices.

Sign languages gestures are considered linguistic-based and are independent from other gestures styles. There are more than a hundred of known sign language in the world [18]. Sign languages are not designable by interface designer; therefore, not testable and, consequently, not included in the scope of this study.

Further, the gesture framework proposed by [16] describes gestural interaction as a composition of intercepting two human-computer interaction (HCI) task artifact cycle [19]. The task cycles comprises four main components from Fig. 1: gestures styles, application domain, enabling technologies and system response; which roles are either to provide possibilities (i.e., methods and medium of interaction) or system responses.

3.2   Gathering of Gesture Usability Heuristics

Once the gesture definition and framework has been determined, the study proceeds to review and gather gesture-related usability heuristics. The selected studies from literature review are: [10], Wach et al. [20], Baudel and Beaudouin-Lafon [21], Wu et al. [22], Yee [23], and Ryu et al. [24].

As mentioned, [10] provides critical analysis of the usability issues in mainstream touch-screen gestural interactions. Six fundamental principles of general interaction design were offered: Visibility, Feedback, Consistency and Standards, Discoverability, Scalability, and Reliability. However, these heuristics overlapped with the generic-purpose usability heuristics of Table 1.

Study in [20] is an older literature on the general state and potential of gestural interaction before the proliferation of smartphone and tablets gestural interaction devices. The set of heuristics outlined were Learnability, Intuitiveness, User Feedback, Low Mental Load, User Adaptability, Reconfigurability, and Comfort. The heuristics are gesture-specific and could be used in a wide range of field from gaming to medical surgery.

In [21], a glove-based gestural interaction named Charade was created. The study proposed a set of heuristics for designing and testing the gestures of the device. Five major heuristics proposed are Fatigue, Non-Self-Revealing, Lack of Comfort, Immersion Syndrome, and Segmentation of Hand Gestures.

Study in [22] has a gestural interaction device based on small table-sized touch-screen surface that utilizes hand and stylus. The study also proposed a set of heuristics for designing and evaluating the gestural interaction. The heuristics are Gesture Registration, Gesture Relaxation, and Gesture and Tool Reuse. Compared to [20], there is more focus on re-using a small set of gestures for multiple functions.

Study in [23] reviews the problem of usability of indirect or abstract gestures which, according to the classification in [16], could be a mixture of gesticulation, and semaphores. The study identified five major needs and the corresponding guidelines for gestural interaction: "achieve high effectiveness", "deviate potential limitation in productivity application", "minimize learning among users and increase differentiation among gestures", "design efficient gestures to increase user adoption", and "maximize the value of finger gestures".

Lastly, [24] conducted a systematic gathering and evaluation of information and guidelines of gesture applicability. The amount of heuristics offered is not necessary gesture-specific. Using the definition of gestural interaction in [16], two gesture-specific heuristics have been identified: Naturalness and Expressiveness.

4 Proposed Heuristics

After gathering the heuristics, the study uses a simple phenomenon or phase-based classification method [25] to group and combine these heuristics. The gesture heuristics are put into four phases: "Before using", "During using", "After using", and "Prolonged using" (as shown in Table 2).

Table 2. Proposed heuristics by phase classification

Phase / Study title	Before using	During using	After using	Prolonged using
Charade: Remote control of objects using free-hand gestures	Non-self-revealing	Segmentation of hand gestures		Fatigue, lack-of-comfort
Gestural interfaces: a step backward in usability	Consistency and standards, Discoverability, Visibility	Feedback,	Scalability	
Vision-based hand-gesture applications	Learnability, Intuitiveness	User feedback, Low mental load	User adaptability, Re-configurability	Comfort
Conditions of Applications, Situations and Functions Applicable to Gesture Interface	Naturalness (sub-items: Communication, Behavioral pattern)	Expressiveness (sub-items: Entertainment, Security, Special manipulation)		
Potential Limitations of Multi-touch Gesture	Deviate potential limitation in productivity application. Minimize learning among users and increase differentiation among gestures.	Archive high effectiveness.	Design efficient gestures to increase user adoption.	Maximize value of finger gestures.
Gesture Registration, Relaxation, and Reuse for Multi-Point Direct-Touch Surfaces		Gesture registration, Gesture relaxation, Gesture reuse		

Table 3. Naming of the four group of gsetures

Phase	Generalized usability concepts	Heuristic Name
Before using	Discoverability, Learnability, Memorability	**Learnability**
During using	Cogntive workload, Segmentation, Feedback	**Cognitive Workload**
After using	Adaptability, Extensibility, Reconfigurability, Scaling	**Adaptability**
Prolonged using	Comfort, Fatigue, Ergonomics	**Ergonomics**

This method of classification is simple to understand and yet comprehensive for all stages of gesture use. Labels are assigned to the classifications based on the generalization of the heuristics inside the classification. The labels are also the names of the four proposed heuristics: Learnability, Cognitive Workload, Adaptability, and Ergonomics (as shown in Table 3).

5 Experiment

An experiment was conducted in order to verify the gesture heuristics. Five usability practitioners were invited to participate in a heuristic evaluation using the gesture-specific heuristics. The participant ages are between 25 to 55 year old, with at least three years of usability-related experience. The number of participant is considered sufficient because heuristics evaluations are usually performed using a recommended three to five evaluators [2].

The testing was carried out on basic touch-screen gestures related tasks on an iPhone 5 running iOS 8.1.1 operating system. The tasks are phone unlocking, internet browsing, map navigation, note taking, and home screen miscellaneous operations. The tasks involves using the gestures available [7].

Initially, the usability practitioners were instructed to perform heuristic evaluation to identify issues and good design features of the gestures used during the tasks. At this point, the practitioners can only rely on existing heuristic guideline in Table 1.

Subsequently, a waiting period of two days imposed in order to eliminate bias from the first session. After that, the GH (gesture heuristics) descriptions and its related literature [10, 20–24] were taught to the practitioners. Then, the usability practitioners perform the heuristics evaluation again with the additional of the new gesture heuristics. From this, the null and alternative hypotheses are as follows:

- $H_0 : \mu_{before\ GH} = \mu_{after\ GH}$ there is no significant difference in the mean numbers of defects for before and after using the gesture heuristics.
- $H_a : \mu_{before\ GH} \neq \mu_{after\ GH}$ there is significant difference in the mean numbers of defects for before and after using the gesture heuristics.

6   Results

Shapiro-Wilk test supports the hypothesis the data is normal for both with GH and without GH (p > 0.05). A paired-sample t-test was conducted using SPSS vs22 to compare the number of defects found before and after the GH knowledge were transferred to the evaluators. Results reveal that there were statistically significant differences in the number of defect before (mean = 4.4, SD = 0.6782) and the defects found after the knowledge transfer (mean = 6.2, SD = 0.6633); t (4) = 4.811; p = 0.009. Hence, it could be concluded that GH intervention provides significantly more defect than heuristic evaluation performed with GH.

On average, there is an increase of 1.8 issues for each participant when GH is used to find issues. Figure 2 shows the amount of issues found per users while Table 4 shows the statistical analysis results.

Among the important findings are that more ergonomics issues were detected with gesture heuristic. This is because the general-purpose heuristics does not involve consideration in prolonged use of a product.

In addition, learnability issues are more likely to be considered valid when using gesture heuristics. This is because the gesture heuristics literature provides better clarity

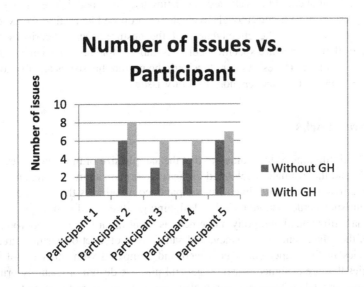

Fig. 2. Experiment result showing number of issues found without and with GH (gesture heuristics).

Table 4. Paired sample t-test analysis results

Paired Sample Statistics	Mean	N	Std. Deviation
Without GH	4.4	5	0.6782
With GH	6.2	5	0.6633
Paired difference	1.8		0.8366
Paired differences	**t**	**df**	**Sig. (2-tailed)**
With GH – Without GH	4.811	4	0.009

and information on past errors. Further, the gesture Learnability heuristic requires user to be able to perform systematic exploration of menu to learn gestures.

Overall, the participants' feedback was that the gesture heuristics provides additional domain-specific knowledge that is useful in heuristic evaluation.

7 Conclusion

The study proposed four usability heuristics for the use of heuristic evaluation specifically on the gesture vocabulary used in human-computer interaction. The heuristics are Learnability, Cognitive Workload, Adaptability, and Ergonomics. These heuristics does not include general-purpose software heuristics or hardware performance based-heuristics that could be evaluated in existing usability model. The study gathered six existing usability heuristics models to create the proposed heuristics. An experiment was conducted to verify the effectiveness of the gesture-specific heuristics and the results show that the gesture-specific heuristics did complement the general-purpose heuristics to find more issues. As hypothesized, the gesture heuristics are able to enable heuristics evaluators to discover more usability issues.

8 Future Works

Some of the limitations of this study are that the sample size of the heuristic evaluators were small, and the evaluators belonged to the same organization, culture, and country. Future experiment with more diverse participants could address these limitations. The gesture heuristics could also be used for designing gestures used in new products such as those that utilize hand and body movement as input in large screen environment. In such case, the effectiveness, efficiency, and satisfaction of a set of gestures created by the heuristics in this paper could be gaged and compared with other set of gesture vocabularies that are designed based on general-purpose design or usability principles. In addition, time taken to modify or replace gestures in later stages of the product development could be documented in order to calculate the amount of timesaving that could be gained from using the gesture heuristics.

References

1. Greenberg, S., Fitzpatrick, G., Gutwin, C., Kaplan, S.: Adapting the locales framework for heuristic evaluation of groupware. Australas. J. Inf. Syst. **7**, 102–108 (2000)
2. Nielsen, J., Molich, R.: Heuristic evaluation of user interfaces. In: SIGCHI Conference on Human Factors in Computing Systems, pp. 249–256. ACM (1990)
3. Nielsen, J.: Enhancing the explanatory power of usability heuristics. In: Proceedings of the SIGCHI Conference on Human Factors in Computing Systems, Boston, Massachusetts, pp. 152–158 (1994)
4. Sivaji, A., Abdullah, A., Downe, A.G.: Usability testing methodology: effectiveness of heuristic evaluation in E-Government website development. In: 2011 Fifth Asia Model Symposium, pp. 68–72 (2011)
5. Subramanian, S.: Dynamically Adapting Design and Usability in Consumer Technology Products to Technology and Market Life-Cycles: A Case Study of Smartphones Libraries. Massachusetts Institute of Technology, Massachusetts (2009)
6. Huberty, K., Lipacis, M., Holt, A., Gelblum, E., Devitt, S., Swinburne, B., Meunier, F., Han, K., Wang, F.A.Y., Lu, J., Chen, G., Lu, B., Ono, M., Nagasaka, M., Yoshikawa, K., Schneider, M.: Tablet Demand and Disruption: Mobile Users Come of Age. Morgan Stanley Research Global, New York (2011)
7. iOS Human Interface Guidelines: Interactivity and Feedback. https://developer.apple.com/library/ios/documentation/userexperience/conceptual/mobilehig/InteractivityInput.html
8. Gestures | Android Developers. http://developer.android.com/design/patterns/gestures.html
9. Use touchscreen gestures on Microsoft Surface | Zoom, scroll, tap, copy, paste. http://www.microsoft.com/surface/en-my/support/touch-mouse-and-search/using-touch-gestures-tap-swipe-and-beyond
10. Norman, D., Nielsen, J.: Gestural interfaces: a step backward in usability. Interactions **17**(5), 46–49 (2010)
11. Windows 8—Disappointing Usability for Both Novice and Power Users. http://www.nngroup.com/articles/windows-8-disappointing-usability/
12. Chuan, N.-K., Sivaji, A.: Combining eye gaze and hand tracking for pointer control in HCI: developing a more robust and accurate interaction system for pointer positioning and clicking. In: IEEE Colloquium on Humanities Science and Engineering, pp. 172–176 (2012)
13. Sivaji, A., Abdullah, M.R., Downe, A.G., Ahmad, W.F.W.: Hybrid usability methodology: integrating heuristic evaluation with laboratory testing across the software development lifecycle. In: 10th International Conference on Information Technology: New Generations, pp. 375–383. IEEE (2013)
14. Neilsen, M., Störring, M., Moeslund, T.B., Granum, E.: A procedure for developing intuitive and ergonomic gesture interfaces for man-machine interaction, Aalborg, Denmark (2003)
15. Henninger, S.: A methodology and tools for applying context-specific usability guidelines to interface design. Interact. Comput. **12**(3), 225–243 (2000). Elsevier
16. Karam, M.: A framework for research and design of gesture-based human computer interactions (2006)

17. Quek, F., Mcneill, D., Bryll, R., Mccullough, K.E.: Multimodal human discourse : gesture and speech. ACM Trans. Comput. Hum. Interact. **9**, 171–193 (2002). University of Illinois at Chicago
18. Deaf sign language | Ethnologue. http://www.ethnologue.com/subgroups/deaf-sign-language
19. Carroll, J.M., Rosson, M.B.: Getting around the task-artifact cycle: how to make claims and design by scenario. ACM Trans. Inf. Syst. **10**, 181–212 (1992)
20. Wachs, J.P., Kölsch, M., Stern, H., Edan, Y.: Vision-based hand-gesture applications. Commun. ACM **54**, 60 (2011)
21. Baudel, T., Beaudouin-Lafon, M.: Charade: remote control of objects using free-hand gestures. Commun. ACM **36**, 28–35 (1993)
22. Wu, M., Shen, C., Ryall, K., Forlines, C., Balakrishnan, R.: Gesture registration, relaxation, and reuse for multi-point direct-touch surfaces. In: 1st IEEE International Workshop on Horizontal Interactive Human-Computer Systems (TABLETOP), pp. 185–192. IEEE, Adelaide (2006)
23. Yee, W.: Potential limitations of multi-touch gesture vocabulary: differentiation, adoption, fatigue. In: Jacko, J.A. (ed.) HCI International 2009, Part II. LNCS, vol. 5611, pp. 291–300. Springer, Heidelberg (2009)
24. Ryu, T., Lee, J., Yun, M.H., Lim, J.H.: Conditions of applications, situations and functions applicable to gesture interface. In: Kurosu, M. (ed.) HCII/HCI 2013, Part IV. LNCS, vol. 8007, pp. 368–377. Springer, Heidelberg (2013)
25. Clancey, W.: Classification problem solving. In: AAAI 1984, pp. 49–55. AAAI, Austin (1984)

Exploring and Experimenting Cooperative Design

Salomão David[(✉)] and Lorenzo Cantoni

Faculty of Communication Sciences, Universita della Svizzera Italiana,
via G. Buffi. 13, 6900 Lugano, Switzerland
{salomao.david.cumbula,lorenzo.cantoni}@usi.ch

Abstract. This paper describes a community co-design approach performed in rural Mozambique. It discusses the experiences and experiments performed in a community multimedia center towards creating services with inherent values for daily community activities. The design approach pursues a holistic interpretation of community needs, and discusses emerging, new and creative applications for future community binding.

Keywords: Community design · Co-design · ICT4D · Development · Tourism · And education

1 Introduction

The sub-Saharan Africa faces development problems, reflected in high unemployment, digital divide, disparities in access to health, and education [1]. To tackle these issues donors and sub-Saharan nations devoted significant human and financial resources to Information and Communication Technologies (ICTs), creating public access venues or ICT venues. Public access venues are locations that provide access to computer and Internet services, open to the public. They are also defined as a place that offers public access to information with services available to everyone, and not directed to one group excluding others [2]. Examples of public access venues established in sub-Saharan Africa are telecentres, community radios, cybercafés, millennium villages, and libraries.

The birth of public access venues was expected to improve efficiency in government service delivery, and to contribute to development, to promote digital inclusion through technology, information access and development of ICT skills [3]. Public access venues have high social impact on users, deliver benefits that touch aspects of users livelihood, including access to culture, education, communication, information, political participation, and leisure.

This paper presents a collaborative approach used to design a solution with inherent value for the community of Morrumbene, in Mozambique. The case shows how involving individuals, social groups, and organizations, can provide conditions to create an environment to produce a social and financial sustainable solution.

The rest of the paper is organized as follows: in the next three sections, we present an overview on public access venues in Mozambique, their context, and the methodological framework used in this action-research. The last two sections present the outcome

© Springer International Publishing Switzerland 2015
A. Marcus (Ed.): DUXU 2015, Part I, LNCS 9186, pp. 149–156, 2015.
DOI: 10.1007/978-3-319-20886-2_15

of the intervention, and provide a discussion, which includes stakeholders, context, ownership, and sustainability.

2 Public Access Venues in Mozambique

Mozambique is a country located in sub-Saharan Africa, bordered by the Indian Ocean on the east, Zimbabwe on the west, Tanzania and Malawi on the north, and South Africa on the south. The country has approximately 70 % of inhabitants living in rural areas [4].

In 1999, Mozambique witnessed the establishment of two public access venues in Manhiça and Namaacha districts. These venues were conceived to provide access to computers, ICT training (word, excel, power point, graphic design), public phone, fax, photocopy and Internet [5].

Communities' information, technology, and leisure needs were somehow met during the first years of implementation; the demand for ICT courses and services were high and exclusive to the telecentre.

With the appearance of mobile technologies in the country, community needs shifted, with mobile phones becoming affordable and socially sustainable compared to telecentres, the mobile industry growth casted shadow on the two existing telecentres [6].

Sustainability of telecentres remained a key challenge, addressed in the year 2000 by a scale-up project funded by UNESCO: the scale-up project consisted in increasing the technological infrastructure in the telecentre, and in merging it with the community radio operating on the same venue [7, 8]. That was the very beginning of CMC: Community Multimedia Centers.

A research and development project called RE-ACT (social Representations of community multimedia centers and ACTions for Improvement), run in 2011-2014 by the Università della Svizzera italiana (Lugano, Switzerland) and by the University Eduardo Mondlane (Maputo, Mozambique), performed in 2011 field trips throughout all provinces of Mozambique to collect data about communities' perception and adoption of CMCs.

CMCs in Mozambique face three common problems: financial sustainability, inability to meet local needs, inability to get technical assistance [2, 9–11].

These problems arise when the income generated doesn't cover operating costs; or other venues do exist close to it providing similar services at a lower cost. In some cases communities are not aware of the services offered by the CMC, or the services are just offered for free.

CMCs are located in rural areas, where to repair, purchase or perform (preventive) maintenance on equipment is financially not feasible.

Community adoption of CMC means how communities perceive it: adoption of CMC services is lower in locations where local communities perceived the CMC as being just a technology provider, adoption is higher in locations where the CMC is perceived as a space for social and cultural exchanges.

3 Morrumbene

The Morrumbene district is located in the center of the Inhambane province, approximately 450 km north of Maputo, the capital of Mozambique. It has a largely dispersed population of 110,817 inhabitants, and a land extension of 2,608 km^2 [12]. The district is known for its wonderful beaches, tranquility, vibrant culture, and resorts built with a mixture of western and local architecture.

District's main economic activities are fishing, tourism, and agriculture. Fishing and agriculture activities are for subsistence (artisanal), while tourism has contributed to develop rural areas, and to rise demand on local agriculture and fishing industry [13].

The Ministry of Science and Technology (MCT) founded the Morrumbene CMC in 2010, and its management has been entrusted to a local association, named *Associaçao Juvenil a Chama.*

The CMC offers basic computer training (word, excel, power point, access, and internet). The Community Radio transmits in Portuguese and Xichangana, and covers the entire Morrumbene district plus the neighboring districts of Maxixe and Homoine. Additionally, information and communication services like newspapers, seminars, and cinema on weekends are also provided [14].

The CMC has 14 volunteers, mostly local teachers pursuing a degree in education and students of 10th and 12th grades, all members of the local association.

The communication infrastructure in the district has several limitations; the telephone line doesn't reach the location where the CMC is established: they rely on mobile phones to acquire information. The Internet broadband is accessed by using a very small terminal (VSAT), with free access up to 6 GB per month financed by the MCT. Other Internet providers such as mobile companies are also available, but more expensive.

4 Methodological Framework

The methodological framework used in this action-research is co-design, following a similar path of participatory design, although it's seen as an evolutionary approach to technology design for socio-economic development.

The methodology is associated with two approaches: inclusion and empowerment, characteristics that gained increased attention in the more mature years of Information and communication technologies for development (ICT4D) research and practice [15].

Co-design refers to the conception or creation of artifacts drawing on a shared vision, social learning and mutual understanding among all key stakeholders, taking into account that all those involved in the design process have somehow different perspectives and expectations, which should be adequately considered [16]. Literature on community design outlines stakeholders, context, ownership, social learning, and sustainability as problem domains to be addressed during socio-technical experiments [16, 17].

To ensure ownership and empowerment, and to provide optimal learning conditions, the implementation followed in every phase three codes of conduct:

1. Communities views and concerns regarding technology had to be taken into consideration;
2. Every participant, regardless of their educational background, social status, was considered an expert on their own domain;
3. The main sources of design ideas and innovations are from within the community;

The co-design process used at the Morrumbene district was a participatory assembly for inclusion and sharing of ideas, only accepted when consensus about a topic was reached [18].

The process followed two distinct phases:

- Focus group sessions; and
- Website design.

4.1 Focus Group Sessions

The RE-ACT project aimed at creating an "improvement action" for the Morrumbene CMC, the goal was to co-design a technological solution with inherent value for the community.

The process to select and implement the improvement action had two distinct focus group sessions, the first session held at the University Eduardo Mondlane (UEM) in Maputo, and the second one at the Morrumbene CMC in the Morrumbene district.

The improvement actions were small-budget projects co-designed such that implementation was to be performed by the CMC overseen by the community, and RE-ACT team. The improvement action envisioned to be implemented by the Morrumbene CMC was a tourism website, idea conceived during the first co-design session held at UEM.

This first co-design session had as participants' nine CMCs directors, as well as representatives of MCT, UNESCO, and UEM entities that performed the establishment and scale-up project of CMCs in Mozambique.

The second stage of the focus group had three sessions held at the Morrumbene district.

The first focus group session held in Morrumbene was devised to build a good relationship between co-design session intervenient, and to acquire knowledge capabilities, area of expertise, contribution, and limitations of participants.

In order not to limit, but to manage expectations and enable participants to voice their views, all sessions in Morrumbene where led by the CMC director, who started presenting the concept of improvement actions, consisting in the tourism website. The local community rejected the idea, voicing concerns about inclusion, and declaring that tourism entrepreneurs and authorities have their websites in English, designed, hosted, and maintained elsewhere.

With unviable conditions to produce a website, a question was raised by the CMC.

"What should we implement that will allow inclusion of all social groups in the district?"

Through the second session discussions, consensus was reached to invite actors with relevant information and knowledge about community core activities; participants comprised then members of police, health service, fisherman association, local entrepreneurs, resort owners, teachers, local youth and religion leaders.

The second session produced a fruitful discussion around the services that have inherent value for district social groups, unanimity was reached to design a website about the Morrumbene district with the aim to connect people from the district living in and outside. The website had to contain information about the education sector, police information (safety and local reports), health information, and information about commerce.

As the website would only connect people from the community with knowledge and access to computers or smartphones, to mitigate this exclusion it was decided to share information on the website using Short Messaging Service (SMS). These messages were to be sent only to people who subscribed to specific website categories; exception was placed on urgent police and health information, which is sent to all registered numbers.

4.2 Website Design

The website design was carried by the CMC, overseen by the community and the RE-ACT team.

The CMC was responsible for defining the website template using joomla; it was also responsible to collect information from the community and to host on the website.

Training and selection of open source technologies for the website and SMS platform was the responsibility of the RE-ACT team. The solution selected for the SMS platform was PlaySMS, compatible with Hypertext Preprocessor (PHP); the RE-ACT team and MCT provided training on those technologies.

The community was responsible for testing de solutions, and evaluates the overall project.

The CMC and RE-ACT team performed the assessment and evaluation, the community was informed about the progresses of the project once a month, through a radio program. The website and the SMS were verified and analyzed using observium network management, and Google analytics.

5 Result

This section will focus on the relevant results related to:

(1) Community participation;
(2) Empowerment;
(3) Ownership; and
(4) Sustainability.

The co-design process resulted in a community website (www.cmcmorrumbene.co.mz), consisting of information about the CMC, community radio, government, police, school results (primary, secondary), local publicity, public opinion quiz, and a webmail.

To include higher number of people in the community, an SMS solution was designed to provide quick information to the community about the local market price (fish, vegetable), health tips, and security-related issues.

The CMC staff was trained in web-design and progressively introduced new features in the website. Such training brought to CMC staff independence, and confidence when it comes to using web design and development tools.

The CMC staff became active and decisive on local practices and use of technologies for social inclusion [19].

As the number of people registered for the SMS service, reached 134 in the first month, to sustain the SMS service the community emphasized the need of selling some of CMC services in exchange for SMS balance or mobile balance transference. The actual number of subscribers for the SMS service is 686, for each community member or house only one number is registered.

As communities best know their life context and therefore are entitled to contribute with finding solutions for local problems [20], the community proposed that services such as cinema tickets, radio announcements and music selection should be charged based on SMS recharge or mobile balance transference. To use alternative types of currency might seem unusual to some people [21, 22], literature on forms of money suggests that what works best is to have a currency that fits a specific purpose or mean for payment of a specific service [23].

6   Conclusion

Community's focus groups sessions undoubtedly provided liberty of expression to participants; the RE-ACT team followed the approach of assembly gathering during the session, as this is a community local and traditional costume. This created conditions for cohesion, and strengthen relations between researcher and community.

Although when working with communities goals are framed and reframed several times, every co-design session produced consensus, and mutual understanding among intervenient. Commitment was observed by how intervenient devoted time, knowledge, attention and patience to design and draft the final solution. Dialog at all social levels to find shared solutions for domain problems is an exploration of spaces to invite possibilities to share past experiences and contextual knowledge.

Ownership of the designed solution was attained thanks to the involvement of all core businesses in the district. It was also achieved by providing freedom to change, veto, and reformulate the final solution.

The inclusive framework on the website design was equality and respect, so to make it visible the collaboration of individuals with social and political differences.

References

1. Oyedemi., T.D.: Social inequalities and the South African ICT access policy agendas. Int. J. Commun. 3, 11–18 (2009)
2. Kuriyan, R., Kitner, K., Watkins, J., Gomez, R., Gould, E.: The 'cool factor' of public access to ICT: Users' perceptions of trust in libraries, telecentres and cybercafés in developing countries. Inf. Technol. People 23(3), 247–264 (2010)

3. Sey, A., Coward, C., Bar, F., Sciadas, G., Rothschild, C., Koepke, L.: Connecting People for Development: Why Public Access ICTs matter (eBook). Technology & Social Change Group, Seattle (2013)
4. W. H. Organization: World health statistics 2010. World Health Organization (2010)
5. Gaster, P.: A pilot telecentres project in Mozambique. In: Latchem, C., Walker, D. (eds.) Telecentres: Case studies and key Issues, pp. 119–121. The Commonwealth of Learning, Vancouver (2001)
6. Sey, A., Fellows, M.: Literature review on the impact of public access to information and communication technologies, Center for Information & Society, University of Washington, Seattle (2009)
7. Vannini, S., Rega, I.: Inbound and outbound information and communication flows: perspectives from community multimedia centres in Mozambique. In: CIRN 2012 Community Informatics Conference: 'Ideals Meet Reality', Monash Centre. Presented at the CIRN (2012)
8. Naidoo, M.: The changing venues for learning. Doc. RESUME, 18 (2001)
9. Van Zyl, I., Vannini, S.: Participatory Re-action: Reflecting on a Design-Based Research Approach in ICT4D (2013)
10. Baia, A., Macueve, G., Rega, I., Cumbula, S.D., Vannini, S., Cantoni, L.: Social Representations of Multimedia Community Centers (CMC) in Mozambique. Electron. J. Inf. Syst. Develop. Countries 65(8), 1–23 (2015)
11. David, S., Vannini, S., Sabiescu, A.G., Cantoni, L.: Commitment, proactivity and trust: ingredients for successful cooperation in community development actions. In: Proceedings of the CIRN 2013 (2013)
12. Kampango, A., Cuamba, N., Charlwood, J.D.: Does moonlight influence the biting behaviour of Anopheles funestus? Med. Vet. Entomol. 25(3), 240–246 (2011)
13. Cardinale, M., Chacate, O., Casini, M., Chaúca, I., Helge Vølstad, J.: CPUE trends of Hilsa kelee and Thryssa vitrirostris exploited by the artisanal finfish fisheries in Mozambique derived from an on-shore sampling of catches by trip. Sci. Mar. 78(1), 55–64 (2014)
14. Rega, I., Cantoni, L., Vannini, S., David, S., Baia, A., Macueve, G.: Community Multimedia Centres in Mozambique: a Map. White Paper (2011)
15. Avgerou, C.: Information systems in developing countries: a critical research review. J. Inf. Technol. 23(3), 133–146 (2008)
16. David, S., Sabiescu, A.G., Lorenzo, C.: Co-design with Communities. a reflection on the literature. In: Steyn, J., Van Vyver A.G. (eds.) 2013 Public and Private Access to ICTs in Developing Regions, Proceedings of the 7th International Development Informatics Association Conference, pp. 152–166, Bangkok, Thailand (2014). ISBN 978-0-620-58040-3
17. Camara, S.B., Noø era, J.A., Dunckley, L.: Exploring the problem domain: a socio-technical ICT design for the developing world. In: Proceedings of the Tenth Anniversary Conference on Participatory Design 2008, pp. 154–157 (2008)
18. Winschiers-Theophilus, H., Winschiers-Goagoses, N., Rodil, K., Blake, E., Zaman, T., Kapuire, G.K., Kamukuenjandje, R.: Moving away from Erindi-roukambe: transferability of a rural community-based co-design. In: IFIIP WG, vol. 9 (2013)
19. Warschauer, M.: Technology and Social Inclusion: Rethinking the Digital Divide. MIT press, Cambridge (2004)
20. Weinberg, T.: The new community rules: Marketing on the social web. O'Reilly Media, Inc., Sebastopol (2009)

21. Krugman, P.: Competitiveness: a dangerous obsession. Foreign Aff. **73**(2), 28–44 (1994)
22. Davenport, T.H., Beck, J.C.: The Attention Economy: Understanding the New Currency of Business. Harvard Business Press, Cambridge (2013)
23. Boyle, D.: More than Money: Platforms for Exchange and Reciprocity in Public Services. NESTA, London (2011)

Prototyping and Testing Throughout all the Design Process as a Methodology for Developing Interaction Design Projects

Lucas Cypriano[✉] and Mauro Pinheiro

Universidade Federal do Espírito Santo, Vitória, Espirito Santo, Brazil
{lucascypriano,mauropinheiro}@gmail.com

Abstract. Based on the experience of developing a mobile app, this paper discusses the prototyping and testing cycles not as final steps of a design process, but as a methodology to be used from the beginning to the end of a project. On the project described in this paper, prototyping was not a tool used only to test the final product, but it was present throughout the design process.

Keywords: Prototyping · Interaction design · Design process

1 Introduction

In this paper we discuss the development of a digital artifact – OpenGates – focusing on the prototyping and testing cycles that occurred throughout the development process. OpenGates is a smart object that provides the connection between garage gates and the internet, consequently letting users control these gates through a mobile app. The Open Gates project was developed by the author of this article at the Federeal University of Espírito Santo (Universidade Federal do Espírito Santo, Brazil).

In the OpenGates project, prototyping and continuous testing were the most important methodologies for its development. Moreover, in each test that was processed, the project lost or gained a new aspect, which means that, to some extent, it was the process that determined the characteristics, features and values of the smart object. In addition, it is important to state that, in this study, we consider prototyping as the development of a functional model of the smart object, and therefore, here we do not discuss low fidelity prototypes, which only simulate few characteristics of the product. The prototype's capacity of performing exactly as the intended final product would perform is the fundamental characteristic of the type of design technique approached in this article.

In this article, we will briefly introduce the interaction design field and discuss different prototyping approaches commonly used. We will then describe the OpenGates project's development process, in order to discuss the implications of using prototyping as a design methodology. Finally, based on this study, we will discuss in general the utilization of this type of methodology in interaction design projects, considering its specificities, its constrains and requirements of use.

© Springer International Publishing Switzerland 2015
A. Marcus (Ed.): DUXU 2015, Part I, LNCS 9186, pp. 157–166, 2015.
DOI: 10.1007/978-3-319-20886-2_16

2   The Interaction Design

Understanding the interaction design field is an important setting stage for this paper. Mainly, for highlighting two characteristics of this area that favor the design methodology discussed in this article: the digital nature of interaction design projects, and the development of devices with new functions.

The emergence of interaction design occurs with the great technological changes of recent decades – with emphasis on digital technologies –, which provided the design a new field. As stated by Pinheiro [1] such advances have not only changed the production methods and tools for the designers, but also their area of expertise, the very nature of the artifacts and systems to be designed. Thus arises, in such scenario, the interaction design.

Moggridge [2] is one of the pioneering authors to use the term «interaction design». The author argues, based on his perception of the new demands of the design market, that there was an opportunity to create such a new area of design that would meet this new context.

"I felt that there was an opportunity to create a new design discipline, dedicated to creating imaginative and attractive solutions in a virtual world, where one could design behaviors, animations, and sounds as well as shapes. This would be the equivalent of industrial design but in software rather than three-dimensional objects. Like industrial design, the discipline would be concerned with subjective and qualitative values, would start from the needs and desires of the people who use a product or service, and strive to create designs that would give aesthetic pleasure as well as lasting satisfaction and enjoyment. [...] so we went on thinking of possible names until I eventually settled on 'interaction design'" [2].

Lowgren [3] also shows that in the beginning interaction design was something marginal. At that time, interaction aspects of computer interfaces were more likely to be decided by engineering and HCI professionals. However, with the popularization of personal computers, the more intense use of pagers, laptops and the advancement of internet, these two fields, engineering and the design, met in order to try to understand, explore and further develop such technological universe [3].

So interaction design becomes, in general sense, the field that aims to study and design digital artifacts for human use. Such definition still doesn't have a consensus among different authors, but in general they tend to point to the same direction. Important to notice that, due to the large scope of the term «interaction», it is possible to question the definitions in that area. However, on this work we focus on the definitions of interaction design that are related to digital technologies. Some of the interaction design definitions considered in this work are:

"Interaction design is about shaping digital things for people's use" [3].

[...] "Interaction Design is: The design of subjective and qualitative aspects of everything that is both digital and interactive, creating designs that are useful, desirable, and accessible." [2].

"Designing interactive systems is concerned with developing high quality interactive systems, products and services that fit with people and their way of living." [4].

"Interaction Design defines the structure and behavior of interactive systems. Interaction Designers strive to create meaningful relationships between people and the products and services that they use, from computers to mobile devices to appliances and beyond." [5].

[...] "By interaction design, we mean designing interactive products to support people in their everyday and working lives." [6].

Given these various interaction design definitions, two features, although not directly or explicit stated in most of these concepts, stand out in this article:

1. The digital aspect, i.e. the interaction design is related somehow to computer technologies;
2. The functional aspect of the discussions in this area: the main concerns that drives interaction design are not limited to typography, color, or visual aspects, but rather the design as a service, a system, a tool - which means that the interaction design somehow has its attention drawn not only to the aesthetic but also to the functional aspects of the systems and artifacts.

These two characteristics were strongly observed during the development of OpenGates, and thus correlated with the prototyping methodology used in this project. The correlation of these features with the methodology will be discussed later on.

3   The OpenGates Project

OpenGates is an interaction design project that was accomplished in 2014 by the author of this paper, Lucas Cypriano, as the final project of the undergraduate design course at the Federal University of Espírito Santo, under the supervision of Prof. Mauro Pinheiro. The project comprises the development of a digital artifact that connects motorized garage gates to the Internet, allowing its users to control the garage gate through a mobile phone app.

The project is not only something from the digital realm and not only a product but something that integrates these two areas. It's an interactive system consisting of a digital interface that controls the user's garage gate and an electronic device (product) that activates the motor the gate.

For this project we used typical prototyping tools, such as a Spark-Core microcontroller, that allowed the gate's connection to the Internet, and also wifi modules and servomotors. Moreover, it was also developed a mobile app that sends the "open" request to the device, which then triggers the gate. All of these technologies are commonly used for prototyping interaction design projects, being these essential tools for the realization of OpenGates.

The OpenGates system can be summarized in two main parts: a physical part, which comprises an object called Trigger Device, and a digital interface, which is the mobile phone app. The Trigger Device is the object that connects the gate to the Internet, allowing this to be triggered. The application is the interface that allows the user to remotely control The Trigger, so he/she can open the garage gate using his/her mobile phone. The right image on Fig. 1 is the Trigger's prototype (a microcontroller, a servomotor and the inside part of the user's garage gate's remote control). The left image shows the application interface – the gate activate screen.

Fig. 1. Digital Interface (app) and Trigger Device, project OpenGates

This project was set in the context of affordable, simple prototyping tools and components that are normally used to create smart objects and to connect them to the Internet. We've used these technologies to allow the users to connect and trigger the garage gate using a mobile phone application.

In this paper we focused on the development of the mobile app interface, mainly because it was easier to prototype the app, and therefore it is also easier to explain the methodology addressed throughout the development of the whole system. So, even though we describe the design process for developing the application interface, the same methodology was used in the development of the Trigger.

4   The Prototyping Methodology

Prototyping can be considered as a secular historical practice [7]. Based on an ancient history of the Roman Empire – where the emperor Julius Cesar had a building demolished because he considered it was not according with what he had previously approved – Leon Batista Alberti, important figure in Architecture of the fifteenth century, already recommended his builders to develop models in wood and other materials before building the final building to avoid this kind of situation [8].

"I will always recommend the time-honored custom, practiced by the best builders, of preparing not only drawings and sketches but also models of wood or any other material" [8].

Prototyping consolidates itself as a technique in several areas and not only in architecture. Michel Lafon and Wendy Mackay [9] indicate that prototyping can have different settings according to each field: in architecture, as in the case of Leon Baptist Alberti, a model on a small scale can be considered a prototype; to fashion designers, the prototype is often a full-scale model, and sometimes at *Haute couture* this prototype is already the final product.

This paper focuses on the discussion of prototypes in the field of interaction design and on prototypes of software and digital artifacts. In addition to having different areas for different perspectives, there are several types of prototyping in the realm of digital products.

"When you hear the term prototype, you may imagine something like a scale model of a building or a bridge, or maybe a piece of software that crashes every few minutes. But a prototype can also be a paper-based outline of a screen or set of screens, an electronic 'picture,' a video simulation of a task, a three-dimensional paper and cardboard mockup of a whole workstation, or a simple stack of hyperlinked screen shots, among other things" [6].

Often different authors present some divisions of types and prototypes characteristics. Hom [10] considers a prototype as an object that allows the realization of test on the final product's attribute before it is ready. He has different categories such as: rapid prototyping – quickly, a prototype is developed, evaluated, and discarded so a new one is produced; Reusable prototyping - also called evolutionary prototyping, in which the prototype is not discarded but modified, and can be used as part of the final product; horizontal prototyping - increases the quantity of the product characteristics but without functioning [10].

It is important to note that the prototype is related more often to the project's final test before the construction of the final product. Leon Baptist in the fifteenth [8] century recommends the construction of the model, so that it could verify, certify and modify the design before construction, the method was more associated with the last phase of the project, prior to the final development of the product. The importance was mainly a kind of last check on the project before producing. The work in Opengates is more related to prototyping methodologies of this technique, not only as a final stage of the project, but also and especially as its own design methodology, being not only a final test design, but also a method of designing and creating.

Michel Lafon and Wendy Mackay [9], more directed to the field of digital technologies, already point prototyping in the design process. Besides categorizing them in different aspects, they still show them not only as tools used in the final stages of the project but since the beginning of it.

"Prototypes are diverse and can fit within any party of the design process, from the earliest ideas to the final details of the design." [9].

We depart from this assumption, seeking not to discuss the prototyping methodology itself, but to highlight its use during the design process.

4.1 The Prototyping Methodology in the OpenGates Project

On the OpenGates design project, prototyping and user testing were the methods most used throughout the development process, from the beginning to the end of the project. We didn't establish any specific prototyping methodology to follow. The main goal was to keep building and testing functional models from the earliest stages of the project.

The first prototype was developed in the beginning of the project, comprising the minimum requirements necessary to perform the artifact's function (open the gate using the phone). We've designed a simple interface in which the user just needed to press a button to have the gate activated - the interface was basically the button, there was no

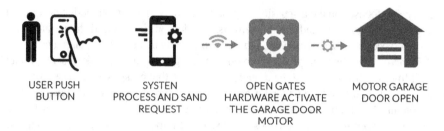

USER PUSH
BUTTON

SYSTEN
PROCESS AND SAND
REQUEST

OPEN GATES
HARDWARE ACTIVATE
THE GARAGE DOOR
MOTOR

MOTOR GARAGE
DOOR OPEN

Fig. 2. System process map to open the gates using the Opengates

system login process, no registration was needed, nor any settings were made. Thus, the first prototype was done, being the first step of the methodology: to determine the minimum functional requirements of the project, and to develop an initial prototype that met those requirements.

From the initial prototype on, begins a constant process: developing and testing a prototype, changing the design based on the tests, testing a new prototype, adjusting again and so on.

Concerning the tests, the main goal was to make a fully functional prototype available to people, in other words, to break the line between the design that mimics an intended action, and a prototype that actually carry out such action. So even if only a small group of users or even a single user performs the test, that is enough for this project humanization. If you can make a broader test, based on a statistical sample of the intended users, it can be applied but often it would take longer to conduct the tests, and also it would probably become more expensive. Moreover, on this particular project, it was not a single test that was planned but several more were meant to be done throughout the process. Furthermore, with an incremental develop-and-test approach using a few users to test your designs, it is possible to do as much testes as you want. Thus, in this project we have conducted tests with small groups of users to make the process quick and agile.

In each test cycle, small changes were made in each prototype tested. Functions and features were added, sometimes removed, made more evidence or modified completely in the project. And so, to some extend the tests guided the design process of the Open-Gates system, determining its features, functions and appearance.

To demonstrate this process, we will present some OpenGates design features, which were determined based on this prototyping process. They are: Click Button and feedback, System Feedback and Full time Feedback, Low Bureaucracy Function, Open the Gates: the center of the interface.

Click Button and Feedback. In the first application interface designed, when the «Open» button was clicked it was expected that the Trigger Device would immediately activate the gate (Fig. 2). But with the first tests we realized that, depending on some conditions such as the quality of the mobile connection to the Internet, there could be a delay between the moment when the user releases the button in the application and the moment when the garage gate starts to open. This resulted that sometimes the users pushed the button multiple times, thinking that this would solve the delay - and in the end the gate was turned on and off several times in a row.

FEEDBACK
SYSTEM
MESSAGE
{system sendig
requesting}

FEEDBACK
SYSTEM
MESSAGE
{garage door
openig}

Fig. 3. Interface Open Button feedback

From these observations, it became necessary to modify the interface implementing a system feedback response, so that when the user clicked the button a "sending request" message was shown, and when the Trigger Device activated the gates, a confirmation message was displayed assuring to the user the successful operation (Fig. 3). Furthermore, a change was made in the button's behavior setup, ensuring that it couldn't be activated before the last request has been completed.

Only after the real tests we realized the importance of informing the state of the system to the user, during the interval between activating the button and opening the gate. With this, the user has a sense of being in control of what is happening. Without the tests, this important aspect of the user experience would not have been considered.

System Feedback, and all Feedback. In some tests happened that the gate didn't open, i.e. the system didn't work. And the user did neither know what was going on, nor what to do. Thus it was clear that some simple conditions were necessary to the system work properly. For example, the mobile Internet connection must be working perfectly to the application connects to the Trigger Device. In addition, the Internet in the user's home used by the Trigger Device also needs to be working, as The Device needs to be online to communicate with the mobile application.

With the tests in which the system didn't work, it was clear that the app's interface needed to inform some basic conditions that should be satisfied, so that the system works and avoid unsuccessful tries. Then it was needed to inform the state of the mobile Internet connection, and if the Trigger Device was also connected. For this we designed icons indicating when there is no mobile Internet connection or no Device connection, informing that the system cannot work (Fig. 4). The test showed that a crucial condition for the product to work is to have Internet connection and thus the user should have the connectivity status information of the system.

Low Bureaucracy Function. A common way to trigger a motorized garage door is using a remote control. When the user is standing near the gate he/she just pushes the remote control button, which almost immediately triggers the gate. Comparing the earlier versions of Open Gates against a traditional remote control, the task of triggering the gate with the application was more time-consuming and bureaucratic. At the beginning of the project, to open the gate the user needed to: pick up the phone, unlock the

Fig. 4. System feedback icons

phone, navigate to the OpenGates application, open the application, log into the application, select the gate, put a password, and press the button (Fig. 5).

Fig. 5. Evolution of the interface according to the bureaucracy and hierarchy

By observing the tests, it was perceived how the opening process was slow. And it became clear the need of reducing the steps, so that the user can open the gate in the most fast and easy way. Thus, the initial login has been optimized – the user just needs to login once, so that in all other times he/she won't need to repeat this task. The system was designed in such a way that the same user can control as many gates as he/she wishes. So in the initial designs the user needed to «choose a garage door» in every use of the app. This step was also changed: in the first login the user defines a default gate, that won't change unless the user explicit does so. Finally, the step of entering a password to release the button was also removed, since the mobile phone already has a locking system password. With these changes, as soon as the user opens the app, he/she goes directly to the screen with the button to trigger the gate.

Open the Gates: The Interface Center. In the early designs there were several elements on the main screen (Fig. 5). However with the tests it was detected that the primary function of the application was to click the button to open the gate. Actions such as «register a new gate», «change user profile information» had a much lower priority compared to the main action. So through testing we changed the interface, in such a way that the emphasis was clearly in the main action, i.e. open the gate by pressing the «open» button. This primary function was also in evidence throughout the other secondary screens.

5 Discussion

This work is completely structured around a case study, based on the experience and discussions aroused during the development of a practical design project - Opengates. It was not intended to perform a extensive survey of the types of design methodologies, or discuss the different prototyping techniques, but it proposes to highlight the findings originated from a design experiment.

In general what became most evident during the OpenGates project was the fact that most of the final characteristics of the product were determined based on actual testing cases of the prototypes. Within this continuous process of prototyping and testing the project was designed. And without these tests we would have most likely designed a product with minimal chances of success. Using this methodology of departing from the minimal functional prototype and reviewing the scope of the product based on continuous prototyping-testing cycles, we achieved a design solution that we believe is consistent with a real context of use.

This study seeks to bring the design field closer to this kind of discussion. In a way, with this methodology, the borders between the project and the product are looser; the use of prototyping reduces the barriers between the design plan, the intermediary mockups, and the final product. This changes not only the role of the project in the development process, but also the role of the designer – emerging as a "digital craftsman", one who not only works on the concept of a product, but somehow builds the product in the process.

In addition, it is important to notice that the OpenGates project is more than the mobile app interface. As stated before, it is a smart object, comprised by a digital interface and a physical object. On this paper we focused on the development of the app interface, but the use of prototyping methods was not limited to that. Although with more difficulties and limitations, prototyping was also used on the development of the physical part of the project, the Trigger Device, since its inception. Michel Lafon and Wendy Mackay [9] note that there is a need to expand the use of prototyping in the design of interactive objects, especially in the context of ubiquitous computing [11]. And although this may be a challenge for the designers, new tools are becoming more common and accessible – like digital fabrication [12], 3D scanners and printers, for example, can powerfully increase the prototyping techniques. We hope that more and more designers embrace prototyping-and-testing as part of the design process, which we believe will bring better products, more close to the user needs.

References

1. Rodrigues, M.P.: Design de interação e computação pervasiva: um estudo sobre mecanismos atencionais e sistemas de informação ambiente, Rio de Janeiro (2011)
2. Moggridge, Bill: Designing Interactions. The MIT Press, Cambridge (2006)
3. Lowgren, J.: Interaction design - brief intro. In: Soegaard, M., Dam, R.F. (eds.) The Encyclopedia of Human-Computer Interaction, 2nd edn. The Interaction Design Foundation, Aarhus (2014). http://www.interaction-design.org
4. Benyon, D., Turner, T., Turner, S.: Designing Interactive Systems – People, Activities, Contexts, Technologies. Pearson, Harlow (2005)
5. Interaction Design Association: Interaction design definition (2014). www.ixda.org
6. Preece, J., Rogers, Y., Sharp, H.: Interaction Design: Beyond Human Computer Interaction. Wiley, New York (2002)
7. Schwartz, E.: Axure RP 6 Prototyping Essentials. Packt Publishing, Birmigham (2012)
8. Alberti, L.: On the Art of Building in Ten Books. The MIT Press, Cambridge (1988)
9. Beaudouin-Lafon, M., Mackay, W.E.: Prototyping tools and techniques. In: Jacko, J., Sears, A. (eds.) Human Computer Interaction Handbook: Fundamentals, Evolving Technologies, and Emerging Applications. CRC Press (2007)
10. Hom, J.: The Usability Methods Toolbox HandBook (1998)
11. Weiser, Mark: The Computer of the 21st Century. Scientific American, Palo Alto (1991)
12. Gershenfeld, Neil: How to Make Almost Anything: The Digital Fabrication Revolution. The MIT Press, Boston (2012)

A Living Labs Approach for Usability Testing of Ambient Assisted Living Technologies

Miguel Sales Dias[1,4], Elisângela Vilar[2(✉)], Filipe Sousa[3],
Ana Vasconcelos[3], Fernando Miguel Pinto[1], Nuno Saldanha[1],
and Sara Eloy[4]

[1] Microsoft Language Development Center, Lisbon, Portugal
{Miguel.Dias,t-fecos,t-nunosa}@microsoft.com
[2] Centre for Architecture, Urban Planning and Design (CIAUD),
Rua Sá Nogueira, Pólo Universitário, Alto da Ajuda, 1349-055 Lisbon, Portugal
elipessoa@gmail.com
[3] Fraunhofer Portugal Research, Porto, Portugal
{filipe.sousa,ana.vasconcelos}@fraunhofer.pt
[4] ISCTE Instituto Universitário de Lisboa, Lisbon, Portugal
sara.eloy@iscte-iul.pt,

Abstract. This paper presents usability tests results with real users during the prototype development phase of two applications for seniors care, AALFred and SmartCompanion. To this aim, usability testing was performed considering a Living Lab approach. Seniors were invited to use the applications in an environment that simulates the one they would use the tested technology during their everyday life. Observation methods, thinking aloud and questionnaires were used to collect data related to the systems' effectiveness and users' satisfaction, namely their expectations, frustrations and difficulties. Evaluations were performed during the initial phases of product development and results were used to improve the applications, considering the development cycle of User-Centered Design methodology.

Keywords: Usability tests · User-centered design · Ambient assisted living · Living labs

1 Introduction

Global projections [1] point to a significant increase in the aging rate. These projections estimate, for instance, that the proportion of people with 60 or more years old will duplicate between 2009 and 2050, reaching two billion in 2050. This trend is also reflected in the increase of chronic diseases incidence such as Diabetes, which should reach more than 340 million people in 2030 [2].

In this context, it is clear that an active intervention to promote the several levels of social integration is needed. Ambient Assisted Living (AAL) is a new approach to the needs of population aging, with the main goal of applying the technologies of ambient intelligence in helping people with specific demands, and in building safe environments for the maintenance of independent living [3]. Considering this, two applications developed and integrated by partners in the scope of the QREN AAL4ALL – Ambient

© Springer International Publishing Switzerland 2015
A. Marcus (Ed.): DUXU 2015, Part I, LNCS 9186, pp. 167–178, 2015.
DOI: 10.1007/978-3-319-20886-2_17

Assisted Living for ALL interoperable and standardized platform [10], are the main focus of analysis in this paper, AALFred, from Microsoft and the PaeLife consortium partners [4], and the Smart Companion [5], from Fraunhofer Portugal AICOS (FhP). To engage real users in the various stages of development, both applications were developed using a user-centered design methodology [6].

The main objective of this paper is therefore, presenting usability testing with real users during the prototype development phase. For this, a Living Usability Labs methodology [7] was used. According to Schumacher [8], the concept of Living Labs is based on a systematic co-creation, directed to the user, which integrates the research and innovation processes. These processes are integrated throughout the development, exploitation, experimentation and evaluation of ideas, scenarios, concepts, products/services in real-life utilization.

In the following sections, this paper will present the usability testing performed with both AALFred and Smart Companion, describing the adopted methodology, main findings and improvements achieved with the applications' re-design.

2   The Applications

Two applications directed for senior's use, were the focus of usability tests, namely, AALFred and Smart Companion.

2.1   AALFred

AALFred is a personal life assistant that helps and guides users in the access to ICT's, developed by Microsoft and the PaeLife consortium partners [3] and improved and integrated on AAL4ALL ecosystem in the scope of AAL4ALL project. Older users interact with AALFred, via speech (in European Portuguese) and touch, using a Windows 8.1 Tablet. With AALFred, messaging with friends and relatives exchanged in social media (Facebook, Twitter), email, agenda (Outlook) and audio-videoconferencing calls (Skype) can be easily accessed and used to make seniors more active, engaged in social and community life and therefore less isolated. Additionally, interesting information such as news and access to nearby services, such as informal and formal healthcare, pharmacies and authorities, is delivered in an integrated way.

2.2   SmartCompanion

Smart Companion is an Android launcher developed by Fraunhofer Portugal AICOS (FhP-AICOS). It is an Android customization that was specially designed to address seniors and caregivers' goals and needs. Its main objective is to facilitate the use of a smartphone by reducing its complexity. In this way, Smart Companion aims to promote the use of smartphones by seniors during their everyday activities, considering several tools, from messages to medication reminders, activity monitoring, fall risk analysis and fall detection.

3 Methodology

For the usability evaluation of the two selected applications (i.e., AALFred and Smart Companion), personas and scenarios were identified and tasks were defined, considering the User-product interaction. The Living Lab methodology was considered in order to make the simulated use closer to the real experience seniors would have, if they were performing the same tasks in their everyday life.

3.1 Data Collection

All data was collected through direct observation and questionnaires. For direct observation, a set of tasks was pre-defined during brainstorming meetings with the development team, and experts in Psychology, Ergonomics and Software Engineering. From this, an observation form was specifically developed to collect metrics such as task execution time, task completion rate (and how easily the participant completed the task), assistances during task completion, and the participant's visible emotional state. All tasks were decomposed into activities that were evaluated separately. Demographic data was collected at the beginning of the usability test through a questionnaire. A satisfaction questionnaire was also developed and applied after the completion of each pre-defined task. These questionnaires were developed by the project team and were pre-tested during the initial phases of the AAL4ALL Project. A Usability Scale, based on the International Classification of Functioning (ICF) was developed by the AAL4ALL partners and was also applied at the end of each task completion.

3.2 Protocol

Usability testing was performed considering a task-oriented analysis in which participants were asked to perform predefined tasks. Before the test, all participants were asked to sign a Consent Form. It was mandatory, in a way that if a participant did not sign the consent form, he/she was not allowed to continue the test.

After signing the Consent Form, participants were asked to fill out the demographic questionnaire together with technology-related and quality of life-related questions.

Then, a facilitator presented to the participants all AAL4ALL products involved in the usability test. In this phase, the facilitator explained to the participants the main functionalities of the products.

After the presentation phase, the facilitator started the task-related phase. At this moment, the facilitator explained to the participants that he/she should accomplish tasks with the presented products without time restrictions. Tasks were given in a sequential manner, in random order, in a way that only after completing one task and fulfilling the satisfaction questionnaire and the usability scale related to that task, the facilitator started with a new task with the participant. Each task was read by the facilitator and also delivered to the participant written on paper. The usability test finished when all tasks were given and completed by the participant.

3.3   Usability Testing with AALFred

The evaluation took place at Microsoft's Living Lab in Lisbon, Portugal. It simulates a regular house living room, in which participants will interact with AALFred through the use of a tablet and a TV, simulating real situations that seniors may face.

Scenarios and Personas. For usability testing of ALLFred, two main scenarios were considered: Monitoring seniors at home and social integration, entertainment and communication of senior users. Personas were defined based on a previous study of the AAL4ALL consortium considering the target market, and participant selection was done based on these persona definitions, which can be seen on Table 1.

Table 1. Personas, characteristics and criteria for participant's selection for usability testing with AALFred.

Personas	Characteristics	Criteria for participants selection
Teresa	She is no longer able to regulate body temperature as before. It occurs because her response to body temperature changes are not normal, consequently she is not able to normally react to hypothermia situations. Some parts of the body such as hands and toes are more critical and need special attention regarding temperature regulation	• Senior (>=70 years old) • Shoe size (42) • No speech impairments • No hearing impairments • With limited mobility
Formal caregiver	Health care professional responsible for seniors' monitoring	• Health care professional • No motor impairments • No visual impairments • Good technological literacy

Participants. For the usability testing four senior participants were recruited considering the selection criteria. The average participant age was 79.50 (SD = 5.74; min. 76, max. 88 years old), and all of them were female. All participants were retired. Half of the participants had an elementary school level education, and others had a high school level. All participants had used a cellphone, but none of them had ever used a smartphone. Half of the participants reported a moderate use of the cellphone while 33 % reported a frequent use. Regarding the usage of a computer, most of the participants (83 %) did not use it.

In addition to the demographic and technology-related data, participants were also asked to self-evaluate their quality-of-life and memory abilities. Most of participants were completely satisfied (33 %) or very satisfied (50 %) with their ability to carry out their daily activities and evaluated their quality of life as good (50 %) or very good (33 %). Considering memory abilities, all participants reported it as good. Most of the participants reported being apprehensive (67 %) before the test. The others stated being motivated to perform the tests (33 %).

Tasks. For AALFred usability tests, three external devices were also used: the Smartshoe, a chestband, and a body temperature and pulse sensor.

The Smartshoe is a device that aims to contribute with feet temperature regulation. It has sensors integrated on the shoes that reads room temperature and humidity (outside the shoes) and regulates feet temperature (temperature inside the shoes) according to the external data. The values can be observed through AALFred's user interface, since it is linked to AALFred via wireless means (Bluetooth).

The Chestband by Plux[1], is a device that enables the remote monitoring of a senior's respiratory rate, electrocardiogram (ECG) and home location (via inertia unit sensing) by a caregiver. It is connected with AALFred via wireless (Bluetooth) and can be accessed also by the caregiver during an AALFred-to-AALFred Skype call over the Internet.

Another device considered for the test was a set of sensors (EXA ALL-in-One[2]) that collect body temperature and heart rate for personal and remote monitoring.

All devices (Smartshoe, Chestband, EXA ALL-in-One) and AALFred communicate over the internet with peer remote ALLFred apps (used by formal or informal caretakers), via the AAL4ALL interoperable and standard service-oriented communication architecture.

Three main tasks were defined and were presented to the participants considering a hypothetical scenario:

Task 1 – "Imagine you arrive home after buying your Smartshoes that regulate the temperature of your feet. Your task is to turn them on, tell me what is the internal temperature of the shoes and the humidity of the environment, and finally charge their battery".

Task 2 – "You have installed at home a system called Chestband that allows your doctor, or a family member to observe some of your vital signs and talk to you through a Skype video call. Your task is to answer a video call on the tablet and put the Chestband so that your data is sent to your doctor/family member".

Task 3 – You need to frequently monitor your vital signs, so you use the "EXA ALL-in-One " device. Your task is to check and inform me about your temperature and your pulse using the "EXA All in One".

3.4   Usability Testing with SmartCompanion

The evaluation took place at Fraunhofer's Living Lab, more specifically in its living room and all participants were volunteers from Colaborar[3] network.

---

[1] http://www.plux.info.

[2] http://www.exatronic.pt/en/home/.

[3] http://colaborar.fraunhofer.pt/en/.

Scenarios and Personas. For the usability testing of Smart Companion five main scenarios were considered: Time management, Time Management with TV, Mobility - Navigation, Mobility – Activity Monitoring and Medication Reminders.

The Personas defined for usability testing with the Smart Companion can be seen on Table 2.

Table 2. Personas, characteristics and criteria for participants'selection for usability testing with the Smart Companion.

Personas	Characteristics	Criteria for participants selection
Ana	Active and healthy, with an autonomous life. She practices exercise everyday	• Senior (>=65 years old) • Active and autonomous life • No speech impairments • No hearing impairments • No mobility limitations
Maria	She lives in a nursing home. She has a chest angina, which requires daily medication. She also has memory loss, so she is afraid of forgetting to take her medicines	• Senior (>=65 years old) • Can read and write • Without severe vision limitations • Without severe speech limitations • Without severe hearing limitations • No experience in dealing with cellphones, computers and internet use

Participants. For the evaluation 12 senior participants were recruited as volunteers. The average participant age was 68.42 (SD = 3.40; min. 64, max. 76 years old), eight male and four female. Almost all participants were retired, with the exception of one participant who was self-employed. Most participants had high-school level education. All participants had a cellphone, 67 % of which were smartphones. 83 % of the participants reported a frequent and moderate use of the cellphone, while 17 % reported little use. Regarding computer use, most of the participants (83 %) were users and only 17 % did not have a computer.

Considering the participants' self-evaluation of their quality-of-life and memory abilities, all participants were completely or very satisfied with their ability to carry out their daily activities, however 50 % of the participants evaluated their quality of life and their memory only as reasonable. All participants but one stated being motivated to perform the tests and were confident on their abilities to work with the tested technologies.

Tasks. All tasks were selected as a representation of the main features of each application and the most frequently used as well. For each task the participants were given instructions on what they were expected to do, given a hypothetical scenario:

Task 1: "Imagine that you decide to invite your friends for a lunch at your house. Your task is to use your smartphone to choose the best day to schedule the lunch, considering the week of the 19th to the 23rd of May, schedule the appointment and invite your friends Maria and Ana."

Task 2: "[The participant was told to watch some TV and let the facilitator know if something out of the ordinary happened] Please read what appeared on the TV and dismiss it when you are ready".

Task 3: "Imagine that you need to go to a new place and you don't know how to get there. You will use your smartphone's navigation system to help you get there. Your task is to introduce the address in the system and try to understand the directions".

Task 4: "In your phone you have an application that monitors your daily activity. One of your doctor's recommendations was that you should do a 30 min walk at least three times a week. To know when was the last time you accomplished this goal you can check your activity history. Your task is to verify if you did a 30 min walk today and how many times you did it last week".

Task 5: "During your last medical appointment the doctor prescribed you a new medication that you are not used to, and therefore you are afraid that you will forget about it. You can use the medication reminder application in your smartphone to ensure that you do not forget to take the medicine. Your task is to create a new medication reminder on the phone".

Task 6: "[The participant was told to watch some TV and let the facilitator know if something out of the ordinary happened] Please read what appeared on the TV and dismiss it when you are ready".

Task 7: "You can't remember if you took the medicine you were supposed to on May 9th. Therefore you decide to check you intake history. Your task is to check your intake history on the smartphone".

4   Results

4.1   ALLFred

Performance Results. The overall performance results suggest that the apps did not present major usability issues, with less than half tasks (n = 2) requesting assistance during the test and a mean unassisted task completion effectiveness of 91.7 % (SD = 13.9; min = 66.7; max = 100). Table 3 summarizes the performance results.

Even though we did not have a comparison threshold for the time needed to perform the tests, the average time of approximately 6 min for all tasks (SD = 2.04; min = 5; max = 10) can be considered a reasonable value.

Each task was divided into activities (A1.. AN) that were scored according to their completion and how easily it was for the participant (easily completed, completed, completed with difficulty, not completed). In general, all activities were completed without a challenge. The only exception that can be noticed happened in task 3, with the activities A4 and A5 not being completed by half of the users.

Activity 4 of task 3 refers to the access, through AALFred's interface, to the "Vital signs" item using touch and/or speech commands. Activity 5 refers to the verbalization of the values for the body temperature and pulse.

Table 3. Summary of performance results for AALFred

User #	Unassisted Task Effectiveness [(%)Complete]	Duration (min)[1]	Assists
P1 – task 2	100	5	0
P1 – task 3	100	5	0
P2 – task 1	83.3	5	1
P3 – task 3	66.7	5	2
P4 – task 1	100	5	0
P4 – task 2	100	10	0
Mean	91.7	5.8	0.5
Standard Deviation	13.9	2.04	0.8
Min	66.7	5	0
Max	100	10	2

The difficulty with task 3 (activities 4 and 5) however could be due to a lack of comprehension about the terms used. According to a user's verbalization, "the terms and icons are difficult to understand". As they were sequential activities, not completing activity 4 would lead to difficulties in completing activity 5.

Main verbalizations were related to failures on voice commands, font size, color scheme, and difficulties on understanding the meaning of terms and icons.

Satisfaction Results. The overall results of the satisfaction questionnaire related to the users' satisfaction with the app and perceived usefulness indicate that all participants understood the service as a potential benefit on their daily lives and something that they would be willing to acquire and learn how to use. All participants considered that the presented solution facilitates the health monitoring and 83 % of the participants agree that it promotes relaxation and would be willing to pay for the service.

Usability Scale Results. The average score for the Usability Scale was 22,5 (SD = 6,12; min = 15; max = 30), which, considering that the maximum score is 30, indicates a successful result. Figure 1 presents the scores attained for all tasks.

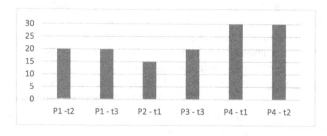

Fig. 1. ICF-Usability scale score by participant

4.2 SmartCompanion

Performance Results. The overall performance results suggest that the products did not present major usability issues, with less than half the users requesting assistance during the test and a mean unassisted task completion effectiveness of 88.1 % (SD = 15.92; min = 57.14; max = 100). Table 4 summarizes the performance results.

Table 4. Summary of performance results for Smart Companion

User #	Unassisted Task Effectiveness [(%)Complete]	Duration (min)[1]	Assists
P1	100	15	0
P2	71.43	17	2
P3	85.71	15	1
P4	100	13	0
P5	100	23	0
P6	100	12	0
P7	100	15	0
P8	100	12	0
P9	57.14	19	4
P10	100	21	0
P11	71.43	21	2
P12	71.43	21	2
Mean	88.10	17	0.92
Standard Deviation	15.92	3.88	1.31
Min	57.14	12	0
Max	100	23	4

The average time for all tasks completion was 17 min for all tasks SD = 3,88; min = 12; max = 23) which can be considered also a reasonable value.

In general, all activities were completed without challenge. The only exception that can be noticed happened in task 1, with the activities A2 and A3 not being completed by half the users. This fact however was due to deviations in the activity flow, i.e., there were different flows that allowed the participants to achieve the same result. In this case, half of the users chose a flow which did not require the completion of these two specific activities but that produced result required to complete the task.

Satisfaction Results. The overall results of the satisfaction questionnaire related to the users satisfaction with the app and perceived usefulness indicate that all participants understood the service has a potential benefit on their daily lives and something that they would be willing to acquire and learn how to use. Participants also indicated the three most valued characteristics of this service as the immediate access to information, the easing of a problem's resolution and the ease of use.

Usability Scale Results. The average score for the Usability Scale was 24.6 (SD = 2,64; min = 19; max = 27), which, considering that the maximum score is 30, indicates a successful result. Figure 2 presents the scores attained for all tasks.

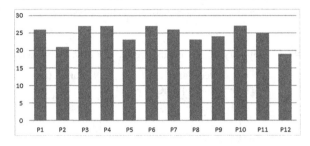

Fig. 2. ICF-Usability Scale score by participant

Fig. 3. Main changes in GUI of ALLFred: left – GUI used during the studies reported on this paper; right – new GUI (darker theme) that took into account the learning from this study.

Fig. 4. Current version of Smart Companion

5   Conclusions

The usability testing during the prototype phase of app development, allowed a better understanding of senior users' needs and expectations. From this analysis some changes were considered for the Graphical User Interface (GUI) and information architecture of both apps.

For AALFred, main changes were made considering the: (i) color scheme and font size/type to improve contrast and legibility, (ii) icons design to a better information comprehension, and (iii) rearrangement of the layout elements to meet users' expectations and to be updated using Windows 8 look and feel and design guidelines. Figure 3 shows AALFred's evolution with re-designed icons and a new with a new layout, with a more comprehensive flow of information. Users were also given choice to customize their user experience by having access to GUI parameters like multiple application themes (dark/light), list orientation (vertical or horizontal scrolling), or speech interaction customization (multiple synthetic voices). This is easily configurable via a step-by-step wizard available when the app first starts and in the preferences screen.

New usability tests performed with most recent version of AALFred, yet to be published, have shown a clear choice of the darker theme when compared to the clearer one. The clearer theme was perceived as harder to read and understand by the seniors.

As for the Smart Companion, the results of this evaluation indicated that the proposed solution meet the criteria to be considered suitable for the target users. Participants' performance did not vary significantly, and the low number of assistances and high completion rate are considered as positive results. The only task including activities that were not completed, only suggests that the alternative flows allow users to also easily complete tasks. Since satisfaction results were also positive, there were no recommendations to change the application design at the time of the usability testing during the prototype phase of development (Fig. 4).

We believe that these results are a direct consequence of the use of a user-centered methodology adopted early in the apps design and development. Since requirements elicitation phase to the early prototype phases, both AALFred and Smart Companion have been built on users' input and according to design guidelines for this target audience [9]. Since the tested design had already gone through a series of iterations that included usability tests and redesign of the user interface, the above presented results validate the current design. Both AALFred and SmartCompanion are currently being used in extensive field trials in various regions of Portugal, in the context of QREN AAL4ALL, whose results will be subject to further publication. Future work for these apps includes the development of new features covering seniors' needs and iterations to improve new designs.

Acknowledgments. Portuguese Project AAL4ALL (http://www.aal4all.org/), co-funded by the European Community Fund FEDER through COMPETE – Programa Operacional Factores de Competitividade (POFC).

References

1. United Nations: World Population Ageing 2009. United Nations, New York (2009)
2. World Health Organization: Diabetes action now. In: W. H. Organization (ed.): World Health Organization and International Diabetes Federation (2004)
3. Kleinberger, T., Becker, M., Ras, E., Holzinger, A., Müller, P.: Ambient intelligence in assisted living: enable elderly people to handle future interfaces. In: Stephanidis, C. (ed.) UAHCI 2007 (Part II). LNCS, vol. 4555, pp. 103–112. Springer, Heidelberg (2007)
4. AAL PaeLife. http://www.aal-europe.eu/projects/paelife/. Accessed 6 Dec 2014
5. Smartcompanion. http://smartcompanion.projects.fraunhofer.pt/. Accessed 6 Dec 2014
6. International Organization for Standardization (ISO): Human-centred design processes for interactive systems. ISO 13407:1999. International Organization for Standardization, Geneva, Switzerland (1999)
7. Pacheco da Rocha, N., Queirós, A., Oliveira, C., Teixeira, A., Pacheco, O., Pereira, C., Martins, A. I.: Integrated development and evaluation of innovative AAL services; A Living Lab approach. Paper presented at the Information Systems and Technologies (CISTI), 2013 8th Iberian Conference on Information Systems and Technologies, Lisbon, Portugal, 19–22 June 2013 (2013)
8. Schumacher, J.: Alcotra Innovation project: Living Labs. Definition, Harmonization Cube Indicators & Good Practices (I. Alcotra, Trans.), Alcotra (2013)
9. Correia de Barros, A., Leitão, R., Ribeiro, J.: Design and evaluation of a mobile user interface for older adults: navigation, interaction and visual design recommendations. Procedia Comput. Sci. 27, 369–378 (2014). Elsevier B.V.
10. QREN AAL4ALL, Ambient Assisted Living for ALL. http://www.aal4all.org/. Accessed 6 Dec 2014

Investigating Synergies Between Interaction Design Methods

Stefano Filippi[1(✉)], Daniela Barattin[1], and Paula Alexandra Silva[2]

[1] DIEGM Department, University of Udine, Udine, Italy
{stefano.filippi,daniela.barattin}@uniud.it
[2] Department of Design Innovation, National University of Ireland, Maynooth Ireland
palexa@gmail.com

Abstract. A successful product provides a pleasurable and straightforward experience. This leads to an increasing importance of the human-computer interaction and user experience issues in design. Despite the wealth of methods and tools available to support the design process, these are frequently incomplete and difficult to use. This research contributes to fill this gap by investigating the possible synergies between two design methods, the BadIdeas method (BI) and the Interaction Design Integrated Method (IDIM). BI is an early design method especially suited for the ideation phase of the design process. IDIM deals with design, evaluation, and innovation forecasting, and covers the first part of the product development process. Two limitations are highlighted in each of these methods and their concepts and tools are mutually exploited to improve the other. Suggestions for integration and improvement are presented with examples that demonstrate the benefits of this research.

Keywords: Interaction design methods · Badideas · IDIM · Design process

1 Introduction

In the last thirty years, human-computer interaction has acquired an increasingly important role in engineering design. One of the reasons why this happened is due to the change in the definition of product quality, nowadays focusing not only on the satisfaction of user needs [1] but also on providing a pleasurable and comprehensive user experience [2]. Thus, classic design methods are no longer suitable and new ones have emerged to put the user experience at the center of the design activities. However, these methods and tools are often incomplete and difficult to use. In this context, the goal of this research is to investigate and exploit the possible synergies between two existing design methods – the BadIdeas method (BI) [3] and the Interaction Design Integrated Method (IDIM) [4], in order to increase their effectiveness. BI is an early design method that aims at nurturing creativity and innovation in the design and development of interactive solutions, exploiting the generation of bad ideas. IDIM covers the first part of the product development process, from gathering user needs to the generation of validated design solutions thanks to the exploitation of different tools working in synergy. Both methods have limitations. This research identifies them and

© Springer International Publishing Switzerland 2015
A. Marcus (Ed.): DUXU 2015, Part I, LNCS 9186, pp. 179–190, 2015.
DOI: 10.1007/978-3-319-20886-2_18

investigates how tools and activities of the other method can be used to address the limitations and improve the effectiveness of the first and vice versa. The paper starts by describing the two methods. Then, it analyses them and two limitations in each method are identified. Afterwards, the paper proposes improvements based on the exploitation of the other method in a mutually beneficial process. The paper then discusses the pros and cons of the proposed integrations and concludes by summarizing the research and suggesting directions for future research.

2   Background

2.1   The BadIdeas Method

BI is a design method that aims at nurturing creativity and innovation in the process of designing novel user interfaces. It initially focuses on the generation of bad ideas, which are then submitted to a critical examination to uncover their good and bad characteristics. This examination subsequently turns the method into a convergent analysis of the bad ideas, finally transformed until they are of good use and have materialized into tangible artefacts or ideas for future implementation [3]. Figure 1 shows the six phases of the method, which are described next.

Fig. 1. The six phases of the BI method

Phase 1 – Presentation of design brief – consists of describing the design problem the facilitator wants the participants to solve to. This includes a clear statement about the domain and the context of use for which participants will be generating ideas.

Phase 2 – Generation of bad ideas – consists of asking participants to generate bad ideas. This phase includes an explanation of what is meant by a bad idea and the provision of a couple of examples of bad ideas (for examples see [3]). A good bad idea has to be purposely bad, silly, crazy, weird and/or impossible; has to be vague enough to allow transformation; is not too detailed, so that it becomes harder to lay aside those details; does not need to be related to anything or to any domain in particular, including the design brief.

Phase 3 – Analysis: what, why and when not – examines the nature of the ideas obtained in phase 2. This improves participants' understanding of the ideas as well as their related concepts, potential of transformation and, ultimately, their design space. To support this process, BI uses a set of prompt questions, such as "what is bad about this idea?" or "are there any other things that share this feature but are not bad?" (for a complete list of prompt questions, please refer to [3]).

Phase 4 – Turning things around – uses a set of strategies to help participants to uncover new dimensions and possibilities for the bad ideas being examined. These strategies are "going back and forth", "change the context", and "role-play". "Going back and forth" consists of alternating between positive and negative aspects of each feature. "Change the context" involves looking at bad ideas from a different perspective and in different circumstances. "Role-play" consists of imagining that the bad idea was deliberately designed as it is by an expert.

Phase 5 – Making it good – has the purpose of turning the bad idea into a good one. This often happens on its own accord during phases 3 and 4, but if not, it is addressed as a separate stage by further analyzing the bad ideas and their singular components, by making use of analogies, by abstracting their main characteristics, or by exploring the potential of transformation. At this stage, participants must produce something that has the beginnings of pragmatics, i.e., a solution that addresses the initial design challenge. This should be performed with the initial design problem brief in mind.

Phase 6 – Selection of outcomes – comprehends the evaluation and selection of the ideas that are going to be further developed into fully working prototypes. A panel of judges should evaluate the generated ideas and the low-fidelity prototypes, if available. Novelty and appropriateness (to the design brief and domain) are two possible evaluation criteria, but the panel of judges should be able to define adequate criteria themselves as well. For more details on how to evaluate creative design methods and the outcomes of a session with BI, please refer to [5].

2.2   Interaction Design Integrated Method – IDIM

IDIM is a design method focused on interaction issues [4]. It covers the first part of the product development process, from gathering user needs, the goals of the design process expressed directly by the people who will use the product, to the generation of validated design solutions. It originates from the combination of three existing methods, the Interaction Design GuideLines (IDGL), the Usability Evaluation Multi-Method (UEMM), and the Interaction Trends of Evolution (ITRE), developed by dealing with interaction design, usability evaluation, and innovation forecasting respectively [6–8]. Figure 2 shows the IDIM architecture and the process data flow.

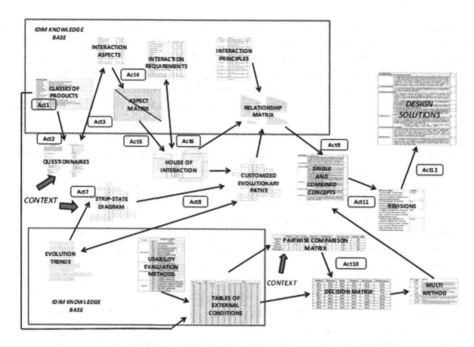

Fig. 2. IDIM architecture and data flow

IDIM exploitation starts with activity Act1, where the product classes are used. These are pieces of information describing functions – what the product is called to perform to achieve the user needs – domains for the application, criteria for user characterization, and features of existing products.

If the class the product under development belongs to already exists in the knowledge base, the designers simply select it; otherwise, designers are required to fill an empty form to create a new class. Then, IDIM supports designers in generating a questionnaire to collect users' characteristics and expectations (Act2). The outcome of this activity is a rough set of user needs that designers transform in an ordered set of interaction aspects (Act3). These represent foreseen and unexpected user needs, processed to make them usable in the forthcoming activities. These interaction aspects are analyzed thanks to the data structure named aspect matrix to highlight implicit user needs (Act4). The aspects are listed as rows in the main IDIM data structure, the House Of Interaction (HOI), derived from the House of Quality of the Quality Function Deployment (QFD) theory [9] (Act5). The HOI allows pieces of information to be collected and related to each other in a structured way. The core of the HOI collects the relationships between inter-action aspects and product requirements (Act6). These are quantitative indices, which aim at making usability concerns as objective as possible, and represent meaningful design constraints corresponding to the data collected during the survey. They are thirty-one collected in IDIM knowledge base for the moment, but these are likely to increase. While exploiting the HOI, IDIM supports designers in highlighting the best evolutionary paths for the product being designed. Eleven trends of evolution are included in the IDIM knowledge base. These are sets of ordered evolutionary stages, describing the interaction characteristics of a product. Every stage has a definition and some examples associated for an easier exploitation. Afterwards, designers classify the product under development against the trend stages (Act7) and this leads to the definition of the so-called Strip-Stage Diagram (SSD). The SSD has eleven strips, one for each trend, containing the trend stages. The strips are rearranged in order to get the stages of every trend depicting the current innovation level of the product aligned vertically. Act8 uses the interaction requirements highlighted thanks to the HOI and the SSD to define the Customized Evolutionary Paths (CEP). A CEP is a guideline that tries to foresee future changes of specific interaction characteristics corresponding to the eleven interaction trends of evolution. A CEP is obtained by mapping the generic definitions of the trend stages appearing to the right of the vertical line of the SSD to the specific product domain, and this is done for every interaction requirement. Each interaction requirement has interaction principles associated. IDIM includes forty-seven interaction principles derived from the forty principles of the Theory of Inventive Problem Solving (TRIZ) [10, 11]. The interaction principles consist of advices on how to implement/solve generic interaction design issues/problems. Starting from these suggestions and from the CEP, designers can easily develop the so-called single concepts (first part of Act9). Possible contradictions or positive connections among interaction requirements are managed and exploited by another data structure, named relationship matrix, derived from the TRIZ contradiction matrix [11, 12]. The rows and columns of this matrix include the list of requirements. The main diagonal contains the links to the principles related to each requirement. The other entries refer to relationships between requirements, suggesting the most suitable interaction principles to solve possible contradictions or enhance positive relationships. These suggestions contribute to the generation of the second half of the design solutions, named combined concepts (second part of Act9). All the concepts are evaluated using the most suitable usability evaluation methods [13], collected in a list named multi-method. IDIM supplies this multi-method thanks to the exploitation of the pairwise comparison matrix and the decision matrix (Act10). The use of the multi-method generates of a list of possible improvements of the concepts (Act11). The last activity (Act12) defines the final design solutions implementing the improvements given in Act11. These solutions are ready to be delivered to production designers.

3 Exploring Synergies Between BI and IDIM

3.1 Exploitation of IDIM Concepts, Activities and Tools into BI

This section analyses BI to identify possible limitations. Then, IDIM concepts, activities, and tools are considered to improve the knowledge and actions required by a design team using BI. Two examples are provided to demonstrate the proposed improvements and their effectiveness.

Analysis of BI. When analyzing the BI phases both from the perspective of the design team activities and the design tools the team has to support the design process, two limitations are identified. The first, labelled from now on as BI_L1, is identified in phase 1 "presentation of design brief". In this phase, the design team is expected to understand the design problem (context of use, goals to achieve, user needs to satisfy, etc.) without any formal support. This is a limitation and this phase can benefit from the use of dedicated activities and tools.

The second limitation – BI_L2 – is identified in phase 5 "making it good", and refers to the absence of guidelines on how to transform the bad aspects of the bad ideas initially generated into good and practical ones. Even if directions are given on how to perform this transformation (e.g., identify the good aspects and keep them, identify the bad aspects and change them or transform them), no specific tools are provided to the design team on how to perform this transformation.

Exploiting IDIM Inside BI. This section describes how the IDIM concepts, activities, and tools can be used to overcome the limitations identified in BI. Figure 3 summarizes how IDIM can contribute to BI.

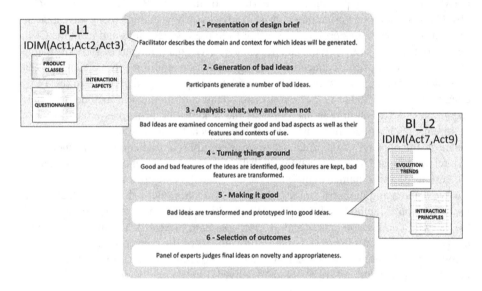

Fig. 3. IDIM contribution to BI

BI_L1 can be addressed by integrating activities and tools supporting the understanding of the design problem in a more precise and systematic way. IDIM manages all of this in its first three activities by exploiting the design team knowledge about the design context and goals – which are expressed in the classes of products (Act1), by generating a questionnaire to collect information from real users (Act2), and by analyzing this information to achieve the interaction aspects (Act3). These activities can then introduced as a complement to the first phase of BI. In this case, the facilitator is expected to create a product class beforehand in order to highlight the context of use as well as the functions involved in the design problem. He/she is also expected to generate a users' questionnaire, through which the users will express their needs and expectations. The execution of these activities will enable the definition of the design problem, which in turn can be expressed in the form of interaction aspects that will provide the facilitator with the means to explain better the design problem to the design team. For example, when considering the design of a container for liquids, such as a bottle or a tank, the first activity would be to generate the product class, if it was not present in IDIM yet. The product class makes the contexts of use clearer, for e.g., by determining if the container is to be used in a domestic or an industrial environments, or if the container should be suitable for edibles or not, etc. Then, the facilitator generates the questionnaire following the empty template provided by IDIM. The resulting questionnaire consists of fourteen questions. Five focused on the users' characteristics (e.g., "do you manage the production of the container?") and the other nine on the interaction between the container and the user (e.g., "do you have some negative or positive aspects to highlight when you use spill the liquid if that is required?"). The data collected from the questionnaire are then transformed into interaction aspects; e.g., difficulty to understand how to start opening the container, difficulty to open the container; too much strength required to open the container; difficulty to hermetically close the container; excessive weight of the container; difficulty to see inside the container given the presence of too many labels, etc. These aspects will form the design problem description to present to the participants of a BI session.

BI_L2 can be addressed by exploiting the potential of guidelines in supporting the design team to put good ideas into practice. Two activities of IDIM are considered for this purpose: the generation of evolutionary paths exploiting the interaction trends (Act7) and the generation of the single concepts, exploiting the interaction principles (first part of Act9). The interaction trends of evolution consist of generic guidelines that help reasoning about the evolution of the interaction aspects without physical or technological limitations. The interaction principles provide suggestions on how to put an idea or an interaction requirement into practice by considering different characteristics (e.g., color settings of the component/interface according to the product state), physical properties (e.g., the mechanical vibration to enhance feedback quality), and user capabilities (e.g., by combining more actions together to avoid mental loads through multiple selections). Because these two IDIM lists of guidelines are generic enough to cover the most of the situations, they can be integrated in phase 5 of BI, without requiring any further adaptations. If we consider again the example of the container for liquids and the bad idea "the container is made of air", the positive aspects are the lightness and transparency of the box and the absence of problems to open it. These aspects have the potential to solve some of the problems highlighted in BI_L1, such as the "difficulty to open the container" and the "difficulty to see inside the container". Likewise, the interaction trends of evolution can support the reasoning about the strategy to deal with the change of context in phase 4. In particular, the last state of the third trend "intermediaries" says that users do not need any type of real container, but they can interact directly with the liquid. This suggests creating walls made by air curtains. This is not possible in the context of a container but consists of a good and innovative idea if considering a fridge. To make this idea real, the interaction principles P2 "taking out – trim functions or components not important from the users' point of view; focus on those that could generate dissatisfaction if missing", and P21 "another dimension – move from a physical interaction to a contact free one" are used. The final good idea becomes "air curtains are used as walls in a fridge, allowing the users to interact directly with the food and see inside the fridge without opening the door, and therefore preserving the quality of food at all times".

3.2   Exploitation of BI Concepts, Activities and Tools into IDIM

In this section the roles of IDIM and BI are inverted; IDIM is analyzed to find possible limitations to be overcome thanks to BI concepts, activities and tools. As it happened before, an example is used to explain better the improvements and their effectiveness.

Analysis of IDIM. A deep analysis of the IDIM-based design process allows two limitations to be highlighted. They deal with the rigorous sequence of activities that have to be performed to obtain the final design solutions. Solutions cannot be found outside the established path and the discarded ones cannot be recovered. The first limitation – ID_L1 – consists in the absence of tools to generate ideas free of guidelines that could limit designers' creativity, and that may negatively affect the number and variety of the design solutions.

The second limitation – ID_L2 – deals with the absence of tools to extract and adapt the good aspects of ideas discarded in the evaluation activity (Act11). These may include details and aspects that could be useful to obtain new/innovative ideas in the same context (thanks to suitable analyses and changes) or in different ones.

Exploiting BI Inside IDIM. The two limitations of IDIM are now observed considering the BI concepts, activities, and tools to discover possibilities to overcome them. Figure 4 summarizes the contribution of BI to IDIM.

ID_L1 requires new activities and tools to generate different kinds of ideas to be considered in the definition of the single and combined concepts. In BI, ideation starts from silly and/or bad ideas. This kind of ideas is completely new in IDIM, which has originally been thought and developed to find exclusively good ideas since the beginning. Moreover, BI is free from any rigid formalism that could limit designers' creativity, unlikely what happens in most of IDIM activities. Therefore, phases 2, 3, 4 of BI can mitigate the rigidity of IDIM and they are used in parallel with Act9 "development of the solution concepts". This way, designers can follow two paths to generate the concepts: from one side, they use the classic procedure based on the interaction principles, the CEP, and the relationship matrix; by the other side, they generate bad and silly ideas (phase 2), convert these into good ones (phases 3 and 4), and add them to the list of the single and combined concepts. For example, consider the redesign of a desk lamp. One of the user needs regards the difficulty to orient the light without burning, because the external surface of the lampshade could be too hot.

A design solution coming from the classic procedure is "a stick covered with insulating material is placed on the external surface of the lampshade and can be safely handled to orient the light". The other path based on the BI contribution suggests thinking wild around this problem and allows the generation of silly ideas, for e.g., "a cooking glove can be put somewhere close to the top of the lamp so that the user introduces the hand inside it and moves the lamp safely, without burns". Then, the BI prompt questions

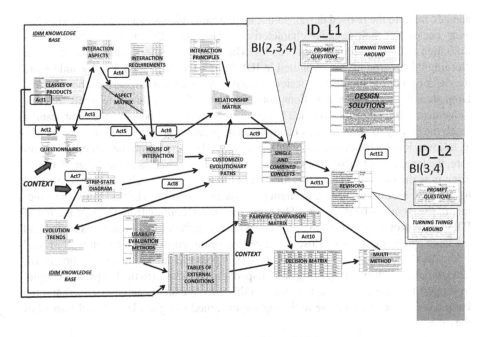

Fig. 4. BI contribution to IDIM

allow the identification of the bad aspects of this idea and the reasons for them. In this case, a bad aspect is that the glove does not cover all the surface of the lamp and if the user does not take care where the glove is, he/she risks burning. Therefore, the use of a glove requires an unnatural user behavior to move the lamp, because he/she needs to look at the lamp. Moreover, a glove on a lamp is unsightly indeed. After this reasoning, other BI prompt questions allow the identification of the positive aspects; e.g., the glove completely prevents the hand from burning if used correctly. Once the bad ideas have been generated and processed, the two separated paths merge again. Interaction principles are involved to transform the positive aspects coming from the bad ideas into design solutions. By considering the positive aspect just highlighted and the principles P7 "nested doll – embed functions in one another in order to perform all of them with the same actions", P26 "harm to benefit – substitute components showing obsolete shapes that recall different actions/functions", and P31 "self-service – avoid exploitation of external help in performing actions, and improve interface components (color, shape, positions, materials, etc.) to enhance affordance", a new design solution can be developed. This is "a moving plate of insulated material is placed on the lampshade. It is small enough to avoid affecting the aesthetic appearance of the lamp. A sensor feels the user's hand approach and the plate moves accordingly, aiming at matching the position of the hand. In this way, the user has not to take care about searching safe places to grab the lamp, the lamp will not burn the user's hand and the user behavior gets enhanced, given that the user is not required to look at the lamp anymore".

ID_L2 needs new activities to deal with the discarded ideas coming from the evaluation activity (Act11), aiming at finding good aspects in these ideas in order to recover and add them to the revised design solutions. Discarded ideas can be considered as bad ideas because of their negative characteristics. Therefore, BI can help addressing this limitation thanks again to phases 3 and 4. The prompt questions and the strategies of "turning things around" are exploited in IDIM, after the evaluation activity and before the definition of the final list of design concepts. As an example, consider the idea "the lamp stem is made of three sections connected to each other thanks to joints to allow movements. It cannot be extended". This idea is discarded because the lamp cannot reach the ceiling to be used as a chandelier. The prompt questions help in recovering it as follows. First, what is bad about this idea is that the stem cannot be extended. Therefore, the lamp cannot satisfy some user needs (e.g., being used as a chandelier). Considering now the good aspects of this idea, the stem is strong enough and easy to manage to allow the user in controlling the light position and direction. Thanks to this, the structure of the stem can be improved. The revised concept, coming from the exploitation of IDIM only, would be "the stem is spring-like shaped; therefore, it can be extended and the lamp can be placed also close to the ceiling or turned to light a lateral wall instead of the desk". An improvement of this concept is possible due to the contribution of BI, and it would be "the stem is spring-like shaped; the part closed to the lampshade is rigid, to support the user in moving the lamp. In this way, the stem can be extended and the lamp can be placed also close to the ceiling or turned to light a lateral wall instead of the desk".

4   Discussion

Thanks to the mutual integrations, the two design methods considered in this research seem notably improved. The integrations of IDIM in BI focused on the description of the design problem help the facilitator to better define the context of use and other design problem details. The context of use is systematically described thanks to the information collected in the product classes. Moreover, the possibility of considering different functions allows the description of more than one context of use for a specific case study, just because functions are related to the context of use. This is demonstrated in the example of the container for liquids, where the context of domestic containers for edibles is related to the function "allow seeing the liquid inside", while the context containers for poisoning liquids is related to the function "contain hermetically the liquid". Problem details are very important for the subsequent phases of the design process, as highlighted by the second limitation (BI_L2) where silly ideas are generated starting from them. Always in the example of the container for liquids, the two interaction aspects "difficulty in opening the container" and "too high strength required to open the container" are solved thanks to the silly idea "the container is made of air" because of the absence of walls. The "making it good" phase is simplified due to the use of interaction principles and interaction trends of evolution. This because the two lists of guidelines help the design team by suggesting alternative contexts where the bad ideas can be turned into good or feasible ones. In both limitations, the IDIM contribution does not bound creativity because only suggestions are given and no restrictions are imposed at all. For example, the generation of bad ideas in the case of the refrigerator demonstrates that the description of the initial context with the IDIM product classes does not limit changes of context on the fly.

Regarding IDIM, the introduction of the bad idea generation concept moves it closer to a think wild approach to design; that is, brainstorming without the reasoning limits imposed by technology, costs, structured design paths, etc. Designers are free to explore their creativity increasing their potential to generate innovation. Moreover, the number of design solutions increases, thanks to the new ideas added by applying the tools of the BI phases 2, 3, and 4. The design solutions are also improved due to the details recovered from the discarded ideas. For example, the design solution that describes the stem of the lamp is improved thanks to the discarded idea considering the lamp stem as rigid. By following the design path suggested by IDIM only, this solution would have been probably lost. Finally, IDIM remains a suitable method for both design and redesign, but design is particularly improved, aimed at maximizing innovative achievements.

However, some limitations remain. For example, more studies need to be conducted to confirm the validity of the integrations this paper proposes. Moreover, sometimes the integration is not direct and requires the modifications of the activities and tools belonging to the other method. This happens for example in IDIM, where the results of the transformation of bad ideas into good ones require them to be elaborated with the interaction principles, because they are not compatible with the single and combined concepts. Design solutions need to be more structured than the ones usually found thanks to the first phase of BI.

5   Conclusions

The human-computer interaction and user experience have acquired an increasing importance in the product development process, with the definition of the product quality being often closely related to these two aspects. Traditional design methods overlook them; therefore, design tools that focus on interaction issues need to be developed. Human-computer interaction approaches put the users, their characteristics and behavior, at the center of the design process. Still, design methods offer different levels of completeness, but important design phases are often missing. This research investigated how the limitations of two design methods – BI and IDIM – could be address by exploiting the potential of the other. In order to do so, each method was first thoroughly analyzed to identify possible limitations, to then investigate how the concepts, activities, and tools of the other method could be used to improve these limitations and vice versa. Two limitations for each method have been highlighted and addressed due to mutual integrations.

In the future, it will be interesting to assess the advantages of these integrations. First, new case studies are required to demonstrate the effectiveness of the results and the improvement of both the methods. These case studies should cover different design fields and compare the results obtained with those performed using the original BI method and IDIM, without integrations. Moreover, further integrations of BI and IDIM with other methods should be considered as well, in order to address remaining limitations. For example, none of the methods considers technological feasibility or the time and budget available while developing the final design solutions. Resorting to different methods not necessarily belonging to the interaction field can be of great help to address these limitations.

References

1. ISO 9000:2005. Quality management principles. http://www.iso.org/iso/home/standards/management-standards/iso_9000.htm
2. Hassenzahl, M.: User experience and experience design. In: Soegaard, M., Dam, R. (eds.) The Encyclopedia of Human-Computer Interaction, 2nd edn. The Interaction Design Foundation, Aarhus (2014). https://www.interaction-design.org/encyclopedia/user_experience_and_experience_design.html
3. Silva, P.A.: BadIdeas 3.0: a method for the creativity and innovation in design. In: 1st DESIRE Network Conference on Creativity and Innovation in Design, pp. 154–162 (2010)
4. Filippi, S., Barattin, D., Cascini, G.: Analyzing the cognitive processes of an interaction design method using the FBS framework. In: ICED13 International Conference on Engineering Design (2013)
5. Silva, P.A., Read, J.C.: A methodology to evaluate creative design methods: a study with the BadIdeas method. In: OzCHI, pp. 264–271. ACM Digital Library (2010)
6. Filippi, S., Barattin, D.: IDGL, an interaction design framework based on systematic innovation and quality function deployment. Int. J. Interact. Des. Manuf. 1–19 (2014). doi: 10.1007/s12008-014-0231-6 (published online)
7. Filippi, S., Barattin, D.: Generation, adoption, and tuning of usability evaluation multi-methods. Int. J. Hum. Comput. Interact. **28**(6), 406–422 (2012)
8. Filippi, S., Barattin, D.: Definition and exploitation of trends of evolution about interaction. Technol. Forecast. Soc. Change **86**, 216–236 (2013)
9. Cristiano, J.J., Liker, J.K., White, C.C.: Customer-driven product development through quality function deployment in the US and Japan. J. Prod. Innov. Manag. 17, 286–308 (2000)
10. Cong, H., Tong, L.H.: Grouping of TRIZ inventive principles to facilitate automatic patent classification. Expert Syst. Appl. 34, 788–795 (2008)
11. Altshuller, G.S.: Innovation Algorithm: TRIZ, Systematic Innovation and Technical Creativity. Technical Innovation Center, Inc., Worchester (1999)
12. Chang, H.T., Chen, J.L.: The conflict-problem-solving CAD software integrating TRIZ into eco-innovation. Adv. Eng. Softw. **35**, 553–566 (2004)
13. Nielsen, J., Mack, R.L.: Usability Inspection Methods. Wiley, New York (1994)

A Posture HCI Design Pattern for Television Commerce Based on User Experience

Rosendy Jess Galabo[⊠] and Carlos Soares Neto

Laboratory of Advanced Web Systems, Federal University of Maranhão, Av. dos Portugueses Campus do Bacanga, São Luís, Maranhão 65080-040, Brazil
rj@fgalabo.com, csalles@deinf.ufma.br

Abstract. Television commerce represents a significant opportunity for worldwide market due to the digital TV transition in several countries. In order to provide a design guidance for these applications, we developed a T-commerce Posture HCI Design Pattern based on user experience research. Three focus groups are composed of twenty-five participants and an experiment with eight volunteers were performed. The results are described as a design pattern template composed of four types of t-commerce applications. Each type presents a recurrent problem, a proven solution and a context. The developed design pattern helps designers to decide the t-commerce main interactions focusing on better user experience.

Keywords: Guidelines · IDTV commerce · Home shopping · T-commerce

1 Introduction

Digital television transition is being implemented in several countries with different deadlines to finish this process. Interactive Digital Television (IDTV) offers many opportunities through interactive applications. One of these opportunities is the electronic commerce or e-commerce known as television commerce or t-commerce. An e-commerce transaction is the sale or purchase of goods or services conducted over computer networks for receiving or placing of orders [1]. In contrast to the e-commerce on websites, the t-commerce business model is not completely defined. It means that the t-commerce remains heavily underexploited. One of the reasons might be the lack of design guidance for this type of service.

In 2012, there were 55 % of worldwide households with digital TV receivers [2]. In absolute terms, 380 million households with digital TV in developed countries. In the same year, worldwide B2C (Business-to-Commerce) e-commerce sales grew 21.1 % to top 1 trillion dollars for the first time and the top five countries were the United States, China, United Kingdom, Japan and Germany [3]. This given scenario presents a potential worldwide market for t-commerce.

In January 2014, the first known integrated t-commerce and advertising was broadcasted [4] and it allowed viewers to purchase the featured products using the TV remote control. It was an experiment with t-commerce interactive advertising. However, this experiment raises a few questions: Is this the first existing t-commerce application? How do users think about the t-commerce? In which contexts can we

© Springer International Publishing Switzerland 2015
A. Marcus (Ed.): DUXU 2015, Part I, LNCS 9186, pp. 191–203, 2015.
DOI: 10.1007/978-3-319-20886-2_19

apply the television commerce? How to choose the best way to sell products in t-commerce applications?

Answers for these questions can be resumed in a HCI design pattern, which helps designers to choose a good solution for their applications. A design pattern is a proven solution for a problem in a context. Each pattern is a three-part rule, which expresses a relation among a certain context, a certain system of forces that occurs repeatedly in that context, and a certain software configuration, which allows these forces to resolve themselves [5].

We purpose a posture design pattern to help designers to choose a t-commerce type for a specific business goal. A posture pattern is a high-level pattern in hierarchy problem scale in interaction design. When we talk about top-down design, it means that, usually, our first activity is to start understanding the users and their tasks, technical environment, business, context etc. Every system or application has a reason for existence [6]. A posture pattern describes what the essentials of that posture are: what kind of application is used consistently, which elements are typically necessary and what are the main experiences that are offered to users.

HCI research has one major aim, which is to create good experiences while interacting with an interface. Research in this area is often referred to as UX research (User eXperience) [7]. In order to achieve positives experiences on t-commerce applications, we developed a t-commerce posture design pattern using a user-centred design approach.

Section 2 presents a background about digital TV and its context. Some related works about television commerce are presented in Sect. 3. In Sect. 4 we present our method and techniques. Section 5 describes the HCI posture design pattern for television commerce developed in this paper. The last section is reserved for conclusions and future work.

2 Background

To develop a design pattern, it is necessary to define quality criteria for identifying proven design solutions. Since we chose the user experience (UX) as quality criteria, three factors [8] affects UX: the context around the user and system, the user's state, and the system properties.

Currently, there are four digital TV distribution technologies [9]: Digital Terrestrial TV broadcasting (DTT), Digital Cable TV (CATV), Internet Protocol TV (IPTV), Direct-to-home Satellite (DTH). To a certain degree, the present t-commerce pattern is for DTT technology, but it may be extended for the other TV distribution technologies. One of the requirements for DTT is a set-top box that allows a viewer to receive digital signal that includes digital data from TV applications.

We have to consider several context of IDTV [10] such as viewing distance, environment, number of user and user engagement. TV is a social tool, in a familiar environment that is watched from long-range distance. All UX aspects were considered in the t-commerce application interaction as we show in the following sections.

3   Related Work

Some researches provide definitions about television commerce [11–13]. These findings describe traditional and interactive application t-commerce categorization from the general to specific.

According to Lin et al. [11], a television commerce comprises all the transaction behaviors via TV including the traditional TV shopping. The authors categorize t-commerce in four types: TV shopping, direct response TV, travel shopping and TV applications. Summing up, they classify t-commerce into these three traditional t-commerce types and one using an interactive TV application.

E-commerce involves transactions of goods or services, t-commerce applications include other types of digital transaction, such as banking, gambling, video on demand, donation services. Yu et al. [12] consider that t-commerce has two types of home services: homeshopping and homebanking.

Ghisi et al. [13] suggest a t-commerce categorization including this other digital transactions and different forms that are linked to advertising. They proposed four presentation models for t-commerce: Sales Channel, Program Related, Interactive Advertising and Other initiatives. This categorization is most suitable to our study because it suggests low-level types for digital television commerce applications. However, the provided elements in this model do not have specific design guidance on development of each t-commerce type and do not include user expectation regarding user experience.

In this paper, we show design guidance for four t-commerce type, which is similar in certain degree to the Ghisi presentation model [13]. Our categorization is based on user expectations and is an improvement on the current model because it better describes each t-commerce type in a pattern. Since interactive advertising were included in these models and there are different ways to attract viewer's attention and to provide specific information [14] (for instance advertising that aim to reward the viewer with coupons or discounts) our study is limited to advertisings that aim at increasing sales and provide online purchase functionality.

Several t-commerce applications were found on Internet from different countries and companies, which the interfaces are illustrated as follow on Fig. 1.

Fig. 1. T-commerces from left to right (Top): YuBuy (Portugal), HSN shop by remote (USA), Brava tcommerce [13] (Brazil), Rovi advertising (USA), CJ TMall (South Korea); T-commerces from left to right (bottom): Domino (USA), H&M (USA), IcueTV (USA), History shop (USA), This.co (South Korea)

We used these t-commerce interfaces as bases for designing prototypes and for exemplifying the posture pattern developed in this paper. In brief, all the presentation models [13] fits to each t-commerce application illustrated, however we notice that some of them have different contexts that could not fit very well to this categorization. We believe that another set of t-commerce types can be better than the current model.

4   Method and Techniques

We developed the t-commerce pattern based on user experience research (focus group & experimental testing with video demonstrations) and existing t-commerce applications. All study volunteers signed consent forms before the beginning of each study and all sessions were recorded using a video camera.

In order to select the appropriate participants (sample) for focus group and experiments, preliminary criteria were defined. The volunteers recruited must have made at least one online purchase, and there were not any distinction on gender, age, education level or income. This profile allowed us to understand the expectations of t-commerce users. It is worth mentioning that the digital t-commerce at Brazil is not as popular as other countries, like UK or USA. Thereby, we believe the selected sampling is good to collect the expectations and responses about the anticipated use of t-commerce.

Useful anticipated experiences were collected, such as expectations on how t-commerce works and how it should behave for users. After this study, we design an experiment in order to validate the users' statements collected.

4.1   Focus Group

Focus group is a technique that collect feelings, beliefs and opinions about a given subject through collective interview composed of seven to twelve participants. It is a discussion led by a moderator using a script with predetermined topics.

There were 25 volunteers for the three focus groups sessions, in which 17 were male and 8 female. The groups are heterogeneous comprising different ages. Half of the participants (50 %) were between the ages of 18–24 years old, more than a third (38 %) were between the ages of 25–30 years old, 8 % were between the age of 31–45 and a very small number (4 %) were over 45 years old. They are from different professional areas (social communication, design, education, architecture, banking, computer science, social science, sales and account executive). Three focus groups sessions were performed as can be seen in Fig. 2 below.

Fig. 2. Focus groups sessions

First, the sessions started with an introduction about t-commerce. Second, participants were asked about their expectations and ideas about the possibility to do shopping on TV using remote control. Then, they were asked about how a t-commerce works for them, questions such as: How to purchase an offer? How to interact and how to pay? Third, the participants wrote keywords or statements about their feelings and requirements that are important to do television commerce on sticky notes. Fourth, participants watched some video demonstrations of t-commerce and commented about them. Finally, participants were thanked for coming and helping.

4.2   Experimental Testing with Video Demonstrations

In order to understand hypothesis about the television commerce types that arouse on the focus group sessions, we designed an experiment that consists of two steps. First, an introduction about t-commerce was presented to a volunteer. Second, a pair of t-commerce videos demonstrations were shown and the participant was enquired to comment about what he had seen on these videos.

In this experiment, the independent variable are the t-commerce types and the users' statements are the dependent variable. The controlled variable are the same goods presented on a set of video demonstrations. For instance, a certain company's jeans is offered in both t-commerce situations sales channel and interactive advertising.

To ensure a fair test, we looked for videos with products that were possible to fit different t-commerce types as possible. Thereby, nine videos demonstrations were designed as illustrated in Fig. 3.

Fig. 3. (A) C&A Fergie Jeans 1 -virtual mall, (B) C&A Fergie Jeans A2 - virtual mall, (C) C&A Fergie Jeans – related TV program 1, (D) C&A Fergie Jeans - related TV program, (E) I-Steamer Conair – virtual mall 1, (F) I-Steamer Conair - interactive advertising, (G) I-Steamer Conair - enhanced infomercial, (H) TopTherm - related TV program, (I) TopTherm - enhanced infomercial

We group the videos in pairs with different t-commerce types, in order to make a contrast among them. Videos were organized in six pairs: (A + C), (E + G), (H + I), (B + D), (C + D) and (F + G).

The experiment was performed using a laptop with a voice recorder software and connected to the HDMI input of digital TV (32" LCD). There were 8 volunteers, in which 4 males and 4 female from different professional area, age and background (computer science, sales, fashion entrepreneur, management, architecture, account executive, designer and advertiser). 3 out of 8 volunteers were between ages 18–24, the same number of volunteers were between ages 25–30 years old and a small minority (2 out of 8) were between 31–45 years old.

4.3   Design Pattern Template

A data analysis was performed using recorded videos from both UX research (focus group and experiment). A transcription of each participants' statement was performed and they were categorized into related groups, then each group of assertions were summarized into a short description of problem or proven solution.

The results were organized on pattern template that we built on the structure of Kunert [15] and Obrist [16]. We describe each result in pattern structure described as follow.

- **NAME:** The name identifies the content presented in the pattern.
- **CONTEXT:** The context describes the use of the design pattern in the workflow of designing a t-commerce application.
- **PROBLEM:** The problem is formulated from user perspective and is related to how do users expect a certain system works. This pattern element is filled with results collected from focus group sessions in this research.
- **SOLUTION:** It provides alternative solutions for the design problem. Each solution is a core of solution that the designer has the freedom to implement in many ways. This field is filled out with user expectations results collected during the experimental testing, literature review and existing t-commerce application analyses.
- **EVIDENCE:** It provides where the solution came from. This field can be filled out with references to other literatures or results UX research results.
- **EXAMPLES:** Screenshots of existing t-commerce application and prototypes that show approaches to solve the design problem addressed.

5   Posture Design Pattern for Television Commerce

In this section, the knowledge gleaned from UX research, existing t-commerce application and other design guidance for t-commerce are summarized and presented on a design pattern template. The main posture pattern is illustrated below and the workflow continues according to the selected proven solution, in the following subsections.

PATTERN: Choose a t-commerce type.

CONTEXT: Designer has to decide how to sell a product on IDTV through a t-commerce application that solve his project and user requirements.

PROBLEM: There are four different t-commerce types for different goals: Related TV program, Interactive Advertising, Enhanced Infomercial, Virtual Mall

SOLUTION: Choose the t-commerce type according to your business goals:

(A) **Related TV Program:** If your goal is to convert a product placement[1] on a direct sell, this type is the solution.

(B) **Interactive Advertising:** If your goal is offer products, which is easy for impulse shopping, such as exclusive offer, air tickets, food, you should follow this type.

(C) **Enhanced Infomercial:** If your goal is increase conversion sales rates during the infomercials,[2] this t-commerce type is the solution for it.

(D) **Virtual Mall:** If your goal focuses on selling offers (products or services), a variety of products and details through a t-commerce application that can be used whenever you want or during a long time interval, then this type of t-commerce is the solution and it can be combined with the other types.

EVIDENCE: Participants of focus group reported the three t-commerce presentation models [13]. They also expect that a t-commerce can be available to interact whenever they want or, at least, for a long time interval (Virtual Mall).

EXAMPLE: (Fig. 4).

5.1 T-Commerce Type (A): Related TV Program

PATTERN: Related TV program.

CONTEXT: The design requirement is to improve the user experience by selling products or services presented on a product placement during a TV program, such as soap operas, movies, series, talk shows, etc.

PROBLEM: A product placement linked to a t-commerce application during a TV show may not satisfy everyone, because the viewer focus might be on the TV show instead of the t-commerce application. However, some of them are willing to buy the offer advertised.

SOLUTION: The application could offer a good or service through a product placement.

---

[1] The integration of advertising material with a TV show.

[2] TV commercial that looks like a television program, including testimonials, which main goal is selling products or services. A telephone number for teleshopping is commonly displayed.

Fig. 4. T-commerce types: (A) Related TV program [13], (B) Interactive advertising, (C) Enhanced infomercial, (D) Virtual mall

- If the TV show has a plot and narrative story such as soap operas, movies or TV series, t-commerce should be done during commercial breaks. A 'saving' (or skipping) key [17] can keep a summary of content related products for later viewing. However, the access to the application for impulse shopping could also be available.
- If the TV show or scene does not need full focus of viewer, such as talk shows, the t-commerce application can be available for viewers during the TV program.

EVIDENCE: 4 out of 8 participants reported that they and other people would not like to change their focus, during a movie or soap opera, for doing shopping. Whereas the other half commented that the possibility to make a purchase during TV shows are interesting. Another evidence is the ad consuming method [17].

EXAMPLE: (Fig. 5).

5.2   T-Commerce Type (B): Interactive Advertising

PATTERN: Interactive advertising.

CONTEXT: The project requirement is to design positive experiences by improving an advertising, in order to increase sales conversion rates through t-commerce application.

PROBLEM: Converting viewers into paying customers through t-commerce application. The time of TV advertising is too short for making a purchase.

Fig. 5. This.co: related TV program t-commerce by Capstone media – South Korea

SOLUTION: An advertisement provides a trigger that can be accessed instantly (typically one-click button) by the viewer. The t-commerce purchase process should have few steps to finish an online transaction. The content of advertising should motivate a viewer to purchase a product at the first few seconds. A t-commerce requires an extended time that can be possible in following ways:

- **60-sec TV commercial:** The traditional 30-sec commercials should have an extended time more than the usual, to allow viewers to purchase an offer.
- **Impulse response:** An advertisement provides a trigger for t-commerce application, which can be accessed as soon as a user presses a button on a remote control. Depending of the TV business model, it does not affect the normal program flow.

EVIDENCE: 2 out of 8 volunteers notice that there is a relationship between TV advertising time and application time.

EXAMPLES: (Fig. 6).

5.3   T-Commerce Type (C): Enhanced Infomercial

PATTERN: Enhanced Infomercial.

CONTEXT: The project requirement is to design positive experiences by improving an infomercial, in order to increase sales conversion rates through t-commerce application.

PROBLEM: Improve the conversion rates by converting viewers into paying customers through t-commerce application.

SOLUTION: The infomercial video should be visible to the viewers during users' interaction with the t-commerce application for sales improvement. In this case, the video should be resized and positioned in one corner of the screen, thereby products'

Fig. 6. H&M: interactive advertising t-commerce by delivery agent and HSM - USA

testimonials and details can continue to inform and motivate the customers to purchase while they are using the IDTV application.

Whereas, infomercial has longer time than a TV advertising, the t-commerce application should present more details such as user reviews and technical product specifications to provide information that help customers to purchase the infomercial's offer.

However, some people does not like this type of TV show and they reported that it is not good to force them to interact with t-commerce application.

EVIDENCE: 5 out of 8 volunteers pointed out the advantages of the convenience of purchasing a product offered on infomercials.

5 out of 8 volunteers reported that they do not like infomercial and to be forced to do an impulse shopping.

EXAMPLES: (Fig. 7).

5.4   T-Commerce Type (D): Virtual Mall

PATTERN: Virtual mall.

CONTEXT: The design requirement is to sell a variety of products like e-commerce websites.

PROBLEM: This t-commerce type can disturb the viewers' attention while they are watching a TV show. There are many possibilities to access a t-commerce virtual mall application. It can be combined with other t-commerce types or it can be available according to TV station business model.

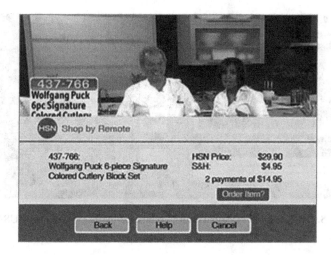

Fig. 7. HSN shop by remote - enhanced infomercial t-commerce by HSN & Comcast - USA

SOLUTION: A virtual mall can sell products from the TV station, TV show or online retail company. It can be presented to users in following ways:

- **Combined with Related TV Program Type**: if the TV show has a plot and narrative story such as soap operas or TV series, the t-commerce can be done during commercial breaks. If the TV show does not need full focus of viewer, the t-commerce application can be available for viewers during the TV program.
- **Infomercial Virtual Mall:** When TV advertisers buy a time to broadcast their infomercial, they can offer a virtual mall in this period with other company's products.
- **TV Station Virtual Mall**: A TV channel can offer their products categorized by TV show during the whole day (24/7), so the viewers can interact whenever they want.
- **Retail Company Virtual Mall**: Since traditional TV business model works selling time for broadcasting TV shows, a TV station could sell time to online retail companies to offer their product through a t-commerce application.

In some cases, the task could be focused on making a purchase, using a full screen application to do this. Since the goal is to do shopping, we can do it better on this interface like we do shopping in e-commerce websites.

EVIDENCE: Existing t-commerce application and UX research insights.

EXAMPLES: (Fig. 8).

Fig. 8. History shop – Virtual mall t-commerce by history channel - USA

6 Conclusions

In this study, we developed a posture design pattern for t-commerce application based on user experience. We improve the Ghisi presentation models [13] adding a virtual mall t-commerce type based on the users expectations. Furthermore, the design pattern developed provides a template that presents a context, problem and proven solution, which help designers to make initial decisions about designing t-commerce applications focusing on good user experiences.

Each context of t-commerce application has different problems and different solutions to achieve positive experiences. We find problems and solutions based on the focus group, experiments results and existing t-commerce applications. These findings provide insights into the first activities of the top-down design for t-commerce applications projects.

Further studies will be necessary to develop a complete pattern language for t-commerce applications. A pattern language is collection of patterns that has a hierarchy structure classified on four levels [6]: Posture, experience, task and action. Our findings only highlight the posture level pattern. Therefore, the other remaining pattern levels will need to be developed further in future studies.

Acknowledgements. CAPES, CNPq and FAPEMA (Brazil) for financial support.

References

1. OECD: OECD Guide to Measuring the Information Society 2011. OECD Publishing, Paris (2011)
2. International Telecommunication Union: Measuring Information Society. Place des Nations, Geneva, Switzerland (2013)
3. eMarketer: Ecommerce Sales Topped $1 Trillion for First Time in 2012. http://www.emarketer.com/Article/Ecommerce-Sales-Topped-1-Trillion-First-Time-2012/1009649

4. Delivery Agent: Delivery Agent Powers the First Shoppable TV Commercial Bringing T-Commerce to Life at CES 2014 (2014). http://www.deliveryagent.com/2014/01/hm-and-david-beckham-are-back-in-action-at-the-super-bowl-with-groundbreaking-campaign
5. Buschmann, F., Henney, K., Schmidt, D.: Pattern Oriented Software Architecture: On Patterns and Pattern Languages. Wiley, Hoboken (2007)
6. van Welie, M., van der Veer, G., Eliëns, A.: Patterns as tools for user interface design. In: International Workshop on Tools for Working with Guidelines, France, pp. 313–324 (2000)
7. Krischkowsky, A., Wurhofer, D., Perterer, N., Tscheligi, M.: Developing patterns step-by-step: a pattern generation guidance for HCI researchers. In: Proceedings of the Fifth International Conferences on Pervasive Patterns and Applications (PATTERNS2013), IARIA, Valencia, pp 66–72 (2013)
8. Law, E.L., Roto, V., Hassenzahl, M., Vermeeren, A., Kort, J.: Understanding, scoping and defining user experience: a survey approach. In: Proceedings of the SIGCHI Conference on Human Factors in Computing Systems (CHI 2009), pp. 719–728. ACM, New York (2009)
9. ITU: Measuring Information Society 2012. International Telecommunication Union, Geneva (2013)
10. Galabo, R.J., Soares Neto, C.S.: Orientações Para O Design de Interface e Interação em Aplicativos de Comércio televisivo. In: Anais do 13º USIHC. Universidade Federal de Juiz de Fora – UFJF (2013)
11. Lin, K., Lin, C., Shen, C.-L.: Evaluation of interactive digital TV commerce using the AHP approach. In: Pagani, M. (ed.) Encyclopedia of Multimedia Technology and Networking, vol. 1, 2nd edn, pp. 2291–2297. Information Science Reference, Hershey (2008)
12. Yu, J., Ha, I., Choi, M., Rho, J.: Extending the TAM for a t-commerce. Inf. Manage. 42(7), 965–976 (2005)
13. Ghisi, B., Lopes, G., Siqueira, F.: Conceptual models for t-commerce in Brazil. In: Proceedings of EuroiTV 2010. Tampere University of Technology, Finland (2010)
14. NDS Business Consulting: Interactive advertising (2000). www.broadcastpapers.com, http://www.broadcastpapers.com/data/NDSInteractiveAD01.htm
15. Kunert, T.: User-Centered Interaction Design Patterns for Interactive Digital Television Applications. Springer, Heidelberg (2009)
16. Obrist, M., Wurhofer, D., Beck, E., Tscheligi, M.: CUX patterns approach: towards contextual user experience patterns. In: Proceedings of the 2nd International Conference on Pervasive Patterns and Applications, Lisbon, pp. 66–65 (2010)
17. Cho, J., Sah, Y., Ryu, J.: A new content-related advertising model for interactive television. In: Broadband Multimedia Systems and Broadcasting 2008, pp. 1–9. IEEE, Las Vegas (2008)

Investigating the Correspondence Between UMUX-LITE and SUS Scores

James R. Lewis[1(✉)], Brian S. Utesch[2], and Deborah E. Maher[3]

[1] IBM Software Group, Boca Raton, FL, USA
jimlewis@us.ibm.com
[2] IBM Software Group, Raleigh, NC, USA
butesch@us.ibm.com
[3] IBM Software Group, Cambridge, MA, USA
debmaher@us.ibm.com

Abstract. The UMUX-LITE is a two-item questionnaire that assesses perceived usability. In previous research it correlated highly with the System Usability Scale (SUS) and, with appropriate adjustment using a regression formula, had close correspondence to the magnitude of SUS scores, enabling its comparison with emerging SUS norms. Those results, however, were based on the data used to compute the regression formula. In this paper we describe a study conducted to investigate the quality of the published formula using independent data. The formula worked well. As expected, the correlation between the SUS and UMUX-LITE was significant and substantial, and the overall mean difference between their scores was just 1.1, about 1 % of the range of values the questionnaires can take, verifying the efficacy of the regression formula.

Keywords: Perceived usability · System usability scale · SUS · Usability metric for user experience · UMUX-LITE

1 Introduction

In 2013, we published the results of an initial investigation into the psychometric properties of the two-item UMUX-LITE questionnaire, and demonstrated that with a regression formula, it was possible to obtain a close correspondence between UMUX-LITE and SUS scores [9]. A limitation of the initial research was that the regression equation was not independent of the data used to evaluate its accuracy. The current study describes a partial replication of the initial research designed to address that limitation.

1.1 The System Usability Scale (SUS)

The SUS is questionnaire that uses 10 five-point scales. Item responses are recoded to compute an overall score that ranges from 0 to 100. Although a self-described "quick-and-dirty" questionnaire [3], the SUS appears to have excellent psychometric properties (reliability around 0.9, significant correlation with outcome measures, and sensitivity to

© Springer International Publishing Switzerland 2015
A. Marcus (Ed.): DUXU 2015, Part I, LNCS 9186, pp. 204–211, 2015.
DOI: 10.1007/978-3-319-20886-2_20

variables such as frequency of use and system/product), and accounts for about 43 % of post-study questionnaire usage [1, 2, 8].

The SUS is available in Standard and Positive versions [12]. The Standard (original) version has items with mixed tone – odd items have a positive tone; even items have a negative tone. In the Positive version, all items have a positive tone. Sauro and Lewis [11] found that the Positive version had advantages over the Standard version with regard to reductions in misinterpretation, mistakes, and miscoding. Both versions had high reliability (Standard: 0.92; Positive: 0.96), and had no significant difference in their mean scores. There was no evidence of acquiescence or extreme response biases in the Positive version.

A relatively recent research development for the SUS has been the publication of normative data from fairly large sample databases [1, 12]. For example, Table 1 shows the curved grading scale published by Sauro and Lewis (SL-CGS) [12], based on data from 446 industrial usability studies (over 5000 completed SUS questionnaires). The SL-CGS provides an empirically grounded approach to the interpretation of mean SUS scores obtained in industrial usability studies. Consequently, the adoption of any alternative metric for the assessment of perceived usability would greatly benefit if it were to not only correlate with the SUS, but would also correspond to its magnitude.

Table 1. The Sauro/Lewis curved grading scale (SL-CGS)

SUS score range	Grade	Percentile range
84.1–100	A+	96–100
80.8–84.0	A	90–95
78.9–80.7	A−	85–89
77.2–78.8	B+	80–84
74.1–77.1	B	70–79
72.6–74.0	B−	65–69
71.1–72.5	C+	60–64
65.0–71.0	C	41–59
62.7–64.9	C−	35–40
51.7–62.6	D	15–34
0.0–51.7	F	0–14

1.2 The Usability Metric for User Experience (UMUX)

The Usability Metric for User Experience (UMUX) [5–7] was designed to get a measurement of perceived usability consistent with the SUS, but using only four (rather than 10) items. The primary purpose for its development was to provide an alternate metric for perceived usability for situations in which it was critical to reduce the number of items while still getting a reliable and valid measurement of perceived usability (e.g., when there is a need to measure more attributes than just perceived usability leading to limited "real estate" for any given attribute).

Like the standard SUS, UMUX items vary in tone but unlike the SUS, have seven rather than five scale steps from 1 (strongly disagree) to 7 (strongly agree). Finstad reported desirable psychometric properties for the UMUX, including its discrimination between systems with relatively good and poor usability, high reliability (coefficient alpha of .94), and extremely high correlation with SUS scores ($r = .96$). The four UMUX items are:

1. This system's capabilities meet my requirements.
2. Using this system is a frustrating experience.
3. This system is easy to use.
4. I have to spend too much time correcting things with this system.

Lewis et al. [9] included the UMUX in their study, and found results that generally replicated the findings reported by Finstad [5]. For the two datasets (one using the standard SUS and the other using the positive version), the UMUX correlated significantly with the SUS (Standard: .90; Positive: .79). Although this is significantly less than Finstad's correlation of .96, it supports his claim of strong concurrent validity. The estimated reliabilities of the UMUX in the two datasets were more than adequate (.87, .81), but like the correlations with the SUS, a bit less than the originally reported value of .97. For both datasets, there was no significant difference between the mean SUS and mean UMUX scores (extensive overlap between the 99 % confidence intervals), consistent with the original data.

1.3   The UMUX-LITE

The UMUX-LITE is a short version of the UMUX, consisting of its positive-tone (odd-numbered) items (maintaining the use of 7-point scales). Thus, for the UMUX-LITE, the items are:

1. This system's capabilities meet my requirements.
2. This system is easy to use.

Factor analysis conducted by Lewis et al. [9] indicated that the UMUX had a bidimensional structure with item alignment as a function of item tone (positive vs. negative). This, along with additional item analysis, led to the selection of the two items for the UMUX-LITE for the purpose of creating an ultra-short metric for perceived usability. Data from two independent surveys demonstrated adequate psychometric quality of the UMUX-LITE. Estimates of reliability were .82 and .83 – excellent for a two-item instrument. Concurrent validity was also high, with significant correlation with standard and positive versions of the SUS (.81, .81) and with likelihood-to-recommend (LTR) scores (.74, .73). Furthermore, the scores were sensitive to respondents' frequency-of-use. UMUX-LITE score means were slightly lower than those for the SUS, but easily adjusted using linear regression to match the SUS scores (Eq. 1).

$$\text{UMUX-LITE} = .65((\text{Item 1} + \text{Item 2} - 2)(100/12) + 22.9) \tag{1}$$

Another reason for including the specific two items of the UMUX-LITE was their connection to the content of the items in the Technology Acceptance Model (TAM) [4], a questionnaire from the market research literature that assesses the usefulness (e.g., capabilities meeting requirements) and ease-of-use of systems, and has an established relationship to likelihood of future use. According to TAM, good ratings of usefulness and ease of use (perceived usability) influence the intention to use, which influences the actual likelihood of use.

1.4   Research Goals

Due to its parsimony (two items), reliability, validity, structural basis (usefulness and usability) and, after applying the corrective regression formula, its correspondence to SUS scores, the UMUX-LITE appeared to be a promising alternative to the SUS when it is not desirable to use a 10-item instrument (for example, when the assessment of perceived usability is one part of a larger survey). Our primary goal for the research reported in this paper was to partially replicate our 2013 study so we could investigate whether the regression formula developed using that data would similarly adjust the data from a completely independent set of data to result in close correspondence with the SUS. A successful replication would lead to greater confidence in using the UMUX-LITE in place of the SUS, while still using the emerging norms (e.g., Table 1) to interpret the results.

2   Method

To follow up on our initial investigation of the psychometric properties of the UMUX-LITE, especially with regard to how well the regression formula would work with an independent set of data, we combined data from four surveys for a total of 397 cases in which respondents completed the UMUX-LITE and the positive version of the SUS [11, 12] (see Figs. 1 and 2). In addition to collecting SUS and UMUX-LITE ratings, participants also provided ratings of likelihood-to-recommend (LTR).

3   Results

3.1   Reliability

Consistent with previous research [9], the UMUX-LITE was reliable as assessed using a standard metric of internal consistency (coefficient alpha of .86).

3.2   Validity

The UMUX-LITE correlated significantly with ratings of Likelihood-to-Recommend ($r(395) = .72, p < .0001$) and SUS scores ($r(395) = .83, p < .0001$), providing evidence

	The System Usability Scale Positive Version	Strongly Disagree 1	2	3	4	Strongly Agree 5
1	I think that I would like to use the website frequently.	O	O	O	O	O
2	I found the website to be simple.	O	O	O	O	O
3	I thought the website was easy to use.	O	O	O	O	O
4	I think that I could use the website without the support of a technical person.	O	O	O	O	O
5	I found the various functions in the website were well integrated.	O	O	O	O	O
6	I thought there was a lot of consistency in the website.	O	O	O	O	O
7	I would imagine that most people would learn to use the website very quickly.	O	O	O	O	O
8	I found the website very intuitive.	O	O	O	O	O
9	I felt very confident using the website.	O	O	O	O	O
10	I could use the website without having to learn anything new.	O	O	O	O	O

Fig. 1. The system usability scale (positive version)

	The UMUX-LITE Version 1	Strongly Agree 1	2	3	4	5	6	Strongly Disagree 7
1	This system's capabilities meet my requirements.	O	O	O	O	O	O	O
2	This system is easy to use.	O	O	O	O	O	O	O

Fig. 2. The UMUX-LITE

of concurrent validity. Note that with a two-item instrument, it is not possible to assess construct validity using analytical methods such as principal components analysis or factor analysis. Thus, the UMUX-LITE is assumed to be a unidimensional metric for perceived usability.

3.3 Correspondence

Most importantly, the overall mean difference between the SUS and regression-adjusted UMUX-LITE scores was just 1.1 – only 1 % of the range of the values that the SUS and UMUX-LITE can take (0–100). Strictly speaking, that difference was statistically significant ($t(396) = 2.2, p = .03$), but for any practical use (such as comparison to norms such as the SL-CGS shown in Table 1), it's essentially no difference, especially for results within a point of the break between grades. When sample sizes are large, it's important not to confuse statistically significant differences with meaningful differences.

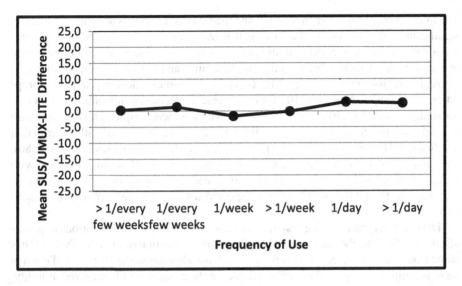

Fig. 3. Difference between mean SUS and UMUX-LITE as a function of frequency of use

3.4 Sensitivity

To assess sensitivity, an ANOVA was conducted on the main effect of Questionnaire (SUS vs. UMUX-LITE), Frequency of Use (Once every few months or less, Once every few weeks, Once a week, Several times a week, Once a day, More than once a day), and their interaction. Consistent with prior research [9], the effect of Frequency of Use was highly significant ($F(5, 390) = 10.2, p < .0001$). The main effect of Questionnaire was not significant ($F(1, 390) = 2.2, p = .135$), and the Questionnaire x Frequency of Use interaction was also not significant ($F(5, 390) = 1.6, p = .158$). Figure 3 shows the differences between the SUS and UMUX-LITE means as a function of Frequency of Use. As shown in the figure, the mean differences hovered around 0, sometimes slightly positive and sometimes slightly negative, and always with an absolute magnitude less than 3.0.

4   Discussion

The broad use of and emerging interpretative norms for the SUS make it an increasingly powerful tool for usability practitioners and researchers. This presents a significant challenge for alternative methods for the assessment of perceived usability. Unless one can establish a correspondence between the alternative metric and the SUS, it may be difficult to justify using the alternative metric because one would not be able to take advantage of the interpretative norms developed for the SUS.

The research presented in this paper is one more step toward establishing such a correspondence between the UMUX-LITE and the SUS. Using a regression formula derived from an independent set of data, the difference between the overall mean SUS score and overall mean UMUX-LITE score was just 1.1 (on a 0–100 point scale).

The linear correlation between the SUS and the UMUX-LITE was not only statistically significant (nonzero), but was also of considerable magnitude ($r = .83$). The correspondence between the two questionnaires was also evident when assessing the nonsignificant interaction between the questionnaires and reported frequency of use.

As in previous research, the UMUX-LITE exhibited excellent psychometric properties. According to Nunnally [10], for instruments that assess sentiments the minimum reliability criterion is .70 (typically assessed with coefficient alpha) and the minimum criterion for predictive or concurrent validity is .30 (typically assessed with a correlation coefficient). The reliability of the UMUX-LITE exceeded .70 (coefficient alpha of .86). Two assessments of concurrent validity, correlation with the SUS and correlation with ratings of likelihood-to-recommend, both exceeded .30 (respectively, $r = .83$ and $r = .72$). Finally, the UMUX-LITE had the expected sensitivity to self-reported frequency of use.

Despite these encouraging results, it is important to note some limitations to generalizability. To date, the data used for psychometric evaluation of the UMUX-LITE has come from surveys. Indeed, this is the primary intended use of the UMUX-LITE when there is limited survey "real estate" available for the assessment of perceived usability. It would, however, be interesting to see if data collected in traditional usability studies would show a similar correspondence between the SUS and the UMUX-LITE. Until researchers have validated the UMUX-LITE across a wider variety of systems and research methods, we do not recommend its use independent of the SUS.

5   Conclusion

These findings add to the emerging literature on the psychometric properties of the UMUX-LITE and increase confidence in its use, but it is still important for the foreseeable future for usability practitioners and researchers to continue to investigate the relationship between the SUS and UMUX-LITE over a wider variety of systems and research methods. Researchers who use the SUS should include at least the two UMUX-LITE items in their work (and if possible, the entire UMUX) to build independent databases for future evaluation of its reliability, validity, sensitivity, and correspondence with the SUS.

References

1. Bangor, A., Kortum, P.T., Miller, J.T.: An empirical evaluation of the system usability scale. Int. J. Hum. Comput. Interact. **6**, 574–594 (2008)
2. Borsci, S., Federici, S., Lauriola, M.: On the dimensionality of the system usability scale: a test of alternative measurement models. Cogn. Process. **10**, 193–197 (2009)
3. Brooke, J.: SUS: a "quick and dirty" usability scale. In: Jordan, P., Thomas, B., Weerdmeester, B. (eds.) Usability Evaluation in Industry, pp. 189–194. Taylor & Francis, London (1996)
4. Davis, D.: Perceived usefulness, perceived ease of use, and user acceptance of information technology. MIS Q. **13**, 319–339 (1989)
5. Finstad, K.: The usability metric for user experience. Interact. Comput. **22**, 323–327 (2010)

6. Finstad, K.: Response to commentaries on "the usability metric for user experience". Interact. Comput. **25**, 327–330 (2013)
7. Lewis, J.R.: Critical review of "the usability metric for user experience". Interact. Comput. **25**, 320–324 (2013)
8. Lewis, J.R., Sauro, J.: The factor structure of the system usability scale. In: Kurosu, M. (ed.) HCD 2009. LNCS, vol. 5619, pp. 94–103. Springer, Heidelberg (2009)
9. Lewis, J.R., Utesch, B.S., Maher, D.E.: UMUX-LITE—when there's no time for the SUS. In: Proceedings of CHI 2013, pp. 2099–2102. ACM, Paris (2013)
10. Nunnally, J.C.: Psychometric Theory. McGraw-Hill, New York (1978)
11. Sauro, J., Lewis, J.R.: When designing usability questionnaires, does it hurt to be positive? In: Proceedings of CHI 2011, pp. 2215–2223. ACM, Vancouver (2011)
12. Sauro, J., Lewis, J.R.: Quantifying the User Experience: Practical Statistics for User Research. Morgan Kaufmann, Waltham (2012)

Experimental Case Study of New Usability Heuristics

Freddy Paz[1]([✉]), Freddy Asrael Paz[2], and José Antonio Pow-Sang[1]

[1] Pontificia Universidad Católica del Perú, San Miguel, Lima 32, Perú
fpaz@pucp.pe, japowsang@pucp.edu.pe
[2] Universidad Nacional Pedro Ruiz Gallo, Lambayeque, Perú
freddypazsifuentes@yahoo.es

Abstract. A widely used method to measure the level of usability of software applications is the heuristic evaluation. In this method, specialists commonly use the Nielsen's heuristics to assess the usability of a software product. However, these principles address to general aspects and become inappropriate when they are used to evaluate new categories of software applications. For this reason, we previously proposed a new set of usability heuristics in the Web transactional domain. In this paper, we present an empirical analysis of our new proposal. For this purpose, fifteen undergraduate students were asked to perform a heuristic evaluation in which the new set of heuristics were employed. A survey was taken in order to capture their perceptions about the heuristics in four dimensions: ease of use, usefulness, intention to use and completeness. The results showed that the new heuristics meet the expectations. In addition, this analysis was compared with the results of a similar study that was performed to the current proposal of Nielsen. The results from this study have allowed to reach promising results in this area.

Keywords: Heuristic evaluation · Usability inspection · Usability heuristics · Experimental evaluation · Perception model

1 Introduction

The continuous growth of Electronic Commerce has led to the development of increasingly dynamic websites [1]. Nowadays, Web applications are embedded of complex components, sophisticated designs, excessive functionality and real-time processing. Although software products have changed their nature, specialists still continue using traditional methods to evaluate quality aspects. However, there is enough evidence in the literature proving that these conventional techniques are no longer suitable for the new categories of software applications that are emerging. They fail to cover aspects from the application domain offering inaccurate results, especially, when they are used to assess the usability of new kinds of software products.

Usability is considered as a critical success factor for the development of Web applications, since this quality attribute contributes to the user goals through the

© Springer International Publishing Switzerland 2015
A. Marcus (Ed.): DUXU 2015, Part I, LNCS 9186, pp. 212–223, 2015.
DOI: 10.1007/978-3-319-20886-2_21

implementation of a friendly and easy to use graphical interface. At this time, software developers are not only concerned about functionality, but also on the user experience. The result of an interaction is as important that can determine if the website will be used again in the future. For this reason, companies have been forced to change their business strategy by focusing on having usable Web applications. This process is only possible if usability evaluation methods [4] or usability techniques [15] are applied during the software development process.

Usability evaluation methods can be classified into two main categories [5]: inspection methods (which involve the participation of usability specialists), and test methods (which involve the participation of end users). Heuristic evaluation is one of the most recognized inspection methods in this field because of the significant advantages it provides. In contrast to usability testing, where a considerable amount of users is required, heuristic evaluations only demand the collaboration of three to five specialists. Additionally, it involves a simple process, that can be performed faster than other methods and during any software lifecycle stage.

Heuristic evaluation is an inspection method which involves the evaluation of a graphical user interface in order to determine whether each dialogue element follows established usability principles [9]. These guidelines are known in Human Computer-Interaction as usability heuristics. Although, the most widely used principles until the present are the ten usability heuristics proposed by Nielsen, there are gaps in the evaluation when they are used for interactive systems such as: video games, mobile applications, transactional Web applications, augmented reality applications and virtual worlds. This new generation of systems has new particular features that were not considered during the elaboration of the conventional principles. The emergence of new software environments leads to the appearance of new usability aspects that come from the application domain. Therefore, are Nielsen's usability heuristics still an appropriate instrument to evaluate usability in these new categories of software applications?

In a previous work [11], we conducted an experimental evaluation in order to determine if the Nielsen's usability heuristics are still valid for the new emerging kinds of software applications of the Web domain, especially, transactional Web sites. The heuristics were evaluated in terms of *perceived ease of use* (PEOU), *perceived usefulness*, (PU), *intention to use* (IU), and *perceived completeness* (PCO). Although Nielsen's heuristics were perceived as usefulness, they were classified as difficult to use, because of the lack of clarity in the interpretation of each of them. Additionally, most of the participants perceived that Nielsen's heuristics do not cover all usability aspects of a transactional Web application, since there are important issues that are not considered during an evaluation. Despite this, people who participated in our experimentation stated that they would use the traditional heuristics in case they become involved in future evaluations. The advantages of the evaluation method and the lack of a more specialized assessment tool encourage the use of the Nielsen's heuristics. However, we have proposed a new set of heuristics for transactional Web applications [10], whose validation is established in this study. The intention of this new proposal is to provide specialists with a tool that is able to entirely examine the usability in this kind of software applications. This paper presents an evaluation of the new usability heuristics based on the same analysis that was considered for the Nielsen's principles. The results between both are compared and discussed.

2   Background

2.1   Usability Heuristics for Transactional Web Sites

In a previous work [10,12], we developed a new set of usability heuristics for transactional Web sites. These principles were established following a systematic and structured methodology proposed by Rusu et al. [14]. During a previous phase, the heuristics were used in a real scenario, proving to be an appropriate assessment instrument. In this study, we validate the proposal through an analysis of perceptions. The usability heuristics that were proposed are:

1. **Visibility and Clarity of the System Elements (F1):** The most important elements of the system must be clearly visible. Some components of the graphical user interface will be more relevant than others according to the purpose of the system. These elements should be established with a high level of visibility and clarity, in order to allow the achievement of the user goals.

2. **Visibility of the System Status (F2):** The user must be aware about the processes that the system performs. The software application must notify users when any kind of response or confirmation is required. The system must keep users informed about the current state of the software application within reasonable wait times.

3. **Match between System and User's Cultural Aspects (F3):** The application design have to be consistent with the cultural aspects of the user. The graphical interface must be oriented to the cultural profile of the users who will use the application. Users should not feel forced to use the system under unfamiliar mechanisms.

4. **Feedback of Transaction (F4):** The system must keep users informed about the final status of transactions. The system should notify users about the success or failure of all transactions that are performed through the use of the application. Users must know the partial and final result of their operations until the achievement of their goals.

5. **Alignment to Web Standards Design (F5):** The system must follow established design conventions in the Web domain. The graphical user interface should be aligned to standardized guidelines, commonly used structures and widely known layout elements. System should be implemented by the use of design patterns that have become an standard due to their extended use over time.

6. **Consistency of Design (F6):** All sections of the system should maintain the same design style and a well organized structure. The graphical interface must be consistent and preserve the logical order of the elements.

7. *Standard Iconography (F7):* The interface design must be implemented by the use of standardized icons that are already part of the user's conceptual model because of their frequent use in several software applications. The icons should be represented by standardized concepts, that besides being known by most users, succeed in communicating their intended purpose.

8. *Aesthetic and Minimalism Design (F8):* The user interface must not only be attractive, but also it must contain the units of information that are relevant to users. The information should be properly distributed, without overloading the interface with extra units of information that will be competing in importance with other units that are indeed essential.

9. *Prevention, Recognition and Error Recovery (F9):* The system must prevent the occurrence of errors. In addition, it must prevent users from taking actions that leads to errors in the application. However, once the error has occurred, the system must help users to recognize and quickly overcome these scenarios by displaying clear messages with appropriate instructions to solve the problem.

10. *Appropriate Flexibility and Efficiency of Use (F10):* The system must provide accelerators that allow expert users to effectively accomplish their tasks, without affecting the normal work flow of novice users. The interface design must allow both, inexperienced and experienced users, to use the software application with flexibility and effectiveness.

11. *Help and Documentation (F11):* The system must provide support options that help users perform specific tasks. These procedures should be clear and specify concrete actions for the achievement of the user goals. Support options must avoid ambiguity and confusion, by providing concise instructions focused on work flow and user's tasks.

12. *Reliability and Quickness of Transactions (F12):* Transactions must be highly reliable. The system must guarantee that all transactions will be successfully completed within the expected time under specific operating conditions. However, in case of errors, the system must be able to correct the issue and undo all changes that are required. The software application must maintain data stability and avoid certain scenarios that negatively affect the user.

13. *Correct and Expected Functionality (F13):* System elements must be correctly implemented, and they should provide the functionality that users are expecting of them. The interface components should run processes related to the purpose that is established in the design.

14. *Recognition Rather than Recall (F14):* The user should not be forced to remember information from a previous state of the current transaction. Instructions for use must be easy to recall, and the Web form design must not be complex. The system should minimize the user's memory load by developing highly intuitive graphical interfaces.

15. *User Control and Freedom (F15):* Users can choose certain system functions by mistake. Therefore, the system must provide mechanisms that allow users to exit from unwanted states and undo their actions. Users should not be affected because of a mistake.

2.2   An Evaluation Model

In order to evaluate the new set of usability heuristics for transactional Web sites, we have adopted part of the Method Evaluation Model that is presented in Fig. 1. This validated theoretical model was proposed originally for evaluating IS design methods. However, it incorporates general aspects of evaluation that can be applied to any kind of software development tool. Despite heuristics are recognized as a usability evaluation instrument, they can also be considered as a design method, in the sense that they are used during all phases of the software lifecycle in the context of a user-centered design for the development highly usable graphical interfaces [6].

The Method Evaluation Model, proposed by Moody [7], was designed considering two important concepts: the Methodological Pragmatism, a theory for validating methodological knowledge [13], and the Technology Acceptance Model (TAM), a theoretical model for explaining and predicting user acceptance of information technology [3]. From these two approaches, it was designed the core of MEM, known as Method Adoption Model (MAM) [2].

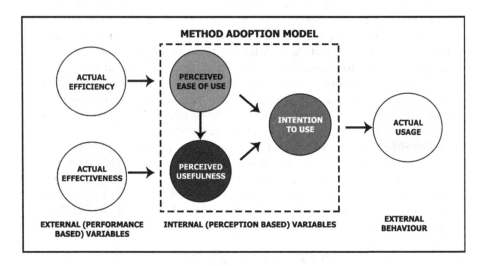

Fig. 1. Method evaluation model

In this study, we have focused on the perception/intention-based variables of the MEM that are defined in the Method Adoption Model. This model establishes the existence of three psychological aspects that are present in any successful method, and whose relationship is defined in Fig. 1. According to this evaluation model, the success of a method is reflected in its adoption in practice. If a design method is currently used in real contexts, is because of its efficiency and effectiveness. However, the acceptability of a method is the result of a set of perceptions and intentions. Only if a method is perceived as easy to use and useful, specialists will be motivated to use the method again in future scenarios.

This intention to use a particular instrument becomes into actual usage of the method. The model establishes that a successful proposal is one that is widely used by the community. Nevertheless, the level of adoption can not be high if the perception about the method is not appropriate.

The variables that were considered for this study are:

- **Perceived Ease of Use (PEU):** The degree to which an evaluator believes that the use of a particular usability heuristic would be free of effort.
- **Perceived Usefulness (PU):** The degree to which an evaluator believes that a particular usability heuristic will achieve its intended objectives.
- **Intention to Use (IU):** The degree to which an evaluator will use the usability heuristics in future evaluations.
- **Perceived Completeness (PC):** The degree to which an evaluator believes that established heuristics cover all aspects of usability in a specific domain.

As a complement to this model, we have considered an additional aspect of evaluation. Our new proposal was developed in order to obtain an appropriate assessment tool of usability in this domain. For this reason, all features of transactional Web applications were studied. In contrast, when traditional heuristics are used to evaluate the usability in new categories of software, the results are inaccurate. Nielsen's heuristics were designed for standard Web interfaces, and they do not cover aspects that may be relevant for some specific systems. This fact has led us to include a variable to determine whether our proposal is considering all aspects that are required in a heuristic evaluation.

3   Research Design

3.1   Participants

The participants of this case study were fifteen undergraduate students from the Information System Engineering program of the National University Pedro Ruiz Gallo. They were randomly selected from a section of Software Quality, a technical mandatory course. All students voluntarily agreed to participate in our study without expecting any kind of compensation for their participation. There were no significant differences in their backgrounds, since they had attended to the same courses of their curriculum.

As part of the requirements of the sixth semester, students had to assess the quality attributes of a software product. This fact encouraged the teaching of usability evaluations during class. However, in order to conduct this study, it was necessary to train students in heuristic evaluations. Despite their lack of experience, participants identified a relevant set of usability problems using the new heuristics we have proposed.

3.2   Method

Our empirical study was focused on the analysis of the students' perceptions about the new set of usability heuristics for transactional Web sites. The study was conducted in classroom settings during the Springer semester of 2014. The broad research questions addressed are:

- **RQ1:** Do the students consider that the new set of usability heuristics for transactional Web sites is easy to use and useful?
- **RQ2:** Would the students use the new set of heuristics in future evaluations?
- **RQ3:** According to the students' opinion, are the heuristics covering all aspects of usability in the transactional Web domain?
- **RQ4:** What is the degree of perceived ease to use and perceived usefulness of each heuristic?
- **RQ5:** Is the perception of usefulness of the new heuristics being influenced by their perception of easy of use?
- **RQ6:** Is the degree of intention to use, perceived usefulness, perceived ease of use and perceived completeness of new set of usability heuristics higher than in the traditional proposal of Nielsen?

The experiment was conducted through a systematic procedure. First, all participants were trained in the main concepts of usability and user experience. When these definitions were fully conceptualized by the students, they were trained in heuristic evaluations. The students had to follow the new set of heuristics and analyze a Web site in order to find usability problems. For this purpose, a transactional Web application for booking accommodation online was selected: *Booking.com*. The students examined the graphical user interface of the application for about two hours. As a result of the evaluation process, each participant reported a list of usability problems in the interface with references to those usability principles that were violated by the design in each case.

Finally, a post-task survey was used to measure the following constructs about the new set of usability heuristics: *perceived ease of use* (PEU), *perceived usefulness* (PU), *intention to use* (IU) and *perceived completeness* (PC). The items of the survey instrument were formulated using a 5-point Likert scale, where 1 was referred to an extremely negative perception of the construct, and 5 to an excellent positive rating of it. Although PEU and PU were measured by heuristic, the set of principles was considered as a single instrument for the evaluation of IU and PC. In the survey, we inquired into the ease of use and usefulness of each heuristic. However, the questions were not formulated by heuristic when we asked for IU and PC. The interest in the use of a particular heuristic without considering the others is not possible. The heuristics have to be used as a single evaluation instrument because of each of them addresses to a specific aspect of usability. For this reason, the survey was focused on determining if the students would use the entire proposal in future evaluations, and if the heuristics, as a single tool, succeed in covering all aspects of usability.

4   Data Analysis and Results

We collected fifteen valid documents which were submitted to analysis. This stage was performed using a standard version of *SPSS for Windows, Release 22.0*. In this section, we present the obtained results for each research question.

4.1   Research Question 1

The purpose of this research question was to determine the *perceived ease of use* (PEU) and *perceived usefulness* (PU) of the new heuristics for Transactional Web Sites. In a previous work [11], we identified that the Nielsen's heuristics, despite being regarded as the most commonly used principles, they are difficult to use by novice evaluators. When specialists use the traditional heuristics for the first time, they fail to correctly interpret each principle. This situation seems to be reflected due to the complexity of the heuristics. However, we consider that the principles should be easy to use by both, experts and novice evaluators, without the necessity of an in-depth study in these guidelines. In addition, the *perceived ease of use* represents a key success factor in a method according to the MAM. For this reason, this aspect was considered during the development of the new heuristics and as a part of this evaluation.

Other important aspect that was addressed in this question is the *perceived usefulness* of the new usability principles. The purpose of this construct was to determine if the new proposal was appropriate and could be used as a useful tool to identify usability problems. During the previous work, we noticed that the usefulness of the Nielsen's heuristics was questioned by the specialists when usability issues out of the scope of the evaluation instrument were identified. Although certain aspects of the interface were considered as usability problems, there was no heuristic that could support these statements. The Nielsen's heuristics, despite being efficient design recommendations, were not longer useful for the transactional Web domain. In this study, we examine if the new set of heuristics meets these requirements.

The scores of all students were averaged in order to obtain a final result for each construct. The descriptive statistics were:

- Perceived Ease of Use (PEU) (mean = 3.37, standard deviation = 0.53)
- Perceived Usefulness (PU) (mean = 3.91, standard deviation = 0.46)

The results show that the mean is greater than 3 (the neutral score in a 5-point Likert scale) in both constructs. In this way, we can conclude that the new set of heuristics is perceived as easy to use and usefulness. However, the mean value is not high enough for PEU. From this result, we can establish that it is still necessary to conduct studies in order to determine the cause of the difficulty of use. Some assumptions we propose are the complexity of the evaluation method and the lack of clarity in the definition of the heuristics. Nevertheless, many efforts were made for the development of understandable heuristics. For this reason, we concluded that the difficulty of the process of heuristic evaluation affects in a way the perception of ease of use of the usability heuristics.

4.2   Research Question 2 and 3

In these research questions, the purpose was to measure the degree of adoption in practice of the new usability heuristics as well as their validity. The students were asked if they would use this proposal in case they had to perform a heuristic evaluation again. The construct of intention to use can be considered as a critical success factor because it determines if the heuristics will be used in the future. Similarly, we included into the evaluation model a construct to validate the completeness of the heuristics from the opinion of the participants. In this variable, we evaluated if our new proposal was covering all aspects of usability of a transactional Web domain.

The scores of all students were averaged in order to obtain a final result for each construct. The descriptive statistics were:

- Intention to Use (IU) (mean = 3.93, standard deviation = 0.93)
- Perceived Completeness (PC) (mean = 4.07, standard deviation = 0.70)

The results show that the mean is greater than 3 (the neutral score in a 5-point Likert scale) in both constructs. Therefore, we conclude there are intentions to use our proposal in future evaluations, and that also the heuristics are covering most of the aspects of usability in this domain. Although the results are appropriate, more studies are required to perform continuous improvements through the feedback of the specialists.

4.3   Research Question 4

In this research question, the purpose was to examine individually each heuristic of the new proposal. For this reason, the survey was designed in order to obtain a score about the ease of use and the usefulness of each heuristic. The scores of all participants were averaged by heuristic and construct. The results are presented in Table 1. From these results, we can conclude that: (1) F8. *aesthetic and minimalism design* is perceived as the easiest to use, (2) F4. *feedback of transaction* is perceived as the most difficult to use, (3) F3. *match between system and user's cultural aspects* is perceived as the most useful, and (4) F14. *recognition rather than recall* is perceived as the less useful.

From the results, it is possible to notice that most of the heuristics which covers aspects of usability that are not considered by the proposal of Nielsen, such as: F1, F3, F5, F6, F7 and F13, obtained high scores greater than 3 (the neutral score in a 5-point Likert scale). However, F4 and F12 were rated with low scores in PEOU. We believe that this fact is due to the inability to complete a entire work flow during the evaluation of the software product. Both heuristics demand the execution of transactions. Given that the transactional Web application was a E-Commerce Web site in operation, it was required to execute a financial transaction to complete a work flow, that obviously was not performed because of the nature of this test.

4.4   Research Question 5

The purpose of this research question was to verify one of the relations established by the MAM in our new proposal of usability heuristics. Due to the design

Table 1. Perceptions of the students about the new set of usability heuristics

Usability Heuristic	PEU	PU
F1. Visibility and clarity of the system elements	4.06	4.27
F2. Visibility of the system status	3.67	4.07
F3. Match between system and user's cultural aspects	3.20	4.73
F4. Feedback of transaction	2.67	4.27
F5. Alignment to Web standards design	3.13	3.73
F6. Consistency of design	3.33	4.13
F7. Standard iconography	3.47	3.93
F8. Aesthetic and minimalism design	4.33	4.20
F9. Prevention, recognition and error recovery	3.20	3.80
F10. Appropriate flexibility and efficiency of use	2.80	3.27
F11. Help and documentation	4.30	3.47
F12. Reliability and quickness of transactions	2.87	3.93
F13. Correct and expected functionality	3.53	4.33
F14. Recognition rather than recall	2.73	2.93
F15. User control and freedom	3.33	3.60

of the survey, we only focused on analyzing if the perceived ease of use had some kind of influence on their perception of usefulness of the heuristics. Therefore, we formulated the following hypothesis:

We calculated the Pearson product-moment correlation coefficient to observe the impact of the perceived ease of use on the perceived usefulness of the new usability heuristics. The assumption of normality was satisfied.

The Pearson correlation coefficient was significant ($r = 0.495$, $p = 0.006$). This result shows a strong relationship according to Mujis [8] and indicates that: 49.5 % of the variance in the perceived usefulness of the heuristics is explained by a linear relationship with their perceived ease of use. Considering a significance level of 5 %, these values allow to conclude that the perceived usefulness of the new heuristics is being influenced by their perceived ease of use.

4.5   Research Question 6

The purpose of this research question was to compare the perception analysis of our new proposal with the results of another study that was performed to the traditional heuristics. In a previous work [11], we conducted a similar case study of the Nielsen's heuristics in the transactional Web domain. The results showed that these principles were not appropriate since they did not cover all usability aspects of this specific kind of software application. This fact encouraged the authors to elaborate a new set of usability heuristics improving all the aspects of the MAM. The results of both studies are presented in Table 2.

Although there is an improvement in all aspects regarding the traditional heuristics of Nielsen, the differences were not highly remarkable. One of the

Table 2. Comparison between the new set of usability heuristics and the traditional proposal of Nielsen

Construct	Usability heuristics for Transactional Web Sites	Nielsen's usability heuristics
Perceived ease of use (PEU)	3.37	3.03
Perceived usefulness (PU)	3.91	3.68
Intention to use (IU)	3.93	3.64
Perceived completeness (PC)	4.07	2.67

most relevant results is the perceived completeness. According to this comparison, the new usability heuristics for transactional web sites would be achieving their purpose by covering most of the aspects of usability in this specific domain. However, it is still necessary to complete more studies with the aim of further improving the other variables of the model. The results of this comparison must only be considered as a reference since the studies were conducted in different contexts. Despite the methodological design was the same and the participants were undergraduate students in both studies, there are aspects that could affect the validity of this comparison, such as: the institutional context, the teaching, the curriculum of the program, the cultural differences between groups, the experiment settings and others.

5   Conclusions and Future Works

In recent years, several categories of software applications have emerged. Systems nowadays are embedded of complex and sophisticated components. However, we keep using the same assessment tools that were developed to measure the level of usability of generic software. In a previous study, we determined that Nielsen's heuristics, a list of principles to assess the usability of software products in heuristic evaluations, were not appropriate in the domain of transactional Web applications. They failed to cover all aspects of usability in this kind of software product. Therefore, a new proposal was developed.

A new assessment instrument of fifteen new usability heuristics for transactional Web sites was proposed. In this work, we validated this new proposal through an perception analysis about the heuristics. The purpose was to determine how the new set of heuristics is perceived by specialists who use it for the first time. This experimental case study was conducted following the Method Adoption Model (MAM) which establishes the study of three dimensions: perceived ease of use (PEU), perceived usefulness (PU) and intention to use (IU). However, an additional construct was considered to verify if the heuristics as a set are covering all aspects that are required: perceived completeness (PC). Fifteen undergraduate students were asked to performed a heuristic evaluation using the new proposal. After the evaluation, a survey was taken to measure the dimensions.

The results showed that the new heuristics were perceived as easy to use and usefulness. Furthermore, participants expressed their intentions to use this new proposal in future evaluations and adopt it in practice. According to the student's opinion, the new heuristics cover many aspects that were not considered by the traditional proposal. Although these promising results, it is still necessary to refine some heuristics that individually scored low results. It would be also convenient to propose a checklist and to conduct more studies in different context. In a final comparison, we determined that our proposal is better perceived than Nielsen's heuristics, however, more experiments should be performed in order to generalize these results.

References

1. Alroobaea, R., Mayhew, P.: How many participants are really enough for usability studies? Science and Information Conference (SAI) **2014**, 48–56 (2014)
2. Davis, F.D.: Perceived usefulness, perceived ease of use, and user acceptance of information technology. MIS quarterly **13**(3), 319–340 (1989)
3. Davis, F.D., Bagozzi, R.P., Warshaw, P.R.: User acceptance of computer technology: A comparison of two theoretical models. Management Science **35**(8), 982–1003 (1989)
4. Fernandez, A., Insfran, E., Abraho, S.: Usability evaluation methods for the web: A systematic mapping study. Information and Software Technology **53**(8), 789–817 (2011)
5. Holzinger, A.: Usability engineering methods for software developers. Commun. ACM **48**(1), 71–74 (2005)
6. Jurca, G., Hellmann, T., Maurer, F.: Integrating agile and user-centered design: A systematic mapping and review of evaluation and validation studies of agile-ux. Agile Conference (AGILE) **2014**, 24–32 (2014)
7. Moody, D.: Dealing with Complexity: A Practical Method for Representing Large Entity Relationship Models. University of Melbourne, Department of Information Systems (2001)
8. Muijs, D.: Doing quantitative research in education with SPSS. Sage (2010)
9. Nielsen, J.: Usability inspection methods. In: Conference Companion on Human Factors in Computing Systems. pp. 413–414. CHI '94, ACM, New York, NY, USA (1994)
10. Paz, F., Asrael Paz, F., Pow-Sang, J., Collantes, L.: Usability heuristics for transactional web sites. In: Information Technology: New Generations (ITNG), 2014 11th International Conference on. pp. 627–628 (April 2014)
11. Paz, F., Villanueva, D., Rusu, C., Roncagliolo, S., Pow-Sang, J.: Experimental evaluation of usability heuristics. In: Information Technology: New Generations (ITNG), 2013 Tenth International Conference on. pp. 119–126 (April 2013)
12. Paz, F.: Usability Heuristics for Transactional Web Sites. Master's thesis, Pontifical Catholic University of Peru (December 2013)
13. Rescher, N.: Methodological Pragmatism: Systems-theoretic Approach to the Theory of Knowledge. Blackwell Publishers, New York, NY, 1 edition edn. (1977)
14. Rusu, C., Roncagliolo, S., Rusu, V., Collazos, C.: A methodology to establish usability heuristics. In: The Fourth International Conference on Advances in Computer-Human Interactions. pp. 59–62. ACHI '11 (2011)
15. Salvador, C., Nakasone, A., Pow-Sang, J.A.: A systematic review of usability techniques in agile methodologies. In: Proceedings of the 7th Euro American Conference on Telematics and Information Systems. EATIS 2014, pp. 17:1–17:6. ACM, New York (2014)

A Usability Study of a Brain-Computer Interface Apparatus: An Ergonomic Approach

Rafaela Q. Barros[✉], Gabriele Santos, Caroline Ribeiro,
Rebeca Torres, Manuella Q. Barros, and Marcelo M. Soares

Department of Design, Federal University of Pernambuco, Recife, Brazil
queirozdebarros@hotmail.com

Abstract. Several studies are being conducted on understanding users' behavior when using the product to analyze if the behavior that users claim to have or to demonstrate is similar to what they are actually doing at the time of the survey. Against this background, this study sets out to examine the usability of the Emotiv EPOC apparatus using heuristic analysis to detect possible problems involved in the interaction between the product and individual users.

Keywords: Electroencephalogram · Neuro-ergonomics · Neuroscience

1 Introduction

Various studies on understanding users' behavior with the product are being carried out using eye-tracking technology to analyze if the behavior that users claim to have or to demonstrate is similar to what they are actually performing at the time of the survey [1]. In general, these technologies do not identify users' real day-to-day behavior. Very often this behavior also differs when a comparison is made between undertaking an experiment and a user's real life.

Recently research studies have been developed in the neuroscience area with a view to analyzing and understanding human behavior [2]. In their studies, researchers are using the system of measures performed by Electroencephalogram (EEG) which analyzes a user's experience in accordance with the record of the electrical signals produced by neurons that are picked up by sensors arranged all over the user's scalps. The data of the electrical activity detected are recorded and stored by a computer via the Brain Computer Interface (BCI) simplified by means of a wireless hardware device called Emotiv EPOC that lets what the user really does and thinks while performing various tasks be observed.

As a result, ergonomics studies associated with neuroscience have led to neuro-ergonomics, namely the study of the brain and its behavior in the various activities of work in the various activities [3]. This area lets human cognition and behavior be analyzed in various locations and activities.

According to Kirkland [4], neuroscience when used in conjunction with knowledge of cognitive science, has led to the emergence of research studies in neurodesign. In this field of research, the user's experience based on cerebral activities can be better understood and it becomes possible to explain whether or not such an experience is satisfactory for a particular individual.

© Springer International Publishing Switzerland 2015
A. Marcus (Ed.): DUXU 2015, Part I, LNCS 9186, pp. 224–236, 2015.
DOI: 10.1007/978-3-319-20886-2_22

In this context, the appearance of new technology has been aiding practice in neurodesign, such as using the EPOC Emotiv headset in research studies associated with product design. The Emotiv EPOC® system (Fig. 1) uses neurotechnology knowledge to perform real-time scanning and storage of the EEG signals emitted by a user's brain so that they can be stored in the software of the apparatus.

Fig. 1. Emotiv EPOC

It is valid to comment that for every activity we perform we have cerebral areas that are respectively activated and which can be studied via the Brain Computer [5] interface. Therefore, the cognitive load of a human being coming from the tasks performed is detected by combining parameters of the power spectrum, of the electroencephalogram (EEG) produced by the Emotiv EPOC.

To do so, the EEG waves are picked up by electrodes that are placed directly on an individual's scalp and which are highly sensitive to the changes of the potential of neural action of the cerebral cortex. Therefore, the registration of cerebral activity is transmitted by the difference of the interval of the voltage time between a connected active electrode and the reference electrode placed in different locations on the body or scalp. The detected signals are amplified and processed in real time using graphs and decoded in accordance with the behavior of the activity.

The voltage coming from a standard brain activity has a sensitivity standard of 7 µV/mm and the average of the voltages close to the sensor area is amplified and combined to establish a rhythmic activity that is classified and combined in the frequencies Delta, Theta, Alpha, Beta and Gamma [6].

The Emotiv EPOC is a headset consisting of 14 data channels that are arranged using stems. The main rod is responsible for fixing the other secondary stems and has the format of a "tiara".

Thus, the product was selected for the study because it has the ability to control objects by using the power of thought and was developed to interact with the computer x human interface. Moreover, the Emotiv EPOC can detect thoughts, feelings, facial expressions via a wireless connection. Thus, to analyze the usability of this equipment is of extreme importance, because the utility and function performed may not be consistent with good levels of usability of the product.

Against this background, this research sets out to analyze the usability of the Emotiv EPOC equipment using heuristic analysis to detect possible problems involved in the interaction between the product and the user.

2 Methodological Procedures

The Emotiv EPOC device was investigated using the following procedures.

In the first part of the study, the product was introduced and a general description of was made in relation to its components and operation. Subsequently, the stage of setting out problematic issues and of analyzing the task associated with video-recording the Methodology for the Systemic Analysis of the Human Task-Machine System - SHTM [7] was engaged on. Additionally, the types of problems and interactions related to the design of the Emotiv EPOC were investigated based on how the SHTM set out the problematic issues.

Thereafter, an analysis of the usability of consumer products was made which examined the supposition, learning, and performance of the user, the potential of the system and re-usability [8].

Finally, the SUS (System Usability Scale) method [9] was applied which had 10 questions and so too was a questionnaire with 26 questions relating to the user's profile, handling of the product, safety and comfort, placement of the sensors and saline solution, place and use of the USB cable, and feedback from the on/charge button. The SUS method invites the user to list tasks such as the activities performed during the process of using the product. This presents a system to the respondent which has questions that should be marked and answered on a scale of satisfaction in accordance with his/her level of agreement or disagreement with each question.

This scale uses scoring that ranges from zero to one hundred by using five response categories: 1- I totally disagree, 2- I disagree, 3- I neither agree nor disagree, 4- I agree and 5-I totally agree. As the sample used in this study was eleven individuals interviewed and the answers to the extreme categories were, in most cases, few in number, it was decided to merge the following categories: I totally disagree, I disagree with I agree, I totally agree.

The ten SUS questions assessed the following categories: use of the system, complexity of the system, ease of use, assistance to use the system, integrated functions of the system, inconsistency of the system, fast learning, user's discomfort and complications while using the system, security and confidence when using the system and knowledge of other information so as to use the system.

The SUS questionnaire invites the user to list tasks such as the activities performed during the process of using the product. This presents a system to the respondent which has questions that should be answered and marked on a scale of satisfaction according to the level of agreement or disagreement to each question.

The data obtained from the survey were analyzed qualitatively for information on the users' performance and attitude while performing the task and for suggestions to solve possible problems.

3 Introduction to and Description of the Product

The Emotiv EPOC is marketed through a web page available on the internet (www. emotiv.com). Since it is a new piece of equipment on the market, users do not have experience with the product and the usability issues were analyzed based on how tasks were undertaken while using the device.

The equipment takes the form of a tiara-like headset. The main rod has an on/charge button and the luminous signal that provides feedback by displaying a blue LED light when turned on and a red one to indicate that the system is being charged via a USB cable connected to the exit of the computer which must have properly installed software. Next to the end of the extremities of the main rod, the other secondary stems are divided into two groups of seven stems each, arranged along the left and right hemispheres of the skull. The material that makes up the equipment allows the stems to have flexible movement so they can be handled and coupling on the skull using a simple and practical interface (Fig. 2).

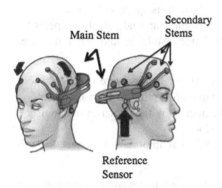

Fig. 2. Description of the components of the Emotivo EPOC Headset on the head as seen from the front and side [10].

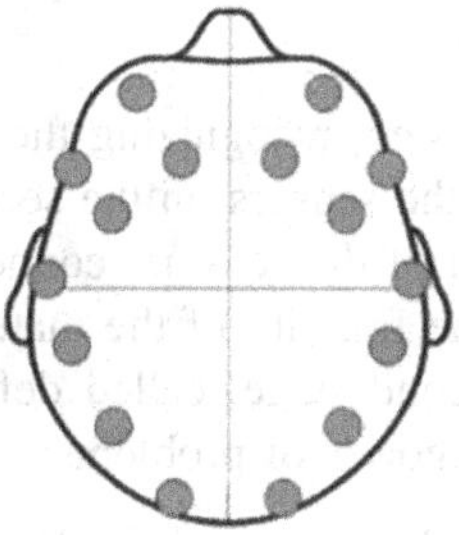

Fig. 3. Arrangement of the electrodes of the Emotiv EPOC Headset [10]

The two reference sensors are fixed below the ears, as shown in Fig. 2, and serve as a reference for identifying the left and right hemispheres of the head and to capture signals from the other sensors arranged on the scalp.

The visual interaction of the Emotiv EPOC in operation is accomplished by using the computer monitor after installing the license for using the program. This interaction is achieved via menus and tabs with different content and information. The Emotiv EPOC offers six different SDK (Software Development Kit) packages that store and save the data and may contain 4 different programs in accordance with the objective of the study. In this study we used the Education edition and the Control Panel in the Headset Setup tab so as to see the connection of the sensors. The software displays an image, in a top view of the human skull with the 16 sensors arranged as shown in Fig. 3.

The electrodes form seven sets of channels are arranged on the scalp. Using the software of the product, each sensor is displayed graphically by circles that appear in different colors in accordance with the quality of the contact. Each sensor is represented by a color code: Black - No signal; Red - Very poor signal; Orange - Poor signal; Yellow - Fair signal; Green - Good signal.

4 Setting Out the Problematic Issues

The investigation of the problem will allow an appropriate analysis in order to identify possible solutions for the dysfunction of the human- task-machine system.

Based on this statement, an investigation was undertaken of the types of problems and interactions and how these relate to the situation of the design of the product by means of a three-stage investigation of the problem [7]:

1. Recognizing the problem: Listing the most serious problems of the product analyzed, in terms of meeting the user's needs
2. Defining the problem: Classifying the situation of the problems by means of the Analysis of Dysfunction of the product-user interface using photographs.
3. Formulating the problem: Describing the most significant and solvable aspects by considering personal competence, the knowledge available and what the user required.

In the first step, recognizing the problem, the following factors were observed: poor fixation of the sensors on the secondary stems; rapid absorption of the saline solution into the felt of the sensors; connection signal hampered by the presence of the user's hair; and the fragility of the materials of the product.

The second stage, called defining the problem, was important to detect the following categories of problems:

- Structural and Movement Problems: Little resistance when moving the sensors on the scalp during handling; Lack of practicality for fixing the sensors when adjusting the signal settings and for preventing their sliding on the scalp; Lack of security and the looseness of the sensors as to fixing them to the secondary stems thus causing failure or absence of the connection signal; Connection failure arising from the lack of sensitivity of the sensors to the presence of hair; The felt of the sensor quickly absorbs the saline solution; The looseness and slanting of the sensors impair the connection signal intermittently and causes transmission error of the connection signal of the system. This failure can be seen when the sensor is not connected to the scalp but the system detects the presence of a connection signal via the Emotiv Control Panel.
- Problems of Resistance: Lack of resistance of the material covering the secondary stems, caused by handling on the scalp, thereby leaving the internal circuitry seen. Lack of resistance of the felt material of the sensors arising from the attrition caused by docking and undocking.

5 Task Analysis Associated with Video Recording

The strategy for assessing the usability of the product was based on the methodology for analyzing a task given by Moraes and Mont'Alvão [7].

To this end, the analysis considered the users' inexperience with regard to using the product. Thus, the evaluators made general comments on the equipment and its use, and also distributed a list with instructions on how to use the task.

The operations of the Emotiv EPOC system were selected and displayed in summary form in the functional action-decision flowchart below (Fig. 4).

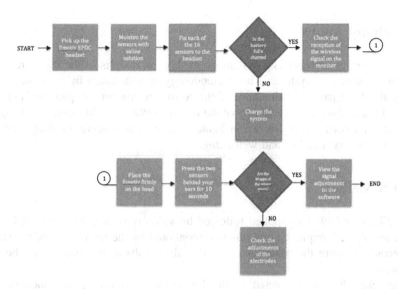

Fig. 4. Action-Decision Flow-chart of the Emotiv EPOC system

The aspects used for the analysis of the task were with regard to ease of use, learning and the user's first impressions during his/her first experience using Emotiv EPOC. These aspects served as a reference to evaluate the following proceedings of the user's interaction: Time spent to carry out the activity; Number of attempts to perform the task; Doubts, questions and comments verbalized during the experiment; Nonverbal aspects perceived because of the user's behavior.

The aspects related to the task procedure were recorded on video and analyzed according to the time taken to performing the following tasks: the average time of the first part of the task which consists of the moistening plus placement of the sensors was five minutes; the time taken in the second part of the activity corresponding to adjusting the connection signal was six minutes. The time spent on the two tasks was eleven minutes.

The main problem observed in the first stage of the video observation was the falling away of the stems of the secondary sensors when they were being placed and when being put on the user's scalp.

In the second observation step, the same problem as in the previous step was observed regarding the falling off of the sensors from the stems and all users required the help of the researchers to adjust the signal on their scalp. The adjustment was made after pressing the two Emotiv reference sensors, which are located behind the ears, for 10 s. Subsequently, the most troublesome activity was that of sliding the sensors gently on the scalp until all the sensors were green on the Emotiv Control Panel. This practice required some sensors to be again moistened, the sensors that came loose and fell off to be replaced and to push aside the hair of the area on the scalp that the sensor was occupying.

6 Usability Analysis

The evaluation of usability is a systematic method of analysis of the user's relations with the product and systems. This methodology is undertaken by gathering information about the particular situations of the consumer products in question [11]. The results of the analysis of the usability of the Emotiv EPOC usability analysis, using the principles of Jordan [8], are shown in Table 1, in order to analyze the user's level of satisfaction, safety, comfort and well-being.

7 SUS Method

The SUS method [9] was applied followed by video recording the users while they performed the task requested and this was monitored by the researchers of the study. The recordings were the basis for comparing the results of the analysis of the task requested.

The research was conducted in the Center for Arts and Communication, the location of the Design course at the Federal University of Pernambuco, and in CESAR (Center for Studies and Advanced Systems of Recife) located in the city of Recife, Brazil. 11 subjects (students, designers and engineers), nine males and two females, aged 20–30 years, were recruited. None of them had some kind of physical disability. An overview was given to each interviewee on the topic of the research and on the purpose of the questionnaire and then the interviewees received some information on how to use the apparatus and the software. Later, they were given some instructions on the task to be performed with the Emotiv EPOC and then asked to answer a questionnaire on evaluating usability. The task performed was the same as that presented in the schema of the action-decision flowchart of the Emotiv EPOC system (Fig. 4).

Volunteers were asked whether they had previously used any similar apparatus and they all said they had not. Because of this they were given some instructions on how to use the product and how to connect the sensors with the software. Even after having read the instructions, users were still uncertain about how to use the product and their questions were answered by the researchers.

Regarding the use of the headset, they were asked if they considered that in their opinion handling and maneuvering the headset was comfortable and safe. Five disagreed, five said they were neutral, another agreed that it was comfortable but not safe and one agreed that it was safe. One person answered twice. On being asked if they had problems in handling and maneuvering the headset, the problems mentioned were: Form of the secondary stems ($n = 6$); Dimensioning ($n = 2$); USB cable docking system ($n = 1$); On/charge button ($n = 2$); Poor dimensioning ($n = 2$); Appears to be fragile ($n = 2$).

When asked if screwing sensors into and removing them from the secondary stems of the headset was easy, one respondent totally disagreed, four disagreed, three marked

Table 1. Result of the analysis of usability as per Jordan [8]

Principles	Results
Consistency	The switch on and charge button is similar to the trigger mechanism of buttons of the push with your finger and slide sideways type. The user's interaction with the buttons is given by viewing the information charge, presented in high relief next to the button as follows: switch on ⏻ and charge 🔌.
Compatibility	The movement of the switch on and charge button is compatible with the stereotype of movement in the sense of pushing to the sides (right and left). The trigger of the button for the desired function is performed by sliding a finger sideways on it.
Considerations on the user's resources	The method of operation of the equipment takes into account the user's visual and tactile aspects when handling and using the product.
Feedback	The button of the equipment is used to fulfill two functions: switch on and charge. A blue light is always on when the Switch on function is selected. When the machine is in the charging mode, a red light comes on. The difference in colors lets the user have feedback about each state of the equipment.
Prevention and recovery from error	The equipment lets the user make online adjustments to the connection signal. This adjustment facilitates the correction of signs considered inadequate for reading brain activity correctly.
Control by the user	The user has control over the set of actions and calibration of the equipment.
Visual clarity	The interface of the software interface is presented via menus with information functions and tab options with different content on the selected activity.
Prioritization of functionality and information	The software has windows that allow the choice and prioritization of the function and desired information.
Transference of technology	The product does not have any technological transferences.
Clarity	The information in the user manual on using the product and software is clear. The language of the information is in English and there is no translation to other languages.

this as neutral, one totally agreed and two agreed. As to screwing the sensors into and removing them from the secondary stems, the problems encountered were: Screwing the sensors in ($n = 3$) and adjusting the sensors ($n = 9$). One person answered twice.

Two participants noted the option of another problem, one reported a threading problem and suggested a plug, while the other referred to the problem of bad contact.

They were asked if it was easy to apply the saline solution on the sensors, One was neutral about this, six agreed it was and four agreed completely with this. Similarly, they were asked if it was easy to moisten the sensors. One marked this as neutral; five agreed it was and five agreed completely with this.

Regarding the effectiveness of moistening, two disagreed it was; three marked as neutral, three agreed and three agreed completely. They were asked if they considered moistening the sensors was practical. Three said they were neutral about this, seven agreed and one totally agreed with this. Another question was about which type of problem was identified when moistening the sensors. The comments were as follows: Little absorption ($n = 2$); Much absorption ($n = 3$); Rapid absorption ($n = 1$). Four people marked the option of other problems and their comments were: "Hair absorbs the liquid and interferes with the moistening"; "Rapid absorption of the solution in the sensors"; "There is no indication of the level of moistening if it has already been wetted"; "Rapid evaporation and deterioration of the sensors" One person did not answered.

When asked if installing and removing the USB cable is considered easy, three respondents agreed it was and six agreed completely. To respondents did not answer. Regarding the type of problem when installing and removing the USB cable, two respondents found it difficult to locate the entry point of the USB cable; another did not identify any problem and eight did not answer this question. They were asked if the information on the switch on/charge button was sufficiently clear enough. Two disagreed, four agreed, and five agreed completely with this. The problems encountered in the Switch on/charge button were: Symbol of switch on/charge is not clear ($n = 2$); the color of the symbol is inadequate for Switch on/charge ($n = 1$); Inappropriate contrast of the symbol for switch on/charge ($n = 1$); Size Three respondents indicated another option and commented as follows: "Location"; "The side of on/off is not identified"; "The place of the symbols are in opposite places" ($n = 3$) and the other did not detect any problems. Three people did not answer.

On aspects related to security, they were asked whether the headset use was safe to use. One disagreed, five were neutral, three agreed and two agreed completely with this. The types of problems identified as to its safe use were: an uncomfortable feeling ($n = 2$), a feeling of being unsafe ($n = 2$), fear of getting a shock ($n = 3$); other, "It looks like it will fall off." ($n = 1$). Some people did not answer all questions.

On aspects related to security, they were asked if they considered it safe to use the equipment. One disagreed with this; five were neutral about it; three agreed and two totally agreed it was. The problems identified in relation to safety were: a feeling of discomfort ($n = 2$); a feeling of being unsafe ($n = 2$); a fear of getting a shock ($n = 3$), and other "It looks as if it´s going to fall off" ($n = 1$). Three people did not give their opinion.

They were asked if the feedback provided by the luminous signal of switch on/charge was effective. Two disagreed with this; one was neutral; three agreed and five totally agreed it was. The problems identified with the feedback of the luminous signal were as follows: Display indication of switch on is not sufficiently clear ($n = 3$);

Display indication of charge is not sufficiently clear ($n = 1$); Other: "small symbols" and "inadequate location" ($n = 2$). Five people did not give their opinion.

On aspects related to comfort when using the headset, they were asked if they considered this was comfortable. Two disagreed; four said they were neutral; four agreed and one totally agreed with this. Regarding comfort, the problems identified were: getting hold of it inadequate ($n = 4$); difficulty in maneuvering it ($n = 5$); the material ($n = 2$); Other, "The sensors keep falling off" and "gripping the neck." ($n = 2$): One people answered twice.

Regarding the placement and removal of the headset, they were asked if they considered this was easy. Two totally disagreed; three disagreed; two said they were neutral; one agreed and three totally agreed. They were asked what kind of problem they had identified when putting on and removing the headset on their head. The problems were: The action of placing the headset on their head ($n = 1$), adjusting the headset on my head ($n = 4$), Other ($n = 1$): The sensor falls easily. "

On aspects related to the use when connecting the headset with the software, they were asked if this was effective (it fulfils the role it is aimed at). Two totally disagreed; two disagreed; two were neutral; one agreed; and three totally agreed. The problems identified when connecting to the software were: Absence of signal ($n = 1$), oscillating signal ($n = 7$) and did not answer ($n = 3$).

Regarding the user's satisfaction with the connection to the software, the users were asked if they considered they would like to use this system frequently. One person strongly disagreed; three disagreed; two were neutral and five agreed.

When questioned if they found the system unnecessarily complex, one person strongly disagreed; four disagreed; three were neutral; two agreed and one strongly agreed. As to the question I thought the system was easy to use, one person strongly disagreed; seven disagreed; one was neutral and two agreed. The participants were questioned about whether they thought that they would need the support of a technical person to be able to use this system.

The answers were: two respondents disagreed, seven agreed and two strongly agreed. As to the question "Did you find the various functions in this system were well integrated", two disagreed; five were neutral; three agreed and one strongly agreed. Next, they were asked if they thought there was too much inconsistency in this system. The answers were: four disagreed; five were neutral; one agreed and another strongly agreed. The next question was "Would you imagine that most people would learn to use this system very quickly" and they answered as follows: two people strongly disagreed, four disagreed, one was neutral and four agreed.

The users were questioned about whether the system is very cumbersome to use, and the answers were: three disagreed; two were neutral; five agreed and one strongly agreed. The question "Did you feel very confident when using the system" obtained the following results: one strongly disagreed and one disagreed; seven were neutral; one strongly agreed and one agreed. Finally, the last question about satisfaction with the software was "Did you need to learn a lot of things before you could get going with this system?" The results were: six disagreed; one was neutral and four agreed.

In the last question, the respondents were asked to write their opinion about the Emotiv EPOC. The comments were compiled and summarized as follows:

- "Interesting and useful but tricky and complicated to use without help. The felts fall off thus making the process difficult." "The adjustment of the equipment is troublesome. The sensors are not sufficiently well docked to the equipment. It takes practice to use it." "It's not practical."
- "Very light and good feeling when being put on because it is something that I had never before had contact with. It was kind of hard to assimilate how to adjust it or use it but nothing at all after a little practice in learning about it; it seems effective and logical. Within three days I would be able to master how to handle it."
- "It's a nuisance to put on if you have a lot of hair. I found it very difficult to get all sensors to stay green." "It does not come up to scratch in its operation due to the sensors." "The connection between the headset and the head was never made and the sensors are difficult to dock."

Analyis of the Results and Suggestions. It was noted that no user had used this equipment before. Most users felt the grip and handling of the equipment is not comfortable and safe and encountered problems especially regarding the form of secondary stems. As for docking and removing the sensors, most users disagree that this is easy and reported problems in adjusting the sensors.

Everyone considered that putting the saline solution on and moistening the sensors are easy, practical and effective tasks. On the other hand, most identified problems as to adjusting the sensor due to the insufficient amount of saline on the sensors.

Most participants also did not identify problems as to the clarity of the information of the switch on/charge button nor in installing and removing the USB cable. However, when they were asked to identify problems in the button, some alternatives were marked.

The respondents were asked if they considered the equipment was safe. Most agreed it was. However, some items related to safety issues were marked. Most considered the feedback provided by the luminous signal of switch on/charge was effective.

Most thought using the equipment was comfortable, but they identified some problems.

Most had difficulty as to installing and removing the headset and also identified some problems such as:

Regarding satisfaction with the connection of the headset to the software, the responses were divided: roughly, half agreed and the other half disagreed. However, most agreed that the connection signal oscillated.

Attention should be drawn to the fact that there is disagreement between most respondents stating that they would use this system frequently and at the same time that that they agree that the system is not complex yet they would require support from a technician to use it. It was the unanimous view that the equipment really needs the help of an experienced user if it is to be used properly.

Almost all of the respondents considered that the system functions were well integrated, that the system was difficult to use and that most people would take a long time to learn to use it. We also believe that the system works properly, but through the experience of using it.

Regarding the classification of the scores of the SUS questionnaire, values below 60 represent satisfactory and poor systems and which cause users to be dissatisfied. Scores from 61 and over represent very good experiences with a good satisfaction rating [9]. According to the usability indices obtained by the SUS score, the equipment analyzed had a usability index of 46.5. This index is indicated below that recommended by the author. In other words, the Emotiv EPOC does not have a good usability. Its system level is considered to be poor and can result in users being dissatisfied.

8 Recommendations

As a suggestion from the usability analysis, it was realized there is a need to improve how to attach the sensors to the secondary stems so that they do not easily become detached from the insertion site.

Regarding the adjustment of the connection signal, the oscillation of the connection signal displayed by changing the color code should be improved in relation to the sensitivity of the sensors so that the adjustment is easier, faster and more effective.

The sensitivity of the sensors should also be reviewed given that the presence of the user's hair interferes with the adjustment of the signal connection.

The practicality of fixing the sensors can be improved by implementing a magnetic locking system.

As for the coating material, it is recommended that the material used in the secondary stems and in the felt be replaced with a tougher one that prevents the internal wiring being seen and that allows a better docking and undocking of the sensors.

9 Conclusion

Usability tests in neuroscience are still in their growth phase but the area has been proving to be quite interesting and promising when developing research to discover solutions for complex problems related to the usability of products.

Therefore, it is important to make clear that research studies in this context can help to analyze the usability of a piece of equipment that furthers understanding of human behavior through the brain as well as to assist the design area with the use of emerging technologies.

The use of SUS [9] proved to be pertinent to the analysis conducted of the product. However, we identified some contradictions in the answers. Therefore, we consider that such contradictions have adversely affected the usability analysis of the product. We believe that this problem could have been minimized if the sample had been larger than that used in the study.

We conclude that the idea of the design of the Emotiv EPOC fulfils facilitating the tests that require EEG analysis. To this end, this study set out to contribute by making suggestions to solve the usability problems so that users may conduct their tests with this equipment in a pleasant and satisfactory manner.

Acknowledgements. The authors thanks to the CNPQ – National Council for the Development of Science and Technology, Brazil – for sponsoring their research at Federal University of Pernambuco, from which this article is extracted and Marcelo Soares for his valuable supervision.

References

1. Redwood, G.: Neuroscience and the online purchase. Internet Retail. **5**(4) (2011). www.internetretailing.net
2. Khushaba, R., Wise, C., Kodagoda, S., Louviere, J., Kahn, B., Townsend, C.: Consumer neuroscience: assessing the brain response to marketing stimuli using electroencephalogram (EEG) and eye tracking. Expert Syst. Appl. **40**(2013), 3803–3812 (2013)
3. Parasuraman, R., Rizzo, M.: Neuroergonomics: The Brain at Work. Oxford University Press, USA (2007)
4. Kirkland, L.: Using Neuroscience to Inform Your UX Strategy and Design (2012). http://www.uxmatters.com/mt/archives/2012/07/using-neuroscience-to-inform-your-ux-strategy-and-design.php
5. Esfahani, E., Sundararajan, V.: Using Brain-Computer Interfaces to detect human satisfaction in Human-Robot Interaction. Int. J. Humanoid Rob. **08**(01), 87–101 (2011). doi:10.1142/S0219843611002356
6. Nunez, P.L., Srinivasan, R.: Electric Fields of the Brain: The Neurophysics of EEG, 2nd edn. Oxford University Press, USA (2006)
7. Moraes, A., Mont'alvão, C.: Ergonomia: conceitos e aplicações. Rio de Janeiro, 2AB (2010)
8. Jordan, P.W.: An Introduction to Usability. Taylor & Francis, London (1998)
9. Stanton, N.A., Young, M.S.: A Guide to Methodology in Ergonomics: Designing for human use. Taylor & Francis, London (1999)
10. Emotiv EPOC: Brain Computer Interface & Scientific Contextual EEG. Emotiv EPOC & Testbench Specifications. https://emotiv.com/product-specs/Emotiv%20EPOC%20Specifications%202014.pdf
11. Roepke, G.A.L. et al.: A importância da ambientação na avaliação da usabilidade de produtos. In: Anais II Conferência Internacional de Integração do Design, Engenharia e Gestão para a inovação, Florianópolis, SC, pp. 21–23 (2012)

User Experience Evaluations: Challenges for Newcomers

Cristian Rusu[1(✉)], Virginica Rusu[2], Silvana Roncagliolo[1],
Juan Apablaza[1], and Virginia Zaraza Rusu[1]

[1] Pontificia Universidad Católica de Valparaíso, Valparaíso, Chile
{cristian.rusu,silvana}@ucv.cl, jjapablaza@gmail.com,
rvzaraza90@hotmail.com
[2] Universidad de Playa Ancha, Valparaíso, Chile
virginica.rusu@upla.cl

Abstract. Human – Computer Interaction (HCI) should be a basic part of the formative process of all computer science professionals. Usability and User Experience (UX) were (re)defined by many authors and well recognized standards. UX is usually considered as an extension of usability. To move from usability to UX seems to be a tendency lately. Forming usability/UX evaluators is a challenging task. Practice is usually more appealing and persuasive than theory. The paper presents a study on the perception of (novice) evaluators over generic and specific usability heuristics.

Keywords: Usability · User experience · Usability evaluation · Heuristic evaluation · Usability heuristics

1 Introduction

The Joint Task Force on Computing Curricula of Association for Computing Machinery (ACM) and IEEE Computer Society establishes Human – Computer Interaction (HCI) as part of the Body of Knowledge in their Computer Science (CS) curricula proposal (CS2013) [1].

Usability was (re)defined by many authors. Usability definitions were also provided by well recognized standards. One of the best known and widely used definitions is the one proposed by ISO 9241: the extent to which a system, product or service can be used by specified users to achieve specified goals with effectiveness, efficiency and satisfaction in a specified context of use [2].

The UX concept was also referred by ISO 9241: a person's perceptions and responses that result from the use or anticipated use of a product, system or service [2]. Some authors consider UX as an extension of the usability concept. Others use the terms usability and UX indistinctly. The UX concept is still under review. The "User Experience White Paper" aims to "bring clarity to the concept" [3].

CS2013 explicitly includes usability as a compulsory core HCI topic. Usability is also recommended as elective topic. User Experience (UX) is not explicitly incorporated as a core HCI topic; however it is implicitly considered in other core and elective topics. It seems that the usability concept is widely accepted not only by the HCI

© Springer International Publishing Switzerland 2015
A. Marcus (Ed.): DUXU 2015, Part I, LNCS 9186, pp. 237–246, 2015.
DOI: 10.1007/978-3-319-20886-2_23

community, but also by the CS community in general. The UX concept is not yet commonly endorsed by the CS community. To move from usability to UX seems to be a tendency lately. Even the former "Usability Professionals Association" (UPA) redefined itself as "User Experience Professionals Association" (UXPA).

Including HCI in the CS curricula is still a challenge in most Latin American (LA) countries [4]. However, when HCI is present usability seems to be a major topic in both teaching and researching.

Forming usability/UX evaluators is a challenging task. The paper presents an empiric study on the perception of (novice) evaluators over generic and specific usability heuristics. Section 2 examines the concept of usability and UX. Section 3 highlights the heuristic evaluation as a fundamental assessment method for both usability and UX, examining the importance of the set of heuristics that are employed. Section 4 presents the results of experiments that were recently made, using both generic and specific usability heuristics. Section 5 points out conclusions and future work.

2 Usability and User Experience

Over more than three decades usability was (re)defined by many authors. Usability definitions were also provided by well recognized standards. Lewis points out that there is still no clear and generally accepted usability definition, as its complex nature is hard to describe in one definition [5].

One of the best known and widely accepted usability definitions was proposed by ISO 9241 standard: "the extent to which a system, product or service can be used by specified users to achieve specified goals with effectiveness, efficiency and satisfaction in a specified context of use" [6]. Updated ISO standards still refer to the ISO 9241 usability definition. ISO/IEC 25010 defines usability as the "degree to which a product or system can be used by specified users to achieve specified goals with effectiveness, efficiency and satisfaction in a specified context of use" [7]. It considers usability as a subset of quality in use consisting of "effectiveness", "efficiency" and "satisfaction".

Nielsen and Loranger define usability as a quality attribute relating to how easy something is to use [8]. More specifically, how quickly people can learn to use it (learnability), how efficient they are using it (efficiency), how memorable it is (memorability), how error-prone it is (errors), and how much users like using it (satisfaction). Sharp, Rogers and Preece affirm that usability is generally regarding as ensuring that interactive products are easy to learn, effective to use, and enjoyable [9]. They denote six "usability goals": effectiveness, efficiency, safety, utility, learnability and memorability. Usability.gov states that usability is about effectiveness, efficiency and the overall satisfaction of the user, a combination of factors including: intuitive design, ease of learning, efficiency of use, memorability, error frequency and severity, and subjective satisfaction [10].

Regardless they are called "attributes", "factors" or "goals", usability dimensions are recurrent in all definitions. They are also referred in ISO standards. New interaction paradigms, new technologies and new kind of software systems are compelling arguments for reviewing the usability concept, characteristics, methods, metrics and methodologies [11, 12].

ISO 9241-210 standard defines UX as a "person's perceptions and responses resulting from the use and/or anticipated use of a product, system or service" [2]. It considers that UX "includes all the users' emotions, beliefs, preferences, perceptions, physical and psychological responses, behaviors and accomplishments that occur before, during and after use".

Sharp, Rogers and Preece point out that one cannot design a user experience, but only design for a user experience; one cannot design a sensual experience, but only create the design features that can evoke it [9]. They enumerate a broad range of UX positive and negative "qualities". Kuniavsky admits that defining UX is difficult, since it can extend to nearly everything in someone's interaction with a product [13]. UXPA. org defines UX as every aspect of the user's interaction with a product, service, or company that make up the user's perceptions of the whole [14].

The UX concept is still under review. The "User Experience White Paper" aims to "bring clarity to the UX concept" [3]. Rather than intending to give a unique UX definition, the document mentions the wide collection of definitions available at All-aboutux.org [15].

Some authors consider UX as an extension of the usability concept. Others use the terms usability and UX indistinctly.

The ISO 9241-210 standard sustains that usability, when interpreted from the perspective of the users' personal goals, can include the kind of perceptual and emotional aspects typically associated with user experience [2]. Usability criteria can be used to assess aspects of user experience.

Usability.gov refers to usability as the quality of a user's experience when interacting with products or systems [10]. UXPA.org makes a direct link between UX and usability, through the human-centered design (HCD) process [14].

Lewis considers user-centered design (UCD) and UX as usability extensions; in his opinion UCD subsumed usability engineering (and ergonomics and human factors engineering), and UX has subsumed UCD [5]. He also points out that in the (near) future UX will probably become part of a larger customer experience effort, as a result of the growing emphasis on service design and the emergence of the service science as discipline. Lewis highlights usability as a stable component throughout the transformations from usability engineering to UCD to UX.

The "User Experience White Paper" considers that UX is not the same as usability, although usability, as perceived by the user, is typically an aspect contributing to the overall UX [3].

Sharp, Rogers and Preece make a distinction between usability goals and UX goals [9]. They consider usability goals concerned with meting specific usability criteria (related to effectiveness, efficiency and the overall satisfaction of the use), and UX goals concerned with explaining the nature of the UX itself. Overall, they consider usability goals more objective than UX goals.

Mitchell acknowledges that many terms are similar to usability [16]. He even considers that for practical purposes they are the same as usability: usability testing, human factors engineering, customer experience management, ergonomics, UCD, human factors, user – friendly design.

To move from usability to UX seems to be a tendency lately. Even the former "Usability Professionals Association" (UPA) redefined itself as "User Experience Professionals Association" (UXPA) [14].

3   Usability and User Experience Evaluation

Lewis highlights two major conceptions of usability [5]:

- Summative, focused on metrics (i.e., "measurement-based usability"),
- Formative, focused on usability problems detection and associated design solutions (i.e., "diagnostic usability").

The concept of summative usability led to ISO usability standard, emphasizing on three key factors: effectiveness, efficiency and satisfaction. Lewis highlights the resemblance of metrics associated to the three key factors to methods and metrics of experimental psychology, instantiated in human factors engineering.

The concept of formative usability focuses on the iterative design process (design – test – redesign). It led to the development of several usability evaluation methods, essentially classified as:

- Empirical usability testing, based on users' participation [17],
- Inspection methods, based on experts' judgment [18].

UX is generally considered an extension of usability; therefore usability evaluation methods may also be applied in order to assess UX. A broad collection of UX evaluation methods is provided at http://www.allaboutux.org/ [15].

Heuristic evaluation is one of the most common usability assessment methods. It involves the participation of usability specialists analyzing every interactive element and dialog following a set of established usability design principles called heuristics [19]. A heuristic evaluation is usually performed by 3 to 5 evaluators.

When selecting the set of heuristics to be used, there are (mainly) two alternatives: choosing generic heuristics or specific heuristics. Specific heuristics may become hard to understand and hard to apply but they can detect many (relevant) usability issues related to the application area. Generic heuristics are easy to understand and to apply, but they can miss specific usability issues [11].

Our research work over the last decade focused mainly on usability/UX and related topics. We came to the conclusion that the traditional usability engineering concepts and evaluation methods should be re-examined. There is a need for new evaluation methods or at least for the use of traditional evaluations in novel ways. Frameworks of usability evaluation, including appropriate methods or combination of methods should be established, in order to get more effective and efficient evaluations on new interaction paradigms. We proposed specific usability heuristics and associated checklists for transactional web applications [20], touchscreen-based mobile applications [21], grid computing applications [22], interactive digital television [23], and virtual worlds [24]. We also developed a cultural – oriented usability heuristics proposal [25]. The experience of developing specific usability heuristics led to a methodology proposal [11, 26].

4   Challenges When Forming Usability Professionals

Including HCI in the CS curricula and forming usability/UX professionals is still a challenge in most LA countries [4]. An appealing way to introduce HCI at all CS curricula levels is by systematically including usability/UX practices [27]. SIGCHI acknowledges the importance of getting down HCI to the practical work [28]. We believe that a strong relationship between HCI theory, research and practice is particularly important in countries were HCI communities are not yet well established.

Teaching HCI in Chile for more than a decade was a challenging intercultural, interdisciplinary, cross-field but very rewarding experience [29]. As practice is usually more appealing and persuasive than the theory, we gradually increased the weight of practical activities, and we came to focus more and more on teaching the students how to put the HCI theory into practice. Forming usability/UX evaluators is a challenging task.

Heuristic evaluations and usability tests are compulsory practice for all our students, at undergraduate and graduate level. As standard practice, at least one heuristic evaluation is performed based on Nielsen's set of 10 usability heuristics [19]. Usually a heuristic evaluation based on domain-specific usability heuristic is also performed. After each heuristic evaluation a standard questionnaire is applied, giving us an interesting and very useful feedback. Some results were previously published [30, 31].

An experiment was made in 2014, involving 54 CS students:

- 25 undergraduate students from Pontificia Universidad Católica de Valparaíso, Chile, 12 of them having some previous experience in heuristic evaluations,
- 29 graduate students from Pontificia Universidad Católica del Perú, all of them novice evaluators.

All participants were asked to perform a heuristic evaluation over a major airline transactional website (www.lan.com), using Nielsen's 10 usability heuristics. Later on a survey was conducted in order to evaluate their perception over Nielsen's heuristics, concerning 4 dimensions: D1 - Utility, D2 - Clarity, D3 - Ease of use, D4 - Necessity of additional checklist. All dimensions were evaluated using a 5 points Likert scale. As samples are independent, observations are ordinal, and no assumption of normality can be made, results were analyzed using nonparametric statistics tests.

A Mann-Whitney U test was performed to check the hypothesis:

- H0: there are no significant differences between evaluators with and without previous experience,
- H1: there are significant differences between evaluators with and without previous experience.

As decision rule was used $p \leq 0.05$. As Table 1 shows, there are no significant differences between the two groups of evaluators (with/without previous experience), excepting the dimension D4 - Necessity of additional checklist. A preliminary explanation could be that novice evaluators do not really understand the purpose of a checklist that complements a set of usability heuristics.

Table 1. Mann-Whitnew U test for the perception of Nielsen's heuristics

	D1: Utility	D2: Clarity	D3: Ease of use	D4: Necessity of additional checklist
p	0.1353	0.1921	0.0908	0.0359

A Spearman ρ test was performed to check the hypothesis:

- H0: p = 0, the dimensions Dm and Dn are independent,
- H1: p ≠ 0, the dimensions Dm and Dn are dependent.

As decision rule was used $p \leq 0.05$. Results show that:

- All dimensions are independent in the case of evaluators with previous experience;
- There are some weak to moderate dependences in the case of novice evaluators (Table 2);
- There are also some weak to moderate dependences when all evaluators are considered (Table 3).

Table 2. Spearman ρ test for novice evaluators (Nielsen's heuristics)

	D1: Utility	D2: Clarity	D3: Ease of use	D4: Necessity of additional checklist
D1	1	0.55	Independent	Independent
D2		1	0.46	0.35
D3			1	Independent
D4				1

Table 3. Spearman ρ test for all evaluators (Nielsen's heuristics)

	D1: Utility	D2: Clarity	D3: Ease of use	D4: Necessity of additional checklist
D1	1	0.53	0.27	Independent
D2		1	0.43	Independent
D3			1	Independent
D4				1

A second experiment was made, involving the 25 undergraduate students from Pontificia Universidad Católica de Valparaíso, Chile. A month after the first experiment they were asked to perform a new heuristic evaluation over the same transactional website (www.lan.com), this time using a set of 14 specific usability heuristics for transactional websites (TW):

- TW1: Visibility of system status,
- TW2: Feedback on transactions' state,
- TW3: Dependability and anticipated functionality,
- TW4: Security and speed of transactions,
- TW5: Match between system and user world,
- TW6: User control and freedom,

- TW7: Consistency in system design,
- TW8: Use of web standards and symbols,
- TW9: Error prevention,
- TW10: Minimize user's memory load,
- TW11: Flexibility and efficiency of use,
- TW12: Aesthetic and minimalist design,
- TW13: Help for error recognition and recovery,
- TW14: Help and documentation.

The set of TW usability heuristics was developed in 3 iterations [11]. It was validated through several experiments and case studies [20, 31].

The website used as case study did not experienced any changes between the two experiments. A new survey was conducted in order to assess evaluators' perception over TW heuristics, concerning the same 4 dimensions and using the same scale as in the case of Nielsen's heuristics. Results were analyzed in similar ways.

As Table 4 shows, there are no significant differences between the two groups of evaluators (with/without previous experience). Apparently TW heuristics are clear enough; there's no significant need for additional checklist.

Table 4. Mann-Whitnew U test for the perception of TW heuristics

	D1: Utility	D2: Clarity	D3: Ease of use	D4: Necessity of additional checklist
p	0.7441	0.1708	0.6020	0.7692

The Spearman ρ test shows that:

- The major dependences in the case of evaluators with previous experience occurs between dimensions D2 – D1 and D2 – D3 (Table 5); if heuristics are perceived as clear (easy to understand), they are also perceived as useful and easy to use;
- There is a very high (and unexpected) opposite dependency between D3 and D1 in the case of novice evaluators (Table 6); a possible explanation would be their lack of experiences, however further analysis is required!
- There are some moderate dependences when all evaluators are considered (Table 7).

Additional (descriptive) statistics offered important feedback in order to refine the set of TW heuristics. Based on the lowest score, heuristics TW1, TW2, TW5, TW6, TW7, TW11, and TW12 definitions need further review.

Table 5. Spearman ρ test for evaluators with previous experience (TW heuristics)

	D1: Utility	D2: Clarity	D3: Ease of use	D4: Necessity of additional checklist
D1	1	0.68	0.49	Independent
D2		1	0.66	Independent
D3			1	Independent
D4				1

Table 6. Spearman ρ test for novice evaluators (TW heuristics)

	D1: Utility	D2: Clarity	D3: Ease of use	D4: Necessity of additional checklist
D1	1	Independent	-0.90	Independent
D2		1	Independent	Independent
D3			1	Independent
D4				1

Table 7. Spearman ρ test for all evaluators (TW heuristics)

	D1: Utility	D2: Clarity	D3: Ease of use	D4: Necessity of additional checklist
D1	1	0.54	Independent	Independent
D2		1	0.59	0.43
D3			1	Independent
D4				1

5   Conclusions

Over more than three decades usability was (re)defined by many authors. UX is generally considered an extension of usability. Some authors use the terms usability and UX indistinctly. New interaction paradigms, new technologies and new kind of software systems are compelling arguments for reviewing the usability and UX concepts, characteristics, methods, metrics and methodologies.

Including HCI in the CS curricula and forming usability/UX professionals is still a challenge in most LA countries. SIGCHI acknowledges the importance of getting down HCI to the practical work; an appealing way to introduce HCI at all CS curricula levels is by systematically including usability/UX practices. A strong relationship between HCI theory, research and practice is particularly important in countries were HCI communities are not yet well established.

Forming usability/UX evaluators is a challenging task. A study on the perception of (novice) evaluators over generic and specific usability heuristics was conducted. There are no significant differences between the groups of evaluators with and without previous experience, except the perceived necessity of additional checklist (when working with general heuristics). When occur, dependencies between the four surveyed dimensions are somehow expected. The only unexpected (very high, opposite) dependency occurs between dimensions "Ease of use" and "Utility", in the case of novice evaluators (when working with specific heuristics for transactional websites).

The study offered an important feedback for both teaching and research. More experiments are necessary in order to validate preliminary conclusions. Quantitative analyze will be complemented with qualitative data, collected through surveys and interviews.

References

1. CS2013: Computer Science Curricula 2013. Curriculum Guidelines for Undergraduate Degree Programs in Computer Science (Final Report). ACM/IEEE-CS Joint Task Force on Computing Curricula, ACM/IEEE Computer Society (2013)
2. ISO 9241-210: Ergonomics of human-system interaction – Part 210: Human-centred design for interactive systems. International Organization for Standardization, Geneva (2010)
3. Roto, V., Law, E., Vermeeren, A., Hoonhout, J.: User Experience White Paper. Bringing Clarity to the Concept of User Experience. http://www.allaboutux.org/uxwhitepaper. Accessed 20 Nov 2014
4. Collazos, C., Granollers, T., Rusu, C.: A survey of human-computer interaction into the computer science curricula in Iberoamerica. In: 8th International Conference on Information Technology: New Generations (ITNG 2011), pp. 151–156. IEEE Computer Society Press (2011)
5. Lewis, J.: Usability: lessons learned… and yet to be learned. Int. J. Hum.-Comput. Interact. **30**(9), 663–684 (2014)
6. ISO 9241-11: Ergonomic requirements for office work with visual display terminals (VDTs) – Part 11: Guidance on usability. International Organization for Standardization, Geneva (1998)
7. ISO/IEC 25010: Systems and software engineering — Systems and software Quality Requirements and Evaluation (SQuaRE) — System and software quality models. International Organization for Standardization, Geneva (2011)
8. Nielsen, J., Loranger, H.: Prioritizing Web Usability. New Riders, Berkley (2006)
9. Sharp, H., Rogers, Y., Preece, J.: Interaction Design: Beyond Human-Computer Interaction. Wiley, Chichester (2007)
10. Usability.gov: Improving the User Experience. U.S. Department of Health & Human Services. http://www.usability.gov/. Accessed 20 Nov 2014
11. Rusu, C., Roncagliolo, S., Rusu, V., Collazos C.: A methodology to establish usability heuristics. In: The Fourth International Conference on Advances in Computer-Human Interactions (ACHI 2011), pp. 59–62. IARIA (2011)
12. Wiberg, C., Jegers, K., Desurvire, H.: How applicable is your evaluation methods – really? In: The Second International Conference on Advances in Computer-Human Interactions (ACHI 2009), pp. 324–328. IEEE Computer Society Press (2009)
13. Kuniavsky, M.: Observing the User Experience: A Practitioner's Guide to User Research. Morgan Kaufmann, San Francisco (2003)
14. UXPA.org: User Experience Professionals Association. http://uxpa.org/. Accessed 20 Nov 2014
15. Allaboutux.org: All About UX. http://www.allaboutux.org/. Accessed 20 Nov 2014
16. Mitchell, P.: A Step-by-Step Guide to Usability Testing. iUniverse, New York (2007)
17. Dumas, J., Fox, J.: Usability testing: current practice and future directions. In: Sears, A., Jacko, J. (eds.) The Human – Computer Interaction Handbook: Fundamentals. Evolving Technologies and Emerging Applications, pp. 1129–1149. Taylor & Francis, New York (2008)
18. Cockton, G., Woolrych, A., Lavery, D.: Inspection – based evaluations. In: Sears, A., Jacko, J. (eds.) The Human – Computer Interaction Handbook: Fundamentals, Evolving Technologies and Emerging Applications, pp. 1171–1189. Taylor & Francis, New York (2008)
19. Nielsen, J., Mack, R.L.: Usability Inspection Methods. Wiley, New York (1994)
20. Quiñones, D., Rusu, C., Roncagliolo, S.: Redefining usability heuristics for transactional web applications. In: 11th International Conference on Information Technology: New Generations (ITNG 2014), pp. 260–265. IEEE Computer Society Press (2014)

21. Inostroza, R., Rusu, C., Roncagliolo, S., Rusu, V.: Usability heuristics for touchscreen-based mobile devices: update. In: First Chilean Conference on Human - Computer Interaction (ChileCHI 2013), pp. 24–29. ACM International Conference Proceeding Series (2013)
22. Roncagliolo, S., Rusu, V., Rusu, C., Tapia, G., Hayvar, D., Gorgan, D.: Grid computing usability heuristics in practice. In: 8th International Conference on Information Technology: New Generations (ITNG 2011), pp. 145–150. IEEE Computer Society Press (2011)
23. Solano, A., Rusu, C., Collazos, C., Arciniegas, J.: Evaluating interactive digital television applications through usability heuristics. Ingeniare 21(1), 16–29 (2013)
24. Rusu, C., Muñoz, R., Roncagliolo, S., Rudloff, S., Rusu, V., Figueroa, A.: Usability heuristics for virtual worlds. In: The Third International Conference on Advances in Future Internet (AFIN 2011), pp. 16–19. IARIA (2011)
25. Diaz, J., Rusu, C., Pow-Sang, J., Roncagliolo, S.: A cultural – oriented usability heuristics proposal. In: First Chilean Conference on Human - Computer Interaction (ChileCHI 2013), pp. 82–87. ACM International Conference Proceeding Series (2013)
26. Jimenez, C., Rusu, C., Roncagliolo, S., Inostroza, R., Rusu, V.: Evaluating a methodology to establish usability heuristics. In: 31st International Conference of the Chilean Computer Science Society (SCCC 2012), pp. 51–59. IEEE Computer Society Press (2013)
27. Rusu, C., Rusu, V., Roncagliolo, S.: Usability practice: the appealing way to HCI. In: The First International Conference on Advances in Computer-Human Interactions (ACHI 2008), pp. 265–270. IEEE Computer Society Press (2008)
28. ACM SIGCHI: ACM SIGCHI Curricula for Human-Computer Interaction. http://old.sigchi.org/cdg/cdg2.html#2_1. Accessed 12 Nov 2014
29. Rusu, C., Rusu, V.: Teaching HCI: a challenging intercultural, interdisciplinary, cross-field experience. In: Ishida, T., Fussell, S.R., Vossen, P.T.J.M. (eds.) IWIC 2007. LNCS, vol. 4568, pp. 344–354. Springer, Heidelberg (2007)
30. Jimenez, C., Rusu, C., Rusu, V., Roncagliolo, S., Inostroza, R.: Formal specification of usability heuristics: how convenient it is? In: 2nd International Workshop on Evidential Assessment of Software Technologies (EAST 2012), pp. 55–60. ACM International Conference Proceeding Series, (2012)
31. Paz, F., Villanueva, D., Rusu, C., Roncagliolo, S., Pow-Sang, J.A.: Experimental evaluation of usability heuristics. In: 10th International Conference on Information Technology: New Generations (ITNG 2013), pp. 119–126. IEEE Computer Society Press (2013)

Lessons Learned in Usability Consulting

Tim Schneidermeier[✉]

Media Informatics Group, University of Regensburg, Regensburg, Germany
tim.schneidermeier@ur.de

Abstract. User-centered design in varying domains and contexts defines the daily routine of (external) usability consultants. Understanding users, their tasks and goals is essential for a successful project. This can be quite challenging, especially in more complex domains. Documenting design decisions and solutions provides a sound basis for efficient and sustainable further development by reusing design knowledge and artifacts.

Keywords: Usability consulting · Return on investment · Sustainability · Design reuse · Documentation

1   The Usability Consulting Profession

A consultant is a professional, usually specialized in a specific area, such as management, finance, science etc., who provides expert advice to clients ("Consultant" 2004). As a usability consultant you are mandated to cater for an overall good user experience (UX) of a product or service. Applying the user-centered design framework in varying fields and domains – including learning the ropes on a daily basis is business as usual. Knowing your users, their tasks and the context of use is essential for effective results. The more complex the domain, the more effort has to be made to truly understand the context, processes and current problems. In order to ensure more sustainable solutions, documenting findings and design decisions is crucial. These results may guide subsequent extensions and enhancements of the product or service. Taking action to redesign an application or service for a better UX in many cases has to be justified considering the return on investment (ROI) by relating the input and the potential benefits of an investment.

This paper is composed as follows: In the first section benefits and the return of investment of usability engineering are described. In the following sections user-centered design activities are characterized and it is argued for an extended framework including the documentation of designed solutions. A description of lessons learned in usability consulting completes the paper.

© Springer International Publishing Switzerland 2015
A. Marcus (Ed.): DUXU 2015, Part I, LNCS 9186, pp. 247–255, 2015.
DOI: 10.1007/978-3-319-20886-2_24

2   The ROI of Usability

Taking a look at the reasons why software projects fail might provide valuable insights and links for optimization: The CHAOS Report[1] is a survey-based study analyzing influencing factors for success and failure of IT projects on a year-on-year basis. It is published and updated by The Standish Group[2]. The most important reasons why projects struggle or fail are incomplete requirements and the lack of user input and involvement (The Standish Group 1994). Yet almost 20 years later, user involvement is still rated under the top two project success factors (The Standish Group 2013). These results already illustrate the general benefits of usability engineering, user research and user involvement being one of the core activities in the user-centered design process.

Defining the ROI of usability engineering and user experience design activities has been subject to numerous studies and has been addressed in several publications and white papers (e.g. Graefe, Keeenan and Bowen 2003; Marcus 2005; Turner 2011; Weinschenk 2005). One of the most influential publication on this topic still is *Cost-Justifying Usability* by Randolph G. Bias and Deborah J. Mayhew (1994)[3]. Even though the accurate calculation of the ROI by means of a precise amount of money is a complex issue (Rosenberg 2004; Weinschenk 2005), there is broad consensus that there are numerous benefits of applying a user-centered design process: "The benefits of usable technology include reduced training costs, limited user risk, and enhanced performance (...). American industry and government will become even more productive if they take advantage of usability engineering techniques." (Gore 1998)

The following list covers some more benefits (Bias and Mayhew 1994, p. 17f.; Weinschenk 2005, p. 3–10):

- Increased ease of use and productivity.
- Increased efficiency and satisfaction.
- Increased sales and conversion rates (e.g. e-commerce).
- Decreased user errors and less frustration.
- Decreased development and maintenance costs.
- Decreased training and support costs.

The Nielsen Norman group collected data from 72 case studies of website redesigns and compared their usability applying the same metrics before and after the redesign (Nielsen et al. 2008). Table 1 shows the average usability improvements after the redesign.

A systematic and iterative user-centered design process is the basis for profiting from the benefits listed above. ISO 9241-210 (2010) provides a basic framework and guidance on activities in the human-centered design process.

---

[1] The Chaos Report was first published in 1994; variants of the Chaos Report under varying names are updated every year ever since (The Standish Group 2015).

[2] http://www.standishgroup.com/.

[3] In 2005 an updated edition was published (Bias and Mayhew 2005).

Table 1. Average usability improvements after website redesign (Nielsen et al. 2008, p. 5).

Metric	Average Improvement Across Web Projects
Sales / conversion rate	87%
Traffic / visitor count	91%
User performance / productivity	112%
Use of specific (desired) features	174%

3   Human-Centered Design Process

The framework describes an iterative process to design and develop interactive products. It is based on comprehensive user involvement and feedback and accepts failure as part of the process (see Fig. 1). It is essentially structured in five activities:

1. Plan the human-centered design process.
2. Understand and specify the context of use.
3. Specify the user requirements.
4. Produce design solutions to meet user requirements.
5. Evaluate the designs against requirements.

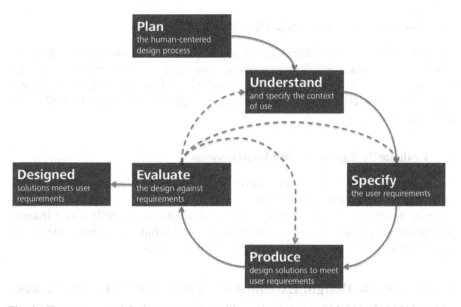

Fig. 1. Human-centered design process (own illustration based on ISO 9241-210 2010, p. 15)

3.1   Plan the Human-Centered Design Process

In the first activity, resources, roles as well as responsibilities are defined, suitable methods to be applied in the design process are preselected, user interface design guidelines are provided (e.g. for a specific operating system), (business) goals are defined and criteria to measure the success of the project (especially regarding the usability) are set (ISO 9241-210 2010, p. 13f.).

3.2   Understand and Specify the Context of Use

It is essential to identify, analyze and describe the user characteristics, tasks, physical and social environment, current problems, as well as user needs and goals (ISO 9241-210 2010, p. 16f.).

3.3   Specify the User Requirements

The goals and needs identified so far are analyzed and requirements are derived. The requirements are prioritized regarding different aspects, including relevance to the user, practicability and economic considerations. User requirements are the basis for the design and evaluation of the interactive system and are most crucial for all following activities (ISO 9241-210 2010, p. 17f.).

3.4   Produce Design Solutions to Meet User Requirements

Based on the context of use, the identified requirements, and in consideration of special domain characteristics and design guidelines suitable design solutions are developed (usually in terms of (interactive) prototypes). This includes information design and architecture, interaction design and the design of the user interface (ISO 9241-210 2010, pp. 18–21).

3.5   Evaluate the Design Against Requirements

User feedback is substantial for an iterative optimization of design solutions. The evaluation can be conducted applying user- or expert-based methods (e.g. heuristic walkthrough), in situ or long-term studies, formative or summative usability tests. Choosing appropriate methods depends on available resources, (non-functional) requirements, and other domain context factors (ISO 9241-210 2010, pp. 22–24).

4   Sustainable Design: Extended Human-Centered Design Process

When the designed solution successfully meets the user requirements, it also marks the end of the development life cycle described in ISO 9241-210. Catering for a more sustainable process, the framework needs to be extended by documenting the design decisions made during the process, the final designs as well as potential guidelines for

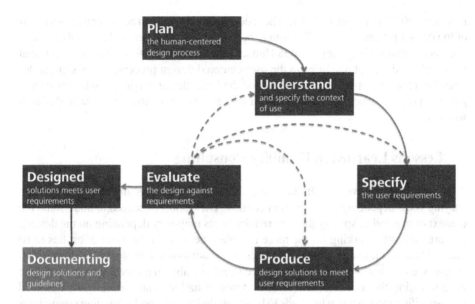

Fig. 2. Extended human-centered design process (own illustration based on ISO 9241-210 2010, p. 15).

further development (see Fig. 2). This is especially crucial if you are working as an external consultant.

"Sustainable development is development that meets the needs of the present without compromising the ability of future generations to meet their own needs." (World Commission On Environment and Development 1990, p. 41)

Sustainable design therefore cares about the responsible and efficient management of available resources (Shedroff 2009, p. 3). Different strategies can be applied to enhance sustainability in product design: Reduce, reuse, recycle, restore, rethink and redesign (Kramer 2012, p. 7f.; Shedroff 2009, p. xi). Documenting design solutions primarily supports reducing the amount of resources and materials needed in the development life cycle and the reuse of design knowledge and artifacts. Design reuse aims at assisting the designer in developing products with a maximum of user satisfaction and a minimum of resources, cost and effort (Sivaloganathan and Shahin 1999, p. 641).

Reusing design knowledge and artifacts requires a well-structured documentation adjusted to its purpose. This can be the reuse of artifacts in future projects for reoccurring problems (e.g. form design, checkout process) or to provide guidance on further development of the designed product or product family (e.g. style guide, corporate identity). This not only ensures consistency throughout the design, but also reduces time and cost as you can rely on the design decisions that already have been made.

There are plenty of different forms of design documentation varying in their applicability (e.g. general or product specific) and the level of detail (e.g. design patterns including a detailed description of the problem and the solution or more superficial design heuristics). The solutions proposed also vary concerning their level of formality from open document formats to formal XML-based description languages (Bolchini and

Randazzo 2005; Feiner et al. 2010). These design documents can be generated as a result of the design process (see Fig. 2) or may be available from other professionals, institutions or companies (e.g. Apple's iOS Human Interface Guidelines). The documents can be useful for different activities in the user-centered design process, e.g. design guidelines for a specific operating system define the basic design language, whereas design patterns provide structured solutions for more generic problems (e.g. how to design a wizard).

5   Lessons Learned in Usability Consulting

As a consultant you work with different clients, in different domains, trying to achieve varying goals depending on the project context. The resources needed to understand the context of use and to specify the user requirements may vary depending on the domain you are currently working in; the more complex the domain the more effort has to be made. Therefore it makes a huge difference if you are asked to evaluate a web shop that an average user without special knowledge should be able to use or if you are in charge of redesigning the user interface of a wind power station control unit that is designed for a specific target group who needs to have detailed domain understanding (sometimes years of training/experience). This is a recurring challenge usability consultants are facing, who naturally do not have long term experience or a specific training in this domain.

In a study conducted by Chilana, Wobbrock and Ko 21 experienced usability professionals (in-house experts, external consultants, managers) that frequently work in complex domains were interviewed concerning their experiences and challenges. They found that all of the interviewees irrespective of their personal experience rated the work in complex domains as challenging: Collaboration and the availability of domain experts was identified as a critical success factor. Hence the best results are achieved when both usability experts and domain experts are part of the design team (Chilana, Wobbrock and Ko 2010).

Although the resources and effort needed may vary regarding the domain the following findings and lessons learned based on my experience might be helpful (independent of the complexity of the domain):

- **The Understanding of the Domain is Depending on the Project Progress:** Based on my experience especially in more complex domains there is a typical confidence and learning curve varying depending on the project progress (see Fig. 3; Schneidermeier, Heckner and Fuchs 2014): At the beginning of the project you are excited about new challenges and design solutions to come (1). After the project honeymoon is over the complexity of the domain becomes clearer (2). First design drafts are sketched based on user requirements and knowledge gained from intense training on the domain (3). In many cases these design drafts fail first user tests and you realize that you only have a superficial understanding of the domain and that it will take much more effort to truly master it (4). Continued exchange with end users and domain experts finally leads to a design that meets the user requirements (5).

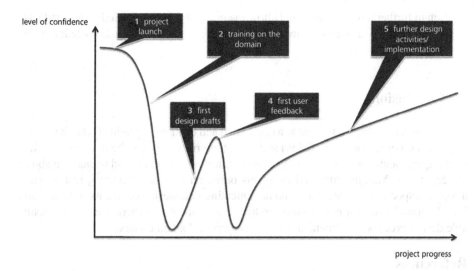

Fig. 3. Level of confidence according to the project progress

- **A General Understanding of the Domain is Required for Successful Requirements Engineering:** Lacking important previous knowledge may lead to a misinterpretation and faulty categorization (important, not important) of results gained e.g. from contextual inquiries or focus groups. Consulting additional resources such as specialist reading material or conducting pre-interviews may be necessary.

- **Clients Tend to Underestimate Time and Effort:** The complexity of the domain and the effort needed for the usability consultant to become acquainted with it often gets underestimated by clients, especially it they are domain experts themselves. For the client the domain is business as usual while the consultant may need to start from scratch.

- **Complex Domains Require More Time and Effort:** In many cases the full extent of complexity is revealed only during the project duration. Therefore it is essential to respond with the right methods and tools. Furthermore important domain knowledge needed to design user-friendly solutions may only be available implicitly and has to be acquired through interviews, feedback loops and user tests.

- **The Better Your Understanding of the Domain and the Context of Use, the Better Your Design Solutions:** A successful project is based on a regular exchange with target users and the availability of domain experts throughout the project. This may be even more important in complex domains.

- **Adapt Your Methods and Toolbox to Domain and Context Factors:** Different domains and contexts may need a customizable set of methods. Be prepared to think outside the box. Managing your resources well is crucial for a successful and smooth course of the project.

- **Document Your Design Solutions:** Whether you are working in-house or as an external consultant, documenting your work and the decisions made during the design process is essential for a more sustainable design. This can be personas, design patterns, prototypes, style guides etc. These documents provide a sound basis to build upon in further developments and allow the reuse of design knowledge and artifacts. Documenting your design knowledge additionally enables tacit knowledge to be made explicit.

6 Conclusion

Working as a usability consultant is a diversified and challenging field: Today you redesign a customer relationship (CRM) software, tomorrow you may be in charge of eliciting requirements for a mobile application for chimney sweepers and wandering above the city roofs. Making informed decisions based on user requirements, testing your designs, respecting user feedback and documenting your design decisions and solutions lays the foundations for easy-to-use products with good user experience and a sustainable design process – independently from project or domain context.

References

Bias, R.G., Mayhew, D.J.: Cost-Justifying Usability. Academic Press, Boston (1994)

Bias, R.G., Mayhew, D.J.: Cost-Justifying Usability. An Update for the Internet Age, Second Edition, 2nd edn. Morgan Kaufmann, San Francisco (2005)

Bolchini, D., Randazzo, G.: Capturing visions and goals to inform communication design. In: Proceedings of the 23rd Annual International Conference on Design of Communication: Documenting & Designing for Pervasive Information (SIGDOC 2005), pp. 131–137. ACM, New York (2005). doi:10.1145/1085313.1085344

Chilana, P.K., Wobbrock, J.O., Ko, A.J.: Understanding usability practices in complex domains. In: Proceedings of the 28th International Conference on Human Factors in Computing Systems (CHI 2010), p. 2337. ACM Press, New York (2010). doi:10.1145/1753326.1753678

Consultant (n.d.): In Wikipedia. http://en.wikipedia.org/wiki/Consultant. Accessed 15 Feb 2015

Feiner, J. Andrews, K., Krajnc, E.: UsabML: formalising the exchange of usability findings. In: Proceedings of the 2nd ACM SIGCHI Symposium on Engineering Interactive Computing Systems (EICS 2010), pp. 297–302. ACM Press, New York (2010). doi:10.1145/1822018.1822065

Gore, Al: A letter from Vice President Al Gore. Common Ground 8(3), 1 (1998)

Graefe, T.M., Keenan, S.L., Bowen, K.C.: Meeting the challenge of measuring return on investment for user centered development. In: CHI 2003 Extended Abstracts on Human Factors in Computing Systems (CHI 2003), p. 860. ACM Press, New York (2003). doi:10.1145/765891.766036

ISO 9241–210: Ergonomics of human-system interaction – Part 210: Human-centred design for interactive systems. Beuth, Berlin (2010)

Kramer, K.-L.: User Experience in the Age of Sustainability: A Practitioner's Blueprint. Morgan Kaufmann, San Francisco (2012)

Marcus, A.: User interface design's return on investment: examples and statistics. In: Bias, R.G., Mayhew, D.J. (eds.) Cost-Justifying Usability, 2nd edn, pp. 17–39. Morgan Kaufmann, San Francisco (2005)

Nielsen, J., Berger, J.M., Gilutz, S., Whitenton, K.: Return on Investment (ROI) for Usability, 4th edn. Nielsen Norman Group, Fremont (2008)

Rosenberg, D.: The myths of usability ROI. Interactions **11**(5), 22 (2004). doi:10.1145/1015530.1015541

Schneidermeier, T., Fuchs, M., Heckner, M.: Über Höhen und Tiefen des Usability-Consulting in komplexen Domänen. In: Usability Professionals 2014 (2014)

Shedroff, N.: Design is the Problem: The Future of Design Must be Sustainable, p. 352. Rosenfeld Media, New York (2009)

Sivaloganathan, S., Shahin, T.M.M.: Design reuse: an overview. Proc. Inst. Mech. Eng. Part B: J. Eng. Manuf. **213**(7), 641–654 (1999). doi:10.1243/0954405991517092

Turner, C.W.: A strategic approach to metrics for user experience designers. J. Usability Stud. **6**(2), 52–59 (2011)

The Standish Group: CHAOS (1994). http://www.standishgroup.com/sample_research_files/chaos_report_1994.pdf. Accessed 19 Feb 2015

The Standish Group: CHAOS Manifesto 2013. Think Big, Act Small (2013). http://www.versionone.com/assets/img/files/CHAOSManifesto2013.pdf. Accessed 19 Feb 2015

The Standish Group: CHAOS Report 2014 (2015). http://blog.standishgroup.com/post/18. Accessed 19 Feb 2015

Weinschenk, S.: Usability: A Business Case (white paper). Human Factors International, Fairfield, IA (2005)

World Commission on Environment and Development: Our Common Future. Oxford University Press, Oxford (1990)

INUIT: The Interface Usability Instrument

Maximilian Speicher[1]([✉]), Andreas Both[2], and Martin Gaedke[1]

[1] Technische Universität Chemnitz, 09111 Chemnitz, Germany
maximilian.speicher@s2013.tu-chemnitz.de,
martin.gaedke@informatik.tu-chemnitz.de
[2] Research and development, Unister GmbH, 04109 Leipzig, Germany
andreas.both@unister.de

Abstract. Explicit user testing tends to be costly and time-consuming from a company's point of view. Therefore, it would be desirable to infer a quantitative usability score directly from implicit feedback, i.e., the interactions of users with a web interface. As a basis for this, we require an adequate usability instrument whose items form a usability score and can be meaningfully correlated with such interactions. Thus, we present INUIT, the first instrument consisting of only seven items that have the right level of abstraction to directly reflect user behavior on the client. It has been designed in a two-step process involving usability guideline reviews and expert interviews. A confirmatory factor analysis shows that our model reasonably well reflects real-world perceptions of usability.

Keywords: Instrument · Metrics · Questionnaire · Usability · Interfaces

1 Introduction

The usability of a website is a crucial factor for ensuring customer satisfaction and loyalty [23]. However, adequate usability testing is often neglected in today's e-commerce industry due to costliness and time consumption. Particularly user testing happens less frequently because it is "heavily constrained by available time, money and human resources" [18]. Hence, stakeholders tend to partly sacrifice usability by requesting cheaper and more efficient methods of conversion maximization (e.g., in terms of clicks on advertisements), also potentially caused by the demand for a short time-to-market. To tackle this shortcoming we require a similarly *efficient* method that is more *effective* in measuring usability. A straightforward approach would be to make use of real users' interactions with a web interface to infer knowledge about its usability. Optimally, such knowledge would be present in terms of a *key performance indicator* (i.e., a usability score) for easier communication with stakeholders who are not usability experts.

To be able to realize such a framework (Fig. 1), it is necessary to build upon an adequate usability instrument for providing a quantitative measure that combines ratings of the contained items. A corresponding formula for such a measure

---

M. Speicher—The contents of this paper were developed while Mr. Speicher stayed at Unister GmbH as an industrial PhD student. An earlier version has been published as [24].

A. Marcus (Ed.): DUXU 2015, Part I, LNCS 9186, pp. 256–268, 2015.
DOI: 10.1007/978-3-319-20886-2_25

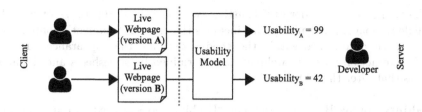

Fig. 1. A model providing a quantitative metric of usability [24].

could be $usability = -(confusion + distraction)$. As usability is a latent variable, we need to define factors thereof that can be meaningfully inferred from interactions, e.g., *faster and more unstructured cursor movements indicate user confusion* ⇒ confusion = 1. Numerous instruments for determining usability have been developed (e.g., [5,8,10,22]), but none has been specifically designed for providing a key performance indicator for usability that can be directly inferred from user interactions.

Thus, we propose INUIT—a new usability instrument for web interfaces consisting of *only seven items* that have the *right level of abstraction* to directly reflect users' client-side interactions. The items have been determined in a two-step process. First, we have reviewed more than 250 usability rules from which we created a structure of usability based on ISO 9241-11 [14]. Second, we conducted semi-structured expert interviews with nine experts working in the e-commerce industry. Based on a user study with 81 participants, results of a confirmatory factor analysis show that INUIT's underlying model is a good approximation of real-world perceptions of usability.

In the following, we give an overview of important background concepts and related work (Sect. 2). After that, we explain the design of our new usability instrument (Sect. 3). Section 4 presents the set-up and results of the evaluation of INUIT. In Sect. 5 we discuss results and limitations before giving concluding remarks.

2   Background and Related Work

Web Interfaces. Low-level user interactions on the *client-side* can be tracked on a per-web*page* basis, i.e., for an HTML document delivered by a server and displayed in a web browser. Such interactions are commonly collected using Ajax technology and are valid only for the given document. Due to the stateless nature of HTTP[1], they are difficult to track and put into context across multiple webpages. Contrary, user interactions in the context of a whole web*site* (i.e., a set of interconnected, related webpages) are of a higher-level nature, such as navigation paths between webpages. They are usually mined from *server-side* logs.

---

[1] ⟨http://www.w3.org/Protocols/⟩, retrieved June 11, 2014.

Thus, in the remainder of this article, we consider a WEB INTERFACE to be a single webpage. Particularly, this includes the HTML document's content and structure as determined within the <body> tag, and the appearance during a user's interaction with the webpage as determined by stylesheets and dynamic scripts that alter the DOM tree[2].

Usability. In [5], Brooke states that "Usability does not exist in any absolute sense; it can only be defined with reference to particular contexts". Thus, it is necessary that we clarify our understanding of usability in the context of our proposed approach. Orienting at ISO 25010 [13], the *internal usability* of a web application is measured in terms of static attributes (not connected to software execution); *external usability* relates to the behavior of the web application; and *usability in use* is relevant in case the web application involves real users under certain conditions. Therefore, given the fact that we intend to infer usability from real users' interactions, *usability in use* is the core concept we focus on. In accordance with this, [12] uses the notions of "do-goals" (e.g., booking a flight) and "be-goals" (e.g., being special) to distinguish between the pragmatic and hedonic dimensions of user experience, a concept that has a large intersection with usability. Particularly, he states that *"Pragmatic quality* refers to the product's perceived ability to support the achievement of 'do-goals' [and] calls for a focus on the product – its utility and usability" [12]. Since a user's interactions with an interface are a direct reflection of what they *do*, for our purpose the *pragmatic* dimension of usability is of particular interest.

Based on the above, in the remainder of this article USABILITY refers to the pragmatic [12] and in-use [13] dimensions of the definition given by ISO 9241-11 [14]. Internal/external usability [13] and the hedonic dimension ("the product's perceived ability to support the achievement of 'be-goals'" [12]) of usability in use are neglected.

Definition 1. USABILITY: *The extent to which a web interface can be used by real users to achieve do-goals with effectiveness, efficiency and satisfaction in a specified context of use (adjusted definition by [14]).*

Instruments for Determining Usability and Related Concepts. Reference [22] has investigated metrics for usability, design and performance of a website. His finding is that the success of a website is a first-order construct and particularly connected to measures such as download time, navigation, interactivity and responsiveness (e.g., feedback options). The data used for analysis was collected from 1997 thru 2000, which indicates that the methods for website evaluation might be out-of-date regarding the radical changes in website appearance and thus also in the perception of usability. In particular, measures such as the download time should be less of an issue nowadays (except for slow mobile connections).

---

[2] ⟨http://www.w3.org/DOM/⟩, retrieved June 11, 2014.

Reference [8] describe a usability instrument that is specifically aimed at websites of small businesses. They evaluated the instrument in the specific case of website navigation and found that navigation impacts ease of use and user return rates, among others. The used questionnaire (i.e., the instrument) features some factors of usability that we have identified for INUIT as well. However, it is rather elaborate and thus potentially not adequate for evaluation of online web interfaces by real users. Moreover, we do not want to focus on a specific type of website—such as small businesses—but instead provide a general instrument.

Reference [10] developed a website usability instrument based on the definition given by ISO 9241-11 [14]. They have chosen five dimensions of usability: effectiveness, efficiency, level of engagement, error tolerance, and ease of learning. Along with these comes a total of 17 items to assess the dimensions. A factor analysis showed no significant difference between their usability instrument and a set of test data. However, like the above approach [8], the instrument seems to be specifically focused on e-commerce websites. In particular, they found that, e.g., error tolerance is a significant indicator for the intention to perform a transaction and that efficacy predicts the intention of further visits.

AttrakDiff[3] measures the hedonic and pragmatic user experience [12] of an e-commerce product based on a dedicated instrument. *UEQ*[4] follows a similar approach based on an instrument containing 26 bipolar items. In contrast to INUIT, both of these are oriented towards measuring the *user experience* of a software product as a whole. More similar to our instrument is the *System Usability Scale* (SUS) [5], which measures the usability of arbitrary interfaces by posing ten questions based on a 5-point Likert scale. The answers are then summed up and normalized to a score between 0 and 100.

There are also numerous instruments in the form of usability checklists, which can be used in terms of spreadsheets that automatically calculate usability scores (e.g., [11,27]). However, such checklists usually contain huge amounts of items that are also very abstract in parts. They are therefore aimed at supporting inspections by experts (cf. [19]) rather than having them answered by users.

The ISO definition of usability [14] states that satisfaction is a major aspect of usability. Reference [1] present a revalidation of the well-studied End-User Computing Satisfaction Instrument (EUCS), which is an instrument for this particular aspect. While certain items of EUCS clearly intersect with those of usability instruments—e.g., in the dimension "Ease of Use"—it is clearly pointed out that EUCS specifically measures satisfaction rather than usability.

Another aspect that is closely related to usability but not mentioned in the ISO definition is the aesthetic appearance of a web interface. Reference [15] present an instrument for the concept and state that aesthetics cannot be neglected in the context of effective interaction design. The instrument is clearly focused on very subjective aspects of design and layout and shows less intersections with existing usability instruments than EUCS.

---

[3] ⟨http://attrakdiff.de/⟩, retrieved July 29, 2014.

[4] ⟨http://www.ueq-online.org/⟩, retrieved July 29, 2014.

3 INUIT: The *In*terface *U*sability *I*nstrumen*t*

The aim of INUIT is to provide a usability instrument that is adequate for the novel concept of Usability-based Split Testing [25]. Particularly, it must be possible to meaningfully infer ratings of its contained items from client-side user interactions (e.g., unstructured cursor movements $\Rightarrow$ confusion $= 1$). Also, the instrument must be consistent with Definition 1 above. All of this poses the following requirements:

(R1). The instrument's number of items is kept to a minimum, so that real users asked for explicit usability judgments through a corresponding questionnaire are not deterred. This helps with collecting high-quality training data.

(R2). The contained items have the right level of abstraction, so that they can be meaningfully mapped to client-side user interactions. For example, "ease of use" is a higher-level concept that can be split into several sub-concepts while "all links should have blue color" is clearly too specific. Contrary, an item like "user confusion" can be mapped to interactions such as unstructured cursor movements.

(R3). The contained items can be applied to a web interface as defined earlier.

Regarding these requirements, existing instruments lack meeting one or more thereof. Instruments such as those described by [5, 8, 10, 22] feature items with a wrong level of abstraction (R2) or that cannot be applied to standalone web interfaces (R3). Similar problems arise with questionnaires like *AttrakDiff* and *UEQ* (R2, R3). Finally, usability checklists (e.g., [11, 27]) usually contain huge amounts of items and therefore violate R1.

To meet the above requirements, the items contained in INUIT have been determined in a two-step process. First, we have carried out a review of popular and well-known usability guidelines that contained over 250 rules for good usability in the form of heuristics and checklists. After we eliminated all rules not consistent with the requirements above, a set of underlying factors of usability has been extracted. That is, we grouped together rules that were different expressions of the same (higher-level) factor. From these underlying factors, we have derived a structure of usability based on ISO 9241-11 [14]. Second, we asked experts for driving factors of web interface usability from their point of view and revised our usability structure accordingly.

3.1 Guideline Reviews

As the first step of determining the items of INUIT, we have reviewed a set of six well-known resources concerned with usability [7, 9, 17, 20, 26, 27]. They were chosen based on the commonly accepted expertise of their authors and contain guidelines by *A List Apart*[5] and Bruce Tognazzini (author of the first *Apple Human Interface Guidelines*), among others. The investigated heuristics and

---

[5] ⟨http://alistapart.com/⟩, retrieved June 11, 2014.

Table 1. Set of items derived from usability guideline reviews

Usability factor	# related rules
Aesthetic appearance	8
Amount of distraction	6
Information density	6
Informativeness	6
Reachability of desired content[a]	4
Readability	5
Understandability	6

[a] With respect to Fitt's Law, i.e., "The time to acquire a target is a function of the distance to and size of the target" [26].

checklists contained a total of over 250 rules for good usability. In accordance with requirements R2 and R3 above, we eliminated all rules that:

- were too abstract, such as "Flexibility and efficiency of use" [20];
- were too specific, such as "Blue Is The Best Color For Links" [7];
- would not make sense when applied to a web interface in terms of a single webpage, e.g., "Because many of our browser-based products exist in a stateless environment, we have the responsibility to track state as needed" [26].

The elimination process left a total of 32 remaining rules, from which we extracted the driving factors of usability. Starting from ISO 9241-11 [14] and Definition 1, one can roughly state that the concept of *usability* features the three dimensions effectiveness, efficiency and satisfaction. Our goal was to find those factors that are one level of abstraction below these main dimensions and manifest themselves in multiple more specific usability rules. Thus, we investigated which of the remaining rules were different expressions of the same underlying principle and extracted the intended factors from these. To give just one example, "The site avoids advertisements, especially pop-ups" [27] and "Attention-attracting features [...] are used sparingly and only where relevant" [27] are expressions of the same underlying principle *distraction*, which is a driving factor of web interface usability. Moreover, distraction is to a high degree disjoint from other factors of usability at the same level of abstraction, e.g., it is different from the factor *confusion*. To complete the given example, distraction can be situated as follows regarding its relative level of abstraction (higher level of abstraction to the right): presence of advertisements → distraction → efficiency → usability.

From the remaining rules, we extracted the underlying factors of usability as shown in Table 1 (more than one related factor per rule was possible). Originally, the factor "reachability" was named "accessibility". To prevent confusion with what is commonly understood by accessibility[6], the factor was renamed lateron. What we understand by "reachability" is how difficult it is for the user to

---

[6] ⟨http://www.w3.org/TR/WCAG20/⟩, retrieved June 12, 2014.

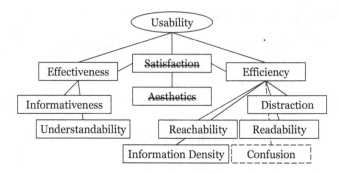

Fig. 2. Structure of usability derived from the guideline reviews. Struck through factors were removed, factors in dashed boxes were added after the expert interviews.

find their desired content within a web interface w.r.t. the temporal and spatial distance from the initial viewport.

Using the seven factors from Table 1, we could describe all of the relevant usability rules extracted from the reviewed guidelines. Subsequently, based on the definition given by ISO 9241-11 [14] and own experience with usability evaluations, we constructed a structure of usability as shown in Fig. 2.

3.2   Expert Interviews

As the second step of determining the items of INUIT, we conducted semi-structured interviews with nine experts working in the e-commerce industry. The experts were particularly concerned with front-end design and/or usability testing. First, we presented them with the definition of usability given by ISO 9241-11 [14] (Fig. 3, bottom left). Based on this, we asked them to name—from their point of view—driving factors of web interface usability with the intended level of abstraction from requirement R2 in mind. That is, showing positive and negative examples on the web, they should indicate factors that potentially directly affect patterns of user interaction. All statements were recorded accordingly (Fig. 3, bottom right).

Second, we presented the experts with a pen and a sheet of paper showing the above structure of usability (Fig. 2) and asked them to modify it in such a way that it reflected their perception of usability (Fig. 3, top middle).

After the interview, the experts were asked to answer additional demographic questions (Fig. 3, top right). On average, they stated that they are *knowledgeable* (m = 3) in front-end design, interaction design and usability/UX (4-point scale, 1 = *no knowledge*, 4 = *expert*). Moreover, they indicated *passing knowledge* (m = 2) in web engineering. Two experts said they have a research background, three indicated a practitioner background and four stated that they cannot exactly tell or have both. The average age of the interviewees was 30.44 years (σ = 2.96; 2 female).

Based on the interview transcripts, we mapped the usability factors identified by the experts to the seven factors shown in Table 1. The experts mentioned all of

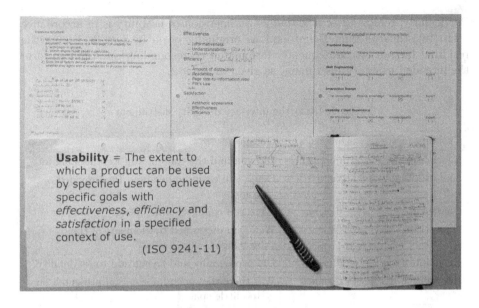

Fig. 3. Set-up of the expert interviews.

these factors multiple times, but a total of 38 statements remained that did not fit into the existing set. Rather, all of these remaining statements were expressions of an additional underlying concept *mental overload* or *user confusion*. During the second part of the interview, the experts made the following general statements:

- Aesthetic appearance goes hand in hand with both effectiveness and efficiency. Thus, it cannot be considered separate from these. Rather, the item "aesthetics" should be a sub-factor of both effectiveness and efficiency.
- An additional factor "ease of use" / "mental overload" / "user confusion" should be added as a sub-factor of efficiency since this concept is not fully reflected by the existing items.
- "Fun" should be added as a sub-factor of effectiveness or a separate higher-level factor "emotional attachment".

Apart from this, the experts generally agreed with the structure of usability that was given as a starting point (Fig. 2).

3.3   Items of INUIT

Based on the findings from the interviews and careful review of existing research [1, 15], we revised the structure of usability given in Fig. 2. That is, we added *user confusion* as a sub-factor of efficiency. Also, following requirement R2, we cleaned up the construct by not considering any potential factors that are higher-level latent variables themselves (i.e., satisfaction, aesthetics, emotional attachment, fun) and cannot be directly mapped to user interactions in a meaningful way.

Particularly, removing *satisfaction* as a dimension of usability is in accordance with [16], thus altering Definition 1 as originally given in Sect. 2. Taking the resulting factors, we subsequently formulated corresponding questions to form the intended usability instrument as given in Table 2.

Table 2. INUIT the interface usability instrument

Usability factor	Dimension	Question
Informativeness	Effectiveness	Did you find the content you were looking for?
Understandability	Effectiveness	Could you easily understand the provided content?
Confusion	Efficiency	Were you confused while using the webpage?
Distraction	Efficiency	Were you distracted by elements of the webpage?
Readability	Efficiency	Did typography and layout add to readability?
Information density	Efficiency	Was there too much information presented on too little space?
Reachability	Efficiency	Was your desired content easily and quickly reachable (concerning time and distance)?

The overall usability metric of INUIT can now be formed either by directly summing up all items or by equally weighting the dimensions *effectiveness* and *efficiency*.

4   Evaluation

To evaluate the new usability instrument, we have conducted a confirmatory factor analysis [2,6] with a model in which all of the seven items directly load on the latent variable *usability*.

Method. The data for evaluation were obtained in a user study with 81 participants recruited via Twitter, Facebook and company-internal mailing lists. Each participant was randomly presented with one of four online news articles about the Higgs boson [3] (CERN, CNN, Yahoo! News, Scientific American) and asked to find a particular piece of information within the content of the web interface[7]. Two of the articles did not contain the desired information (Yahoo! News, Scientific American). Having found the piece of information or being absolutely sure the article does not contain it, the participant had to indicate they finished the task. Subsequently, they were presented with a questionnaire containing the items from Table 2 and some demographic questions. As a first simple approach,

---

[7] We intended to choose a topic an average user would most probably not be familiar with to ensure equality among the participants.

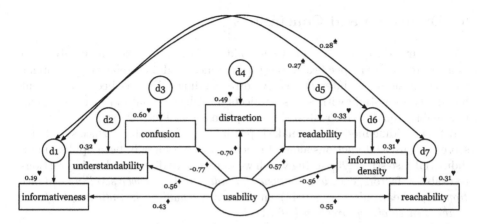

Fig. 4. Model with standardized estimates (correlations♣, squared multiple correlations♥, regression weights♦)

the INUIT questions could only be answered with "yes" or "no" (i.e., the overall usability score has a value between 0 and 7) rather than providing a Likert scale or similar. We believe this is reasonable since it reduces the user's perceived amount of work, which might increase the willingness to give answers in a real-world setting. It was possible to take part a maximum of four times in the study, being presented a different article each time.

To make the evaluated model more realistic, we introduced covariances between the residual errors of informativeness and information density as well as between the residual errors of informativeness and reachability. This is a valid approach [2,6] and in this case theoretically grounded since users who cannot find their desired content due to a high information density or bad reachability will probably (incorrectly) indicate a bad informativeness and vice versa.

Results. Of the 81 non-unique study participants, 66 were male (15 female) at an average age of 28.43 ($\sigma = 2.37$). Only two of them indicated that they were familiar with the news website the presented article was taken from.

Using IBM SPSS Amos 20 [2], we performed the confirmatory factor analysis as described above. Our results (Fig. 4) suggest that the model used is a reasonably good fit to the data set, with $\chi^2 = 15.817$ (df $= 12$, p $= 0.2$), a comparative fit index (CFI) of 0.971 and a root mean square error of approximation (RMSEA)[8] of 0.063.

Demo. For the complete set-up of the study and reproducing the confirmatory factor analysis, please visit ⟨http://vsr.informatik.tu-chemnitz.de/demo/inuit⟩.

---

[8] According to [2], an RMSEA value of 0.08 or less is "a reasonable error of approximation". For detailed descriptions of the measures of fit and their shortcomings, the interested reader may refer to [2].

5 Discussion and Conclusions

We have introduced INUIT—a novel usability instrument consisting of only seven items that has been specifically designed for meaningful correlation of its items with client-side user interactions. A corresponding CFA has been carried out based on a user study with 81 test subjects. It indicates that our instrument can reasonably well describe real-world perceptions of usability. As such, it paves the way for providing models that make it possible to infer a web interface's usability score from user interactions alone. In fact, INUIT has already been applied in an industrial case study [25] during which we were able to directly relate interactions to usability factors, e.g., *less confusion is indicated by a lower scrolling distance from top* (Pearson's $r = -0.44$) and *better reachability is indicated by fewer changes in scrolling direction* (-0.31).

Yet, we are aware of the fact that INUIT has several limitations. First, complex concepts like satisfaction and aesthetics have been removed from our set of items to keep the instrument simple according to the posed requirements. Particularly, INUIT can only measure the specific type of usability described in Sect. 2, which is a rather pragmatic interpretation of the concept leaving out potential hedonic qualities (cf. [12]). Second, usability itself is a difficult-to-grasp concept that cannot be forced into a structure consisting of yes/no questions in its entirety. Therefore, the mapping between our model of usability and the real world should be investigated with additional scales comprising more than two points (e.g., a Likert scale). Third, for the CFA performed we have chosen a set-up in which all factors directly load on the latent variable usability. Yet, it would be desirable to also explore set-ups in which, e.g., the factors load on the two dimensions *effectiveness* and *efficiency*, which then again load on the latent variable with equal weight. This could unveil models that even better describe real-world perceptions of usability than the one described above.

In accordance with the above, future work includes the investigation of INUIT based on different scales as well as CFAs with different set-ups. In fact, the instrument has already been applied in a separate user study [25] based on a three-point scale. The gathered data will be prepared to further investigate INUIT as intended and to confirm the good results of our CFA described in Sect. 4.

Acknowledgements. We thank our interviewees and all participants of the Unister Friday PhD Symposia. This work has been supported by the ESF and the Free State of Saxony.

References

1. Abdinnour-Helm, S.F., Chaparro, B.S., Farmer, S.M.: Using the End-User Computing Satisfaction (EUCS) Instrument to Measure Satisfaction with a Web Site. Decision Sci 36(2) (2005)
2. Arbuckle, J.L.: IBM® SPSS® Amos™ 20 User's Guide. IBM Corporation, Armonk, NY (2011)

3. ATLAS Collaboration: Observation of a new particle in the search for the Standard Model Higgs boson with the ATLAS detector at the LHC. Phys Lett B 716(1) (2012)
4. Atterer, R., Wnuk, M., Schmidt, A.: Knowing the User's Every Move - User Activity Tracking for Website Usability Evaluation and Implicit Interaction. In: Proc. WWW. (2006)
5. Brooke, J.: SUS: A "quick and dirty" usability scale. In: Jordan, P.W., Thomas, B., Weerdmeester, B.A., McClelland, A.L. (eds.) Usability Evaluation in Industry. Taylor and Francis (1996)
6. Byrne, B.M.: Structural Equation Modeling With AMOS: Basic Concepts, Applications, and Programming. CRC Press (2009)
7. Fadeyev, D.: 10 Useful Usability Findings and Guidelines, riptsize http://www.smashingmagazine.com/2009/09/24/10-useful-usability-findings-and-guidelines/
8. Fisher, J., Bentley, J., Turner, R., Craig, A.: A usability instrument for evaluating websites - navigation elements. In: Proc. OZCHI. (2004)
9. Goldstein, D.: Beyond Usability Testing, http://alistapart.com/article/beyond-usability-testing
10. Green, D., Pearson, J.M.: Development of a Website Usability Instrument based on ISO 9241–11. JCIS 47(1) (2006)
11. Harms, I., Schweibenz, W., Strobel, J.: Usability Evaluation von Web-Angeboten mit dem Web Usability Index [Usability evaluation of web applications using the Web Usability Index]. In: Proc. 24. DGI-Online-Tagung. (2002)
12. Hassenzahl, M.: User Experience (UX): Towards an experiential perspective on product quality. In: Proc. IHM. (2008)
13. ISO: ISO/IEC 25010:2011 Systems and software engineering - Systems and software Quality Requirements and Evaluation (SQuaRE) - System and software quality models. (2011)
14. ISO: ISO 9241–11:1998 Ergonomic requirements for office work with visual display terminals (VDTs) - Part 11: Guidance on usability. (1998)
15. Lavie, T., Tractinsky, N.: Assessing dimensions of perceived visual aesthetics of web sites. Int J Hum-Comput St 60(3) (2004)
16. Lew, P., Olsina, L., Zhang, L.: Quality, Quality in Use, Actual Usability and User Experience as Key Drivers for Web Application Evaluation. In: Benatallah, B., Casati, F., Kappel, G., Rossi, G. (eds.) ICWE 2010. LNCS, vol. 6189, pp. 218–232. Springer, Heidelberg (2010)
17. Mandel, T.: The Elements of User Interface Design. John Wiley & Sons, Hoboken, NJ (1997)
18. Nebeling, M., Speicher, M., Norrie, M.C.: CrowdStudy: General Toolkit for Crowdsourced Evaluation of Web Interfaces. In: Proc. EICS. (2013)
19. Nielsen, J., Molich, R.: Heuristic Evaluation of User Interfaces. In: Proc. CHI. (1990)
20. Nielsen, J.: 10 Usability Heuristics for User Interface Design, http://www.nngroup.com/articles/ten-usability-heuristics/
21. Nielsen, J.: Putting A/B Testing in Its Place, http://www.nngroup.com/articles/putting-ab-testing-in-its-place/
22. Palmer, J.W.: Website Usability, Design, and Performance Metrics. Inform Syst Res 13(2) (2002)
23. Sauro, J.: Does Better Usability Increase Customer Loyalty? http://www.measuringusability.com/usability-loyalty.php
24. Speicher, M., Both, A., Gaedke, M.: Towards Metric-based Usability Evaluation of Online Web Interfaces. In: Mensch & Computer Workshopband. (2013)

25. Speicher, M., Both, A., Gaedke, M.: Ensuring Web Interface Quality through Usability-Based Split Testing. In: Casteleyn, S., Rossi, G., Winckler, M. (eds.) ICWE 2014. LNCS, vol. 8541, pp. 93–110. Springer, Heidelberg (2014)
26. Tognazzini, B.: First Principles of Interaction Design, http://www.asktog.com/basics/firstPrinciples.html (accessed Mar 22, 2013)
27. Travis, D.: 247 web usability guidelines, http://www.userfocus.co.uk/resources/guidelines.html

Are We Testing Utility? Analysis of Usability Problem Types

Kimmo Tarkkanen[✉], Ville Harkke, and Pekka Reijonen

Information Systems Science, University of Turku, Turku, Finland
{kimmo.tarkkanen,ville.harkke}@utu.fi

Abstract. Usability problems and related redesign recommendations are the main outcome of usability tests although both are questioned in terms of impact in the design process. Problem classifications aim to provide better feedback for designers by improving usability problem identification, analysis and reporting. However, within the classifications, quite little is discussed about the types and the contents of usability problems as well as the types of required design efforts. We address this problem by scrutinizing the findings of three empirical usability tests conducted in software development projects. As a result, 173 problems were classified into 11 categories. Specific focus was placed on the distinction between the utility and usability types of problems, in order to define the correct development phase and method to fix the problem. The number of utility problems varied from 51 % to 74 %, which shows that early usability testing with a think-aloud protocol and an open task structure measure both utility and usability equally well.

Keywords: Usability problem · Utility problem · Problem classification · Usability testing

1 Introduction

Usability testing is a popular method to evaluate early designs during product development. Usability problems and related redesign recommendations are the main outcome of usability tests. Much of the critic towards usability testing pinpoints the role of usability problems both in method development and in method deployment in the design process [1, 2]. Particularly, problem identification, extraction, documentation, and value for design have been challenged. Both industry and research cases report that usability problems are rarely fixed and redesign proposals are not very influential in the short term development [3, 4]. Therefore, research efforts have been put to study usability practitioners' analysis practices [5], evaluation results downstream utility [6], use of usability method ingredients [7] as well as further developing problem report formats [8] and problem classifications [9]. In their CUP (Classification of Usability Problems) Scheme Hvannberg and Law identify several attributes of problems, the most important of which are, for the purpose of giving better feedback to designers and measuring the design influence of usability testing, 'failure qualifier' and 'expected phase' [10]. The former problem attribute helps designers to see the real problem whereas the latter makes them think about how to fix the problem [11]. However, quite little is known about these

© Springer International Publishing Switzerland 2015
A. Marcus (Ed.): DUXU 2015, Part I, LNCS 9186, pp. 269–280, 2015.
DOI: 10.1007/978-3-319-20886-2_26

attributes i.e. the types and the contents of usability problems as well as types of required design efforts. We address this problem by scrutinizing the findings of three industrial usability tests. Using the grounded theory methodology, we form a categorization of problem types with the data derived from three empirical usability tests that were performed with open test tasks. All the tested systems were of professional nature and were to be used as tools in the actual work of the users. The testing was a part of systems development effort and conducted on prototypes simulating new systems.

The categories of problem types were further analyzed to reveal what the problem types are measurements of. Specific focus was placed on the distinction between utility and usability issues, the former being issues that are related to the functions/offerings of the systems i.e. whether it is possible to do with the system what the user expects to get done, and the latter being a measure of how effective, efficient and pleasant it is to use the system in doing the needed things. In their study on usability testing results, Norgaard and Hornbaek [12] found that utility problems are much less frequently explored than usability problems. By separating usability and utility types of problems, we are able to help designers to address the correct development phase and method to fix the problem.

2   Utility vs Usability

Nielsen [13] made in his early definition of usability a clear distinction between usability and utility which are the constituents of usefulness, i.e. "whether the system can be used to achieve some desired goal" (p. 24) [13]. According to this definition, utility concerns the functionality of the system and usability is the question of how well users can use this functionality. In other words, usability is concerning with 'how the system is operated' and utility with 'what the system can do'. The distinction between utility and usability is not always that straight forward: The examples of the benefits of usability engineering given by Nielsen (see [13] p. 2) point more to utility than usability. Usability has no meaning without appropriate functionality and utility is not realized without good system usability [14]. The distinction can even be seen as superficial and a mere result of different disciplines focusing on different aspects. Already in 1988, Whiteside et al. stated that: "usability and functionality are linked inseparably in design and implementation" [15]. This was supported by Grudin [16]: "It is notoriously difficult to separate the function of interactive software from its form, to draw a line between software functionality and its human-computer interface." In a broader view, as in the ISO definition of usability [17], usability takes into account the context of use and usefulness aspects [18].

Despite the fact that it is difficult to distinguish between utility and usability in a real-world implementation, it is vital that both aspects of usefulness are addressed in evaluations. Furthermore, the two aspects lead to different types of problems and, ultimately, different types of possible solutions to them. As Mahmood et al. [19] describe: "It seems that end-users primarily adopt an application based on perceived benefits, and secondly on how easy or hard it is to achieve those benefits (...) no amount of use can compensate for lack of needed functionality." Johannesen and Hornbaek [20] again point out that utility is about building the right system.

For usability testing findings, this distinction would translate to that a usability problem is one that makes it difficult, cumbersome or unpleasant to achieve one's goal, but a utility problem makes it impossible. Utility problems may occur regardless of the users' knowledge of the system usage. The origin of impossibility is then in the fit between the system properties and the test users' way of work in the specific context. Although the definition of a usability problem by [8] includes such "an aspect of the system and/or a demand on the user" that makes it "impossible for the user to achieve their goals in typical usage situations", the interpretation is that usability can prevent task completion, but do not necessarily imply that the system is useless in the work tasks, if the usability problems are corrected.

3   Usability Problem Classifications

There are numerous of ways to classify usability problems. The roots of the problem classifications lay in the software defect tracking models at the beginning of the 90's [21]. For example, the Orthogonal Defect Classification (ODC) classified software defects in order to give useful feedback to developers and managers on the progress of the development project [22] and to steer development in reactive or proactive manner [23]. ODC concentrates on the problem causes on the system's side i.e. it describes what is wrong with the design and what should be fixed by the system designers. For that purpose, the defect qualifiers (the values for different types of defects) (1) missing, (2) incorrect (and later also irrelevant) were introduced [22].

One of the first holistic usability problem classifications, the User Action Framework (UAF) by [24] is "a classification scheme for usability problems based upon the type of problem in terms of its cause within the interaction cycle" ([24], p. 112). UAF organizes human activity into several phases finally locating the found problem into a node in a hierarchical tree, for example under "font size and contrast" ([24] p. 127), which is then considered as the root cause for the classified problem. Thus, UAF follows a classification taxonomy, namely the UPT (the usability problem taxonomy by [25]), which defines the problem in the artifact component or in the task component at very detailed level (28 categories). In design recommendations, UAF relies on the cumulative knowledge about the problem types collected into the database rather than on describing how something is a problem in the first place, like ODC does. In other words, if we want to know how the problem appears in the system or what kind of problem it is to the developer, the classifiers that describe that some named system element is "missing" or "irrelevant" would probably be in many cases more informative and practical for designers than a statement: "The usability problem is a high-level planning issue involving the user's model of the system in order to understand the overall concept" (see [24] p. 132). Nevertheless, the positive effects of such taxonomy for learning and steering purposes are undeniable within a longer time frame.

The most recently refined usability problem classification is the Classification of Usability Problems (CUP) scheme by [9, 10]. It has its basis in ODC. In the CUP terminology, the attribute explaining "how the user/expert experienced" a usability problem is called a failure qualifier (defect qualifier in ODC). In the most recent version of CUP [10] a usability problem is something that is being (1) missing, (2) incongruent, (3) irrelevant, (4) wrong, (5) better way or (6) overlooked (i.e. the possible values of the qualifier attribute). As these failure qualifiers were deemed useful by designers to understand problems [11], our following analysis aims first to classify usability problems by qualifiers arising from empirical data from prototype tests, and second to separate usability and utility types of problems in order to provide better feedback for designers.

4 Research Method

4.1 Data Collection

For this study, we collected and analyzed data from three different usability tests. The tests were conducted during 2012-2013 by the authors for the responsible for the design of prototypes. Our tests were the first usability tests with future users for each of the prototypes. The prototypes were designed for professionals in the health care domain and the test participants represented the current users and customers of the company's products. Two systems were tested as paper prototypes (cases 2 and 3) one involving over 170 and the other 38 printed screens on A4 sized papers. The prototype in case 1 was implemented on a tablet computer, which allowed more feasible and effortless navigation than the paper versions in other cases. All tests applied a think-aloud method and had at least two administrators present. In the case 1, also two of the designers followed the sessions. The number of participants in cases varied from four to six professionals. Video and audio were recorded in all test sessions.

Despite the differences in the purposes and use contexts of the prototypes, all the test tasks were designed in similar manner avoiding the too detailed presumptions of the work tasks of the users: High-level and open-ended tasks were given to users in each session (see [26]). For example, in case 1 the test task was (translated into English): "You have just arrived at your workplace and you begin to prepare your work shift. This [prototype name] is a new application that you can use during your shift. You have already logged in." The open task approach was supplemented with pre-defined lower level tasks, for example in situations where designers had some open design questions and users did not work on that question during the open task. Otherwise, the tests followed common problem identification strategies of think aloud testing. The origins of problems lay in users' verbal and non-verbal behavior observed as well as in the evaluators' interpretations of these actions, the combinations of similar problems and system-initiated malfunctions. The problems are thus based on, for example, users negative feelings and negative expressions about the aspects of the system and their conscious or unconscious lack of understanding of the system features and objectives. Problems based on non-verbal indications were related, for example to time (e.g. slowness, delay, number of tries), errors (wrong path, randomness, slips) and task completion (giving up, wrong result, impossibilities). The found problems were documented to the final report delivered to the responsible system designers in each case. The findings and reported usability problems in the cases are based on our participatory involvement in the design and evaluation of the usability of the system, which follows loosely the tradition of action research (see [27]).

4.2   Data Analysis

The individual evaluation results, the reported usability problems of the cases were approached with a grounded theory methodology [28] retrospectively for this study. The procedure started with one researcher who reviewed usability problems and gave each problem a code, either existing from previously reviewed problems or creating a new one. Codes were abstractions of real findings and newly invented during the research process. We were not following any pre-existing problem classifications or values of failure qualifiers, in order to keep the origins of the analysis purely in our empirical data. However, we wanted to increase our understanding about the underlying characteristics of the problems in terms of how something is a problem. Therefore, the coding was done in relation to the system and users' work. The fundamental question followed in the coding was "what is wrong with the system from the viewpoint of users' work". The question is relevant particularly in the early usability evaluations, because the assumption of lean user experience studies is that the initial designs will be wrong, and what is wrong, needs to be found as soon as possible [29].

As the categories are built and formulated on the basis of the question above, the problem categories represent design faults from the users' and their work point of view, and are thus values of the failure/defect qualifier attribute. For example, users' were reported as "confusing the meaning of the symbols of isolated and inert patients" as well as "misinterpreting the meaning of the numeric value related to laboratory results", which were then encoded under the same category of (the system feature is) "misinterpreted". The categories are exclusive i.e. the same problem was located in only one category. During the coding, a criterion for each category was iteratively refined. The related design decisions (e.g. misinterpreted features need to be explicated more clearly in the next version of the design) were not considered but were attached after the whole coding process. After coding the first case, another researcher performed the same analysis and coding with the existing scheme, yet including, excluding or altering categories, criteria or both. After both researchers had coded the case, the codes were combined and each problem and coding category was discussed to achieve mutual understanding about the codes and the placement of problems in categories. The same procedure was applied to each of the three cases. The final number and description of categories and problems in categories are discussed in the next chapter.

5   Results

In our analysis, 11 different problem types were identified (i.e. failure qualifiers in CUP terms) from the total of 173 reported problems analyzed. The problem types are described below in the numbered list (1–11). Our categorization is not intended to function as a tool for usability evaluations as such, but is merely a tool for dissecting the information we have collected. The purpose is to help us define the attributes of human-system interaction that are classifiable as problems in order to highlight areas of high relevance. This categorization does not require a content/functionality dichotomy but is applied to findings regarding both the functions of the tested system prototypes and the information form and content provided by the prototypes. The categories below contain the most obvious and typical design improvement suggestions and a distinction where in the typical development cycle of the user-centered design process the problem should be addressed (see [30] for phases: *understand* context of use, *specify* requirements, *produce* design solution and *evaluate* solution [not applied]).

1. Missing information or functionality:

- An element of the system that is necessary for the users' work is not available at all. The task/work cannot be performed with the presented system. Information or functionality has not been implemented, designed or planned to be designed, yet after the test identified as a user requirement and critical for performing the work.
- Design decisions: Add new feature.
- Development phase: Understand.

2. Misinterpreted information or functionality:

- The terminology or symbols/functions are not correctly understood by the user. She thinks about a different meaning for the symbol, feature, function or information from the designed purpose.
- Design decisions: Clarify feature.
- Development phase: Specify.

3. Positive information or functionality:

- The feature or information is found good, pleasant or effective.
- Design decisions: Implement feature.
- Development phase: Produce.

4. Inadequate information or functionality:

- A required element of the system is present but the implementation is not sufficient for the task at hand. Information or functionality has been designed and implemented into the system, but it lacks a proper fit with the work and practices of users preventing or significantly hindering the performance.
- Design decisions: Refine feature.
- Development phase: Specify.

5. Unexplored design issue:

- The function or information provided by the system could be used to increase the effectiveness of work but the exact changes in requirements are unclear. A need or possibility for positive change in the current work practice is identified, which can lead to new design issues. Not necessarily critical for work performance (at this stage), yet could drastically improve UX or result in other value for the users.
- Design decisions: Consider designing a feature (i.e. invent feature).
- Development phase: Understand.

6. Misplaced information or functionality:

- The needed element is available and adequate but in a cumbersome format or requires unnecessary effort to find and use. The feature or information is implemented somewhere or somehow, but not available at a required place and point in time. This covers misplacing or replicating information under certain features and representing information in unfamiliar terms and inappropriate forms.

- Design decisions: Duplicate feature (or delete and add).
- Development phase: Produce.

7. Unnecessary information or functionality:

- Users do not use, notice, behaviorally or verbally ignore a function or a piece of information that has been implemented.
- Design decisions: Remove feature.
- Development phase: Produce.

8. Technical deficiencies or carelessness in implementation:

- The design is implemented with errors/bugs. These are mostly due to the technical development phase of the system i.e. due to unpolished prototypes.
- Design decisions: Repair feature.
- Development phase: Produce.

9. Problematic change of work practice:

- Using the system as planned would change the work patterns in such a way that causes problems elsewhere. This may not realize only benefits but also major drawbacks. Users point to the problematic effects and uncertain benefits of a feature. A feature may cause a change in work that is experienced as problematic and questionable.
- Design decisions: Re-consider feature.
- Development phase: Understand.

10. Preferenced information or functionality:

- A way of doing something in the system is preferred to an alternative way.
- Design decisions: Implement feature and create a design pattern.
- Development phase: Produce.

11. Misaligned information or functionality:

- The feature or the information would require a change in the work practice to be useful. The way in which information or functionality is meant to be used differs from the existing or traditional use. This may or may not be intentional, depending on whether the change in work practice is one of the purposes of the new system implementation. Features that are implemented for instance based on legislation generate this type of problems.
- Design decisions: [Out of control of the system design process].
- Development phase: Understand.

The number of problems in each category is presented in Table 1. The categories Missing (no. 1), Inadequate (4), Unexplored (5), Unnecessary (7), Problematic (9) and Misaligned (11) are primarily utility problems i.e. these problems can render doing the job simply impossible (categories 1 and 4), be prone to cause unfavorable (9) and uncontrollable consequences (11), be useless (7), or worth to explore for more benefits (5). The rest of the categories (no. 2, 6, 8 and 10) are more dependent on the interface design and as such must be seen as usability problems. Problems in these categories may prevent task completion, but are not in contradiction to the goals and tasks of the users. For example, system features that are misinterpreted by the users can be redesigned without altering the purpose and goal of the feature.

Table 1. Numbers of usability and utility problems and problems in each category

Category name:	1. Missing	2. Misinterpreted	3. Positive	4. Inadequate	5. Unexplored	6. Misplaced	7. Unnecessary	8. Technical	9. Problematic	10. Preferenced	11. Misaligned	Total	Utility problems	Usability problems
Case 1	20	4	0	7	8	5	3	6	4	0	0	57	42	15
Case 2	20	9	8	7	7	6	3	1	2	2	0	65	39	18
Case 3	12	15	10	2	1	3	3	1	0	1	3	51	21	20
Total	52	28	18	16	16	14	9	8	6	3	3	173	102	53

Problems in the Positive category (no. 3) are not counted either as utility or usability problems. Findings in the positive category implicate that users have liked system features, which do not need to be altered in the design. Moreover, positive usability findings would form a classification of their own (like problems do), if analyzed in more detail, which was not the purpose of this analysis. Definitely, positive findings would cover both usability and utility issues. Thus, the total number of problems included is 155. Table 1 shows that 34 % (53) of the reported problems were usability observations, while 66 % (102) of reported problems concerned utility issues. Percentages of utility problems in individual cases vary from 51 % (Case 3) to 74 % (Case 1).

6 Discussion

Compared with other studies, our analysis required five more categories than the ODC-based CUP scheme [10] but 17 less than UPT-based [25] classifications. The categories of *Missing* and *Unnecessary* are commonly found in other classifications (e.g. over-looked, extraneous, irrelevant). *Misplaced* has similarities with incorrect and *Misinterpreted* with incongruent in the CUP. *Inadequate* has no direct correspondence in CUP. In our interpretation the *Unexplored, Misaligned* and *Problematic* categories are distinct, whereas the CUP scheme assigns only one category, better way, for these types of problems. However, we find this distinction valuable, because the subsequent design decisions are also very different.

If the results are compared with a specific evaluation method, which is designed to support substantial re-design and improvement of system utility [31], we find that our categories *Missing, Unnecessary* and *Inadequate* cover the possible combinations of the misfits presented by the CASSM method (see example 1 in [31]. From the study by Norgaard and Hornbaek [12] we can find at least implicit correlation in the categories *Missing, Unnecessary,* and *Positive* as well as in the work-based categories *Problematic, Misaligned* and *Unexplored.* Moreover, their exploration of utility issues is also in line with our usability and utility distinction of the categories above. For them, utility problems included the tasks the system did not support, the notions of unrealistic test tasks as well as users' actual and desired usage flows dissimilar to flows implemented into the system [12]. For example, a statement of user "I would use Phonebook [which is not implemented]" was then identified as a utility problem. However, Norgaard and Hornbaek [12] found that utility problems are much less frequently explored than usability problems in think aloud usability test sessions. Utility issues were discussed in 10 out of 14 think-aloud sessions analyzed, yet in 13 sessions, usability was favored over problems relating to the utility of the system. In contrast, our results show that utility problems can and indeed will be found in usability testing.

7 Conclusions

We set out to analyze the findings of our usability tests to identify different types of usability problems. In our data-based analysis, we were able to distinguish a set of categories, which differ from each other in terms of how they manifest themselves and how the problems can be addressed in further software development. The number of findings in each category and division of those into usability and utility issues indicate that formative usability tests conducted with open task approach measure equally well utility, "what the product should do", and usability, "how the product is operated". Despite our similar interpretation of distinction between utility and usability, our results are inconsistent with the findings by [12]. Currently, our best guess for the inconsistency is that open test tasks produce more utility related findings than predefined test tasks, which were presumably applied in their study. In addition, the early stages of the development in our tests may have brought out more utility problems.

The utility related problem types are very context-dependent and rely heavily on the procedure of testing with real users in actual usage context. This is positive in a sense that the fit of the proposed system to the actual usage patterns and needs can be verified within the tested context. However, the generalizability of the results to different usage situations and contexts is compromised. One interesting aspect of our findings was the relatively high amount of problems and categories that demand further exploration of the work patterns and contexts of the users (*Missing, Unexplored, Problematic* and *Misaligned* cover 45 % of the problems). Especially interesting is the type of finding where an attribute of the tested system is potentially beneficial but works only if the work patterns and organization of work are radically changed (*Misaligned*). This leads to situations where the design team might not have the power or even right to make decisions about whether the system or organization of work should be changed. This highlights the necessity of software developers' cooperation with the users on different levels in order to realize the full potential of new information systems design.

Our findings add to the recently started development of utility evaluation methods as well as theoretical discussion of researching utility distinct from usability (see [20]). In addition, problem classifications and their potential feedback for design are again being upgraded [10, 21, 32]. One of the benefits of this research for HCI practitioners lies in the clarification of which issues can be improved by redesigning the systems and which would be better addressed by changing the work patterns or the social/organizational constructs where the systems are to be used. The distinction of usability and utility problems will help making such design decisions.

The prototypes tested were all employer-provided professional systems, i.e. their use is not voluntary for the user and the higher level goals of usage are set by the employing organizations and not the users themselves. Furthermore, the systems and their usage can be seen as complex in a sense that the order and desired outcome of system tasks can vary (see [33]). In this type of environment the majority of found problems are utility-related, suggesting that the development and requirements elicitation methods used previously in the design process do need support from this form of testing (45 % of our findings denote lack of knowledge of the context of use). On the other hand, the context may also be a threat to the validity of the developed categories and the overall study as the complexity of the use context may lead to an exceptional number of utility related problems. Furthermore, the evaluator effect is present in a usability study [34], which implies that the following design recommendations have no scientifically constructible relation to observed problems. This is a validity and reliability problem of not only this research but all practical usability evaluations. The validity and reliability of the categories should be tested with more evaluators, different empirical data and formal methods. Moreover, in the future, we consider it important to study how the problem categories are valued in design, what are the practical benefits to, and how feasibly the categories can be exploited in the design process.

References

1. Wixon, D.: Evaluating usability methods: why the current literature fails the practitioner. Interactions 10(4), 28–34 (2003)
2. Hornbæk, K.: Dogmas in the assessment of usability evaluation methods. Behav. Inf. Technol. 29(1), 97–111 (2010)
3. Molich, R., Ede, M.R., Kaasgaard, K., Karyukin, B.: Comparative usability evaluation. Behav. Inf. Technol. 23(1), 65–74 (2004)
4. Hornbæk, K., Frøkjær, E.: Comparing usability problems and redesign proposals as input to practical systems development. In: Proceedings of the SIGCHI Conference on Human Factors in Computing Systems, pp. 391–400. ACM (2005)
5. Følstad, A., Law, E.L.-C., Hornbæk, K.: Analysis in usability evaluations: an exploratory study. In: Proceedings of the 6th Nordic Conference on Human-Computer Interaction: Extending Boundaries, pp. 647–650. ACM (2010)
6. Law, E.L.-C.: Evaluating the downstream utility of user tests and examining the developer effect: a case study. Int. J. Hum.-Comput. Interact. 21(2), 147–172 (2006)
7. Woolrych, A., Hornbæk, K., Frøkjær, E., Cockton, G.: Ingredients and meals rather than recipes: a proposal for research that does not treat usability evaluation methods as indivisible wholes. Int. J. Hum.-Comput. Interact. 27(10), 940–970 (2011)

8. Lavery, D., Cockton, G., Atkinson, M.P.: Comparison of evaluation methods using structured usability problem reports. Behav. Inf. Technol. **16**, 246–266 (1997)
9. Hvannberg, E.T., Law, E.L.-C.: Classification of usability problems (CUP) scheme. In: Proceedings of the INTERACT 2003, pp. 655–662. ACM Press (2003)
10. Vilbergsdottir, S.G., Hvannberg, E.T., Law, E.L.-C.: Assessing the reliability, validity and acceptance of a classification scheme of usability problems (CUP). J. Syst. Softw. **87**, 18–37 (2014)
11. Vilbergsdóttir, S.G., Hvannberg, E.T., Law, E.L.-C.: Classification of usability problems (CUP) scheme: augmentation and exploitation. In: Proceedings of the 4th Nordic Conference on Human-Computer Interaction: Changing Roles, pp. 281–290. ACM (2006)
12. Nørgaard, M., Hornbæk, K.: What do usability evaluators do in practice? an explorative study of think-aloud testing. In: Proceedings of the 6th Conference on Designing Interactive Systems, pp. 209–218, ACM (2006)
13. Nielsen, J.: Usability Engineering. Academic Press (1993)
14. Goodwin, N.: Functionality and usability. Commun. ACM **30**, 229–233 (1987). ACM
15. Whiteside, J., Bennett, J., Holtzblatt, K.: Usability engineering: our experience and evolution. In: Helander, M. (ed.) Handbook of Human-Computer Interaction. North Holland, Amsterdam (1988)
16. Grudin, J.: Utility and usability: research issues and development contexts. Interact. Comput. **4**(2), 209–217 (1992)
17. ISO 9241-11: Ergonomic Requirements for Office Work with Visual Display Terminals (VDTs)–Part II Guidance on Usability (1998)
18. Bevan, N.: Usability is quality of use. Adv. Hum. Factors/Ergon. **20**, 349–354 (1995)
19. Mahmood, M.A., Burn, J.M., Gemoets, L.A., Jacquez, C.: Variables affecting information technology end-user satisfaction: a meta-analysis of the empirical literature. Int. J. Hum.-Comput. Stud. **52**(4), 751–771 (2000)
20. Johannessen, G.H.J., Hornbæk, K.: Must evaluation methods be about usability? devising and assessing the utility inspection method. Behav. Inf. Technol. **33**(2), 195–206 (2014)
21. Ham, D.-H.: A model-based framework for classifying and diagnosing usability problems. Cogn. Technol. Work **16**(3), 373–388 (2014)
22. Chillarege, R., Bhandari, I.S., Chaar, J.K., Halliday, M.J., Moebus, D.S., Ray, B.K., Wong, M.-Y.: Orthogonal defect classification-a concept for in-process measurements. IEEE Trans. Softw. Eng. **18**(11), 943–956 (1992)
23. Grady, R.B.: Software failure analysis for high-return process improvement decisions. Hewlett Packard J. **47**, 15–24 (1996)
24. Andre, T.S.: Rex Hartson, H., Belz, S.M., McCreary, F.A.: The user action framework: a reliable foundation for usability engineering support tools. Int. J. Hum.-Comput. Stud. **54**(1), 107–136 (2001)
25. Keenan, S.L., Hartson, H.R., Kafura, D.G., Schulman, R.S.: The usability problem taxonomy: a framework for classification and analysis. Empirical Softw. Eng. **4**(1), 71–104 (1999)
26. Tarkkanen, K., Reijonen, P., Tétard, F., Harkke, V.: Back to user-centered usability testing. In: Holzinger, A., Ziefle, M., Hitz, M., Debevc, M. (eds.) SouthCHI 2013. LNCS, vol. 7946, pp. 91–106. Springer, Heidelberg (2013)
27. Baskerville, R.L.: Investigating information systems with action research. Commun. AIS **2**(3es), 4 (1999)
28. Strauss, A., Corbin, J.M.: Basics of Qualitative Research: Grounded Theory Procedures and Techniques. Sage Publications, Newbury Park (1990)
29. Gothelf, J.: Lean UX: Applying Lean Principles to Improve User Experience. O'Reilly Media, Inc. (2013)

30. International Organization for Standardization: ISO 9241-210:2010. Ergonomics of Human-system Interaction - Part 210: Human-centred Design for Interactive Systems. ISO (2010)

31. Blandford, A., Green, T.R., Furniss, D., Makri, S.: Evaluating system utility and conceptual fit using CASSM. Int. J. Hum.-Comput. Stud. **66**(6), 393–409 (2008)

32. Geng, R., Chen, M., Tian, J.: In-process usability problem classification, analysis and improvement. In: 14th International Conference on Quality Software 2014, pp. 240–245. IEEE (2014)

33. Campbell, D.J.: Task complexity: a review and analysis. Acad. Manag. Rev. **13**(1), 40–52 (1988)

34. Hertzum, M., Molich, R., Jacobsen, N.E.: What you get is what you see: revisiting the evaluator effect in usability tests. Behav. Inf. Technol. **33**(2), 144–162 (2014)

DUXU Management and Practice

Supply Chain Risk Management in the Era of Big Data

Yingjie Fan[1,2(✉)], Leonard Heilig[1], and Stefan Voß[1]

[1] Institute of Information Systems (IWI), University of Hamburg,
20146 Hamburg, Germany
{fan.yingjie,leonard.heilig,stefan.voss}@uni-hamburg.de
http://iwi.econ.uni-hamburg.de
[2] Xuzhou Institute of Technology, Jiangsu 221008, China

Abstract. The trend of big data implies novel opportunities and challenges for improving supply chain management. In particular, supply chain risk management can largely benefit from big data technologies and analytic methods for collecting, analyzing, and monitoring both supply chain internal data and environmental data. Due to the increasing complexity, particular attention must not only be put on the processing and analysis of data, but also on the interaction between big data information systems and users. In this paper, we analyze the role of big data in supply chains and present a novel framework of a supply chain risk management system for improving supply chain planning and supply chain risk management under stochastic environments by using big data technologies and analytics. The process-oriented framework serves as a guideline to integrate and analyze big data as well as to implement a respective supply chain risk management system. As such, this paper provides a novel direction of utilizing big data in supply chain risk management.

Keywords: Supply chain risk management · Big data · Cloud computing · Framework · Supply chain management system

1 Introduction

The complexity of global supply chain (SC) environments and the lack of relevant information resulted in unpredictable and uncontrollable SC uncertainties in the past. Existing quantitative research about SC risk management is mostly based on the assumption that parameters of SC risks are known [7], but does not mention how to retrieve and process these values in practice. In today's big data era, more and more shop floor and SC data are measured by integrating SC actors and external data sources (e.g., traffic data, weather forecasts) as well as by adopting advanced technologies such as sensor, identification, and positioning technologies. SCs become more visible to executives, but also more complex due to information overload. The increasing volume, velocity and variety of globally available data imply that SC planning requires accessible, on-demand, and

© Springer International Publishing Switzerland 2015
A. Marcus (Ed.): DUXU 2015, Part I, LNCS 9186, pp. 283–294, 2015.
DOI: 10.1007/978-3-319-20886-2_27

near real-time information retrieval techniques and decision support. Big data is defined as a collection of data (sets) so large and complex that they are difficult or impossible to process with traditional database management tools or data processing applications [23]. In recent years, advanced data processing technologies for handling big data have become available, often using the well-known approach of divide and conquer applied in scalable IT infrastructures. In this context, cloud computing offers novel options to flexibly and economically use scalable technologies and services forming a basis for cloud-based decision analytics [11]. Thus, low computation time and high quality solutions of optimization methods, which were mutually exclusive in former research [2,24], are able to get along in harmony by using cloud computing. While the data and advanced technologies are available, we identify a lack of integrative approaches to facilitate real-time monitoring and more accurate forecasting of SC risks for designing flexible SCs under uncertain environments. According to Tang [22], collaborative planning, forecasting, and replenishment (CPFR) strategy improves SC resiliency. The CPFR system generates common demand forecasting for SC partners, shares inventory information, and adopts a common ordering rule which will be promoted by incorporating big data technologies and analytics. Although more and more companies realize the importance of adopting big data techniques into supply chain management (SCM), a lack of research in this area can be identified.

In this paper, we present a framework for integrating big data into supply chain risk management (SCRM) based on analytic methods, such as multi-stage stochastic optimization techniques and cloud infrastructures. We focus on handling SC operational risks and low frequency high impact SC disruption risks. Scenario-based analysis [18], which has been successfully used in SC planning problems [25,27], will be used to support decision making. Thus, the proposed framework provides guidelines of handling SC risks in the era of big data. To the best of our knowledge, this is the first approach to incorporate big data into SCRM. According to this framework, global SC will be able to handle SC risks with low SC costs. The framework also facilitates real-time monitoring, emergency planning, and decision support immediately when incidents happen. As such, the paper is a first step towards a new direction in SCM and interdisciplinary research in respect of information systems research and operations research.

The remainder of this paper is organized as follows. Section 2 provides a theoretic background on SCRM, big data, and reasons for using cloud technologies. SCRM relevant big data is analyzed and classified in Sect. 3. In Sect. 4, the overall framework and main modules are introduced in detail. Finally, a conclusion is presented in Sect. 5.

2   Background

SC risks are generated from SC internal and external uncertainties. SC internal uncertainties are mostly foreseeable based on SC internal data, which is collected by advanced technologies within the production and transportation systems. SC external uncertainties stem from SC external environments, such as from social, economic, and natural environments. Obviously, external uncertainties are more complicated and multifaceted so that advanced analytic methods and decision support systems are required for external uncertainty analysis. Due to the increasing complexity of global SCs, decision support systems are indeed becoming indispensable tools for SCRM. In this context, Dadfar et al. present global SC risk mitigation strategies [5]. In order to manage disruptions and mitigate risks in manufacturing SCs, Giannakis and Louis [9] propose a framework of a multi-agent based SC decision support system. An interesting viewpoint is that SC risks come from a lack of confidence in the SC [4]. Two main elements of improving SC confidence are visibility and control. Visibility is strengthened by SC information sharing, control could be enhanced through SC event management, which involves collection and exchange of data on events from and between SC partners, respectively. Both visibility and control require information and communication technologies (ICT) to retrieve relevant information. Several works focus on an efficient use of information in SCs.

For analyzing risks in the context of SCM, a widely used technique is scenario analysis. Scenario analysis is regarded as a thinking tool and a communication device that aids the managerial mind rather than replacing it [20]. A scenario is an internally consistent view of what the future might turn out to be – not a forecast, but one possible future outcome [17]. The uncertainty of the future can be appraised through the number of possible scenarios within the field of probables [10]. For instance, SC stochastic scenarios are indicated by a group of scenario indexes [7], such as possible victim locations (SC nodes or transportation links) and their possibilities, reconstruction times after risk events, extra times and extra costs for adopting alternative planning after the event, etc. The first step of scenario analysis is scenario design. According to the "iceberg" metaphor in [3], a series of factors should be thought through during the process of scenario building which includes resources, culture, information, technology, policy, policy distribution, regulation, demography, legislation, ecology, society, and territory. Since a wide range of unstructured and real-time changing data is incorporated, the scenario design process becomes a big data analysis process. Consequently, these processes must be supported by appropriate big data infrastructures and analytic methods, such as the Progressive Hedging Algorithm (PHA) [18].

Similar to other methods, the computing time of PHA is quite high for large amounts of data and respective scenarios [26]. A cloud-based infrastructure could be used to economically deploy scalable computing clusters when needed, enabling a near real-time computation of large scale problems [26] as well as on-demand applications that provide decision support for SC planners and decision makers.

Big data technologies are defined as a new generation of technologies and architectures. They are used to economically extract useful values from very large volumes of a wide variety of data. High-velocity and real-time capture, discovery, processing, and/or analysis are supported by big data technologies and analytic methods [8]. Further, an important aspect of big data technologies and analytic methods is a user-oriented presentation and visualization of data and results for supporting decision making.

The number of unpredictable "black swans [21]," which is used to describe low-frequency and high-impact events, is getting smaller with big data analytics [19]. The authors of [19] also propose that one of the most significant aspects of big data analytics is to foresee events before they happen by sensing small changes over time. "JD.com," one of the most frequently used Chinese e-commerce companies, is forecasting customer demands 28 days in advance through big data technologies which is one of JD.com's critical success factors [14]. Historical records see a remarkable relationship between JD.com products' customer demand and its advertisements' click rate. Thus, demand can be forecast through tracking products' advertisements click frequencies. By forecasting demand four weeks in advance, the company maintains a low inventory level as well as short delivery lead time. Amazon is another example of using advanced technologies and analytics for predicting demands, such as based on the pattern of products searches [19]. These case studies demonstrate that both companies and customers can benefit from big data analytics. The more companies characterize themselves as data-driven, the better they perform on objective measures of financial and operational results [16]. According to an investigation in [1], however, most companies are far from accessing all the available data. Often, companies do not have the expertise and processes to design experiments and extract business value from big data.

Big data technologies and analytics, however, rely massively on flexible ICT infrastructures. As computational requirements of analytical systems heavily fluctuate, especially in SCM where those systems are mainly used for planning purposes, a flexible ICT infrastructure can be a huge cost saver. The effect is increased by a growing amount of data to be processed and analyzed. In recent years, cloud computing has become popular as a way of using ICT infrastructure and services on-demand. These scalable cloud services are offered through a network, mostly based on a usage-based pricing model. Cloud services are grouped into three categories: infrastructure as a service (IaaS), platform as a service (PaaS), and software as a service (SaaS) [15]. Consequently, computing resources can be automatically adopted to the needs of analytical tasks in SC planning and replanning processes as well as released to reduce expenses. Moreover, the accessibility and standardized interfaces of cloud services allow a better collaboration and information sharing among SC actors. Although concerns and issues, such as related to the interoperability of cloud services, are still discussed in practice and research (see, e.g., [12]), we consider cloud computing as a promising solution for supporting flexible big data analytical systems in the area of SCM.

3   Big Data in SCRM

In the background of fast development of information technologies, the amount of acquirable SC data increases over time. In our framework, SCRM will be improved by collecting, analyzing, and monitoring SC real-time data. SC data, which will be used to support SCRM, is classified into two categories: SC internal data and SC external data. SC internal data refers to data collected from SC partners. The multi-source internal data is unstructured due to being collected from different organizations and different data terminals, such as point of sales (POS) terminals, global positioning system (GPS), and sensors. Table 1 lists applications of SC internal data and big data in SCRM. Potential SC risks,

Table 1. Examples of SC internal data and big data

(Big) data sources	Potential SC risks	Description
Purchasing records	Product quality issues	Date and time, product_id, supplier_id, purchasing quantity
Production records	Product quality issues	Date and time, product_id, facility_id, process
Bill of materials	Product quality issues	Date and time, product_id, material_id, supplier_id of the material
Packing records	Packing and transportation issues	Date and time, container_id, product_id
Delivery records	Transportation issues	Date and time of loading, container_id, vehicle_id
GPS of vehicles	Transportation issues	Date and time, vehicle_id, location
Container sensor records	Product quality issues	Date and time, container_id, temperature
Sales records	Demand fluctuation	Date and time, product_id, customer_id, quantity
Customer complaints	Product quality issues	Date and time, customer_id, focus, content
Financial records	Financial issues	Balance sheet, income statements, financial statements, liquidity etc
Crucial facilities records	Facility issues	Date, facility_id, performance
Human resources records	Personnel issues	Personnel_id, time phases, duty, salary, rewards and punishments, further notes

such as product quality issues and transportation delays, are able to be forecast in advance and traced afterwards based on the analysis of SC internal data. Important data, which should be collected from each big data source is depicted in the column "Description." The volume of SC internal data is positively related to the scale of a SC, such as the number of SC partners, products and services. SC internal data grows frequently and is required to be stored for a number of periods, such as several months, in order to trace causes after failures and predict risks. Thus, SC internal data, which is relevant for SCRM, may use different structures and increase over time.

SC external data refers to data collected from public news, social media, etc. Table 2 depicts applications of SC external big data in SCRM. SC external data is larger and more complicated than SC internal data. It reveals potential disasters and uncertainties in external environments. For instance, exchange rate movements can be forecast from time series of Tweet counts [13]. Twitter messages

Table 2. Examples of SC external big data

Big data sources	Potential SC risks	Description
Public news	Disasters and uncertainties	Date, focus, contents, sources, potential risks
Policies of economics, politics, industries, etc.	Policy changes	Date, regions, focus, contents, sources, potential risks
Weather records	Extreme weather	Date and time, regions, weather, future weather forecasts, sources
Natural disasters records	Natural disasters	Date, regions, pre-disaster forecasts, real situation
Social networks and other social media	Disasters and uncertainties	Date, focus, contents, sources, impacts to SC

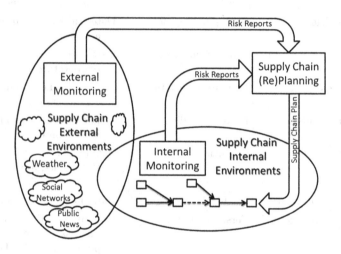

Fig. 1. Module overview

can also be used for rapid detection and qualitative assessment of earthquakes [6]. Information from media is diversified not only in its formats and contents, but also in its languages and reliabilities. Furthermore, media data increases faster than SC internal data. These bring about toughness for information discrimination and analysis. Our intention is to find out potential risks and ongoing disasters from SC external big data as early as possible. Due to the requirements of SC external big data collection and analysis, we suggest to outsource SC external big data processing tasks to professional third-party analysis (3PA) companies.

4   Framework

The focus of our framework is to make a robust SC plan under stochastic environments. Monitoring and planning are two crucial parts of the framework. Environment monitoring and analysis provide stochastic parameters for the SC

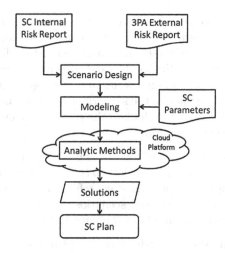

Fig. 2. SC planning/replanning module

planning process. As depicted in Fig. 1, the SCM system in our framework includes three main modules: SC planning module, SC internal module, SC external module. A SC plan is generated from a SC planning module. SC internal and external modules monitor SC internal and external environments, respectively. Once an emerging risk is detected by an internal or external module, a new risk report is generated based on risk analysis and is sent to the SC planning module. The SC planning module will be activated and a renewed SC plan is generated based on the renewed risk report. The whole process runs in a circle to maintain flexibility of a SC under stochastic environments. The functions of each module will be demonstrated in the following.

4.1   SC Planning/Replanning Module

As SC flexibility is decided at the planning stage, we start to consider related tasks before regarding risks. In order to design a flexible SC plan allowing a smooth supply under stochastic environments, SC risks should be taken into account at the SC planning phase (see Fig. 2). The process of the SC planning module and the SC replanning module is the same. Scenarios, which represent SC uncertainties, should be designed based on SC internal and external risk reports. Then, a stochastic model is built based on proposed scenarios. Analytic methods are applied to solve the model after putting SC parameters into the model. Solutions of the model are used to support the SC plan at last. The whole process is demonstrated in detail in the following.

SC internal reports should be provided by companies of the SC since internal data is normally privately owned. The process of how to generate a SC internal risk reports will be introduced in detail in Sect. 4.2. SC external reports should be provided by 3PA companies since external data processing work is complicated and will be a waste of resources and energies for a single SC or company to do. The detailed process of how to generate a SC external report will be demonstrated in Sect. 4.3.

Scenario Design. The scenario analysis, as a common approach to deal with stochastic problems in practice, is adopted. Scenarios are designed based on SC internal and external risk reports. Each scenario refers to a distinguished kind of consequence after disruptions. Probability and costs are two essential features for each scenario. The costs depend on a series of factors: geographic areas involved in the scenario, time of duration of the scenario, extra costs under the realization of each scenario, etc. In order to calculate the costs, an emergency plan is taken into consideration for each scenario.

Modeling. A two-stage multi-scenario model is built based on proposed scenarios and scenario features. The first stage refers to the safe period of a SC without any disruption or catastrophe. The second stage refers to the uncertain period when a SC may suffer any of the proposed scenarios. Values of scenario parameters and other SC parameters are inputs of the model.

Analytic Methods. Analytic methods, such as optimization, simulation, heuristics, and metaheuristics, can be chosen to solve the model. Due to the complexity of multi-scenario models, metaheuristics seem to be good approaches to be adopted in our framework. PHA is an option for solving the proposed two-stage multi-scenario model. For models with simple SC structures and a small amount of scenarios, solutions are generated in tolerable amount of time. A cloud platform serves as the underlying computing infrastructure and can be flexibly adopted to the computational requirements of solvers, in particular important for complex SC structures with a large amount of stochastic scenarios. That is, computational tasks are sent to a cluster of computing nodes in order to accelerate solving the model. The related cloud computing nodes are purchased and released on-demand. An SaaS solution provides an interface for setting up the model and presenting results in different views for different stakeholders. A set of two-stage solutions will be generated for the two-stage model. The first stage solution refers to the safe period SC plan. Second stage solutions refer to the emergency plans, which are related to the realization of scenarios.

SC Plan. Based on the solutions of the multi-scenario model, a two-stage SC plan, including a safe period plan and emergency plans for uncertain periods, can be generated.

4.2   SC Internal Module

A SC internal risk in the SC internal monitoring and risk analysis framework (see Fig. 3) refers to foreseeable risks based on analysis of SC internal data (see Table 1). SC internal risks can be forecast based on the analysis of SC internal data. SC monitoring is used to detect emerging risks. The corresponding emergency plan is adopted immediately after a stochastic event is detected. The SC internal risk report will be renewed and sent to the SC replanning module if the stochastic event is not a short-term event. SC internal data refers to purchasing, production, transportation, final demand, etc. (see Table 1). Detailed data is helpful for forecasting and controlling. For example, an Intelligent Maintenance

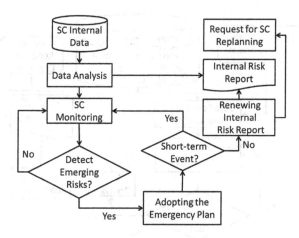

Fig. 3. SC internal monitoring and risk analysis

System (IMS) is able to predict and prevent machines' potential failures by an analysis of collected data from the machinery. In the following, components of the SC internal module are explained briefly.

Data Analysis. Data analysis provides a risk report and benchmarks of SC parameters for the SC monitoring process. Data analysis methods, such as data mining and machine learning, can be adopted at this stage.

SC Monitoring. SC real-time monitoring is used for sensing SC changes and foreseeing SC risks. Monitoring helps SC managers to figure out sudden events and forecast SC risks as early as possible.

Adopting the Emergency Plan. Once sudden events or potential uncertainties are detected, the corresponding emergency plan, which is specified in the SC planning module, is utilized in order to get more available time. For short-term disruption events, SC restores the original SC plan after the short disruption period.

Renewing Internal Risk Report. For long-term impact events, the SC internal risk report is modified in order to activate the SC replanning module. An internal risk report should at least contain probabilities and a description of uncertainties for each SC partner, impacts, duration, and costs of each uncertain event.

Request for SC Replanning. Once the internal risk report is renewed, the SC replanning module is activated. A new SC plan will be generated and launched afterwards.

4.3   SC External Module

SC external big data is mostly unstructured and growing fast since it has a wide range of aspects from various channels, such as public media, social networks, and professional databases (see Table 2). Professional infrastructures and personnel are needed for big data processing and forming an external risk report.

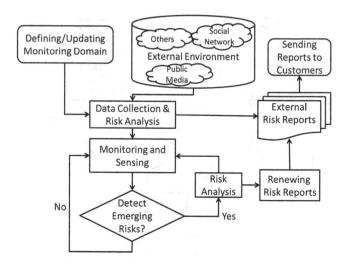

Fig. 4. SC external monitoring and risk analysis

However, a company's external risks depend on its geographic location and industry background. It means that external risks for companies, which locate at the same geographic area and provide similar products, are similar. In order to fully utilize resources, the SC external risk analysis in our framework (see Fig. 4) is outsourced to a professional 3PA company that monitors the environment based on data mining and data analysis. The domain of the external environment should be defined by the 3PA company according to its customers' background at first. SC external risk reports are formed based on external data collection and risk analysis. Monitoring and sensing are used to detect emerging risks in the external environment. Risk analysis is adopted again once an emerging risk is captured. The renewed risk reports will be sent to customers after risk analysis. The SC replanning module will be activated once a new risk report is achieved. Explanations of main processes of the SC external module are listed as follows.

Defining/Updating Monitoring Domain. In order to abstract valuable data efficiently, a domain of external environments should be defined at first. Only data which will have explicit impacts on a SC is analyzed.

Data Collection and Risk Analysis. The characteristics of external environments data are large volume, unstructured, and increasing over time. Thus, data collection techniques, such as web crawling and text mining, are used to extract information from websites and web services. Advanced data analysis technology is required for analysis of SC external big data. The purpose of external risk analysis is to find out external threats and parameters of each threat. External threats include bad weather, policy changes, economic changes, social changes, terrorist attacks etc. Parameters of each threat may refer to its geographic region, possibility, and severity.

Monitoring and Sensing. Real-time monitoring and sensing of external data is required to detect emerging risks by 3PA companies. The risk analysis task is triggered once an emerging risk is discovered.

Risk Analysis. The risk analysis process is used to form new risk reports for customers of 3PA companies. External risk reports should at least include information on uncertainties at the location of SC partners and during transportation of products. This encompasses parameters of probabilities, duration, impacts of uncertain events. The cost for each uncertain event should be designed and calculated by the SC itself since it depends on emergency plans, which should be decided by companies of the SC.

Sending Reports to Customers. Risk reports are sent to customers of 3PA companies after being renewed. Once a renewed external risk report is received by the SC planning module, the SC planning module is triggered to generate a new SC plan.

5 Conclusion

SC risks relevant big data is analyzed and classified into SC internal big data and SC external big data. Based on the SC big data classification, a framework that incorporates big data technologies into the SCRM system is proposed. Research about the application of big data in SCM is very rare. This paper provides a guidance of utilizing big data to improve SCRM. Big data technologies provide opportunities of prediction and detecting potential SC risks as early as possible so that the SC becomes more visible and flexible. Further research needs to be done for the implementation of our framework into practice. Technologies and approaches for abstracting valuable information efficiently and accurately from big data resources should be applied. In this context, we plan to implement and evaluate a prototype that provides decision support for SCRM by utilizing the proposed framework. For this purpose, cloud technologies should be combined with PHA.

References

1. Bughin, J., Chui, M., Manyika, J.: Clouds, big data, and smart assets: ten tech-enabled business trends to watch. McKinsey Q. **56**(1), 75–86 (2010)
2. Caserta, M., Voß, S.: Metaheuristics: intelligent problem solving. In: Maniezzo, V., Stützle, T., Voß, S. (eds.) Metaheuristics, pp. 1–38. Springer, USA (2010)
3. Chermack, T.J., Lynham, S.A., Ruona, W.E.: A review of scenario planning literature. Futures Res. Q. **17**(2), 7–31 (2001)
4. Christopher, M., Lee, H.: Mitigating supply chain risk through improved confidence. Int. J. Phys. Distrib. Logistics Manage. **34**(5), 388–396 (2004)
5. Dadfar, D., Schwartz, F., Voß, S.: Risk management in global supply chains - hedging for the big bang? In: Mak, H.Y., Lo, H. (eds.) Transportation and Logistics Management Proceedings of the 17th International HKSTS Conference (HKSTS 2012), pp. 159–166. Hong Kong (2012)

6. Earle, P.S., Bowden, D.C., Guy, M.: Twitter earthquake detection: earthquake monitoring in a social world. Ann. Geophys. **54**(6), 708–715 (2012)
7. Fan, Y., Schwartz, F., Voß, S.: Flexible supply chain design under stochastic catastrophic risks. In: Kersten, W., Blecker, T., Ringle, C. (eds.) Next Generation Supply Chains, pp. 379–406. Epubli, Berlin (2014)
8. Gantz, J., Reinsel, D.: The digital universe in 2020: big data, bigger digital shadows, and biggest growth in the far east. IDC iView: IDC Analyze Future **2007**, 1–16 (2012)
9. Giannakis, M., Louis, M.: A multi-agent based framework for supply chain risk management. J. Purchasing Supply Manage. **17**(1), 23–31 (2011)
10. Godet, M.: The art of scenarios and strategic planning: tools and pitfalls. Technol. Forecast. Soc. Chang. **65**(1), 3–22 (2000)
11. Heilig, L., Voß, S.: Decision analytics for cloud computing: a classification and literature review. In: Newman, A., Leung, J. (eds.) Tutorials in Operations Research - Bridging Data and Decisions, pp. 1–26. INFORMS, Catonsville (2014)
12. Hofmann, P., Woods, D.: Cloud computing: the limits of public clouds for business applications. IEEE Internet Comput. **14**(6), 90–93 (2010)
13. Janetzko, D.: Predictive modeling in turbulent times - what Twitter reveals about the EUR/USD exchange rate. Netnomics **15**(2), 69–106 (2014)
14. Lang, X.P.: Lang Said - Headache Hotspot. Oriental Press, Beijing (2013)
15. Marston, S., Li, Z., Bandyopadhyay, S., Zhang, J., Ghalsasi, A.: Cloud computing - the business perspective. Decis. Support Syst. **51**(1), 176–189 (2011)
16. McAfee, A., Brynjolfsson, E.: Big data: the management revolution. Harvard Bus. Rev. **90**(10), 60–68 (2012)
17. Porter, M.E.: Competitive Advantage: Creating and Sustaining Superior Performance. Free Press, New York (1985)
18. Rockafellar, R.T., Wets, R.J.B.: Scenarios and policy aggregation in optimization under uncertainty. Math. Oper. Res. **16**(1), 119–147 (1991)
19. Sanders, N.R.: Big Data Driven Supply Chain Management: A Framework for Implementing Analytics and Turning Information into Intelligence. Pearson Education, New Jersey (2014)
20. Schoemaker, P.J.: When and how to use scenario planning: a heuristic approach with illustration. J. Forecast. **10**(6), 549–564 (1991)
21. Taleb, N.N.: The Black Swan: The Impact of the Highly Improbable Fragility, 2nd edn. Random House, New York (2010)
22. Tang, C.S.: Perspectives in supply chain risk management. Int. J. Prod. Econ. **103**, 451–488 (2006)
23. Voß, S.: Interview with Daniel Dolk and Christer Carlsson on decision analytics. Bus. Inf. Syst. Eng. **6**(3), 181–184 (2014)
24. Voß, S., Fink, A.: Hybridizing reactive tabu search with simulated annealing. In: Hamadi, Y., Schoenauer, M. (eds.) LION 2012. LNCS, vol. 7219, pp. 509–512. Springer, Heidelberg (2012)
25. Voß, S., Woodruff, D.L.: Introduction to Computational Optimization Models for Production Planning in a Supply Chain, 2nd edn. Springer, Berlin (2006)
26. Watson, J.P., Woodruff, D.L., Hart, W.E.: PySP: modeling and solving stochastic programs in Python. Math. Program. Comput. **4**(2), 109–149 (2012)
27. Woodruff, D.L., Voß, S.: Planning for a big bang in a supply chain: fast hedging for production indicators. In: Proceedings of the 39th Annual Hawaii International Conference on System Sciences (HICSS 2006), vol. 2, pp. 40–46. IEEE (2006)

Practice What We Preach – Checking the Usability of HCI Conference Websites

Franziska Hertlein(✉), Bastian Hinterleitner, Matthias Voit,
Tim Schneidermeier, and Christian Wolff

Media Informatics Group, University of Regensburg, Regensburg, Germany
{franziska.hertlein,bastian.hinterleitner,
matthias.voit}@student.ur.de,
{tim.schneidermeier,christian.wolff}@ur.de

Abstract. Today many conferences invite human-computer interaction and usability professionals for presentations, discussions and networking. Dedicated conference websites offer general information on the conference, on the submission process as well as on practical aspects of attending the conference. Considering the domain expertise of the audience, these websites should have extraordinary usability and offer a formidable user experience (UX). In order to evaluate this hypothesis, we have conducted a comparative usability study of three international conference websites with novice and expert users. The results show that previous experience has a slight influence on task efficiency, but also that the findings vary strongly from site to site. Independently from their experience, all participants rated the websites' overall usability moderate to low.

Keywords: Usability evaluation · User experience · Conference websites · Novice versus expert users · System usability scale · Attrakdiff

1 Introduction

Usability is a crucial factor for easy-to-use interfaces and websites. Many conferences in the field of human-computer interaction (HCI) discuss new approaches, case studies and methods in usability engineering and user experience design. Considering the domain expertise of the audience these websites should be extraordinarily usable and offer a positive user experience (UX). In this paper, we probe this hypothesis and present results of a comparative usability study with expert and novice users. Our findings show that previous experience with different conference websites has no significant influence on task performance or perceived usability. We have evaluated three conference websites, namely the platforms of HCII 2014[1], CHI 2014[2] and MobileHCI 2013[3]. Although the results show no notable differences regarding the usability of the sites, the CHI 2014 website performed best with respect to usability.

---

[1] http://2014.hci.international/.
[2] http://chi2014.acm.org/.
[3] http://www.mobilehci2013.org/.

© Springer International Publishing Switzerland 2015
A. Marcus (Ed.): DUXU 2015, Part I, LNCS 9186, pp. 295–305, 2015.
DOI: 10.1007/978-3-319-20886-2_28

Although only a few severe problems could be identified during the tests, all sites show room for improvement regarding their usability and UX.

The rest of this paper is organized as follows: In Sect. 2, the selection of conference websites as objects of study is introduced. Section 3 explains the design of the study, the metrics used as well as the actual execution of the study. Major results are presented and discussed in Sect. 4, and finally Sect. 5 gives a short summary of our findings.

2   Conference Websites

Three international human-computer interaction conference websites served as object of investigation: CHI 2014, HCII 2014, and MobileHCI 2013. These sites were chosen according to the following requirements:

- Relevance in the field of HCI (measured by the number of publications and citations).
- International conference including an English website.

According to a list of top conferences in the field of human-computer interaction published by the Microsoft Corporation (2013) concerning publications and citations, the CHI conference can be identified as the biggest conference in this field. Because of its high popularity and its many participants the website of the HCII conference was chosen (HCI International Conference, 2015) as second object. Using a conference website may be relevant in three points in time:

- **Interest:** Looking for submission deadline and general information
- **Submission:** Submitting the paper
- **Attending:** Looking up accommodation and program information if the paper got accepted

In order to map this procedure over time from submitting an abstract to actually attending the conference during the usability test we used the *Wayback Machine*[4] as a powerful tool to retrieve all states of a website over time.

Completing the list of websites to be tested we had to choose between the platforms of IUI[5], UXPA[6], Interact[7] and MobileHCI.

Examining and verifying the feasibility of possible tasks, the *Wayback Machine* and the archived states of the websites turned out to be another selection criterion. The website of MobileHCI 2013 therefore completed the list.

---

[4] http://archive.org/web/.

[5] International Conference on Intelligent User Interfaces, http://www.iuiconf.org/.

[6] User Experience Professionals Association conference, http://uxpa2014.org/.

[7] INTERACT International Conference, http://www.interact2013.org/.

3   Study Design

3.1   Identifying Tasks

In order to identify relevant tasks we interviewed expert users and asked them about their typical procedure to submit a paper at a conference. As a result, we found out that the process to actively attend a conference can be divided in three steps. In the first step, potential authors may be interested in submitting a paper. In the second step, the user has to submit the paper or abstract. In the third step, the user is interested in information about accommodation and the conference program.

We could identify the following tasks for our usability study (see Table 1). Submitting a paper usually works through the conference management system (CMS). As these systems are independent from the actual websites we excluded them from our study as it was not our intention to evaluate conference management systems[8]. Finding the link to the CMS therefore is the only task in step two. Following a realistic timeline in the study, all participants had to execute the tasks shown in Table 1 in the same exact order. We are aware that this may have led to learning effects and may have influenced the rating of the system's usability.

Table 1. Task description

Step	Task	Description
Interest	1	Find submission deadline for full papers
	2	Download template for Microsoft Word
Submission	3	Find link to Conference Management System for uploading the paper
Attending	4	Find registrations fees for default conditions
	5	Find certain hotel, which is advertised on the website
	6	Find paper presentation date by author and paper title

The usability of the conference websites was measured using a between-subject study design with novice and expert users. Novice users had no experiences in submitting a paper, but as students could possibly do so in the future (6 female, 14 male, avg. age 24.2). We defined expert users by having at least submitted three papers in the last three years (5 female, 15 male, avg. age 31.5).

Because we used the *thinking aloud* method (Nielsen Norman Group, 2015) as a method to gather more user insights and because of the extended loading times during the use of the *Wayback Machine*, tracking the task time to measure the efficiency was not suitable. Instead, we used a key logger developed by Fimbel (2013) to track interactions and calculated – based on the KLM model by Card, Moran and Newell (1980) – the time on task without interruptions. The KLM provides different estimation

---

[8] We are aware of the fact that there is no clear dividing line between a specific conference website and the conference management system used for the conference. For example, the registration and payment process can be part of the conference website, while in other cases an external service provides this function or it is part of the conference management system.

times for different types of interaction; a keystroke for an average typist for example is estimated with .2 s, a click interaction with .1 s.

In order to handle the key logger, we implemented a local website, which showed the current tasks and started the key logger in the background as soon as the user decided to start a task (see Table 1). All data was stored in a local database.

3.2 Study Execution

The websites were tested on a 15.6″-laptop with an additional external mouse. The test was recorded using the usability software Morae (TechSmith, 2015). In addition to the test conductor, a transcript writer took notes during the test.

The order of the websites to be tested was randomized. Each participant had to solve all six tasks on each website. A new tab that showed the currently needed *Wayback Machine* version of the website was opened. When the task was solved, the user closed the tab and the key logger stopped tracking and restarted when the next task-tab was opened. The selection screen (1.) and the screens for task 1 on the website of CHI2014 (2.-4.) are shown in Fig. 1. After completing the tasks on one site, the website showed a follow-up questionnaire. Thereafter the next conference website was loaded and the participants were asked to start over.

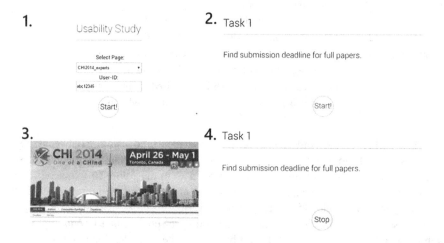

Fig. 1. Important steps of the test website for the execution of our study

As follow-up questionnaires we used the *system usability scale* (SUS) and the *AttrakDiff*. The SUS is a fast method to measure the usability of a product (Sauro and Lewis, 2012, p. 198). It consists of ten questions answered on a 5-point Likert scale. The results can be summed up to a non-linear scale from zero to 100 points. A system with 100 points has the most suitable usability. In addition to the measurement of usability, user experience is an issue that is inevitable when it comes to the evaluation of websites. In order to quantify the UX of the conference websites the *AttrakDiff* was chosen. It is an established questionnaire developed to measure the user experience of a product (Hassenzahl, Burmester and Koller, 2008). It is based on 28 bipolar, seven-stage items, which can be mapped onto different qualities (pragmatic quality, hedonic quality (stimulation), hedonic quality (identity) and attractiveness). The results of the *AttrakDiff* questionnaire are shown in a coordinate system with a pragmatic and hedonic axis. A product positioned in the top right corner can be seen as most pragmatic and hedonic and therefore offers a good user satisfaction (User Interface Design GmbH, 2015).

3.3   Data Evaluation

Besides the study-website, which guided the participants through the test and managed the key logger, we implemented two further websites: one website for analysis, which conducted statistical tests and one website for result presentation that dressed up the results in graphs and tables. To analyze the time-on-task between the different websites, a t-test for unpaired samples was used, to compare the time of the different samples we used a student's t-test (Sauro and Lewis, 2012, p. 63ff). All tests are based on a significance level $\alpha = 0.05$.

The results of the SUS were drawn by the results-website in a diagram; the results of the *AttrakDiff* are analyzed and presented in a pdf by the *AttrakDiff* website.

4   Results

4.1   Differences Between Expert and Novice Users

In order to verify if domain knowledge and previous experience increases the task efficiency we took a look at the time needed for each task and each website and compared the two groups.

The first task was completed faster by expert users on each conference website but only significantly faster on the page of the MobileHCI (see the value highlighted in Table 2). With 28.05 % (df = 39, t = 1.9724), the experts needed less time than the novice users. On the CHI website, the experts were 22.11 % faster and on the HCII website 14.64 %.

Similar results were measured for the second and third task. The expert group was always faster than the first user group. That means for task two 17.89 % faster on the CHI website, 29.55 % faster on the HCII website and 11.64 % faster on the MobileHCI website. For task three 17.13 % faster on the CHI website, 20.78 % faster on the HCII website and 37.11 % faster on the MobileHCI website. Because of a quite large variance, none of those differences are significant.

A slight difference occurs on task four where again the experts were faster than first users by 15.33 % on the CHI website and 21.63 % on the MobileHCI website but only slightly faster on the HCII website (with 3.25 % less time needed).

For task five, results are quite different when compared to the first four tasks: Here, first users were faster than the experts on all pages. For the CHI website experts needed 28.80 % more time, for the HCII website 14.75 % and for the MobileHCI website 18.48 %.

That means that on a single sided t-test the null hypothesis could not be neglected. Because of the big amplitude of the t-value (t = −1.9938) we considered conducting a two-sided t-test which did not deliver any significant results.

For the last task we found out that the expert group was faster for the CHI website by 7.28 % and the HCII website by 11.10 %, but for the MobileHCI website the first user group was faster by 25.91 %.

Overall, there are clear differences between times for first users and experts depending on website and task. Because of that, a closer look at the different pages is worthwhile to find out which page is better at which task.

Table 2. Differences in task times (in seconds) between experts and novice users. The table shows the results from the experts' point of view.

| Tasks | Conferences | | |
	CHI2014	HCII2014	MobileHCI2013
1	- 4.18s	- 3.27s	- 4.85s (t = 1.97)
2	- 6.73s	- 15.48s	- 3.77s
3	- 5.91s	- 4.21s	- 17.37s
4	- 5.34s	- 0.52s	- 8.96s
5	+ 8.6s	+ 5.17s	+ 8.54s
6	- 4.59s	- 10.08s	+ 10.48s
Aggregate	- 18.13s	- 28.39s	- 15.95s

4.2 Differences Between the Websites

To find out which website is designed as the most suitable for a task, we compared the times needed for each task and each group.

The first task was completed fastest with the MobileHCI website in both groups with non-significant differences to the other websites.

Task two was conducted fastest on the MobileHCI website again and even significantly faster in comparison to the HCII website (experts: t = 2.4181, first users: t = 2.1940).

This tendency does not last for task three. In this task, the MobileHCI website was the slowest for both groups with the HCII website being the fastest. These differences were significant for the first user group compared to the MobileHCI website (t = 2.5297) and the CHI website (t = 2.7709).

The same goes for the next task. In task four, the HCII website was the fastest and the MobileHCI the slowest. This time the differences were significant for both test groups. The HCII website was significantly faster than the CHI website (t(first users) = 4.7419, t(experts) = 3.3512) and the MobileHCI website (t(first users) = 4.0098, t(experts) = 3.0331).

Only for task five, the CHI website was the fastest. However only the differences to the MobileHCI website were significant (t(first users) = 3.1625, t(experts) = 3.0136). For this task the MobileHCI website was overall the slowest with also significantly higher times than the HCII website for the expert group (t = 2.6695).

In contrast to task five, the MobileHCI website was the fastest for task six. The differences for the first user group in comparison to the HCII website (t = 4.7284) and the CHI website (t = 3.7367) were significant. The HCII website was the slowest for this task. The expert group needed significantly more time on this website than on the MobileHCI website (t = 2.4017).

Overall, no page was always faster than the others but the MobileHCI website was the fastest in three of six tasks (see Table 3). To find out which problems slowed down the users mostly the next section will list the most important usability problems found.

Table 3. Most efficient website by user group (significant differences are highlighted)

Task	Experts	Novice Users
1	MobileHCI	MobileHCI
2	MobileHCI significant only to HCII	MobileHCI significant only to HCII
3	HCII	HCII significant
4	HCII significant	HCII significant
5	CHI significant only to MobileHCI	CHI significant only to MobileHCI
6	MobileHCI significant only to HCII	MobileHCI significant

4.3   Most Important Usability Problems

In step one, the biggest problem was to find the right template for the paper. Not only the position and the style of the link, which lead to the download of the file, but also the labeling of the function caused problems to the users. A second problem in this phase was to find the right submission date. Many users overlooked the information because of its positioning (HCII website) and especially first users had problems recognizing which of the given submission dates is the right one.

The next test phase consists of the task to find the link to the Conference Management System (CMS). The HCII provided a link to the CMS represented by an icon, but most of the participants could neither identify the icon as representation of the CMS nor identify the icon as a link. The other websites did not show a link on the landing page and the users had to look for it quite a while.

During the last phase – the phase in which the users want to attend the conference – the main problem was the layout of the conference program. All websites presented the program in a different way (only session titles or all papers, all at once or with pop ups), but in fact, the users had problems with every version. On the website of the HCII conference, the display of the time slots were more or less hidden and the long list overwhelmed the users. The CHI website presented sessions only in its program, with papers popping out after a click on a session. Most of the users did not recognize that the entries shown represent sessions, not papers. Finally, the MobileHCI site showed only a list with session titles, again without any notice of their status as sessions. To get an overview of the paper in a session, one had to click on the session – this was not clear to the users. Altogether, the CHI had a huge advantage in this step, because it provides a search function. This would be desirable for the other two programs too.

The presentation of the recommended hotels on the MobileHCI website was another problem. The website presented the hotels in different lists with a lot of text in between and no headers. It was not clear to the users that the different lists show different price categories and without scrolling, they did not even find the further (cheaper) hotels. Therefore, they often did not find the cheapest hotel.

For all phases in the study, the differences between the menu entries "Venue", "Attending" and "Participate" was not clear enough so that the test users opened the wrong page when executing several tasks concerning content related to these menu items. This problem occurred mostly on the MobileHCI website, but there were several problems with the wording in the menus on the other websites, too. Figure 2 summarizes all problems found. It shows the usability findings grouped by category over all websites. Table 4 gives an overview of the observed usability problems along with their severity ranking and their relative occurrence for the two user groups.

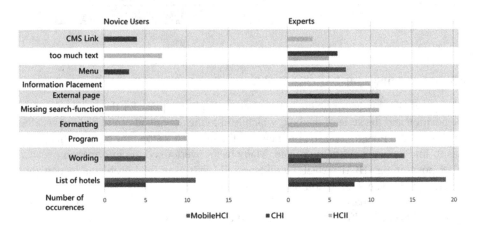

Fig. 2. Usability findings by category

4.4 System Usability Scale and AttrakDiff

According to the System Usability Scale questionnaire, none of the websites show *good* usability (see Fig. 3). For both user groups, the CHI website was the most usable one, but still with merely acceptable results. Big differences exist between results of the first

Table 4. Severity rating of usability problems.

Usability problem	Conference	Severity-rating	Percentage of occurrence (experts /novice users)
Presentation of multiple lists of hotels irritating	MobileHCI	4	95 % /55 %
Confusing presentation of the program	HCII	4	65 % /50 %
Separation of the program in days confusing because of badly formatted links	HCII	4	30 % /45 %
Unclear difference between "venue", "attending" and "participate"	MobileHCI	3	70 % /25 %
Missing search function for program content	HCII	3	55 % /35 %
Complicated and strange wording like "camera ready", "proceedings" or "proposal submission"	HCII	3	45 % /20 %
Bad menu placement for items belonging together ("participate" and "attending")	MobileHCI	3	35 % / <15 %
Bad placement and wording for the link to upload in the conference management system	CHI	3	< 15 % /20 %
Submenu doesn't always show the current position of the user in the menu	CHI	3	< 15 % /15 %

user group and the experts group concerning the MobileHCI website. Experts judged it only four points worse than the CHI website whereas first users said it to be the worst of the three websites with eleven points behind the CHI website on the SUS scale. Overall, the expert group always gave the websites a higher rating than the first users. However, with a two sided t-test only the difference between the two groups was significant ($t = 2.1680$) and the difference of the websites among themselves were not significant.

According to the *AttrakDiff*, the CHI website again was able to score the best results. Its confidence interval partially overlaps the "task-oriented" area that is the best of the three pragmatic results a product can score. All websites are considered "neutral" which means that none shows especially good user experience and each website needs improvements.

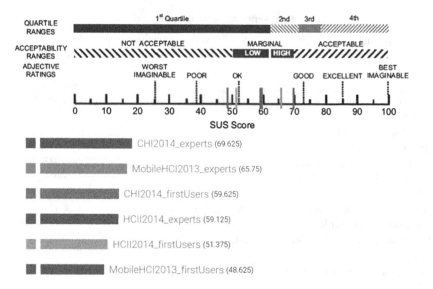

Fig. 3. SUS results

5 Conclusion

The findings of the study presented in this paper show that expert users were in average more efficient in completing the tasks. Yet the comparison of the results of expert and novice users predominantly do not show significant differences. It can be said that previous experience does not make a big difference concerning task success and task time. Depending on the task, each website showed strengths and weaknesses. An outstanding website with respect to tasks, steps, and measures could not be identified.

Some limitations of this study are obvious: The usage of the *Wayback Machine* influenced the selection of the test website: As not all conference websites are archived to the same extent, the number of possible sites was constrained. Another critical point is that the study should be conducted over a longer period, appropriately accompanying the actual conference participation progress of the participants. This approach would allow for a free choice, as every conference website would be suitable to be tested.

Practice what we preach: The study results show that there is ample room for improvement concerning usability and UX of HCI conference websites. It might be suitable to focus even more on the different steps (see Table 1) in the attending process and adapt the website to the users' need over time.

References

Card, S., Moran, T., Newell, A.: The keystroke-level model for user performance time with interactive systems. Commun. ACM **23**(7), 396–410 (1980). Accessed from http://dl.acm.org/citation.cfm?id=358895

Google Scholar: Top-Publikationen - Human Computer Interaction (2015). https://scholar. google.com/citations?view_op=top_venues&vq=eng_humancomputerinteraction. Accessed 15 Jan 2015

Fimbel, E.J.: Predicting the performance of skilled computer users without knowing their strategies. Technical report, rejected 7 times (2013). https://sites.google.com/site/skilledusers/ home. Accessed 19 Feb 2015

Hassenzahl, M., Burmester, M., Koller, F.: Der User Experience (UX) auf der Spur Zum Einsatz von www.attrakdiff.de. In: Brau, H., Diefenbach, S., Hassenzahl, M., Koller, F., Peissner, M., Röse, K. (eds.) Usability Professionals, pp. 78–82. German Chapter der Usability Professionals Association, Stuttgart (2008)

HCI International Conference: HCI International News, Number 66, July 2014 (2015). http://www. hci.international/index.php?module=newsletter&CF_op=view&CF_id=73#h1. Accessed 15 Jan 2015

Microsoft Corporation: Top conferences in human-computer interaction (2013). http://academic. research.microsoft.com/RankList?entitytype=3&topDomainID=2&subDomainID=12&last=5. Accessed 8 Jan 2015

Nielsen Norman Group: Thinking Aloud: The #1 Usability Tool (2015). http://www.nngroup. com/articles/thinking-aloud-the-1-usability-tool/. Accessed 7 Jan 2015

Sauro, J., Lewis, J.R.: Quantifying the User Experience, p. 312. Elsevier/Morgan Kaufmann, Amsterdam (2012)

TechSmith: Morae (2015). http://www.techsmith.com/morae.html. Accessed 10 Jan 2015

User Interface Design GmbH: AttrakDiff (2015). http://attrakdiff.de/sience-en.html. Accessed 4 Jan 2015

Learning from Experience Oriented Disciplines for User Experience Design

A Research Agenda

Simon Kremer[(✉)] and Udo Lindemann

Institute of Product Development, Technische Universität München, Munich, Germany
{kremer,lindemann}@pe.mw.tum.de

Abstract. The emergence of positive User Experience (UX) is gaining in importance for convincing and satisfying customers with technical products. Yet, User Experience Design (UXD) is a rather young discipline within product development. Methods are not well established and traditional aspects predominate. On the other hand, other disciplines are traditionally focused on creating experiences (e.g. sports, film, gaming, etc.). The paper sets out a roadmap for transferring practices and insights from experience focused industries to User Experience Design. Analyzing these experience oriented areas, we suggest supporting UXD in three categories. Requirements for UX are derived studying experiences in other fields. Approaches how these experiences are designed enhance the process on the way to the final experience product. Analysis of persons that take part in the development of experiences in other disciplines can help definingroles to be introduced into product development.

Keywords: User Experience · Management of DUXU processes · Product development processes · Emotional design · UX methods and tools

1 Introduction

1.1 Motivation

In recent years crucial changes concerning the expectation of users towards interactive products and their assessment of user product interactions can be observed. Besides traditional aspects like functionality and usability, emotional aspects are gaining in importance: How is a user experiencing a product? What is the user experiencing with the product? User Experience (UX) describes the individual expectation, cognition, evaluation and communication of a product interaction by the user [1]. When disregarding the prospective User Experience during the development of products even technically mature products can fail on market. But by purposefully designing positive experiences in product development it is possible to create potentials for exciting products and emotional customer loyalty.

User Experience Design (UXD) aims at creating products which enable exciting interactions, memorable moments and enjoyable stories [2]. This goal can be

© Springer International Publishing Switzerland 2015
A. Marcus (Ed.): DUXU 2015, Part I, LNCS 9186, pp. 306–314, 2015.
DOI: 10.1007/978-3-319-20886-2_29

achieved by creating products which trigger emotions of the user [3] and satisfy customer needs [4]. While UXD is a rather young discipline within product development other disciplines are traditionally focused on creating experiences (e.g. sports, film, gaming, etc.). There are great opportunities for profiting from those areas for designing the User Experience with technical products. This paper presents a research agenda towards this integration.

1.2   Initial Situation

Analyzing real development projects in industry, we observed that product developers often struggle with designing experiences. This is due to several reasons:

Focus on Technical and Economic Aspects. Product developments are mostly technology-driven. Products are optimized regarding technical and financial aspects. The user is mostly considered under ergonomic aspects and there are great potentials in using technological improvements to optimize the User Experience, and thus increase product value.

Accordingly Designed Product Development Processes. Processes are planned to analyze and solve problems concerning the aspects described before. It is a main challenge to include UX factors besides conventional aspects. Traditional approaches, like requirement lists, have to be enriched and supplemented with new methods and tools when designing inspiring User Experiences.

Competences Specified for These Goals. Furthermore, development teams are compiled accordingly, being experts in their field but finding it hard to design emotions. Required competences and roles on the way to UX have to be specified.

Other Disciplines Ahead of UXD. UXD addresses the described challenges by providing theoretical models for experiences and methods to keep the user in focus throughout the development process [1]. Yet, UXD is still facing great challenges when designing experiences in the field of product development, while other disciplines from the area of entertainment are traditionally oriented at and specialized on generating experiences. It is the very own core competence of these experience related disciplines to fascinate their "users". Examples are people supporting their favorite sports team, or a person watching a movie immersing completely into a fictional world experiencing something special and telling it to friends afterwards.

Other disciplines are far ahead of product development concerning the design of experiences. These circumstances raise the question which is discussed in this paper. What aspects can UXD learn from experience oriented disciplines for designing successful products?

1.3   Goal

UXD aims at creating fascinating products and providing methods and tools on the way to these products. In this field we aim at enhancing traditional processes in product development with new approaches. The goal of the approach presented in this paper is the development of support for designing experiences with interactive products by learning from experience oriented disciplines. This main goal is divided into the following sub goals.

Identification of Relevant Disciplines. First of all, it is important to define criteria for disciplines to be looked at and accordingly identify relevant disciplines for further research.

Analysis and Comparison of Disciplines. We analyze the identified disciplines, extracting how experiences are described and developed compared to each other as well as compared to product development.

Development of Experience Model and Experience Requirements. Coming out of the analysis we develop a model for User Experience and transfer it to the design of technical products – defining requirements for experience products.

Integration into User Experience Design Process. Finally, we develop support for the design of User Experience. This support is anchored in a User Experience Design process.

2   Approach

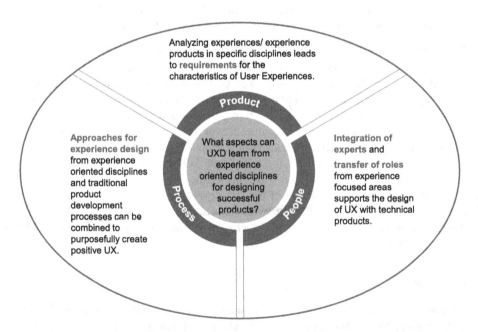

Fig. 1. Framework of research approach

Our approach is based on the question: What can UXD learn from experience oriented disciplines for designing successful products? In product development three areas of application for profiting from experience disciplines have been identified by systematically comparing potentials of the relevant domains with gaps in UXD: products, processes and people (see Fig. 1). In the following, the three areas are described and illustrated with an example – also highlighting challenges in each area.

2.1 Product

Example. It is the final of the football world cup 2014. Millions of people around the globe have followed the event for the last four weeks – experiencing joy, excitement, fear, etc. Now after the final win of Germany the crowd in the stadium, people at home or on the streets are celebrating with the winning team, others suffering with defeated Argentina or again others just following the spectacle, but all being fascinated and thrilled, experiencing something special.

What are the important aspects behind these experiences? It is possible to describe them as an adventure that is shaped by three factors [5] (Fig. 2): (1) experiencing "controlled danger" (e.g.: Is your favorite team going to lose and exit from the tournament?); (2) different forms of surprises (e.g.: When are the goals scored? How many? By whom?); (3) various modifications of the new and foreign (e.g.: Atmosphere, supporters, stadiums, participating teams, media, etc. are different every four years when the world cup takes place.). The criteria of newness, surprise and danger together lead to an increased experience of the moment, an escape from daily life and the experience of "flow". Besides, aspects like the world cup history, prestige, expectations of supporters, connected emotions etc. can also play an important role and intensify the experience.

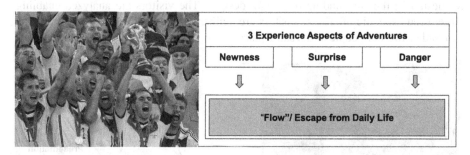

Fig. 2. Award ceremony of the FIFA world cup 2014 (© by Agência Brasil) and aspects of adventure experience in sports [5].

Description. It is not the goal to create a second football world cup. Yet, we can learn a lot for User Experience Design by studying the characteristics of occurring experiences, such as the ones explained before. By analyzing "products" from specific experience oriented areas (e.g. sports event, sports activity, movie, computer game etc.) via observations, interviews and literature review we can derive important characteristics of experiences that emerge in these fields. We transfer these aspects to product development, defining requirements for the characteristics of User Experiences and providing patterns to purposefully design UX. Thus, product developers are supported, knowing which aspects to consider in experience design and being guided by successful examples from other disciplines.

Questions. When analyzing experiences in certain fields and transferring explanations to User Experience Design several questions occur: Can various experiences be unified in one model, defining the main requirements for User Experience? Which aspects of experiences in other areas can be transferred into technical products? Are experiences emerging in certain areas related to specific target groups and therefore limited in their transferability? Besides our main analysis we address these questions as well as challenges in the following categories as part of our research.

2.2 Process

Example. You enter a big hotel in the mountains. But it feels like entering a new world, a place you want to stay. The surrounding makes you experience the big hotel like a traditional cottage. Although the hotel is almost fully booked it does not seem there are many people around. It feels cozy and of high quality at the same time. You do not feel the daily rush. Every detail seems to fit – the wine bottles stored next to your table, the stony floor…

How is this experience designed? According to the model shown in Fig. 3 in tourism defining a theme (e.g. mountain cottage) is the first step towards an intended experience. Based on this theme the presentation concept is an instrument for strategically planning the holistic experience and adjusting different elements to each other (e.g. rooms arranged similar to traditional cottages). Within this concept attractions create various experience potentials (e.g. wine cellar) whereas the setting is the aesthetic instrument for designing the surrounding (e.g. light design). The visitors are analyzed enabling target group specific offerings. Visitors are deliberately guided in between attractions to avoid crowds of people at the same place.

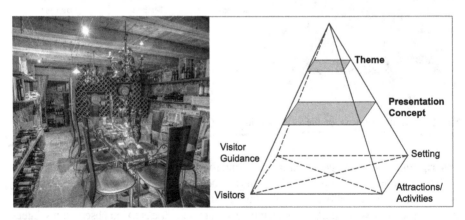

Fig. 3. Wine Cellar at Angerer Alm (© by Angerer Alm) and tourism experience production model [6].

Description. Not only the "products" differ in product development and experience oriented disciplines. Also the processes that produce these products and possibly lead to experiences are remarkably different. Product development processes are traditionally product oriented. Problems occur in maintaining initial experience ideas throughout the development process and accordingly designing consistent User Experiences [7]. In contrast, e.g. processes in tourism or film production processes have the explicit goal of and succeed in creating experiences. We analyze processes in the experience domains and combine advantages of approaches keeping the product in focus but integrating new elements to keep the story behind the product alive (e.g. presentation concept).

Questions. Challenges on the way of adapting processes from other disciplines to UXD are among others: To which degree are experiences in other areas designed systematically or rather are emerging randomly? Do adaptions affect the whole product development process or only certain development phases (e.g. idea generation)?

2.3 People

Example. A young man is playing a video game of the Indiana Jones series on his computer. He is absolutely fascinated by the interplay of several aspects: the thrilling story, the amazing sound, the great design and the convincing gameplay. Not recognizing the world around him at this moment, he is taking the role of the game character, experiencing an artificial adventure.

Which competencies are essential to design such a gaming experience? Figure 4 shows the team around the creative director who communicates the overall creative vision within the game development team and takes care that this vision is realized with every aspect of the game. He interacts with several team members with different backgrounds: production (producer), art (concept artist), design (lead designer, world builder, writer) and engineering (sound designer). The roles vary from team to team. One role is not necessarily performed by one person but each role brings in a specific expertise on the way to designing gaming experiences.

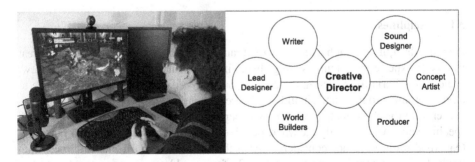

Fig. 4. Gamer immersing into fictional world (© by Laura Hordern) and team members in game development [8].

Description. People involved in the design process are the third category that is concerned in our approach. By analyzing team compositions and established roles in experience oriented disciplines, we extract new roles to be introduced in UXD. Experts from other areas can also bring their expertise into development teams directly, generating ideas that are out of scope of traditional developers. For example a creative director or a film director could be integrated in an interdisciplinary UX team to keep the intended story behind a technical product. The right level of integrating experts from experience oriented disciplines into development teams has to be defined, finding a balance between challenges of diverse teams and improved creativity for potential UX innovations.

Questions. Concerning this category, it is important to analyze the following questions: Which existing roles in product development and User Experience Design [9] can be enhanced with aspects from other disciplines? Which new roles should be introduced? What is the reason for improved experience design when integrating people into design teams – participation of an expert from an experience oriented field or just the presence of someone who has the ability and right to think different?

2.4 Integration

The three categories are not analyzed completely separately. Aiming at the development of support on the way to UX, all models, methods etc. are integrated into a User Experience Design process: (1) the "product" as the target to enable positive UX at the end of the process, (2) the "process" building the framework for the way towards the target and providing support on this way and (3) "people" in the form of UX team roles realizing the product in the process. This work builds on a User Experience Design process (www.designingexperiences.org) that was developed in an interdisciplinary research project [9]. We aim at enhancing and adapting this process according to findings of the systematic approach explained in this paper.

3 Research Design

3.1 Disciplines

Potential disciplines which address a broad range of potential users and provide a great variety of experience potentials are gathered in a user survey and by literature review. We define criteria for selecting the areas to be analyzed. Relevant disciplines have to offer a certain "product" and should also address economic aspects. The second important criterion is the orientation towards experiences. These should be the aim in the specific fields. Areas of daily life where positive or negative experiences occur randomly (e.g. road traffic) are not considered. Also the transferability of characteristics into product development is a main criterion. So far we address sports, gaming industry, tourism, film industry, marketing, arts, music, experiential education and events management. The disciplines are ranked, promising the biggest impact on UXD in product development and offering a realistic extract for the research agenda.

3.2   Analysis

The Analysis can be divided into two parts – theoretical and practical investigation. By reviewing literature, we derive theoretical models and processes in experience focused disciplines. In addition, we interview experts which are deeply involved in the specific fields (e.g. sports psychologist, film director) revealing substantial insights. By this means we gather triggers for experiences (e.g. possibility to win or lose in sports) and theoretical models and approaches that exist for these specific experiences. On the other hand we analyze "products" from the specified areas (e.g. sports event, sports activity, movie etc.) and emerging experiences by observations as well as by interviewing involved persons. Considering the growing popularity and evidence base for design thinking approaches much can be learned from engaging with people committed to a certain discipline (e.g. game players, sports enthusiasts and film connoisseurs) when attempting to construct a new framework for effective User Experience Design.

3.3   Demand

With our approach we want to overcome existing shortcomings in User Experience Design. Therefore, we analyze the status quo in research and industry of product development concerning the design of UX. Finding and addressing requirements of UX theory and needs of industry partners we aim at building our approach on a profound basis and providing useful support. Industry partners assess the potentials of new ideas and various sources are used to evaluate new approaches, methods and processes.

3.4   Background

Supporting our approach, we look at basics of some specific fields, besides UX and general psychological background of experiences. The field of bio-inspired design is analyzed, revealing challenges to be faced when integrating ideas and approaches from another discipline into the field of product development. Design Thinking provides the background for integrating "users" of other disciplines into our analysis. Gamification is examined as an approach which already introduces gaming elements into technical products.

3.5   Development of Support

Ultimately support for the conscious design of UX is developed regarding the three categories: products, processes and people. Therefore, we compare approaches from the different disciplines and extract main findings. Analyzed mechanisms are transformed into patterns to be used in product development, supporting designers in purposefully creating experience products: a requirements model and according checklists for experience products, a process for purposefully designing these products supplemented with necessary methods and specifications of roles needed on this way. Finally, models and methods have to be presented and communicated in an understandable and appealing way for developers (e.g. integrating experience examples from the original discipline and linking them to technical application).

4   Conclusion

While User Experience Design is a rather young discipline within product development other disciplines are traditionally focused on creating experiences. The originality of the approach is the systematic analysis of experience related disciplines to extract concrete recommendations, guidelines and design patterns for UXD. It aims at the creation of support for product designers. Demand has been identified in research and industry regarding three categories – being optimized concerning technical implementation (products), systematic approaches (processes) and engineering competences (people) but requiring external input to create inspiring experience products. We want to enhance existing approaches in UXD with identified and specified mechanisms of designing experiences and evaluate these new methods and tools in student projects at university and real development projects in industry.

References

1. Roto, V., Law, E., Vermeeren, A., Hoonhout, J.: User experience white paper - bringing clarity to the concept of user experience (2011). www.allaboutux.org/files/UX-WhitePaper.pdf
2. Hassenzahl, M.: Experience Design – Technology for All the Right Reasons. Morgan & Claypool Publishers, San Francisco (2010)
3. Norman, D.: Emotional Design - Why We Love (or Hate) Everyday Things. Basic Books, New York (2005)
4. Kim, J., Park, S., Hassenzahl, M., Eckoldt, K.: The essence of enjoyable experiences: the human needs. In: Marcus, A. (ed.) HCII 2011 and DUXU 2011, Part I. LNCS, vol. 6769, pp. 77–83. Springer, Heidelberg (2011)
5. Schleske, W.: Abenteuer – Wagnis – Risiko im Sport. Struktur und Bedeutung aus pädagogischer Sicht. Hofmann, Schorndorf (1977)
6. Müller, H.R., Scheurer, R.: Tourismusdestinationen als Erlebniswelt – Ein Leitfaden zur Angebots-Inszenierung. Forschungsinstitut für Freizeit und Tourismus, Universität Bern (2004)
7. Kremer, S., Michailidou, I., von Saucken, C., Lindemann, U.: User experience milestones – structuring the development of experience products. In: Marcus, A. (ed.) DUXU 2014, Part IV. LNCS, vol. 8520, pp. 308–318. Springer, Heidelberg (2014)
8. Chandler, H.: The Game Production Handbook. Jones & Bartlett Learning, Burlington (2014)
9. Bengler, K., Butz, A., Diwischek, L., Frenkler, F., Körber, M., Kremer, S., Landau, M., Loehmann, S., Lindemann, U., Michailidou, I., Norman, D., Pfalz, F., von Saucken, C., Schumann, J.: CAR@TUM: The Road to User Experience (2014). www.designingexperiences.org

On Chinese Online P2P Lender's Model Building on the Macro, Micro and Industry Level

Qiwei Liang[✉]

Shanghai DianRong Financial Information Service LLC, Shanghai, China
fredjoyliang@gmail.com

Abstract. Only in a few years, P2P lending prospered in China, with the annual growth rate over 300 %. But in China, the extension and innovation of P2P industry is not mature yet. Especially, there is little innovation attempting from the lender-side. This paper studies on the macro, industry and micro level to investigate the Chinese lender's preference and its causes and try to dig out the opportunities in the market. On this basis, this paper gives out a typical lender's model in P2P in China. The results are worthwhile for related practitioners to innovate new financing products for lenders in China.

Keywords: Chinese online P2P · Lender-side · Macro level · Micro level · Industry level

1 Background

1.1 Online P2P's Origin and Current Situation

P2P (peer-to-peer) lending is a kind of individual debit and credit behavior besides the governmental financial organizations or systems. With the development of internet and the matureness of credit situation, the linkage of internet makes numerous borrowers and lenders break the offline limits of area and community of acquaintance. The scope of peer-to-peer debtor-creditor relationship largely expanded, coming up with the online credit platforms.

Since 2005, represented by Zopa, Lending Club, Prosper, P2P lending marketplace has grown up in the Occident, followed with the whole industry's upsurge in the world. P2P online credit platform develops rapidly in the Occident while is still at its initial stage in Europe and Asia.

1.2 P2P in China

In May 2006, CreditEase was established, entering the P2P industry from the angle of petty loan. In August 2007, the first real online P2P platform PaiPaiDai was formed. Since 2011, there came up an influx in the P2P industry, with the amount of platforms and annual trading volume rising up 4–5 times per year. In the aspect of industry volume, online P2P in China has already exceeded the one in UK or US [3, 4].

© Springer International Publishing Switzerland 2015
A. Marcus (Ed.): DUXU 2015, Part I, LNCS 9186, pp. 315–327, 2015.
DOI: 10.1007/978-3-319-20886-2_30

1.3   Extension and Innovation of P2P Industry

As a peer-to-peer lending model, generally P2P lending includes three stakeholders at least, which are borrower, lender and platform.

The extension and innovation of the P2P lending model are conspicuous. For example, in the US, Lending Club appeared as an app on Facebook social media, in order to achieve information and dig its values. Prosper once tried to use the online auction system to match its lenders and borrowers.

In China, in regard of lender, there are different segments, from the acquisition of customers to the design of investment products, as shown in Table 1.

Table 1. Lender-side segmentation in China [2]

Stakeholder			Details	Feature
Lender-Side	The acquisition of customers	Online	Acquire lenders via non-offline way, e.g. online marketing, tele-sales, etc	• Low acquisition cost • High demands of projecting, publicizing, and promoting
		Offline	Acquire lenders via offline way, e.g. offline events, ground-sales, etc	• High acquisition cost • KPI can be easily quantified and copied • Apply to specific groups
	The design of investment products	Manual-investment	Lender should choose loan and set investing amount by himself/herself.	• Lender has the right to select on his/her own • The operation might be complicated • The loan of excellent quality might be hard to buy
		Auto-investment	Lender sets the investing rules, such as loan type and total investment amount, and entrust the P2P platform to choose the final loans automatically	• The operation is simple. • Lender has no right to select on his/her own • The auto-investment model might cause controversy
		Automatic Investment Plan (AIP)	Lender invest automatically in the way of automatic investment plan, by setting standardized loan type, interest rate and investing period	• The operation is simpler • There is an implication of tough cashing. • If the platform operates wrongly, there would be controversy of funding pool, and other violation problems

The extension and innovation of P2P industry is not mature yet. Most of the innovating attempts start from the borrower-side or the platform's turnover itself. There is little innovation attempting from the lender-side.

1.4   Research Necessity

Nowadays, the number of middle class and the rich in China is increasing rapidly. Their demand of managing wealth is becoming stronger and stronger. The contradictory between the product's homogenization and lender's strong financing requirements puts the research on lender in the fore. The results are worthwhile for related practitioners to innovate new financing products for lenders in China.

2   Research Methods

2.1   Research Framework

This paper studies on the macro, industry and micro level to investigate the Chinese lender's preference and its causes.

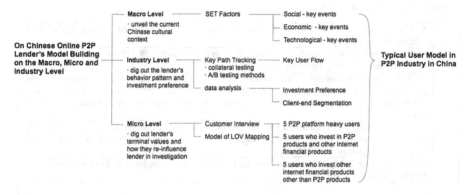

Fig. 1. Research framework

On this basis, this paper gives out a typical lender's model in P2P in China (Fig. 1).

2.2   Macro Level

On the macro level, this paper uses Cagan and Vogel's SET Factors (Social – Eco-nomic - Technological) to unveil the current Chinese cultural context. "The

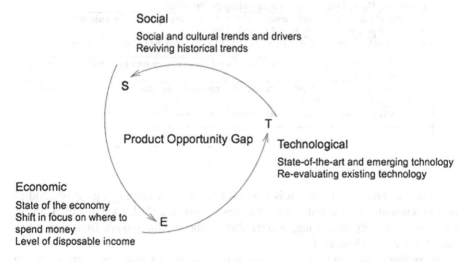

Fig. 2. Scanning SET Factors leads to POGs by Cagan and Vogel [1]

changes in Social, Economics, and Technological Factors that produce new trends and create Product Opportunity Gaps (POGs)." (Cagan, Vogel) (Fig. 2) Table 2 lists part of Social, Economic, and Technological key events and governmental policies happened or announced around 2014.

Table 2. Part of Social, Economic, and Technological key events and governmental policies happened or announced around 2014 in China.

Society	• China started the third time of economic census on Jan. 1st 2014, using the modern information technology
	• Postal services kept rapid developing. Its volume exceeds 268 billion. Express exceeded 9.2billion times, ranking the 2nd in the world
	• The State Council issued *Advices on establishing a unified basic endowment insurance system for rural residents*, combined the new one for rural residents and the one for city residents, coming out 4 unification in system's name, policy standards, management services, information system
	• The State Council issued *Instruction advices on speeding up the productive services accelerate the work of adjusting and upgrading the industrial structure*, suggesting that the government will guide the market main body behavior
	• On Sep. 19th 2014, Alibaba was listed on the NYSE. The trade became the one of the largest IPO trading in the world
	• ......
Economy	• Lenovo and Google reached a significant agreement that Lenovo would purchase Motorola's smart mobile phone businesss at the price of 2.9 billion USD
	• The number of Alipay's identificated real users exceeded 300million. The company became the largest payment company in the world
	• The World Intellectual Property Organization Office in China opened in Beijing on Jul. 10th 2014. The Number of international applications received by State Intellectual Property Office of the P.R.C as the receiving office has exceeded Germany
	• ......
Technology	• China Gold Association released that China produced gold 428.163 ton, growing to record levels, ranking 1st in the world for seven consecutive years
	• The People's Bank of China published social financing statistics for the first time. Figures showed that Guangdong, Beijing, Jiangsu ranking the first three.
	• National Bureau of Statistics announced that the consumer price of the residents nationwide increase 2.6 percent, below the annual target of 3.5%
	• China ranked first in global goods trading in 2013, exceeded the US for the first time
	• China Securities Regulatory Commission issued the three measures to strengthen the process supervision of IPO
	• National Bureau of Statistics showed the narrowing increase trend of Sales Price of Commercial Residential Housing
	• Chinese agricultural insurance market ranks 1st in the Asia, 2nd in the world
	• ......

From the above key events, it is obvious that China is keeping a positive trend of modern development. Central Bank continues to follow a slack fiscal policy. Chinese economy is steadily increasing, mainly due to the wealth growth from real estate market and the stock market.

According to Boston Consulting Group [5], Mainland China per capita net worth increase rapidly since 2000, and the number of middle-class has already exceeded

300 million. Financial assets share a high percentage (49 %) of household assets, especially the high savings ratio. As figures from National Development and Reform Committee, China regional economy has shown two positive changes. The one is the Narrowing decline in economic growth in the eastern area. The other is that the central region actively undertakes regional and international industrial transfer on the East Coast area and its fixed-asset investment growth ranks first in all regions.

The three basic laws of Internet provide the technology foundation for the rapid increase of basic internet finance: Moore's Law (more powerful computing search ability),More than Moore(MtM)(more faster information exchange), and Metcalfe's Law(more wider social linkage). All these technology developments make/lead:

- The appearance of internet indirect financing activities. The traditional indirect banking financing is exerted a negative impact while the mode of online P2P is prospering.
- The decrease of information asymmetry of provision and requirement and the weakening of offline financial intermediaries. Moore's Law and MtM led a high decrease in modern information technology cost.
- The decrease of borrower's credit risks by means of Big Data and new credit analysis system. Take Alibaba as an example, it quantizes the data within its own network (customer purchase data, credit data, distribution data, authentication info, competitive data, etc.), combining with third party organization (such as the Customs, taxation, water and electricity.) to get a model of identification and control standards. The default rate gets lower thanks to the credit analysis of data exchange.
- The realization of petty loan and inclusive finance by reducing transaction costs. In the Internet Era, the long tail theory attracts people's attention. Numerous small markets resemble together to compete with the mainstream market. The loan amount of online credit platform is comparatively small, which is propitious to risk control and is the result of focusing on the financing requirements of small and micro businesses. As to lender, the minimum of online investment amount is smaller than any one of the traditional ways ever.

2.3   Industry Level

On the industry level, this paper takes Dianrong.com, a typical P2P lending platform in China, as the research sample, using heatmap, collateral testing and A/B testing methods, via the 3rd party online data analysis tools to dig out the lender's behavior pattern and investment preference. The details are listed as follows:

- Use Google Analytics (GA) to get lender's page flow on web site.
- Use Baidu Fengchao System to observe new lender's click heatmap of main pages to see which parts attracts new lender more.
- Use Optimizely to do A/B testing to eliminate the design causes.
- Use Flurry to do collateral testing on mobile app.
- Use company raw data to make up for the deficiency.

After 5 months' data tracking, this research gets 2,740,373 pieces of data and finishes 15 A/B testing. It came out several obvious conclusions: (Due to Non-Disclosure Agreement, some raw data or graphs might not be listed here, which did not affect obtaining the conclusions.)

1. According to GA, new user's bounce rate is 54.11 %, while old user's bounce rate is 23.00 %. The conversion rate is 4.16 % without promotion. The most successful promotion led to a 23 times higher conversion rate.
2. According to Baidu Fengchao System:

   - Compared with old user, potential new user (who register and become lenders later) stay much longer on the home page and About-Us page.
   - The Leadership Page has the most hits among the information pages, closely following the Partnership Page. New user is more interested in the platform level information such as Platform Operation Mode, Leadership Introduction and News Reports.
   - The hottest part on the home page is Principal Protection Plan, following the Platform Operation Mode.

3. GA shows a most important key-user-flow on the PC Web (shown in the Fig. 3).

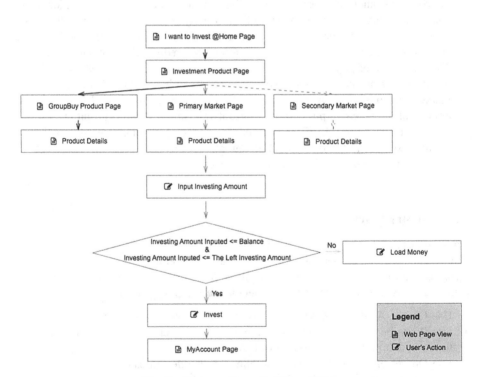

Fig. 3. Key user flow - Investment Flow

4. Data from GA and inside the company show lender's investment distribution in Tables 3 and 4.

   Instructions: New-user Group is a kind of product containing a package of loans in Dianrong, which provides a definite annualized return of 7 % and is both principal and interest guaranteed. AB means loans with a safer loan grade with annualized return range from 9.49 % to 13.99 %, usually is principal-guaranteed by a third-party company. CDEF means loans with higher interest rate (14.49 %-23.99 %) but higher risk at the same time.

Table 3. Total investment amount of different loan product (RMB) from Aug. 2014 to Dec. 2014

Month	New-user Group	AB	CDEF
2014-08	4005500	18970800	5989700
2014-09	6027800	14826600	1845100
2014-10	15237100	16202300	1111900
2014-11	43334600	29246300	7400
2014-12	45517300	24965300	700

Table 4. Number of notes invested in different loan product from Aug. 2014 to Dec. 2014

Month	New-user Group	AB	CDEF
2014-08	3284	6635	20172
2014-09	5864	9154	6309
2014-10	5759	8510	4415
2014-11	7708	14794	17
2014-12	12786	15095	3

From above, it is obvious that **New-user Group** enjoys a swift increasing trend. **AB** shares a slower increasing trend. **CDEF** decreases rapidly. Thus, we can come to conclusion that most lenders prioritize security over than higher interest.

Obviously, security factor is more attractive to lender than the interest rate factor.

5. Data from Optimizely and Flurry provided lenders' distribution on client platform (shown in Table 5).

Once H5 is released, the number of unique visitors balloons. According to the collateral testing data collected on Flurry, the subsistence users of the mobile app are exponentially higher than these of the PC web. This might attribute to smart phone's mobility and the convenience of promotion ways, such as pushing notifications accordingly, etc.

Table 5. Unique Visitors in different client-end from Aug. 2014 to Dec. 2014

Month	iOS	Android	PC Web	H5[a]
2014-08	6419	2016	128472	–
2014-09	11195	7462	153603	–
2014-10[b]	10613	8124	111884	25
2014-11	17508	15685	219729	13264
2014-12	24209	21230	258149	179565

[a]DianRong released H5 website on the last day of November. Before that, user will see PC web if he/she open the website on the mobile.

[b]The little decrease in October might be caused due to the golden week during the China National Day.

2.4 Micro Level

On the micro level, this paper chooses 15 end users, including 5 P2P platform heavy users, 5 users who invest in P2P products and other internet financial products, and 5 users who invest other internet financial products other than P2P products, and separately have one on one deep customer interview on each of them to get the insights of end-users and map them to the model of LOV(List of Values) [6–11] to dig out lender's terminal values and how they re-influence lender in investigation.

Interview Design

Get Customers. First, put a notice on WangDaiZhiJia (The biggest P2P portal website in China) forum to recruit customers who are qualified for the deep customer interview, and then randomly choose 15 end users, including 5 P2P platform heavy users, 5 users who invest in P2P products and other internet financial products, and 5 users who invest other internet financial products other than P2P products (Table 6).

Interview Process. Each interview involves 1 host(author), 1 note-taker, and 1 interviewee, and is taken in a ordinary café. The interview process includes Welcome Interviewee, Collect Demographics, Tell a story(Let interviewee imagine that he/she has some spare money and think what he/she will do with it.); Demo Financing Products(three typical consumer-oriented financing products on www.yooli.com is shown to interviewee, which contain of normal P2P loans, products containing a package of loans, and money fund products), Simulate a Fake Investment, Dig Insights, Documentation;

Analysis and Insights. After documentation, elimination of similar factors, comparing the model of LOV (List of Values) [6], this paper get 45 Attributes, 6 Consequences and 6 Values, listed as follow:

Attributes

1. Animation Effect; 2. Infographic Illustration; 3. Auditing; 4. Auto-investment Products; 5. Bank Card Binding; 6. Charging Fees; 7. Company Brand; 8. Company News;

Table 6. Part of customer interview documentation[a]

Interviewee[b]	A1	A2	A3	A4	A5
Gender	female	male	male	male	male
Age	30	27	34	29	32
Job	Designer	Marketing Specialist	Software Developer	Product Manager	Software Architecture
Investing experience	• RenRenMoney • Yooli • DianRong	• RenRenDai • iTouZi • YongLiBao	• JimuBox • DianRong	• Yooli • RenRenDai • DianRong • WaCai	• JimuBox • Lufax
Financial habits	put 20 % salary into investment	put a quarter of salary into investment	depend on promotion	diversify his investments on every platform	put 30 % salary into investment, invest more if there is a promotion, the maximum percentage is 50 %
Three main factors considered when they choose a P2P platform	1. Security 2. Interest Rate 3. Investment Period	1. Company Authentication 2. Guarantee System 3. CRM	1. Principal Guarantee Plan 2. Platform Operation Mode 3. Loan Details	1. Company Reliability 2. Loan Details 3. Liquidity	1. Security 2. Interest Rate 3. Payment Reliability
......	......	......	......	......	......

[a]The table only lists part of documentation due to limited paper length.
[b]A group members are 5 P2P platform heavy users.

9. Company Performance; 10. Company Popularity; 11. Company Reliability; 12. Company Size; 13. Company's Profit Mode; 14. Compensation System; 15. CRM; 16. FAQ List; 17. Friend's Reference; 18. Principal Protection Plan; 19. Highness of Loan Risk; 20. Interest Calculation Method; 21. Interest Rate; 22. Investment Period; 23. Investment Strategy; 24. Liquidity; 25. Loan Amount; 26. Loan Description/Details; 27. Loan Period; 28. Loan Verification; 29. Minimum Investment Amount; 30. New User Tutorial; 31. Company Office Address; 32. Package Investment Products; 33. Payment Reliability; 34. Platform Operation Mode; 35. Policies and Regulations; 36. Principal Guarantee Plan; 37. Promotion; 38. Repayment Method; 39. Repayment Process; 40. Risk Control; 41. Risk Model; 42. Capital Security; 43. Third-party Guarantee; 44. Third-party Payment Channel; 45. Withdraw Time.

Consequences

46. Easy to Operate; 47. Easy to Understand; 48. Increase of Efficiency; 49. Money-Saving; 50. Creativity; 51. Superiority; 52. Increase of Wealth

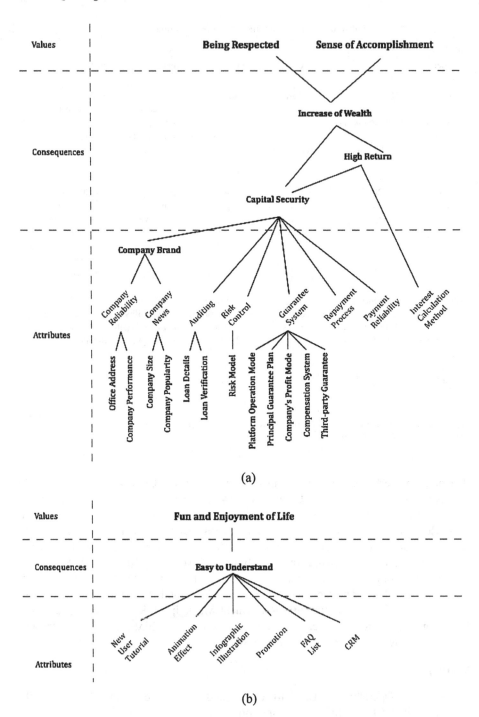

Fig. 4. (continued)

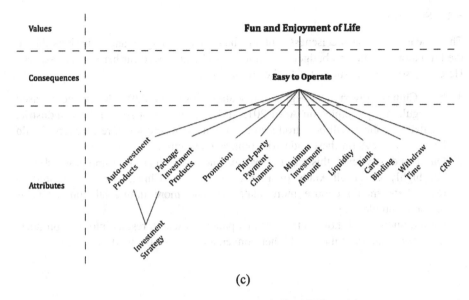

(c)

Fig. 4. The three widest chains in the MEC model

Values

53. Self-repect; 54. Being Respected; 55. Self-fulfillment; 56. Security; 57. Fun and Enjoyment of Life; 58. Excitement; 59. Sense of Accomplishment

Then map the factors to the model of LOV via the Means-End Chain methods. During the one on one interview, author try to get how the interviewees meet their self-value via P2P products' attributes. After the interview, author use means-end-method to get the hierarchical value map (HVM) to illustrator these relationships.

The attributes displayed in each chain reveal a certain group's preference. The more often the factor is being mentioned, the wider the chain is. The three HVMs in Fig. 4 show the widest chains in the model.

3 Conclusions and Suggestions

3.1 Conclusions

This paper studies on the macro, industry and micro level to investigate the Chinese lender's preference and its causes. On this basis, this paper gives out a typical lender's model in P2P in China. On the macro level, it comes with inspirations of creating breakthrough products by means of the SET Factors. On the industry level, it turns out obvious preferences and trends of lenders when they do some investment. On the micro level, it finds lender's concerns and deep values. Based on the above results, P2P product strategy maker can refer to the results above to map out the product strategy for lender, including choosing the target market, positioning the final customers, designing a appropriate products for them, etc.

3.2   Suggestions

This research aims at preciseness, but still has some oversights and omissions due to the limitation of time and budget, which needs to be improved further in some aspects. Here lists some suggestions for further researches:

1. Now Chinese government begins to pay attentions to the P2P industry and released 10 regulatory principles on April 2015. It is believed that some related industrial regulatory polices will be introduced soon. On the macro level, researchers should keep a close eye on these industrial polices constantly.
2. On the industry level, this paper only uses one platform as an example, which may not highly cover all kinds of P2P companies in China. For further studies, researchers should choose more platforms and more influential companies as research samples.
3. On the micro level, how to transfer this paper's research results into new products innovation and contribute to higher conversion rate is also worth of study.

Announcement

The author holds the post of User Experience Designer in Shanghai DianRong Financial Information Service LLC.

The paper focuses on the academic research and does not constitute investment advice.

References

1. Cagan, J., Vogel, C.M.: Creating Breakthrough Products: Innovation from Product Planning to Program Approval, p. XXXI. FT Press, New Jersey (2002)
2. Caijing, L.Y., Shuju, L.Y.: 2014 China P2P Debit and Credit Service Industry White Book, p. 11. China Economic Publishing House, Beijing (2014)
3. CBN New Economic Research Center: 2013 China P2P Debit and Credit Service Industry White Book. China Economic Publishing House, Beijing (2013)
4. Fang, W.Z., Jiang, Z.S., Guo, Y.H., Zhou, T.L., Dong, C.K.: On Theories, Practices and Regulations on Internet Finance. China Economic Publishing House, Beijing (2014)
5. Beardsley, B., Becerra, J., Burgoni, F., Holley, B., Kessler, D., Muxi, F., Naumann, M., Tang, T., Zakrzewski, A.: Global Wealth 2014: Riding a Wave of Growth, BCG Prospectives (2014). https://www.bcgperspectives.com/content/articles/financial_institutions_business_unit_strategy_global_wealth_2014_riding_wave_growth/
6. Kahle, L.R.: Social Values and Social Change: Adaptation to Life in Amercia. Praeger, New York (1983)
7. Kahle, L.R.: Attitudes and Social Adaptation: A Person-Situation Interaction Approach. Pergamon, Oxford (1984)

8. Kahle, L.R.: The value segmentation debate continues. Mark. News **18**(14), 2 (1984)
9. Kahle, L.R.: Social values in the eighties: a special issue. Psychol. Mark. **2**(4), 231–237 (1985)
10. Kahle, L.R.: The nine nations of north america and the value basis of geographic segmentation. J. Mark. **50**, 37–47 (1986)
11. Veroff, J., Douvan, E., Kulka, R.A.: The Inner American. Basic Books, New York (1981)

Twenty Years on: A Second Look at 10 Important Social Impact Characteristics of Computer Technology

Blaise W. Liffick[✉]

Department of Computer Science, Millersville University,
Millersville, PA 17551, USA
Blaise.liffick@millersville.edu

Abstract. Twenty years ago, Liffick [38] explored 10 characteristics of computer technology that contributed to their impact on societal issues of that era. The purpose of this exploration was to "anticipate the social consequences of a new product and mitigate any potential negative effects it may have on society." Furthermore, "the intent of developing a list of these characteristics is that it could lead to a better understanding of the nature of the social impact of computers. In this way, it might be possible to examine a new computer project at the time of its design ... to determine its potential impacts as a social change agent". The purpose of this current paper is to review the characteristics originally proposed to determine whether they are more or less relevant, given the enormous changes in computer technology (CT) in the last 20 years.

Keywords: Human-computer interaction · HCI · Social impact · Computers and society

1 Introduction

What was the state of computer technology (CT) in 1995? Cell phone technology was just beginning its second generation (with about 33 M subscribers in the US, 10 % of today's subscribership). Wi-Fi was still too new a technology to be available and mobile devices were limited to the new technology of unconnected personal data assistants. The typical personal computer configuration in 1995 was 8 megabytes of RAM, 33 MHz processor, 1 gigabyte hard drive, and a 28.8 K-bit modem. Today's system is about 1000 times more powerful, following Moore's Law quite closely. The first web browser was released in 1993 and the World Wide Web Consortium was formed in October 1994, so the WWW was still relatively new in 1995. Current estimates are that there are now 4.36 billion web pages [15].

Also consider that 20 years represents about ¼ to ⅓ of the entire history of modern computing. Furthermore, this timeframe represents a growth in the technology by approximately 10-fold, so this 20-year timespan is a convenient length of time for us to use for this comparison.

The list of social impact characteristics discussed in 1995 were (in no particular order):

© Springer International Publishing Switzerland 2015
A. Marcus (Ed.): DUXU 2015, Part I, LNCS 9186, pp. 328–338, 2015.
DOI: 10.1007/978-3-319-20886-2_31

1. *ubiquity* – CT is pervasive.
2. *magnification* – CT magnifies the amount of information available, through both collection and generation, as well as magnifying the effects of errors.
3. *accessibility* – the increased availability of information, devices, etc.
4. *reproducibility/distributability* – exact duplication of information artifacts (e.g. videos) and the ability to distribute them widely (e.g. broadcast).
5. *lack of accountability* – the link between the creator/supplier of information and the consumer of that information is masked through many layers of separation by networks, software, and lack of human participation.
6. *temporality* – CT affects both time (in both real and perceived ways) and timeliness.
7. *spatiality* – distances increasingly no longer matter.
8. *surviellability* – the ability to not only gather massive amounts of data about someone, but to watch them in near-real time.
9. *shifting relationships/changes in intercommunication protocols* – how we interact with one another on both personal and professional levels.
10. *illusion of precision* – the many ways that what is truly imprecise is masked by CT to appear precise.

2 The Characteristics Today

As can be seen in the discussion below, these issues have increased in significance right along with the increasing power of the technology that affects them.

2.1 Ubiquity

It is not difficult to recognize that with computer technology having advanced so significantly since 1995, the penetration of computers into our environment would enjoy a correlative increase, to the point that a new term has been coined along the way: pervasive computing. The numbers are staggering: by mid-2013, Apple claims to have shipped over 600 million iOS devices (iPhones, iPads, iPods), while Google claims over 900 million Android devices [27]. Considering that the first iPod was introduced in 2001, it means on average about 125 million devices per year are purchased. There is currently nearly one mobile phone subscription per person in the world. There were 296.0 million PCs/laptops sold in 2013, and 195.4 million tablets [5]. And these are just the independent mobile devices. There are countless additional embedded devices in our cars, appliances, and in every electronic device in existence.

Wearable computers appear to be the next evolutionary step, with recently introduced devices such as FitBit [23], the Samsung smartwatch [16], and Apple smartwatch [3]. Beyond the current landscape of such devices lies "implantables, disposable wearables, ingestibles, and smart prosthetic devices" [22, pp 20–22].

What's different after 20 years is certainly the penetration of CT into our everyday lives. The reality is that we now expect computers to be everywhere. More importantly, thanks to cell technology and WiFi, we expect to be connected to the entire world of computing from nearly everywhere.

2.2 Magnification

It is easy to demonstrate the power of CT to magnify, as there are examples in our daily news. On the dark side of this characteristic is the ability of a single individual (or a small group) to disrupt society, including hacks that deny the use of services as well as those that steal data [25, 42, 47, 55]. The potential for devastation is enormous.

The concept of *virality* [52] has been coined to encompass those situations that, whether by design or accident, have ended up being transmitted throughout social media on a widespread scale. On the most negative side are examples of cyberbullying, identity theft, and deliberate attempts to harm someone through projecting negative information throughout cyberspace, such as through the use of revenge porn sites [11].

All this is not to say that computer technology doesn't magnify an individual's power in a number of positive ways as well. The success of George Takei to use first Twitter and then Facebook as platforms of personal promotion is a prime example. With a rise from obscurity a few years ago to some 3 million Facebook followers, Takei has used the potential virality of social media to create a distinct voice amongst the cacophony of the millions who are striving to be heard [52].

2.3 Accessibility

In 1995 the discussion centered on the ability to access unlimited information from unlimited locations, despite the fact that transmission speeds were relatively slow, graphics were still crude, and video streaming was still years away. Shopping online had yet to be realized [39]. The number of web pages available was still only in the hundreds of thousands. Most public records had not yet been digitized. Print media was still strong.

Twenty years later online shopping is a major force in the economy, with Amazon alone accounting for nearly $68 billion of total online sales of nearly $7 trillion in 2013 [17]. The number of available web pages indexed by Google tops 4 billion [15].

Another area of digital accessibility that didn't exist in 1995 is ebook publishing. Barely 8 years old, today ebooks are a $6 billion industry, with projections of overtaking print books in total sales within the next two years [43]. Ebooks provide unprecedented access to not only literature but every form of information, with interactive features impossible with printed books.

The most negative side of accessibility has been the explosion of hacking incidents, where personal information, credit card numbers, etc. are frequently stolen [1, 25, 55]. With more of our lives being lived online every day (with online shopping, banking, communication, record keeping, utilities control, social media, etc.), we have all but lost the ability to control information about ourselves. This loss of privacy is a major source of anxiety in the modern age [29].

2.4 Reproducibility/Distributability

As media has shifted toward the digital, the ability to exactly duplicate artifacts has increased so that nearly any form of publishing in text, photographic, audio, or video form can be copied as many times as one would like, nearly instantly with the push of a button. The big fear of the media world in 1995 was digital audio tape (DAT), a technology that was quickly eclipsed and made obsolete (as a general consumer product) by compact disks (CDs). Now, CDs have been made nearly irrelevant by flash drives and through digital distribution systems such as Apple's iTunes, introduced in 2003 [37]. The ease of downloading ebooks onto mobile devices has completely changed the field of publishing, but didn't really take off until the introduction of Amazon's Kindle device in 2007 [29, 43].

Finally, the advent of the social media era has spawned a special language that encapsulates this characteristic. Terms such as retweeting or reposting indicate an ability to distribute a message to a wide audience. Even more significantly, the phrase going viral (or, as George Takei has coined, virality) demonstrates clearly one goal of those who post or tweet [52]. The new concept of the meme is another term that exists solely to describe a social media artifact that has been distributed to an enormous audience.

2.5 Lack of Accountability

The original concern revolved around customer service, where the increasing use of voice menus gave rise to the voice-mail labyrinth, from which there was little hope of escape. This allowed companies to hide from customers while the computerized system gave the appearance of providing quick, accurate service for the most mundane of customer queries. Such automated customer service systems have become somewhat more sophisticated over the last 20 years, improving the delivery of service, but in addition companies have moved customer service centers overseas.

A number of additional examples of a lack of accountability have developed over the past 2 decades. One of the more insidious is social media lurkers, known as trolls, who anonymously post nasty comments [24]. By being anonymously, the poster feels emboldened to say whatever they want, and the post is frequently intended to upset people or to start an argument. Many sites end up shutting down all comments in order to eliminate such a situation.

Similarly, the Internet has also been used to seek revenge, typically anonymously. Revenge porn sites allow ex-boyfriends (and a few ex-girlfriends) to post nude photos of their exes online, along with nasty comments and, frequently, addresses of their targets [11]. Such cyber-stalking has become an increasing problem.

Spam may be the ultimate example of a lack of accountability. An entire industry has been created just to try to filter out spam email.

2.6 Temporality

Computer technology has a great impact on our perceptions of time. In 1995 it was nothing to wait upwards to a minute or more for a web page to load, and many minutes for the typical download, with a maximum transfer speed of 56.6 K bps. Still, our ability to actually transfer files in a relatively short amount of time (compared to sending disks through the mail) was considered a significant improvement in efficiency.

Today, with speeds measuring in gigabits, we routinely expect near instantaneous data transfers and page loads. Our sense of time has become somewhat warped by our ability to place an order for a product and have it delivered the next morning. Indeed, it seems that now, in the era of 3-D printing, we don't even need to wait that long [54]. This "instant consumerism" already pervades our thinking. We expect every transaction to result in instantaneous access to the product we just bought (or at least instantaneous shipping). When we have medical tests, we expect the results to be available, if not immediately, then within a relatively few days. Online, we can instantly not only purchase but compare products, services, and prices that in 1995 still required traveling to possibly multiple stores to accomplish.

One of the most significant changes in society is the immediacy of communication. With cell and Wi-Fi technologies, one can be in continuous communication (text, voice, or video) with anyone. The mobility of devices introduced in just the last 10 years has made it possible to carry our communications devices with us at all times. The delay of communicating by mail, or even email, has all but disappeared. Our modern expectations include being able to access nearly all of our accounts (banking, phone, utility, car, insurance, taxes, medical records, etc.) at any time we choose, any day we choose.

2.7   Spatiality

Just as with temporality, distances have continued to shrink in a number of ways. While in 1995 it was already easy to make a long-distance phone call, such calls still cost extra money at the time. Today, the ability to call nearly anywhere in the world for the base cost of a phone plan is fairly standard.

We have also been able to collaborate with colleagues even more easily than in 1995, when about the only option was to transfer files back and forth. Today collaborative systems such as Google Docs, Dropbox, and the like make it easy to "write, edit, and collaborate wherever you are" [6]. Other tools make it possible to attend meetings using "web conferencing" instead of being physically present [7].

Perhaps the most dramatic example of the spatiality characteristic is when NASA "emailed a tool" to the International Space Station [55]. Of course, what they emailed was instructions that could be used to construct the tool using a 3D printer. But 3D manufacturing shows great promise as a technology that brings buyers and sellers even closer together [12].

2.8   Surveillability

There were few public concerns about digital privacy in 1995, since in general the public was still not very connected. The Electronic Privacy Information Center had just been founded "to focus public attention on emerging civil liberties issues" [4], but with the public being almost entirely computer illiterate, their impact was limited at the time. In the past 20 years, however, issues of privacy have become a significant public concern. In 2008, EPIC released a report on a proposal from Homeland Security for a national ID program [4]. Concerns about the commercial mining of data has grown [20], [48]. The revelations about massive government surveillance programs continue to surface [31]. Even celebrity watching has been enhanced to the point of electronic stalking [18].

2.9   Shifting Relationships/Changes in Intercommunication Protocols

The way we communicate has changed significantly since 1995. At that time the main form of electronic group interaction was still bulletin board systems [26]. But it would be nearly ten more years before social networking websites became popular, with Facebook finally being introduced in 2004.

With the introduction of more sophisticated social media, a more indirect form of mass communication has become commonplace. Rather than sending direct messages to individuals as is generally done with email, these new tools provided a different model of communication: multicasting (posting to a group). This one-to-many form of communication uses networks of "friends" to create a "personal and private community" [9]. This dynamic is much more like a party than traditional forms of communication (one-to-one). Concepts of posting, having followers, creating channels, and using likes, shares, and ratings as a means of communicating interest have all been introduced within the last 10 years.

Another way in which CT has changed channels of communication is through "computer-mediated communication and interaction", where context is often missing or altered [33, p. 8]. Developing trust through computer mediation has become a commonplace occurrence online [21, 28, 51].

2.10   Illusion of Precision

In 1995 I wrote about the general lack of understanding by lay persons regarding how computers actually work, specifically that most people don't understand that computers in reality are amazingly imprecise in several important respects. This concern was based on many years of experience working with computer novices who had no idea that (1) there was finite space in which to store numbers, and that therefore many numbers were approximations, and (2) because numbers are actually stored in binary, some decimal numbers cannot be accurately represented. One textbook demonstrates this to beginning programming students by showing how Java calculates the sum of 0.1 and 0.2 as 0.30000000000000004 [46], but for the vast majority of computer users this fact is unknown.

Today there are many more examples of how the computer supports the illusion of precision. Consider Auto-tune, which "corrects intonation and timing problems in vocals or solo instruments" [2]. This tool gives musical performances the illusion of precise playing or singing. Not that adjustments to recordings didn't happen before auto-tuning; errors such as a missed note were often fixed manually by manipulating the various tracks to add or subtract sounds. With auto-tuning, however, the automatic forcing of notes to be perfectly on pitch can lend an artificial quality to the sound, and many listeners consider the process cheating to make up for an artist's lack of skill [41]. Regardless, its use still pervades pop music.

Search engine results are another example of the illusion of precision. Those who provide search engines use various algorithms to present results to searchers, ranked in what is hoped will be the most relevant pages at the top of the list [40, 44]. To users, this presented ranked list gives the appearance of precisely finding those pages that will be of most interest to the searcher and ordering the list from most to least relevant. However, in fact there is nothing precise about such searches, and biased results are a frequent problem [53]. Indeed, one of the significant imprecisions about this process is the fact that users typically look at only the first page of results, even when more relevant pages might be further down the list [36].

3   Where Things Stand

Twenty years ago I compiled the list of what I felt were the 10 most obvious characteristics of computer technology in an attempt to get a handle on how CT impacts society. Upon the above reflection of the state of computing today, these characteristics are clearly even more prevalent, and represent deep issues related to how computing affects society. Even the characteristics for which there was perhaps minimal evidence in 1995 (e.g. the lack of imprecision or the changes in communication) have advanced to the point where there is more than ample evidence for them – in some cases almost too much evidence, as countless examples are available from which to choose.

4   So What's New

In researching the characteristics above, one additional area quickly surfaced as a major issue related to the social impact of computer technology: the computer as weapon. There are two meanings to this. The first is weapon systems that would not be possible without the computer as an integral component. Nearly all modern weaponry, from rockets to smart bombs, to aircraft and drones, incorporate computer technology to assist in the delivery control systems. There is no doubt that modern weapons would not be possible without computer technology.

The second sense in which "computer as weapon" is meant is in using computers to attack an opponent's digital infrastructure. Some of these attacks are clearly being perpetrated for financial gain, creating substantial economic losses for hacked companies and loss of confidence by consumers [42]. Rather than robbing banks, these criminals are looking for vulnerable companies to loot.

Of perhaps greater concern, however, is the use of hacking as an actual tool of warfare, as a means of causing terror and attempting to destabilize entire countries. This latter form of "computer as weapon" has been in evidence for just the past 10 years [8]. Cyberwarfare is playing an increasing role in how wars are being fought globally [32].

5 Conclusions

There is no doubt that computer technology continues to have a tremendous impact on society, for a number of reasons. The characteristics noted above provide a clear picture of many of the sources of that impact. Revelations of widespread effects of the failure of technology are a weekly, and sometimes daily, occurrence. It is somewhat surprising that the ten characteristics described twenty years ago are not only still relevant, but are actually much easier to articulate – they have become increasingly important rather than having been resolved. And certainly the added eleventh characteristic – the computer as weapon – is the most anxiety-inducing of them all. Does this mean that the future looks bleak, considering that computer technology will continue to have an increasingly negative impact on society?

That is not a preordained conclusion. Indeed, the intent of this list is to try to gain a deeper understanding of the ways in which this technology provides the means of influencing society so that safeguards might be designed into systems rather than just added on once an emergency prompts a response. Future research in this area can focus on providing remedies for each of these characteristics. At the very least, it should be possible to anticipate what social impact a potential computer product might have by mapping its features to these characteristics. In this way, it may be possible to minimize the negative impacts that plague our current use of computer technology.

References

1. 13 Revelations from the Sony hack. Seth Rosenblatt. C/Net, 13 December 2014. http://www.cnet.com/news/13-revelations-from-the-sony-hack/. Accessed 17 Dec 2015
2. www.antares.com
3. Apple Watch Unveiled. C/Net, 11 September 2014. http://www.cnet.com/products/apple-watch/. Accessed 20 Oct 2014
4. www.EPIC.org
5. Global mobile statistics 2014 Part A: Mobile subscribers; handset market share; mobile operators, 16 May 2014. http://mobiforge.com/research-analysis/global-mobile-statistics-2014-part-a-mobile-subscribers-handset-market-share-mobile-operators
6. https://www.google.com/intl/en/docs/about/
7. http://www.gotomeeting.com/online/
8. The history of cyber attacks – a timeline. NATO Review Magazine. http://www.nato.int/docu/review/2013/cyber/timeline/EN/index.htm. Accessed 17 Dec 2014
9. The history of social networking. Digital Trends. http://www.digitaltrends.com/features/the-history-of-social-networking/. Accessed 9 Jan 2015
10. iPhone, iPad and iPod Sales from 1st Quarter 2006 to 4th Quarter 2014. Statista. http://www.statista.com/statistics/253725/iphone-ipad-and-ipod-sales-comparison/. Accessed 27 Dec 2014
11. Misery Merchants. The Economist, 5 July 2014. http://www.economist.com/news/international/21606307-how-should-online-publication-explicit-images-without-their-subjects-consent-be. Accessed 20 Dec 2014
12. Print me a Stradivarius. The Economist, 10 February 2011. http://www.economist.com/node/18114327?story_id=18114327. Accessed 8 Jan 2015

13. REAL ID Implementation Review: Few Benefits, Staggering Costs. EPIC, May 2008. https://epic.org/privacy/id_cards/

14. www.reputation.com

15. The size of the World Wide Web (The Internet). http://www.worldwidewebsize.com/. Accessed 21 Dec 2014

16. The Smartwatch that's also a Smartphone. C/Net, 17 November 2014. http://www.cnet.com/products/samsung-gear-s/. Accessed 1 Dec 2014

17. Statistics and Facts about Online Shopping. Statista. http://www.statista.com/topics/871/online-shopping/. Accessed 3 Jan 2015

18. Ahuja, G.: Does web site promote celebrity stalking? ABC News, 15 March 2006. http://abcnews.go.com/GMA/story?id=1729270. Accessed 4 Jan 2015

19. Anderson, L.: Seduced by 'perfect' pitch: how Auto-Tune conquered pop music. The Verger, 27 February 2013. http://www.theverge.com/2013/2/27/3964406/seduced-by-perfect-pitch-how-auto-tune-conquered-pop-music. Accessed 9 Jan 2015

20. Angwin, J., Valentino-DeVries, J.: Google's iPhone tracking. Wall Street J., 17 February 2012

21. http://www.wsj.com/news/articles/SB10001424052970204880404577225380456599176 Accessed 19 Dec 2014

22. Araujo, I., Araujo, I.: Developing trust in internet commerce. In: Proceedings of the 2003 Conference of the Centre for Advanced Studies on Collaborative Research, pp 1–15. IBM Press (2003)

23. Baker, M., Hong, J., Billinhurst, M.: Wearable computing from jewels to joules. Pervasive Comput. **13**(4), 20–22 (2014). doi:ieeecomputersociety.org/10.1109/MPRV.2014.81

24. Biggs, J.: TC50: FitBit, A Fitness Gadget that Makes Us Want to Exercise. TechCrunch, 9 September 2008. http://techcrunch.com/2008/09/09/tc50-fitbit-fitness-gadget-the-makes-us-want-to-exercise/. Accessed 27 Dec 2014

25. Campbell, T.: Internet Trolls. Internet Archives, 13 July 2001. http://web.archive.org/web/20011026130853/http://members.aol.com/intwg/trolls.htm. Accessed 6 Jan 2015

26. Condon, B.: Sony Hacking Fallout Explodes as Theaters Cancel 'The Interview' Showings. The Huffington Post, 17 December 2014. http://www.huffingtonpost.com/2014/12/17/sony-hack-theaters_n_6338246.html

27. Curtis, A.: The Brief History of Social Media. http://www2.uncp.edu/home/acurtis/NewMedia/SocialMedia/SocialMediaHistory.html. Accessed 9 Jan 2015

28. Cutler, K.: Apple Has Sold 600 M iOS Devices, But Android Is Not Impressed. TechCrunch. http://techcrunch.com/2013/06/10/apple-android-2/. Accessed 27 Dec 2014

29. Ferenstein, G.: The science of building trust with social media. Mashable, 24 February 2010. http://mashable.com/2010/02/24/social-media-trust/. Accessed 10 Jan 2015

30. Fitzgerald, B.: Social Media is Causing Anxiety, Study finds. Huffington Post. http://www.huffingtonpost.com/2012/07/10/social-media-anxiety_n_1662224.html. Accessed 3 Jan 2015

31. Flood, A.: Where did the story of ebooks begin? The Guardian, 12 March 2014. http://www.theguardian.com/books/2014/mar/12/ebooks-begin-medium-reading-peter-james. Accessed 4 Jan 2015

32. Greenwald, G., MacAskill, E.: NSA Prism program taps in to user data of Apple, Google and others. The Guardian, 7 June 2013. http://www.theguardian.com/world/2013/jun/06/us-tech-giants-nsa-data. Accessed 19 Dec 2014

33. Gross, M.J.: Silent War. Vanity Fair. July 2013. http://www.vanityfair.com/culture/2013/07/new-cyberwar-victims-american-business. Accessed 17 Dec 2014

34. Grudin, J.: Has the ice man arrived? tact on the Internet. IEEE Intell. Syst. **14**(1), 8–9 (1999)

35. Hearst, M.A.: When information technology "goes social". IEEE Intell. Syst. **13**(1), 10–15 (1999)
36. Hochheiser, H., Lazar, J.: HCI and societal issues: a framework for engagement. Int. J. Hum. Comput. Interact. **23**(3), 339–374 (2007). Lawrence Erlbaum Associates
37. Kassner, M.: Search engine bias: What search results are telling you (and what they're not). TechRepublic, 23 September 2013. http://www.techrepublic.com/blog/it-security/search-engine-bias-what-search-results-are-telling-you-and-what-theyre-not/. Accessed 9 Jan 2015
38. Knapp, E.: A Brief History of Apple's iTunes. Wall St. Cheat Sheet, 16 June 2011. http://wallstcheatsheet.com/breaking-news/a-brief-history-of-apples-itunes.html/. Accessed 3 Jan 2015
39. Liffick, B.: Social impact characteristics of computer technology. In: Proceedings of ETHICOMP95 International Conference, De Montfort University, Leicester, March 28–30 (1995)
40. Liffick, B.: Cruising the E-Mall: Shopping by Computer. In a Reader in Ethical Computing and Business. Blackwell Publishers, London (1997)
41. MacCormick, J.: Nine Algorithms that Changed the Future. Princeton University Press, New Jersey (2013)
42. McDonald, S.N.: Everyone hates Auto-Tune. The Washington Post, 31 October 2014. http://www.washingtonpost.com/news/morning-mix/wp/2014/10/31/everyone-hates-auto-tune-t-pain-may-have-finally-put-us-all-out-of-our-misery/. Accessed 9 Jan 2015
43. McGregor, J.: The Top 5 Most Brutal Cyber Attacks of 2014 So Far. Forbes, 28 July 2014. http://www.forbes.com/sites/jaymcgregor/2014/07/28/the-top-5-most-brutal-cyber-attacks-of-2014-so-far/. Accessed 17 Dec 2015
44. Owen, L.H.: PwC: The US consumer ebook market will be bigger than the print book market by 2017. Gigaom Research, 4 June 2013. https://gigaom.com/2013/06/04/pwc-the-u-s-consumer-ebook-market-will-be-bigger-than-the-print-book-market-by-2017/. Accessed 3 Jan 2015
45. Peng, W., Lin, Y.: Ranking web search results from personalized perspective. In: Proceedings of the International Conference on E-Commerce Technology. IEEE Computer Society, San Francisco, June 26–29 (2006)
46. Ramanathan, L.: High-tech gifts: You should love them. If only you knew how to use them. Washington Post, 26 December 2015. http://www.washingtonpost.com/lifestyle/style/high-tech-gifts-you-should-love-them-if-only-you-knew-how-to-use-them/2014/12/26/9d7c6adc-8d35-11e4-8ff4-fb93129c9c8b_story.html. Accessed 30 Dec 2015
47. Reges, S., Stepp, M.: Building Java Programs, 4th edn. Addison-Wesley Publishing, Boston (2014)
48. Rosenblatt, S.: Revelations from the Sony hack. C/Net, 13 December 2014. http://www.cnet.com/news/13-revelations-from-the-sony-hack/. Accessed 17 Dec 2015
49. Shaer, M.: Google gets $25 K fine for 'impeding' FCC probe into Street View, 17 April 2012. The Christian Science Monitor. http://www.csmonitor.com/Innovation/Horizons/2012/0417/Google-gets-25K-fine-for-impeding-FCC-probe-into-Street-View. Accessed 19 Dec 2014
50. Shneiderman, B.: Universal usability. Commun. ACM. **43**(5), 84–91 (2000). http://dl.acm.org/citation.cfm?id=332843
51. Stephanidis, C.: Adaptive techniques for universal access. User Model. User-Adap. Inter. **11**, 159–179 (2001)
52. Stossel, J.: How the Internet helps society be more trusting. The Washington Examiner, 6 January 2015. http://www.washingtonexaminer.com/how-the-internet-helps-society-be-more-trusting/article/2558247. Accessed 10 Jan 2015

53. Takei, G.: Oh, Myyy (There Goes the Internet). Limited Liability Company (2013)
54. Tavani, H.: Search engines and ethics. The Stanford Encyclopedia of Philosophy (Spring 2014 Edition). http://plato.stanford.edu/entries/ethics-search/. Accessed 9 Jan 2015
55. Temperton, J.: NASA just emailed a wrench to space. Wired, 19 December 2014. http://www.wired.co.uk/news/archive/2014-12/19/3d-printed-space-wrench Accessed 20 Dec 2014
56. Van Natta, D., Becker, J., Bowley, G.: Tabloid Hack Attack on Royals, and Beyond. The New York Times Magazine, 1 September 2010. http://topics.nytimes.com/top/reference/timestopics/organizations/n/news_of_the_world/index.html. Accessed 17 Dec 2014

Startup Rio: User Experience and Startups

Adriano Bernardo Renzi[1](✉), Adriana Chammas[2], Luiz Agner[3], and Jacob Greenshpan[4]

[1] Escola Superior de Desenho Industrial, UERJ, Rio de Janeiro, Brazil
adrianorenzi@gmail.com
[2] Pontifícia Universidade Católica, Rio de Janeiro, Brazil
chocolight@gmail.com
[3] Faculdades Integradas Helio Alonso/FACHA, Rio de Janeiro, Brazil
luizagner@gmail.com
[4] UXUX Inc., Tel Aviv, Israel
yaakov@uxux.co.il

Abstract. UX design and UX research play an important role in startups and their projects. The expressive growth of startups around the world encouraged the Rio de Janeiro State government to foment entrepreneur culture in the city in an attempt of transforming Rio de Janeiro in a digital technology center of reference and created the Startup Rio to encourage startups' growth in the city. This paper presents the launchpad method used around the world as well as the experience and results collected during UX mentorship on the 5-day Google event (startup launchpad) with 50 startups in Rio de Janeiro, showing the close connection between startup culture and user experience.

Keywords: User experience · Startups · UX mentorship

1 Introduction

Startup is a term that has been used widely on the business market around the world. Many consider that any small company that starts with a great idea is entitled to receive the denomination startup. As companies with low maintenance costs, startups has advantages over traditional companies and can grow rapidly with high lucrative results, if balanced with the right mix of products, services, tools and processes. According to the Brazilian Association of Startups (abstartups - www.abstartups.com.br), startups are companies in the beginning stage that develops innovative products or services, with potential fast growth. Eric Ries [1], in his book *the lean startup*, defines it as "a human institution designed to create a new product or service in conditions of extreme uncertainty". New resources like cloud storage, digital distribution, crowd-sourced funding, global outsourcing are some of the tools that can contribute to manage and fight these uncertainties.

The author proposes that startups should optimize productivity and make quick tests throughout the development process. The iteration cycles have to be fast and with low costs in order to the startup validate and discard hypothesis on the new product or service. The lean startup proposal, derived from the lean methodology, endorse the idea of

© Springer International Publishing Switzerland 2015
A. Marcus (Ed.): DUXU 2015, Part I, LNCS 9186, pp. 339–347, 2015.
DOI: 10.1007/978-3-319-20886-2_32

creating fast low fidelity prototypes to validate market hypothesis and investigate users' feedback to involve them as part of the development process. The idea of using low fidelity prototypes with the minimal number of features is to identify flaws in a fast (with low money investment) pace and iterate fast to solve the pointed problems.

There has to be more than just develop a new smart product ou increment something that already exists. The startup needs to consider a number of integrated factors, like hypertexts of Levy's [2] semantic connections, that goes far beyond features and functions of a new product in order to fascinate users and make them fall in love with it. It must be planned to bring experiences to the user. Even with innovative solutions in daily routines, needs and processes change faster and faster in a dynamic market. The reputation of a product derived from the experience of users is imperative to the success of the product or service.

The entrepreneurs need to find balance between technology, process and market expectations. They need to identify and involve people and find what delights them and them transform them in users. To achieve users' delight, projects have to be proposed, conceptualized and developed focusing in good usability experience and great user experience (UX). Braden Kowitz [3] (Google Ventures) during the startup panel at Form SF 2014, points out that even if every startup experience is unique, the fastest you can test the idea of your project, the better: the entrepreneur have a fast feedback and can make decisions on what is working and what is not. And adds: find a mentor.

2   User Experience Design

Nielsen and Norman [4] summarize the concept of UX as "User experience encompasses all aspects of the end-user's interaction with the company, its services, and its products". Following how the authors distinguish between usability and UX, where usability covers whether the system is easy to learn, efficient to use, pleasant and objective; UX covers a much broader concept.

As usability covers the easiness of using and learning a specific system by a user, the research on user experience analyses the whole experience of the user outside the system, the scenario and circumstances in which the user may open the system and what happens during the interaction, inside and outside the system.

Leaving the system scenario, Jared Spool [5] on his lecture regarding mobile and UX, compares the usability of performing tasks (activities) with user experience, using theme parks to portray the idea. The theme park known as Six Flags can be found on few states (of USA) and it is possible to see a pattern of use: people get in the park, choose the closest ride, get in a long line, ride the roller coaster and then choose another ride and re-start the cycle. The map distributed at the entrance helps customers to find themselves and make these choices showing all rides that exists in the park. The goal of the map is to pin point where the users are and which choices of activities (tasks) they have. Each individual activity is enjoyable and fun.

On the other side the author shows the Disney Magic Kingdom's map where is hard to understand specific rides unless you are a fan and recognize the architectural structures drawn on the map. The rides are not pointed out as in the six flags' map because Disney doesn't think of themselves as a place with rides, but a place people take their kids for an adventure. Disney focus on things to construct this adventure: breakfast with characters, lunch with princesses, princess beauty shop, photographers throughout the park taking pictures from people's adventures for later download and the day ends with lightning parade and lots of fireworks. After it, parents carry their very tired children back to the Disney Resort and as entering the room, the first thing to notice is that there are animals and characters made of towels on the bed. The Disney's slogan is seen by everyone as they reach the entrance: let the memories begin.

Using Spool's examples, activities are distinct things (tasks) that happens (are performed); experience is making sure everything blends, everything is connected, even afterwards when people leave the park. The concept of the whole Disney experience of building new memories goes far beyond specific tasks, it considers the whole "adventure" that starts even before the arrival at the airport. As shown in Garret's diagram, UX design research englobes many field studies of design, as it has to understand what happens with the users from different points of view and knowledge.

The UX design approach could diminish the risks of new enterprises, financially and timely, for startups when conceptualizing new products or services. There are many things happening, a sequence of moments, outside the app that determine the user's interest and flow of interaction within the app. The user experience design can be the key to make users fall in love with a new product and help filter ideas that seemed incredible at first (Fig. 1).

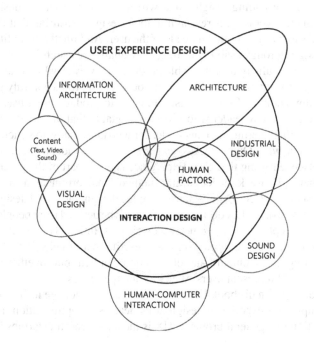

Fig. 1. J.J. Garret graphic representation of user experience field of studies compared to other disciplines related to design

Daniel Szuc [6], Principal and Cofounder of Apogee Usability Asia Ltd., and Jo Wong, Principal and Cofounder of Apogee Usability Asia Ltd., point a few factors that should be considered to create great UX design:

- meets user needs that a business fully understands and nurtures
- maps to business needs, whose improvement we can track over time
- connects to data points that speak to the product or service story
- uses a well-defined and well-understood design framework that scales well and promotes consistent and usable interactions
- leverages design patterns that promote useful, usable, and delightful interactions
- maps to well-defined design principles that connect to brand principles and business goals and directions
- undergoes continuous improvement through customer and business feedback
- tries out new ideas and conducts experiments that do not disrupt the core value
- is led and owned by people who are well educated and grounded in deep knowledge of design foundations
- is visible and improves through structured and balanced critique

In the same article by UX matters [6], Jim Nieters (Global Head, User Experience, of HP's Consumer Travel Division, UX matters columnist) adds "The large majority of well-designed products have been designed following a user-centered design (UCD) approach. In this process, user researchers first identify user task flows, challenges, and emotional triggers, providing insights that will inform the proposed design solution. Then UX designers leverage this research in their designs, ensuring that they are both easy to use and satisfy the emotional needs of the user. And finally, usability specialists validate the designs through usability testing, or evaluative research. This basic approach pretty consistently results in useful, usable products. However, while usability is absolutely necessary, it's not always sufficient. If you want to produce a truly great design, you'll need a few additional ingredients… Finally, to produce great user experiences repeatedly, you need a UX leader whose voice is equal to that of the leaders in Product Management and Engineering. You need a leader who knows how to structure an organization in the right way. One of a UX leader's goals is to identify and put the right processes in place, ensuring that User Experience is a key part of the process."

UX designers [7] use knowledge and methods that originate from psychology, anthropology, sociology, computer science, graphic design, industrial design and cognitive science. The role of the UX design should always be derived from people's problems and aim at finding a pleasurable, seductive, inspiring solution. The results of that work should always be measurable through metrics describing user behavior. Many methods of usability testing, questionnaire and observation can help put together the pieces of the puzzle that could represent users' scenario of experiences.

Marcin Trader [8], in his book UX design for startups, indicate its importance in the world of startups: user experience design at its heart is an optimization: an iteratively improved solution to a general problem. UX is the air successful startups breathe.

3 The Startup Rio Program

The expressive growth of startups around the world encouraged the Rio de Janeiro State government to foment entrepreneur culture in the city in an attempt of transforming Rio de Janeiro in a digital technology center of reference. From a public-private initiative, it was created then the Startup Rio program (http://www.startuprio.org/). According to the official site, entrepreneurs with digital projects could apply to be part of the program. The 50 selected startups would receive financial help from the government as well as a co-working space (with auditorium, conference rooms, wifi, lounges, skype rooms and coffee shop) and an educational program to help the entrepreneurs develop abilities and knowledge for digital tech to act in the Brazilian and foreign markets and develop business, generate knowledge for the execution of digital tech prototypes, act in an environment of innovation and entrepreneurship and develop an entrepreneur mindset and culture.

As part of the educational program offered, the startups would participate in the first Google Startup Launchpad in Brazil. The launchpad, developed by Google Inc., is spread around the globe with successful results "provides startups in all stages with the platform, resources, online content, mentorship and training they need to succeed. From first idea to successful implementation and growth, its mission is to help startups worldwide become successful on the Google Developers platform and open-source technologies".

The Startup Launchpad event had the duration of 5 days in Rio de Janeiro and had organizers, presenters and mentors flight in from several different countries. The 50 startups were separated by 9 themes: multi-sided platforms, B2B, Education, e-commerce and retail, events and social, health, media, tourism and entertainment and tourism and entertainment 2. Each group formed with 4–6 startups. The event where divided by time schedule and after first introductions, offered lectures on UX, web and mobile development, tips, monetization, pitch preparation during the mornings and individual mentorship in the afternoons.

Four types of mentoring were offered for the afternoon sessions: UX, Product, marketing and Tech. Each theme group had at least one of each type of mentor to show the projects, receive feedback and knowledge lecture focused on each specific topic. At the final day, 10 startups were sorted out to present a pitch video and have feedback from real investors.

4 The Google Startup Launchpad Model

The Google's Startup Launch program provides startups in all stages with the platform, resources, online content, mentorship and training they need to succeed. As shown in its webpage, the program offers coaching in three basic steps: Start, Build and Grow. The three stages include startup launchpad events worldwide, online trainings, online sections for designing and developing apps, free resources and credits, mentorship from startup launch's network, UX review by google's developers, early access to upcoming product releases, access to developer relations and startup's mentor network and online section on distribution and monetization.

The Startup Launchpad events have until now occurred in London, Paris, Barcelona, Tel Aviv, Berlin and Rio. And from organizers' observation and experience, although events at different parts of the world, there is much in common regarding the startups and the involved challenges to help prepare them:

- Usually, startups don't know much what UX is exactly – thinking it is all about graphics/buttons locations etc.
- most of startups don't know their users – in many cases startups has only vague idea of who their users are and don't invest enough time in checking it out.
- startups think they know their users, but they don't. In this case, they think they know who they are, but they don't. UX wise, they use "personas" technique without any research done. Which in many cases, is even worst then not knowing their users.
- afraid to meet their users – in many cases, they don't feel comfortable getting out there, talking to users.
- don't use any Lean/agile methodologies. This results in a long in-startup design, development and only then, they find out that the customers don't need this and that.

The Startup Launchpad events tries to introduce the UX concept to the startups in four approaches: (1) give them an introduction lecture to UX, even as a very general talk, it has been noted that it helps focus them; (2) give user research lectures and talks; (3) provide them with the self–use UX document we have created; (4) give them mentorship by UX experts.

The self use UX document gives a general idea of what is UX research: what is used for, when to use it and how to use the kit. It is divided in five tasks to help startups re-think and test their products:

Task 1: defining the users and usage-model – In order to fit the product to its user's needs and abilities, it is important to first know them. Define the users, refer to all the listed criteria and be specific ("everybody" is not a good answer).

Task 2: defining the main processes and workflow - using a product does not end with one click. It is important to identify the main processes which the users will be going through. Whether having detailed design at this stage or not, it is important to be able to identify the main logical stages users should be going through, such as: registration, selecting a route etc.

Task 3: identify hidden assumptions - Startups assume a lot about who their users are, what do they want to do with the product and what are their needs. Actually, you have a bunch of assumptions about how your product is going to be used. These assumptions are already shaping the product, but if some of the assumptions are wrong, that would mean that the Startuo is either building the wrong product or building it in the wrong way. So in comes UX research helping you to validate these assumptions.

Task 4: find people/places who fit the profile – Starting with a list of people, places and/ or online communities who fit the profile and context you described in the previous tasks, methods of information collection might be interviews, observations, surveys and similar products analysis making sure what they want to learn.

Task 5: collecting information about relevant behavior – From this point, Startups
should initiate contact with at least 3 names/groups of the list and plan finding
ways to quantifiably measure users' behavior. How to measure it and what would
be considered a success should be decided in advance. All must be documented
and analyzed in comparison with previous assumptions.

The tool kit provided by google developers add 10 golden rules to help collect information, since the way you collect the information heavily influences what it is learned:

- Your target is to collect relevant information. Not to sell your product. You should
  be listening/observing, not talking.
- In any direct interaction, both you and the people you are collecting information from
  are always biased. Avoid using phrases like "Why don't you" "Shouldn't you" or
  any other phrasing that will influence the other person by revealing what you think
  and what answer you expect to receive.
- Analytics help you understand what the behavior is. Direct contact lets you understand motivation for behavior.
- Do not use the observations/interviews to ask people what they think of you product.
  It is not a good indication of their future behavior.
- If you are talking to people ask them to describe the last time they did whatever it is
  you are collecting information about (this is focus on behavior rather than opinions).
  For example, for Drively I would ask about the last time they had a long drive, and
  ask them to describe before during and after in detail.
- Help them expand upon relevant points by asking "why/when/who/what/how" questions.
- The aim of the observations/interviews/analytics is to map relevant behavior. The
  more maps you have, the more you can compare real behavior to your assumptions.
  A good minimum is 5–8 people. You want to keep going until you recognize some
  patterns that help you group the users into archetypes. Each archetype or profile (also
  known as persona) has its own needs and motivations.
- Document the conversation/observation/analytic report. Later go over it with your
  team and discuss its details and how they compare to your assumptions.
- Map the tools and surroundings that are used/present during the relevant behavior.
- Prepare a list of points of interest in advance. Use your assumptions list as a basis.

5   Mentoring UX for the Startups

The objectives of the Launchpad event were not to turn the startups into UX experts,
but to have them better understand what UX is all about, gain an understanding of what
user research is, get a grasp on the processes underlying UX design, receive some limited
tools, including our document and build better UX.

During the 5-day launchpad event, each UX mentor was responsible for at least 2
themes groups of startups (previously each mentor had to choose a minimum of 3
different preferred themes), resulting in a group of at least 10 startups for counseling.
Due to the size of the audience, there were more presentations in the beginning of each

day to get people prepared for the task at hand. As an introductory move, UX mentors were suggested to evaluate the startups by asking the CEOs to introduce their startup and answer questions relevant to your mentorship topic. Although suggested to choose 2–4 startups that show the highest potential for improvement and work with them as an example for the whole group, it was possible to focus on a few startups with more complex problems in group sessions and act individually with each startup on specific problems and approaches. All startups were given research homework, based on each startup's specific problems, to develop after the mentoring sessions and return the next day with preliminary results and more questions for a follow up.

During the group mentoring sessions, startups were encouraged to work together and share opinions on each other's projects. Projects that were in beginning of conceptual phase were lectured on specific research tools for understanding better their future users and their cultural conventions and interaction expectations. Projects with more advanced development were lectured on usability tests and user research according to each particularity. Startups were suggested to approach startups from other groups to apply the tests. On the final mentoring day during the launchpad event, UX mentors changed theme groups in order to give a different point of view on the projects.

6   Results

It was possible to perceive positive results after the Startup Launchpad event and the UX mentoring. At least 3/4 of the startups didn't have knowledge about what would be UX design and almost the totality of the participants didn't any basic knowledge on how to include it as part of the conceiving and building processes of their new product.

The lectures on affordance, UX Design, usability and user-centered design, even if presented with generalized information, helped get the attention and focus of the groups and set the ground for the UX mentoring later on. As the mentoring occurred at the same time as programming lectures, startups divided themselves in order to attend everything. At least one member of each startup participated in the UX mentoring, but mostly more than one member participated if the event schedule permitted.

Getting more specific on the startups and their process, it was observed during the UX mentoring that 1/3 of the startups felt the need to re-think the whole basic concept of their main product from a new approach: the users' point of view. On the last day of mentoring these startups had at least planned out how they would research and see how much they would need to alter the concept and the project. It was also perceived that at least 3/4 of the startups understood they didn't have enough data on their future users nor on the experience that happens inside and outside their product. The experience exchange and UX mentoring they understood the necessity of doing more research to map the users' expectations and the situations in which the product would be used and needed.

Only 1/4 of the startups began the event with advanced concept and development. In theses few cases, the mentoring brought up some new questions about their product experience and helped test usability and affordances. These influenced a few changes (some structural) on the final product and helped the creation of new plans.

7 Conclusion

After applying the startup launchpad in 6 cities from different countries (London, Paris, Barcelona, TLV, Berlin and Rio), the challenges with the startups have much in common. On the first day of the launchpad, User Experience seems out of the process in most startup cases. Lectures on the subject (even generalized ones) can bring startups to turn everything around on their products/services concepts and re-start from the beginning.

The individual and group UX mentorship helped the different startups exchange experiences and brought new points of view to each entrepreneur about their projects/ services and made each startup re-think their approach. The tutoring and testing demonstrations brought a base knowledge for them to investigate their future users.

Although the participants didn't leave the event as UX experts (as it was not intended to), it was important to observe that they changed their way of thinking and planning after the launchpad. Each one of them understood the importance to include UX design in the process of product/service creation and development in order to make it work. Some of the startups shared their future plans of having one of the team members to start a UX design or usability specialization or at least to integrate an UX designer as an employee of the startup or as a consultant. Each and every participant entrepreneur understood the need to include UX research into their process to increase the probabilities of their success.

The process of investigating users' expectations and needs, the fast iteration cycles during development, understanding the tools to test the product in several stages of its construction can minimize the risks and uncertainties of the new product and help diminish financial and time losses. As Braden Kowitz [3] (Google ventures) indicated on 2014 San Francisco Forms, every startup experience is unique, you should find mentors. The fastest you can test the idea of the project, the better.

References

1. Ries, E.: The Lean Startup. Crown Publishig Group – Ramdom House, New York (2011)
2. Levy, P.: Tecnologias da inteligência: o futuro do pensamento na era da informática. Editora 34, São Paulo, SP (1993)
3. Kowitz, B.: Panel: Startup Design. San Francisco Forms, CA (2014)
4. Nielsen, J., Norman, D.: Definition of User Experience (2015). http://www.nngroup.com/articles/definition-user-experience
5. Spool, J.: Mobile & UX: Inside the Eye of the Perfect Storm. Interaction South America, Recife (2013)
6. Six, J.M.: Fundamental Principals of Great UX Design | How to Deliver Great UX Design. UX matters (2014). http://www.uxmatters.com/mt/archives/2014/11/fundamental-principles-of-great-ux-design-how-to-deliver-great-ux-design.php
7. Hartson, R., Pyla, P.: The UX Book: Process and Guidelines for Ensuring a Quality User Experience. Elsevier, Amsterdam (2012)
8. Trader, M.: UX Design for Startups. UXPin, Mountain View (2013)

Innovation, Exceptional Experience and Sustainable Success Made Easy: The NI© Needs Innovation Model

Johannes Robier[✉]

Youspi Consulting Gmbh, Graz, Austria
johannes.robier@youspi.com

Abstract. The NI© Needs Innovation Model is a structured customized approach for product and service development.

Keywords: Innovation · Design · Thinking · User experience · UX toolbox · Customer experience

1 Introduction

Is it magic or a jack of all trades? The Needs Innovation Model can best be understood as a combination of various established concepts, models and maps, aiming to provide a holistic and reliable way to achieve long-lasting success on the market. The NI©Model was created to help practitioners gather and assess a comprehensive set of customer needs, thereby determining the critical areas for improvement. In order to identify customer needs and opportunities for value improvement the NI©Model analyses the "Main task & the surrounding journey" that customers are trying to get complete when they use products, services or interact with a company.

2 The Model

The seven steps of the Needs Innovation Model are defined as follows:

NI© "NEEDS INNOVATION MODEL"

1. Specify the market and the problem.
2. Elicit all needs along the journey in a qualitative research.
3. Quantify needs and ask for satisfaction, importance, KPIs and emotions.
4. Create the "Needs Prioritization Matrix" and determine the needs with the highest impact and value.
5. Create, iterate, draft and design solutions.
6. Evaluate your new solutions through the previously defined KPIs.
7. Design structured experiences building on the emotions/satisfaction map.

We deployed this model to speech processing systems and redesigned the Philips LFH 9600. It is a high-end device for quality voice recording. Since competitors released

© Springer International Publishing Switzerland 2015
A. Marcus (Ed.): DUXU 2015, Part I, LNCS 9186, pp. 348–355, 2015.
DOI: 10.1007/978-3-319-20886-2_33

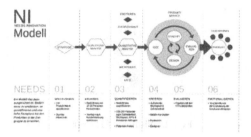

Fig. 1. NI© "NEEDS INNOVATION MODEL" by youspi

new products, Philips had to follow and innovate as well. Through the consequent redesign according to the NI© Needs Innovation Model, Philips achieved an increase of 15 % market share on a global basis with the new Philips DPM 8000 (Fig. 1).

Furthermore, the model was put into practice to develop, evaluate and optimize a new product for Dewetron, a market leading provider of test and measurement systems showcasing state-of-the-art data acquisition instruments & solutions. Together with Youspi a new multitouch analyzing soft-hardware combination called "Trendcorder" was developed. This product was awarded by NASA as the product of the year 2014 within the industrial sector.

To better illustrate the NI© "NEEDS INNOVATION MODEL", the individual parts of the model are explained below with examples from the Philips DPM 8000 redesign process.

NI© "NEEDS INNOVATION MODEL" used at Philips DPM 8000

'kfg ,sdgb

2.1 Specify the Market and the Problem

At a beginning of every project the first step is an interdisciplinary workshop, where the market and the user group for the envisioned redesigned product are clearly defined. In the case of Philips the following targets were set (Fig. 2):

– Optimize the experience for the actual user.
– Enable Philips to enter a new market of analogue voice-recording users.
– Driving market growth within the displacement market.
– Create and integrate 3 core innovations within the redesigned product.

It is paramount for the targets to be precisely defined as a first step as this creates the foundation the NI© "NEEDS INNOVATION MODEL" builds up on. With unclear targets, true optimization cannot be achieved, regardless of the effort.

2.2 Elicit the Needs Along the Journey

At the beginning the initial user journey for every target group has to be specified in order to define unique user groups for observation and in-depth interviews. In the case

Fig. 2. Philips LFH 9600

of Philips, Youspi visited lawyers and doctors around Austria and was able to obtain a comprehensive list of **various actual needs** associated and clustered to the recorder journey. The qualitative study included key stakeholders from 5 hospitals, 5 private doctors, as well as 10 lawyers from different company sizes and their transcriptionists. All interviews and observations were completed within a 3 week time frame, during which the user input led to valuable insights, in turn enabling Youspi to thoroughly optimize the entire journey. Recommended methods at this stage comprise in-depth interviews, observations, or daily diary entries. This step is one of the most crucial ones throughout the presented process (Fig. 3).

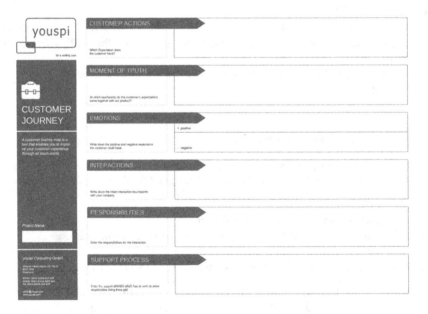

Fig. 3. Customer journey Map by youspi

Combined with a service blueprint, the needs customer journey map is a tool to evaluate the internal processes.

In the case of Philips, the customer journey was defined through a qualitative user research and completed with internal workshops for the service blueprint. For C-level management qualitative research is often not sufficient, which is why it was decided to quantify the needs of our research studies with 10 times the number of people in our qualitative study.

Some of the identified need are as follows:

Target group	Customer journey	Need
Analogue user	During recording	Data security, no changes
Lawyers	Before buying	High quality product design
Young lawyers	All the time in use	Send dictate to transcriptionist, regardless of the location (train, home etc…)
Lawyers	Tribunal	Long recording time (no possibility to charge)
Hospitals	Before buying	Easy connection to their internal system
Traditional lawyers	After recording on screen	Fewer, more comprised information
Transcriptionist	Listening to the recorded information	High quality recording
Doctor	Room tour/Visit	Speed

2.3   Quantify Needs

As a next step, a large-scale interview phase throughout a time span of three additional weeks was initiated to gather further intelligence for Philips. For the interviews a survey was prepared, which collected

- Satisfaction degree
- Importance
- KPIs
- Emotions

for all clustered needs.

Each interview conducted in this step will last for about two hours and will gather key information on Satisfaction, Importance and Emotions for all needs, which is indispensable to create the Need Prioritization Matrix. The identified Users KPIs are employed to evaluate the optimization of the process at a later stage and are of prime importance for the needs prioritization. This is a great possibility to quantify and prove Usability & User Experience!

2.4   Create the Needs Prioritization Matrix and Determine the Needs with the Highest Potential

The "Needs Priorisation Matrix" shows all needs with the potential for innovation. Simply put, this means that a high importance and lower satisfaction rate indicate a noteworthy potential. At this stage, a third layer, shown as size and color of a circle will be introduced, representing emotions, which will ultimately allow you to determine the innovation potential.

It may be possible that some needs have a high satisfaction rate and score low in importance (right graphic area), which enables a possible reduction in functionality or service quality. In fact, reducing unnecessary innovation to create space and simplicity can be a prime way of creating and conveying the added value to the target user, making the product of service itself easier comprehensible, more usable and consequently more attractive for the end-user.

The third dimension "emotion" provides an additional key evaluation possibility on top (Fig. 4).

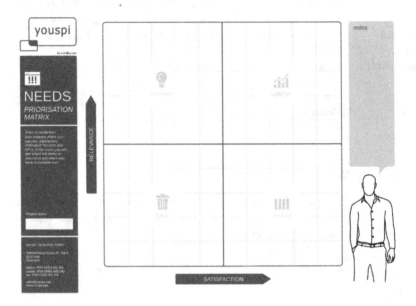

Fig. 4. Needs priorisation map by youspi

This model thence allows you to concentrate on exactly those needs that exhibit a high acceptance level. In case of the Philips DPM, one prime need for the analogue user was "DATA SECURITY". Users connect a tape with reliability and trust, knowing that their spoken words will be archived and will thence always be available, which is not possible through usage of a digital device. In addition, they know that the recording is happening through looking at the turning tape and thus have a visual input they may be lacking with a digital device.

2.5   Create, Iterate, Draft and Design Solutions for the Needs with the Highest Potential

The next step in the NI© "NEEDS INNOVATION MODEL" is to create, iterate, draft and design solutions based on the previously identified needs with the highest potential.

For Philips, Youspi now started its creative processes to define and visualize all defined needs with the attempt to find new technical and User Interface solutions.

Needs	Solution
Analogue user: data security, no changes	– Classic mode for clear and simple operation
Fewer, more comprised information	– Integrated motion sensor for automatic microphone selection
High quality recording	– Integrated motion sensor for automatic microphone selection
Speed	– Docking station for quick battery charging and hands-free recording
Speed data security	– Integrated barcode scanner for optimization in the documentation

At the iterative development process Mock-UP testing, ergonomic testing and usability optimization testing was included to achieve the best possible solution (Fig. 5).

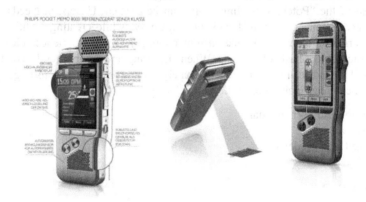

Fig. 5. New features, and simulated analogue screen at the DPM 8000

2.6 Evaluate Your New Solutions with the Defined User KPIs

As a last step in the usability testing the pre-defined user KPIs were tested and evaluated. The results were outstanding. For the medical use in hospitals the process duration of two days was compressed to a few hours, showcasing a huge innovation in the working process (Fig. 6).

During the entire development process all functionalities were checked according to the needs in the previously created needs feature matrix. The needs and functionalities were thence prioritized so the reasoning for the specific design of various processes became clear for all stakeholders. The most important needs had to match the most important features, while being as intuitive as possible.

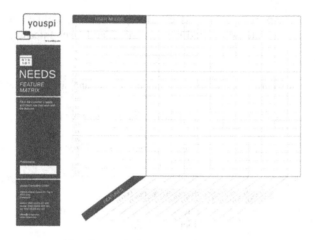

Fig. 6. Needs feature matrix by youspi

2.7   Design Experiences Building on the Emotions/Satisfaction Map

While the main product, process or service is being redesigned, much more experiences on the base of the "Potential Feeling Map" can be created. Unspoken Needs or less important needs can be complied with fast and easy, while creating additional surprising experiences along the whole customer journey. Such experiences clearly can also be created on the basis of big data. When clustering and combining different target groups, similar needs can be identified, ultimately leading to a tremendous target group.

Experiences may include the following:

- Simple first-use user manual
- First-use wizard
- Optimized service delivery.

3   Conclusion

The NI© NEEDS INNOVATION MODEL provides the tools and a structured process to design, develop and optimize customized products and processes along the entire customer journey.

Given the fact that the NI© NEEDS INNOVATION MODEL relies on both quantitative and qualitative data and is optimizes products, services and processes to suit their exact target audience, end users will showcase very high acceptance rates. At the same time different types of innovations can be achieved based on various identified user needs.

In the case of Philips the following innovations were created:

Emotional Innovations

- Analogue Design
- First-Use Wizard/Olympus User & Analogue & Non User

- Product Design.

Functional Innovations

- New scanner tool
- Improved noise-canceling
- Automated switching of microphones.

Process Innovations

- Optimized process duration compressed from 1–2 days to a view hours
- Direct transfer to external transcriptionist.

The procedure and method proved us right where the market was grateful. Within the first six months, Philips achieved a worldwide market share increase of more than ten percent, with further market gains in the subsequent years.

Software Project Management Combining Agile, Lean Startup and Design Thinking

Bianca H. Ximenes[(✉)], Isadora N. Alves, and Cristiano C. Araújo

Department of Informatics (CIn), Universidade Federal de Pernambuco (UFPE),
Recife, PE, Brazil
{bxhmm,ina,cca2}@cin.ufpe.br

Abstract. This paper describes a project management model named Converge, that combines Agile, Lean Startup and Design Thinking with the aim of producing user-centered software and sustainable innovation through empathy with users. The model is based on previous works combining the aforementioned methodologies and adjusted considering needs that arose from teams inside the lab, observed empirically. In order to test the method's validity in a real project, an undergraduate team part of an experimentation lab followed the proposed model to guide the development of a homonymous data storage app.

The app was built in 8 weeks and, at the time of release, 80 % of testers considered it a better solution compared to ones they already used. Overall test results suggest that it is productive to combine the methodologies. The model met its aim since it guided the development of a novel software solution highly regarded by users.

Keywords: Project management · Agile methodologies · Lean Startup · Design Thinking · Model · Software development · Innovation · Case study

1 Introduction

The software development industry has gone through great changes in the last decade. The shift from computer to mobile devices, alongside the popularization of ubiquitous computing, internet of things and wearables have expanded markets and changed the industry. All these factors combined offer many opportunities in innovative new market niches.

But how can software development teams lead an innovative process, create a five-star product and still deliver in time? Methodologies such as Agile (using techniques such as Extreme Programming, Scrum, Kanban) have become more common and attempted to change this scenario, preparing teams to be more adaptive and coming to closer contact with clients and customers. However, some issues are still left unresolved or not satisfactorily handled. Griffith [1] appoints the most prominent reason for software project failure as being building something for which there is no market – essentially, products nobody wants. This is most likely due to the fact teams become too focused on technical aspects and entrapped in their own product vision, as seen in [2], which also highlights the products built do not solve real problems. Furthermore, [3] also indicates no go-to market strategy and lack of competitive research

© Springer International Publishing Switzerland 2015
A. Marcus (Ed.): DUXU 2015, Part I, LNCS 9186, pp. 356–367, 2015.
DOI: 10.1007/978-3-319-20886-2_34

as common problems. Finally, [4] explains the major pitfall is the teams' inability to put themselves in the users' shoes, truly understanding the way they think and what they need, a concern echoed by all other authors.

Two recent movements that have become popular in the technology and software industries are Lean Startup and Design Thinking. Lean Startup brings a market focus to project development and was conceived inside a software development company. The Lean Startup movement begun with Eric Ries, who defined a startup as being "a human institution designed to create a new product or service under conditions of extreme uncertainty" [5]. Its philosophy is to transform teams into efficient learning units that do not build products nobody wants to use. Design Thinking, made popular by Tim Brown [6] conveys that the methodology employed by designers when approaching problems can be applied in all areas of knowledge in order to achieve innovation. True innovation lies in working out a creative solution that is desirable for the consumer, economically viable and technically feasible. Thus, Design Thinking is a tool that helps develop new products, services, processes and strategies. These two movements address common problems identified by specialized literature regarding IT project failure, in both the business and the user aspects. Besides, they encourage an environment where it is possible to transform uncertainty into new products, generating innovation.

For all reasons presented above, the idea of combining them in the software development scenario and making a unique model with the state-of-the-art methods for software and startup developments, and user experience design with the aim of fostering innovation appeared to be worthy of further investigation.

2 The Converge Model

The model had its inspiration in previous works combining Agile, Lean Startup and Design Thinking, as well as empirical observations inside the experimentation lab. Converge model is applicable to development teams in need of creative solutions. In this scenario, the solution is not yet known; in reality, several times the problem itself is complex and not yet defined. Such characteristics are typical of Design challenges (which address wicked problems) [6, 7] and common in the startup scenario as well, which deals with extreme uncertainty according to the definition present in the Lean Startup philosophy [5]. Its graphic representation is depicted in Fig. 1.

Agile provides the necessary structure to coordinate software development and deployment. It reminds every one of the time constraints and breaks tasks into small portions members can approach and tackle effectively; Scrum meetings keeps the team bounded and informed of each other's tasks. Agile's iterative approach to software development also provides the necessary basis for developers to change and rebuild fast, in case it proves necessary – a culture in which it is admissible to pivot [8]. All team's tasks are described and fit into weekly or 2-week sprints maximum, be the member a developer, a designer or from any other area of expertise that comes to be involved in the project. Since the main output of the lab is software, the organizational structure was conceived to support its development at best. Requirements exist, but they do not come from a single client; the team themselves establish the requirements based on potential customers pull and extreme users, crossing their references with their own product vision (a Lean Startup characteristic).

Fig. 1. The converge model graphic representation

A feature-by-feature implementation is followed strictly; some other Extreme Programming values such as pair programming and collective code ownership [9] are also part of the model fundamentals. A complete project would last a complete cycle – from concept to publishing - and lasts the sum of all sprints, hence the Agile being represented by the bigger outside circle, with the estimated duration of three months [10]. As it was previously mentioned, lab members were too young and inexperienced to constitute a self-organizing team. One of the authors worked as a Scrum Master, closely to a Project Leader (PL), responsible for the project vision. This Leader came from inside the lab and was supervised until he gained independence and understood the process well enough to operate as a Scrum Master himself, if needed. Each project has their own Scrum meeting the first day of the week, done separately. Tasks were registered and managed using Asana. Because of students working only part time in the lab and their schedules not always matching, there were no daily Scrum meetings.

Since the model is to be applied in innovative projects which are not always funded, the model is also concerned with approaching the product development issue, following Lean Startup precepts. Lean is based on the constant validation or rejection of hypothesis one has about an unclear problem, while trying to achieve an unclear solution [5]. Every week, the teams must go through a build-measure-learn loop, learning more about the product and maturing its concept, being able to adjust to demand and pivot strategies. It is essential to establish key metrics to assess learning – otherwise, loops do not exist. Lean focuses on building an MVP and arriving fast to market, which works especially well for mobile application development, since quantitative and qualitative consumer feedback is available at ease on application markets on all platforms. These help continue the learning cycles and product improvement.

In the first week, team defines their strategy and fill in the Lean Canvas [11] to have a holistic perspective of the project. Like Agile, Lean Startup (and development) also focuses on delivering working code often [12]. Unlike Agile, however, a Lean Startup team has a product vision [13], hence the Project Leader role advocated in the model – it is not only meant to facilitate training. This Project Leader has a lot to do with the Scrum's Product Owner [14]; however, Converge's PL is not the client. Instead, they must motivate the team to find users and clients (early adopters) for their products. The early adopter is not necessarily a single person or company, but rather a market niche. That is why software requirements in the Converge model are a mix of what the team believes and what they can find while talking to or observing potential users. Lean Startup is also important because, due to the exploratory aspect and the focus on learning, it teaches students to balance their views with what is feasible and desirable for the market (a concern present in DT as well.) Moreover, for Lean Startup, the user (who uses the software) and client (who pays for software, service of information) are not necessarily the same thing, forcing students to start to consider business models.

A direct consequence of this was that students were free to work on projects before the introduction of the Converge model and remained so; they had, nevertheless, to prove qualitatively there was a demand for that type of app and that they were addressing a real need. This was done following [11]: they had to validate problem and idea separately with at least 5 people outside the lab, independently. Finally, to prepare students to presentations with investors and to pitch their projects, a Results meeting was held weekly, on the last day of the week. In it, a team member from each project (usually, three different projects were running simultaneously in the lab) would present the problem, the solution, the activities and the working code produced in the week. At these meetings, all lab members helped their colleagues from other projects improve their presentations and establish the hypotheses each team would have to validate or reject the following week.

The loops presented in the model follow through the whole extension of the structure circle. They never stop, for hypothesis validation and learning are always present, guiding the decisions. Their repetition is meant to indicate their continuity.

For the last part, some challenges present in software development projects are neither technical nor market-related; they concern the ability to understand the user, their limitations and needs, and to come up with different creative solutions beyond technical issues. Those challenges are represented by the "knots" and may appear at any point of a project. When they appear, the main reason for the hold-up is diagnosed and Design Thinking techniques applied to overcome those problems and come up with solutions. Those techniques are applied in DT rounds, which fit in weekly sprints, and last 1–2 h. Therefore, in the model, to each knot identified, there is a correspondent DT round. Just like the loops, their existence throughout the whole process is indicated by their repetitive presence in the model.

Following the model, which is inspired by d.school [15] and depicted in Fig. 2, knots are catalogued in five categories: Empathizing, Problem Definition, Ideation, Prototyping and Testing. They may occur in any order and must be recognized and addressed.

The relevance of Design Thinking mindset and techniques are not only about overcoming project challenges, but also about adding value because it allows for real insight on users' needs. That is why Design Thinking is also present during the first week of the project, as seen in the model – techniques are applied to the problem identification and idea validation phases preached by Lean, but also to explore and understand the nature of the project and users' reality – empathize – which sometimes may be completely different from developers' experience. A key feature in the Converge model is that the team responsible for the idea and design is also fully responsible for the development of the final product. This is relevant as the budget and time constraints encompass the project as a whole, from conception to delivery to the app store. Besides, all team members take part in the creative process from the very beginning until the end – developers do not receive ready-made requirements from others, taking part in the making of the product concept, being able to innovate. This follows suggestions from [16]. The following subsections explain what is done in each phase:

Empathizing: This phase is important to reduce the time spent in discussion and hypothesizing inside teams. It was observed that the students had a tendency to make decisions without inputs from customers and users, based only on their own perceptions of the product. At times, when it comes to a dead-end, members will take a vote to decide what to do next. This practice helps them see the customer as the person who has the final word. It is very focused on research and interviewing, and meant to allow team members to learn about their competitors, monetization and market, besides user behavior. Most used technique in this phase inside the lab: interviews with extreme users [17].

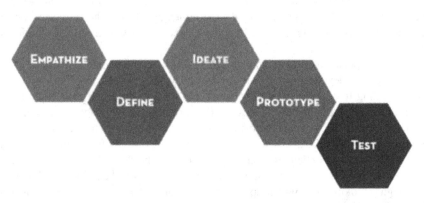

Fig. 2. Stanford's d.school Design Thinking flow

- **Problem Definition:** This phase is more commonly necessary when the team cannot find common ground and lacks alignment. It is noticed when there are no clear goals; team members define the project in different ways; functionalities implemented are of little importance to the product or do not complement each other. Defining the problem makes sure everyone knows what they want to achieve and work towards it, providing focus. Most used technique in this phase inside the lab: five whys method [18].

- **Ideating:** It is a very comprehensive phase, ranging from techniques to choose names of applications to the conception of a whole new project idea. Teams learn to think in new ways, be less judgmental and generate a great range of ideas to choose from. Every time someone in a company suggests a brainstorm, this actually means they are in need of an ideating phase. Brainstorm is, although widely accepted and renowned, simply one technique that corresponds to this phase. Most used technique in this phase inside the lab: triggered brainwalking [19].
- **Prototyping:** In Agile, prototypes are almost always a simpler version of the final code. This is important, but here the main focus are wireframes, mock-ups and paper prototypes. The main function of such prototypes is to allow quick testing of a tangible idea, even if it is low-fidelity. Prototypes provide quick feedback from potential customers and are fast to make as well as inexpensive. In the Converge model, the initial validations are done with paper prototypes and Rabiscapp[1] application, one of the lab's products, to assemble the screen flow. Prototyping knots also cover creating more than one prototype for split tests, allowing to better test hypotheses. Prototyping always happens in the first-week loop and afterwards as many times as prototyping knots are identified. Most used technique in this phase inside the lab: representation sketches [20].
- **Testing:** Every test round is an empathy round as well, for teams learn a lot by observing their users interact with the product. The difference is that testing has the development team necessarily offer a version of the product (be it on paper, code or any other applicable medium) for the user to interact. Testing reduces clashes inside the team. It makes it clear what works best for the user. Tests for a creative software project are much like requirement engineering for agile – the client chooses what they prefer. In the Lean Startup mindset, testing is what allows teams to assess whether they are working on a potentially successful product or failing. It validates the project existence. Every test round happens because there is a hypothesis to be proven or rejected. Therefore, whenever there is a hypothesis, there is a test knot. Teams must be trained to understand when they are making hypothesis and assuming things that should otherwise be tested. Most used technique in this phase inside the lab: interaction with application of Likert-scale questionnaire.

3   Validating the Model Empirically

This section narrates the development of a data storage app as a case study, exemplifying how the Converge model works in practice and describing project repercussions.

The First Immersion

First Week: In the beginning, all students in the lab became familiar with the current lab design challenge "How may we refine user's data collection and storage experience?". In order to empathize and understand users' needs, the first step was a 30-minute brainstorm. At first, students had to think of people to whom they had access

---

[1] To read more about and get to know Rabiscapp, access http://rabiscapp.net.

that they considered extreme users concerning data storage and collection. After coming up with some names, students had to explain to the group why they considered that person an extreme user, and the group decided whether they agreed or not. When the 30 min were up, there was a list of 6 people that were to be interviewed in the next 2 days. They were a young entrepreneur, an engineer that supervised construction works, a national energy agency manager, a public school director, an oral surgeon and the president of a junior enterprise. They were chosen because of the amount of data they had to gather and organize, the diverse types of medias and files they handled, the quantity of people of things the data they collected helped monitor and the high frequency in which that happened (many times every day). This characterizes an Empathy round. Students had two days to interview the people they identified as extreme users.

All interviews were recorded with users' consent. They were later transcribed and brought back to further discussion in the lab, on the 3rd week day. The initial questions were the same for all people, but everyone was free to elaborate if they thought they could get more relevant information. During 2 h, students became aware of the users' work routines, the type of data they had to store and consult, the instruments they used to help them, what they perceived as challenges in their daily lives and how easily they considered to storage, organize and retrieve data. This characterizes another Empathy round.

At that point, the team got wary: they realized interviewees had different needs and tasks to address. It seemed impossible to build an app with high UX and usability standards that tended to all users' expectations, particularly considering the time constraint suggested in the model (3 months). However, they understood that they were not yet aware of the problems underneath, and that those problems could maybe be the same.

It was then time for the Define round, which occurred on the same day. Using the 5-whys technique, students focused on the challenges and difficulties the users described trying to get to the root causes that made users experience the issues they mentioned. By the end of the round, they were able to synthesize common root causes for all challenges users mentioned, identifying 3 problems the app could address:

1. Data is geographically trapped.
2. Data is spread out.
3. Other people have my data.

On the 4th day, it was time for the Ideation round. In this phase, only half the original team continued to work on this project, and others resumed working on other ongoing products. Team used triggered brainwalking to write about how they thought an app could treat the underlying user problems they identified. At first, they thought about functionalities the app could have – natural for a technical team. Ideas were mostly to provide organization by tags, date, native search for content, offline storage of chosen files, automatically group similar files. After the first 20 min, a new constraint was introduced in the brainwalk to allow students to focus on the macro aspects of the project: they could not write down functionalities, but rather describe the ideal digital environment to organize users' data. In the end, students perceived people organized their lives in what the team named "projects", which could be personal or work-related, private or shared. All data related to a specific life "project" should therefore be stored together. The app would offer the same functionalities to everyone, but be able to adapt to each user's own reality, according to their personal activities, with varying degrees of granularity. For example, each one of a doctor's patients could be a separate project. A yearly company budget could also be a project, albeit of a different nature. A holiday trip planning, a wedding, could all be projects as well, and shared with as many people as deemed necessary by the user. The project would be a grand central for all data concerning that topic.

Having understood what the app should offer, it was time to translate the concept into an app interface, in a Prototyping round. The team used representation sketches mixed with the 6-3-5 design technique. This part was more focused on experience and functionalities. Common aspects proposed on screens were passed on to a prototype synthesizing best features (not by functionality, but by ease to use). Aspects deemed good by the team were also passed on. The main app flow consisted of 4 screens. None of what was built was final, and students understood that – it was a rough draft they would test with potential users.

On the 5th day, the team's designer started transforming the low-fidelity prototypes on high-fidelity screens, to be imported into Rabiscapp and tested the following week. The final project team was defined, consisting of two developers and one designer. The other students resumed working on other lab projects. Those three members started filling in the Lean Canvas – the areas of Key Metrics, Cost Structure and Revenue Streams were left blank, for the moment. Team also defined what would constitute the MVP and what could be added later; finally, they discussed the hypothesis they had to validate the following week, in the first learning loop.

The Learning Loops

Second Week: Ideally, Lean preaches the validation of the problem decoupled of the solution, in two separate moments. However, as the high-fidelity screens were ready, the team took them on Rabiscapp for a Test round with the extreme users previously interviewed. All 6 extreme users liked the project organization and functionalities, and considered the app flow intuitive. They pointed out some improvements such as enhancing header and text contrast, modifying visual assets as well as changing the color pallete. The best qualitative measurement, nevertheless, was the fact all users demanded new and more screens to test the complete app flow, thus playing the part of early adopters. The app solution and the hypothesis that users organize their lives in projects was validated. At that point, developers started to set up the database tables and enabling projects to be saved in the database. Besides, part of developers' work contemplated studying to overcome their technical limitations, such as implementing animations in Cascades, BlackBerry 10 native language.

Third Week: At this point, the team reassessed the Lean Canvas. They improved the Unique Value Proposition (adding "a structured Dropbox"). It was also necessary to propose a business model to generate revenue, but team did not have ideas because they did not know much about other data storage solutions. This characterized an Empathy knot – it was necessary to learn more about how to monetize in that market niche. Team listed all the competitors they identified besides the ones the extreme users cited as options they used to store data. Students conducted an extensive research and shared their findings amongst themselves. An Ideation knot followed suit, in which the team considered how to offer advantages when compared to their competitors, in a way that also allowed them to reach a break-even point. In the end, team decided Converge would sell monthly subscriptions of USD 5.99, which allowed for sending 10 GB of data each month, and unlimited storage. To do so, team also had to consider their cost structure. That way, two more fields of the Lean Canvas were also filled in. Besides, the business model still needed validation. In the development sprint, developers implemented the functionality of saving files and displaying the ones saved. They also created the different categories for saving files (images, documents, and notes) and a native text composer for the notes section. The designer altered the color pallete and made as visual assets, typography and icons uniform. The team put off validation to the following week. For the first time, Converge app took part in the weekly results meeting and the Project Leader pitched the project to the lab colleagues, who posed questions and gave suggestions for the team to explain and reply, dealing, on a lower scale, with the pressure of presenting a product.

Fourth Week: A Test round validation with the extreme users had them pull two new features – a file preview screen, expanding information available to help them decide whether they wanted to download the file; quick access buttons. Project's folders had icons displayed next to its name on the main screen to showcase which type of files were stored there inside it. The users wanted it to become a direct access to a specific type of file (i.e. images). They also highlighted the real-life elements look (e.g. cork-textured mural, pins, Polaroid frames for images, paper folders), remarking them positively. They were to be present on all screens. The well-known elements made them feel a sense of familiarity. Half the users declared they would pay the price for Converge. The other half said they did not subscribe to digital services, which is a rather common challenge for mobile services is Brazil. The team considered they needed further validation before rejecting or accepting their business model. The final comment in the validation was that the first screen picture and the app logo were not appealing. For that reason, a Prototyping round was set up with the members and other lab designers, to sketch different options until a final layout was reached. The development progressed, creating a synchronization protocol and implementing sync server $\rightarrow$ app and the other way around. Downloading files from server was enabled. The validated interface started to be implemented on code. The team pitched the project and shared their week findings in the results meeting at the end of the week.

Fifth Week: New screens were put forth on a Test round in Rabiscapp – some just created, like the file preview, some refactored, like the image upload screen. The extreme users/early adopters were extremely pleased; however, they felt the lack of file history could make it difficult to keep up with many updated, especially when projects were shared among many people. Beyond that, they were impressed with the app concept and flow. The history functionality was not part of the MVP. The app could be released without it, and have it added a posteriori. Notwithstanding, the team felt the history provided a unique opportunity to make Converge stand out from its competitors. The team's vision prevailed, and a Prototyping round took place in order to decide what the history would include. For that round, two people with the Converge user profile, from Business, were invited to join in. The final prototype result included complex features, such as being able to restore the last 5 deleted files, also present in history. Anyone could restore a file on the list, but the only ones able to delete would be the person who uploaded or the project manager (the person who created the project by default). Another added feature to make uploading files easier was an automatic filter. The system was able to identify the extension and send the file to the correct sub-folder in a given project. The upload button became a single one. This was aligned with the UVP of making it as easy as possible for users to share and store files. The server was set up on Heroku and the file storage on Amazon. Multiple accounts were enabled, and support to shared projects added.

Sixth Week: The first screen and history screen high fidelity prototype got ready, completing the entire app flow. Before implementation of the file history, file owner-ship and deletion/restauration logic, the complete flow was taken for a final Test round. All six extreme users rated the final result (showed in a high fidelity prototype, not in the real app) 5/5 points. The history screen and functionalities were greatly responsible for the high ratings. The development sprint contemplated providing support for tag-ging and displaying tags on files in-app, as well as editing or removing them; tags were enabled within the server, to be used when searching for a file; the screens for notes and documents preview were implemented following the validated design.

Seventh Week: At this moment, enough tests and iterations were conducted, allowing for launching. Key Metrics, however, were not yet defined. That required an Empathize round to decide how it was possible to measure whether Converge was fulfilling its UVP and delivering value to users, as well as retaining them. Number of downloads and subscriptions, number of projects and average number of users per project was something obvious to monitor. Besides that, team concluded that to assess whether Converge was accomplishing its UVP, users should use it every day. Daily users were considered active users. To validate their business model and prove it was sustainable, it was important to monitor the number of files uploaded per user (average), uploading frequency (average), and file size (average). Development sprint covered syncing tags. The history screen, with the recent activity list, was implemented alongside the vali-dated interface. Push notifications and images' thumbnails on the main project page were implemented.

Eighth Week: The development sprint included implementing and supporting regis-tration and login, as well as e-mail invitations for collaborators who were not already registered. Other details, such as "share from Converge" (export) and "save to Con-verge" (import) were added. The final task was implementing metric monitoring inside the app through Flurry and an IAP system. The final Test round before release was carried out on week 8. After 8 weeks of development, final tests with 17 potential users yielded positive results; they were all-new testers, no longer the extreme users who guided the team throughout the process. Even though none of the testing volunteers opted exclusively for mobile storage, in spite of Converge being a mobile-exclusive application, after testing 80 % of volunteers found Converge application provided a superior data storage experience than the one they currently employed and 40 % affirmed they would be willing to pay a monthly subscription to use it. The ones who did not agree with the price suggested that further development combining mobile and computer-based clients would make them more willing to pay for the subscription. This was handled as a possible project development post-MVP. The application was set up for sale in BlackBerry World in the following week, closing the Converge project development cycle and getting to market.

4 Conclusion

The complete cycle was pursued and closed in two months. In spite of the app produced being developed exclusively by undergraduates with little experience, the qualitative validation showed high acceptance of testers and gathered positive remarks. This corroborates the notion that the Converge model operates well in guiding software projects conception and development, until the product arrives to market.

On the other hand, there was not enough time to observe a market experience of the product and try to escalate it. It remains unassessed whether Converge can be adapted to projects already in market and help in quantitative product development.

The case study results suggest that it is possible to combine the methodologies and approach Design Thinking in rounds. The model seems to enable innovation and good product rapport with users. It was possible to make Computer Science undergraduates see beyond requirements and tasks, identifying mental models and real needs. Even though inexperienced developers and designers conducted the project, they were able to understand users and change their behavior by proposing a new way to approach data storage and providing a memorable experience.

The Converge model can be applied and tested in similar settings, those of experimentation labs and incubators. It benefits teams in need of creative solutions that can build and release the product into market fast and cheaply, as it is the case for the mobile content industry.

References

1. Griffith, E.: Why startups fail, according to their founders (2014). http://fortune.com/2014/09/25/why-startups-fail-according-to-their-founders/
2. Tobak, S.: 9 Reasons why most startups fail (2014). http://www.entrepreneur.com/article/231129
3. Deeb, G.: The unlucky 13 reasons startups fail (2013). http://www.forbes.com/sites/georgedeeb/2013/09/18/the-unlucky-13-reasons-startups-fail/
4. Aulet, B.: Disciplined Entrepreneurship: 24 Steps to a Successful Startup. Wiley, New York (2013)
5. Ries, E.: The Lean Startup: How Today's Entrepreneurs Use Continuous Innovation to Create Radically Successful Businesses. Crown Business, New York (2011)
6. Brown, T.: Change by Design: How Design Thinking Transforms Organizations and Inspires Innovation. Harper Business, New York (2009)
7. Brown, T.: Design thinking. Harv. Bus. Rev. **86**(84–92), 141 (2008)
8. Nelson, E.: Extreme programming vs. interaction design (2002)
9. Bird, J.: Code ownership – who should own the code? (2011). http://swreflections.blogspot.com.br/2013/04/code-ownership-who-should-own-code.html

10. Poppendieck, M., Poppendieck, T.: Lean Software Development: An Agile Toolkit. Addison-Wesley Professional, Boston (2003)
11. Maurya, A.: Running Lean: Iterate from Plan A to a Plan That Works. O'Reilly Media, Sebastopol (2012)
12. Widman, J., Hua, S., Ross, S.: Applying lean principles in software development process–a case study. Issues Inf. Syst. **11**(1), 635–639 (2010)
13. Nobel, C.: Teaching a lean startup strategy (2011). http://hbswk.hbs.edu/
14. Moe, N.B., Dingsøyr, T., Dybå, T.: A teamwork model for understanding an agile team: a case study of a scrum project. Inf. Softw. Technol. **52**, 480–491 (2010)
15. Virtual crash course in design thinking http://dschool.stanford.edu/dgift/
16. Lindberg, T., Meinel, C., Wagner, R.: Design thinking - a fruitful concept for IT development? In: Meinel, C., Leifer, L., Plattner, H. (eds.) Design Thinking: Understand - Improve - Apply, pp. 3–18. Springer, Heidelberg (2011)
17. Lafreniere, D.: Extreme user research (2008). http://boxesandarrows.com/extreme-user-research/
18. Serrat, O.: The five whys technique (2009)
19. Mattimore, B.W.: Idea Stormers: How to Lead and Inspire Creative Breakthroughs. Jossey-Bass, San Francisco (2012)
20. Beaudouin-Lafon, M., Mackay, W.E.: Prototype development and tools. In: Sears, A., Jacko, J. (eds.) Human Computer Interaction—Development Process, pp. 122–142. Lawrence Erlbaum Associates, Hillsdale (2003)

Integration of Usability and Agile Methodologies: A Systematic Review

Claudia Zapata[⊠]

Doctorado en Ingeniería Escuela de Posgrado, Pontificia Universidad
Católica del Perú, Lima, Peru
zapata.cmp@pucp.pe

Abstract. Nowadays, Agile Methodologies are widely used and accepted among software development teams. These methodologies allow speeding up the development process while permitting less documentation and more flexible processes. Moreover, Usability is a measure of software quality and has become more important with the changes that users have experienced. This paper aims to answer how usability and agile methodologies have been integrated into the various stages of software development through a systematic review.

Keywords: Usability · Agile methodologies · Systematic review · User centered design · Software engineering

1 Introduction

Currently software users are increasingly demanding and not only have a clearer understanding of their needs but, upon using an application, require a certain degree of usability. Usability is defined as the extent to which a product can be used by specified users to achieve specified goals with effectiveness, efficiency and satisfaction in a specified context of use [18].

Agile methodologies have allowed, as its name emphasizes, to speed up the process of building software. However, different authors agree that, despite facilitating the development and adjusting easily to usability techniques, more industrial applications must be developed to validate the proper way to integrate both philosophies [38].

The Agile manifesto [10] consists of four values:

- Individuals and interactions over processes and tools.
- Working software over comprehensive documentation.
- Customer collaboration over contract negotiation.
- Responding to changes over following a plan.

These values and its twelve principles are funded through incremental, cooperative, and adaptive methods [2].

The main agile methods are: Extreme Programming (XP), Scrum, DSDM (Dynamic Software Development Method), AM (Agile Modeling), ASD (Adaptive Software Development), Crystal series, FDD (Feature Driven Development [2]. The first three are the most used as seen in the results of the review.

© Springer International Publishing Switzerland 2015
A. Marcus (Ed.): DUXU 2015, Part I, LNCS 9186, pp. 368–378, 2015.
DOI: 10.1007/978-3-319-20886-2_35

On the other hand we have user-centered design (UCD) whose life cycle is very similar to that of agile methodologies. UCD is a set of techniques, methods, procedures and processes that places the user at the centre of the development process. The ISO 13407 defines UCD as an iterative process composed of four basic design activities [18]:

- Understand and Specify Context of Use. Know the user, the environment of use, and the tasks that he or she uses the product for.
- Specify the User and Organizational Requirements. Determine the success criteria of usability for the product in terms of user tasks, e.g. how quickly a typical user should be able to complete a task with the product.
- Determine the design guidelines and constraints. Produce Design Solutions. Incorporate HCI knowledge (of visual design, interaction design, usability) into design solutions.
- Evaluate Designs against Requirements. The usability of designs is evaluated against user tasks.

Based on the significant similarity of the objectives sought by the UCD and agile methodologies, it would seem that the problem could be reduced to developing soft-ware using an agile methodology and UCD in the design stage, in order to ensure a usable software product.

For Salah, Paige and Cairns [36], Agile and User Centered Design Integration gained increased interest due to three reasons:

- The reported advantages of UCD on the developed software as it enables developers to understand the needs of the potential users of their software, and how their goals and activities can be best supported by the software thus leading to improved usability and user satisfaction.
- The Agile community hardly discusses user needs and user interface design. Moreover, none of the major Agile processes explicitly include guidance for how to develop usable software.
- There are differences between Agile methods and UCD in: focus, evaluation method, culture and documentation, that suggest that their integration will be fundamentally challenging.

Could it occur that a software product designed using UCD fulfills the requirements proposed by users but does not have a high degree of usability? These and other questions are discussed in this systematic review about integrating agile methodologies and techniques of usability as a complete process of software development to fulfill the requirements of the user through an easy to use tool.

2 Systematic Review

The systematic review is a research method widely used in medical sciences and adapted by Kitchenham to software engineering. In contrast to traditional reviews, systematic reviews allow us to find the best available evidence by methods to identify, evaluate and synthesize relevant studies on a research topic. The methods used are pre-defined and documented, so that other researchers can evaluate them critically and can be replicated later [20].

2.1   Research Questions

The definition of research questions is the most important part during a systematic review, because they will appropriately focus the research. In order to determine these questions, criterion called "PICOC" (Population, Intervention, Comparison, Outcome and Context) was used.

As the objective of this systematic review is not to find comparisons between usability techniques and agile methodologies, the Comparison criteria of PICOC was not used. Table 1 shows the results obtained by applying the other criterion.

These terms were compared to systematic reviews found in this review as they cover similar issues but with different objectives.

The research questions that were defined for the review were:

Table 1. PICOC results

Criteria	Description
Population	Agile software development
Intervention	Usability techniques
Outcomes	Integrating methods
Context	Academic and business context

- Question 1: What usability methods are integrated into software development methodologies?
- Question 2: What agile methodologies have integrated usability techniques throughout the complete software development process?
- Question 3: What new frameworks or methods have been proposed for the integration of agile processes and usability engineering?

2.2   Search Strategy and Selection

In order to perform the search and selection of papers, a strategy was defined. First, the search terms were defined in the databases; then the phases of the search; and finally, the criteria that would be used to include or exclude the resulting papers.

Search Terms. Based on information obtained by applying the PICOC criterion, search terms were defined and thus the following search string was derived.

> ("software development" OR "software construction" OR "software project" OR "software projects" OR "software process" OR "software processes" OR "software engineering") AND
> agile AND
> (method OR technique OR process OR practice OR procedure OR approach) AND
> (usability OR "user-centered" OR "user centre")

Search Process. The search was performed using three online databases that contained references for scientific articles and journals, conference proceedings and technical papers: Scopus, ISI Web of Science, and IEEE Xplore.

Criterion of Inclusion and Exclusion. We defined a set of precise selection criteria (inclusive and exclusive) to select the most appropriate studies for the systematic review. The inclusion of studies was determined by the following criteria: the study presents integration of usability methods/techniques and agile methodologies.

However, studies that fulfilled either of the following criteria were excluded:

- The study only presents usability techniques applied in post production
- The study is not written in English or Spanish
- The study is a book or conference review

Additionally, the studies published before 2010 were excluded because this review includes four previous systematic reviews [19, 36–38] that cover earlier years.

2.3   Search

The search was conducted on December 19th, 2014, which allowed finding 2015's papers, but after applying the criteria for exclusion were not considered.

The search string found 693 papers. After reviewing the title, keywords and abstract, 96 articles were obtained and finally after the full reading 37 were selected. These results are shown in Tables 2 and 3.

Table 2. Amount of papers classified by database

Database	Found papers	Duplicated papers	Selected papers
Scopus	682	0	37
ISI Web of Science	11	11	0
IEEExplore	40	25	0
Total	693	11	37

3   Results

In order to answer each of the research questions, the selected items were classified according to the method used for the study, the agile methodology employed and the usability techniques applied. This classification is shown in Table 4.

Table 3. Complete list of seleted studies

ID	Authors	Year
1 [2]	Abdelouhab K.A., Idoughi D., Kolski C.	2014
2 [5]	Bertholdo A.P.O., Da Silva T.S., De O. Melo C., Kon F., Silveira M.S.	2014
3 [8]	Ferrario M.A., Simm W., Newman P., Forshaw S., Whittle J.	2014
4 [11]	Ganci A., Ribeiro B.	2014
5 [12]	Garnik I., Sikorski M., Cockton G.	2014
6 [17]	Isa W.A.R.W.M., Lokman A.M., Aris S.R.S., Aziz M.A., Taslim J., Manaf M., Sulaiman R.	2014
7 [19]	Jurca G., Hellmann T.D., Maurer F.	2014
8 [21]	Kropp E., Koischwitz K.	2014
9 [22]	Larusdottir M., Cajander A., Gulliksen J.	2014
10 [26]	Liikkanen L.A., Kilpio H., Svan L., Hiltunen M.	2014
11 [27]	Lizano F., Sandoval M.M., Stage J.	2014
12 [31]	Peres A.L., Da Silva T.S., Silva F.S., Soares F.F., De Carvalho C.R.M., De Lemos Meira S.R.	2014
13 [32]	Plonka L., Sharp H., Gregory P., Taylor K.	2014
14 [36]	Salah D., Paige R.F., Cairns P.	2014
15 [37]	Salvador C., Nakasone A., Pow-Sang J.A.	2014
16 [1]	Abdallah A., Hassan R., Azim M.A.	2013
17 [3]	Adikari S., McDonald C., Campbell J.	2013
18 [6]	Davies M., Chamberlain A., Crabtree A.	2013
19 [13]	Gonzalez C.S., Toledo P., Munoz V., Noda M.A., Bruno A., Moreno L.	2013
20 [14]	Grigoreanu V., Mohanna M.	2013
21 [28]	Losada B., Urretavizcaya M., Lopez J.-M., Fernandez-Castro I.	2013
22 [29]	Maguire M.	2013
23 [33]	Prior S., Waller A., Black R., Kroll T.	2013
24 [34]	Raison C., Schmidt S.	2013
25 [7]	Felker C., Slamova R., Davis J.	2012
26 [16]	Hussain Z., Lechner M., Milchrahm H., Shahzad S., Slany W., Umgeher M., Vlk T., Koffel C., Tscheligi M., Wolkerstorfer P.	2012
27 [24]	Larusdottir M.K., Cajander A., Gulliksen J.	2012
28 [30]	Moreno A.M., Yague A.	2012
29 [38]	Da Silva T.S., Martin A., Maurer F., Silveira M.	2011
30 [9]	Ferreira J., Sharp H., Robinson H.	2011
31 [15]	Humayoun S.R., Dubinsky Y., Catarci T.	2011
32 [25]	Lester C.Y.	2011
33 [35]	Salah D.	2011
34 [39]	Sohaib O., Khan K.	2011
35 [4]	Benigni G., Gervasi O., Passeri F.L., Kim T.-H.	2010
36 [40]	Sohaib O., Khan K.	2010
37 [41]	Xiong Y., Wang A.	2010

Table 4. Classifcation of studies

Research question	Possible answer	Papers	Percents of total
Question 1: What methods of usability are integrated into software development methodologies?	Informal Cognitive Walkthrough	1	2.7 %
	Usability Design	4	10.8 %
	User-centered Design	22	59.5 %
	Usability Evaluation	7	18.9 %
	User Experience Design and Evaluation	3	8.1 %
Question 2: What agile methodologies have integrated usability techniques throughout the complete software development process?	Agile Requirements Engineering	1	2.7 %
	Agile-UX	1	2.7 %
	DSDM	1	2.7 %
	eXtreme Scenario Based Design	1	2.7 %
	Agile Methodologies	21	56.8 %
	InterMod	1	2.7 %
	Lean UX	1	2.7 %
	Scrum	7	18.9 %
	XP	3	8.1 %
Question 3: What new frameworks or methods have been proposed for the integration of agile processes and usability engineering?	Case Study	9	24.32 %
	Exploratory	6	16.22 %
	Literature Review	1	2.70 %
	Systematic Review	4	10.81 %
	Framework/Method	17	45.95 %

Systematic reviews found [19, 36–38] were used for tuning the review process applied to define the years that were considered and check if the search string was adequate.

Exploratory studies [9, 11, 16, 23, 24, 34] are the outcomes of observation or applying questionnaires or interviews to development teams about using agile methodologies integrated with usability. They allow us to understand the point of view of developers, designers and usability experts who every day face the construction of software.

The methods and frameworks [2–5, 8, 12, 14, 15, 21, 26, 28–31, 35, 39, 41] were set forth by the authors as proposals of specific procedures to follow according to a determined type of software development. In all of these studies the proposed or adapted method or framework is described, and include at least one case study where its application is shown.

The selected case studies [1, 6, 7, 13, 17, 25, 27, 32, 33] include the intent of integrating usability techniques and methods to agile methodologies. Case studies that used usability techniques in an isolated manner with regard to the methodology without forming a unified process were excluded.

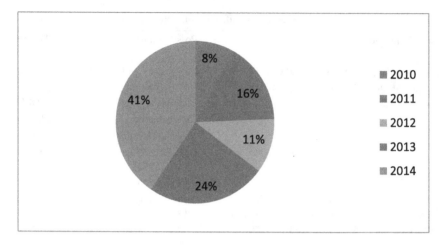

Fig. 1. Papers per year

It was also observed, as can be appreciated in Fig. 1, that the concern for integrating Usability and Agile Methodologies in a unified process, that would allow the development of a usable software product, has grown considerably in the last two years.

3.1   Integration of Usability and Agile Methodologies

The objective of Isa et al. in [17] is to demonstrate the applicability of agile user-centered design in software applications developed in a rural community. In said article, it is stated that particular issues regarding information use exist, and that these are influenced by the culture and environment in this scenario. Using Extreme Programming (XP), interviews, prototypes and feedbacks in the two proposed iterations, software was developed for the commercialization of handcrafts. Lastly, the satisfaction with the fulfillment of functional and non-functional requirements was verified, but no usability evaluations were applied that could demonstrate that this integration aided the construction of a usable software.

On the other hand, Lizano et al. [27] propose applying Remote Synchronous User Testing (RS) to projects developed using Scrum. The case study included RS in the different development stages as a tool to evaluate usability, with the principal contribution being the feedback obtained in these evaluations. The authors propose that RS should be applied by developers. This last statement can be related to [32] where it is mentioned that the low cohesion between designers and developers must be mitigated. This presents the challenge of verifying the technical viability of the design proposed by the designers and the prioritization of the agile methodology proposed by the developers.

Despite being the integration of UCD and Scrum similar to the previously mentioned case studies, [13] obtains additional results specific to the type of software developed. Being an educational tool, besides being usable it must also be accessible, and thus includes tests with kids affected by Down Syndrome. This case study again emphasizes the cohesion among the different actors that participate in software creation and the importance of the communication among them. In [33] a tool is also developed that must be usable and accessible, but aimed at elder adults. Additionally the authors observed that Agile Methodologies are more flexible than others because they allow reevaluating the requirements in the different software development stages, allowing the system to be adapted.

Finally, the exploratory studies [9, 11, 16, 23, 24, 34] confirm what has been said in the different case studies: the integration of Agile Methodologies and Usability is convenient and totally possible. In order to realize that integration the usability experts (designers and testers) must share a common objective: to satisfy the needs of the user. The diverse stages of Agile Methods complicate the labor of the designers, since they may lose the general vision of the software product due to the incremental and iterative process. This situation can be mitigated by the adequate formation of future professionals in both design and computing, in such a way that both disciplines find common grounds. These studies also reveal the need of a unified and clear process that allows the team members (analysts, designers, programmers and testers) to follow precise steps and techniques. In the following subsection the different proposed methods and frameworks are discussed.

3.2   Frameworks and Methods

Bertholdo et al. [5] present a series of usability patterns applied during agile development. Examples and recommendations are given to clearly identify the situations in which to apply each pattern and solution example. As in [3, 21, 30] these methods propose applying different usability techniques in the early stages of software development to establish the software requirements.

Methods that describe in detail the integrated usability and software engineering activities and techniques applied throughout the software development process exist for the benefit of development teams. Papers [1, 2, 4, 8, 15, 26, 29, 31, 35, 39, 41] propose well defined and detailed methods that integrate agile methodologies and usability in the different stages unlike [14, 28] where the emphasis is placed on the use of different types of usability evaluations to obtain user feedback in the iterations.

Some of the frameworks, such as those proposed in [2, 4] were developed to be applied in specific types of software.

4   Conclusions and Future Works

Agile methodologies are the most accepted in current development teams due to their level of flexibility and speed but must be integrated with different techniques and methods that will permit validating and verifying requirements compliance and the generation of usable software.

Designers, usability experts and developers must improve their communication and cohesion, acknowledging themselves as actors in the same process, and participating in different stages.

A different professional education may be required so that the different actors of the software development process see usability design as not only an aesthetic issue, but the development of a pleasant user interface, natural interaction and simple processes that aid the user in the fulfillment of his objectives.

Emphasis must be made in designing strategies that permit combining the general vision of the software product, realized during the design stage, with the modular vision produced when applying Agile Methodologies.

Although the methods and frameworks that propose the integration of usability and agile methodologies in a single unified process are facilitators for the work of development teams, more case studies of their use is needed to validate their applicability in the industry.

Finally, the systematic review is a powerful tool for the visualization of a subject, however the vast difference in the paper formats demands a significant time investment during their selection. Hopefully this issue will eventually be overcome with initiatives such as those of ELSEVIER to include specific elements in the abstracts like: goals, methods and results, among others.

References

1. Abdallah, A. et al.: Quantified extreme scenario based design approach. In: Proceedings of the ACM Symposium on Applied Computing, pp. 1117–1122 (2013)
2. Abdelouhab, K.A. et al.: Agile & user centric SOA based service design framework applied in disaster management. In: 1st International Conference on Information and Communication Technologies for Disaster Management, ICT-DM 2014 (2014)
3. Adikari, S., McDonald, C., Campbell, J.: Reframed contexts: design thinking for agile user experience design. In: Marcus, A. (ed.) DUXU 2013, Part I. LNCS, vol. 8012, pp. 3–12. Springer, Heidelberg (2013)
4. Benigni, G., Gervasi, O., Passeri, F.L., Kim, T.-H.: USABAGIL_Web: a web agile usability approach for web site design. In: Taniar, D., Gervasi, O., Murgante, B., Pardede, E., Apduhan, B.O. (eds.) ICCSA 2010, Part II. LNCS, vol. 6017, pp. 422–431. Springer, Heidelberg (2010)
5. Bertholdo, A.P.O., da Silva, T.S., de O. Melo, C., Kon, F., Silveira, M.S.: Agile usability patterns for UCD early stages. In: Marcus, A. (ed.) DUXU 2014, Part I. LNCS, vol. 8517, pp. 33–44. Springer, Heidelberg (2014)
6. Davies, M., et al.: Issues and understandings for rural HCI systems development: Agile approaches "In the wild". In: Stephanidis, C. (ed.) HCI International 2013 - Posters' Extended Abstracts, Part I. Communications in Computer and Information Science, vol. 373, pp. 22–26. Springer, Heidelberg (2013)
7. Felker, C., et al.: Integrating UX with Scrum in an undergraduate software development project. In: SIGCSE 2012 - Proceedings of the 43rd ACM Technical Symposium on Computer Science Education, pp. 301–306 (2012)
8. Ferrario, M.A., et al.: Software engineering for "social good": integrating action research, participatory design, and agile development. In: 36th International Conference on Software Engineering, ICSE Companion 2014 – Proceedings, pp. 520–523 (2014)
9. Ferreira, J., et al.: User experience design and agile development: Managing cooperation through articulation work. Softw. Pract. Exp. 41(9), 963–974 (2011)

10. Fowler, M., Highsmith, J.: The agile manifesto. Softw. Dev. **9**(8), 28–35 (2001)
11. Ganci, A., Ribeiro, B.: Becoming a team player: the evolving role of design in the world of agile development. Int. J. Des. Manag. Prof. Pract. **7**(2), 11–23 (2014)
12. Garnik, I., et al.: Creative sprints: an unplanned broad agile evaluation and redesign process. In: Proceedings of the NordiCHI 2014: The 8th Nordic Conference on Human-Computer Interaction: Fun, Fast, Foundational, pp. 1125–1130 (2014)
13. González, C.S., et al.: Inclusive educational software design with agile approach. In: ACM International Conference Proceeding Series. pp. 149–155 (2013)
14. Grigoreanu, V., Mohanna, M.: Informal Cognitive Walkthrough (ICW): paring down and pairing up for an agile world. In: Conference on Human Factors in Computing Systems – Proceedings, pp. 3093–3096 (2013)
15. Humayoun, S.R., Dubinsky, Y., Catarci, T.: A three-fold integration framework to incorporate user–centered design into agile software development. In: Kurosu, M. (ed.) HCD 2011. LNCS, vol. 6776, pp. 55–64. Springer, Heidelberg (2011)
16. Hussain, Z., et al.: Practical usability in XP software development processes. In: ACHI 2012 - 5th International Conference on Advances in Computer-Human Interactions, pp. 208–217 (2012)
17. Isa, W.A.R.W.M., et al.: Engineering rural informatics using agile user centered design. In: 2014 2nd International Conference on Information and Communication Technology, ICoICT 2014, pp. 367–372 (2014)
18. Jokela, T., et al.: The standard of user-centered design and the standard definition of usability: analyzing ISO 13407 against ISO 9241-11. In: Proceedings of the Latin American Conference on Human-Computer Interaction, pp. 53–60. ACM, New York (2003)
19. Jurca, G., et al.: Integrating agile and user-centered design: a systematic mapping and review of evaluation and validation studies of agile-UX. In: Proceedings - 2014 Agile Conference, AGILE 2014, pp. 24–32 (2014)
20. Kitchenham, B., Charters, S.: Guidelines for Performing Systematic Literature Reviews in Software Engineering (2007)
21. Kropp, E., Koischwitz, K.: User-centered-design in agile RE through an on-site user experience consultant. In: 2014 IEEE 2nd International Workshop on Usability and Accessibility Focused Requirements Engineering, UsARE 2014 – Proceedings, pp. 9–12 (2014)
22. Larusdottir, M., et al.: On the integration of user centred design in agile development. In: Proceedings of the NordiCHI 2014: The 8th Nordic Conference on Human-Computer Interaction: Fun, Fast, Foundational, pp. 817–820 (2014)
23. Lárusdóttir, M., et al.: Informal feedback rather than performance measurements - user-centred evaluation in Scrum projects. Behav. Inf. Technol. **33**(11), 1118–1135 (2014)
24. Lárusdóttir, M.K., et al.: The big picture of UX is missing in Scrum projects. In: CEUR Workshop Proceedings, pp. 42–48 (2012)
25. Lester, C.Y.: Combining agile methods and user-centered design to create a unique user experience: an empirical inquiry. In: ACHI 2011 - 4th International Conference on Advances in Computer-Human Interactions, pp. 16–21 (2011)
26. Liikkanen, L.A., et al.: Lean UX - the next generation of user-centered agile development? In: Proceedings of the NordiCHI 2014: the 8th Nordic Conference on Human-Computer Interaction: Fun, Fast, Foundational, pp. 1095–1100 (2014)
27. Lizano, F., Sandoval, M.M., Stage, J.: Integrating usability evaluations into Scrum: a case study based on remote synchronous user testing. In: Kurosu, M. (ed.) HCI 2014, Part I. LNCS, vol. 8510, pp. 500–509. Springer, Heidelberg (2014)

28. Losada, B., et al.: Applying usability engineering in InterMod agile development methodology. a case study in a mobile application. J. Univers. Comput. Sci. **19**(8), 1046–1065 (2013)
29. Maguire, M.: Using human factors standards to support user experience and agile design. In: Stephanidis, C., Antona, M. (eds.) UAHCI 2013, Part I. LNCS, vol. 8009, pp. 185–194. Springer, Heidelberg (2013)
30. Moreno, A.M., Yagüe, A.: Agile User Stories Enriched with Usability. In: Wohlin, C. (ed.) XP 2012. LNBIP, vol. 111, pp. 168–176. Springer, Heidelberg (2012)
31. Peres, A.L., et al.: AGILEUX model: towards a reference model on integrating UX in developing software using agile methodologies. In: Proceedings - 2014 Agile Conference, AGILE 2014, pp. 61–63 (2014)
32. Plonka, L., Sharp, H., Gregory, P., Taylor, K.: UX design in agile: a DSDM case study. In: Cantone, G., Marchesi, M. (eds.) XP 2014. LNBIP, vol. 179, pp. 1–15. Springer, Heidelberg (2014)
33. Prior, S., et al.: Use of an agile bridge in the development of assistive technology. In: Conference on Human Factors in Computing Systems – Proceedings, pp. 1579–1588 (2013)
34. Raison, C., Schmidt, S.: Keeping user centred design (UCD) alive and well in your organisation: taking an agile approach. In: Marcus, A. (ed.) DUXU 2013, Part I. LNCS, vol. 8012, pp. 573–582. Springer, Heidelberg (2013)
35. Salah, D.: A framework for the integration of user centered design and agile software development processes. In: Proceedings - International Conference on Software Engineering, pp. 1132–1133 (2011)
36. Salah, D., et al.: A systematic literature review for agile development processes and user centred design integration. In: ACM International Conference Proceeding Series (2014)
37. Salvador, C., et al.: A systematic review of usability techniques in agile methodologies. In: ACM International Conference Proceeding Series (2014)
38. Da Silva, T.S., et al.: User-centered design and agile methods: A systematic review. In: Proceedings - 2011 Agile Conference, Agile 2011, pp. 77–86 (2011)
39. Sohaib, O., Khan, K.: Incorporating discount usability in extreme programming. Int. J. Softw. Eng. Its Appl. **5**(1), 51–62 (2011)
40. Sohaib, O., Khan, K.: Integrating usability engineering and agile software development: A literature review. In: 2010 International Conference on Computer Design and Applications, ICCDA 2010, pp. V232–V238 (2010)
41. Xiong, Y., Wang, A.: A new combined method for UCD and software development and case study. In: 2nd International Conference on Information Science and Engineering, ICISE2010 – Proceedings (2010)

Research on the Correspondence Between Designer End Expressions of Product Semantics with the Cognition of User End

Liqun Zhang[(⊠)]

School of Media and Design, Shanghai Jiao Tong University, Shanghai, China
zhanglq@sjtu.edu.cn

Abstract. For ICT product, the importance of the functional property of a product speaks for itself. However, as an important method of defining the product differentiation, the influence of product appearance on that whether the product property can be perceived correctly. As the engineer of human-computer cooperative relationship in product location, if the product appearance can't provide service for the macro planning and strategy made by an enterprise to the company, it will brings negative effect on the healthy development of the product system. The paper tries to provide a method to help enterprises to evaluate the appearance design scheme before putting the product into production to check the matching degree with the product planning. Then the product appearance design will conform to the product strategy of an enterprise. The evaluation method uses physical projection method to obtain the user cognitive image data about product appearance from the user end. Then using the Correspondent Analysis method, the perpetual method shows analysis result. Finally, according to the overall analysis of product system, it forms the evaluation of the new product appearance. The research shows that there are defects in the company's product system planning. And these mainly are similar perceptual location, without characteristics, inconsistency of user end cognition of appearance result with the designed definition, hard to attract the consumers' and users' interests.

Keywords: Product appearance design · Cognitive image of users · Perceptual location map

1 Introduction

According to different innovative impetuses, Dosi puts forward two opposite innovative methods: market demand innovation and technology push innovation [1]. Market demand innovation considers the new product development activity as the reflection of clear client demand. In market demand innovation, market is the core resource of innovation; in technology push innovation, the usability of new technology is the pusher. In technology push innovation, innovation is the R&D behavior of enterprises and enterprises develop new products through new technology.

In the traditional product development, enterprises attach great importance to the function, efficiency and style of products. As the world of man-made materials

© Springer International Publishing Switzerland 2015
A. Marcus (Ed.): DUXU 2015, Part I, LNCS 9186, pp. 379–391, 2015.
DOI: 10.1007/978-3-319-20886-2_36

becomes more and more colorful, the pursuance of humans to products isn't limited to product function and style any more. The emotional value and symbolic value (product meaning) shown by color, line, material and architectural appearance can meet the deep demands of users. The development of new products also notices that the product with the user value and meaning has bigger advantage than other products under the fierce market competition environment. Users not only pay attention to the practical function and style, but the product meaning too. It's because that function meets the demand of users to use the product and product meaning pleases consumers' emotion and social culture demand.

Verganti proposes the third innovative method: design-driven innovation. He thinks that the motivation of innovation is to understand, acquire and influence the meaning of new products [2]. Design-driven innovation is a breakthrough innovation in product language and meaning. Technology push is a breakthrough innovation in technological function. Market demand innovation is the incremental innovation of technological function and product language. For these innovation methods and strategies, market demand innovation is the innovation with consumers as the center (including users which have special meaning of consumers) and it's an incremental innovation. Technological push innovation focuses on the improvement of product function and property and no product language appears. However, the design-driven innovation or language-driven innovation creates new product language, then designers can provide the breakthrough products.

Since the design philosophy of taking humans as the center has been widely recognized in the field of new product development, the researchers, designers and engineers of product design many technologies and methods to help the research on human factors [3] in order to build a more complete product stricture to meet users' physiological, cognitive, social, cultural and emotional demand, wish and preference and to achieve good user experience [4]. Then it can realize the sustainable development of product, brand and even enterprises. Product appearance activity is an important process to reflect the expected user experience to visual and touchable product.

At present, the philosophy that "product design is actually the design of user experience has become a consensus of companies and organizations at the leading edge of product and service design innovation. On this basis, how to understand the formation of user experience, how to change the user understanding into design specification and standard, how to evaluate the product concept and scheme with the principle of user experience have become the research topics in recent years.

Usually the success rate of product innovation in enterprises is low and 46 % of new product development will fail. The research shows that 60 % of the faults lies in the design and further statistical data also shows that these 60 % of faults result from demand and analysis activity, which means it's caused by the faults of early stage of innovation. The input and quality to (market and user value) demand analysis in the Fuzzy Front End of new product development determines the success of the final product [5].

The product development and design process based on the philosophy focuses on the exploration and analysis of user experience. It builds product structure according to it. Every periodic decision in the whole design process introduces the design quality evaluation of user experience factors of periodic results by all means. Then many new methods have taken shape, such as participating design or co-creation design. As the product classes are different and different understandings of the design team to user experience may affect the final quality of the experience design, the costs of changing the design is high when problems appear after making the design evaluation as the completion of product structure and design. So the earlier the user experience evaluation is, the better the design quality can be guaranteed and the higher the cost-effectiveness is.

Although the design philosophy of UCD has proved its meaning by many design projects, the knowledge obtained from user research still needs designers to make design conversion. Some cases have shown that although we have obtained some valuable design knowledge in the Fuzzy Front End, we can't guarantee the success of the final product. Some research results show that designers design products with the precondition of enterprise profit and it's the compromise and balance of the connected factors such as technology, economic value and business enterprise; the users' understanding and experience of products are based on the realization of user value. It's the balance of product function, the relation with related system, products and the usage on the user meaning (Fig. 1) [6]. As the objectives and influence factors are different, the encoding information in the process of design in the design end on the basis of design knowledge is inconsistent with the decoding information in the process of connecting and using the product in the user end, i.e. the product knowledge obtained by users are inconsistent with the product knowledge which the designers try to express through encoding. This makes it hard to realize the presupposed objective of product development. For example, it will lead to the location to appear objective offset in front of the market and product, the difference between different products in the same product line will be not clear enough, even the internal competition will appear among products. Then the effective realization of product strategy in an enterprise will be influenced, even the enterprise will suffer from loss of competitive capacity in the market as a whole.

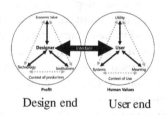

Design end   User end

Fig. 1. Design knowledge composition of design end encoding and product knowledge composition of user end decoding.

Design encoding - the semantic expression process taking product as the physical medium to product meaning has always been considered as a black box process. There is no effective method to guarantee the high quality of encoding by some obvious mechanism at present. But by measuring the cognition of users to the design result, i.e. the spread effect of appearance to product meaning, and evaluating the match of cognition content and design location and specification is an effective method of finding the problem of design encoding and promoting the optimization of design iteration. The objective of this research is to build a method to match the index of the cognition decoding in the user end to product and the semantic information encoding to product meaning in the design end and then to provide methods and tools of the periodic design evaluation involved in the participating design process which takes users as the center.

2   Research Objective and Method

Research Objective. The research objective is to build a method to help designers evaluate the appearance design in two directions: 1- whether the property described by product location in the appearance design can deliver to consumers/users; 2- considering from the angle of product line planning, whether the appearance design can become an effective tool to differentiate the product with the other products in the product line. In addition, the methods provided by the research can be used to evaluate the quality of product line planning. It helps enterprises understand the product line/system structure based on the understanding of consumers/users and provides the basis or reference for enterprises to adjust or optimize the product strategy.

Research Method. The research adopts the participating evaluation method and uses physical projection method to obtain the subjects' cognitive image data of users. With the help of statistical analysis method, it uses perceptual location map to show the analysis result. Finally, it forms the evaluation on the concept of new product through the overall analysis of the product system [7]. Besides, to reveal the product line structure from the angle of the product line and product system of the enterprise and check that whether the structure meets the product strategy of the enterprise and the problems provide inspiration and suggestions for the subsequent design activities and the product strategy behavior of the enterprise.

The analysis of the research data adopts the Correspondent Analysis method. Correspondent Analysis is a multiple statistical analysis technology and it helps to reveal the relationship between the variables through researching the summary table of interaction composed by qualitative variables [8]. The information of interaction table is shown in pictures. It's mainly used for the qualitative variables with several types and it can reveal the difference of one variable among different types and the correspondence relation of different variables among different types. It's applicable to the analysis of two or more qualitative variables. The Correspondent Analysis technology has widely used for concept development, new product development, market refining, competition analysis, advertisement research at present. It helps the researchers and designers who are engaged in product strategy research and market research to solve many problems: product user and its property, competitor, product location. The detailed data analysis is completed by SPSS (statistical analysis software).

3   Research Process

The research takes a new product development of H Company as an example to do research.

3.1   Case Review

H Company is an enterprise which develops and producing network Router as the leading products. It has many subsidiaries in the world. After the operation of more than 10 years, the company has completed the transformation from an ODM enterprise to an OBM enterprise. At the meantime, the product chain has spread from network equipment to mobile communication system such as smart phone. The research object is the wireless Router product for home use. The design activity of the design team in H Company usually bases on the new product location of the Market Research Department of the company. The design team combines the materials and data in user research to determine the design direction. There will a symbolic semantic word in the early stage of design to generalize the user cognition which the product is expected to achieve. For example, the descriptive semantic words of three products are "light and handy", "active and strong", and "noble and graceful". As the generality and importance of the descriptive semantic words to design guidance, the research takes 7 products and 1 conceptual product under the stage of R&D to analyze the match relation of design location (product appearance) of products of different types in the product chain and the corresponding descriptive semantic words (for the purpose of standardization, it's called as "semantic words of product appearance"). And with the analysis of product specification, we find the suitable direction.

3.2   Acquisition of Research Data

The following are the detailed procedures of data acquisition:

Experiment Preparation. H Company provides all the products and a high fidelity concept product model for the research of the cognitive image of users. Relatively speaking, the product has more real and abundant product information, it's easy to make subjects to have user experience. Therefore, the experiment bases on the physical projection method to adopt data using the match of physical stimulus and semantic words of product appearance. The experiment design is as following:

1- Choice of subjects. Limited by the research grant, the research only samples the undergraduate in College of Design of Media & Design Institute in Shanghai Jiao Tong University. The research uses cluster random sampling method to classify the students by grade and sex for random sampling (Table 1). There are 86 subjects taking part in the experiment.
2- 2–7 physical products and 1 high fidelity concept product model are put on 8 desks in random order. The desk surface is white non-reflective material in order to reduce the interference of background to the stimulus; in order to reduce experiment noise, the brand logo of H Company is removed;

Table 1. Examinee distribution of random sampling based on layer

	Grade 1	Grade 2	Grade 3	Grade 4
Male	10	10	10	10
Female	12	12	10	12

3- According to the description of key words of design objective when design the product, the research acquires 8 semantic words of product appearance. Taking the basic standard of easy to recognize in normal distance, 8 semantic words of product appearance are used to make standard cards. The character is Song typeface and 3 black font. The product semantic words come from the key words of product orientation from the design stage of H Company. They are light and handy, active and strong, elegant and classic, HiTech and Fashionable, exquisite and noble, implicit and flexible, free and convenient, noble and graceful. The correspondence relation between 8 products (including a high fidelity concept product model) and 8 semantic words (Table 2):

Table 2. Correspondent relationship between product and product type and semantic word

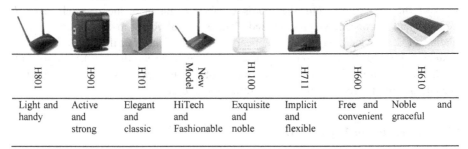

H801	H901	H101	New Model	H1100	H711	H600	H610
Light and handy	Active and strong	Elegant and classic	HiTech and Fashionable	Exquisite and noble	Implicit and flexible	Free and convenient	Noble and graceful

Experiment Process. 1- The subjects undertake the observation and free operation of 30 s to every object and then the subjects are offered 8 semantic word cards to match one pair by one pair. The researchers take photos of the matching results and record the data.

According to the consumer orientation of the product, we find 86 subjects. There are 78 effective samples through the experiment. After the Correspondence Analysis operation, we get the following perceptual location map (Fig. 2):

Note: in order to show the result intuitively. Figure 2 attaches the pictures of the product and the model on the basis of SPSS output result. Also two axes are added at the 0 point and there is no further change.

The analyzed data forms a contingency table of 8 × 8. The smallest dimensional is 1 and the 7th dimensional can explain 100 % of the contingency table. The first dimensional explains 59.4 % and the second 18.3 %. These two explain 77.7 % of the contingency table (Table 3). In general, the result is ideal.

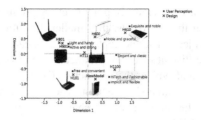

Fig. 2. Perceptual location map

Table 3. Abstract of Correspondent Evaluation

Dimensional	Singular value	Inertia	Chi-square	Significance	Inertia ratio		Confidence singular value	
					Situation	Accumulation	Standard deviation	Correlation 2
1	.572	.328			.594	.594	.009	.129
2	.318	.101			.183	.777	.013	
3	.267	.071			.129	.906		
4	.210	.044			.080	.986		
5	.077	.006			.011	.997		
6	.038	.001			.003	.999		
7	.018	.000			.001	1.000		
Total		.552	3312.225	.000[a]	1.000	1.000		

[a] 49 Degree of freedom

4 Data Analysis

The following is the further analysis of the results.

Overall Observation. We can see that 8 products distributing spread in the location map and the distribution of 8 semantic words of product appearance are widely spread too. It shows that there are differences among these products (including a design scheme model) from the view of the subjects, i.e. there is product orientation difference (Fig. 3).

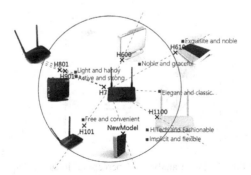

Fig. 3. Vector analysis of perceptual location map

To make the vector from the reference point to every product orientation point. The smaller the angle between the vectors is, the smaller the difference between the correspondent products in subjects' user perception, which means the product similarity is bigger. Besides, the more distant of every product orientation point from the original point, the more particular and typical the product is. Otherwise, it is less characteristic and it's harder to attract consumers' attraction. Therefore, it's much harder to form unique user experience. The above analysis chart shows that comparing with other products, H801, H610 and H1100 are considered as more typical. The interview after the event also shows that these products leave a deep impression on the subjects. The most undistinguished product is H711. Its locating point is almost located in the original point and it will be explained in details in the later analysis.

Observe the Neighboring Area. In 8 products, H801 and H901 are close; H101and New Model (New Concept) are close; and other product relations are relatively far. As to the semantic words of product appearance, "light and handy", "active and strong", "HiTech and Fashionable", "implicit and flexible" are considered as closer by subjects. This can be explained by comparing the meaning of these two groups of words.

To observe the Psychological Distance Perceived by Subjects of Semantic Words and Different Types of Products. 8 semantic words of product appearance directly come from the design department of H Company. According to the design intent, the product plan hopes that every product can deliver the user experience described by these key words to consumers. The correspondence map shows that the design objective of most products has consistent relevance with the subjects' cognitive image of users stimulated by the stimulus. The next is to analyze the distance relation between every semantic words of product appearance and the location of every product in the subjects' cognitive image of users. The detailed analysis method is: to draw a reference line OWi from the original point O(0,0) to every product semantic word (taking free and convenient as an example). Then to make a vertical MjQj from every product locating point to OWi, and the distance |WiQj| which is from the foot point to the current semantic word (free and convenient) is the distance from the cognitive image of users to product semantic word. It's shown in the following chart (Fig. 4):

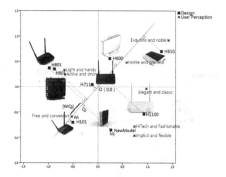

Fig. 4. Pedal analysis of perceptual location map

The distance relation between 8 semantic words of product appearance and 8 product types is as following (Figs. 5 and 6):

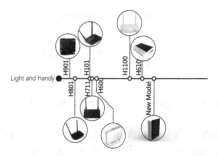

Fig. 5. Pedal projection figure of the semantic word "Light and Handy".

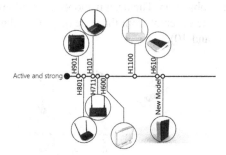

Fig. 6. Pedal projection figure of the semantic word "Active and Strong".

Light and handy: the closest semantic words of product appearance of this product are H901 and then H801 - the original type.

Active and strong: consistent with the design objective, H901 becomes the type which is the closest one to the semantic word in the subjects' mind (Figs. 7 and 8).

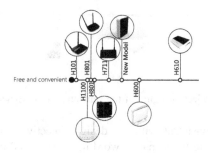

Fig. 7. Pedal projection figure of the semantic word "Free and Convenient".

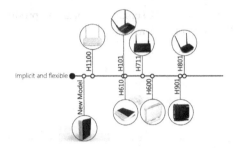

Fig. 8. Pedal projection figure of the semantic word "Implicit and Flexible".

Free and convenient: under this semantic word, H101 becomes the closest type, which is consistent with the design objective. The distance between the other types is close as well and that shows that the difference isn't huge.

Implicit and flexible: New Model is the closest one to the semantic word, and this is consistent with the design objective. The design adopts the random honeycomb support form. Its appearance is quite different from the style of all the other types. However, its color is implicit (Figs. 9 and 10).

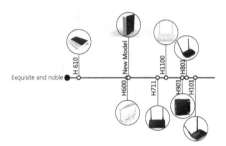

Fig. 9. pedal projection figure of the semantic word "Exquisite and Noble".

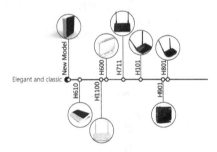

Fig. 10. Pedal projection figure of the semantic word "Elegant and Classic".

Exquisite and noble: consistent with the design objective, H610 becomes the type which is the closest one to the semantic word in the subjects' mind, while other types are distant from the semantic word.

Elegant and classic: being elegant and classic is the design objective of H711, but the data shows that H711 is quite distant from the semantic word. The interview finds that the subjects are antipathetic to H711 as its modeling language is considered as has intimating some competitive product, even though its overall modeling is great. As its unique design, New Model is considered by the examinees as the closest to the feeling of "elegant and classic" (Figs. 11 and 12).

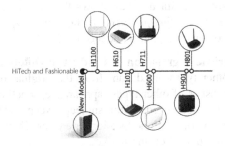

Fig. 11. Pedal projection figure of the semantic word "HiTech and fashionable".

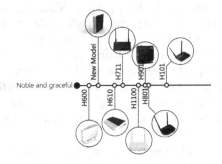

Fig. 12. Pedal projection figure of the semantic word "Noble and Graceful".

HiTech and Fashionable: New Model is the closest one to the semantic word and this consistent with the design objective. It is closely connected with the new visual language and high technological modeling language.

Noble and graceful: consistent with the design objective, H610 becomes the type which is the closest one to the semantic word in the subjects' mind and New Model ranks the second.

Analysis on Product Similarity Reflected by the Subjects' Cognitive Behavior. Referring to Fig. 2, to make vectors from the original point to the points of products of 8 types, then we can get 8 vectors. Comparing in pairs, if the angel between vectors is an acute angle, then the subjects' cognitive difference between these two products is small. The smaller the acute angle is, the smaller the difference of subjects' cognition between these two products is. We can see from the figure that the cognitive distance between H801 and H901 is small, then we can deduce that although the appearances of these types are different, the subjects' overall cognition reflects huge similarity. We can find from analyzing the product property that the the products' configuration and function are similar. The main difference lies in the appearance (and size). In addition, H600 and H610 are similar too. However, besides the difference in some functional configurations, their biggest difference is that they use different surface materials and processes. According to the prediction of researchers, the cognitive distance between these two types is smaller than that between H801 and H901 and researchers think that they are the closest products. But the data shows the influence factor of appearance plays a role in differentiating the products in these two types. The psychological cognition distances of other types can be deduced from it.

Analysis of Characteristic Segregation of Product in Different Types. We can see from the figure that other types are distant from the original point except H711. It shows that the characteristics of other types (appearance, functional configuration and interaction) can be easily recognized by the subjects except H711, i.e. the characteristics of these types are obvious and the locations are clear. They can easily recognized by consumers after being placed on the market.

Analysis of Market Location and Product Refining. Referring to Fig. 1, the correspondence map shows that: the key word of the product located in the first quadrant is noble which means focusing on the high grade product; the product in the second quadrant focuses on "light" and "strong" and it can be understood as portable and good performance; that in the third quadrant focuses on function integration and it supports users to complete many tasks; that in the fourth quadrant focuses on high technology and fashion, such as the product responses quickly in operation and go along the fashionable appearance language. The internal information reflected by the correspondence map shows the consumption appeal of the subjects (or consumers of products) to these products and it's also one of the bases for enterprises to develop products.

At the same time, the small cognitive distance between H801 and H901 shows that these two products are competitors. This is what enterprises should avoid when make the product planning.

5   Conclusion

We can easily discover from the above analysis that using the technology and procedures provided by the research can predict the consumers'/users' cognitive image of users to the product. With the help of corresponding data exploration technology, it can help designers to evaluate the semantic spread effect of the appearance design activity under the direction of product planning and help enterprises and the design department to undertake management and quality control in every link in the whole innovative design process as early as possible. It also helps the design team to make effective segregation through appearance to the product location among different types from the consumers' cognition characteristics at the beginning of product planning in order to achieve the integrity and complementarities of product line and reduce the huge risks brought by blind development; meanwhile, introducing the potential users of the product to take part in the concept development, plan design and decision, and prototyping can effectively guarantee the design philosophy of taking humans as the center in the whole development process until the realization of the final product.

Acknowledgement. This paper is sponsored by Shanghai Jiao Tong University Humanity and Social Science Research Innovation Fund 2012 (TS09). Moreover, we thank to the students of Shanghai Jiao Tong University who contributed to this research.

References

1. Dosi, G.: Technological paradigms and technological trajectories: a suggested interpretation of the determinants and directions of technical change [J]. Res. Policy **11**, 147–162 (1982)
2. Verganti, D.: Design Driven Innovation Changing the Rules of Competition by Radically Innovating What Things Mean. Harvard Business Press, Boston (2009)
3. Liqun, Z.: Theory, Principles and Methodology of UCD. Mach. Des. Res. **19** (2003). CN31-1382/TH
4. Kumar, V., Whitney, P.: Faster, Cheaper, Deeper User Research, spring 2003. Des. Manag. J. **14**, 50–57 (2003). Design Management Institute. BusinessWeek, October 2007
5. Cagan, J., Vogel, C.M.: Creating Breakthrough Products: Innovation from Product Planning to Program Approval. FT Press, Upper Saddle River (2001). ISBN 0-13-969694-6
6. Heskett, J.: Ten Steps to Heaven (Keynotes), D2B - The 1st International Design Management Symposium – Shanghai (2006)
7. Participatory design. http://en.wikipedia.org/wiki/Participatory_design
8. Huixin, K., Hao, S.: Statistical Analysis Methods in Survey Research, 2nd Version. China Media Agency, Beijing (2005). ISBN 7-81085-261-2

Emotional and Persuasion Design

OBDEnergy

Making Metrics Meaningful in Eco-driving Feedback

Sumayyah Ahmed[✉] and Angela Sanguinetti

Consumer Energy Interfaces Lab, University of California, Davis, USA
sahmed@ucdavis.edu, angelasanguinetti@gmail.com

Abstract. This paper describes an eco-driving feedback system, OBDEnergy. Twenty-six drivers described their understanding of environmental impacts of driving before and after using OBDEnergy. Before OBDEnergy, participants discussed impacts in abstract, global terms (pollution, global warming). After OBDEnergy, participants appealed to concrete reference points (gallons of gas, trees required) with calculations and comparisons. We conclude that user-centered eco-driving feedback can contribute to pro-environmental behavior via increased awareness of the concrete environmental impacts of driving.

Keywords: Eco-driving · Feedback · Integrated technology · Carbon emissions

1 Introduction

Fuel economy estimates posted on every car sold in the US state the caveat, "Actual results will vary for many reasons, including driving conditions, and how you drive and maintain your vehicle." Eco-driving is strategically taking advantage of this variability through driving and maintenance practices (e.g., by minimizing braking and hard accelerations, ensuring proper tire inflation, and avoiding traffic). Estimates of fuel economy improvements and concomitant carbon emission reductions resulting from eco-driving range from 5 % to 20 % [1].

1.1 Eco-driving Feedback: The Technology

In-vehicle feedback displays are becoming more prevalent and increasing in variety (Fig. 1), especially in hybrid, plug-in, and electric vehicles; gas vehicles typically have at most a numeric indicator for real-time and average fuel economy (Fig. 2). Eco-driving feedback systems are also available after-market via devices and web or mobile applications. A search in iOS and Android app stores revealed more than 40 eco-driving apps (at least 24 originating outside the US).

Some apps integrate with a device that plugs into a vehicle's OBD (OnBoard Diagnostic) port, usually located underneath the steering wheel and standard for all cars after 1996. Use of OBD improves accuracy by collecting data directly from the engine

© Springer International Publishing Switzerland 2015
A. Marcus (Ed.): DUXU 2015, Part I, LNCS 9186, pp. 395–405, 2015.
DOI: 10.1007/978-3-319-20886-2_37

Fig. 1. Lincoln MKZ (Hybrid)

Fig. 2. Mazda CX-5 (ICEV)

Fig. 3. Drivee

(e.g., fuel level, Mass Air Flow), whereas app-only feedback is limited to factors external to the engine (e.g., GPS, speed, acceleration) and user input. Examples of app-only feedback systems include Geco and Drivee (Fig. 3). Systems with OBD include Metromile, Torque, Dash, and CaroO Pro (Fig. 4).

Fig. 4. CaroO Pro

1.2   Eco-driving Feedback: The Psychology

Research suggests eco-driving feedback results in average fuel and emissions savings of 5 %, ranging from 0 % to 18 % [3]. Some of this variation is undoubtedly due to variation in the feedback itself in terms of information provided and design, which have implications for its effectiveness in shaping and motivating behavior.

Schwartz's Norm Activation Model (NAM) [4] contends pro-environmental behavior is supported by awareness of the consequences (AC) of one's behavior, perhaps especially concrete consequences: "A person who becomes aware intensely and in detail of how his potential actions may affect others is likely to experience activation of moral norms" (p. 357). Raising awareness of concrete consequences via eco-driving feedback may involve quantification of environmental impacts. In scientific and popular climate change discourse, kilograms (kg) of CO_2 is commonly used to convey environmental impact (Fig. 2). Eleven of the 40 + eco-driving apps we found report carbon emissions, typically in kilograms. Whether such a specific, quantified consequence is meaningful may depend on how familiar or tangible the metric is; for example, icons of clouds or power plants are sometimes paired with quantifications of carbon (Fig. 2). In perhaps yet another sense, concrete consequences might be personal or emotionally evocative; e.g., nature imagery (e.g., Fig. 1) is often used in eco-driving feedback.

Relational Frame Theory (RFT) [2] is a behavior analytic theory of language and cognition applicable to this predicament of fostering awareness of concrete consequences. This theory focuses on the phenomenon of framing events relationally, which means responding to (thinking about or speaking about) some event in terms of another event (a relational frame). Relational frames of coordination are based on identity or similarity (e.g., fuel combusted equates to carbon emitted). Comparative relational frames involve comparing one event to another in terms of a specific dimension (e.g., one gallon of gas weighs less than the carbon emissions from its combustion). Temporal relations are a special case of comparative frames whereby someone understands an event in terms of its relationship to time.

An important property of every relational frame is *transformation of stimulus functions*, which refers to a change in the functions of a stimulus as a result of its relation to another stimulus; e.g., given a frame of coordination between kilograms of carbon and trees required to offset emissions, if trees required evokes an emotional response and motivates conservation, kilograms of carbon will have a similar effect. Eco-driving feedback systems are operating with assumptions that align with RFT and NAM. They attempt to change how drivers understand (i.e., respond to) abstract environmental impacts by framing them in relation to concrete concepts, such as money, time, or trees.

1.3   Present Research

We present a behavioral study of the effectiveness of an integrated mobile app and OBD eco-driving feedback system called OBDEnergy in promoting awareness of concrete environmental consequences of personal vehicle travel. The system's user interface (UI) juxtaposes abstract and concrete metrics for trip-level and historical data. Based on RFT and NAM, we hypothesized that users' awareness of consequences would become more concrete. OBDEnergy does not directly prompt specific behavior through real-time feedback, but to the degree that it enhances awareness of consequences we anticipated some effect on behavior and intentions in accordance with NAM.

2   Method

2.1   OBDEnergy

An Android application was programmed to communicate with vehicle engines via a Bluetooth-enabled OBD-II plug-in device. The engine is queried constantly throughout a drive for Fuel Level and Mass Air Flow. At the end of a drive, a formula for each parameter is used to calculate gallons of gasoline used for that drive and the two numbers are cross-checked. Gallons of gas used is multiplied by the EPA's constant (8.9 kg CO_2) to estimate kilograms of carbon emissions.

The UI has three screens. A 'Drive' screen is hands-off to prevent driver distraction; this screen simply has prompts to activate the system. Pressing 'START' activates data collection and the button changes to 'STOP'. Pressing 'STOP' at the end of a drive activates the 'Metrics' screen (Fig. 5), which presents metrics with corresponding icons. The third screen, 'Graphs' (Fig. 6 and 7), presents metrics accumulated over time. Clouds accumulated much faster than trees since it requires only 0.026 trees to offset 1 kg of carbon; therefore we visualized trees in terms of accumulations of 10 leaves for greater sensitivity. 'Graphs' can be viewed anytime and is the most interactive screen.

2.2   Study Design, Participants, and Recruitment

In a within-subjects, pre-posttest, quasi-experimental design, 26 University of California, Davis, students (23), staff (2), and faculty (1) were recruited via department listservs and exposed to the same feedback. They completed a survey before and after using OBDEnergy for at least one month (M = 36 days, min. = 28, max. = 42). Participants were male (15) and female (11), ranging from 19 to 47 years old (M = 25.87 years,

Fig. 5. Metrics screen

Fig. 6. Trees in 'Graphs'

SD = 7.21 years). They were required to have a valid driver license, Android phone, and personal vehicle—1997 or newer, and to confirm driving at least 20 times per month on average. Participants received a $30 gift card.

2.3 Procedure

The lead researcher installed an OBD-II plugin in each participant's vehicle, emailed them a link to download the app to their phone, tested the system to ensure valid data

Fig. 7. CO_2 in 'Graphs'

communication between the engine, OBD, and app, and oriented participants to the app. Both pre-test and post-test surveys were paper-based and administered in an office building at the University of California, Davis. The pre-test survey consisted of seven open-ended questions, one closed-ended question, and prompts for demographic information; it took approximately 10 min to complete. The post-test survey consisted of 12 open-ended questions, one closed-ended question, and included items regarding system usability; it took approximately 20 min to complete.

Awareness of concrete consequences was gauged by asking participants to describe the environmental impact of one gallon of gas (priming a relational frame between a tangible, familiar metric and a more abstract concept). Similarly, we queried participants about their understanding of carbon emissions and their personal energy footprint. The post-test survey included one item about behavior change, inquiring how, if at all, OBDEnergy affected participants' behavior.

3 Results

We organize our analysis around four lines of questioning. Three relate to awareness of consequences and relational framing, in general and specific terms (carbon emissions broadly versus kilograms of carbon and one gallon of gas), and impersonal and personal terms (impact of gas and carbon versus personal footprint). A fourth line of inquiry concerns self-reported behavior change. Responses to these sets of questions were coded separately according to emergent themes. Each response could yield multiple codes; all participants answered all questions.

3.1   Impact of One Gallon of Gas

Before and after using OBDEnergy, participants were prompted to consider the environmental impact of one gallon of gas. In the pre-test survey, 17 of the 26 participants indicated that they did not know and did not venture a guess. Four participants cited general impacts, including mention of smog, pollution, or global warming (e.g., *I imagine the carbon entering the atmosphere adds to the global warming problem*). Two made a vague normative observation about emission being "bad" (e.g., *I just know that carbon emissions are bad*). Even participants who seemed well-versed in the climate change discourse were unable to specify a concrete impact in relation to this familiar metric:

> *I do realize that it's more polluting than simply releasing the CO2 into the atmosphere (...) there is a huge amount of energy that goes into getting the gas out of the earth, processing, packing, and transporting it to the gas station. And then of course there's all the energy and materials required to build each gas station... So the impact depends on where one draws the life cycle parameters, but I really have no idea what impact one gallon of gas used by my car has on the atmosphere.*

Five participants implied that they should know or want to know (*I would like to see just how much an impact just one gallon has*); two of these were inferred by the fact that they qualified their "no" with "honestly", but others were more explicit (*Sadly, I do not know; I unfortunately do not - I routinely dismiss it as negligible*). One participant was able to quantify a specific impact of one gallon of gas in a relational frame of coordination, although it was not an environmental impact: *1 gal is about a 1 way trip to work*. In sum, the pre-test survey revealed that none of the participants could provide a specific impact of one gallon of gas on the environment.

In the post-test survey, participants described environmental impact in relation to metrics provided in the feedback. Four participants described the impact in terms of the trees (e.g., *Needs ~ 1/4 of a tree to offset its carbon emission; I know we don't have nearly enough trees!*). Two referenced weight of carbon emissions—neither explicitly in kilograms, however, and both rather tentatively (*I'm pretty sure that one gallon of gas releases more weight than the actual gallon of gasoline; For every gallon of gas my car used it generated close to 20 lbs of CO2?*). Six expressed surprise that the impact was greater than anticipated (e.g., *It is quite a large impact!*). In contrast to the pre-test survey, there was no mention in the post-test surveys of general impacts concerning pollution and global warming.

Just eight participants still reported very little understanding of the impact of a gallon of gas at the end of the study (e.g., *I have a vague idea after looking at the app*). Of these, four had technical difficulties that prevented them from viewing retrospective feedback and two reported minimal app use (e.g., *I don't think I drove enough to really understand the impact of a single gallon of gas*). Some affirmative responses were too vague to interpret (e.g., *Now I do, I had almost no idea of the impact before!*). One response very clearly affirms our hypothesis regarding increased awareness of consequences: *This app just made me more aware of what I'm releasing into the environment.*

3.2   Carbon Emissions

Participants were asked about their understanding of carbon emissions, the metric of kilograms of carbon, and the environmental impact of carbon emissions. Again, we looked for differences in awareness of specific consequences and relational frames before and after using the app. In the pre-survey, most participants (19) described general impacts (e.g., *I know carbon emissions play a role in global warming*), frequently using the terms *global warming* (6), *greenhouse gas* (5), *ozone* (6), and *climate* (6). Other responses were vague (e.g., *It adds up*) or offered a general normative statement (e.g., *Carbon emissions are bad. Beyond that I have very little understanding*).

Despite the prevalence of climate change language to describe general consequences of carbon emissions (19 participants), 6 of those participants qualified their response to indicate uncertainty or a limited understanding (e.g., *Emissions contribute to global warming and thinning of the atmosphere? Is that even right[?] I just know that they are bad and we are always trying to reduce our carbon footprint*). Seven participants related carbon to fossil fuels (e.g., *My understanding is that carbon emissions come from fuel and energy usage?; Carbon as a fuel source isn't infinite; burning fossil fuels...*). Three participants referenced trees but not in terms of negative environmental impact of carbon emissions (*Trees take in CO2 and output O2 during photosynthesis; forest loss; cutting down our environment*). None quantified the impact of carbon emissions or mentioned a specific carbon metric (e.g., kilograms or pounds).

The post-test survey item asked participants directly about any change in their understanding of kilograms of carbon compared to the beginning of the study. Nine participants related kilograms of carbon to metrics in the feedback in frames of coordination or comparison (trees, gallons of gas, trip distance) and/or time (trip comparison or accumulation across trips). There were six relations to time or distance (e.g., *It doesn't take a lot of driving to rack up a lot of kg of carbon; I got a much better understanding of how the ways I drive changes the emissions of my car on a drive-by-drive basis*). There were two relations to trees (*I had no clue of how much is 1 kg, but over time I started comparing "trees required"; It is like using up a lot of trees! It showed me how much carbon I use when I drive compared to using trees*). There were three relations to gas (e.g., *I have more of an idea of how gas used compares to CO2 emitted*).

Two participants quantified relations between carbon and other metrics or time (*I had generated over 400lbs of CO2 over the month study period; I was driving under 9 kilograms of carbon per day*). Five participants expressed surprise at the amount of kilograms of carbon their vehicle emitted (e.g., *I realized I use more kilograms of carbon than I would think; ... at times it felt like I was killing off a whole forest!*). Two participants implied that social comparisons in the feedback would increase their understanding of kilograms of carbon (e.g., *It would be more helpful if I could compare my results with other users or avg American driving similar cars*). Six participants had technical difficulties and/or low driving frequency so their responses were not applicable and five others reported no change in awareness of kilograms of carbon or their answer revealed misunderstanding (e.g., *Trees required to make the gas?*).

3.3   Energy Footprint

We asked participants to discuss their understanding of their personal energy footprint before and after using the app. All but two participants listed or implied some of their energy-related behaviors, often focusing on energy-responsible behaviors (e.g., *I use energy efficient bulbs, try to turn off lights, have solar on my roof*). Sixteen of these participants mentioned personal transportation behaviors (e.g., *I am conservative with gas too, won't take a long route or drive wastefully all over town; I probably destroy the environment with my driving habits. Deep footprint!*).

Many participants ranked themselves in relation to others (e.g., *Maybe slightly less than average*), perceived norms (e.g., *Probably quite a bit since I commute a lot*), or even other time periods (*... more than I would have if I'd been born 100 years ago!*). A few participants also used self-comparison, considering their footprint in terms of different energy-use domains (e.g., *I don't try to save gasoline so much but I am very conservative with energy in the home*). Only one participant provided a quantitative assessment: *I recall taking an online carbon footprint/test and the results stated if everyone lived as I did we would need about two earth's worth of resources.* A few participants explicitly noted their inability to quantify their footprint (e.g., *I couldn't really give an accurate description of my energy usage/carbon footprint, because there's nothing that measures how much I use*), and one participant remarked: *I would love to be even better and hopefully this app will know* [my footprint] *better.*

In the post-test survey, twelve participants explicitly reported or clearly implied an increased quantitative understanding of the energy footprint associated with their personal vehicle travel (e.g., *I can quantify it now. I'm still not sure of the impact; I gained a better idea of what my energy consumption is*). Some responses were too vague to ascertain any change as a result of the app (e.g., *I could do better*). Five participants reported no understanding or a vague understanding of the concept after using the app; of these, three reported technical problems.

Again, participants described environmental impact in terms of metrics provided in the feedback (trees, gallons of gas, trip distance) and/or time (trip comparison or accumulation across trips) to explain their carbon footprint (e.g., *This app made me realize that all those short distances add up; I was able to visually see my carbon footprint and that my footprint does add up over time.* One participant offered a quantified relational frame: *Every 50–60 gallons or so I would need an entire tree to offset my carbon usage.* Another recurring theme was that of surprise (e.g., *My CO2 contributions to the environment are much higher than I thought*), though this time one participant was surprised by using less than she imagined. Two participants made inferences to the population at large based on their feedback (e.g., *There couldn't possibly be enough trees to get rid of all that was created from my driving plus the rest of the population*).

3.4   Behavior and Intentions

In response to the post-test survey item inquiring after behavior change, as well as in responses to other items, participants did reveal some interesting insights about how the app affected their behavior or intentions. Three themes emerged in the data related to behavior and intentions, though none was present in more than three responses. One reported behavior change was to drive less (i.e., *I have already taken steps to drive less*; *It definitely has taught me to only drive when super necessary*; *Because of this, I have tried and found a carpool system to reduce my carbon*). Another indicated influence over participants' next vehicle purchase (e.g., *Although it didn't change my driving habits, it did change my considerations on my next vehicle purchase*). Finally, one participant reflected on goal-setting in relation to the carbon metric in the feedback: [regarding kilograms of carbon:] *it's now the unit I try to keep down because it's what I am putting into the world*.

4 Discussion

Several common themes emerged from the pre-test survey data related to a lack of awareness of concrete consequences. Before using OBDEnergy, participants were unanimously unaware of any concrete environmental impact of one gallon of gas, a highly familiar metric. Instead, their explanations circled abstract (general, global) impacts (climate change, Ozone degradation, and pollution) and norms ("bad"). Regarding their personal carbon footprint, participants cited travel mode choices, frequency of driving, and driving style; they qualitatively assessed the impact of their behavior (e.g., as minimal, average, or significant), comparing it to some standard.

The post-test survey data revealed an increase in awareness of concrete consequences after using OBDEnergy. Instead of echoes of scientific explanations and climate change discourse about abstract phenomena, participants' explanations of environmental impact involved relational frames of coordination and comparison across metrics (carbon, trees, gallons of gas, trip distance) and temporal relations (trip comparison or accumulation across trips). Another pervasive theme related to increased awareness is participants' surprise upon learning about concrete impacts of their personal vehicle travel. Finally, participants reported changes or intentions toward more conservative driving styles, travel mode choices, and even next vehicle purchase decisions, supporting the contention of NAM [4] that awareness of consequences contributes to pro-environmental behavior.

Trees and gallons of gas featured heavily in post-test survey relational frames; that is, participants referenced them in their explanations of the environmental impacts. Temporal relations were also apparent as participants calculated and compared metrics across time, often based on the historical comparisons available in the app. The kilograms of carbon metric, however, did not seem to become concrete for users in the sense of adopting it into relational frames of environmental impact. For example, of the three instances where a specific carbon measurement was provided, two translated kilograms into (or misinterpreted them as) pounds. Pounds likely would have been more successful since it is more familiar among our population. One participant translated gallons of gas into money in a relational frame of coordination.

Six users reported either infrequent app use or technical problems. Frequency of use was not controlled and varied among participants. Future research should include frequency of use as a moderating variable. Future research with eco-driving apps and

OBDs should also take care to ensure uninterrupted and accurate technical performance through rigorous initial setup and pre-testing with each participant as well as regular communication with participants.

We have just scratched the surface of the opportunity to apply RFT and the concept of awareness of concrete consequences to the field of eco-driving feedback. Further conceptual work is needed to disentangle the multiple meanings of *concrete* (specific, local, tangible, familiar, quantifiable, emotional) in this context. Further research should systematically investigate the relative effectiveness of different metrics and iconography as measured by relational responding in users reported understanding of environmental impacts.

References

1. Barkenbus, J.N.: Eco-driving: an overlooked climate change initiative. Energy Policy **38**, 762–769 (2010)
2. Barnes-Holmes, Y., Hayes, S.C., Barnes-Holmes, D., Roche, B.: Relational frame theory: A post-Skinnerian account of human language and cognition. Adv. Child Develop. Behav. **28**, 101–138 (2002)
3. Kurani, K.S., Stillwater, T., Jones, M., Caperello, N.: EcoDrive I-80: A Large Sample Fuel Economy Feedback Field Test Final Report. ITS UC Davis Working Paper (2013)
4. Schwartz, S.H.: Awareness of consequences and the influence of moral norms on interpersonal behavior. Sociometry **31**, 355–369 (1968)

Emotion-Centered-Design (ECD) New Approach for Designing Interactions that Matter

Eva de Lera[✉]

Av Marqués de La Argentera 17, Barcelona, Spain
edelera@gmail.com

Abstract. The emotional dimension of users of information and communications technologies (ICT) is a key aspect in user experience (UX), as designers' main objective is to ensure users are happy (satisfied, engaged) with their interaction designs. However, current UX design methods focus on ensuring that efficacy (success achieving a specific task) and efficiency (in the fastest, best way possible) are successfully achieved. The satisfaction of the user is evaluated at the end of the process, and evaluated in reference to the efficacy and efficiency of their experience. In this paper, the author presents a new approach (Emotion-Centered-Design, or ECD) in which the key to successful interaction design (happy users) is brought about by placing emotions at the center of the design process, versus doing so at the end. By doing so, designers can deliver more significant experiences, increase user experience satisfaction, and identify new ways to innovate in interaction design, as well as add more value to users.

Keywords:: Emotions · Usability · Design processes · Design methodologies · User experience · Human-computer interaction · User centered design · Affective computing

1 Introduction

The "happiness" (satisfaction) of a user during an ICT interaction will depend on the efficacy and efficiency of the interaction with the device, the context of use (location-specific) and, in the "moment of use" (emotional/stress level at a specific point in time). Nowadays, UX methods ensure working designs, and technology is already adapting to the users' context, but is ICT adapting to user's "moments"? UX designers are designing for people, considering a unique emotional dimension or "moment" for each person or user, when in fact, each has many "moments", and their satisfaction levels (evaluation of interactions) will differ depending on these. Then, how can ICT adapt to user's many "moments" and make users happy all the time? The objective of this paper is to introduce Emotion-Centered Design as a way to begin considering the importance of this dimension, and does so by proposing initial solutions and potential designs for the near future.

In other words, and as an initial example, depending on the user's available time, specific limitations (special needs and context included) and emotional state (level of stress and anxiety), he or she may choose a different route to go front point A to point B.

© Springer International Publishing Switzerland 2015
A. Marcus (Ed.): DUXU 2015, Part I, LNCS 9186, pp. 406–416, 2015.
DOI: 10.1007/978-3-319-20886-2_38

- When in a hurry, time is this person's priority and the best route is the fastest route, a time-efficient solution.
- When this person decides to begin to ride a bicycle to work, the same person, may be afraid of riding next to cars and choose a route with bike paths, away from danger, this being an effective solution, yet less time-efficient.
- And when the person is on holidays and wanting to feel good, a scenic route may be chosen, looking for a more engaging, stimulating and interesting experience, rather than a simply effective or efficient one.

There isn't a unique design path for one same individual, but a range of solutions, to adjust to each of this person's preferences, needs and overall emotional state, at a very specific time of use of the technology ("moments of use").

The Emotion-Centered-Design (ECD) approach places the level of stress and relaxation of the user at the center of the design process of any digital interaction. This means that, depending on this stress/relaxation level at the time of the interaction, the user's preferred interaction will be different. As technology has evolved, it is now possible to design for the user's emotional states at any given time, and there's no need anymore to have users adapt to the technologies, but for the technologies to adapt to users.

To help clarify this further, we bring this example to the field of human-computer interaction [21] and use the case of online travel booking as it is one of the industries that grew faster and it's quite consolidated worldwide. This example shows how ECD can bring about more satisfactory results, both to end users and the company's running online bookings, when applied.

According to Statistics Brain [27], in 2013 there were 148.3 million of travel bookings made on the Internet. Out of all of these:

- 65.4 % of hotel bookings where done on the brand website (operated and managed by the brand)
- 19.5 % of hotel bookings where done on the merchant website (e.g. Expedia/Hotels.com,)
- 11.3 % of hotel bookings took place through opaque websites where the customer does not know the brand of the supplier (e.g. Priceline)
- 3.7 % of hotel bookings are done through retail websites where hotels pay distributors a commission (e.g. HRS or Bookings).

The statistics clearly show consumers preference for using brand websites. There are several hypotheses for explaining such difference; the following are just a couple of possibilities:

- Brand websites usually project a lifestyle and a higher-level option to either (1) find out the rates or (2) make a reservation, a time-saver to user and a less frustrating experience.
- Merchant, opaque and retail websites are similar to a marketplace, quite cluttered, confusing, and therefore, perceived as overwhelming at first sight, frustrating in many occasions, and promoters on increased stress or anxiety levels.

As we cannot here go deeper into the business decision variables that may affect consumer choices, the ECD approach tries to over-ride these potential hypotheses and be proactive, by allowing consumers to choose the user experience they need at that particular moment and context in time.

The ECD approach applied to any of the above online booking websites helps understand the user's needs further, and deliver the best solutions for them. For example:

- An entrepreneur with family responsibilities and working long-hours needs to book a flight for a business trip and any time used in searching for this flight is time that he or she does not apply to the actual work or family. In this case, the person needs the fastest (and cheapest) option. In ECD terms, the person's level of stress or anxiety is higher than usual and needs an interaction that saves him or her time.

- The same entrepreneur planning the Summer holidays with a romantic partner may choose to do so after dinner, while comfortably sitting down in the sofa, lights dimmed, fireplace on. In ECD terms, the person's level of stress or anxiety is low, time is not an issue, but the contrary, the person is relaxed and needs the type of interaction that would allows them both to savor what the next holiday would be like: discover options, explore ideas, compare rooms, amenities, find friends, forums, etc. These two people (as web interactions are not only done individually) may prefer to take the "scenic" online route (path) for planning a holiday, and they may be on the travel website for hours that night, enjoying the experience of having multiple choices.

In the above scenarios we see one same person using online booking with two different experiential needs. Current human-computer interaction and user-centered design processes do not contemplate the importance of the emotional dimension in the design process, and it is key to reach a fuller and more impactful user satisfaction and engagement, while also contributing to the online travel business, as more satisfied consumers usually mean gaining new clients and maintaining loyalty.

2   Identifying Stress and Relaxation Levels

There are several ways for knowing the stress or relaxation level of a user. In the Emotion-Centered-Design approach we focus on the following two methods:

- Self-reporting assessments: the person tells us how he or she feels at the end of the interaction, or task requested by the evaluator. These measures are subjective and therefore non-correlational or fully unreliable. The efficacy of self-reported assessments has been questioned throughout the year and these may usually need to be supported and accompanied by other measures (both qualitative and quantitative) [18, 29].

- Automatic measures: through affective wearables [25], the person wears a sensor that captures the neurological or physiological response of the user during the interaction with the specific interface; or a facial recognition software can help co-relate facials to emotions (most of these systems still based on Paul Ekman's FACS) [11]. Even though these are objective measures, these still offer many limitations, such as their intrusive aspect, its inability to discriminate between negative stress and positive stress (e.g. happy) or to specifically correlate measures to exact emotions. Once again, these measures serve as a guide to help designers in their design processes and still will need to be accompanied and supported by other qualitative and quantitative measures (usability, questionnaires, etc.).

Both of this stress and relaxation reporting levels are still fully unreliable, but do serve as "red" or "green" flags to designers, to aid in their design process.

Red flags are used to identify what should be a specific time or place in the interaction design, indicating further evaluation and study is needed in that particular part of the design process. Green flags indicate that a particular part of the interaction design is both, not an obstacle and also adds value to the user.

3 Limitations of User-Centered Design

The User-centered design (UCD) process has mostly been focusing on integrating the human characteristics and capabilities of users, and their needs at a specific point in time [26]. Moreover, new approaches, such as Designing for Situation Awareness, have proposed improvements for the UCD, such as the Emotion-centered design process is doing: "The operational concept, environmental constraints, user characteristics and operational requirements" as the basic input of the design process [5]. In this paper, the Emotion-Centered Design process proposes a more dramatic change in the design process as it's not a mere new set of data that requires to be gathered (which it also does), but it creates a need to place emotion at the center of the design process, to direct the process, calling for multiple designs of a one desired person's interaction, working simultaneously.

The large success and impact of UCD, applied to the newer design of new technologies, interfaces and multiple devices, has made it possible for technology products with interfaces to be used by a much wider audience, and also by those who did not necessarily know much about technology, or even feared it.

One of the key processes of UCD was the creation of Personas, the creation of fictitious user profiles based on real yet grouped characteristics, attributes and needs of a variety of users [3]. These Personas have been extremely useful as a way to design processes and have served guide the design of interfaces, as they identified the most common needs or preferences of users, ensuring that all profiles incorporated the basic characteristics of all target users. Personas help define needs, tasks and also evaluate the interaction throughout an iterative process. Its success has been fully documented in the literature [2, 17, 20]. Personas however are limiting in that it tries to identify the most commonly used profile (set of needs and preferences).

Moreover, the successful promotion by UCD of the need for continuous participation of the users in the design process, through multiple iterations in the design and development phases brought about a major change in the Usability and HCI field. Such iterative participation (also seen in agile development) has allowed the users to become active participants and continuous evaluators of the product or website being designed, ensuring a reduction of errors and frustration once the produce was launched. Its success is clearly documented in multiple case studies and scientific publications [28, 32]. However, participating participants are non-representative of a diverse society and people's self-diversity.

The current user-centered design approach and its many variants do not incorporate the users' global needs and preferences, as temporary and permanent, in terms of access (include disabilities, as short as a minute as long a years), context, and emotional as well, as their emotional state at the time of the interaction (stressed or relaxed, in terms of time or other variables influencing the emotional state) can be a major influencer in the satisfaction or frustration level of the user, and their sense of happiness or frustration with the given experience.

Some of the hypothesized reasons why the emotional dimension was not incorporated in the UCD approach and design process point to:

- Overall focus on removing frustration of navigation as opposed to focusing on generating increased satisfaction or engagement ("satisfaction" used as a measure of ensuring the quality of the end-design as opposed to a measure to help guide the design, before the tasks are even set up, or the concept created).
- Lack of tools and methods to assess the "satisfaction" of users, as these are unreliable and do not provide accurate objective measures (surveys, questionnaires and interviews). Such subjective measures being unreliable based on a conflict of certain variables: the context of evaluation, the actual profile of people willing to participate in an evaluation and the recurrent lack of well-wished dishonesty, possibly to please the researchers [9].
- Lack of non-intrusive wearables capturing objective measures and producing reliable results.

It is also understandable that the changes in the technology allow for different methodologies to be set in place, as these depend on the technological solutions available, and affordable. With the current technological landscape, the growth of the online population and the removal of the initial fear brought about by non-tech users, we are now at a new cornerstone in which the user-centered methodologies can now integrate the emotional dimension into the design process, and go even further, have these emotions direct the design process.

As before human computer interaction, usability, user-experience, user-centered design and related others focused on the efficacy and efficiency of use, followed by a satisfaction-of-use assessment measuring "the feedback of user's attitude, perceptions, and feelings about the service" [4], the current landscape allows for a major change in the design process to incorporate this "satisfaction" measure at the center and beyond the satisfaction of that interaction scenario, to help guide designers in the design process, and creating different interactions based on the different satisfaction or emotional dimension levels.

4 The Emotion-Centered Design (ECD) Approach

The Emotion-Centered-Design approach is inspired on the "satisfaction" measure objective used-to-date in HCI, UCD and other user experience methods, and aims at going beyond these past practices to deliver more impactful interaction experiences and designs. ECD proposes to do so by placing emotions in a central phase of the design process in which these serve to guide the design process, as opposed to evaluate it, guaranteeing more significant and valuable results.

Emotions are not new to user experience; it is an area of expertise that several UX professionals have been flirting with for the past years. The emotional dimension of users has long been a focus of interaction designers [12, 22, 23] and research clearly shows that such variable is a key to a successful interaction design. The challenge being that there are no clear methodologies or sets of methodologies that help incorporate such dimension in an objective, easy and efficient way. The ECD approach aims to ensure that the concerns, intuitions and knowledge in regards to the importance of this dimension in the interface design field finds a way to reach professionals around the world that are craving for solutions to help, not only improve their products, but the satisfaction level of their users in a way beyond removal of frustration, and in a more engaging and added-value way. And to do so, emotion has to be looked at from a bigger distance, from a global point of view for the experience, and not as only a part of a concrete designed interaction.

5 Opening-up to the Emotional Dimension

Just as designers must understand their users' needs, characteristics and behavior, is also necessary to understand designers themselves. Human beings tend to do what had previously worked for them, insist in their practices and ways of doing things and many times find themselves resistant to change [24]. As the need to understand and integrate the emotion dimension has well documented and alive for decades, the user experience community has only entered superficial or peripheral stages, and not seriously enough to make the leap that user experience needs to make, to innovate in user experience by looking at the design process from an emotion-centered perspective, instead of a task-centered perspective which incorporates the user at the center.

Integrating the emotional dimension requires for all of those involved in the design process to be open to new ways of doing things, challenge current methods and incorporate new ideas (often meaning people with different talents and experiences).

5.1 The Case of Mobile Phones

A great example of the above-described situation is what has taken place in the mobile industry during these past years, since these were able to access the Internet and the many services offered through them (e.g. email).

Most mobile manufacturing companies (often lead by engineers) have designed and competed with similar products (Nokia, BlackBerry, Samsung, Erikson, Etc.). During the annual Mobile World Congress, a gathering of the top mobile industry players became a showcase of similar products trying to compete amongst themselves. During the mobile fair, visitors are able to confirm that mobile devices have been designed for similar Personas and for the tasks these had been planned to execute. The phones displayed and showcased during the 2002 Mobile World Congress:

- Were mostly black
- Had small buttons with multiple functions each
- Used the same number keyboard to type text
- Lacked interface color and aesthetics
- Used technical language
- Hard to set up (settings)
- Displayed cluttered menus
- Displayed as luxurious items (following a display design similar to those found in New York Fifth Avenue jewelry stores)
- Supported by visual materials representing the young and mature executive world (suits, success, beauty, perfection, etc.)
- Geared to executive professionals
- Geared to men.

When the first Apple's iPhone was launched in 2007 [1], it was mentioned by Time Magazine as the "Invention of the Year" [13]. This new mobile phone had broken with what had been done to-date and for the past 9 years has been rated the highest in user satisfaction: "For the ninth consecutive study, Apple ranks highest among manufacturers of smartphones in customer satisfaction. Apple achieves a score of 855 and performs particularly well in physical design and ease of operation". [15]. What had apple done differently? Apple challenged the status quo of the mobile industry and made its initial breakthrough by making the following changes:

- Geared to a much wider population through ease-of-use characteristics.
- Integrated aesthetics into the physical design of the device and the interfaces.
- Used a simple terminology, easy to understand by a wide variety of users, mostly non-technologically savvy.
- Understood the basic needs of this wider audience and provided easy-to-use functions (e.g. photo/video camera, applications and games).
- Amongst other improvements related to performance, features, operations and customization.

Up until that time the mobile industry had been implementing UCD methodologies in their design processes in such a way that it actually limited their capability to really satisfy and engage the user, and expand their market reach. The narrow focus in target, effectiveness and efficiency became an obstacle to growth and innovation. Evaluating "satisfaction" of the interaction was not a guarantee of "satisfaction of the user". In part, most mobile brands had focused on the executive work force and the technology savvy, party because it was unthought-of that other type of users would pay a large sum for such a device. For years, their assumptions, possible fear to risk and lack of multi— disciplinary teams, impeded mobile brands from identifying a major gap in the mobile industry, the people:

- The grandparents wishing to receive current photos from their loved ones.
- The teenagers wishing to exchange photos with their peers.

- The lovers wishing to send love texts and visuals to each other.
- The impatient wishing to entertain themselves while waiting in line, on the bus or at the doctor's office.
- And every person who wished something more personable was available to them (a daily horoscope app, a driving-test app, an cloud-expense recording tool, etc.).

iPhone not only delivered a new brand of mobile phone, but a personalized experience that would add value to their wide range of users, would bring perceived happiness. The App Store allowed for the existence of multiple solutions, providing a vast variety of choices ensuring that each person would find some solution, service or product that would adapt to his or her personal needs.

When the emotional dimension is placed at the center of the design process, and before (such as Apple did with the iPhone), the experience becomes richer and more engaging, not only removing user experience obstacles but also actually adding new values to the user experience. Variables such as graphic design, use of specific colors, layouts and other visual aspects (aside from actual physical aspects of the product) are key in user experience and not just a layer that is used to paint over a lo-fidelity prototype, but also the layer directing the design of prototypes. By also taking into account the user's emotional dimension (including lifestyle preferences, psychographics and stress/relaxation state levels), the ECD approach brings about a need to re-think the design process and methodologies used to date, and generate new experiences, enhanced experiences, interactions and products.

5.2 The Case of Online Learning

Some early approaches to integrating the emotional dimension of users into the design process are found in the field of online learning, and virtual environments, as such is the case at the Universitat Oberta de Catalunya [30] and their research toward the Joy of Learning [7, 8, 10]. At UOC, the researchers developed different approaches for measuring the affective dimension of learners in an objective manner, to account for this dimension and incorporate it in the design of the online learning environment, including a study that incorporates a method of triangulation of pupil-size data, emotion heuristics and self-assessment methods [31]. The Ten Emotion Heuristics, the Enjoy Guidelines and the Joy of Learning have been early efforts for integrating these emotional variables into the design process of online learning experiences. Emotion-Centered-Design represents an evolved approach based on the previous work done in online learning [9, 10], one in which incorporates the previous emotion research, findings and experiences, and proposes a new methodology for ensuring that emotions take the leading role it needs to ensure that designs go beyond satisfying users and into enriching them.

6 One Person, Multiple Paths

The Emotion-Centered-Design approach presents a new design process that changes the diagram of a design methodology process in which the "pieces" or elements stop looking like a circle or spiral indicating the need of iteration, and the graphic begins to look like a tree that sprouts several branches, a tree being a metaphor for a given person. ECD proposes that design methods do not use unique paths but multiple paths for moments of use, as opposed to profiles. A need to design different experiences for different moments, and people will convene and coincide in their choice of experience depending on their "moment".

According to ISO 9241-201:2010's definition (formerly known as ISO 13407) [14, 16], user experience includes all the users' emotions, beliefs, preferences, perceptions, physical and psychological responses, behaviors and accomplishments that occur before, during and after use. The ISO also list three factors that influence user experience: system, user and the context of use. However, this definition does not contemplate the variability of emotions over time (and this may be within an hour), being this key to Emotion-Centered-Design. This "emotional" variability must be taken into account before initiating a design process, defining and prioritizing goals, tasks and needs. Assuming that people's emotional dimension stays at one same level throughout the person's day, or life, is unrealistic and will lead to limiting the designer's knowledge and therefore, negatively influence the design, and the user experience. Understanding the inconsistency and variability of users will help provide the measures that allow them to either choose their preferred experience for that moment/time/context or to be automatically offered (prompted) the right design, or interaction path, matching their emotional scale at the time of use.

The Emotion-Centered-Design approach invites UX designers to continue applying their design methods, yet to moments, levels of stress and other emotional related potential interactions, as opposed as to the people or users (Fig. 1).

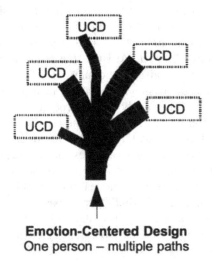

Emotion-Centered Design
One person – multiple paths

Fig. 1. Visual representation of the Emotion-Centered-Design approach, multiple paths for one same user at any given time.

7   Conclusion

The Emotion-Centered-Design approach here introduced presents a new method for designing highly satisfactory user experiences, by taking into account people's range of "moments" throughout their days and lives, as opposed to designing interactions for a person's profile. By doing so, this approach invites user experience professionals to undertake a major revision in their methods, to introduce the necessary design needs, technologies and solutions to ensure that people's variability and diversity is taken into account.

Implementing ECD can be done today by offering users the option to choose the way they feel, so their choice provides them with the right interaction. In the future, this could be done through sensors, and other existing – of future – technologies. The way to implement such call-for-action from the user can be as creative and innovative as designers design, from a pop-up window, to a top-left button, or through an app that pushes that information onto all devices and effects behavior, or via a new key added to all keyboard, or. What's important is that the users' moments are taken into account and that they enjoy, and are really satisfied, with their online experiences.

Acknowledgments. We thank the all research, professionals and colleagues, who throughout the year supported and provided helpful comments on previous revisions of this document.

References

1. Apple, http://www.apple.com/
2. Aoyama, M.: Persona-scenario-goal methodology for user-centered requirements engineering. In: 15th IEEE International Requirements Engineering Conference, RE 2007. IEEE, (2007)
3. Billestrup, J., et al.: Persona usage in software development: advantages and obstacles. In: The Seventh International Conference on Advances in Computer-Human Interactions, ACHI 2014 (2014)
4. Bratati, C., Roy, S., Pattnaik, P.K.: User satisfaction metrics for cloud computing environment. Eur. J. Acad. Essays 1(3), 63–69 (2014)
5. Silva da Silva, T., et al.: User-Centered design and agile methods: a systematic review. In: Agile Conference AGILE 2011. Salt Lake City, UT (2011)
6. De Lera, E., Almirall, M.: ENJOY: guidelines for designing engaging eLearning environments. In: proceedings of iLearning Forum (2008)
7. De Lera, E., Fernàndez, C., Almirall, M.: Emotions: the forgotten key success in online learning. In: 13th UNESCO-APEID International Conference and World Bank-KERIS High Level Seminar on ICT in Education, Hangzhou, China (2009)
8. De Lera, E., Fernandez, C., Valverde, L.: The emotional gap in virtual online environments. In: Abas, Z., et al. (Eds.), Proceedings of Global Learn 2010, AACE. pp. 67–70 (2010)
9. De Lera, E., Muriel, G.: Ten emotion heuristics: guidelines for assessing the user's affective dimension easily and cost-effectively. In: Proceedings of the 21st British HCI Group Annual Conference on People and Computers: HCI… but not as we know it-Vol. 2. British Computer Society, (2007)

10. De Lera, E., Mor, E.: The joy of e-learning: redesigning the e-learning experience. In: Proceeding of HCI 2007 workshop: Design, Use and Experience of e-Learning Systems (2007)

11. Ekman, P., Rosenberg, E.L., (eds.).: What the face reveals: basic and applied studies of spontaneous expression using the facial action coding system (FACS). Oxford University Press, Oxford (1997)

12. Fogg, B.J.: Persuasive technology: using computers to change what we think and do. Ubiquity 2002. December 2002. doi:10.1145/764008.763957

13. Grossman, L.: Invention of the year: The iPhone. Time Magazine. 1 November 2007

14. ISO. http://www.iso.org/iso/home/store/catalogue_ics/catalogue_detail_ics.htm?csnumber= 52075

15. JDPower. http://www.jdpower.com/press-releases/2013-us-wireless-smartphone-satisfaction-study-volume-1-and-2013-us-wireless

16. Jokela, T., et al.: The standard of user-centered design and the standard definition of usability: analyzing ISO 13407 against ISO 9241–11. In: Proceedings of the Latin American Conference on Human-computer Interaction. ACM, (2003)

17. Khalayli, N., et al.: Persona based rapid usability kick-off. In: CHI 2007 Extended Abstracts on Human Factors in Computing Systems. ACM, (2007)

18. Levenstein, S., et al.: Development of the perceived stress questionnaire: a new tool for psychosomatic research. J. psychosom. res. **37**(1), 19–32 (1993)

19. McDonagh, D., et al. (eds.): Design and Emotion. CRC Press, Boca Raton (2004)

20. Nielsen, L., Nielsen, K., Stage, J., Billestrup, J.: Going global with personas. In: Kotzé, P., Marsden, G., Lindgaard, G., Wesson, J., Winckler, M. (eds.) INTERACT 2013, Part IV. LNCS, vol. 8120, pp. 350–357. Springer, Heidelberg (2013)

21. Norman, D.A., Draper, S.W.: User centered system design: new perspectives on human-computer interaction. L. Erlbaum Associates Inc., Hillsdale (1986)

22. Norman, D.: Emotion and design: attractive things work better. interactions **9**(4), 36–42 (2002)

23. Norman, D.A.: Emotional Design: Why We Love (or Hate) Everyday Things. Basic books, New York (2007)

24. Park, R.E.: Human nature and collective behavior. Am. J. Sociol. **32**, 733–741 (1927)

25. Picard, R.W., Healey, J.: Affective wearables. Personal Technologies **1**(4), 231–240 (1997)

26. Ritter, F.E., Baxter, G.D., Churchill, E.F.: Introducing user-centered systems design. In: Ritter, F.E., Baxter, G.D., Churchill, E.F (eds.) Foundations for Designing User-Centered Systems. pp. 3–31. Springer, London (2014)

27. Statistics Brain. http://www.statisticbrain.com/internet-travel-hotel-booking-statistics/. http://www.adobe.com/products/acrobat/

28. Sy, D., Lynn, M.: Optimizing agile user-centred design. In: CHI 2008 Extended Abstracts on Human Factors in Computing Systems. ACM, (2008)

29. Oscar, T., Marc, P., Joaquim, L.: Analyzing the role of constructivist psychology methods into user subjective experience gathering techniques for product design. In: Proceedings of the 16th International Conference on Engineering Design ICED07, (2007)

30. Universitat Oberta de Catalunya (UOC). http://www.uoc.edu/portal/en/index.html

31. Valverde, L., Eva de, L., Fernàndez, C.: Inferencing emotions through the triangulation of pupil size data, facial heuristics and self-assessment techniques. In: Second International Conference on Mobile, Hybrid, and On-Line Learning, 2010. ELML 2010. IEEE, (2010)

32. Williams, H., Ferguson, A.: The UCD perspective: Before and after agile. In: Agile Conference (AGILE), 2007. IEEE, (2007)

Rhetoric of Interaction: Analysis of Pathos

Barbara Emanuel[✉], Camila Rodrigues, and Marcos Martins

Escola Superior de Desenho Industrial – UERJ, Rio de Janeiro, Brazil
design@barbaraemanuel.com,
{falecomkamy,marc.a.martins}@gmail.com

Abstract. The study of rhetoric evolved from focusing solely on discourse, in Ancient Greece, to the inclusion of audiovisual elements in the 20th century. Today, a ubiquitously digital world opens a new field of research, which might be called "rhetoric of interaction". The purpose of this work is to explore rhetorical possibilities of interactive features, that is, how different interactive design solutions may influence the apprehension of messages and help the building of arguments. Based on Aristotelian concepts of classical rhetoric, this study concentrates on the presence of the appeal of pathos, that is, an appeal to the emotions of visitors, with analyses of three websites: "Pablo the Flamingo", "World Under Water", and "Sortie en Mer".

Keywords: Interaction · Rhetoric · Pathos · Interface design

1 Introduction

Mostly connected to persuasion, rhetoric can be defined as guidelines to construct effective communication. It can also be seen as a means to provide the audience with motivation for adopting a new attitude or taking a new course of action. It is a tool for achieving goals, generating responses. In that sense, rhetoric is present in all kinds of communication. Gui Bonsiepe [1] affirms, "informative assertions are interlarded with rhetoric to a greater or lesser degree. (…) 'Pure' information exists for the designer only in arid abstraction. As soon as he begins to give it concrete shape, the process of rhetorical infiltration begins."

Digital pieces such as websites, accordingly, have rhetorical aspects as well. They aim to persuade visitors to purchase goods or contract a service, participate in a project, admire a brand, or believe that their content is relevant, interesting and true. At the very least, they try to convince visitors that it is worth to stay connected for a while.

Text and images play an important part in building arguments and influencing visitors, but there is another important rhetorical element, especially in digital communication: interaction. The very ways through which in which users interact with websites influence the apprehension of messages, as tools of persuasion. Still, while much has been studied about verbal rhetoric since Ancient Greece and about visual rhetoric since the mid-20th century, the same does not apply to the rhetoric of interaction. This work aims to contribute to this field, using a classical principle from the Aristotelian study of discourse: the rhetorical appeal of pathos.

© Springer International Publishing Switzerland 2015
A. Marcus (Ed.): DUXU 2015, Part I, LNCS 9186, pp. 417–427, 2015.
DOI: 10.1007/978-3-319-20886-2_39

Based on principles of classical rhetoric, we can analyze the presence of three appeals: ethos, logos and pathos. Ethos focuses on attributes of the speaker, such as character and credibility; logos, on the message and the use of reasoning to construct an argument; and pathos appeals to emotions of the audience [2]. The purpose of this paper is to explore rhetorical possibilities of interactive features that appeal to visitors' emotions, through the analysis of three websites: Pablo The Flamingo, promoting the adoption of flamingos, World Under Water, warning about dangers of global warming, and Sortie en Mer, that works as a drowning simulator.

2   Rhetoric

Rhetoric is a dynamic, polysemic term, of which implications vary with time and author. Classical rhetoric focused in speech and, later, in written text. In the twentieth century, authors such as Barthes [3], Bonsiepe [1] and Durand [4] have expanded the study of rhetoric, including visual arguments. Later, Buchanan [5] examined rhetoric in products. In the twenty-first century, authors such as Bonsiepe [6] and Joost [7] initiated studies of rhetoric in audiovisual media.

Aristotle defined rhetoric as "the faculty of observing in any given case the available means of persuasion" [2]. Barthes [8] identifies six sides of rhetoric: (1) a technique, that is, an art in the classical sense of the word: "art of persuasion, body of rules and recipes whose implementation makes it possible to convince the hearer of the discourse (and later the reader of the work)"; (2) a teaching: since the art of rhetoric, initially transmitted by personal means, was introduced into institutions of learning; (3) a science, that is, a field of observation and classification of language phenomena; (4) an ethic, as a group of rules with a practical goal and moral code; (5) a social practice, since rhetoric is a power that allows privileged classes to hold ownership of speech; and (6) a ludic practice, with what Barthes calls *black rhetoric*: "games, parodies, erotic or obscene allusions".

According to Eco [9, 10], Aristotle defined the difference between dialectic and rhetoric discourses in the fact that the former looks for rationally accepted conclusions, while the latter articulates its own rhetorical syllogisms—the enthymemes—, in order to obtain not only rational agreement, but also emotional adherence from the audience. The rationale of enthymemes does not have the same degree of certainty as logical syllogisms have, but its intention is to serve as evidence. For this sake, there are proofs provided by the discourse, which, according to Aristotle, lie in three areas: the character of the speaker (ethos), discourse itself (logos) and emotions aroused in the audience (pathos).

Rhetoric concentrates on provoking decisions, which are based on more than logical arguments. By addressing audience's emotions, the speaker can bring them into the appropriate mindset to agree with his arguments. Aristotle [2] commented on the importance of influencing audience's emotions: "When people are feeling friendly and placable, they think one sort of thing; when they are feeling angry or hostile, they think either something totally different or the same thing with a different intensity: when they feel friendly to the man who comes before them for judgment, they regard him as having done little wrong, if any; when they feel hostile, they take the opposite view. Again, if they are eager for, and have good hopes of, a thing that will be pleasant if it happens, they think that it certainly will happen and be good for them: whereas if they are indifferent or annoyed, they do not think so."

3 Interaction

Carolyn Handler Miller [11] indicates that there are only two possible ways for visitors to connect with content: interacting or watching it passively. By interacting, visitors becomes participants. "You can manipulate, explore, or influence it in one of a variety of ways. As the word 'interactive' indicates, it is an active experience. You are doing something" [11]. The sensation of being an active part of the process enhances the possibility of visitor engagement to any idea advocated by the website. The mere presence of interactive features indicates a disposition to transfer some control to the visitor, which may contribute to an overall friendliness.

The sense of participation is influenced by how much control visitors are convinced to have, that is, how much they feel that what happens on screen is a direct result of their inputs. Engagement can also be increased by promoting a sense of immersion in the piece. Using multimedia cues, such as sound and video, a website can go from resembling a document to be read, to simulating a space to be explored, something to be experienced. Immersive websites bring visitors into the action, the narrative, or the message. As pointed out by Miller [11], it is like, instead of merely watching a movie, becoming a character in it.

An important aspect to consider in immersive experiences is the choice of point of view (POV). There are two possible ways of experiencing interactive material: through first or third-person POV [11]. In the first-person POV, visitors look at the action as if really being there, that is, seeing through their own eyes. Visually, that is represented by the view of parts of the body, like arms and hands, the way a person usually sees them, and by movements that resemble the way heads usually move. The third-person POV shows facial expressions, which can be effective to communicate emotions, but hinders the sense of immersion.

4 Methodology

Several components are instrumental to the rhetoric of websites, like text, images, multimedia content, aesthetic appeal, technological refinement and usability. While using some of these elements as support for the analyses, this work concentrates on interactivity and its connection to the rhetorical appeal of pathos, that is, to emotions aroused in visitors.

The first step of the analysis is to identify the communicated function of the website, namely, what the website wants to achieve. The study of the function follows the methodology proposed by Foss [12], based on the piece's function as perceived by the critic, that is, the person conducting the analysis. Foss defends the use of the term function, rather than purpose, in order to dissociate the judgment from any possible intention of the object's creator. In opposition to the intentionalist view, "which suggests that a creator's intentions are relevant to or determine the correct interpretation of a work", this methodology proposes that "a work, once done, stands independent of its production and the intentions of artists or creators are irrelevant to critics' responses to their works" [12]. The function considered in the analysis is not, then, the one intended by the creator but rather the one communicated by the object, as interpreted by the critic.

Having identified the communicated function, the analysis goes on to examine the interactive features of the website and their contribution to the engagement of visitors. The degree of engagement depends considerably on the perceived extent of control visitors have over what happens in the website. It may vary from having no control at all, as in non-interactive websites, to co-authorship, where visitors are active in the construction of the content.

The final step is to analyze how the interactive features of the website and the degree of engagement relate to the emotions of visitors, and how they support the fulfilment of the communicated function. Does the interaction induce fear? Tenderness? Laughter? Anger? How may these emotions lead to action, inspire reflection, change opinions? How does it contribute to the accomplishment of the website's goals?

5   Analysis

5.1   Pablo the Flamingo

Flamingos are endangered species, and the World Wildlife Fund (WWF) receives donations, directed to worldwide conservation activities around the world, including preservation of these animals. One way of collecting donations is by selling "adopt a flamingo" kits, including items such as plush flamingos, photos and cards with species information. Art director Pascal Van der Haar, being an admirer of WWF efforts, decided to combine flamingo preservation with a project that experiments with code, illustration, animation and interaction. Along with illustrator Jono Yuen and developer Nathan Gordon [13], Van de Haar created Pablo the Flamingo (http://pablotheflamingo.com).

Instead of images of flamingos or information on endangered species, the website presented a fun way to connect with these animals. As the visitor enters the website, the loading page shows an egg with headphones, bouncing up and down, and the caption "turn up your sound…". After the page loads, we see Pablo, the flamingo, eyes closed, dancing to Eve's song "Let me blow ya mind" (Fig. 1). On the left side, there are three buttons: *sound off/on*, *share Pablo* (links to social media), and *adopt a flamingo* (leading to the WWF flamingo adoption store). If the visitor clicks on the first one, turning the music off, Pablo stops dancing, stares alarmed at the visitor and at the button, then reaches to the button with his beak and turns the music back on, resuming his dance moves (Fig. 2).

The main communicated function of the website is to promote donations, by generating an emotional response from the user. The main interactive feature here is turning the music off, which controls Pablo's reaction. Therefore, the visitor can interact directly with the character, in a playful way.

The turn-off/turn-in game visitors play with Pablo mimic repetitive games we play with pets, like throwing a ball so they can catch it again and again. This interaction

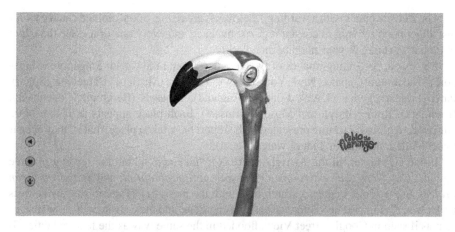

Fig. 1. Pablo dancing (Source: pablotheflamingo.com)

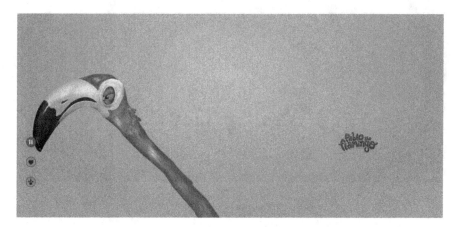

Fig. 2. Pablo turning the music back on (Source: pablotheflamingo.com)

creates therefore a personal, emotional bond with a flamingo in a way we would have with a dog or a cat. This emotional connection stimulates the purchase of the adoption kit, fulfilling the website's function.

5.2   World Under Water

In May 2004, the U.S. Global Change Research Program (USGCRP) released the National Climate Assessment, a report that summarizes present and potential impacts of climate change on the United States. CarbonStory, a crowdfunding platform for projects that reduce or remove greenhouse gas emissions, commissioned BBDO and Proximity Singapore to create a website that would make the findings of the report more accessible and real for the public. The piece, World Under Water (http://worldunderwater.org), calls attention to the issue by showing what real places would look like if flooded by rising sea levels.

The website opens with a warning: "Sea levels are rising. Soon, climate change won't just affect people living in coastal regions, but each and every one of us. See the effect of global warming in your neighborhood" (Fig. 3).

It goes on, presenting images of twelve cities around the world: Singapore (Singapore), Kakamura (Japan), New York (USA), Yucatan (Mexico), Barcelona (Spain), Paris (France), Dubai (UAE), London (England), Brussels (Belgium), Copenhagen (Denmark), Rome (Italy), and Moscow (Russia). Each place appears as if the future effects from global warming presented in the report have taken place, that is, they appear to be flooded, deep in six feet of water (Fig. 4).

In the site footer, in the far right, there is a "take action" button, leading to three options: *Calculate your emissions*, *Offset your carbon footprint*, and *Support a green project*. In the footer center, a search field with the message: "Type to see any address under water" (Fig. 5) The visitor can enter any address, and the website will show images of it as if seen in Google Street View, flooded in the same way as the featured cities. If

Fig. 3. Opening page, with warning (Source: worldunderwater.org)

Fig. 4. London under water (Source: worldunderwater.org)

Fig. 5. Website footer (Source: worldunderwater.org)

the entered address does not have a usable corresponding image from Street View, the website shows any working image within a larger radius from the initially searched-for location.

The website does not depict an accurate demonstration of what each city will look like if, as predicted, sea levels rise six feet in this century. It actually uses a sphere created with Three.js, where Google Street View images are stitched together and composed with simulated six feet of water. The site hacks into street view using WebGL, a Java-Script application program interface that renders three-dimensional graphics within browsers without installing plug-ins [14].

The main function communicated by the website is to lead visitors to take action against global warming, by inciting fear of its consequences. That is, its goal is, primarily, to make visitors aware of the problem, then make them afraid that it might affect their lives, and, finally, bring them into taking at least one of the suggested actions against global warming.

The main interactive features supporting these goals are the rotating view and the input of any address by the visitors. The Street-View-style feature of rotating the view around (sideways, upwards and downwards) enhances the feeling of reality and the sense of presence. Being able to look around makes the images more tangible than if they were static photographs. The possibility of entering any address to see under water brings the threat closer to visitors. If they can see their own house, it makes the danger seem more real and imminent for them than it could ever seem from simply reading a report. This way, the interactive features support the rhetorical strategy of focusing on the emotion of fear.

Aristotle [2] observes that, in order to provoke fear in the audience, it is important that they feel danger is close, that whatever the threat at hand, it can happen to them: "Of destructive or painful evils only; for there are some evils, e.g. wickedness or stupidity, the prospect of which does not frighten us: I mean only such as amount to great pains or losses. And even these only if they appear not remote but so near as to be imminent: we do not fear things that are a very long way off: for instance, we all know we shall die, but we are not troubled thereby, because death is not close at hand. From this definition it will follow that fear is caused by whatever we feel has great power of destroying or of harming us in ways that tend to cause us great pain. Hence the very indications of such things are terrible, making us feel that the terrible thing itself is close at hand; the approach of what is terrible is just what we mean by 'danger'."

5.3 Sortie en Mer

The website "Sortie en Mer" (http://sortieenmer.com) shows an interactive video that simulates the steps of drowning. It starts on a sailboat, in open sea, where two friends are talking. Julien gives Charles the control of the rudder, and then ends up falling off the boat. From the water, Julien asks for help, but the boat sails away. He finds himself in the water, alone and not wearing a life jacket (Fig. 6). A message shows up on the screen, telling visitors to scroll up (or swipe, if using a touch screen device) in order to stay on the water's surface (Fig. 7).

If visitors do not scroll, Julien sinks and drowns. As long as they do, he stays afloat. Similarly to what would happen to someone in open sea, Julien goes through different struggles: he takes off his shoes in other to swim better and the cold water causes numb-

Fig. 6. Julien falls off the boat (Source: sortieenmer.com)

Fig. 7. "Scroll without stopping" (Source: sortieenmer.com)

ness to his limbs until a fingernail peels off (Fig. 8), exhaustion gives him hallucinations, from strange birds to rescue teams that never come (Fig. 9).

Nevertheless, the efforts of visitors, scrolling repeatedly, are in vain. After five minutes, even if there is no pause in scrolling, the man inevitably gets too tired, sinks to the bottom of the sea and drowns. A text appears on the screen stating for how long the struggle went on, and then the video ends with a message that explains the point of it all—"At sea, you tire faster than you think. Whenever you go out to sea, wear your life jacket"—, followed by the name Guy Cotten, a French company specializing in outdoor apparel and nautical safety gear.

The main goal of the video is to persuade people to wear a life jacket every time they go out to sea. The central message is that trying to keep the head above water is more tiresome than one might think, so wearing a life jacket may be the difference between

Fig. 8. Fingernail peels off (Source: sortieenmer.com)

Fig. 9. Hallucinations (Source: sortieenmer.com)

life and death. This is obviously related to the fact that a company that sells life jackets commissioned the piece.

Throughout the whole video, visitors have a first-person POV, even during hallucinations, enhancing the connection with the man's struggles. The sense of participation is also physical, since visitors control, by scrolling or swiping, if the character stays on the surface. The interaction connects their real physical actions and the character's virtual movements, making visitors actually feel tired. The immersive storytelling creates a connection between that physical tiredness and possible consequences of being exhausted while at sea.

The appeal of the video is essentially emotional, evoking feelings in order to persuade. The main argument—that it is important to wear a life jacket—is not made by convincing that Guy Cotten is a respectable and efficient company, that sells well-made safety gear (which would be ethos), nor by listing logical reasons why a person needs help to float on open sea (which would be logos). Here, visitors are influenced by the emotions they feel: fear of being left behind, physical exhaustion of fighting to stay afloat, shock of watching fingernails peel off, frustration of sinking no matter how hard you try to avoid it, resignation of inescapable death. Emotions make the experience more immersive and compelling, increasing the connection between user and message.

6   Conclusion

If last century was the age of persuasion through texts and images, this century looks as if it is going to be the time of digital media rhetoric. The way visitors interact with digital content influence its apprehension and its impact, working in a rhetorical fashion. The investigation of rhetorical possibilities of interaction is relevant for researchers, in order to advance the field, not only theoretically, but also when it comes to practical applications, broadening capabilities of interface designers as to building arguments. The analysis of websites can be an instrument for establishing a framework for evaluating digital pieces within a rhetorical perspective, thus contributing to an emerging theory of interaction rhetoric.

Concepts established in classical rhetoric can be the basis for such analyses, providing some guidance when it comes to establishing parameters of investigation. The Aristotelian appeals—ethos, logos and pathos—present an interesting possibility of identifying different strategies, focusing on character, logic or emotions. By concentrating on each one separately, analyses can recognize more clearly the roles played by interactive features in the rhetorical plan.

References

1. Bonsiepe, G.: Visual/verbal rhetoric. Dot Zero **2**, 37–38 (1966)
2. Aristotle: Rhetoric. http://classics.mit.edu/Aristotle/rhetoric.html
3. Barthes, R.: Rhetoric of the image. In: Barthes, R. (ed.) Image Music Text. Fontana Press, London (1977)
4. Durand, J.: Rhétorique et image publicitaire. Communications **15**, 70–95 (1970)

5. Buchanan, R.: Declaration by design: rhetoric, argument, and demonstration in design practice. Des. Issues **2**(1), 4–22 (1985)
6. Bonsiepe, G.: Design as a tool for cognitive metabolism: from knowledge production to knowledge presentation (2000). http://www.guibonsiepe.com/pdffiles/descogn.pdf
7. Joost, G., Scheuermann, A.: Audiovisual rhetoric: a metatheoretical approach to design. In: Proceedings of the Design Research Society. IADE, Lisboa (2006)
8. Barthes, R.: L'ancienne rhétorique [Aide-mémoire]. Communications **16**, 172–223 (1970)
9. Eco, U.: A Estrutura Ausente. Perspectiva, São Paulo (2007)
10. Eco, U.: Tratado Geral De Semiótica. Perspectiva, São Paulo (2009)
11. Miller, C.H.: Digital Storytelling: A Creator's Guide to Interactive Entertainment. Elsevier, Oxford (2004)
12. Foss, S.K.: A rhetorical schema for the evaluation of visual imagery. Commun. Stud. **45**(3–4), 213–224 (1994)
13. Gordon, N.: Pablo the flamingo, case study: the birth of a party animal (2014). https://medium.com/@gordonnl/pablo-the-flamingo-75a21bf8ea12
14. World Under Water from BBDO and Proximity Singapore Wins FWA/Adobe Cutting Edge Project of the Year (2014). http://digitallabblog.com/post/100778979743/world-under-water-from-bbdo-and-proximity

Emotions Logging in Automated Usability Tests for Mobile Devices

Jackson Feijó Filho[(⊠)], Wilson Prata, and Thiago Valle

Nokia Technology Institute, Av. Torquato Tapajós, 7200 - Col. Terra Nova,
Manaus, AM 69093-415, Brazil
{jackson.feijo,wilson.prata,thiago.valle}@indt.org.br

Abstract. This work proposes the use of a system to perform emotions logging in automated usability tests for mobile devices. Our goal is to efficiently, easily and cost-effectively assess the users' affective state by evaluating their expressive reactions during a mobile software usability evaluation process. These reactions are collected using the front camera on mobile devices. The analysis of three different emotions - happiness, surprise and anger – and two "emotional events" – spontaneous smile and gazing away from screen – performed through server software. This automated test generates a graphical log report, timing (a) current application page (b) user events e.g. tap (c) emotions levels e.g. level of happiness and finally (d) emotional events e.g. smiling or looking away from screen.

1 Introduction

Due to the present saturation in the mobile software market, consumers frequently find themselves unable to decide which application to acquire, considering that many of them have the very same functional features. It is very likely they will prefer the application that presents their functionalities in the most usable and efficient manner [9].

In [8] Harty discuss how many organizations do not perform any usability or accessibility testing. It's seen as too expensive, too specialized, or something to address after testing all the "functionality" (which is usually prioritized because of time and other resource constraints). For these organizations, good test automation can be of great benefit.

Usability testing tends to be time consuming and hard to scale when it requires human observation of the people using the software being measured [8].

Most of the usability methodologies (e.g. usability inspection, heuristics, etc.) are both applicable to desktop as well as to mobile software, it is more difficult for mobile context to achieve relevant results with conventional assessment methods. The reason is that the emulation of real-world use during a laboratory based evaluation is only feasible for a precisely defined user context. Therefore, due to physical restrictions, it is difficult to generalize from quickly changing and possibly strongly varying user context [5].

The evaluation of usability in mobile software provides valuable measures about the quality of these applications, which assists designers and developers in identifying opportunities of improvement. But analyzing the usability of mobile user interfaces can be a tiresome assignment. It might be extensive and require expert evaluation

A. Marcus (Ed.): DUXU 2015, Part I, LNCS 9186, pp. 428–435, 2015.
DOI: 10.1007/978-3-319-20886-2_40

techniques such as cognitive walkthroughs or heuristic evaluations, not to mention often expensive usability lab equipment.

Relevant and recent work has been published concerning tools for low-cost, automated usability tests for mobile devices. In [1] such tools have been reported to aid small development teams to perform fairly accurate suggestions on user interface improvements. However, these tools do not consider emotional feedback of users towards mobile software.

1.1   Emotions and Usability

Emotional feedback is a significant aspect in user experience that chronically goes unmeasured in several user-centered design projects. [2] Human emotions are indispensable to understanding users, as these can enable the increase of persistence and strengthen interest in a subject or task. The examination of this affective aspect through well-known empirical user-centered design methods supports software creators in engaging and motivating users while using their systems [3]. The gathering of emotional cues will provide an additional layer of analysis for collecting user data, augmenting common evaluation methods and resulting in a more accurate understanding of the user's experience.

1.2   Automated Tests and Unsupervised Field Evaluations

Furthermore, it is essential to mention the importance of automated tests, while being executed through and for mobile devices. In contrast to desktop applications or web sites, mobile applications have to compete with external stimuli, as users might not be sitting in front of a screen for considerable amounts of time [4]. Due to the very nature of mobility in this scenario, in a real-world context, users might as well be walking on the street or sitting on a bus when interacting with mobile software. Therefore, it is imperative not to ignore the differences of such circumstances and desktop systems in isolated usability laboratories without distractions [5].

This contrasts with Kaikkonen et al. [11] and is supported by Lettner [1] which narrates that conducting unsupervised and automatic field studies will result in more in-depth results than supervised field studies. This statement is also supported by Hertzum [10], who confirms that the results of field studies differ between field tests and laboratory-based tests. Hertzum showed that conducting unsupervised field studies is inexpensive and does not require much preparation. Moreover, supervisors could influence the study by excluding interaction possibilities [1].

2   Related Work

Significant work has been published concerning automated software usability tests, specifically for mobile devices. Lettner et al. [1] approach the present matter implementing a framework to do user interaction logging as basis for usability evaluation on mobile devices. This paper compares commercial frameworks for logging user statistics on mobile devices, such as Flurry1, Google Analytics2, Localytics3 or User-Metrix4. However, these frameworks focus on descriptive user statistics such as user growth, demographics and commercial metrics like in-app purchases. These solutions approach automation of usability tests, but ignore emotional feedback.

Some techniques and methodologies have been reported in significant publications about gathering affective data without asking the users what and how they feel. Physiological and behavioral signals such as body worn accelerometers, rubber and fabric electrodes can be measured in a controlled environment [6, 7]. It is also feasible to evaluate users' eye gaze and collect electrophysiological signals, galvanic skin response, electrocardiography, electroencephalography and electromyography data, blood volume pulse, heart rate, respiration and even, facial expressions detection software [2]. Most of these methods face the limitations of being intrusive, expensive, require specific expertise and additional evaluation time.

2.1 UX Mate

UX Mate [12] is a non-invasive system for the automatic assessment of User eXperience (UX). In addition, they contribute a database of annotated and synchronized videos of interactive behavior and facial expressions. UX Mate is a modular system which tracks facial expressions of users, interprets them based on pre-set rules, and generates predictions about the occurrence of a target emotional state, which can be linked to interaction events.

Although UX Mate provides an automatic non-invasive emotional assessment of interface usability evaluations, it does not consider mobile software contexts, which has been widely differentiated from desktop scenarios [5, 9, 11].

3 Contribution

Our proposal supplements the traditional methods of mobile software usability evaluation by monitoring users' spontaneous facial expressions automatically as a method to identify the moment of occurrence of adverse and positive emotional events. Identifying those events and systematically linking them to the context of interaction is clearly an advance towards overcoming design flaws and enhancing interfaces' strengths.

The automated test generates a graphical log report, timing (a) current application page (b) user events e.g. tap, (c) emotions levels e.g. level of happiness and finally (d) emotional events e.g. smiling or looking away from screen. The gazing away from the screen [2] may be perceived as a sign of deception. For example, looking down tends to convey a defeated attitude but can also reflect guilt, shame or submissiveness. Looking to the sides may denote that the user was easily distracted from the task.

This research has also produced a toolkit for automated emotions logging for mobile software that, in contrast to existing frameworks, is able to trace emotional reactions of users during usability tests and relating them to the specific interaction that is being performed. This framework can be added to mobile applications with minor adjustments.

3.1 System Structure

The basic system structure is displayed in Fig. 1.

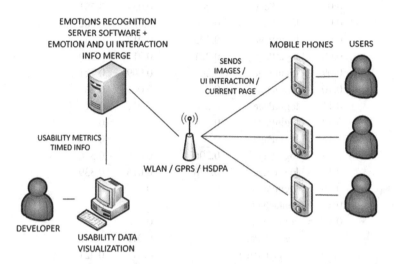

Fig. 1. System infrastructure

The running application uses the front camera to take photos of the user every second. This image is converted to base64 format and is sent via HTTP to the server. The server decodes the base64 information into image and runs the emotion recognition software, which returns the numerical levels of happiness, anger, surprise, smile (true/false) and gaze away (true/false). This information is sent back to the phone via HTTP and written to a text file, with a set of other interaction information. When the user exits the application, the log file is sent to the server, which stores and classifies the test results in a database, which can be browsed via a web front-end.

3.2 Interaction Information Logging

The applications to be tested are written using the library (.dll) we implemented. When the application is started by the user, a log file is created, marking the time, current page, level of happiness, level of anger, level of surprise, smile (0–1), gazing away (true or false) and tap/click (true or false). When tap is true, logs position of tap and name of the control object tapped e.g. button, item on a list, radio button, checkbox, etc.

The generated log file is comma separated value format, enabling visualization in tables, as displayed in Tables 1 and 2.

Table 1. Generated log (part 1)

Time	Page	Happiness	Anger	Surprise
0:00	mainPage	0.204	0.01	0.446
0:01	mainPage	0.252	0.017	0.421
0:02	mainPage	0.252	0.014	0.342
0:03	mainPage	0.276	0.013	0.389
0:04	loginPage	0.216	0.021	0.305
0:05	loginPage	0.204	0.034	0.281
0:06	loginPage	0.226	0.02	0.282
0:07	loginPage	0.223	0.017	0.243
0:08	loginPage	0.221	0.013	0.239
0:09	loginPage	0.204	0.009	0.221
0:10	loginPage	0.24	0.009	0.235
0:11	loginPage	0.214	0.011	0.273
0:12	loginPage	0	0	0
0:13	loginPage	0	0	0
0:14	loginPage	0.206	0.018	0.316
0:15	loginPage	0.276	0.015	0.339
0:16	loginPage	0	0	0
0:17	contactsPage	0	0	0
0:18	contactsPage	0	0	0
0:19	contactsPage	0.324	0.019	0.398
0:20	contactsPage	0.396	0.01	0.421

3.3   Emotion Recognition Software

The emotion recognition software was developed using the well documented Intel RealSense SDK [13]. Among many features, this software development kit allows face location and expression detection in images. This paper does not focus on analyzing any particular image processing algorithms to detect emotions.

3.4   Usability Information Visualization

The front-end web software display one test session as in Fig. 2. It is meant to supplement the traditional usability tools and methods.

4   Experiments

In order to perform early system functioning check, we planned a test session that would induce negative and positive emotions, not necessarily related to the interface design.

To gather negative feedback, we asked one male adult (32 yo) to login to one of his social networks account and post one line of text to his timeline. During this task, we

Table 2. Generated log (part 2)

Smile	Gazing away	Tap	X	Y	UI object
0.17	FALSE	FALSE	0	0	none
0.21	FALSE	FALSE	0	0	none
0.21	FALSE	FALSE	0	0	none
0.23	FALSE	TRUE	245	467	btnConnect
0.18	FALSE	FALSE	0	0	none
0.17	FALSE	TRUE	201	359	txtUser
0.19	FALSE	TRUE	0	0	keyboard
0.19	FALSE	TRUE	0	0	keyboard
0.18	FALSE	TRUE	0	0	keyboard
0.17	FALSE	TRUE	211	420	txtPassword
0.2	FALSE	TRUE	0	0	keyboard
0.18	FALSE	TRUE	0	0	keyboard
0	TRUE	TRUE	0	0	keyboard
0	TRUE	TRUE	0	0	keyboard
0.17	FALSE	TRUE	237	476	btnLogin
0.23	FALSE	FALSE	0	0	none
0	TRUE	FALSE	0	0	none
0	TRUE	FALSE	0	0	none
0	TRUE	FALSE	0	0	none
0.27	TRUE	FALSE	0	0	none
0.33	FALSE	FALSE	0	0	none

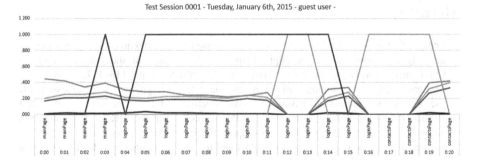

Fig. 2. Emotions log automatically generated chart

turned the WLAN connection on and off, in intervals of 30 s. After 5 min of not being able to execute a considerably simple task, the test subject was clearly upset. The emotional feedback logged by our system was in successful accordance to the test session.

To gather positive feedback, we asked one male adult (27 yo) to complete an online quiz with charades and funny answers. The emotional feedback logged by our system was in successful accordance to the test session, as the user smiled and even laugh about the funny text and imagery.

The test session displayed in Table 1 and Fig. 2 show an example of one test session we have run. The user was asked to login to one communications application in development stage in a research institute.

5 Future Work and Discussions

This work presents an early approach to emotional feedback logging for mobile software usability evaluation. The problem space was narrated through referencing other usability automation research. Some relevant related work was described and distinguished from the present proposal. A system was developed as a proof-of-concept tool to our hypothesis and experiments where performed to raise argumentation topics to provoke advances on the current matter.

Our system logs emotional feedback from users, using the front camera on mobile devices. It stands as a solution for automated mobile software usability evaluation.

The system functional features were tested for negative and positive emotional feedbacks by test sessions that where planned to fail and succeed/provoke smiles, respectively.

Future work will investigate a more in-depth applicability of the logged interaction information. For example, our system is not yet detecting and identifying usability problems. It is strictly logging emotional feedback and UI interactions, merging this information on a timeline, to aid usability evaluation.

References

1. Lettner, F., Clemens H.: Automated and unsupervised user interaction logging as basis for usability evaluation of mobile applications. In: Proceedings of the 10th International Conference on Advances in Mobile Computing & Multimedia, pp. 118–127. ACM (2012)
2. de Lera, E., Garreta-Domingo, M.: Ten emotion heuristics: guidelines for assessing the user's affective dimension easily and cost-effectively. In: Proceedings of the 21st British HCI Group Annual Conference on People and Computers: HCI... but not as We Know It, vol. 2, pp. 163–166. British Computer Society (2007)
3. Spillers, F.: Emotion as a Cognitive Artifact and the Design Implications for Products that are Perceived as Pleasurable. http://www.experiencedynamics.com/pdfs/published_works/Spillers-EmotionDesign-Proceedings.pdf. Accessed 18 Feb 2007
4. Madrigal, D., McClain, B.: Usability for mobile devices, September 2010. http://www.uxmatters.com/mt/archives/2010/09/usabilityfor-mobile-devices.php
5. Oztoprak, A., Erbug, C.: Field versus laboratory usability testing: a first comparison. Technical report, Department of Industrial Design - Middle East Technical University, Faculty of Architecture (2008)
6. Picard, R.W., Daily, S.B.: Evaluating affective interactions: alternatives to asking what users feel. Presented at CHI 2005 Workshop 'Evaluating Affective Interfaces' (Portland, OR), 2–7 April 2005

7. Anderson, R.E.: Social impacts of computing: codes of professional ethics. Soc. Sci. Comput. Rev. **10**(2), 453–469 (1992)
8. Harty, Julian: Finding usability bugs with automated tests. Commun. ACM **54**(2), 44–49 (2011)
9. Madrigal, D., McClain, B.: Usability for mobile devices, September 2010. http://www.uxmatters.com/mt/archives/2010/09/usabilityfor-mobile-devices.php
10. Hertzum, M.: User testing in industry: a case study of laboratory, workshop, and field tests. In: Proceedings of the 5th ERCIM Workshop on 'User Interfaces for All' (1999)
11. Kaikkonen, A., Kallio, T., Kekäläinen, A., Kankainen, A., Cankar, M.: Usability testing of mobile applications: a comparison between laboratory and field testing. J. Usability Stud. **1**, 4–16 (2005)
12. Staiano, J., Menéndez, M., Battocchi, A., De Angeli, A., Sebe, N.: UX Mate: from facial expressions to UX evaluation. In: Proceedings of the Designing Interactive Systems Conference (DIS 2012), pp. 741–750. (2012)
13. Intel RealSense SDK. https://software.intel.com/en-us/intel-realsense-sdk

Motivators of Energy Reduction Behavioral Intentions: Influences of Technology, Personality Characteristics, Perceptions, and Behavior Barriers

June A. Flora[1]([⊠]) and Banny Banerjee[2]

[1] Human Sciences and Technologies Advanced Research Institute and Solutions Science Lab in Department of Pediatrics, Stanford University, MSOB 1265 Welch Road, Stanford, CA 94305, USA
jflora@stanford.edu
[2] Human Sciences and Technologies Advanced Research Institute and ChangeLabs, Building 550, Room 159, 416 Escondido Mall, Stanford, CA 94305, USA
banny@stanford.edu

Abstract. Motivating behavior change for energy reduction using technological solutions has led to the development of hundreds of technological products in less than a decade. Technology design in the energy reduction field is often characterized by two perspectives; "build and they will come" and "begin with human need, motivation, and desire." Using a human centered design perspective – we experimentally evaluated the role of three personality specific motivations, in the usability and behavior change intentions of three motivationally frame energy reduction applications. We found significant usability effects with both the affective and sociability technology have greater usability. There we no difference between technologies on behavioral measures and no interactions of outcomes with personality measures. However, both NFA and NFC have independent effects on differing behavioral outcomes. Discussion called for more research on the role of personality and motivationally framed technologies along with larger samples, and longer times between pre and post assessments.

Keywords: Behavior change · Technology · Energy behavior · Personality · Motivation

1 Introduction

Motivating energy reduction behavior by using technological solutions (such as mobile applications, websites, and in home feedback devices) is an exciting and challenging research and product design endeavor. Hundreds of household energy feedback technology products have been developed in less than a decade [1]. Technology design in the energy reduction field is often characterized by one of two perspectives; "build and they will come" and "begin with human attributes, motivations, and ability." From the human centered design perspective – human characteristics and perceptions precede

© Springer International Publishing Switzerland 2015
A. Marcus (Ed.): DUXU 2015, Part I, LNCS 9186, pp. 436–446, 2015.
DOI: 10.1007/978-3-319-20886-2_41

and iteratively refine product design. Specific human considerations motivating the use of specific technologies include personality factors, demographics, and perceptions about the focal technology such as trust in content and source, topic involvement, and perceived functionality. These perceptions about a technology are often assessed by the SUS, measures of "stickiness" or usability or other newer indices such as the UPscale [2–4]. While usability perceptions can influence continued technology refinements, judged technology effectiveness cannot stop at user's perceived usability. Prior to scaled deployment, technologies must be assessed with regard to higher order outcomes such behavioral intention, perceived behavioral barriers and actual behavior. Understanding the potential for impact is key to technology scaling.

In this randomized controlled trial (RCT), we examine the effects of three prototype motivationally framed energy reduction Facebook applications on perceived usability, behavioral intention, and perceived barriers to behavior. Further, we investigate whether three human personality characteristics that have the potential to be drivers of motivation to change behavior are related to technology impact. Specifically we investigate if when human motivations "match" the motivational frames of the technology prototype behavioral outcomes are enhanced. For example, do individuals high in the need for positive emotion perform better with the affectively framed technology?

1.1 Relevant Literature

Rarely do technologies aimed to engage users to reduce energy focus on emotional content, or differentiate the emotional content from other frames such as need for thought or cognitions and need for affiliation or social comparison such as game play with others [1]. In fact, most energy reduction technologies focus on feedback regarding cost and kWh savings, at times combined with incentives and behavioral principles such as goal setting and social comparison [5]. Yet, few technologies and intervention studies compare the effects of different motivationally framed applications or perhaps even more importantly, examine the extent to which the frames are even more (or less) effective when matched to individual personality characteristics and motivations.

Human Personality Characteristics, Persuasion, and Behavior Change. There is a long history of research into human motivations and personality characteristics and their role in persuasive communications; from ads, to narratives to stories. Much of this research literature is steeped in theoretical perspectives regarding dual system processing of information.

One well researched human personality characteristic theorized to play a role in persuasion and behavior is the need for cognition (NFC). NFC is defined by Cacioppo and Petty [6, 7] as the inclination to engage in and like thinking and problem solving, this tendency is well studied in many different areas of inquiry, from attitudes and persuasion, judgment and decision making, interpersonal and group interactions and applied settings [7]. People high in need for cognition are more likely to form their attitudes and actions by paying close attention to relevant arguments (i.e., via the central route to persuasion). People lows in need for cognition are more likely to rely on peripheral cues such as speaker or message attractiveness and credibility or is more likely to use stereotypes to judge others. NFC is correlated with numeracy skill, which is intuitively linked to the commonly used energy feedback interface – graphic displays of energy consumption [8]. We argue that individuals high in NFC would be more likely to prefer and engage in interfaces that require thinking and analysis, such as energy feedback graphs.

Need for affect (NFA) has been proposed as the affective counterpart to the NFC [9]. Need for affect is defined as the "general motivation of people to approach or avoid situations and activities that are emotion inducing for themselves and others." (p. 586). In particular, NFA may be most persuasive in certain emotion evoking contexts, such as story telling where it has been demonstrated that transportability and NFA moderate the effects of stories on attitudes [10]. Maio and Esses [9] developed a two part need for affect instrument, the seeking out of emotions (approach subscale) and the avoidance of emotional situations. The approach subscale has been shown to predict selection of emotional versus non-emotional movies, and the emotionality of respondents' favorite television shows. Parallel to the message tailoring results for NFC, that is, those high in NFC are more persuaded by factual information; those high in NFA when exposed to emotional content were more likely to be persuaded [10, 11].

This personal motivation and message type interaction points to the conceptual importance of "motivational message tailoring," indicating that this conceptual per-suasion profiling (e.g. rather than demographic tailoring) shows promise for the out-comes of energy reduction technologies. To date persuasion profiling is not widely used in energy reduction or climate change action and advocacy.

A third potential human motivator is the need to affiliate with others. Hill [11] conceptualized and built a five factor scale of human motivation regarding people. Given recent attention to competition via game play [12] and norm interventions involving comparisons of energy consumers to their "neighbors," an affiliation need that is social comparison based could future improve the development of "social" energy reduction interventions. That is, individuals high on the social comparison scale may be more receptive to interventions that involve competition, self-monitoring, and comparison to others. Human responses to normative comparison feedback are one of the more widespread behavioral principles in current use [13]. Recent experiments regarding "neighbor" comparison feedback may be potentially related social compar-ison affiliation, even though in this case the normative feedback is a pseudo non-interactive social engagement. Results typically show 1–3 % energy reduction in response to neighbor feedback comparison reports [5, 13]. In Hill's [11] work the social comparison index was related to measures of sociability, self-monitoring, and public self-consciousness and not related to two empathy scales.

In this paper we argue that personality characteristics can play an independent and interactive role in user engagement with technologies to reduce energy consumption.

Previous research on advertising appeals suggests that persuasive appeals tend to be more effective when the nature of the appeal matches, rather than mismatches, indi-viduals preferred processing style. Ruiz and Sicilia [14] showed that when individuals were exposed to ads congruent with their processing styles, in terms of affect and cognition, higher advertising effectiveness was obtained. Other experimental work on the persuasive effects of story, show that the magnitude of a person's need for affect determined whether and to what extent the person's experiences transportation into the story work and is persuaded by the information presented in the narrative.

The three technology prototypes designed for this study have been infused with user feedback beginning with ethnography [15], investigation of application images and graphic feedback of electricity use [8]. The results of the ethnography stimulated the creation of motivationally framed energy reduction applications that are affective, cognitive, and engage sociability.

2 Research Questions and Hypotheses

We posited one broad research question (RQ) and four primary research hypotheses (HYP). We used research questions to examine relationships among variables and assess questions that we had little or no theoretical reason to posit directional outcomes.

RQ: What are the relationships among demographic, outcome, and mediating variables?

a. What are the relationships among the three personality measures?

b. What are the relationships among the current behavior and future behavioral intentions?

c. What is the role of gender in current behavior, change in behavior change intentions and perceived barriers to behavior change?

HYP1: Motivationally framed technologies will not differ in user perceptions of application function, involvement and satisfaction from a control energy reduction technology but will differ from the control technology.

HYP2: Motivationally framed technologies will improve energy reduction behavioral intentions and number of behaviors changed more than a control technology.

HYP3: Personality characteristics, NFA, NFC, and NFS, will interact with their matched motivationally framed application, Kidogo, Powerbar, and Power tower respectively.

3 Methods

3.1 Research Design

We used a randomized controlled design where volunteer student participants were randomly assigned to one of five conditions (three *treatments* and two controls). **Because of a problem in the second control where post survey measures were only collected for 17 participants, we examine here three energy reduction application** conditions and one "traditional" control of a utility website.

3.2 Participants

Participants were 162 community college students who received course credit for were participation. Their average age was 23 years, 69 % were female, and with an average of two years of college courses completed. 39.3 % of students were Asian, 30.6 % were white, 15 % Hispanic, 4.6 % African American, and 9.8 % other demographic groups.

3.3   Procedures

Community college student study participants were part of a research experience program whereby they received credit for participating in university approved studies.

Prior to participation in this study, all student participants, as part of their credit for participating in research program answered a one hour long survey of a diverse array of questions, for this study NFA, NFC, and NFS questions. Participation in the current study after completion of the course required survey, took approximately 1.hour with ranges from 45 min to 1.5 h. Participants were sent a link to the Qualtrics platform which hosted the study. Once in Qualtrics, participants were randomly assigned to one of the five conditions. Upon assignment, they consented via clicking a link to a university approved IRB form, rated their current performance on and current intentions to perform 22 energy saving behaviors. They then saw a three minute video describing the energy reduction application (condition videos ranged from 2.8–3.2 min). Immediately after viewing the video, participants answered a series of questions on application stickiness, and intention to perform the same behaviors shown in the pretest questionnaire.

3.4   Study Treatment Materials

There were three motivationally framed energy reduction technologies; the affective application, Kidogo, used a stealth intervention strategy [16] whereby human engagement in emotions such as the altruistic desire to help global social entrepreneurs to succeed framed the behavior changes necessary to reduce energy. Kidogo turned the low cost of electricity and thus low financial return into more engaging values. The cognitively framed application, Powerbar, attempted to evoke the need of self-monitoring, interest in numeracy using graphs and journaling to engage users. The sociability framed application, Powertower, used a game structure, to engage users with one another in teamwork and competition, with behavior changes and electricity reduction yielding more "blocks" to build a stable and high tower. Embedded in all applications was the ability to collect real electricity data, to set goals, report behavior commitments, receive feedback, and receive reminders, and to "live" in the ambient Facebook environment (see Table 1 below).

There were three "App Treatment conditions," a prototype – video produced for each of three "*treatment*" applications: affective, cognitive, and social motivationally framed energy reduction applications (Table 1 below). The applications are titled: *Kidogo* (Swalhi meaning a little bit*), Powerbar,* and *Powertower.*

To create the stimulus materials: first, we created screen shots of the current development status of the three energy applications, Table 1 below shows screen shots used in video and indicates the behavioral components embedded in the applications. Next, three minute videos with a voice over were created. Each voice over told an energy story relevant to each application; for example, in Kidogo, the narrator, states that she has a relative in one of the target social entrepreneur countries and will donate to the social entrepreneur from that country. The same person generated all of the voice overs for the videos. Previously we have published research that determined the most

Table 1. Images of each energy reduction application indicating key components of Kidogo, Powerbar and Powertower.

motivational images for Kidogo, and the most comprehensible graphs for Powerbar [8, 15]. In addition there was a control condition; a typical treatment; images of a typical utility graphing of electricity information. The video of the typical condition paralleled that of the three treatment applications.

3.5 Measures

There were three dependent measures, application stickiness, energy behavior intentions, energy behavior barriers, and based on theory and examination of variables related to the dependent variables there were four mediator variables, need for affect, cognition, sociability, current behavior, and gender.

Dependent measures. The primary dependent measures were application "stickiness" and energy reduction behavior intention change from pre to post-test.

The application stickiness questions were asked only at posttest and adapted from twenty two questions previously used to measure website stickiness [4]. The questions originally factored into seven factors, we used six of the factor questions which were modified from website to application (a total of thirteen questions were used): (1) five content questions (such as; *The content of this application is; useful, complete, clear, accurate*), (2) two context questions (*This application looks organized, uses fonts properly*), (3) two positive attitude questions (such as; *This application has personal meaning to me, I like using this application*), (4) two trust questions, (such as, *I trust this application*), (5) two infrastructure questions (such as, *This energy application looks easy to navigate through*), and (6) four sticky questions (such as, *I intend to visit this application as often as I can, I intend to stay a longer time on this website than other websites*). In addition we supplemented the measure with five additional questions: *This energy application would motivate me to reduce my electricity consumption; I would invite others to visit this site, I would like to share personal experiences with energy reduction with users on this site, this energy application looks professional, I like this energy application.* All questions were measured on a one to five scale with one being strongly disagree and five being strongly agree. Because the function, involvement and satisfaction questions all factored as a single scale, we combined them into a single index – overall app usability scale (Cronbach's α = .95).

Energy Reduction Behavior Performance: Energy reduction behaviors were a set of 22 low cost, moderate to low kWh energy saving impact and easy to perform behaviors such as limit showers to less than 8 min, use "task" lighting instead of overhead, line dry clothes, set hot water temperature to 120 degrees F., shut windows/blinds in AM to capture cool air. At pretest only, participants also were asked on a 1–5 scale (never to all of the time) how often they currently performed each behavior. The 22 behaviors factored into a single index with a Cronbach's α = .85.

Energy Reduction Behavioral Intention: At pre and posttest, participants were asked to rate each behavior on a 1–10 scale (not at all – absolutely will) which of the behaviors they intended to performed next week. The single factor behavioral intention measure had a Cronbach's α = 92. at pretest and .94 at post-test.

Energy Reduction Behavior Barriers: At posttest, participants were also asked for each behavior, Which of the following would prevent you from performing each of the following actions? Participants could check all that apply of seven barriers; it is too hard, it costs money, I will not remember, it will make me uncomfortable, it will interfere with my lifestyle, I do not think it is necessary, and there are no barriers. The order of all questions within an index; stickiness, performance, and intention was randomized continuously at pretest and posttest.

Mediator measures. There were three hypothesized personality mediator variables; NFA, NFC and NFS.

Need for Affect: Need for Affect (NFA) questions were selected from a previously validated measure [9]. In the original studies there were two indices, approach affect and avoidance (negative affective). We used eight of the fourteen affect approach questions. We selected all questions that have a previously assessed factor score above .51. Individual predisposition to approach emotions questions included; *It is important to me to be in touch with my feelings, I approach situations in which I expect to experience strong emotions, Emotions help people get along in life.* Questions were measured on a –3 to a +3 (*strongly disagree* to *strongly agree*) scale. In our sample of participants, the NFA measure had a Cronbach's α = 0.79.

Need for cognition: NFC was measured exactly as assessed in the original short form (18 questions) of the NFC Scale (NFC) by Caccippo and colleagues [6]. Questions such as, *I would prefer complex to simple problems, Thinking is not my idea of fun, I find satisfaction in deliberating hard and for long hours* were measured on a one-five Likert scale; 1 is *extremely uncharacteristic of you (very much like you)* to 5 *extremely characteristic of you.*

Need for Social Comparison: Social comparisons questions were from a five factor Affiliation Motivation Scale [10] In Hill's original research social comparison (a five item subscale) had a Cronbach's α = .71. Questions included *I find that I often look to certain other people to see how I compare to others; I prefer to participate in activities alongside other people rather than by myself because I like to see how I am doing on the activity.* Participants rate themselves on a 1–5 Likert scale, with 5 being *not at all true* to 1 being *completely true.*

Because the study took place over 3 quarters of a college school year, the personality measures did not get asked over summer quarter, thus our sample size on those measures was reduced by one third.

4   Results

We examined the distributions of gender, ethnicity, political ideology, age, and percent who reporting paying their own utility bill. There were no differences between the groups (*Kidogo* view group N = 47; *PowerBar* group, N = 38, *PowerTower*, N = 41, *Utility website* control, N = 36). There were also no significant differences between groups in NFA, NFC, NFS, mean current behavior performance, mean pre-test behavioral intention, indicating that randomization worked.

In RQ1a, we asked about the relationships among the three personality measures, NFA, NFC, and NFS. NFA and NFS were significantly correlated ($r = .21$; $p < .01$). In RQ1b we examined the relationships between the current behavior, pre and post behavioral intentions, and increase from pre-to-post behavioral intentions. Current behavioral performance and pre next week behavioral intention and post behavioral intentions, were significantly correlated ($r = .56$; $p < .01$; $r = .62$; $p < .01$, respectively). Pre and post intention were also significantly related ($r = .86$; $p < .01$) and pre-post intention increase was correlated with pre and post intentions ($r = .20$; $p < .05$; $r = .27$; $p < .05$, respectively).

RQ1c asked about the relationship between the personality measures and behavior. NFA was not significantly related to any behavior measures. NFC was significantly related to current behavioral performance, pre behavioral intention and number of no barriers ($r = .17$, $p < .05$; $r = .16$, $p < .05$, respectively). NFS was significantly negatively correlated to pretest behavior intentions and number of behaviors with no barriers ($r = -.14$, $p < .05$; $r = -.16$, $p < .05$ respectively).

RQ1d: What is the role of gender in current behavior, change in behavior change intentions and perceived barriers to behavior change? We found that women reported a higher mean of no barriers to behaviors (women X = 9.86, SD 5.58 versus men X = 7.84 SD 6.75) but that men made greater behavior change than did women.

We also note the usability index is unrelated to all other measures.

To test HYP 1, we used a one-way analysis of variance and found an overall significance ($F = 3.325$; $p < .02$). Contrast tests revealed significant differences in the overall application usability perception scale, with Kidogo ($p < .03$) and Powertower ($p < .01$) being significantly different from the control app. HYP1 was partially confirmed.

HYP 2 was not confirmed, there were no significant differences between applications in behavioral intention, number of behaviors with no barriers, and number of behaviors changed.

HYP 3 was also not confirmed none of the personality characteristics, NFA, NFC, and NFS, significantly interacted with their matched application. However, in an analysis of covariance controlling for pre-test behavioral intention, there was an independent effect for NFA on post behavioral intention ($p < .05$). In addition, in the Kidogo condition, participants with higher NFA increased more behaviors in the post test ($r = .24$, $p < .10$).

There was also an independent effect of gender on the mean number of behaviors increased from pre to post, with men changing more behaviors. The interaction of NFC and gender in the post measure of mean number of behaviors with no barriers; women and those with high NFC perceived more *no barriers* to behavior ($p < .02$ and $p < .009$ respectively).

5 Discussion and Future Research

In this randomized controlled test of motivationally framed energy reduction applications, we find differences among applications on a multi-faceted measure of application usability, with both the affective and sociability technology being significantly different from the control condition. However, there were no differences between conditions in behavioral intention and number of behaviors increased.

Notably, the usage perception measures were unrelated to change in behavior intentions, raising the question of the utility of usability measures such as application function and involvement as primary outcomes of tests of online energy reduction applications. More research is needed to examine the role of usability measures as interim assessments of technologies and their ability to assess engagement and impact.

Personality measure results did not show the predicted interactive effect with their "matched" technology. However, there are indications that both NFA and NFC need further research to determine and clarify their role in profiling and matching human motivations to technological frames. NFA did have an independent effect on post behavioral intention. NFC was correlated significantly with current behavior performance and pre-test behavioral intentions. NFS was negatively correlated with pre-behavior intentions. Previously, we were able to see marginal interactive effects of NFA and Kidogo and here within the Kidogo condition, NFA was significantly correlated with the number of behaviors increased from pre-posttest.

Gender also played an independent role in application behavioral intention, with males showing more positive increase in behavioral intentions.

Individual motivational personality measures assessed here intriguingly point to the need to assess individual personality factors related to energy reduction technology effectiveness.

The lack of effects of the applications to differentially influence behavioral intentions is noteworthy. While we used an RCT design, touted as a means of developing theory within the HCI field, the measurement, time span, selection of controls, and audience are obviously critical features of a robust design [17]. Our results do not allow us to tease out the role of these additional considerations of technology prototyping. However, the loss of already small samples per condition (loss from no personality variables from the summer sample) deterred out ability to detect significant interactions. Further, a no or other topic control may be a better option in the future. Finally, this online study would have benefited from a delayed post assessment. While logistics, loss of sample, and costs are considerations, a one-two week delay of the posttest would have allowed participants time to think and consider what they are being asked and how they want to respond.

We conclude by pointing out that while there few predicted significant results, there are results that are in predicted directions and small and consistent results that indicate the potential for fruitful investigation of personality based motivations to spur investigating tailored technology interventions.

Acknowledgements. This research was funded in part by the Department of Energy ARPA-E under award number DE-AR0000018, the California Energy Commission under award number PIR-10-054, and Precourt Energy Efficiency Center. We acknowledge the data analysis assistance of Dave Voelker and the programming and implementation assistance of Ann Manley, Annie Scalmanini, Brett Madres, Nicole Greenspan, and Nikhil Rehendra.

References

1. Karlin, B., Ford, R., Squiers, C.: Energy feedback technology: a review of products and platforms. Energy Eff. **7**, 377–399 (2014)
2. Brooke, J.: SUS: a 'quick and dirty' usability scale. In: Jordan, P.W., Thomas, B., Weerdmeester, B.A., McClelland, I.L. (eds.) Usuability Evaluation in Industry, pp. 9189–9194. Taylor and Francis, London (1996)
3. Karlin, B., Ford, R.: The usability perception scale (UPscale): a measure for evaluating feedback displays. In: Marcus, A. (ed.) DUXU 2013, Part I. LNCS, vol. 8012, pp. 312–321. Springer, Heidelberg (2013)
4. Lin, J.C.-C.: Online stickness: its antecedents and effect on purchasing intention. Behav. Inf. Technol. **26**(6), 507–516 (2007)
5. Delmas, M., Fischlein, M., Asensio, O.: Information strategies and energy conservation behavior: a meta-analysis of experimental studies from 1975-2011, Institute of the Environment and sustainability, UCLA (2013)
6. Cacioppo, J.T., Petty, R.E., Kao, C.F.: The efficient assessment of "need for cognition". J. Pers. Assess. **48**, 306–307 (1984)
7. Cacioppo, J.T., Petty, R.E., Feinstein, J.A., Jarvis, W.G.B.: Dispositional differences in cognitive motivation: the life and times of individuals varying in need for cognition. Psy. Bulletin. **119**(2), 197–253 (1996)
8. Flora, J., Banerjee, B.: Energy graph feedback: attention, cognition and Behavioral Intentions. In: Human Computer Interaction & Interactivity Design Workshop, Crete, Greece (2014)
9. Maio, G.R., Esses, V.M.: The need for affect: individual differences in the motivation to approach or avoid emotions. J. Pers. **69**, 583–615 (2008)
10. Appel, M., Richter, T.: Transportation and need for affect in narrative persuasion: A mediated moderation model. Media Psych. **13**(2), 101–135 (2010)

11. Hill, C.A.: Affiliation motivation: people who need people …but in different ways. J. Pers. Soc. Psychol. **52**(5), 1008–1018 (1987)
12. Haddock, G., Maio, G.R., Arnold, K., Lindsay, D.S.: Should persuasion be affective or cognitive? the moderating effects of need for affect and need for cognition. Pers. Soc. Psychol. Bull. **34**, 769–778 (2008)
13. Reeves, B., Cummings, J.D., Scarborough, J.K., Yeykelis, L.: Increasing energy efficiency with entertainment media: an experimental and field test of the influence of a social game on performance of energy behaviors. Environ. Behav. **47**, 102–115 (2015)
14. Alcott, H.: Social norms and energy conservation. J. Public Econ. **95**(9–10), 1082–1095 (2011)
15. Ruiz, S., Sicilia, M.: The impact of cognitive and/or affective processing styles on consumer response to advertising appeals. J. Bus. Res. **57**, 657–664 (2004)
16. Flora, J., Sahoo, A., Liptsey-Rahe, A., Scalamnini, A., Wong, B., Stehly, S., Banerjee, S.: Engaging the human in the design of residential energy reduction applications. In: Human Computer Interaction and Interactivity Design Workshop, Denver, CO (2012)
17. Robinson, T.N.: Stealth interventions for obesity preventions and control: motivating behavior change. In: Dube, L., Becharra, A., Dagher, A., Drewnowski, A., LeBel, J., James, P., Richard, D., Yads, R. (eds.) Obesity Prevention: The Role of Brain and Society on Individual Behavior, pp. 319–327. Elsevier Inc, New York (2010)

Soft Computation in the Public Sphere: Enhancing Social Dynamics with Wearable Networks

Raune Frankjær[✉]

Department of Design, University of Applied Sciences Trier, Trier, Germany
raune@frankjaer.de

Abstract. The use of clothing as a vehicle for communication is as old as the garment itself. Over the last few centuries the signaling function of dress has declined into the symbolic and anonymous. Increasing privatization of society, has led to nearly half of its population suffering from debilitating loneliness. Positioned within Positive Computing, this paper examines the possibilities of non screen-based digital personal artifacts, in the form of Soft User Interfaces, to enhance social dynamics. This paper provides a case study on the use of non-verbal signaling as the foundation for soft computation deployed in the public sphere. The proposed technology is aimed at strengthening social capital, by freeing up situated user attention and facilitate the formation of wearable networks upon establishment of mutual sympathy during chance encounters in public space.

Keywords: Photonic displays · Smart fashion · Embedded electronics · Wearable networks · Interactive technology · Soft user interface · Physical computing · Soft computation · Social dynamics · Public sphere · Positive computing · Non-verbal signaling · Proximity · Artifactics

1 Introduction

Clothing has been described as the first public display, both in terms of the individual, but also in the history of humanity as a whole. Whilst theories diverge, recent studies imply that clothing developed from adornments as a medium of communication, most likely for ritual or prestigious purposes [1, 2].

The communication and signaling that emerge from personal objects, such as dress or fashion accessories, is described as artifactics and plays an important part of dress even today. The choice of garment is not just a way of communicating who someone is as a person and which station he or she holds, but is also a tool which can be directly manipulated, as to how a member of society wishes to establish their identity. Clothing acts as an extension and expression of the self and communicates a wide array of meanings, encompassing not just identity, gender and political and social standing but also temporary mood and attitude, as well as the moral and aesthetic standards of both the individual and society [3, 4].

Over the last centuries the way clothes have been used in public has undergone extreme changes. Up until the seventeenth century, garments were used to mark the

© Springer International Publishing Switzerland 2015
A. Marcus (Ed.): DUXU 2015, Part I, LNCS 9186, pp. 447–457, 2015.
DOI: 10.1007/978-3-319-20886-2_42

place a member held in society and consisted of a system of clearly understandable and discernible signs. With the advent of mechanization, clothing became standardized and people became indistinguishable from each other. The signaling became very symbolic, that is the reading and deciphering of the signals sent by the clothes, were only readable by the initiated, who was able to discern amongst the subtly send cues [5]. Concurrently societal structures shifted from predominantly public and clearly demarcated, to increasingly private and anonymous, a development that has had an immensely detrimental effect on the public sphere [6]. At present increasing urban loneliness is becoming a major public health concern, with the amount of sufferers predicted to increase to fifty percent by 2028 [7]. Loneliness is one of the paradoxical hallmarks of contemporary existence. Never in history has humanity been as connected and as adrift, as today. Modern technology, in this respect, seems to be both curse and cure. Individualized media technology on one hand lets everyone retreat into their individualized bubble and private space seems to completely displace the public, with everyone immersed into the screen of a mobile device, yet the same technology has time and again proved itself invaluable in bringing about civic engagement and involvement. The potential of Information and Communication Technology (ICT) and the Internet Of Things (IoT) to address complex issues and foster civic engagement, has been demonstrated by numerous smart applications developed in recent years. Among the first and most prominent is the often cited app *Citizen Connect* developed by MIT's Media Lab for the city of Boston. The app basically allows users to report issues online to local authorities, who will then alert whichever team responsible for attending to the problem at hand. The app vastly super-ceded the developers initial expectations, as the workers assigned to tend to the city's maintenance, simply started watching the online feed and respond immediately, without waiting for instructions from the central authorities [8]. This is just one case illustrating how the infrastructure these technologies provide allows the individual access to peer-to-peer resources almost instantaneously and at a scale previously impossible to mobilize [9].

2   Research Focus

It is the focus of this paper to examine the potential of soft computational technology to improve social dynamics, by extending the inherent signaling abilities of clothing, from passive one-to-many type broadcasting of wearer identity to an interactive technology, which engages its wearers into a relationship of exchange with each other and the environment, without the sensory and cognitive overload and lack of attention and situated awareness, which often accompanies screen-based devices [10]. Besides some technical challenges remaining to be resolved, such as cumbersome batteries and maintenance, one of the biggest challenges facing the development and adoption of computational clothing into existing channels of communication and use in public space, is the amount of functionality to include in the textile and how to properly approach the integration of information flow. Users today are already overwhelmed by the ever-increasing amount of data supplied by their mobile devices, which are detachable from the body. Adding a constantly pinging and buzzing garment, which cannot easily be removed, can quickly be perceived as more of a nuisance that an asset to the wearer. Therefore the proposed technology strives to limit attention requiring user-garment interaction, yet still ascertain the wearer an option of control to ensure instant opt-out at any given time.

Secondly, most users have no interest in complicating basic daily occurrences such as dressing. Hence the focus is on pre-attentive data and single pixel type displays, subtly integrated into the fashionable expression of a garment with reduced functionality, gently extending existing technologies to ensure user acceptance. As the focus of application is within public space and previous research has shown users to be generally apprehensive towards publicly using exposing technology, any sort of display of bio-data has been omitted.

3 Applied Methods

The presented case study *enLight* is part of a bigger research project on the potential of digitally enhanced clothing, as a means to enable communication in the public sphere. Photonic materials, near proximity awareness and non-verbal communication cues, as basis of operating mechanisms applied to extend existing channels of human communication, has previously been explored in the *Lightning Bug*, a case study resulting in the development of Soft User Interfaces (SUI). These previous findings constitute the foundation of the research presented in this paper [11, 12].

Coming from a creative and studio-based background, this and previous research was conducted in a very hands-on fashion, where initial hypothesis is stated in the form of a prototype design. Based on the emerging findings, the design is then successively improved upon [13]. The first prototype in this series utilized luminous fibre integrated in knitwear for signaling. Iterating on this design, a fabric based computational interface, in the form of a jacket with a prefabricated photonic inlay, was developed. The interface was designed to adhere to the principles of a SUI, i.e. it has no screens or other way of using text or image-based communicative tools, it's operation relies on biometric and contextually relevant data, in conjunction with nonverbal communication cues, it has a flexible substrate and is as easy to wear as a conventional garment and does not require any additional training or configuration [14]. For prototyping and testing purposes, a total of five jackets were fashioned in a unisex design and a preliminary study was conducted including both students and older users from mixed occupational backgrounds.

4 The enLight System

The jacket is the wearable part of a mixed platform device, working in conjunction with a mobile app. Configured with the user's preferences, the jacket is able to facilitate interaction between wearers, upon detection of a certain compatibility. Controlling the jacket requires no direct action of the wearer, as it utilizes data from integrated sound and proximity sensors, to analyze it's wearers nonverbal cues and subsequently takes action based there-on. Visual feedback to operations taking place as well as notifications are iconically expressed using the jackets luminous fabric as a single pixel display, supported by a small vibration motor adding tactile stimuli. A zipper switch is integrated into the design, serving as a "kill switch" in order to ensure full user control of the wearable at any given time.

4.1 The enLight App

Before first usage the system is configured with the wearers preferences and interests via a mobile app, which was designed for minimum interaction. Users can enter their name and email and state their interests and skill-sets, picking from three dropdown menus. Additional interests can be added to the system and a picture upload is optional. This establishes an online profile and filters all subsequent interaction facilitated by the system. As the user establishes contacts, the app can then further be used to message, endorse and search among contacts (Fig. 1).

Fig. 1. *enLight* app prototype (Illustration Frankjær)

4.2 The enLight Wearable

The *enLight* jackets are fashioned from neoprene, with an inlay of polychrome fiberoptic fabric, which effectively renders the wearable a single pixel display. The jackets operate in six different modes (Fig. 2):

4.2.1 Listening Mode

In listening mode the garment scans the surrounding environment for *enLight* wearables in proximity. Depending on conditions (inside/outside/crowded/build-up) the radius of the scan is about one hundred meters. This space correlates with the perceptual abilities of the human senses[1].

The jacket and the fabric display is dormant and will show the base color of the fibre-optical fabric. In the background the returned data from the area scan is analyzed to find SUIs with corresponding preferences.

4.2.2 Active Mode

Upon detection of a SUI with corresponding preferences the fibre-optic panel starts slowly emitting pulsing light in the color of the fabric inlay. The rhythm of the pulse gives the impression of breathing, i.e., the jacket is visually "coming to life". In addition to the pulsing light of the luminous fibers, a short vibration directs the wearers attention to the jacket and supports the photonic signal in brightly lit situations.

4.2.3 Interactive Mode

Informed by the activation of the SUI, the attention of the wearer can now be directed towards the surrounding physical space to detect the trigger. The speed of the pulse will increase correspondingly to decreasing distance between two interacting SUIs. When entering social space, i.e., talking distance at about two meters distance the SUIs engage and take on each others color in a loop, which can include an indefinite amount of collocated SUIs [15].

4.2.4 Connected Mode

Upon disengagement of the collocated SUIs the system will calculate if the wearers of the system spend any noteworthy amount of time in each others social space and whether conversation took place during that time-period. These two datasets provide the basis for the system to assess whether sympathy ensued out of the encounter. If so, wearers will be added to each others contact lists and their data can be accessed for skills and name based search, messaging and endorsement.

4.2.5 Panic Mode

Panic mode can be triggered by a slight manipulation of the zipper head on the front of the jacket during the SUI's active states, i.e., 4.2.4–4.2.5 and will result in the system aborting all operations and shutting down. To start the system up again the zipper must be returned to its original position.

4.3 Technical Details

Each *enLight* jacket is powered by a 5 Volt rechargeable power supply and fitted with a Spark Core micro-controller driven by an ARM Cortex M3 and Texas Instruments SimpleLink CC3000 Wi-Fi chip (Fig. 3).

---

[1] Humans are incapable of scanning an area greater than 100 m, which explains the uneasy feelings generally caused by vast open spaces. As this emotion is caused by a physiological trait, it is true independently of cultural preferences [16].

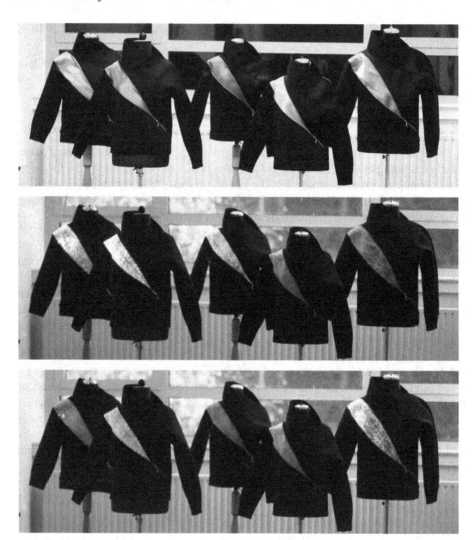

Fig. 2. *enLight* jackets in various states of display (Photo: Frankjaer)

The RSSI of an Xbee radio module is used to establish proximity and orientation, whilst a MEMS microphone detects oratory signal. A vibration motor supports the visual signal from the Lumitex fabric, which has had it's monochrome LED replaced with an RGB LED to fashion a material capable of color-change.

4.4   User Interaction

The *enLight* system is designed in such a way that the user does not have to become active for it to work, but simply uses it as a conventional garment. By gathering simple sensor values, proximity, orientation, timeframe of collocation and use of voice can be

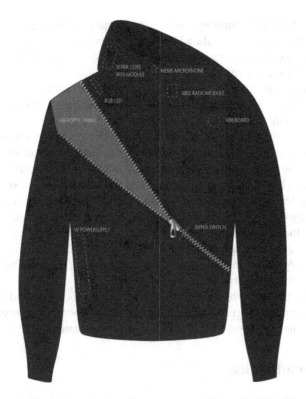

Fig. 3. The *enLight* jacket with components (Illustration: Frankjaer)

established. These make up a large part of the users non-verbal signals, which the system analyzes to gauge user intentions, on which it then bases its operations. The only exception to this is the zipper switch, which allows the user to manually override the system.

5   Related Work

The idea of automating relationships between interactants using digital agents dates back at least thirty years with early visionary works, such as *Liveware,* which lacked the wireless infrastructure, required its members to physically carry and exchange floppy disks during encounters [17]. The research of the Wearable Computing Group at the University of Oregon at the turn of the century, aimed to develop wearable and mobile computing technology for facilitating and augmenting trust-based human collaboration and has been very influential on the development of the *enLight,* as has Howard Rhinegold's notion of seeking ways to 'reunite social space and physical place' and Ariana de Souza e Silva's work on Hybrid Space [18–20]. More recently a great deal of applications have been developed within ICT, utilizing locative systems to enable and encourage direct citizen engagement, as in the mentioned *Citizen Connect* in Boston. Other initiatives include *Adopt a Hydrant,* a gamified web application, where citizens take responsibility for keeping a particular fire hydrant free of snow in the winter-months, whereby any hydrant that is spotted uncleared can be claimed by others using an online map [21]. A similar initiative has been implemented in Honolulu addressing maintenance of tsunami-sirens [22]. In Aarhus the *City Bug Report* functions similarly to *Citizens Connect* but with an added public display on the city's city hall tower [23].

Recently the term *Positive Computing* has emerged, defined as 'the design and development of technology to support wellbeing and human potential' [24]. This project can be assigned to this category.

In the field of Smart Fashion a few wearable devices and garments have been proposed, which in some way or other, address social networking, often in the form of bracelets signaling when a like-minded person would be in proximity. One project suggests scanning Facebook for common interests and subsequently send friend requests [25]. The Ping Dress by Electric Foxy, can receive Facebook notifications and the Twitter Dress by Cute Circuit displays the wearers feed [26, 27]. Another project by Cute Circuit is the Hug Shirt, which through the use of actuators allows users to send each other hugs [28]. Although not having reached any kind of commercial significance, these kind of projects do indicate a growing awareness of the possibilities of Smart Fashion deployed in social space.

In the mobile market there is a plethora of apps based on GPS, to find nearby people, mainly for dating purposes such as Tinder, Blendr and Badoo but also more serious apps like Smacktive, helping users to find nearby partners for platonic activities [29–32].

6   Discussion/Results

It is estimated that 70–90 percent of inter-human communication takes place using non-verbal cues, yet screen based devices rely exclusively on text and voice input, which effectively means a loss of the majority human expression [33]. The focus required to interact in this manner demands complete attention and so people tend to "disappear" into the screens of their mobile devices. Private space thus effectively invades and displaces the public [34].

Largely removing the screen by integrating simple sensing technology into clothing, and analyzing users' non-verbal cues, such as phonetics, proxemics and chronemics, opens up new possibilities of developing algorithms that can act upon users emotional propensities, without them having to direct their attention to the system.

In the study the *enLight* was met with a considerable amount of skepticism from users, who either doubted its accuracy or felt uncomfortable with an automated agent basing its actions on what might be perceived as unconscious and not really wanted on their part. Here the challenge of the designer lies in designing the system in such a way to ensure the user feels safe and in control at all times. Demonstrating the function of the zipper-switch and clarifying that the system is based on active physical signaling, which will naturally not occur if a situation is not desired, to a large extend alleviated the doubts. Having moved beyond these initial difficulties, user reaction was generally very positive towards the factually non-existent interaction with the garment, however the "creepiness" which accompanies any sort of automation remains an area which has to be firmly addressed to ensure user acceptance of such products on a larger scale.

The aim of the *enLight* is to enhance the public sphere, by augmenting the distinct skill-base and interests of the user and present them to the world in such a way that interaction with others is only initiated in case of similarities, i.e., it is likely that mutual benefit will arise from the relation,

As with any filter function this may have the negative effect of increasing the social 'bubbling', where the only others who are allowed in are like-minded, that do not disrupt personal comfort zones.

Yet in order for the public sphere to function it is important that the exchange that happens is within a heterogeneous population, bringing people from different backgrounds together. Here the *enLight* can provide a safe space, since no data will be exchanged if interactants have not developed mutual sympathy. In conjunction with strong user control at any given time, these parameters of interaction open up new possibilities for strangers to engage with each other in an anonymous environment, without the danger of unpleasantly encroaching on or breaching each others personal space, or feeling pressured to make unwanted commitments.

It could be argued, that by introducing an app interface into the system, the enLight is not a SUI in that the garment itself may be devoid of any screens, yet screens are still present within the system. However, as it is the intention of the project to free up situated user attention, by delegating those functionalities to the periphery, which do not necessarily require direct interaction or user engagement, the enLight exploits the strengths of each medium. For conducting tasks such as the original configuring of the garment and later search, messaging and endorsements, the screen interface has proved superior as these activities denote reflective cognitive processes. Navigating the app proved without any difficulty. The low entry-level barrier and restricted functionality lets the user switch effortlessly between the two platforms and ensures an aesthetic interaction experience across the different platforms.

7   Future Development

Following a bigger study into user acceptance and integration into daily life, the next iteration of the *enLight* will aim to improve the sympathy algorithm by deploying more sensors and a more complex algorithm. Immediate plans are to analyze the voice input to establish emotion in the pitch, as well as accelerometers to gauge posture, in order to integrate kinesics into the system, which are very effective in establishing a wearers attitude towards an occurring situation [35]. Expanding on the design of the SUI itself, integrating the *enLight* technology in various kinds of garments are planned and the project will be published under a Creative Commons license, encouraging anyone to develop their own *enLight* capable device to suit their taste and needs.

Further iterations will expand on the capabilities of the garments to integrate location-based services. For instance reminding users to shop for a certain item when in the vicinity of the appropriate shop and developed to incorporate the community, by the agent asking if a user could acquire a certain item needed by a contact, who happens to be on that users route. In this way contacts are of increased benefit to each other, without exerting much additional effort. In addition to increasing points of interaction and non-monetary exchanges, new habits of acting outside the purely personal realm are shaped, leading to an enhanced social dynamics and thereby increases social capital.

Acknowledgements. The *enLight* project and ensuing research was funded by the Media and Film Grant of Rhineland-Palatinate (Medienförderung). The jackets (excluding wiring) were designed and manufactured by Kerstin Anders from the Department of Fashion Design, Trier University of Applied Sciences.

References

1. Toups, M.A., Kitchen, A., Light, J.E., Reed, D.L.: Origin of clothing lice indicates early clothing use by anatomically modern humans in Africa. Mol. Biol. Evol. **28**(1), 29–32 (2011)
2. McCracken, G.D., Roth, V.J.: Does clothing have a code? empirical findings and theoretical implications in the study of clothing as a means of communication. Int. J. Res. Mark. **6**(10), 13–33 (1989)
3. Stone, G.P.: Appearance and the self: a slightly revised version. In: Brissett, D., Edgley, C. (eds.) Life as Theater: A Dramaturgical Sourcebook, pp. 141–162. Transaction Publishers, New Jersey (1990)
4. Roach-Higgins, M.E., Eicher, J.B.: Dress and identity. Cloth. Text. Res. J. **10**(4), 1–8 (1992)
5. Sennett, R.: The Fall of Public Man, p. 165. WW Norton & Company, New York (1992)
6. Gehl, J.: Cities for People, pp. 3–6. Island Press, Washington, DC (2010)
7. Ferguson, L.: The campaign to end loneliness. Working Older People **15**(2), 66–70 (2011)
8. Cityofboston.gov - Official Web Site of the City of Boston (n.d.). http://www.cityofboston.gov/doit/apps/citizensconnect.asp. Accessed 20 Feb 2015
9. Rifkin, J.: The Zero Marginal Cost Society: The Internet of Things, the Collaborative Commons, and the Eclipse of Capitalism. Macmillan, New York (2014)
10. Bawden, D., Robinson, L.: The dark side of information: overload, anxiety and other paradoxes and pathologies. J. Inf. Sci. **35**(2), 180–191 (2009)
11. Frankjaer, T.R., Gilgen, D.: Wearable networks, creating hybrid spaces with soft circuits. In: Marcus, A. (ed.) DUXU 2014, Part II. LNCS, vol. 8518, pp. 435–445. Springer, Heidelberg (2014)
12. Gilgen, D., Frankjaer, T.R.: From wearables to soft-wear: developing soft user interfaces by seamlessly integrating interactive technology into fashionable apparel. In: Marcus, A. (ed.) DUXU 2014, Part IV. LNCS, vol. 8520, pp. 253–260. Springer, Heidelberg (2014)
13. Frankjaer, T.R., Flanagan, P.J., Gilgen, D.: Employing creative practice as a research method in the field of wearable and interactive technologies. In: Stephanidis, C. (ed.) HCII 2013, Part I. CCIS, vol. 373, pp. 31–35. Springer, Heidelberg (2013)
14. Gilgen & Frankjaer. From Wearables to Soft-Wear
15. Hall, E.T.: The Hidden Dimension. Doubleday, Garden City (1966)
16. Gehl, J.: Cities for People, pp. 3–6. Island Press, Washington (2010)
17. Witten, I.H., Thimbleby, R.W., Coulouris, G., Greenberg, S.: Liveware: a new approach to sharing data in social networks. Int. J. Man Mach. Stud. **34**(3), 337–348 (1991)
18. Schneider, J., Kortuem, G., Preuitt, D., Fickas, S., Segall, Z.: Auranet: trust and face-to-face interactions in a wearable community. Informe técnico WCL-TR 15 (2004)
19. Cyborg Swarms and Wearable Communities. http://www.thefeaturearchives.com/topic/Culture/Cyborg_Swarms_and_Wearable_Communities.html
20. de Souza e Silva, A.: From Cyber to Hybrid Mobile Technologies as Interfaces of Hybrid Spaces. Space and culture **9**(3), 261–278 (2006)

21. Adopt a Hydrant. http://www.adoptahydrant.org/
22. Adopt a Siren. http://sirens.honolulu.gov/
23. Korsgaard, H., Brynskov, M.: City bug report: urban prototyping as participatory process and practice. In: Proceedings of the 2nd Media Architecture Biennale Conference: World Cities, pp. 21–29, ACM (2014)
24. Calvo, R.A., Peters, D.: Positive Computing: Technology for Wellbeing and Human Potential. The MIT Press, Cambridge (2014)
25. Firefly - the next social phenomenon. https://www.kickstarter.com/projects/1446565822/firefly-1?ref=category
26. Ping. http://www.electricfoxy.com/ping/
27. Twitter Dress. http://cutecircuit.com/collections/twitter-dress/
28. The Hug Shirt. http://cutecircuit.com/collections/the-hug-shirt/
29. Tinder - It's how people meet. http://www.gotinder.com/
30. Meet People on Blendr, Make New Friends, Chat, Flirt. http://blendr.com/
31. Meet People on Badoo, Make New Friends, Chat, Flirt. http://badoo.com
32. Smacktive.com. http://www.smacktive.com/
33. Hogan, K., Stubbs, R.: Can't get Through 8 Barriers to Communication. Pelican Publishing Company, Gretna (2003)
34. Groening, S.: From 'A Box in the Theater of the World' to 'The World as Your Living Room': cellular phones, television, and mobile privatization. New Media Soc. **12**, 1331–1347 (2010)
35. Mota, S., Picard, R.W.: Automated posture analysis for detecting learner's interest level. In: Conference on Computer Vision and Pattern Recognition Workshop, 2003, CVPRW 2003, vol. 5. IEEE. (2003)

Re-sequencing the Ludic Orchestra

Evaluating the Immersive Effects of Dynamic Music and Situational Context in Video Games

Hans-Peter Gasselseder[(✉)]

Department of Communication and Psychology, Aalborg University,
Aalborg, Denmark
hpg@hum.aau.dk

Abstract. A growing number of video games utilize structural and expressive methods to implement music dramaturgy 'dynamically' into a non-linear and immersive format. Nevertheless little is known about these musically supported immersive experiences and their processing at the user end. Accordingly, this paper studies the effects of dynamic music on attention allocation and subsequent cognitive-emotional involvement. Self-report data is presented from 60 subjects playing an action-adventure in dynamic as well as static music conditions with low and high arousal expression. The dynamic condition systematically affected imaginary components of immersive experience. Design recommendations for flow and self-location are given with regards to task context and regulatory effects of emotion experience.

Keywords: Dynamic music · Games · Immersion · Presence · Flow · Emotion

1 Introduction

Think of playing a game. You play the game, and the game plays you. The same should apply for its music. However, when trying to create music for video games, developers face the challenge of having to implement dramaturgic conventions of linear story-telling into an interactive non-linear framework. To make matters worse, the complexity of narratives in video games promises to surpass those of traditional audio-visual media in the near future [10]. Factor in the need for supporting challenge-based motives and satisfying aesthetic expectations of the audience, and it becomes apparent: A pre-recorded music loop won't do. It will either become annoying or make you turn off the game completely. What happened? You certainly were not 'transported' to that fictional setting, which was encingly promised in the game's marketing material. Nevertheless, if music can destroy that much of your gaming experience, what potential will it hold when it follows your actions, and even more, what if it could express why to perform these actions? These premises form the motivation of the present paper. Dynamic music, while trying to fulfill the above-mentioned shortcomings by adaptively reacting to game events, not always aligns perfectly to the remaining modalities presented in a video game. However, its most important function, as will be argued here, may be seen in the ability to establish

A. Marcus (Ed.): DUXU 2015, Part I, LNCS 9186, pp. 458–469, 2015.
DOI: 10.1007/978-3-319-20886-2_43

an awareness of situational context; a cognitive representation of how we relate to our surroundings. Knowing what situation one is present in lays out the purpose of an action that will have it appear in a different light when contextualized in the virtual. These non-mediated or immersive experiences arise from a holistic experience of congruent multisensory input [24, 30]. To achieve this congruency in musical terms, standard implementations in the genre action-adventure deploy structural and expressive characteristics of dynamic music. Here, structure refers to the design of horizontal sequencing, which retrieves music cues in a way to match the general, narrative and mood of a scene. In contrast, expression is handed over to the design of vertical re-orchestration that adds and removes individual music tracks according to the portrayed intensity in gameplay. Despite these rather sophisticated techniques, relatively little is known about the involved perceptual processes in playing games with (dynamic) music [10]. The present paper intends to fill this gap by providing an empirical validation of the hypothesized facilitatory effects of dynamic music on attention allocation and emotional involvement. In addition, by covering the aforementioned challenges in the course of the discussion, game designers may gain an empirically founded insight in what ways audio implementations can potentially improve game experience – and what's more – keep their players in front of the screen.

2 Music Set in Situational Context

Research on non-mediation has seen many descriptions of experiencing situational awareness within a virtual scenario. Terms such as 'immersion', 'presence', 'involvement', 'absorption', 'suspension of disbelief' as well as 'self-location' and 'flow' form examples of overlapping constructs that sometimes are used interchangeably and merely denote a specific application, such as virtual reality or challenge-based video games. However divergently defined, it may be argued that common ground is found in the notion of specific motivational states and altered cognitive representations of situational factors. Here, imaginary aspects found in constructs such as absorption and suspension of disbelief are discerned from embodied, sensory-spatial aspects found in flow, self-location, and perceived possible actions. The multiconstruct 'immersive presence' [10] aims to consolidate these imaginary and sensory-spatial aspects of non-mediation within a unified framework that incorporates the notion of relational differentials during agency detection. In this view, immersive experiences arise from perceptual processes that juxtapose expected and incoming sensory data as a function of situational demands [5, 10, 23]. Hereby relational differentials operationalize an agent's current and future state as well as realm of interaction in the environment with regards to expected outcomes for the user. Ascribing purpose and relevance to surrounding events in relation to our own beliefs and desires appears to be a ubiquitous process of perception [32]. Research on theory of mind supports this view in that activity of the mirror neuron system is only observed when actions are attributed to agents but not to non-agents (see [8]). In order to assess a situation, these relational differentials are subsumed to a syntax or reference frame that determines the situational context, which is further projected to subsequent cue juxtapositions and awareness of the range of possible actions. Relational differentials may then be seen in connection to intrinsic motivation, which in turn is believed to support the experience of flow and the exploration of the environment. It is hypothesized that music achieves immersive experiences by altering relational differentials as a result of directing selective attention and retrieving schemata in function to varying levels of expression-congruency. In doing so, connotations based on prior experiences and cultural codes drive expectations and evaluative functions of music [6, 11]. Applying this information to relational differentials enhances the validity and predictive value of individual cues. The attribution of a reference frame and its associated situation model then emerges from sensations caused by corresponding audio-visual accent structures [3, 6, 21].

The first step of achieving immersive experiences through music in multimedia may be seen in the primal urge of humans to synchronize incoming stimuli [18]. When initializing selective attention and searching for salient cues in the environment, other senses are taken over by the superior temporal resolution of sonic dimensions [18, 27]. At this, a first set of filters directs subsequent hypotheses testing towards congruent percepts [5]. Synchronization ensures the assessing of audio-visual accent structures at contact with visual and other stimuli. If music and the remaining modalities are found to follow similar structural features causing analog sensations, multisensory expectations on emotional congruency towards the situation at focus are formed. If matching combinations of stimuli are found to be congruent to a hypothesis of perception, attention allocation to the media content is intensified [10]. While at this point connotations of music are processed on an extramedial level, that is a conscious integration into relational differentials within the situational context of media reception (e.g. sitting in front of a PC and knowing that music is played back by speakers placed in the room), the emerging reference frame (e.g. defining challenge-based motives) is attributed towards the situational context implied by the media content. This process of 'situational context localization' sets the stage for experiencing imaginary immersion by giving access to portrayed intentions and motivations [9, 10, 30]. At this point only expressive features reach the processing of relational differentials. Previous work by the author suggests that expressive features related to emotional valence may play a dominant role during extramedial processing [10]. This may be due to a basal matching process of synchronization that yet does not fully account for momentary changes. Accordingly, valence is less likely to change spontaneously; suggesting that the potential of music in modulating emotional valence, as for example by the means of minor keys and dissonance, may provide an efficient way of establishing mood and situation. The associated connotations are integrated consciously, meaning that the perceiving subject is still able to discern the presence of music as well as its surface features from the remaining modalities of the media content. This is of relevance for the attribution process of agency, which is negotiated between a subpersonal automatic level for action identification and a more conscious level for sensing agency related representations about intentions, plans and desires [8]. While this hierarchy is asserted for real-life social interactions, it is the contention of the here presented situational context model that in media reception this sequence may be reversed [10]. Hence, the conscious sense of agency pre-exists and is followed by covert automatic processing that couples pre-motor action with a virtual avatar. Compared to automatic bottom-up, the conscious top-down path processes information slower, making it more susceptible to information that is carried by the valence potential of music. For the faster bottom-up path, however, a more efficient source of information may be seen in the changing levels of arousal potential in music. Having reached extramedial localization, the basal matching process of synchronization may be extended by momentary changes. The gained relevance of the latter allows for lower latency in action identification so that varying levels of music expressed arousal take a dominant role in driving multisensory expectations on emotional congruency. If proportional to the arousal potential of remaining modalities, an increase of arousal in music leads to an intramedial localization of schemata recall. Arising connotations are now unconsciously integrated into relational differentials attributed to the situational context implied in the media content. However, the transition to intramedial localization is gradual insofar as it depends on the latency that music takes to follow the remainder of the accent structure. This latency determines the degree of attributing a particular event or action to an agent, such as the user itself. Note that due to constraints in terms of syntactic structure and scoring conventions, music expression rarely mimics on-screen action directly [6]. Within pre-motor activation, however, music may affect expectations directed towards action readiness or 'forward models' at a higher level that encodes global specifications of the action with the controlling and adapting to their goals and underlying motivations [8, 14]. This synchronization of pre-motor activity marks the point when intramedial localization has been reached and the self has become aware of its physical extension towards the possible realm of action and its location. Since an action may become an intrinsic motivator in its own right, it is more likely to be attributed to the self. Within the context of the flow model [7], the additional information provided by music affects the assessment of task demands, while also modulating self-perception of skills [10]. For presence, previous studies have found a correlation between varying levels of induced arousal and self-location [23]. Moreover, forward models may also contribute to discern one's own thoughts and emotions apart from others, providing the foundation of cognitive empathy [8]. This discrimination may allow relational differentials to become emotionally contagious. Finally, schemata recall and emerging relational differentials are contextualized beyond those motivational ties that were ascribed to the usage situation (e.g. playing for fun in the living room). The situational context model thus operationalizes immersive presence as a mediated perspectivation of situational characteristics that are represented by the media content and its expressed meaning structures [4].

3   Method

60 subjects (23 female, 37 male) aged 18-30 years (M = 23.72, SD = 3.4) answered self-report questionnaires and rated their emotional state each time after playing a 3rd-person action-adventure video game for 10 min in three randomized conditions accounting for (1) dynamic music, (2) static music/low arousal potential and (3) static music/high arousal potential. Subjects spend on average 2.37 h (SD = 1.68) at 2.81 days per week (SD = 1.78) with playing digital games. None of the included subjects had played the game 'Batman: Arkham City' [25] before. Also note that no subjects identified the experimental manipulation.

3.1   Materials

Because of its guided navigation allowing free movement, the challenge map 'Penguin Museum' of the critically acclaimed 3rd person action-adventure 'Batman: Arkham City' [25] was set as a stage for investigating immersive experiences. The game's demands set as per instruction allow the player 10 min of time (as shown on a countdown) to distract enemies from chasing escaping hostages before challenging them in a final battle. The provided timeframe has been shown to be sufficient for immersive experiences to manifest [20]. The orchestral score of 'Arkham City', written by Nick Arundel and Ron Fish, makes use of a horizontal sequencing mechanism that reflects calm and confrontational situation changes by musical expression of low and high arousal potential. In addition, the score utilizes a vertical mechanism that reflects dramaturgic aspects ranging from danger to task progress by adding and removing four orchestral stems to the mix relative to the actions and performance of the player. For example, if the avatar subdues henchmen by using stealth strategies, the orchestration dims down to strings only. Additional layers of brass and percussion will be introduced when further enemies are attacked in secret or evolve to a tutti arrangement when the player is being discovered by surprise.

3.2   Instruments

EMuJoy. The emotion software measurement instrument 'EMuJoy' [19] operationalizes the circumplex model of emotion [26] in an intuitive visual interface. Here the emotional space is represented as a coordinate system between degree of valence (pleasure-displeasure, X-axis) and arousal (Y-axis). Ratings are given by moving a cursor and pressing a controller. Previous applications have found high re-test and construct correlations of about $r > 0.8$ as well as high consistency between continuous and distinct measures. The present study makes use of distinct measures before and after game presentation as to prevent interference with immersive experience.

iGEQ. Two dimensions taken from the 'In-Game Experience Questionnaire' [13] were used to measure subjects' experience of immersion and flow while playing the game. Each dimension contains a pair of items, which were order-randomized and rated on a Likert-type scale scored from 0–4. Good internal consistencies of about $\alpha = .80$ attest reliable measures for the German translation in use [16]. The dimension 'imaginative and sensory immersion' aims to measure narrative elements and associated empathic responses while also considering sensations caused by the audio-visual quality and style of the game. 'Flow' describes a holistic sense of absorption and its intrinsic gratification when merged in performing an activity, though it has been found that iGEQ item operationalization primarily address autotelic experiences [22].

MEC-SPQ. Three dimensions taken from the 'MEC Spatial Presence Questionnaire' [29] add to the measurement of immersive presence. Each dimension contains four items presented in randomized order and rated on a Likert-type scale scored from 0–4. Prior studies demonstrate good internal consistencies of the questionnaire, $\alpha = .80$ to $\alpha = .92$ [29]. The dimension 'self location' refers to a sense of physical projection when interacting with the game. Herein the dimension 'possible actions' measures perceived interactive qualities. 'Suspension of disbelief' bears on the cogency of the medium. Here, item operationalization appears to refer on the plausibility of the presentation, in this way accommodating links to absorption and imaginary immersion [10].

3.3   Procedure

The game was displayed on a 15.6'' notebook running at 1366×768 pixels, 32-bit, 60 Hz, and second highest graphic settings. Sound was provided on closed stereo headphones (AKG K270 Studio) connected to an audio interface (MOTU 828 mk1) at 30 percent volume. Sound-fx were fed to the monitoring input of a DAW (Apple Logic Pro set at 128 samples buffer) and, for static conditions, mixed with the pre-recorded original music tracks (A-weighted volume matched). Prior testing, subjects pass a 30 min training session involving game mechanics and EMuJoy. Before starting the game, EMuJoy ratings on current emotional state were recorded. Following this, a controller button was pressed to start the game excerpt. The game excerpt is presented in three sessions of 10 min length, each reflecting one out of three music modalities contrasting dynamic/static mechanisms and arousal potential characteristics in randomized order. At the end of each game excerpt an animation of five seconds length signaled successful completion, which marked the point when sound was faded out gradually. Following this, subjects were asked to provide ratings on EMuJoy and to fill out the 'iGEQ' and 'MEC-SPQ' questionnaires.

4   Results

As shown in Table 1, music accompaniment systematically affected both ratings on imaginary and sensory-spatial aspects of immersive presence in the video game. As against static conditions, Friedman's test showed significantly higher ratings on 'imaginary and sensory immersion' when playing the game with dynamic music, $\chi^2(60) = 6.23$, $p = .04$, while 'suspension of disbelief' closely approached significance, $\chi^2(60) = 5.14$, $p = .07$. A more differential result emerged for sensory-spatial components. On the one hand, 'flow' saw significantly higher ratings following the low arousal potential versus the high arousal potential and dynamic conditions, $\chi^2(60) = 5.88$, $p = .05$. On the other hand, ratings on 'possible actions' approached significance when static music with high arousal potential was presented, $\chi^2(60) = 5.22$, $p = .07$. However, no statistically meaningful differences were observed in ratings on 'self-location'. Looking at emotion as rated on EMuJoy, reports of valence approached significance after playing the game in static high arousal-potential versus low arousal-potential conditions, $F(59) = 3.83$, $p = .06$. Contrary to expectations, no differences were observed when putting ratings on arousal in low against high arousal-potential conditions, $F(59) = 0.48$, $p = .49$. For the following correlations between latent variables such as emotion and immersive presence, attention is drawn to prior studies in music and social psychology where mean effect sizes range between $r = .21$ and $r = .40$ [15]. Also note that this analysis draws on a local significance level of $p = .017$ (Bonferroni-corrected). Based on Spearman-ranks, a moderate to strong

Table 1. Mean rankings (Friedman's test statistics), arithmetic mean, standard deviation (sd), median, and interquartile range (iQ) of ratings on dimensions from iGEQ and SPQ. 'AP' denotes arousal potential. Asteriks in brackets (*) denote approached statistical significance.

		Dynamic	Non-D. Low AP	Non-D. High AP
Imag. & Sens. Immersion (iGEQ)		2.23 *	1.87	1.90
	Mean (sd)	3.59 (.83)	3.22 (.86)	3.18 (.88)
	Median (iQ)	3.50 (1.37)	3.50 (1.50)	3.50 (1.50)
Suspension of Disbelief (SPQ)		2.23 (*)	1.89	1.88
	Mean (sd)	4.12 (.71)	3.79 (.82)	3.86 (.90)
	Median (iQ)	4.00 (1.25)	3.75 (1.25)	4.00 (1.25)
Flow (SPQ)		1.88	2.23 *	1.88
	Mean (sd)	3.23 (.98)	3.58 (.83)	3.22 (.91)
	Median (iQ)	3.25 (1.50)	3.50 (1.00)	3.50 (1.50)
Self Location (SPQ)		.90	.90	.90
	Mean (sd)	2.48 (1.07)	2.45 (1.03)	2.53 (1.07)
	Median (iQ)	2.25 (1.63)	2.25 (1.75)	2.38 (1.69)
Possible Actions (SPQ)		1.96	1.83	2.21 (*)
	Mean (sd)	3.30 (.79)	3.15 (.87)	3.58 (.83)
	Median (iQ)	3.50 (1.25)	3.25 (1.00)	3.75 (1.25)

correlation between post-gameplay arousal and self-location appeared when the game had been played with dynamic music, $r = .37$, $p = <.01$, and static music with low arousal potential, $r = .32$, $p = .01$, but was not present in the high arousal potential condition, $r = .22$, $p = .09$. Further analysis indicates no significant difference between dynamic music and static music in low arousal potential due to the inclusion of zero within the confidence interval, 95 % CI $l = -.27$ and $u = .17$. In contrast to these results, a Spearman-based moderate correlation between the pre-post difference measure of arousal and self-location emerged only in the dynamic music condition, $r = .31$, $p = .01$, but did not meet significance in static conditions including low arousal-, $r = .22$, $p = .09$, and high arousal-potential, $r = .23$, $p = .08$.

5   Discussion

Overall, the results indicate enhanced immersive experiences following gameplay with dynamic as compared to static music with low and high arousal potential. In the dynamic condition, subjects reported higher imaginary and sensory immersion. For suspension of disbelief, however, this effect was only observed when contrasting dynamic music with static low arousal potential music, but not with its high arousal potential variant. In this regard it shall be noted that MEC-SPQ suspension of disbelief item wording does not distinguish between narrative and sensory aspects of immersive experiences. Accordingly, it is to be expected that item responses on suspension of disbelief are more susceptible to expressive characteristics carried over by the music score as well as its interaction effects with other modalities, such as sound-fx and gameplay controls. One of these effects could entail changes in the perceived degree of realism. Differences in arousal potential of music result in differing relative volume of sound-fx, leading to an increase in saliency of perceptually realistic cues that, amongst others, are held responsible for spatial-sensory states of immersion [31]. Combining the results obtained on imaginary and sensory immersion and suspension of disbelief, it is suggested that dynamic music exerts a strong influence on the narrative-dramaturgic premises during situational context localization. As will be shown below on self-location, such an effect would seem to indicate the presence of a progressive modulation of arousal experience corresponding to gameplay and its integration into dramaturgy, rather than the outcome of stringing together multiple pre-defined cues alone [10]. However, during extramedial localization one may presume the valence potential of music to take the leading role in determining mood and situation. Demonstrating this effect on the current data proves difficult due to the construct discrimination used in the iGEQ. The ambiguous item operationalization of sensory immersion, such as "I found it impressive" confounds both imaginary and sensory aspects of immersion, and may be understood as an overall evaluation of the presentation. Conversely, the scales' imaginary aspect is clearly marked out when rating "I was interested into the narrative of the game". The better-defined notion of narrative may explain subjects' higher ratings following the presentation of dynamic music, suggesting the involvement of other factors apart from arousal potential. Future explorations of this issue may provide a final answer to the interpretation given above. Nevertheless, the differences in the findings on imaginary and sensory immersion as well as suspension of disbelief give reason to presume a dominating role of relatively stabile cues, such as implied valence potential in horizontal re-sequencing, during the first steps of extramedial localization.

Moving on to sensory-spatial components of immersive presence, the situational context model stipulates higher sensitivity regarding sensory inputs in contrast to the more abstract nature of imaginary components. For the experience of flow, similar circumstances as found for the ratings on suspension of disbelief seem to have contributed to the obtained results. One aspect of perceptual realism could be seen in the naturalness of environmental feedback [31]. Depending on the perceived latency between an event and an incoming stimulus, subjects are more likely to ascribe an action to agents corresponding to either the avatar or external/extroavatar characters. This effect may have contributed to higher ratings of flow following presentation of static music with low arousal potential as opposed to high arousal and dynamic conditions. In relation to conditions featuring high arousal potential music, sound-fx appear at higher volume when arousal expressed in the music scenery is low, preventing overshadowing from music and thus boosting saliency of immediate feedback. Subsequently, sound-fx operationalize player skills and task difficulty by affording moment-to-moment synchronization of the sense of control over action and environment. Where Csikszentmihalyi's original model [7] identifies feedback and control as essential components of flow experience, a similar facilitatory effect may be at work in the agent-based action-identification achieved by sound-fx. Here, actions are identified and attributed according to their perceived latency within subpersonal automatic processing structures. The latter may be associated to 'forward models' and their subsequent synchronized pre-motor activation, leading to autotelic stages of flow [14]. Having reached an autotelic state, the purpose of the action is fully intrinsically motivated, suggesting that goals have been clearly defined and taken over by the user [7, 10].

As pointed out previously, the role of music is seen in the suggestion of motivational cues and associated goals, but may be limited in terms of following momentary changes within the accent structure of the media content. Thus, in order to achieve emotional congruency towards momentary changes, music would have to mimic several key actions as to underline their meaning within the progress of a subtask. By adding and subtracting orchestral stems in the progress of moving between opponents, typical implementations of dynamic music, like the one used in the present study, rely on a more general abstraction of the task. Consequently one may expect music to influence only top-down processes that relate to corresponding intentions, plans and desires [10]. The goals of these motivational ties must be contextualized in a way that matches narrative and dramaturgic levels, or when put in flow typology, the global and local goals. While the used game excerpt presents the vigilante fight against crime as well as the protecting of the innocent in a grandiose light as global goals, its local goals, as suggested per instruction, involve the not being discovered and distraction of opponents for a 10 min time window. This constellation follows a better match of music cues referring to stealth behavior, which suggests low arousal potential music to be a better fit for mastering local goals as presented in the used game extract. Whenever changes to higher arousal potentials are introduced, a shift from local to global goals may be suggested to the user who subsequently is inclined to readjust the centering of attention so that a fluid course of action is broken. In view of this, special attention must be paid on integrating global and local goals so as to ensure recall of matching musical connotations. Music then can help to contextualize local goals within the main narrative and potentially prevent unwanted sensibility towards weaknesses of game design, such as in striking cases of gamification [10].

A somewhat different pattern of results comes to light when inspecting self-location. Regardless of the music condition used, no differences were found in subjects' ratings. At first sight this would indicate that music does not affect the sense of being physically located into a virtual environment. However, when consulting correlations with responses on experienced arousal, moderate to relatively strong effects appear in conditions featuring dynamic and static music with low arousal potential. Again these effects may be linked to autotelic states arising from pre-motor activation. Forward models facilitate not alone the intrinsic motivation of an action, but also its attribution to the self. By establishing top-down representations of an action from the encoding of global specifications, matching information from bottom up processes are compiled at lower latencies and thus more likely to be attributed to the self [8, 10, 14]. Combined with perceptual realism, which is gained through sound-fx in conditions including low arousal potential, the actual experience of arousal varies with self-location. This result goes in line with predictions made in the situational context model as well as prior studies that identify correlations between felt arousal and presence [24]. Though, it does not explain why subjects experience similar levels of self-location across music conditions. Some of this inconsistency may be due to inhomogeneous qualitative modes of presenting visual and auditory channels [20]. Another viewpoint is provided when looking at the pre-post measure of arousal. Being more sensitive to in-game changes, pre-post arousal is more likely to capture variations of expression in music dramaturgy as opposed to single measurements [10]. In line with this, reports of self-location correlate significantly with pre-post arousal only in the dynamic music condition. Forward models may account for this insofar as the pre-processing of top-down cognitive empathy affects relational differentials when it is met by the bottom-up processing of emotionally salient cues. If matching arousal expression appears synchronized, spread activation linked to music cognition (e.g. syntactic structure) will be forwarded for integration into the currently active forward model (see [6, 10]). Corresponding to this, the present results indicate a covarying influence of dynamic music on arousal and self-location, albeit with absence of changes in either measure when being rated after gameplay. For the reasons given above as well as the findings obtained from imaginary components, it is presumed that dynamic music holds the potential for protective applications aimed at regulating arousal correlates and cognitive dissonance linked to post gameplay short-term, aggressive tendency without impairing the experience of self-location [for an overview see 1]. While at the time of this writing a follow-up study is in the works, support for this hypothesis may be seen in previous efforts by Grimshaw and colleagues [12] who find combined presentations of sound-fx and music to result in ratings higher on immersion and lower on tension, negative affect as compared to the presentation of either alone. However, it remains to be seen to what extend interactivity in music can contribute to better emotion regulation following gameplay.

Beyond self-location, the present study also asked subjects to report possible actions perceived during gameplay. In line with prior work relating spatial-presence with emotions, the high arousal potential condition received significantly higher ratings compared to low arousal potential and dynamic conditions [24]. Even so, no changes in arousal were observed following the static condition with high potential music. Instead, this condition sees significantly elevated reports of valence, indicating that subjects experience more positive emotions compared to conditions featuring music with low arousal potential. As these measures were taken immediately after having finished gameplay, recency effects may have influenced retrospective reports [2]. Where most prior empirical efforts on the subject fail to ensure consistent feedback to performance across conditions, the present study ensured that subjects completed each game extract successfully. This positive feedback was signaled by a short animation at the end of each trial, but would be translated musically only in the dynamic music condition. Static conditions continued in their pre-defined arousal potential characteristic while fading out slowly (a standard convention in games utilizing static music engines). Though one may expect dynamic music to reinforce positive feedback of the animation, its relieving character and change of tonality suggests lower arousal potential than the continuing music scenery of the high arousal potential condition. Moreover, when consulting expressive parameters reported in the literature and comparing them across conditions, music with high arousal potential shows considerable overlap to the emotion category 'fun', suggesting higher likelihood of experiencing positively valenced emotions when matched with other stimuli [15]. Stevens and Raybould [28] bring up the notion of 'fiero', a high arousal state emerging from the overcoming of obstacles. Being an important source of fun, fiero is likely to appear when high arousal potential characteristics meet the positive reinforcement implied by the visuals [17]. Applying this view on the current findings, it is suggested that the original valence potential in music expression may have given way to congruent percepts of expressed arousal. This could have led to altered schemata recall as a function of situational context [10]. However, in order to study these interactions in more detail, future work will have to check for effects on valence when game excerpts are not completed successfully and accompanied by congruent music stimuli.

The present study demonstrated dynamic music as an efficient tool to enhance immersive experience in the action-adventure video game genre and has given an outlook in what ways future implementations can profit from strategically utilizing horizontal and vertical mechanisms. This is exemplified in that subjects were unaware of the experimental manipulation, though reports indicated differing game experiences. To these belonged perceived changes in difficulty and appearances of characters as well as objective measures of the number of performed combo moves [see 10]. Consequently, given the growing number of commercial titles featuring suitable audio engines, ludopsychology is in need to gain more knowledge on the emotional experience and semantic processes involved in procedural aesthetics.

References

1. Anderson, C.A., et al.: Violent video game effects on aggression, empathy, and prosocial behavior in Eastern and Western Countries. Psychol. Bull. 136(2), 151–173 (2010)
2. Atkinson, R.C., Shiffrin, R.M.: Human Memory. In: Spence, K.W., Spence, J.T. (eds.) The Psychology of Learning and Motivation, vol. 2. Academic Press, New York (1968)
3. Boltz, M.G., Ebendorf, B., Field, B.: Audiovisual interactions: the impact of visual information on music perception and memory. Music Percept. 27(1), 43–59 (2009)
4. Bruner, J.: Actual Minds, Possible Worlds. Harvard University, Cambridge (1986)
5. Bruner, J.S., Postman, L.: On the perception of incongruity. J. Pers. 18, 206–223 (1949)
6. Cohen, A.J.: Music as a source of emotion in film. In: Juslin, P., Sloboda, J. (eds.) Music and Emotion. Oxford University Press, Oxford (2001)
7. Csikszentmihalyi, M.: Flow. Harper and Row, New York (1991)
8. Decety, J., Grèzes, J.: The power of simulation: imagining one's own and other's behavior. Brain Res. 1079, 4–14 (2006)
9. Ermi, L., Mäyrä, F.: Fundamental components of the gameplay experience. In: de Castell, S., Jenson, J. (eds.) Proceedings of the 2005 DiGRA Conference, pp. 15–27 (2005)
10. Gasselseder, H.-P.: Re-orchestrating game drama. Diploma Thesis, Department of Psychology, Paris-Lodron University of Salzburg, Austria (2012)
11. Gaver, W.W., Mandler, G.: Play it again. Sam. Cogn. Emot. 1, 259–282 (1987)
12. Grimshaw, M., Lindley, C.A., Nacke, L.: Sound and immersion in the first-person shooter. In: Proceedings of Audio Mostly, Piteå, Sweden, 22–23 October 2008
13. IJsselsteijn, W., et al.: Characterising and measuring user experiences. In: ACE Conference 2007, Salzburg, Austria, 15–17 June 2007
14. Jeannerod, M.: The Cognitive Neuroscience of Action. Blackwell, Oxford (1997)
15. Juslin, P.N., Lindström, E.: Musical expression of emotions. Music Anal. Musical Expr. Emot. 29(1–3), 334–364 (2011)
16. Klimmt, C., et al.: Identification with video game characters as automatic shift of self-perceptions. Media Psychol. 13(4), 323–338 (2010)
17. Koster, R.: Theory of Fun for Game Design. Paraglyph Press, Phoenix (2005)
18. Maasø, A.: Synchronisieren ist unnorwegisch [Dubbing is atypical norwegian]. Montage AV 9(1), 147–171 (2000)

19. Nagel, F., Kopiez, R., Grewe, O., Altenmüller, E.: EMuJoy. Behav. Res. Methods **39**(2), 283–290 (2007)
20. Örtqvist, D., Liljedahl, M.: Immersion and gameplay experience. Int. J. Comput. Games Technol. **2010**, 1–11 (2010). Article ID 613931
21. Petrini, K., Crabbe, F., Sheridan, C., Pollick, F.E.: The music of your emotions. PloS One **6**, 4 (2011). http://dx.plos.org/10.1371/journal.pone.0019165.pdf
22. Poels, K., de Kort, Y., IJsselsteijn, W.: It is always a lot of fun! In: FuturePlay Conference, Toronto, Canada, 15–17 November 2007
23. Popper, A.N., Fay, R.R.: Evolution of the ear and hearing. Brain Behav. Evol. (Issues and questions) **50**(4), 213–220 (1997)
24. Robillard, G., Bouchard, S., Fournier, T., Renaud, P.: Anxiety and presence during VR immersion. CyberPsychol. Behav. **6**(5), 467–476 (2003)
25. Rocksteady. Batman: Arkham City. Warner Bros. Interactive, Burbank, CA (2011)
26. Russell, J.A.: A circumplex model of affect. J. Pers. Soc. Psy. **39**, 1161–1178 (1980)
27. Spence, C., Driver, J.: Audiovisual links in exogenous covert spatial attention. Percept. Psychophys. **59**, 1–22 (1997)
28. Stevens, R., Raybould, D.: Designing a game for music. Integrated design approaches for ludic music and interactivity. In: Collins, K., Kapralos, B., Tessler, H. (eds.) Oxford Handbook of Interactive Audio. Oxford University Press, Oxford (2012)
29. Vorderer, P., et al.: Development of the MEC Spatial Presence Questionnaire, MEC-SPQ. Report for the European Comission. IST Programme 'Presence Research Activites' (2004)
30. Wirth, W., et al.: A process model of the formation of spatial presence experiences. Media Psychol. **9**, 493–525 (2007)
31. Witmer, B.G., Singer, M.J.: Measuring presence in virtual environments. Presence Teleoperators Virtual Environ. **7**(3), 225–240 (1998)
32. Zwaan, R.A.: Situation models. Current Dir. Psy. Sci **8**, 15–18 (1999)

Exploring Digital Service Concepts
for Healthy Lifestyles

Jonna Häkkilä[1(✉)], Ashley Colley[2], Virve Inget[2], Mira Alhonsuo[1],
and Juho Rantakari[2]

[1] University of Lapland, Laajakaista 3, 96400 Rovaniemi, Finland
{jonna.hakkila,mira.alhonsuo}@ulapland.fi
[2] Center for Internet Excellence, University of Oulu, 90014 Oulu, Finland
{ashley.colley,virve.inget,juho.rantakari}@cie.fi

Abstract. In this paper, we report our findings charting the user interfaces
(UI) design trends of current mobile phone wellness applications (n = 39), and
report e.g. that whereas features related to sharing are already quite common,
conversational UIs and gamification still play a minor role. In addition, we
present the service design based development of future concepts for ubiquitous
wellness services and UIs, and evaluate the concepts in an online survey based
user study with 89 participants. The salient findings show that concepts that
were embedded into everyday life routines and which contained clearly presented interpretation of the data were the most appreciated.

Keywords: Digital health services · Wellness · Service design · Mobile
applications · Ubiquitous computing · User studies

1 Introduction

The health and wellness sector is constantly growing in importance in the field of
public digital services. Whereas conventional health services, e.g. hospitals and
occupational healthcare, are transferring information and services online, also commercial wellness and lifestyle related digital services are rapidly expanding. The digital
age provides enormous possibilities for new, ubiquitous consumer services. Data
related to individuals is no longer collected only through centralized services, but as a
byproduct of the numerous interactions we have through, e.g. smart phones, Internet
use and credit cards. All this creates a digital footprint of our everyday life. Our digital
footprint consists of a vast amount of data from different sectors of our lives, and
contains much lifestyle information that could be utilized by health and wellness
related digital services.

Amongst mobile and ubiquitous computing research, the design of wellness
applications has been quite intensively addressed. Examples of research in the area
include persuasive and playful UI design [1, 2], user experiences with outdoor sport
tracking [3], and enhancing sports experiences with social cues [4]. In this paper, we
approach the area by presenting design reflections on current commercial mobile UI
design trends, and present our approach to the design of a service concept which goes
beyond the scope of currently available services.

© Springer International Publishing Switzerland 2015
A. Marcus (Ed.): DUXU 2015, Part I, LNCS 9186, pp. 470–480, 2015.
DOI: 10.1007/978-3-319-20886-2_44

We first introduce our background study on mobile UI designs with current wellness applications. Then we describe our concept design process in detail, introduce the five digital service concepts created, and present the results from a survey based evaluation of them. We also discuss the role of UI design in public digital services related to wellness and health, and how the availability of our digital footprint and lifestyle data can influence the future services in this domain area.

2 Related Work

According to the WHO, in 2014, globally 39 % of adults aged 18 + years were overweight, and 13 % were obese [5]. Technology has been suggested as one enabler that can motivate people to follow and improve their health and wellness. Prior research on health and wellness related application concepts and user interfaces is vast. Often the topic is investigated from the motivation point of view, as persuading people to do more physical exercise and live a more healthy lifestyle are key problems to address at both individual and societal level in urban cultures. Consolvo et al. [6] list four key design requirements for technologies that encourage physical activity, namely (1) Give users proper credit for activities; (2) Provide personal awareness of activity level; (3) Support social influence, and (4) Consider the practical constraints of users' lifestyles.

Whereas specialized equipment set-ups are used in both research and commercial sectors, mobile phone based wellness applications are very popular amongst large user groups. Research on mobile phone related wellness topics has been extensive, e.g., Ahtinen et al. [3] present a user study on tracking outdoor sports with a mobile phone application. The results report that the form factor of a mobile phone was found sometimes challenging, although its benefits include that people did carry it around anyway, easing its integration to the sports activity. Mobile phones have a strong social function, and thus their use for communicating wellness data is easy both in technical as well as in behavioral sense. Examples of these kinds of concepts are presented, e.g., in [7, 8]. Here, in [7], a game where groups were competing against each other by measuring the team's cumulative step count was designed and implemented, and in [8] Anderson et al. introduce a mobile phone application which tracks the user's activity and enables sharing it with friends. In a study on collaborative context information in social media, received as status updates via mobile phone, updates containing information about physical exercise were found interesting and motivating [9]. Also mobile wellness diaries have been reported to be well received [10], although the effort of typing in and recording the entries has been found burdensome [11]. Mobile phone applications have also been used as a tool to monitor and learn the movements or pace of an exercise, as in RunRight system for runners [12].

In addition to mobile phones and other off-the-shelf gadgets for health and wellness monitoring, such as heart rate monitors, research in the area of ubiquitous computing has provided a variety of user interfaces (UIs) for wellness applications. The concept 'jogging over a distance' makes the person jogging aware of the speed of a peer jogging in a remote location, through headphones and spatial audio [13]. In [14], a person's run is visualized in a playback with an avatar in an imaginary virtual world, and in [15], the running distance on a treadmill is shown on a virtual 3D model of the local city, together with previous runner's achievements.

In the following, we investigate both the user interfaces of current commercial mobile wellness applications, and after that explore user perceptions of wellness concepts utilizing ubiquitous computing technologies.

3   Charting UI Design Trends

3.1   Study Procedure

In order to chart the current user interface (UI) design trends in mobile wellness apps, we investigated the most downloaded free Health and Fitness category iPhone mobile applications during September 2014. The study sample of the 20 most downloaded applications per selected country was taken on 31st of September 2014 and contained listings from 4 different sales areas; United States, United Kingdom, Australia and Singapore. Here, the sales areas were chosen as countries that provided apps in English. The download charts were taken from the AppAnnie charting service (www.appannie.com). From the initial sample size of 80 applications, duplicates that were present in more than one country were removed. Additionally, apps that were purely advertisements, selling health or fitness related products were removed from the list. Hence, the final sample consisted of 39 applications that were targeted to enhancing personal wellbeing.

Fig. 1. Screenshots of 12 of the 39 wellness applications evaluated.

For application comparison purposes, selected applications were firstly reviewed at a general level by walking through their user interfaces and identifying their main functionality and features. Based on the initial findings a detailed question based checklist was created to make a deeper assessment of each of the 39 applications. The checklist consisted of 31 items related to e.g. data presentation style, target setting, data sharing, gamification and accessory usage. For each application, it was identified if an item or feature in question was present or not. In all cases except one, where the application features were checked from information available in the app store, the applications were downloaded to the researcher's device to validate the feature set. To illustrate the selection of application UIs screenshots of selected evaluated applications are presented in Fig. 1.

3.2 Results of the UI Analysis

The results of the analysis of the 39 mobile wellness applications are illustrated in Figs. 2 and 3, where different features are grouped according to common themes. These trends illustrate the current status of the commercial applications, and show that the penetration level of conversational UIs and wearable accessories is still low. These findings suggest that there is much unexplored potential in the design of such UIs. This was exploited in the service design exercise for future wellness application concepts utilizing ubiquitous computing, reported in the next section.

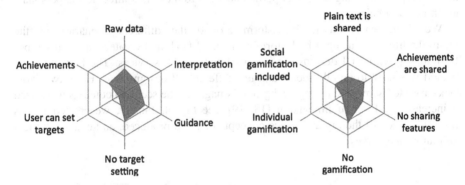

Fig. 2. Number of applications (n = 39) containing UI features related to wellness target setting (left), and sharing and gamification (right).

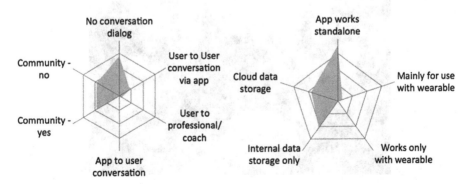

Fig. 3. Number of applications (n = 39) containing features related conversational UIs and user community (left), and data storage and accessories (right).

4   Creating Future Health Concepts via Service Design

4.1   Design Process

In order to create concepts around future wellness services and applications, we organized a design workshop, which utilized various service design methods. Seven participants (three researchers and four university students) took part in the two-day workshop.

At the beginning of the design process, we created a persona to describe our target user. A persona, a concept introduced by Alan Cooper in [16], is an (imaginary) caricature of a target user, and a well-used design tool to help the designers to look the design problem from the end-user point of view, in decision making, and as a communication tool. We then drafted a stakeholder map that described the various wellness related companies and organizations that the persona interacted with in her life, for example dentist services or workplace healthcare providers. The stakeholder map was used as a reference tool, and to focus the target of the design process. A day-in-the-life story was then created to give a comprehensive picture of the persona's activities during a typical working day, with particular focus to those that affect to the persona's health and wellbeing.

We then proceeded to brainstorm around the different scenarios in the day-in-the-life story using a bodystorming method [17], and created rapid prototypes illustrating possible UI designs for various future health services. The bodystorming method was used to rapidly ideate and test different UI design ideas. Here, two large back-projected screens showing background images of the scenario contexts were used to increase the level of immersion [18, 19], see Fig. 4. Finally, we created videos illustrating each of the digital service concepts that had produced, and evaluated them with an online survey.

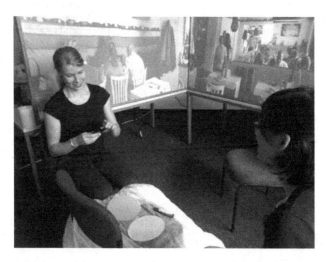

Fig. 4. Two workshop participants prototyping a service using a bodystorming method in a back-projected display environment.

4.2   Persona and Concept Designs

Concept 1 – Shopping Receipt Guidance

This concept aims to affect shopping habits when buying food. When you buy unhealthy groceries, suggestions of some healthier alternative products are printed on your paper shopping receipt. Hence the target is to affect your purchasing patterns next time you shop.

Concept 2 – Health Money

The prices of food items are displayed in 'health money' as well as normal currency. In health money, food is priced based on its unhealthiness. If you have signed up for the health money scheme you will have to pay the higher 'health money' price for unhealthy food. This concept gives a direct financial incentive to purchase healthier food.

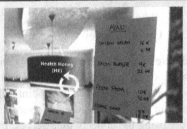

Concept 3 – Intelligent Scales & Mirror

This concept comprises of an interconnected bathroom mirror visual display and bathroom scales. The mirror display shows your weight loss or gain trend as a projected vision of how your silhouette will look, e.g. in 1 year's time, if you continue with you current lifestyle.

Concept 4 – Feedback for tooth brushing

Here a smart toothbrush to assess the quality of your brushing and gives feedback based on your brushing performance, e.g. which areas of your teeth you are cleaning poorly. The data is presented on a bathroom mirror display with the aim used to help you brush your teeth better.

Concept 5 – Connected Dentist

Brushing data from your smart toothbrush is passed directly to your dentist, who can assess your brushing habits and guide you towards a better dental care.

Fig. 5. Created wellness application and service concepts

476   J. Häkkilä et al.

Persona. The target user persona created was that of "Sarah" a 29 year old professional woman, working in the business sector and living a busy career-focused life. The target persona was interested in her health, but often had trouble keeping up with it in her daily life. Sarah's main point of contact with health care providers is through her workplace medical care facilities, which provides her with a yearly health check-up. The persona's eating habits were rather inconsistent, often related to her busy career.

Design Concepts. Altogether five different concepts were created. These were described in the form of short, approximately 1 min long, video clips. The videos were created from photos taken during the bodystorming sessions with a voiceover added, describing each concept. The concepts are introduced in Fig. 5.

4.3 Online Survey

All five concepts were evaluated in an online survey, which was open for 28 days. Each concept was presented as a video clip with an explanatory voice over. Respondents were asked to rate, on a 7-point Likert scale, how useful, innovative, easy to use, and fun they perceived each concept. Participants were also asked if they would consider using the concept themselves. In addition, participants were asked to provide free textual feedback on their positive and negative perceptions related to each concept. At the end of the survey respondents were asked to rank the concepts from the best to the worst, and provide the reason for selecting their favorite.

Altogether, there were 110 participants in the survey, where, after dropouts, 89 proceeded to evaluate the scenarios. Of the 89, 48 were female and 41 male, representing different fields of education and occupation. The age distribution of the participants was, 18–24:6, 25–34:36, 35–44:23, 45–54:12, 55–64:10 and 65–:1. The majority of the participants (82/89) were from Finland. Figure 6 presents the mean evaluation ratings received for each concept.

Considering the ranking of the concepts, the tooth-brushing concept (concept 4) was ranked as the best concept, with 32/89 participants ranking that as they favorite one. The shopping receipt concept (concept 1) was the second most liked concept, being ranked first by 23/89 participants. Only one participant selected the connected dentist (concept 5) as the best concept.

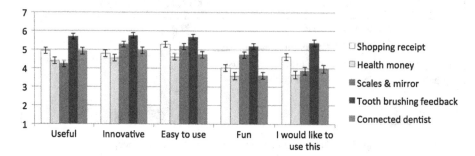

Fig. 6. Mean ranking for each concept. 7 = very much so, 1 = not at all. Error bars show standard error of the mean.

Shopping Receipt (Concept 1). The shopping receipt concept received positive free text comments from 55/87 participants. Particularly 22/87 highlighted that it was a simple and easy idea to motivate them to buy healthier food, reflected e.g. in the comment *"A really good idea and will certainly encourage everyone view their consumption habits."* (Participant #59). Many participants felt the idea was somewhat educational and would awaken their understanding of the health consequences of the food they are buying. A typical comment in this direction being *"This is a good idea. It makes you think more about the healthiness of your purchases than you otherwise would have."* (#84.). On the negative side, some participants (11/87) felt that they would not read the receipt and just throw it into the trash, whilst others (11/87) were concerned that it would affect their enjoyment of the food they had already bought, or not have on effect on their behavior - *"This would barely lead a change of shopping habits, everybody knows that potato chips are unhealthy"* (#8).

Health Money (Concept 2). Here, positive comments (47/87) focused mainly on the power of price to change what they buy, and how the 'health money' concept would guide them in an understandable way to make healthier food purchases. A typical comment in this respect was as follows: *"Could work for people who are just starting a healthier life, so they would understand how unhealthy/healthy something is."* (#107). However, the main challenge with the health money concept was that many people couldn't understand how it would work in practice, or felt it was unrealistic, with altogether 12/87 comments reflecting this opinion. For others (17/87) it was rather a form of economic punishment, rather than providing positive motivation to change: *"Not so funny for people who do not have that much financial resources to use. Where does the money go?"* (#2).

Intelligent Scales and Mirror (Concept 3). This was ranked as the third best concept overall, and was rated particularly highly in terms of *innovation* and *fun*. Many users (24/97) liked the very visible and concrete nature of the concept, and thus considered it could be effective in weight control, for instance *"Makes the change visible and more concrete. I would love to use this."* (#2). Three participants were interested to see not only fat, but also muscles displayed in the mirror display. Some participants were concerned about technological issues, e.g. how to make it realistic and accurate (commented by 10/87 participants). For others (9/87) the idea was seen as frustrating and depressing, because changes in the body can be very slow. A typical comment being *"Changes in the body can be very slow to show and this might lead to frustration"* (#44).

Feedback for Tooth Brushing (Concept 4). This concept was considered as the best overall by the majority of participants, and was the highest ranked in all of the rating criteria. Altogether 45/87 participants responded that they would like to use this concept 'much' or 'very much': *"It would be nice to "see" how you're brushing your teeth, and to do it better."* (#16). The idea was considered good, especially for children's tooth brushing (7/87) and visual feedback was regarded motivating and preventive. For example participants commented *"This is an excellent idea if the implementation would really work! Would help small children to learn how to brush* *their teeth and remind adults to be more precise;)"* (#17). On the negative side, issues such as technology challenges (5/87) and cost (7/87) were raised. Some participants (4/87) also mentioned that a reminder to brush one's teeth should also be included as part of this concept.

Connected Dentist (Concept 5). This concept was ranked as the least liked, but still was rated relatively well in terms of its usefulness and innovativeness. Many participants (4/87) focused on the positive cooperation with the dentist this would enable, perhaps lowering the barrier to visit the dentist regularly. Here one user commenting: *"Basic idea of smoothing the path to go to the dentist and getting more information on the cost of sessions is ok..."* (#44). On the other hand, several participants (8/87) were concerned about privacy aspects, both in terms of data storage and the fact that someone was watching an intimate part of their life, for example *"I wouldn't like that my dentist would know my every brushings, although he could have time to observe me. [...] it would feel like someone is watching me all the time"* (#69).

5 Discussion

The analysis of the UI design of 39 currently popular mobile phone based wellness applications has shown, that so far conversational style UIs are little used. Whereas sharing is supported in several applications, the level of involving community and adding gamification to the UI design is still low. Moreover, the variety of standalone smartphone applications is currently far larger than those utilizing wearable accessories together with the mobile applications. By evaluating the existing user interface designs, visualization patterns and features of popular mobile applications, we anticipate that new service concepts can be better grounded.

Until now, the de facto UI design solutions for wellness applications have focused on presenting the data to the user with less interpretation and contextualization. When developing imaginary wellness service scenarios for the future, we wished to create more conversational dialogs with the user, and offer a higher level of interpretation and guidance rather than simply presenting data. Whereas in 17/39 of current apps data was mostly displayed as it is measured without further interpretation or guidance on actions to take, our futuristic scenarios sought to provide meaningful interpretations and predictions, and proactively suggest actions which would lead to a healthier lifestyle. Compared to current wellness services which still rely on collecting data from a focused source, e.g. a mobile phone or tracker device, the power in the future digital health and wellness services will be driven by the ability to combine data from broader sources.

In creating the concepts, we utilized design methods derived from the fields of service design, user centric design and participatory design. We sought to take into account both experience design [20] as well as usability aspects in our service concepts. The most favored future scenarios in our survey related to straightforward concepts, where the users could identify value for their everyday life. Here, we believe that fitting the scenarios in the context of daily routines, such as shopping and brushing teeth was valued. As a methodological note, compared to typical online survey formats, we believe the acting out the scenarios and presenting them as video clips helped people to comprehend the futuristic wellness concepts. The rich feedback gained on the scenarios provides viewpoints that help in developing the concepts further, and to both add and prune their features.

As a limitation of our work, we acknowledge that selection of the most downloaded applications does not guarantee them to be the best in visual quality, user experience or feature content. However, analyzing a large set of popular mobile applications provides a good overview of the current design trends. We also acknowledge that an online survey is limited in its capability to capture authentic first-hand responses. However, we believe it provided our study with a tool to collect valuable feedback for further development of ubiquitous wellness interfaces.

6 Conclusion

In this paper, we have charted the UI design features of 39 popular mobile phone wellness applications against a checklist of 31 parameters. The salient findings show that although sharing aspects are present in many applications, gamification, conversational UIs and community involvement play still a minor role. To explore futuristic concepts for wellness applications and services, we created five different concepts, and created voice-over video presentations describing them. Our online survey based results indicate that people appreciated contextual feedback embedded in everyday routines and clearly presented interpretation of data.

Acknowledgements. We thank the University of Passau, Germany and prof. Matthias Kranz for hosting the service design workshop. This research has partially been supported by a grant from Tekes – the Finnish Funding Agency for Innovation as part of Digital Health Revolution programme.

References

1. Consolvo, S., McDonald, D.W., Toscos, T., et al.: Activity sensing in the wild: a field trial of UbiFit garden. In: Proceedings of the CHI 2008. ACM (2008)
2. Lin, J.J., Mamykina, L., Lindtner, S., Delajoux, G., Strub, H.B.: Fish 'n' Steps: encouraging physical activity with an interactive computer game. In: Dourish, P., Friday, A. (eds.) UbiComp 2006. LNCS, vol. 4206, pp. 261–278. Springer, Heidelberg (2006)
3. Ahtinen, A., Isomursu, M., Huhtala, Y., Kaasinen, J., Salminen, J., Häkkilä, J.: Tracking outdoor sports – user experience perspective. In: Aarts, E., Crowley, J.L., de Ruyter, B., Gerhäuser, H., Pflaum, A., Schmidt, J., Wichert, R. (eds.) AmI 2008. LNCS, vol. 5355, pp. 192–209. Springer, Heidelberg (2008)
4. O'Brien, S., Mueller, F.: Jogging the Distance. In: Proceedings CHI 2007, pp. 523–526. ACM (2007)
5. WHO World's Health Organization. http://www.who.int/mediacentre/factsheets/fs311/en/. Accessed 13 Feb 2015
6. Consolvo, S., Everitt, K., Smith, I., Landay, J.A.: Design requirements for technologies that encourage physical activity. In: Proceedings of the CHI 2006. ACM (2006)

7. Ahtinen, A., Huuskonen, P., Häkkilä, J.: Let's all get up and walk to the north pole: design and evaluation of a mobile wellness application. In: Proceedings of the NordiCHI 2010, pp. 3–12. ACM (2010)
8. Anderson, I., Maitland, J., Sherwood, S., Barkhuus, L., Chalmers, M., Hall, M., Brown, B., Muller, H.: Shakra: Tracking and Sharing Daily Activity Levels with Unaugmented Mobile Phones. Mob. Netw. Appl. **12**(2–3), 185–199 (2007)
9. Sarjanoja, A.-H., Isomursu, M., Isomursu, P., Häkkilä, J.: Integrating collaborative context information with social media – a study of user perceptions. In: Proceedings of the OzCHI 2013. ACM (2013)
10. Mattila, E., Parkka, J., Hermersdorf, M., Kaasinen, J., Vainio, J., Samposalo, K., Merilahti, J., Kolari, J., Kulju, M., Lappalainen, R., Korhonen, I.: Mobile diary for wellness management—results on usage and usability in two user studies. IEEE Trans. Inf. Technol. Biomed. **12**(4), 501–512 (2008). IEEE
11. Andrew, A. H., Borriello, G., Fogarty, J.: Simplifying mobile phone food diaries: design and evaluation of a food index-based nutrition diary. In: PervasiveHealth 2013. ICST (2013)
12. Nylander, S., Jacobsson, M., Tholander, J.: Runright: real-time visual and audio feedback on running. In: CHI 2014 Extended Abstracts, pp. 583–586. ACM (2014)
13. Mueller, F., O'Brien, S., Thorogood, A.: Jogging over a distance: supporting a "jogging together" experience although being apart. In: CHI EA 2007. ACM (2007)
14. Laaki, H., Kaurila, K., Ots, K., Nuckchady, V., Belimpasakis, P.: Augmenting virtual worlds with real-life data from mobile devices. In: Proceedings of the 2010 IEEE Virtual Reality Conference, VR 2010, pp. 281–282. IEEE (2010)
15. Häkkilä, J., Ventä-Olkkonen, L., Shi, H., Karvonen, V., He, Y., Häyrynen, M.: Jogging in a virtual city. In: Proceedings of the MUM 2013. ACM (2013)
16. Cooper, A.: The Inmates are Running the Asylum: Why High-Tech Products Drive Us Crazy and How To Restore the Sanity. Sams Publishers, Indianapolis (1999)
17. Oulasvirta, A., Kurvinen, E., Kankainen, T.: Understanding contexts by being there: case studies in bodystorming. Pers. Ubiquit. Comput. **7**, 125–134 (2003). Springer-Verlag
18. Rontti, S., Miettinen, S., Kuure, E., Lindström, A.: A laboratory concept for service prototyping – service innovation corner (SINCO). In: Proceedings of the ServDes 2012 (2012)
19. Häkkilä, J., Miettinen, S., Rontti, S., Alhonsuo, M.: Utilizing Large Screens in Experience Prototyping. Workshop paper ARea 14 – Future City as Open Mixed Reality Space. Oulu University of Applied Sciences, 12–13 June 2014 (2014)
20. Miettinen, S., Rytilahti, P., Vuontisjärvi, H.-R., Rontti, S., Kuure, E.: Experience design in digital services. J. Res. Econ. Bus. Cent. East. Eur. **6**(1), 29–50 (2014)

A User Study of Netflix Streaming

France Jackson[1(✉)], Rahul Amin[2], Yunhui Fu[2], Juan E. Gilbert[1],
and James Martin[2]

[1] CISE Department, University of Florida, Gainesville, FL, USA
{france.jackson, juan}@ufl.edu
[2] School of Computing, Clemson University, Clemson, SC, USA
{ramin, yfu, jmarty}@clemson.edu

Abstract. Netflix and Hulu are examples of HTTP-based Adaptive Streaming (HAS). HAS is unique because it attempts to manage the user's perceived quality by adapting video quality. Current HAS research fails to address whether adaptations actually make a difference? The main challenge in answering this is the lack of consideration for the end user's perceived quality. The research community is converging on an accepted set of 'component metrics' for HAS. However, determining an objective Quality of Experience (QoE) estimate is an open issue. A between-subject user study of Netflix was conducted to shed light on the user's perception of quality. We found that users prefer to receive lower video quality levels first with marginal improvements made over time. Currently, content providers switch between the highest and lowest level of quality. This paper seeks to explain a better method that led to higher user satisfaction based on Mean opinion score values (MOS).

Keywords: Perceived video quality · Internet video streaming · HTTP-based adaptive streaming · Simulation modeling · Home network · Video performance assessment · User-Experience assessment

1 Introduction

Sandvine's recent Internet usage report estimates that 65 % of downstream traffic during peak usage times for fixed access networks is 'real-time entertainment' [1]. This traffic category represents streamed content that primarily consists of Netflix and YouTube traffic. Ten years ago the term video streaming implied UDP transport. Now, video streaming typically refers to HTTP-based adaptive streaming (HAS). Various, similar approaches for HAS have evolved from companies such as Netflix, Microsoft, Apple, and Google. This evolution motivated the development of the Dynamic Adaptive Streaming Over HTTP (DASH) Protocol. DASH provides a standard method for containing and distributing video content over the Internet [2, 3]. While it is not clear when or if the current set of HAS applications will converge towards a single standard, it is clear that HAS applications will be the dominant consumer of bandwidth in broadband access networks in the foreseeable future. Given its popularity, we chose Netflix as the video content delivery system to use in our study.

The idea behind HAS is that matching the video content bitrate to the available path bandwidth leads to a better user experience and to reduced bandwidth consumption

© Springer International Publishing Switzerland 2015
A. Marcus (Ed.): DUXU 2015, Part I, LNCS 9186, pp. 481–489, 2015.
DOI: 10.1007/978-3-319-20886-2_45

compared to if the video was streamed at a fixed bitrate. This implies that the application voluntarily gives up available TCP bandwidth with the assumption that this improves the end user experience. This behavior is rationalized throughout the literature. For example, the work in [4] suggests that buffer stalls have the biggest impact on user engagement; the work in [5] suggests that frequent adaptations are distracting; and the work in [6] suggests that sudden changes in video quality trigger poor subjective scores. In addition, there are several recent performance studies of HAS (e.g., [7–9]) that do consider Quality of Experience (QoE). However, determining the perceived QoE of a video streaming session is very complex as the assessment depends on many factors including the viewer, the video encoding details, and the content.

This study explores techniques content providers can use to positively influence user perception and investigate the power of setting user expectations. Our work focuses on two research questions. First, we address the issue of how quickly video rendering should start. The tradeoff may seem trivial: should HAS buffer content when network conditions are excellent while showing the user a fairly high resolution video content, or should HAS use up all the bandwidth to show the user the highest resolution video content and not waste any bandwidth on buffering for the time when network impairments are experienced?

To provide an insight to this complex question, we investigate two relatively simpler questions. If video quality degradation is necessary; it is not beneficial for video content providers to provide content at two extremes, (i.e. starting a video at a lower quality and eventually moving to the highest quality or the converse, starting the video at the highest quality and degrading overtime) or if the user's expectation is set low; by low video quality in the beginning, are the users ok with a sub-par, but slightly better, quality for the rest of the video? Additionally, do users have different video quality expectations if they are told that the video they are watching is online content such as Netflix versus TV Cable provider content such as On-Demand movies?

This work is a continuation of a previous study where user satisfaction with an online game was evaluated. In the previous study, end user's home networks were emulated, including network impairment such as packet delay by utilizing the Linux network emulator netem. While under observation, users played a popular online game Call of Duty: Modern Warfare 2 on Xbox 360. Survey responses were used to calculate a Mean Opinion Score (MOS). It was concluded that although more experienced gamers are more sensitive to network delays compared to novice users, they are still unable to adequately quantify the amount of degradation they experience. Because online videos are also a large source of bandwidth consumption in homes today, we evaluated the online video streaming space in this study [1]. In the research presented in this paper, a subjective evaluation of HAS in the presence of controlled levels of network impairment was performed by conducting actual user studies. Research done by [21] supports the argument that QoE for multimedia services should be driven by the user perception of quality rather than raw engineering parameters such as latency, jitter, and bandwidth.

2 Related Work

The networking community is just beginning to study DASH-like protocols. Most of the recent work has focused on characterizing widely deployed applications like Netflix or YouTube [7–9, 14–17]. The work in [7, 8] is similar to this work as they incorporate QoE assessment in the analysis methodology. Jiang, Sekar, and Zhang introduce an instability metric in [7] that quantifies the level and relative weight of bitrate switches.

Also, there are very few studies that assess the perceived quality of modern Internet protocol television (IPTV) video distribution systems. The art of perceived quality assessment of video broadcasts is well established; however, the majority of this work focuses on traditional broadcast technology. The majority of techniques that are used assume a methodology involving reference streams. The deviation of the received content from the original content is assessed based on numerous standard metrics [19, 20].

Assessing the perceived quality of video without a reference is much more challenging. The 3GPP community has identified several quality metrics for DASH including HTTP request/response transaction times, average throughput and initial playout delay [3GPP]. In [4], the authors explore measures that impact perceived quality of Internet broadcasts and found that the percent buffering time has the largest impact on user engagement although the specific impact varies by content genre. Other metrics that are established in the Internet broadcast communities are:

- Zapping time: The time required for a new stream to begin rendering.
- Rate of re-buffering: This is the rate of re-buffering events.

The work in [8] performed subjective tests to determine which bitrate adaptation behaviors led to the highest overall perceived quality. The work in [18] evaluated three commercial HAS products (Microsoft Smooth Streaming, Adobe Dynamic Streaming, and Apple Live Streaming) as well as an open source HAS implementation. They determine that in vehicular scenarios neither method will always achieve the maximum available bandwidth with a minimal number of quality switches.

To date, there has not been a human factors study that correlates the impacts of the network with perceived quality by end users viewing HAS-based streamed content.

3 Methodology

Video content type could make a difference in the perceived quality. For this study an action movie because the special effects in an action movie allows for easier detection of visual artifacts. An artifact is an anomaly found during visual representation of digital graphics and imagery. Using the action movie video content, preliminary studies were conducted to determine the appropriate level of packet loss for the actual study. In selecting the correct packet loss rate, one of the requirements was that a buffering message should not appear on the screen during the study. When a packet loss rate of 12 % was used, a buffering message appeared; therefore, it was determined that the worst packet loss setting had to be below 12 %. Expert viewers from the University's Digital Production group watched the movie clip at various packet loss levels below

12 % to determine the correct packet loss settings for the actual study where artifacts could be detected.

3.1 Experiment Setup

The action video clip used in the study was 10 min in length. For the actual experiment, 3 settings were consided based on the findings from the preliminary study. See Table 1 for the packet loss settings used for the study.

Table 1. Packet loss settings

Setting	1st 5 min	2nd 5 min
1. Bad to Good	9 %	0 %
2. Good to Bad	0 %	9 %
3. Bad to Ok	9 %	6 %

3.2 Study Design

A between subject approach was taken where each user viewed only one setting. In an attempt to have more control over the video content, each setting described in Table 1 was pre-recorded. For each setting, the video was played with the appropriate beginning and appropriate end setting, and a screen capture software, Fraps,[1] was used to capture the video. Therefore, each participant scheduled to view Setting 1 video, saw the exact same video clip. The same is true for Settings 2 and 3.

A total of 56 experiments were performed, which resulted in 112 survey responses. To test one of the hypotheses related to online vs. on-demand content, half of the participants were told that they were watching a free online movie by the experimenter, while the other half were told they were watching a paid on-demand style movie. During each experiment, no more than four users would participate in the study. The number was kept below four to preserve a fairly straight viewing angle for each user. The distance between the viewers and the 32' 1080p HD TV where the video content was displayed was approximately 6 feet which is a typical distance used by viewers in a home setting.

3.3 Experimental Procedure

Prior to watching the movie clip, participants completed a pre-survey questionnaire where demographic information as well as information related to their movie watching behavior was collected. Following the movie, a post survey questionnaire was completed where users used a 5 point Likert scale to assess their "Level of Frustration", "Video Clarity" and "Distortion" for the beginning and end of the video clip as well as

---

[1] More details about the screen capture software available at: www.fraps.com.

their overall experience. Video clarity was defined as the crispness of the image, while distortion was defined as the presence of artifacts in the image. They were also asked about sound distortion.

There were two additional questions that were very important to our stakeholders. We asked users how much they would be willing to pay for a movie with the current video quality and how likely would they be to switch service providers if they continuously received service at this level. These responses were recorded and analyzed to determine if there was a correlation between willingness to pay and whether the user was told they were watching an online movie versus an on-demand movie.

Finally, there was an oral question. Each user was asked if they prefer to have bad quality in the beginning or at the end of a movie. There was also an option to indicate that any degradation in quality is unacceptable.

4 Results and Analysis

4.1 Calculating Mean Opinion Scores (MOS)

The responses to the post-survey questions were used to calculate a Mean Opinion Score (MOS) value. The MOS metric was used to quantify the user's QoE. Participant responses were first categorized by on-demand or online perception. Next they were categorized by the setting (bad to good, good to bad, and bad to ok) as illustrated in Fig. 1.

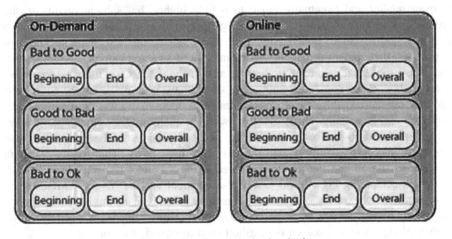

Fig. 1. Results categorization logic

Within each of these categories, the responses for the reported level of frustration at the beginning of the video, the responses for the video clarity at the beginning of the video, and the responses for the distortion at the beginning of the video were all averaged. This created three MOS values. These values were averaged to create the overall MOS for the beginning of the video. The same process was used to caluculate the MOS for the end of the video, as well as the overall opinion(see Fig. 1). The MOS calculation breakdown can be seen in Fig. 2. The process shown in Fig. 2 was repeated for each setting. Each setting under the online condition was also used to calculate MOS values.

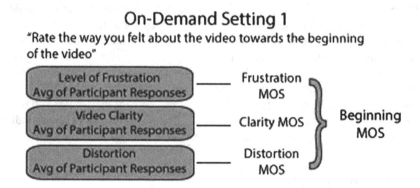

Fig. 2. MOS calculation breakdown

4.2   Interpreting Mean Opinion Scores

Based on the results, the bad to ok setting has the highest "overall" MOS. So, starting with low video quality and then improving it a little satisfied most of the users. The bad to ok overall MOS results support our first hypothesis that video quality should start at a lower quality and eventually move to a little higher, but sub-par quality in the presence of network congestion. Both settings that involved the two extremes (Good to Bad and Bad to Good) resulted in lower MOS values, this also supports our first hypothesis, that content providers current method of showing extremes is not beneficial. The responses to two extreme settings result from the fact that users get to see the "best quality". They know the quality they should have been obtaining the entire time and they can more visibly see the drastic change, as opposed to a less drastic difference. Since the user expectation is set low by low video quality in the beginning, the users actually prefer a sub-par (but slightly better) quality for the rest of the video rather than going to the best quality which supports our hypothesis. The results for both on-demand and on-line studies are illustrated in Figs. 3 and 4 respectively.

When comparing Figs. 3 and 4, it is also apparent that the "overall" MOS for all three settings is lower for online study compared to on-demand study. This supports our second hypothesis that users' perceived level of quality can be influenced by setting a level of expectation based on the method used to provide the content.

The MOS results from the "Willingness to Pay" metric, seen in Fig. 5, also support this hypothesis by showing that the MOS of each setting is lower for the online study compared to the on-demand study.

When asked if they prefered degradation in quality in the beginning or end of the video, the majority (45 %) reported that any degradation in quality is unacceptable.

Of the people that would accept degradation, they preferred that it occur in the beginning. This supports the hypothesis that starting at poor quality and slightly improving over time is beneficial.

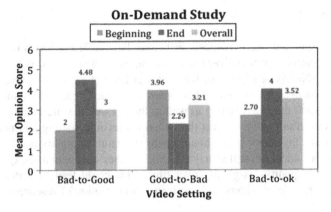

Fig. 3. On-demand MOS results

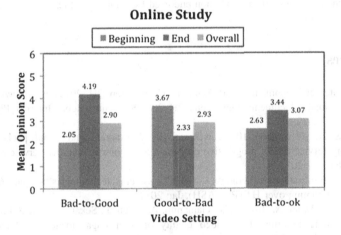

Fig. 4. Online MOS results

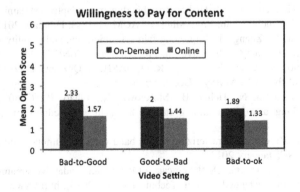

Fig. 5. Willingness to pay MOS results

5 Conclusion

Our analysis supported our hypothesis that users have different levels of expectation based on the method used to deliver the video content. When users watch online movie content such as Netflix or Hulu, they have a lower level of expectation than when they are watching on-demand content. This preset expectation influences the way they perceive and assess the video quality as well as the amount they are willing to spend on the content. Our results also suggest that when a stream is starting and network conditions impair quality, the system should begin at a reduced quality and improve over time. Content providers can still satisfy customers if they start with a bad quality stream and improve the quality marginally over time. This could lead to better bandwidth management for cable providers and result in a conservation of resources.

Acknowledgements. This material is based upon work supported by CableLabs, Inc. Opinions or points of views expressed in this document are those of the authors and do not necessarily reflect the official position of, or a position endorsed by CableLabs, Inc.

References

1. Global internet phenomena report. Sandvine Corporation, 2H (2012). http://www.sandvine.com/downloads/-documents/Phenomena_2H_2012/Sandvine_Global_Internet_Phenomena_Report_2H_2012.pdf
2. GPP TS 26.247 version 10.1.0 Release 10: Transparent end-to-end packet switched streaming service (PSS); progressive download and dynamic adaptive service over HTTP, 3GPP, January 2012
3. ISO/IEC: Information technology — MPEG systems technologies — part 6: dynamic adaptive streaming over HTTP (DASH), Jan 2011
4. Dobrian, F., Awan, A., Joseph, D., Ganjamm, A., Zhan, J., Sekar, V., Stoica, I., Zhang, H.: Understanding the impact of video quality on user engagement. In: Proceedings of SIGCOMM 2011, August 2011
5. Cranley, N., Perry, P., Murphy, L.: User perception of adapting video quality. Int. J. Hum. Comput. Stud. **64**(8), 637–647 (2006)
6. Muller, C., Timmerer, C.: A testbed for the dynamic adaptive streaming over HTTP featuring session mobility. In: Proceedings of ACM MMSys, February 2011
7. Jiang, J., Sekar, V., Zhang, H.: Improving fairness, efficiency, and stability in HTTP-based adaptive video streaming with festive. In: Proceedings of CoNEXT 2012, December 2012
8. Mok, R., Luo, X., Chan, E., Chang, R.: QDASH: a QoE-aware DASH system. In: Proceedings of the ACM MMSys, December 2012
9. Huang, T., Handigol, N., Heller, B., McKeown, N., Johari, R.: Confused, timid, and unstable: picking a video streaming rate is hard. In: Proceedings of the IMC 2012, November 2012
10. Martin, J., Fu, Y., et al.: Characterizing netflix bandwidth consumption. In: Proceedings of the IEEE CCNC, January 2013
11. Martin, J., Fu, Y., Hong, G.: On the efficacy of the dynamic adaptive streaming over HTTP (DASH) protocol – extended version. Technical report (2013). http://www.cs.clemson.edu/~jmarty/papers/EfficacyDASHExtended.pdf

12. Balachandran, A., Sekar, V., Akella, A., Seshan, S., Stoica, I., Zhang, H.: A quest for an internet video quality-of-experience metric. In: Proceedings of the ACM HotNets 2012, October 2012
13. Oyman, O., Singh, S.: Quality of experience for HTTP adaptive streaming services. IEEE Communications Magazine, April 2012
14. Akhshabi, S., Begen, A., Dovrolis, C.: An experimental evaluation of rate-adaptation algorithms in adaptive streaming over HTTP. In: Proceedings of ACM MMSys, February 2011
15. Liu, C., Bouazizi, I., Gabbouj, M.: Rate adaptation for adaptive HTTP streaming. In: Proceedings of ACM MMSys, February 2011
16. Lederer, S., Muller, C., Timmerer, C.: Dynamic adaptive streaming over HTTP dataset. In: Proceedings of ACM MMSys, February 2012
17. Akhshabi, S., Anantakrishnan, L., Dovrolis, C., Begen, A.: What happens when HTTP adaptive streaming players compete for bandwidth. In: Proceedings of ACM NOSSDAV 2012, June 2012
18. Muller, C., Lederer, S., Timmerer, C.: An evaluation of dynamic adaptive streaming over HTTP in vehicular environments. In: Proceedings of ACM MoVid 2012, February 2012
19. Wang, Z., Bovik, A., Sheikh, H., et al.: Image quality assessment: from error visibility to structure similarity. IEEE Trans. Image Process. 14(12), 2117–2128 (2005)
20. Xia, J., Shi, Y., Teunissen, K., Heynderickx, I.: Perceivable artifacts in compressed video and their relation to video quality. Signal Process. Image Commun. 24, 548–556 (2009)
21. Agboma, F., Liotta, A.: Addressing user expectations in mobile content delivery. Mob. Inf. Syst. 3(3), 1 (2007)

Engaging Experience with Physical Activity Tracking Products

Armağan Kuru[1](✉) and Jodi Forlizzi[2]

[1] Department of Industrial Design, TOBB University of Economy
and Technology, Ankara, Turkey
a.kuru@etu.edu.tr
[2] Human Computer Interaction Institute, Carnegie Mellon University,
Pittsburgh, USA
forlizzi@cmu.edu

Abstract. Many people use physical activity tracking products to gather personal behavioral data, make better decisions, and make changes to their behavior. While the proliferation of new products on the market makes collecting personal data easier, how to help people engage with these products over a long period of time remains an open question. To uncover which features of physical activity tracking products lead to engaging experience, we conducted a study with people who use physical activity tracking products to support or track behavior change. We conducted baseline interviews and had participants interact with either a BodyMedia armband or a FitBit activity tracker. Participants rated their experience with the product daily for a period of four weeks and reflected on their engagement at the end of the study. Through synthesis and analysis of the study findings, we draw out four characteristics for engaging experience in physical activity tracking product use: *connectivity, curiosity, personalization, and motivation.*

Keywords: Design · Experience · User experience · Interaction design engaging experience · Physical activity tracking

1 Introduction

Physical activity tracking products that can potentially help people improve the quality of their lives and their general well-being are on the rise. These products are special class of products that track data about their users, either automatically or through user input. A variety of physical activity tracking products exist in the form of commercial products. Currently, apps exist for counting steps, monitoring heart rate, and tracking sleep, among others. Others, such as Daily Burn [www.dailyburn.com], Endomondo [www.endomondo.com], and Runkeeper [www.runkeeper.com] are web sites with easy to access interfaces. Still others take the form of products along with mobile apps or web sites to offer more opportunities to engage with the data that is collected. In the past year, the market has proliferated with products from Body Media [www. bodymedia.com], Fit Bit [www.fitbit.com], Nike [www.nike.com], and Philips [http:// www.p4c.philips.com] among others.

© Springer International Publishing Switzerland 2015
A. Marcus (Ed.): DUXU 2015, Part I, LNCS 9186, pp. 490–501, 2015.
DOI: 10.1007/978-3-319-20886-2_46

There is also a growing body of research that explores the design, uptake, use and effect of physical activity tracking products. In hopes of improving the interaction between technology and people, HCI researchers have explored the ways in which people interact with physical activity tracking products and how these provide feedback. Early research explored aesthetic and game-like visualizations of activity to motivate people to engage with the system [1–6]; others focused on the social and motivational aspects of sharing data [7, 8]. Physical activity tracking products may be helpful in setting tangible goals and relaying process towards that goal.

Yet, little design knowledge has been formalized about how to design physical activity tracking products to sustain use over time. Designers can take inspiration from legacy products such as jewelry, cars, and antiques to understand how relationships with products evolve over time [9]. The meanings attached to these products prolong their lifetime of use, but what about the more mundane technological products of daily life? The issue becomes even more important as apps, services and products continue to enter the market. More and more of these products are developed each month, competing for market share and the possibility of sustaining use over time.

As a community, we have yet to understand the trajectory of long-term experience with physical activity tracking products, to better support designing for *engaging experience*. To address this gap in design knowledge, we need to understand how interactive products can create engaging experience. This knowledge can help designers understand how to design physical activity tracking products that motivate people to use them over time, and positively affect their long term use [10].

In this paper, we explore the topic of engaging experience in physical activity tracking products, by first providing an overview of the literature. We then conducted a study comparing two products, the BodyMedia SenseWear device and the FitBit activity monitor. Through synthesis and analysis of the study findings, we draw out four characteristics for engaging experience in physical activity tracking product use: *connectivity, curiosity, personalization,* and *motivation.* We provide an initial framework to show the connection between these characteristics. Our goal is to help the design community design for engaging experience in future physical activity tracking products.

2 Engaging Experience with Physical Activity Tracking Products

Design researchers have been focused on how to design products that offer engaging experience for several decades. Early interaction design research asserted that products should engage people through their physicality, and be fun to use [11]. The goal of the designer in creating an engaging experience was to design a product that is fun to interact with. Subsequent research drew out specific dimensions of engagement to be considered in design, including challenge, positive effect, endurability, aesthetic and sensory appeal, attention, feedback, variety/novelty, interactivity, and perceived user control [12]. When these product dimensions work together, the result is a product or product that attracts and sustains people through aesthetics, interaction, and use.

User engagement is not a single phenomenon; it evolves with the experience of product use over time. It is a longitudinal process in which reactions towards the product can evolve over time. This process covers engagement, non-engagement-disengagement and reengagement [12]. When the novelty effect of using a product passes, people may disengage with the product. If, after a while, the user desires the experience and starts using the product again, reengagement occurs.

Other research defined engaging experience as a product's ability to inspire more frequent, active and intense interaction [13]. To do so, the product needs to attract the user's attention, keep her interest, and make her think about the product more frequently. Flow Theory [14, 15] is the state of high involvement in certain activities; these can involve product use. The skills of the individual and the challenges of the activity define the level of flow: If these two are at equally optimal levels, then the individual will be in flow. People feel anxiety if the level of challenge is high, but their skill level is not high enough to match these challenges. On the other hand, people feel bored while performing an activity if the challenges of the activity are low but their skill level is higher than the activity requires. It is evident that the level of flow increases when the user has the control of the activity.

Understanding how people experience products over time can provide insights. Chou and Conley [16] define engaging experience as an aspect of a product in addition to usability and aesthetics. We define *engaging experience* as the ability to inspire and motivate people, allowing repeated interaction with a thing over time. In product and interaction design, this has translated into the consideration of functional, aesthetic, social, and emotional needs of people during the design process [17, 18]. Products that feature regular feedback keep people engaged in using the product over time [7]. For example, a pedometer shows steps taken over the course of a day, and this information alone can motivate us to continue to use the product. Interactive products can command our attention, draw us in, and build curiosity [8]. Aesthetics must be considered, too, so the product fits with the notion of who we are and sustains use over time [19]. The quality of the data collected and how it is presented data is also an important factor for preventing the product abandonment [20]. For example, the Nike Fuelband [www.nike. com] features a dynamic visualization display and sleek form that invites sustained interaction.

As a community, we have yet to understand the trajectory of *engaging experience* with physical activity tracking products, to better support designing for sustained usage. To address this gap in design knowledge, we need to understand how these products can create engaging experience. This knowledge can help designers understand how to design new physical activity tracking products that motivate people to use them over time, and positively affect their long term use [10].

3 Methodology

To better understand engaging experience in physical activity tracking product use, we recruited participants by advertising the study on Craigslist and a campus recruiting web site. We sampled for people who had concrete goals related to becoming more active, or a desire to become more active. People who were interested in the study were asked to complete a screening questionnaire in which we asked their age, type of phone, number of hours they are active per week, and whether they would be traveling or on vacation in the next five weeks. In total, 16 people (8 female; 8 male, ranging in age from 23–57, M = 33.58) participated in the study. Nine participants wanted to lose weight and six of them expected to increase their physical activity level.

3.1 Product Selection

To select the physical activity tracking products for the study, we reviewed 15 mobile and seven standalone products that were on the market at the time. We compared them through their abilities of mobility, interaction with data and perceptions of usefulness. Ultimately, two products were selected (Fig. 1): the BodyMedia wearable armband and the FitBit activity tracker. The BodyMedia and FitBit products were chosen because they both show activity in real time, which might be critical for long-term product use.

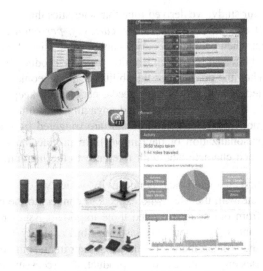

Fig. 1. BodyMedia and FitBit products

3.2 Data Collection

We conducted semi-structured initial interviews with participants, lasting 60–90 min. Here, we gathered details about their typical day, their daily activity level, and their general physical condition. During the initial interview, participants were asked to talk about their goals as participants of this study. Next, participants were given either the FitBit or the BodyMedia product, and were given a week to gain familiarity with the product. We asked participants to use the product for five weeks and after five weeks, we conducted semi-structured debriefing interviews with participants lasting between 45–60 min. All the interviews were voice recorded with the permission of the participants.

3.3 Analysis

We coded interview data thematically to provide qualitative information about the experience of using the product. We drew out characteristics from our data that described product qualities that contributed to long-term use, and therefore, engaging experience. To analyze the qualitative data, each voice record was transcribed into Excel sheets. Then, open coding was conducted where product characteristics, qualities and participants' interactions, needs and expectations were identified [21]. Each sentence of participants was combinations of several sentences; thus they were divided into meaningful utterances. In total 4 main product-quality codes were defined in with 37 sub-codes in total. After the content analysis, product and user related comments of the participants were separated from each other to emphasize the product-related dimensions of engaging experience.

3.4 Results

From the results of our study, we derived four characteristics that we believe contribute to engaging product experience: *connectivity, curiosity, personalization, and motivation*. We suggest that when people feel curious about some kind of information coming from the product and have an interest in learning from the product, they start to engage with the product. When the product has the ability to allow people to make changes to how data is presented to better meet their needs, people will keep using the product. The experience then becomes continuous and engaging over time (Fig. 2). We think that curiosity and motivation are behaviors that are triggered by product interaction. Connectivity and personalization of data move from product back to user. In what follows, we define each characteristic with reference to the literature.

Connectivity. The first characteristic is connectivity, which we define as the "product's ability to communicate with the user, who expects to connect to the product whenever they desire." Data from our study revealed three important issues related to connectivity: (1) People want to see their data instantly, but usability problems related to connecting them to the product meant that they lost their interest in product use. Seeing data instantly increases engagement with the product. (2) Accessibility of data through multiple devices is critical in order to make the process of accessing data less complicated. (3) People expect that products prompt the user to connect by providing analyzed data along with meaningful suggestions and achievable goals.

Our data showed that staying connected to the product whenever people desire is vital to sustain engagement over time. When participants were able to connect to the product with the product's interface, the web, or a mobile app, their engagement increased as they began to draw knowledge from their data. For example, one of the participant's mobile apps used to access the system did not work well during the study, and he devised a way to get data from his device without connecting the device to a computer. He described this as a usability problem, and lost interest in using the product over time. This example shows how connectivity is an important aspect of engaging physical activity tracking products, as it enables sustained interaction with data and meaningful interpretations of the data over time.

Technology has made it easy to connect to an interactive product or service using any number of devices. Using a number of devices such as a smartphone, a wearable sensor, and a web site, products can determine where someone is, what they are doing, and how long they have engaged with a product or service [22]. These conditions also make it possible to access relevant data at all times. Interactive products can effectively sustain engagement by reacting according to the a person's changing contexts of use [23]. Today, people use wireless connections, RFID tags and GPS applications in daily life, all of which can serve as points of connectivity. Many means for staying connected are readily available; well-designed products can take advantage of this to support engagement with products over time.

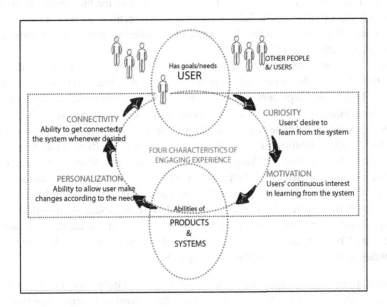

Fig. 2. Four characteristics of engaging experience.

In order to further explore connectivity as it affects engaging experience, physical activity tracking products should enable users to access and analyze data about themselves immediately. Products should support multiple points of data access and data interaction. There should be several simple and direct ways to access data, and data access should transfer seamlessly from one access point to another.

Personalization. The second characteristic is personalization, which we define as "the product's ability to allow the user to make changes in the functionality, interface, information content or distinctiveness of a product" [24] to best support individuals' needs.

In our study, we discovered three findings related to personalization: (1) People wanted the product to "talk to" them specifically, rather than just collecting data and analyzing it according to pre-defined parameters. (2) People wished for the product to make suggestions for behavior change based on analyzing their data. (3) People expected the product to adapt to users in relation to their changing needs and goals.

In general, our study participants expected that the product would offer better adaptation and personalization to their individual needs. For example, one of the participants was initially motivated to use the product. However, she became bored over time, exclaiming that the product was just like a parrot, showing her the data exactly as it was recorded. Instead, she expected the product to be more adaptive and interpretive, to intervene by presenting additional information to the recorded data. Our participants described how personalization is important for interactive products, because personalized interaction strengthens the feeling of ownership of the product and inspires extended use.

Personalized data takes the form of tailored offerings from a service provider to its customers. Products and services are customized relative to the knowledge provided by customers to best fit their needs [25, 26]. Personalized technology can in this way have a persuasive effect on customer, for example by offering personalized messages to improve their well-being [27].

Future physical activity tracking products could go beyond the simple display of information to include personalized prompts for individual users or case-specific solutions. They could represent a person's ideal self in terms of who they want to be, satisfy them emotionally, and prevent them from becoming bored with using the product. They could offer features that people can customize to their personal needs and taste. By understanding the specific user, the product needs to adopt itself to user expectations. For example, tracking whether a purchase was shipped to the customer herself or to someone else might better be tailored Amazon's recommendations. In this way, a product can analyze personal data and make suggestions accordingly.

Personalization cannot be entirely product-driven; it should be a combination of user input and approximations made by the product. For example, a personalized product could be a transition to being a personal coach or helper, where the product coordinates with the user to improve their quality of life.

Curiosity. The third characteristic is curiosity, which we define as "the desire to learn about and keep interest in product data." Our data revealed several important issues related to curiosity: (1) At first, learning about something that people don't know about makes them curious. For example, seeing sleep data at the beginning of the study was novel and people described their curiosity to make sense of this data. (2) A person's curiosity can be satisfied by having instant access to their data. (3) As people understand their data, the process of accessing it becomes more repetitive. They need suggestions about how to break the monotony, which results in decreased curiosity about their data.

In our study, we saw that some of our participants' curiosity decreased over time. We reasoned that this was partly due to the static information displayed by the product. For instance, one of the participants stated that she was curious to interact with her new product at the beginning of the study, but after a while she felt less motivated to interact with the product when the data became more repetitive. She hoped that future versions of the product would be more interactive and offer ways to sustain curiosity. She expected the product to describe "what the data means" and "what it represents". We interpreted this to mean that a product's functionality is highly related a user's curiosity and that adaptability of a product can greatly enhance curiosity and engagement.

We also learned that product breakdowns can negatively affect curiosity and therefore engagement. For example, one participant was curious about her data when doing yoga, yet another was curious about his data when he was walking from home to campus. In both cases, the product was expected to be always readily accessible to address any desire to fulfill one's curiosity. These examples show that curiosity is important in the early stages of product use; when curiosity is satisfied during the early stages of product use, sustained engagement with the product is more likely to occur. Curiosity might also be sustained over time, for example through prompts and suggestions about the user experience of the product and the change in the user results.

Keeping people curious depends highly on the dynamism of their actions. As a very basic example, people feel curious when they start reading a very fascinating novel. The trigger of curiosity is the answer to the question of "what comes next?" [28]. Thus, curiosity is not simply a one-time phenomenon, but instead unfolds over time. In the literature, curiosity is defined as the *"provocative and intentional behaviors"* that people elicit in response to any activity with inherently novel and uncertain properties [29]. Other literature has described curiosity as having *"an appetite for information"* [30]. Curiosity is a very strong feeling that makes people feel enthusiastic about learning something that is unknown. As we now live in a world where a proliferation of products can collect and make a variety of dynamic information about an individual available at any time, it is possible to create curiosity over time and therefore support engagement over time.

To sustain curiosity, products should offer dynamic views of data and allow the data to be easily accessed on demand. Designers of interactive products should facilitate constant and easy updates for the data over time. In addition, the product should provide incentives and content to sustain curiosity.

Motivation. The final characteristic is motivation, which we define as "the product's ability to stimulate people's interest in order to make them continually interested in using the product for reaching a specific a goal."

Our data revealed some important findings about motivation: (1) Participants expected the product to prompt the user to motivate them to do more physical activity. However, when it did, they were disappointed to see only information displayed, rather than a motivational message. Simply looking at the data was not motivating. (2) In order to stay motivated, participants wanted to see more than a record of their activity. (3) If data is inaccessible, or the product is offline, it affects motivation negatively. (4) Positive feedback about one's behavior seems to sustain motivation and product use.

Some of our participants said that the products used in the study did not motivate them at all. They related this lack of motivation to the way that they interacted with the product. They wanted to be prompted with new behavioral suggestions and goals; instead, the products simply presented information about their activities and sleep patterns. Therefore, they lost motivation. Some participants desired for the product to give them suggestions for new physical activities based on an analysis of their daily activities, calories burned and calories eaten. For others, receiving notifications about progress and rewards for the good progress were found to be motivating. If data were inaccessible, or there were problems in interacting with the product, it negatively affected motivation. Collectively, these findings indicate that motivation is an important aspect of engaging experience with interactive products, because it affects how people use the product and can ultimately affect whether and how people change their behavior.

Motivation influences the way people behave [31]. This behavior indicates "...how hard people are willing to try and how much effort they are planning to exert in order to perform the behavior [32]". Motivation also plays a vital role in changing both attitude and behavior [33]. It can be an individual process, but often it is evaluated in terms of external outcomes. Social Cognitive Theory [31] describes the process by which people affect their behavior by evaluating outcomes. The theory defines a motivational process in which people affect their behaviors by self-evaluation of outcome behaviors. The Theory of Reasoned action [34] also defines motivation as a prominent factor in one's behavior. When people are motivated and appreciate the outcome of the behavior, the behaviors are more likely to change. Setting an intention, articulating a goal, making progress towards that goal, and achieving the goal are all interrelated and connected to motivation [34]. If a goal is perceived to be valuable for one's self, people will more readily change their behavior by doing something new and continuing to do it [35, 36]. Thus, without the desire and intention to change one's behavior actually carrying through a plan will be difficult.

Technology can be designed to persuade people to increase their motivation and to trigger a certain behavior [37]. When human abilities are enhanced with aspects of technology, human behavior is more likely to change [37]. By looking at how technology can positively increase motivation, new challenges are revealed for product developers. Researchers are striving to understand how products might be adapted as user interactions are streamlined, people change their behavior, and learn things about themselves.

One potential drawback of products that motivate people is that they run the risk of misleading users by asking them to work towards goals that they can't achieve. This can lead people to stop using the product when the goals are unattainable. By giving motivating, but not unrealistic messages, an interactive product has the potential to provide an engaging experience. Otherwise, interest in the product will wear off, and users will likely abandon it.

4   Conclusion

Developments in technology contribute to the success or failure of interactive products and products. Yet many of these products and products are abandoned after a short time, and fail to help people realize their goals in using the product. In this paper, we explored how to offer engaging experience in interactive product use by helping to create products that inspire curiosity, motivate people, and adapt to their individual needs and changes in goals over time. With this research agenda, we hope to explore how to better design products to offer engaging experience and to improve people's lives.

In the study, we found two product-related (connectivity and personalization) and two behavioral qualities (curiosity and motivation) that led to extended use of the product and contributed to engaging experience. Some of the participants described merely having the device as a motivating factor. Others expected the product motivate them to do more physical activity through prompts and other motivational messages. They were disappointed in the pure information display. People liked the ability to see data instantly; they found it to be motivating and the availability of data in turn affected their curiosity. When product and data could be connected to a desktop computer, it positively affected people's motivation and curiosity. It provided a means of comparing one's data over time and to other users. This also prompted suggestions about tailoring to personal needs.

We believe that the dimensions will be stronger when we are able to observe product use over time. For this reason, interaction with other information resources such as GPS, personal health records, knowledge on types of exercise and benefits, cause-effect relationships etc. is required so as to allow the user to personalize all the aspects of the system. Other concerns are also critical, such as integrating information coming from other resources, or integrating information and data related to health-related concerns. These will ensure prolonged usage, as people will believe that the system is "really" useful to them.

References

1. Fujiki, Y., Kazakos, K., Puri, C., Buddharaju, P., Pavlidis, I., Levine, J.: NEAT-o-games: blending physical activity and fun in the daily routine. Comput. Entertain. 6(2), 1–22 (2008)
2. Consolvo, S., Everitt, K., Smith, I., Landay, J.A.: Design requirements for technologies that encourage physical activity. In: Proceedings of the SIGCHI Conference on Human Factors in Computing Systems, Montreal, Quebec, Canada, ACM (2006)
3. Consolvo, S., Klasnja, P., McDonald, D.W., Avrahami, D., Froehlich, J., LeGrand, L., Libby, R., Mosher, K., Landay, J.A.: Flowers or a robot army? Encouraging awareness and activity with personal, mobile displays. In: Proceedings of the 10th International Conference on Ubiquitous Computing, Seoul, Korea, ACM (2008)
4. Consolvo, S., McDonald, D.W., Toscos, T., Chen, M.Y., Froehlich, J., Harrison, B., Klasnja, P., LaMarca, A., LeGrand, L., Libby, R., Smith, I., Landay, J.A.: Activity sensing in the wild: a field trial of ubifit garden. In: Proceedings of the Twenty-sixth Annual SIGCHI Conference on Human Factors in Computing Systems, Florence, Italy, ACM (2008)
5. Lin, J.J., Mamykina, L., Lindtner, S., Delojoux, G., Strub, H.B.: Fish 'n' Steps: encouraging physical activity with interactive computer game. In: Proceedings of the UbiComp 2006, Orange County, CA, USA (2006)
6. Arteaga, S.M., Kudeki, M., Woodworth, A., Kurniawan, S.: Mobile system to motivate teenagers' physical activity. In: Proceedings of the 9th International Conference on Interaction Design and Children, Barcelona, Spain, ACM (2010)
7. Ahtinen, A., Isomursu, M., Huhtala, Y., Kaasinen, J., Salminen, J., Häkkilä, J.: Tracking outdoor sports – user experience perspective. In: Aarts, E., Crowley, J.L., de Ruyter, B., Gerhäuser, H., Pflaum, A., Schmidt, J., Wichert, R. (eds.) AmI 2008. LNCS, vol. 5355, pp. 192–209. Springer, Heidelberg (2008)
8. Fialho, A.T.S., Van den Heuvel, H., Shahab, Q., Liu, Q., Li, L., Saini, P., Lacroix, J., Markopoulos, P.: ActiveShare: sharing challenges to increase physical activities. In: Proceedings of the 27th International Conference Extended Abstracts on Human Factors in Computing Systems, Boston, MA, USA, ACM (2009)
9. Forlizzi, J., Disalvo, C., Hanington, B.: On the relationship between emotion, experience and the design of new products. Des. J. 6(2), 29–38 (2003)

10. Klasnja, P., Consolvo, S., Pratt, W.: How to evaluate technologies for health behavior change in HCI research. In: Proceedings of the 2011 Annual Conference on Human Factors in Computing Systems, Vancouver, BC, Canada, ACM (2011)
11. Overbeeke, K., Djajadiningrat, T., Hummels, C., Wensveen, S., Frens, J.: Let's make things engaging. Funology, pp. 7–17. Kluwer Academic Publishers, Norwell (2004)
12. O'Brien, H.L., Toms, E.G.: What is user engagement? A conceptual framework for defining user engagement with technology. J. Am. Soc. Inf. Sci. Technol. **59**(6), 938–955 (2008)
13. Chou, C.-J., Conley, C.: Engaging experience: a new perspective of user experience with physical products. In: Kurosu, M. (ed.) HCD 2009. LNCS, vol. 5619, pp. 31–40. Springer, Heidelberg (2009)
14. Csikszentmihalyi, M.: Flow: The Psychology of Optimal Experience. Harper and Row, New York (1990)
15. Csikszentmihalyi, M., Csikszentmihalyi, I.: Introduction to Part IV. Cambridge University Press, Cambridge (1988)
16. Chou, C.-J., Conley, C.: Identifying products that enable engaging experiences: searching cases for theory development. Paper presented at the International Association of Societies of Design Research, Seoul, South Korea (2009)
17. Rafaeli, A., Vilnai-Yavetz, I.: Instrumentality, aesthetics and symbolism of physical artifacts as triggers of emotion. Theor. Issues Ergon. Sci. **5**(1), 91–112 (2004)
18. Forlizzi, J.: The product ecology: understanding social product use and supporting design culture. Int. J. Des. **2**(1), 11–20 (2008)
19. Consolvo, S., McDonald, D.W., Landay, J.A.: Theory-driven design strategies for technologies that support behavior change in everyday life. In: Proceedings of the 27th International Conference on Human Factors in Computing Systems, Boston, MA, USA, ACM (2009)
20. Consolvo, S., Klasnja, P., McDonald, D.W., Landay, J.A.: Goal-setting considerations for persuasive technologies that encourage physical activity. In: Proceedings of the 4th International Conference on Persuasive Technology, Claremont, California, ACM (2009)
21. Strauss, A.L., Corbin, J.: Basics of Qualitative Research. Sage Publications, London (1990)
22. Abowd, G.D., Dey, A.K.: Towards a better understanding of context and context-awareness. In: Gellersen, H.-W. (ed.) HUC 1999. LNCS, vol. 1707, pp. 304–307. Springer, Heidelberg (1999)
23. Baldauf, M., Dustdar, S., Rosenberg, F.: A survey on context-aware systems. Int. J. Ad Hoc Ubiquitous Comput. **2**(4), 263–277 (2007)
24. Blom, J.: Personalization: a taxonomy. In: Proceedings of the CHI 2000 Extended Abstracts on Human Factors in Computing Systems, The Hague, The Netherlands, ACM (2000)
25. Adomavicius, G., Tuzhilin, A.: Personalization technologies: a process-oriented perspective. Commun. ACM **48**(10), 83–90 (2005)
26. Ashman, H., Brailsford, T., Brusilovsky, P.: Personal Services: Debating the Wisdom of Personalisation. Springer, Heidelberg (2009)
27. Berkovsky, S., Freyne, J., Oinas-Kukkonen, H.: Influencing individually: fusing personalization and persuasion. ACM Trans. Interac. Intell. Syst. (TiiS) **2**(2), 9 (2012)
28. Roth, C., Vorderer, P., Klimmt, C.: The motivational appeal of interactive storytelling: towards a dimensional model of the user experience. In: Iurgel, I.A., Zagalo, N., Petta, P. (eds.) ICIDS 2009. LNCS, vol. 5915, pp. 38–43. Springer, Heidelberg (2009)
29. Kashdan, T.B., Rose, P., Fincham, F.D.: Curiosity and exploration: facilitating positive subjective experiences and personal growth opportunities. J. Pers. Assess. **82**(3), 291–305 (2004)
30. Loewenstein, G.: The psychology of curiosity: a review and reinterpretation. Psychol. Bull. **116**(1), 75 (1994)

31. Bandura, A.: Social cognitive theory: an agentic perspective. Asian J. Soc. Psychol. **2**(1), 21–41 (1999)
32. Fogg, B.: Persuasive Technology: Using Computers to Change what We Think and Do. ACM, New York (2002)
33. Petty, R.E., Cacioppo, J.T.: The elaboration likelihood model of persuasion. Adv. Consum. Res. **11**(1), 673–675 (1984)
34. Fishbein, M., Ajzen, I.: Beliefs, attitudes, intentions and behaviour: an introduction to theory and research. Addison-Wesley, Reading (1972)
35. Fishbein, M., Ajzen, I.: Predicting and Changing Behavior : The Reasoned Action Approach. Psychology Press, New York (2005)
36. Bandura, A.: Social cognitive theory: an agentic perspective. Annu. Rev. Psychol. **52**(1), 1–26 (2001)
37. Fogg, B.: A behavior model for persuasive design. In: Proceedings of the 4th international Conference on Persuasive Technology, Claremont, California, USA, ACM (2009)

Personal Museum

A New Museum that Focus on Emotional Relationship Between People and Belongings

Lei Guo[1(✉)], Yipei Shen[2], Shiqiang Yang[1], and Huanbo Luan[1]

[1] Department of Computer Science and Technology, Tsinghua University,
Beijing, China
{millifrog, luanhuanbo}@gmail.com,
yangshq@mail.tsinghua.edu.cn
[2] Academy of Arts and Design, Tsinghua University, Beijing, China
sypl3@mails.tsinghua.edu.cn

Abstract. As human skills of creating and crafting improved rapidly, human and material civilization has developed, thus the man-made objects become the record of the development of human capacity of creating. The museum is an institution that demonstrates such a process. We propose the concept of a novel personal museum in this paper. Different from a traditional museum, a personal museum not only shows personal belongings but also combines personal experiences and emotions with the objects. Apart from time dimension of life, other dimensions of life will be kept in the personal museum forever, thus each person will feel his or her existence and value in the world through this personal museum. The paper contains introduction, methodology, design and insights from user study under this research topic.

Keywords: Human-computer interaction · Emotional memories · Digital museum · Human-objects relationships · Belongings

1 Introduction

Before the birth of human beings, there was no artifacts exist in the world. The appearance of artifacts comes along with the emergence of human beings. Moreover, the development of material civilization has a synchronized pace with the human civilization. As an intellectual creature, the human continue to improve their skills of creating and crafting, thus the man-made objects become the record of the development of human capacity of creating. Before the Industrial Revolution, the development of human creation was at an early stage with a steady slow growth, most of the making demands were driven by survival needs, the emotional relationships between human and objects were long-lasting and simple.

The Industrial Revolution dramatically increased the availability of consumer goods, the manufacturing demands were not only from survival, but also from capital and spiritual needs. The advent of the department store represented a paradigm shift in the

A. Marcus (Ed.): DUXU 2015, Part I, LNCS 9186, pp. 502–512, 2015.
DOI: 10.1007/978-3-319-20886-2_47

experience of shopping. For the first time, customers could buy an astonishing variety of goods, all in one place, and shopping became a popular leisure activity. While previously the norm had been the scarcity of resources, the Industrial era created an unprecedented economic situation. For the first time in history products were available in outstanding quantities, at outstandingly low prices. And the newly emerged e-commerce makes products available to virtually everyone. Various personal items have different function and characteristics, recording its owner's stories, experiences and memories; hence they gradually formed emotional connection with their owner. However, this human—object relationship allows people to scatter emotions and memories on different belongings, thus belongings lost or obsoleted would bring people the loss of emotion and memory.

Museum is institution that cares for a collection of artifacts and other objects of scientific, artistic, cultural, or historical importance and makes them available for public viewing through exhibits that may be permanent or temporary. Throughout the history of museum, the museum development is closely tied with the human civilization. Before the Industrial Revolution, the human's awareness of museum was in its infancy, while there were only a few museums with several types all over the world. After the Industrial Revolution, the museum amount and types increase rapidly, but most of the museums are traditional public museums, only a small number of museums are specific on keeping ordinary people's personal history.

The vigorous development of the Internet has promoted popular culture onto a new stage. Public awareness of self-expression and civic participation has been improved. Internet allows ordinary people to generate their own contents and spread it all over the world. By sharing and social interaction, people influence each other, gaining encouragement and inspiration. The use of mobile Internet gives an additional boost to the use of Social Media, making information sharing and spreading faster and more convenient. In KPCB analyst Mary Meeker's annual Internet Trends report states that all internet-connected citizens share over 1.8 billion photos each day in 2014 [1].

The rest of the paper is organized as follows: the next section we list other related works. The third section summarizes our user research of active users who share their belongings regularly. Following that, we present the two other contributions of this paper. The first is Wu Personal Museum, a novel form of virtual museum for recording and displaying personal belongings and the related stories that was designed based on findings from the qualitative user research. The second contribution is a MVP (Minimum Viable Product) test of this design and the lessons we learned. The user study demonstrates that Wù Personal Museum supports users to record their belongings, enables users to display their memory and emotion linking to the belongings, and encourages users to get emotional consolation and resonance from their records and social interaction.

2   Related Works

2.1   Online Virtual Museum

Online virtual museum is a digital entity that draws on the characteristics of a museum, in order to complement, enhance, or augment the museum experience through personalization, interactivity and richness of content. Most physical museums now have an online presence. These online museums provide simple background information, a list of exhibitions, and the photo of the collections in their exist museums with multimedia, searchable or browsable features. It is a simple mirror of physical museums.

2.2   Nice

Nice is an app that told story of the picture. It allows people to see into the lives of people all over the world. Snap a picture from any moment of life and add a sticker to personalize photo. Use photo tagging feature to tell a story within picture. The picture people snap or tag can related everything, such as people's favorite brands, places, and activities! So the needs of users is very different from each other, and the pictures shows to us is very different. It focus on tag, and tag is more useful to displayed the brands, people's name, place, but not suitable to tell story. The purpose of Nice is more about content consumption, rather than a precipitate emotion, what we think is very important to people, and hope to people to obtain more.

3   Methodology

We were interested to explore the attitudes of people towards various ways of keeping and sharing their belongings, which could be valuable reference and inspiration for our personal museum. To better understand this new form of personal museum, we conducted a series of design research including (1) desktop research and social network immersion to gather basic information and real user sharing (2) a questionnaire study involving 80 active users to share their views and behaviors about keeping belongings; and (3) follow-up semi-structured in-depth interviews with 9 representative users to further study the emotional relationship behind their private belongings and personal story.

We investigated more than 30 online forums and mobile Apps and then chose 2 social networks to conduct our user observation: the Douban and the Weibo. Douban is a Chinese social networking service that offers "lifestyle and culture" products and services for urbanites and college students. Weibo is a Chinese microblogging website. Akin to a hybrid of Twitter and Facebook, it is one of the most popular sites in China, in use by well over 30 % of Internet users, with a market penetration similar to the United States' Twitter. In Douban, the user group *Fetishism* had 12716 group members with approximately 2000 posts. While in Weibo, the hashtag *Do Not Want To Throw Away Old Belongings* had 3.2 billion reads, 13 thousands discussions and 1400 fans. People shared their personal belongings and commented with each other actively in these 2 topic groups. We immersed into these 2 topic groups and interacted with users.

The first author registered on Douban and Weibo and started by posting her own belonging stories under the topic groups. Her post got active responses from the members, thus triggered social interactions, both within and out of the post. She also posted a recruitment message under the topic groups, which disclosed our intention of conducting user research about personal museum, as well as her WeChat information for further contact. Based on the impressions gained from observations and social interactions in the groups, we got basic findings of people disposing belongings as well as actively reached out for more members who appeared active and interesting for questionnaires and interviews. Among these members, we conducted 80 questionnaires and from which we picked out 9 members as our in-depth interviews.

The aim of questionnaire was not to get a quantitative data but to better understand the qualitative basic information of users and their relationship between their belongings. In the questionnaire, we collected the primary information about the people's attitudes towards old belongings, belongings disposing methods and willingness of sharing story behind their belongings. In addition, we were filtering out the proper in-depth interviewees. Details about our in-depth interview participants are shown in Table 1. In in-depth interview, we asked about the details of how they had first started capturing their belongings, sharing the story about this item, how specifically they interacted with the people who interested and left comments with their sharing. When some valuable view points came up, we followed up for further details and concrete examples. Interviews were conducted via WeChat App which is available for live video and audio chat and photo transferring. All interviews were conducted in Mandarin, audio or text recorded, and were later transcribed into Chinese.

Table 1. In-depth interview participants' information

Name	Age	Gender	Job	IP	Location	LH
Xun	23	F	Student	37	Hangzhou, Zhejiang	N
Mengxin	23	F	Student	31	Mianyang, Sichuan	Y
Lee	32	M	Manager	29	Wuhan, Hubei	N
Huizhong	24	F	Student	27	Haidian, Beijing	N
Xuanchen	28	M	Employee	22	Xicheng, Beijing	Y
Zhirong	24	M	Employee	22	Haidian, Beijing	N
Ann	28	F	Manager	21	Shenzhen, Guangdong	N
Jun	27	F	Employee	20	Haidian, Beijing	N
Alex	34	M	Manager	19	Dongcheng, Beijing	N
Zhi	27	M	Employee	19	Haidian, Beijing	N
Lianlun	23	M	Student	19	Hexi, Tianjin	N
Jing	27	F	Employee	19	Pudong, Shanghai	N
Danni	20	F	Student	18	Nanjing, Jiangsu	N
Heli	22	F	Student	16	Qinghuangdao, Hebei	Y
Meng	31	F	Employee	15	Changping, Beijing	Y
Lei	26	F	Student	15	Chengdum, Sichuan	Y
Chao	28	M	Employee	13	Baoshan, Shanghai	N
Qinyi	33	M	Manager	13	Chongqing, Sichuan	N
Pingping	29	F	Employee	11	Putian, Fujian	Y
Jia	29	M	Employee	9	Xianyang, Shannxi	Y

*LH, Currently Living In Hometown
*IP, Photos Show Belongings In 3 Months In His/Her Mobile Phone

4 Findings

Our research participants represent a small percentage of the population in China. Nonetheless, for this particular user group, recording and sharing their emotional memories with belongings has become their very important regulation. Thus these users can be targeted ass the typical user for us to research and gain findings for our further design.

4.1 Personal Belongings as a Record of Life Trajectory

Emotional memory has strong relation with physical memory. In our research, the people who moved out of their hometowns take childhood belongings as the token of remembering the hometown and old times. In addition, when experiencing their lives' "big moment", they usually kept an object as the monuments, such as a trophy, a wedding photo or the first fallen teeth. Therefore, those important monuments composed their lives' trajectory or atlas.

4.2 Belonging-Related Record Behaviour Is Triggered by Emotion

People interact with lots of goods everyday, only a few are important enough to be recorded or documented, so as the memorable people and experience. Moreover, to record these things are trivial and hard to remember. Most of the participants told us, the very moment they came up with recording important things was touched by something when doing housekeeping or at the emotional climax. We argue that the recording behaviour is triggered by emotion and we need to lower the threshold of enabling user to record the moment.

4.3 People Share Belongings to Seek Emotional Consolation and Resonance

Once wrote a story about their belongings, the people are aim at writing down the details of the feeling or the story. They wanted to keep the emotional memories. Some of them just wanted to keep the memories in their deeper heart, but if anyone who wanted to share the story, they were seeking to make the story listened by others. Moreover, if there were feedback from the audience, they would feel happier and accepted by others.

5 The Design of Personal Museum

Our design research helped us define a set of user-driven design goals for a personal museum to record human-object emotion. These goals include: (1) be easy and friendly to use, facilitating item and emotion recording, collecting and sharing, (2) focusing on user-generated content with proper management view, (3) encouraging item-based social interaction to enhance emotional resonance. Based on existing research of online virtual public museum and picture-based interests social network, to provide a better user experience, we decided to utilize mobile device in our design. We thereby created Wù Personal Museum, a mobile phone app supports users to record their belongings with least effort and more useful information, display their memory and emotion linking to the belonging, and get emotional consolation and resonance from their records and social interaction.

5.1 Record the Owner-Belonging's Emotion Information and Relationship

Wù Personal Museum supports user to record emotional information of belongings, simplifies user process of recording information. When taking a photo, users can give tags and description, choose different types of filters to beautify the photo and better express the emotions related to the item. Meanwhile, users can set specific time and location of the item as the start point of the item's virtual life tree, after that, they can keep logging the item's latest status to expand its lifeline. With image recognition technique, key features of the item would be extracted to help the system make recommendation. While other users log the same or similar item, they will be shown up in the item page. By correlating the relevant people who own the same or similar item, more stories and emotion would be expressed and shared. When the item is added into a museum, people can give their like and comments to this item. In such organization form, the item is no longer a stand-alone object, but strongly linked to its product family, owner groups and specific time with the string of emotional proximity (Fig. 1).

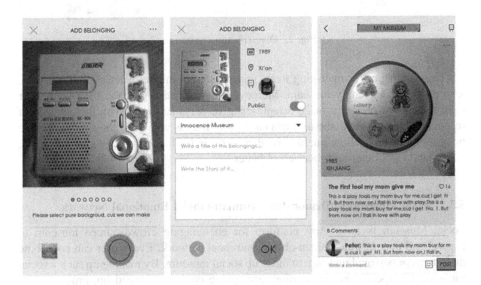

Fig. 1. Belongings emotional information

5.2   Varied Museum to Present Personal Style

Wù Personal Museum provides 2 layouts for user to manage and view their belonging collection. In timeline layout, the items are displayed in chronological order. By swiping upward and downward, the user can review his or her life trajectory by the items. For instance, once the user adds his or her textbooks into Wù Personal Museum, a museum named "My Student Life" would be set up to display the user's primary school, middle school and high school. In Sudoku (3 × 3 grid) layout, users can show their style and taste directly along with the items' appearance and emotional tones (Fig. 2).

Fig. 2.   Diversification museum

This is a better for managing items under different themes, such as doll museum, love museum and family museum. Moreover, the users can pick out their favorite or most meaningful items to make a representative personal page. With the advance of recommendation system, the user can easily find friends who have the similar life line or taste. With this fellow-interaction, they can establish friendship with same topic, understand each other and themselves better.

5.3   Social Museum to Demonstrate Human-Obejct Emotional Network

Social Museum is an in-App platform for encouraging crowdsourced museum to expand and demonstrate human-object emotional network. Every user can contribute their items or personal museum to make up social museum. By making up such a social museum, the specific emotion-driven user group could be formed up, providing the possibility of emotional consolation and resonance. For example, when a user propose a game console museum of 1990s, other users who have recorded the eligible item can add their game consoles and emotional memory into this crowdsourced museum, everybody can visit this museum and leave comments. The visitor will not only read the stories about the items but get to know about the owners who have such a special memory (Fig. 3).

Fig. 3. Social museum

6   User Study by MVP Testing

To evaluate the value of our design, we conducted a first- use study of Wù Personal Museum (WPM). In particular, we were interested in validating that: (1) WPM supports users to record their belongings with least effort and more useful information, (2) WPM enables users to display their memory and emotion linking to the belonging, and (3) WPM encourages users to get emotional consolation and resonance from their records and social interaction.

We use MVP(Minimum Viable Product) to test our design. In this MVP, the user can take photos with enhanced filter, text note, hashtag and location label, manage and view belongings in Sudoku or timeline layout, share their own belongings and comment on the others' item. We sent the MVP to the 20 in-depth interviews, asking them to choose 9 belongings and shot 1 photo for each of them. In addition, they were required to mark out a favorite item and write the story behind this item. Meanwhile, we observed their operating process and asked them to say whatever they are looking at, thinking, doing, and feeling as they go about their tasks when using the MVP. We gathered their feedback and synthesized the insights (Fig. 4).

Fig. 4. MVP testing result

7   Discussion

Our user study insights have illustrated a rich picture of how users record their emotional link with their belongings through our personal museum. While users use this app for various purposes and indeed received more or less emotional resonance, the benefit of this emotional communication channel is still need to explore. In this section, we will discuss the insights and reflections of this novel personal museum.

7.1 Human-Computer Interaction Technology Enhances the Human-Object Emotional Relationship

In old times, it was not easy to capture an object or a moment by using multimedia. With the advance of HCI technology and smartphone, people can shot a photo or video, write notes and share the very moment instantly. Therefore, by using Wu Personal Museum, the threshold of recording human-object emotional memory has been much lowered which provides more possibilities for human interacting with the objects. As a result, the quantity, quality and frequency of human Human-Object emotional interaction are all improved with help of HCI Technology. The human's attitude towards objects would also be changed with the development of HCI technology.

7.2 Abstract Emotion Becomes Tangible and Trackable on Objects

Emotion itself is abstract and intangible, and can only be felt by people via human interactions or pathetic affordance. By recording, visualizing and keeping human-object emotional memories, the emotion is embodied with the object and can develop with the object. In addition, with the form of a belonging-related photo, the memory can be brought with the owner and being recalled anytime. When looking at the photo captioned with user's note, the owner and the audience can feel the relationship between human and object.

7.3 Personal History Should not be Ignored

In human history, the ordinary people's personal history is an important branch with lots of under-discovered value and ignored status. Typically, building a public museum cost much social resource which make it mainly focus on displaying public history relic, while a dedicated personal museum is too expensive for ordinary people. The virtual personal museum with advantage of low cost, friendly use and easy spread could be a very promising exploring for documenting the personal history and fulfill the human history database. The Wu Personal Museum is just a primary trying and there are lots of possibilities for other researchers and practitioners to explore.

8 Conclusion and Future Study

This paper makes three contributions. First, we described a design research of investigating the attitudes of people towards various ways of keeping and sharing their belongings. Second, we described Wu Personal Museum, a mobile phone app supports users to record their belongings with least effort and more useful information, display their memory and emotion linking to the belonging, and get emotional consolation and resonance from their records and social interaction. As a result, it lowers the threshold for recording and sharing human-object emotional memories and encourages social interaction driven by the emotional memories. Finally, we presented insights from a MVP test study of Wu Personal Museum.

We plan to iterate Wu Personal Museum so it will be suitable for use wider range of users, including the elder citizens. This includes improving Wu Personal Museum's user interface through responsive design adapted to multiple devices, as well as more simple and intuitive workflow to suit user's mind model. We intend to further evaluate Wu Personal Museum's strengths and limitations in recording and sharing human-object emotional memories. We also plan to conduct a longitudinal study in both research and educational settings.

Acknowledgements. We would like to thank the study participants for their valuable time and insights. We also acknowledge Pro. Zhiyong Fu and Pro. Yingqing Xu for their advice to our work.

References

1. Mary Meeker's Annual Internet Trends Report (2014). http://www.kpcb.com/internet-trends
2. Alexander, E.P., Alexander, M.: Museums in Motion: An Introduction to the History and Functions of Museums. Rowman & Littlefield, Plymouth (2008)
3. Conn, S.: Museums and American Intellectual Life, 1876-1926. University of Chicago Press, Chicago (1998)
4. Bennett, T.: The Birth of the Museum. Routledge Press, New York (1995)
5. Butcher-Younghans, S.: Historic House Museums: A Practical Handbook for Their Care, Preservation, and Management, p. i, 1, 5. Oxford University Press, New York (1993)
6. Hobbs, S.D.: Exhibiting antimodernism: history, memory, and the aestheticized past in mid-twentieth century America. The Public Historian **23**, 39–61 (2001)
7. Williams, P.: Memorial Museums: the Global Rush to Commemorate Atrocities, pp. 8, 20–21. Berg, Oxford (2007)
8. Bowen, J.P.: A brief history of early museums online. Rutherford Journal **3** (2010)
9. Schweibenz, W.: The Development of Virtual Museums. ICOMNEWS (2004)
10. Wright, R.: A Short History of Progress. Anansi, Toronto (2004)
11. British Museum. http://www.britishmuseum.org/
12. Usher, A.P.: An Introduction to the Industrial History of England. University of Michigan Press, Ann Arbor (1920)
13. Snooks, G.D.: Was the Industrial Revolution Necessary? Routledge, London (2000)
14. Smelser, N.J.: Social Change in the Industrial Revolution: An Application of Theory to the British Cotton Industry. University of Chicago Press, Chicago (1959)
15. De Bono, E.: Eureka! An Illustrated History of Inventions from the Wheel to the Computer. Thames & Hudson, London (1974)
16. Platt, R.: Eureka!: Great Inventions and How They Happened. Kingfisher, London (2003)
17. The Four Great Inventions. (2007). http://www.China.org.cn
18. Brown, T.A.: Human evolution: stranger from Siberia. Nature **464**, 838–839 (2010)
19. DeSalle, R., Tattersall, I.: Human origins: What Bones and Genomes Tell us About Ourselves, p. 146. Texas A&M University Press, College Station (2008). ISBN 978-1-58544-567-7
20. Mellars, P.: Why did modern human populations disperse from Africa ca. 60,000 years ago? Proc. Natl. Acad. Sci. **103**(25), 9381 (2006)

The Marriage Machine: Mobile Persuasion/Behavior Change

Aaron Marcus[(⊠)]

Aaron Marcus and Associates, 1196 Euclid Avenue, Berkeley, CA 94708, USA
Aaron.Marcus@AMandA.com

Abstract. The author's firm undertook the Marriage Machine project aimed to persuade couples to open themselves up towards techniques of daily practice and interaction with their partners, with the objective of making their relationships with each other deeper, more enjoyable, more personally enriching, and educational. In a user-centered design process, we planned, researched, analyzed, designed, implemented (sample screens), evaluated, documented, and prepared training documents for a mobile phone application conceptual prototype. The Marriage Machine combines marriage/bonding theories with information design/visualization and persuasion design. This paper explains the development of the Marriage Machine's user-experience design. A more complete description appears in [22].

Keywords: Bonding · Couples · Culture · Dashboard · Design · Development · Emotion · Experience · Incentives · Information · Interface · Marriage · Mobile · Persona · Persuasion · Social · Scenario · User

1 Introduction

Marriage is a significant component of all cultures. Despite the abundance of marriage theories and training oriented to turning theory into practice, people often fail to adhere to principles due to increasing economic, social, and political pressures and consequent stress. In the US, 37.5 % of the US population between 15 years and older are married, according to [2]. More importantly, 11.7 % of the population are separated or divorced, according to [3]. By combining information design and persuasion/motivation theory, with a particular focus on the works of Maslow's theory of basic human needs [24] and Fogg's theory of persuasion [6, 7], the use of the Marriage Machine could prompt couples to change their behavior to make relationships with each other more enjoyable and personally enriching. The success and effectiveness of the described approach, *i.e.*, the combination of information design with persuasion design in order to promote behavioral change of mobile application users, has already been studied and realized in several previous projects of the author's company: the Green Machine [23], the Health Machine [12], the Money Machine [13], the Story Machine [14], the Innovation Machine [15], the Driving Machine [16], the Learning Machine [17], the Travel Machine [18], the Happiness Machine [19], and the Marriage Machine [21]. All of the past Machine projects rely on the conceptual design of an application through a user-centered user-experience development-process, as defined and explained below.

© Springer International Publishing Switzerland 2015
A. Marcus (Ed.): DUXU 2015, Part I, LNCS 9186, pp. 513–523, 2015.
DOI: 10.1007/978-3-319-20886-2_48

2 UX Design: User-Centered Design, and Persuasion Theory

User Experience (UX), user-centered design (UCD), use scenarios, and persona concepts/practice are described well by Hartson and Pyla [9]. The science of persuasion in Cialdini [4] concentrates particularly on psychological aspects of persuasion. In alignment with Fogg's research of persuasion [6, 7], we have defined six key steps to achieve behavioral change with requirements for each step:

- Attract user via business marketing
- Increase frequency of using application
- Motivate changing some habits: interaction with and openness towards others, experience and observation of differences, ways of journaling or diary documentation
- Teach how to change habits
- Persuade users to change habits (short-term change)
- Persuade users to change general approach to objectives, people, objects, contexts, obstacles (long-term, or life-style change).

We also drew on Maslow's theory of human needs [24] adapted to the Marriage Machine context: Safety and security is met by the assistance of an advisor and by the provision of obstacles-, fun-, human-contact-, and other-related information and tips. Belonging and love is expressed through friend, family and social sharing, and support. Esteem can be satisfied by social comparisons that display progress and destination expertise, as well as by self-challenges suggested by an advisor that displays goal-accomplishment processes. Self-actualization is fulfilled by being able to follow/retrace continuous progress/advancement in a personal diary.

3 Theoretical Background and Research

Marriage exists in most cultures, but has changed over the centuries. The traditional term refers to a solemn act between a woman and a man, empowered with religious and/or civil legitimacy. Today it also includes couples who may opt for a serious relationship, without gender, legal, and/or religious sanctions. We adopt the latter definition, intending our application for committed couples. Marriage is highly subjective, requiring an interdisciplinary approach to issues, e.g., positive psychology, marriage theory, philosophy of marriage, and emotional design. We examined [1, 5, 8, 10, 11, 25] and developed healthy-marriage principles, insights/design principles:

Principle 1. Enhance Your Love Map: Use periodic marriage checkups. Know each other's objectives, goals, hopes, and worries.

Principle 2. Nurture Fondness and Admiration: Remind users of partner's positive qualities and express fondness and admiration. Enhance users and partner's physiological intimacy. Enhance users and partner's emotional connection.

Principle 3. Turn Toward Each Other: Make "bids" for partner's attention, affection, humor, or support.

Principle 4. Let Your Partner Influence You: Share power and decision-making.

Principle 5. Resolve Conflict: Avoid conflicts. Solve solvable problems.

Principle 6. Create Shared Meaning/Value: Marriages with shared sense of meaning result in less conflicts and decrease likelihood of gridlock.

Principle 7. Cultivate Excitement: Try new and exciting activities together to rekindle feelings.

Insight 1. Marriage Improvement is an Objective: Assist users to achieve specific goals/steps in a "journey through marriage." Directions should be "chunked," so people can easily remember what to do.

Insight 2. Marriage is Discipline, a Constant Reminder to Change Attitude: Remind people to be mindful. Expedite change by helping users to reflect.

Insight 3. Marriage is in a Constant State of Flux: Customize to different users in different life stages. Directions should be adaptable to each user at time of use.

Insight 4. Balancing Engagement and Persuasion is Key: Persuade users to do certain activities with the least friction possible.

Tactics for Marriage Machine: Based on our research, we developed the following measures that could be considered relevant and practical:

- Involvement
- Personalization
- Goal/habit-centered
- Entertainment
- Connectedness
- Accomplishment.

4 Market Research

AM+A did market research with potential customers using graduate marketing students, University of California at Berkeley Extension's International Diploma Program, to know more about people's general usage of smartphones and mobile applications and specifically "relationship behaviors" with them. Market research included secondary, qualitative, and quantitative research. Details appear in [22].

5 Competitive Product Analysis

We compared 10 smartphone applications' screens and customer reviews to derive their benefits/drawbacks. This analysis helped us to develop detailed functions, data, information architecture (metaphors, mental model, and navigation), and look-and-feel (appearance and interaction). Details appear in [22]. Most mobile applications emphasize private connection between the couple. Few if any take a holistic approach to help users realize and achieve success in their relationships.

6 Personas and Scenarios

We used use scenarios for different kinds of marriages functions and personas. Personas were "double personas," rare in UX literature. Our details appear in [22].

7 Information Architecture

The Information Architecture (IA) derived from a model in previous Machines with five primary "modules." We altered details to fit our needs/requirements (Fig. 1).

Dashboard: This landing page provides an overview of the user's behavior change status. The user gets a view of his/her goals and where s/he stands in achieving them.

Roadmap: The Process View module shows a "road map" of the process with details of each objective/goal. The user sees the goal-progress, as well as next steps.

Social Network: Focused, subject-matter-based connections with friends, family, and/or like-minded people sharing similar goals or eager to support others.

Tips/Advice: Provides focused knowledge about a given topic to give users insight into the habits they wish either to get rid of or adopt.

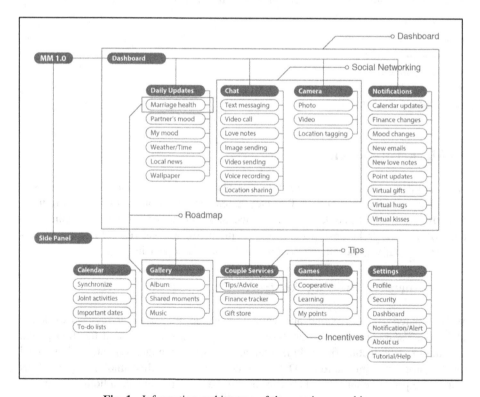

Fig. 1. Information architecture of the marriage machine.

Incentives: Fun-filled, engaging ways to change behavior, e.g., gamification and leaderboards, as powerful tools to motivate users, with virtual of real incentives.

The Marriage Machine groups key components/functions grouped into three "tabs":

Tab 1: Dashboard: The 'homepage' contains the most important information users may need at any time. All of the elements are optional and customizable.

Current Time and Date/Daily Updates: An in-app "news"-source for users:

Marriage health: Depicts the relative "health" of a couple's marriage, 0 % to 100 %, based on an algorithm taking into account finances, frequency of app use, performances on games and quizzes, number of items purchased in the gift store, number of love notes sent, average mood of each partner, and number of virtual kisses/hugs sent. Percentages in the marriage health can stimulate users to discover ways to improve that number, and to proceed in their learning process.

Partner's mood: Allows the user to view his/her partner's mood.

My mood: Allows the user to edit his/her own mood.

Weather/Time/Local News: Displays user's/*partner's* weather, time, and local news.

Shared Wallpaper: User can edit shared wallpaper on their dashboards.

Chat: Supports the following modes of communication:

Text messaging:

- Doodle
- Virtual displays of affection (virtual hugs/kisses)
- Screen Freeze: temporarily "freezes" the partner's screen, such as during a heated argument, forcing the partner to tap on the screen repeatedly until the ice is broken
- Send offline messages
- View availability status.

Video Call: Users can quickly swipe to toggle between text messaging to video calls.

Love Notes: Users can create custom templates by writing/typing/drawing.

Image Sending: Send images from phone to your partner.

Video Sending: Send videos from phone to your partner.

Voice Recording: Send videos from phone to your partner.

Location Sharing: Share your location via GPS.

Camera: Captures and shares marriage moments via beautiful photos and videos.

Notifications: Updates user regarding partner's activities:

- Calendar updates
- Finance changes
- Mood changes
- New emails
- New love notes
- Point updates
- Virtual gifts
- Virtual hugs
- Virtual kisses

Tab 2: Side Panel: Provides access to other functions of the Marriage Machine.

Calendar:

Synchronize: Automatically syncs the user's calendar activities with partner's.

Joint Activities: Just-in-time detection of free time slots, prompting users to engage in joint activities, *e.g.*, dining, entertainment, sports, travel, volunteering.

Important Dates: Just-in-time reminders partner's birthdays, anniversaries, etc.

To-do lists: Multiple lists, with deadline-prompts, for shopping and other tasks that allow the couple to divide chores and signal when finished.

Gallery:

Album:

- Search/save photos/videos in folders with option to title, date, tag, and describe events
- Enable photo upload or download
- Add filters/frames on images
- Create slide show with music.

Shared Moments: Users can "look back" on memories they have shared together, with prompts to create albums after completing joint activities, with categories according to media type, with doodles sent via text messaging, and all other media on Chat.

Music: Send and save music files. Create shared playlists.

Couple Services: The Marriage Machine offers a suite of services designed to help couples in many aspects of their marriage:

Tips/Advice: Provides expert knowledge to couples on ways they can:

- Enhance their love map
- Nurture fondness
- Turn toward each other
- Resolve conflicts
- Create shared meaning
- Cultivate excitement
- Impeocw communication.

Finance Tracker: Users link their credit cards to app to track spending patterns. They can set long-term/short-term objectives and goals, and view metrics to measure these objectives and goals. The app supports just in time functionality to notify users when credit goals/limits are approaching.

Gift Store:

- Purchase gifts from online merchandise store.
- Link to existing online shops (e.g. retail, romantic gifts, music, books, etc.)
- Deliver products in romantic gift wrap
- Create wish lists

- Earn points for discounts
- Just-in-time tip: suggest gifts based on partner's browsing/purchase history, and
- partner's favorites from wish list and preferences.

Games: Games will stimulate/increase users' motivation to create/share marriage moments. For example, the attribution of points to redeem at the gift shop represents a strong incentive and increases use frequency. Games also add fun/play/entertainment.

Cooperative Games: These games are played together in real-time

- Drawing-guessing game: random word generated based on category
- Hangman: user inputs word; partner guesses.

Learning Games: These games are played individually

- Crossword puzzle: decode puzzle made up of info about partner
- Quiz: answer personal questions about partner and his/her family.

My Points: Users can view a scoreboard to check their current points.

- The app supports just-in-time functionality to prompt users to buy virtual gifts when points are sufficient
- Earn points via completed joint activities, to-do lists, love notes, games, virtual hugs/kisses, and finance tracker
- Earn points to buy virtual gifts such as Flowers, Diamond rings, Romantic balloons, Cakes, Teddy bears
- Earn points to upgrade fun interactions and virtual gifts.

Settings:

Profile:

- Edit profile photo
- Input personal data and preferences

Security:

- Change password
- Mobile security for credit card details
- Shared password

Dashboard:

- Change wallpaper
- Location (GPS/Manual)/News
- My mood, Partner's mood
- Weather/Time

Notification/Alert:

- Alert sound/vibrate
- Lock screen alert
- Message alert pop-up
- Message preview

About us:

- Developer info
- Version info

Tutorial/Help:

- Contact us/Feedback
- FAQ/Troubleshooting
- How to use
- Introductory tutorial
- Privacy/security policy
- Terms of service

Tips: Marriage Machine users will be assisted and accompanied by a mobile marriage "advisor." Based on users' characteristics, needs, and preferences; on usage behaviors;

and on the respective usage environment, the advisor provides personalized and tailor-made offers and recommendations.

8   Screen Designs

Based on the information architecture, AM+A prepared initial design sketches of some key screens and, based on internal reviews, revised them (see Fig. 2(a)–(h)).

Fig. 2. (a) and (b) Landing and Side panel menu screen, (c) and (d) Shared Calendar screens, (e)–(h) Chat Love Note screens

Landing Screen: Typifies main menu and app instruction throughout.

Side Panel: Provides primary features. Screens swiped at any time to reveal them.

Shared Calendar: Allows both parties to view partner's schedule. It also acts as a personal assistant by sending date suggestions if both parties are free.

Chat: Besides typical functions, allows user to send customized interactions, such as Love Notes and Virtual Hugs and Virtual Kisses.

9   Usability Testing

We recruited users from the UC Berkeley Extension. In each of three 15-min sessions we explained the test and asked participants to view the Marriage Machine perceptual screens. We asked questions about their impressions of the application's purpose, screen designs, and organization. We gave them navigation tasks to accomplish and asked the participants these follow-up questions: Their overall impression of the Marriage Machine, whether some section(s) seemed confusing whether they would like to use the mobile application, whether they would recommend this app for someone, *and t*heir overall rating of the app.

Participants: All participants were undergraduate students from UC Berkeley Extension. Eight were scheduled over three test sessions. Six completed the test. Of the six participants, three were male and three were female.

Evaluation Tasks/Scenarios: Participants attempted to complete the following tasks:

- *Task 1* Navigating from the dashboard find the side panel
- *Task 2* Finding the settings and activating the "shared password" function
- *Task 3* Returning to the dashboard from the settings;
- *Task 4* Navigating to the chat function
- *Task 5* Finding the button that leads to the chat screen to add a "love note"
- *Task 6* Choosing a love note template
- *Task 7* Adding a kiss sticker and typing a message in the picture.

Results: All successfully completed Task 1, 2, 3, 4, and 6. One could not complete Task 5. One user could not complete Task 7, requiring use of two different functions.

10   Conclusions

The Marriage Machine is conceived to motivate and persuade couples to open themselves up towards techniques of daily practice and interaction with their partners, with the goal of making their relationships with each other deeper, more enjoyable, more personally enriching, and educational. The application incorporates persuasive and motivational elements in order to stimulate users to reflect on and change their behavior. Based on user tests, we found that App Rating 67 % of our participants rated the app "very good" and 33 % rated the app "excellent." With this information in mind, AM+A plans to continue development of the Marriage Machine.

Acknowledgements of Assistance and Related Publications. The author acknowledges Kia Hwee Chew, Vivian Lemes, and Kenneth So, AM+A Designer/Analysts; Prof. Bob Stein, University of California/Berkeley Extension, International Diploma Program; and graduate students Fernando Bittar, Caroline Verghote, and Aditi Arora. This paper, based on [20, 21] appears longer in [22].

References

1. Achor, S.: The Happiness Advantage: The Seven Principles of Positive Psychology that Fuel Success and Performance at Work. Crown Publishing Group, New York (2010)
2. American Community Survey (2012). http://www.census.gov/acs/www/data_documentation/2012_release/. Accessed 30 Dec 2014
3. America Fact Finder (2012). http://factfinder.census.gov/faces/nav/jsf/pages/index.xhtml. Accessed 30 Dec 2014
4. Cialdini, R.B.: The science of persuasion. Sci. Amer. **284**, 76–81 (2001)
5. Córdova, J.V., Gee, C.G., Warren, L.Z.: Emotional skillfulness in marriage: intimacy as a mediator of the relationship between emotional skillfulness and marital satisfaction. J. Soc. Clin. Psychol. **24**, 218–235 (2005)
6. Fogg, B.J.: Persuasive Technology: Using Computers to Change What We Think and Do. Morgan Kaufmann, Amsterdam (2003)
7. Fogg, B.J., Eckles, D., Bogost, I., Consolvo, S., Holmen, E., Spasojevic, M., White, S.: Mobile Persuasion: 20 Perspectives on the Future of Behavior Change. Stanford University Press, Palo Alto (2007)
8. Gottman, J., Gottman, J.: How to keep love going strong: 7 principles on the road to happily ever after. YES! Mag. **56**, 38–39 (2011)
9. Hartson, R., Pyla, P.S.: The UX Book. Morgan and Kauffmann, New York (2012)
10. Karney, B.: Keeping marriages healthy, and why it's so difficult, February 2010. http://www.apa.org/science/about/psa/2010/02/sci-brief.aspx
11. Luo, S., Klohnen, E.C.: Assortative mating and marital quality in newlyweds: a couple-centered approach. J. Pers. Soc. Psychol. **88**(2), 304–326 (2005). Shanhong Luo and Eva C. Klohnen, University of Iowa
12. Marcus, A.: The health machine. Inf. Des. J. **19**(1), 69–89 (2011)
13. Marcus, A.: The money machine. Helping baby boomers retire. User Exp. **11**(2), 24–27 (2012)
14. Marcus, A.: The story machine: a mobile app to change family story-sharing behavior. Workshop paper presented at CHI Conference on Human Factors in Computing Systems. ACM, New York, 5–10 May 2012
15. Marcus, A., Chiou, M., Narula, C., Yu, A.: The innovation machine: mobile UX design combining information and persuasion design to change behavior. In: Marcus, A. (ed.) DUXU 2013, Part IV. LNCS, vol. 8015, pp. 67–76. Springer, Heidelberg (2013)
16. Marcus, A., Abromowitz, S.: The driving machine: mobile UX design that combines information design with persuasion design. In: Marcus, A. (ed.) DUXU 2013, Part III. LNCS, vol. 8014, pp. 140–149. Springer, Heidelberg (2013)
17. Marcus, A., Peng, Y., Lecca, N.: The learning machine: mobile UX design that combines information design with persuasion design. In: Marcus, A. (ed.) DUXU 2013, Part II. LNCS, vol. 8013, pp. 247–256. Springer, Heidelberg (2013)
18. Marcus, A., Schieder, T.K., Cantoni, L.: The travel machine: mobile UX design that combines information design with persuasion design. In: Marcus, A. (ed.) DUXU 2013, Part IV. LNCS, vol. 8015, pp. 696–705. Springer, Heidelberg (2013)
19. Marcus, A.: The happiness machine: mobile behavior change. In: Marcus, A. (ed.) DUXU 2014, Part II. LNCS, vol. 8518, pp. 258–268. Springer, Heidelberg (2014)
20. Marcus, A.: The marriage machine. White Paper, Aaron Marcus and Associates Inc., 11 April 2014
21. Marcus, A.: The marriage machine. In: Proceedings, User Friendly 2014 Conference (UXPA China), Wuxi, China, File HY23, 13–16 Nov 2014

22. Marcus, A.: Mobile Persuasion Design. Springer, London (2015, in press)
23. Marcus, A., Jean, J.: The green machine: going green at home. User Exp. **8**(4), 20–29 (2009)
24. Maslow, A.H.: A theory of human motivation. Psychol. Rev. **50**, 370–396 (1943)
25. Tsapelas, I., Aron, A., Orbuch, T.: Marital boredom now predicts less satisfaction 9 years later. Psychol. Sci. **20**(5), 543–545 (2009)

A Study of the Fault Tree Human in Aviation

Edgard Thomas Martins[1(✉)], Isnard Thomas Martins[2], and Marcelo M. Soares[1]

[1] Universidade Federal de Pernambuco Recife, Pernambuco, Brazil
{edgardpiloto,soaresmm}@gmail.com
[2] Universidade Estácio de Sá, Rio de Janeiro, Brazil
isnardthomasmartins@gmail.com

Abstract. The emotional stability and physical health of workers on board aircraft are faced with the factors and conditions that enable professionals to carry out their activities and develop normally, despite the fact that these conditions may present themselves to professionals in adverse conditions [1]. The modern history of aviation with its great technological complexity has pilots as redundant components that integrate embedded controls in modern aircraft. This leads us to say that the value of the worker as a permanent social group in society does not receive, currently, the proper priority. In research on the health of the pilot, there are three major perspectives that have been investigated that influence his stability, as well as the mental and emotional development of the modern airline pilot [2]: The previous life of the individual directly tied to experience, age, genetic and physiological vectors, The social environment, cultural environment and formal education leading to the final result, manifested by the ability, personality, strength and character and The verifiable standards of quality and quantity of life desired, ambition and achievements and its effects.

Keywords: Automation · Manual procedures · Human factor

1 Introduction

The Digital technology advances, has changed the shape and size of instruments used for navigation and communication. This has changed the actions of pilots, especially in relation to emergency procedures. There are few studies that correlate the reduction of accidents with the cognitive and technological changes. The increased cognitive load relates to these changes and requires assessment. The benefits presented by new technologies do not erase the mental models built, with hard work, during times of initial training of the aircraft career pilots in flying schools. The public must be heeded when an aircraft incident or accident becomes part of the news. In search of who or what to blame, the pilot is guilty and immediately appointed as the underlying factors that involve real evidence of the fact they are neglected.The reading of the *Black-Boxes* notes that 70 % to 80 % of accidents happen due to human error, or to a string of failures that were related to the human factor [3]. We can mention stress and the failure to fully understand the new procedures related to technological innovations linked to automation. Complex automation interfaces always promote a wide difference in philosophy

© Springer International Publishing Switzerland 2015
A. Marcus (Ed.): DUXU 2015, Part I, LNCS 9186, pp. 524–534, 2015.
DOI: 10.1007/978-3-319-20886-2_49

and procedures for implementation of these types of aircraft, including aircraft that are different even manufactured by the same manufacturer. In this case, we frequently can identify inadequate training that contributes to the difficulty in understanding procedures by the crews. Accident investigations concluded that the ideal would be to include, in the pilot training, a psychological stage, giving to him the opportunity of self-knowledge, identifying possible "psychological breakdowns" that his biological machine can present that endangers the safety of flight. Would be given, thus, more humane and scientific support to the crew and to everyone else involved with the aerial activity, minimizing factors that cause incidents and accidents. Accident investigators concluded that the ideal situation for pilot training should include a psychological phase [4], giving him or her, the opportunity of self-knowledge, identifying possible "psychological breakdowns" that biological features can present and can endanger the safety of flight. It should be given, thus, more humane and scientific support to the crew and everyone else involved with the aerial activity, reducing factors that can cause incidents and accidents. Accidents do not just happen. They have complex causes that can take days, weeks or even years to develop [5]. However, when lack of attention and/or neglect take place resulting in a crash, we can be most certain there was a series of interactions between the user and the system that created the conditions for that to happen [6]. We understand that human variability and system failures are an integral part of the main sources of human error, causing incidents and accidents. The great human effort required managing and performing actions with the interface as the task of monitoring, the precision in the application of command and maintaining a permanent mental model consistent with the innovations in automation make it vulnerable to many human situations where errors can occur.

The human variability in aviation is a possible component of human error and we can see the consequences of these errors leading to serious damage to aircraft and people. It is not easy, in new aviation, to convey the ability to read the instruments displays. This can conduct to the deficiency and the misunderstanding in monitoring and performing control tasks: lack of motivation, the fact that it is stressful and tiring, and generate failures in control (scope, format and activation), poor training and instructions that are wrong or ambiguous. The mind of the pilot is influenced by cognition and communication components during flight, especially if we observe all information processed and are very critical considering that one is constantly getting this information through their instruments. There is information about altitude, speed and position of one's aircraft and the operation of its hydraulic power systems. If any problem occurs, several lights will light up and warning sounds emerge increasing the volume and type of man-machine communication which can diminish the perception of detail in information that must be processed and administered by the pilot. All this information must be processed by one's brain at the same time as it decides the necessary action in a context of very limited time. There is a limit of information that the brain can deal with which is part of natural human limitation. It can lead to the unusual situation in which, although the mind is operating normally, the volume of data makes it operate in overload, which may lead to failures and mistakes if we consider this man as a biological machine [6, 7].

Today there are only the pilot and co-pilot in the cockpit and modern automated. Only two men just to control a Boeing 777. This is a large modern aircraft carrying hundreds of passengers and so much faster. Now a days, the tasks of the pilots were multiplied and increased the weights of aircraft, and the number of passengers, speeds takeoffs and landings were more significant, decreasing the number of men in the cockpit. However, the biological machine called human being is not structurally changed in the last thousands of years to support the increased cognitive and emotional overload. How to know your limits? The professional called Mechanics of Flight (the third man in the cockpit), was extinguished when computers arrived. Until the 70 s there was a work station flight engineer. In a modern station with only the pilot and co-pilot, two men just to control a Boeing 777, a huge and modern aircraft carries hundreds of passengers much more quickly. Several procedures were loaded to the pilots that were executed by the Flight Engineer (O terceiro piloto no cockpit - extinto). Several procedures were loaded to the pilots that were executed by the extinguished Flight Engineer (Op.cit).

2   Fundamentation

The following factors are an integral part of cognitive activity in the pilot: fatigue, body rhythm and rest, sleep and its disorders, the circadian cycle and its changes, the G-force and acceleration of gravity, the physiological demands in high-altitude, night-time take-offs and the problem of false illusion of climbing. But, other physiological demands are placed by the aviators. It is suggested that specific studies must be made for each type of aircraft and workplace, with the aim of contributing to the reduction of incidents arising from causes so predictable, yet so little studied. We must also give priority to airmen scientists that have produced these studies in physiology and occupational medicine, since the literature is scarce about indicating the need for further work in this direction. Human cognition refers to mental processes involved in thinking and their use. It is a multidisciplinary area of interest includes cognitive psychology, psychobiology, philosophy, anthropology, linguistics and artificial intelligence as a means to better understand how people perceive, learn, remember and how people think, because will lead to a much broader understanding of human behavior. Cognition is not presented as an isolated entity, being composed of a number of other components, such as mental imagery, attention, consciousness, perception, memory, language, problem solving, creativity, decision making, reasoning, cognitive changes during development throughout life, human intelligence, artificial intelligence and various other aspects of human thought [8].

The procedures of flying an aircraft involve observation and reaction to events that take place inside the cabin of flight and the environment outside the aircraft [4]. The pilot is required to use information that is perceived in order to take decisions and actions to ensure the safe path of the aircraft all the time. Thus, full use of the cognitive processes becomes dominant so that a pilot can achieve full success with the task of flying the "heavier than air".

With the advent of automated inclusion of artifacts in the cabin of flight that assist the pilot in charge of controlling the aircraft, provide a great load of information that must be processed in a very short space of time, when we consider the rapidity with which changes occur, an approach that cover the human being as an individual is strongly need. Rather, the approach should include their cognition in relation to all these artifacts and other workers who share that workspace [9]. The deployment of the accidents are usually generated by bad-planned-tasks.

A strong component that creates stress and fatigue of pilots, referred to the design of protection, detection and effective handling of fire coming from electrical short circuit on board, is sometimes encountered as tragically happened on the Swissair Airlines flight 111, near Nova Scotia on September 2, 1998. The staff of the Federal Aviation Administration (FAA), responsible for human factors research and modern automated interfaces, reports a situation exacerbated by the widespread use an electrical product and a potentially dangerous wire on aircrafts, called "Kapton" [4].

If a person has to deal with an outbreak of fire, coming from an electrical source at home, the first thing he would do is disconnect the electrical power switch for the fuses. But this option is not available on aircraft like the Boeing B777 and new Airbus. The aviation industry is not adequately addressing the problem of electrical fire in flight and is trying to deal recklessly [10] The high rate of procedural error associated with cognitive errors, in the automation age, suggests that the projects in aviation have ergonomic flaws. In addiction, is has been related that the current generation of jet transport aircraft, used on airlines, like the Airbus A320, A330, A340, Boeing B777, MD11 and the new A380, that are virtually "not flyable" without electricity. We can mention an older generation, such as the Douglas DC9 and the Boeing 737.

Another factor in pushing the pilots that causes emotional fatigue and stress is the reduction of the cockpit crew to just two. The next generation of large transport planes four engines (600 passengers) shows a relatively complex operation and has only two humans in the cockpit. The flight operation is performed by these two pilots, including emergency procedures, which should be monitored or re-checked. This is only possible in a three-crew cockpit or cockpit of a very simple operation. According to the FAA, the only cockpit with two pilots that meets these criteria is the cabin of the old DC9-30 and the MD11 series. The current generation of aircraft from Boeing and Airbus do not fit these criteria, particularly with respect to engine fire during the flight and in-flight electrical fire. The science of combining humans with machines requires close attention to the interfaces that will put these components (human-machine) working properly.

The deep study of humans shows their ability to instinctively assess and treat a situation in a dynamic scenario. A good ergonomic design project recognizes that humans are fallible and not very suitable for monitoring tasks. A properly designed machine (such as a computer) can be excellent in monitoring tasks. This work of monitoring and the increasing the amount of information invariably creates a cognitive and emotional overload and can result in fatigue and stress.

According to a group of ergonomic studies from FAA [11] in the United States this scenario is hardly considered by the management of aviation companies and, more seriously the manufacturers, gradually, introduce further informations on the displays of Glass cockpits. These new projects always determine some physiological, emotional and cognitive impact on the pilots. The accident records of official institutes such as the NTSB (National Transportation Safety Bureau, USA) and CENIPA (Central Research and Prevention of Accidents, Brazil) show that some difficulties in the operation, maintenance or training aircraft, which could affect flight safety are not being rapidly and systematically passed on to crews worldwide. These professionals of aviation may also not be unaware of the particular circumstances involved in relevant accidents and incidents, which makes the dissemination of experiences very precarious.

One of the myths about the impact of automation on human performance: "while investment in automation increases, less investment is needed in human skill". In fact, many experiments showed that the progressive automation creates new demands for knowledge, and greater, skills in humans. Investigations of the FAA [11], announced that aviation companies have reported institutional problems existing in the nature and the complexity of automated flight platforms. This results in additional knowledge requirements for pilots on how to work subsystems and automated methods differently. Studies showed the industry of aviation introduced the complexities of automated platforms flight inducing pilots to develop mental models about overly simplified or erroneous system operation. This applies, particularly, on the logic of the transition from manual operation mode to operation in automatic mode. The process of performing normal training teaches only how to control the automated systems in normal but do not teach entirely how to manage different situations that the pilots will eventually be able to find.

This is a very serious situation that can proved through many aviation investigation reports that registered the pilots not knowing what to do, after some computers decisions taken, in emergences situations [10]. VARIG (Brazilian Air lines), for example, until recently, had no Boeing 777 simulators where pilots could simulate the emergence loss of automated systems what should be done, at list, twice a month, following the example of Singapore Airlines. According to FAA [11], investigations showed incidents where pilots have had trouble to perform, successfully, a particular level of automation. The pilots, in some of these situations, took long delays in trying to accomplish the task through automation, rather than trying to, alternatively, find other means to accomplish their flight management objectives. Under these circumstances, that the new system is more vulnerable to sustaining the performance and the confidence. This is shaking the binomial Human-Automation compounded with a progression of confusion and misunderstanding. The qualification program presumes it is important for crews to be prepared to deal with normal situations, to deal with success and with the probable. The history of aviation shows and teaches that a specific emergency situation, if it has not happen, will certainly happen.

The future work makes an assessment in systemic performance on pilots. Evaluating performance errors, and crew training qualifications, procedures, operations, and regulations, allows them to understand the components that contribute to errors. At first sight, the errors of the pilots can easily be identified, and it can be postulated that many of these errors are predictable and are induced by one or more factors related to the project, training, procedures, policies, or the job. The most difficult task is centered on these errors and promoting a corrective action before the occurrence of a potentially dangerous situation. The FAA team, which deals with human factors [12], believes it is necessary to improve the ability of aircraft manufacturers and aviation companies in detecting and eliminating the features of a project, that create predictable errors. The regulations and criteria for approval today do not include the detailed project evaluation from a flight deck in order to contribute in reducing pilot errors and performance problems that lead to human errors and accidents. Neither the appropriate criteria nor the methods or tools exist for designers or for those responsible for regulations to use them to conduct such assessments. Changes must be made in the criteria, standards, methods, processes and tools used in the design and certification. Accidents like the crash of the Airbus A320 of the AirInter (a France aviation company) near Strasbourg provide evidence of deficiencies in the project. This accident highlights the weaknesses in several areas, particularly when the potential for seemingly minor features has a significant role in an accident. In this example, inadvertently setting an improper vertical speed may have been an important factor in the accident because of the similarities in the flight path angle and the vertical speed in the way as are registered in the FCU (Flight Control Unit).

This issue was raised during the approval process of certification and it was believed that the warnings of the flight mode and the PFD (Primary Flight Display-display basic flight information) would compensate for any confusion caused by exposure of the FCU, and that pilots would use appropriate procedures to monitor the path of the vertical plane, away from land, and energy state. This assessment was incorrect. Under current standards, assessments of cognitive load of pilots to develop potential errors and their consequences are not evaluated. Besides, the FAA seeks to analyze the errors of pilots, a means of identifying and removing preventively future design errors that lead to problems and their consequences. This posture is essential for future evaluations of jobs in aircraft crews. Identify projects that could lead to pilot error, prematurely, in the stages of manufacture and certification process will allow corrective actions in stages that have viable cost to correct or modify with lower impact on the production schedule. Additionally, looking at the human side, this reduces unnecessary loss of life.

3   Contextualization

On April 26, 1994, an Airbus A300-600 operated by China Airlines crashed at Nagoya, Japan, killing 264 passengers and flightcrew members. Contributing to the accident were conflicting actions taken by the flightcrew and the airplane's autopilot. The crash provided a stark example of how a breakdown in the flightcrew/automation interface can affect flight safety. Although this particular accident involved an A300-600, other accidents, incidents, and safety indicators demonstrate that this problem is not confined to any one airplane type, airplane manufacturer, operator, or geographical region. This point was tragically demonstrated by the crash of a Boeing 757 operated by American Airlines near Cali, Columbia on December 20, 1995, and a November 12, 1995 incident (very nearly a fatal accident) in which a American Airlines Douglas MD-80 descended below the minimum descent altitude on approach to Bradley International Airport, CT, clipped the tops of trees, and landed short of the runway.

As a result of the Nagoya accident as well as other incidents and accidents that appear to highlight difficulties in flightcrews interacting with the increasing flight deck automation, the Federal Aviation Administration's (FAA) Transport Airplane Directorate, under the approval of the Director, Aircraft Certification Service, launched a study to evaluate the flightcrew/flight deck automation interfaces of current generation transport category airplanes. The following airplane types were included in the evaluation: Boeing: Models 737/757/767/747-400/777, Airbus: Models A300-600/A310/A320/A330/A340, McDonnell Douglas: Models MD-80/MD-90/MD-11, Fokker: Model F28-0100/-0070 [5].

The Federal Aviation A chartered a human factors (HUMAN FACTOR) team to address these human factors issues, with representatives from the FAA Aircraft Certification and Flight Standards Services, the National Aeronautics and Space Administration, and the Joint Aviation Authorities (JAA), assisted by technical advisors from the Ohio State University, the University of Illinois, and the University of Texas. The HUMAN FACTOR [11]. Team was asked to identify specific or generic problems in design, training, flightcrew qualifications, and operations, and to recommend appropriate means to address these problems. In addition, the HUMAN FACTOR Team was specifically directed to identify those concerns that should be the subject of new or revised Federal Aviation Regulations (FAR), Advisory Circulars (AC), or policies. The HUMAN FACTOR Team relied on readily available information sources, including accident/incident reports, Aviation Safety Reporting System reports, research reports, and trade and scientific journals. In addition, meetings were held with operators, manufacturers, pilots' associations, researchers, and industry organizations to solicit their input. Additional inputs to the HUMAN FACTOR Team were received from various individuals and organizations interested in the HUMAN FACTOR Team's efforts [11].

When examining the evidence, the HUMAN FACTOR Team found that traditional methods of assessing safety are often insufficient to pinpoint vulnerabilities that may lead to an accident. Consequently, the HUMAN FACTOR Team examined accident precursors, such as incidents, errors, and difficulties encountered in operations and training. The HUMAN FACTOR Team also examined research studies that were intended to identify issues and improve understanding of difficulties with flightcrew/automation interaction. In examining flightcrew error, the HUMAN FACTOR Team recognized that it was necessary to look beyond the label of flightcrew error to understand why the errors occurred [10].

We looked for contributing factors from design, training and flightcrew qualification, operations, and regulatory processes. While the HUMAN FACTOR Team was chartered primarily to examine the flightcrew interface to the flight deck systems, we quickly recognized that considering only the interface would be insufficient to address all of the relevant safety concerns. Therefore, we considered issues more broadly, including issues concerning the functionality of the uderlying systems. From the evidence, the HUMAN FACTOR Team identified issues that show vulnerabilities in flightcrew management of automation and situation awareness and include concerns about:

- Pilot understanding of the automation's capabilities, limitations, modes, and operating principles and techniques. The HUMAN FACTOR Team frequently heard about automation "surprises," where the automation behaved in ways the flightcrew did not expect. "Why did it do that?" "What is it doing now?" and "What will it do next?" were common questions expressed by flightcrews from operational experience.
- Differing pilot decisions about the appropriate automation level to use or whether to turn the automation *on* or *off* when they get into unusual or non-normal situations

(e.g., attempted engagement of the autopilot during the moments preceding the A310 crash at Bucharest). This may also lead to potential mismatches with the manufacturers' assumptions about how the flightcrew will use the automation.

Flightcrew situation awareness issues included vulnerabilities in, for example:

- Automation/mode awareness. This was an area where we heard a universal message of concern about each of the aircraft in our charter.
- Flight path awareness, including insufficient terrain awareness (sometimes involving loss of control or controlled flight into terrain) and energy awareness (especially low energy state).

These vulnerabilities appear to exist to varying degrees across the current fleet of transport category airplanes in our study, regardless of the manufacturer, the operator, or whether accidents have occurred in a particular airplane type. Although the Team found specific issues associated with particular design, operating, and training philosophies, we consider the generic issues and vulnerabilities to be a larger threat to safety, and the most important and most difficult to address. It is this larger pattern that serves as a barrier to needed improvements to the current level of safety, or could threaten the current safety record in the future aviation environment. It is this larger pattern that needs to be characterized, understood, and addressed. In trying to understand this larger pattern, the Team considered it important to examine why these vulnerabilities exist [4]. The Team concluded that the vulnerabilities are there because of a number of interrelated deficiencies in the current aviation system:

- Insufficient communication and coordination. Examples include lack of communication about in-service experience within and between organizations; incompatibilities between the air traffic system and airplane capabilities; poor interfaces between organizations; and lack of coordination of research needs and results between the research community, designers, regulators, and operators.
- Processes used for design, training, and regulatory functions inadequately address human performance issues. As a result, users can be surprised by subtle behavior or overwhelmed by the complexity embedded in current systems operated within the current operating environment. Process improvements are needed to provide the framework for consistent application of principles and methods for eliminating vulnerabilities in design, training, and operations.
- Insufficient criteria, methods, and tools for design, training, and evaluation. Existing methods, data, and tools are inadequate to evaluate and resolve many of the important human performance issues. It is relatively easy to get agreement that automation should be human-centered, or that potentially hazardous situations should be avoided; it is much more difficult to get agreement on how to achieve these objectives.
- Insufficient knowledge and skills. Designers, pilots, operators, regulators, and researchers do not always possess adequate knowledge and skills in certain areas related to human performance. It is of great concern to this team that investments in necessary levels of human expertise are being reduced in response to economic pressures when two-thirds to three-quarters of all accidents have flightcrew error cited as a major factor.

- Insufficient understanding and consideration of cultural differences in design, training, operations, and evaluation. The aviation community has an inadequate understanding of the influence of culture and language on flightcrew/automation interaction. Cultural differences may reflect differences in the country of origin, philosophy of regulators, organizational philosophy, or other factors. There is a need to improve the aviation community's understanding and consideration of the implications of cultural influences on human performance.

4   Conclusion

A few decades ago, in my early life entering the airlines, we were taught to fly the Authomatic Control in the Throttle Quadrant (TQ) course, with SOP's (*Standard Operating Procedure)* attached. The line operations were refined during line training. The initial emphasis was knowing how the automated new system worked and how to fly it. The line training refined these skills and expanded how to operate it within the airways system and a multitude of busy airports and small visual airfields. Understanding the complexities of the systems came with our 'apprenticeship', which had started. When automation became readily available we used it to reduce workload when we felt like it. We didn't really trust it but we used it knowing we could easily disconnect it when it didn't do what we wanted. Now some airliners want everything done on autopilot because it can fly better than any pilot. Airlines hire young pilots with little experience and they are shown how you don't need to hand fly any more because of automation. Labor is cheap. We developed a study focusing on the guilt of pilots in accidents when preparing our thesis. In fact, the official records of aircraft accidents blame the participation of the pilots like a large contributive factor in these events. Modifying this scenario is very difficult in the short term, but we can see as the results of our study, which the root causes of human participation, the possibility of changing this situation. The cognitive factor has high participation in the origins of the problems (42 % of all accidents found on our search). If we consider other factors, such as lack of usability applied to the ergonomics products, the choise of inappropriate materials and poor design, for example, this percentage is even higher. Time is a factor to consider. This generates a substantial change in the statistical findings of contributive factors and culpability on accidents. The last consideration on this process, as relevant and true, somewhat later, must be visible solutions. In aviation, these processes came very slowly, because everything is wildly tested and involves many people and institutions. The criteria adopted by the official organizations responsible for investigation in aviation accidents do not provide alternatives that allow a clearer view of the problems that are consequence of cognitive or other problems that have originate from ergonomic factors. We must also consider that some of these criteria cause the possibility of bringing impotence of the pilot to act on certain circumstances. The immediate result is a streamlining of the culpability in the accident that invariably falls on the human factor as a single cause or a contributing factor. Many errors are classified as only "pilot incapacitation" or "navigational error". Our research shows that there is a misunderstanding and a need to distinguish disability and pilot incapacitation (because of inadequate training) or even navigational error.

Our thesis has produced a comprehensive list of accidents and a database that allows extracting the ergonomic, systemic and emotional factors that contribute to aircraft accidents. These records do not correlate nor fall into stereotypes or patterns. These patterns are structured by the system itself as the accident records are being deployed. We developed a computer system to build a way for managing a database called the Aviation Accident Database. The data collected for implementing the database were from the main international entities for registration and prevention of aircraft accidents as the NTSB (USA), CAA (Canada), ZAA (New Zealand) and CENIPA (Brazil). This system analyses each accident and determines the direction and the convergence of its group focused, instantly deployed according to their characteristics, assigning it as a default, if the conditions already exist prior to grouping. Otherwise, the system starts formatting a new profile of an accident.

This feature allows the system to determine a second type of group, reporting details of the accident, which could help point to evidence of origin of the errors. Especially for those accidents that have relation with a cognitive vector. Our study showed different scenarios when the accidents are correlated with multiple variables. This possibility, of course, is due to the ability of Aviation DataBase System [6, 7], which allows the referred type of analysis. It is necessary to identify accurately the problems or errors that contribute to the pilots making it impossible to act properly. These problems could point, eventually, to an temporary incompetence of the pilot due to limited capacity or lack of training appropriateness of automation in aircraft. We must also consider many other reasons that can alleviate the effective participation or culpability of the pilot. Addressing these problems to a systemic view expands the frontiers of research and prevention of aircraft accidents.

This system has the purpose of correlating a large number of variables. In this case, the data collected converges to the casualties of accidents involving aircraft, and so, can greatly aid the realization of scientific cognitive studies or applications on training aviation schools or even in aviation companies. This large database could be used in the prevention of aircraft accidents allowing reaching other conclusions that would result in equally important ways to improve air safety and save lives.

References

1. Eugenio, C.: Automação no cockpit das aeronaves: um preciosoauxílio à operação aérea ou um fator de aumento de complexidade no ambiente profissional dos pilotos, vol. 1, pp. 34–35, 1rd ed.. São Paulo (2011)
2. Henriqson, E.: A coordenação como um fenômeno cognitivo distribuído e situado em *cockpits* de aeronaves. Coordination as a distributed cognitive phenomena situated in aircraft cockpits Aviation in Focus (ago/dez. 2010), vol. 1(1), pp. 58–76. PortoAlegre, (2010)
3. FAA- Federal Aviation Administration: DOT/FAA/AM-10/13, Office of Aerospace Medicine, Causes of General Aviation
4. Dekker, S.: Illusions of explanation- a critical essay on error classification. Int. J. Aviat. Psychol. **13**, 95–106 (2003). New Jersey
5. Rasmussen, J.: Human errors: a taxonomy for describing human malfunction in industrial istallations. J. Occup. Accidents **4**, 311–333 (1982)

6. Martins, E.: Study of the implications for health and work in the operationalization and the aeronaut embedded in modern aircraft in the man-machines interactive process complex, Estudo das implicações na saúde e na operacionalização e no trabalho do aeronauta embarcado em modernas aeronaves no processo interativo homemmáquinas complexas. Thesis, Centro de Pesquisas Aggeu Magalhães, Fundação Osw Cruz, Perna, Brazil, pp. 567–612 (August, 2010)

7. Martins, E.: Ergonomics in Aviation: A critical study of the causal responsibility of pilots in accidents, Ergonomia na Aviação: Um estudo crítico da responsabilidade dos pilotos na causalidade dos acidentes, Msc. Monography. Universidade Federal Pernambuco, Pernambuco, Brasil

8. Henriqson, E.: Coordination as a Distributed Cognitive Phenomena Situated in Aircraft Cockpits- Aviation in Focus, A Coordenação Como Um Fenômeno Cognitivo Distribuído e Situado em Cockpits de Aeronaves, UFRGS edit., vol. 12, pp. 58 –76. Porto Alegre, (December, 2010)

9. Federal Aviation Administration Human Factors Team Report on: The Interfaces Between Flightcrewsand- Modern Flight Deck Systems, 18 June 1996

10. Reason, J.: Human Error, 2nd edn, pp. 103–107. Cambridge University Press, Cambridge (1990)

11. FAA - Federal Aviation Administration: DOT/FAA/AM-10/13, Office of Aerospace Medicine, Causes of General Aviation Accidents and Incidents: Analysis Using NASA Aviation, Safety Reporting System Data. Department of Transportation Press, Washington, DC (2010)

12. Green, R.G., Frenbard, M.: Human Factors for Pilots. Avebury Technical, Aldershot (1993)

Scenario Analysis as a Tool for Informing the Design of Behaviour Change Interventions

Luis Oliveira$^{(\boxtimes)}$, Martin Maguire$^{(\boxtimes)}$, Val Mitchell, and Andrew May

Loughborough Design School, Loughborough University,
Leicestershire LE11 3TU, UK
{L.Oliveira, M.C.Maguire, V.A.Mitchell,
A.J.May}@lboro.ac.uk

Abstract. This article presents the design process behind the specification of a behaviour change intervention method to promote energy saving. The amount of energy used for food preparation is highly influenced by people's behaviours. A user-centred design approach based on scenario analysis was applied to provide understanding of context of use and specification of user requirements. This knowledge was applied to the design of behaviour change interventions to motivate sustainable behaviours.

Keywords: Scenarios · User-centred design · Behaviour change · Temporal tensions · Sustainability · Energy saving

1 Introduction

Societies have been increasingly concerned about the amount of carbon released into the atmosphere and the consequences of energy use. The housing sector accounts for more than one third of the energy consumption [1]. It is possible to build domestic products that use less energy via better product engineering, and to reduce the energy consumption by the way people use these products and perform their daily activities [2]. The energy efficiency of appliances has been increasing in recent years [3]. However, owning efficient appliances or living in energy efficient homes is not a guarantee that the energy use will reduce [4, 5]. Furthermore, consumers are buying more appliances and having more standby devices [6].

The role of behaviour in domestic energy use is often the subject of research focusing on different appliances. Verhallen and Raaij [7] presented a study of the energy used for home heating, showing that occupant behaviours explain 26 % of the variance of energy use. They demonstrated that levels of awareness, commitment to energy saving measures and personal preferences varied enormously from one person to another [7]. One study on washing up methods showed that people behave in diverse ways, and on average use more detergent, water, energy and time than a regular dishwasher [8]. But when a set of 'best practice tips' were given to consumers as instructions, they "used around 60 % less water, 70 % less energy and 30 % less detergent compared with the average everyday behaviour the other subjects used. Additionally, they achieved a slightly better cleaning result" [9]. Cultural differences were shown to be an important factor on user behaviours for dish washing, influencing

© Springer International Publishing Switzerland 2015
A. Marcus (Ed.): DUXU 2015, Part I, LNCS 9186, pp. 535–547, 2015.
DOI: 10.1007/978-3-319-20886-2_50

water and detergent usage [10]. Laundry and dish washing energy use was reported to be highly influenced by lifestyles, and "results show a variation of a factor of five between a more sustainable and a more careless behaviour" [11]. For cold appliances, video evidence shows that families have particular ways of storing and retrieving food from the fridge, and the frequency and length of interactions with the appliance can affect the energy consumption [12]. One user observation study demonstrated that people who perform their daily activities with a high level of interaction with kitchen appliances, sometimes cause unnecessary energy usage [13].

The amount of energy used for food preparation is highly influenced by people's behaviours. Cooking demands several interactions between users and appliances, the user is in close proximity during operation, and there are numerous energy saving behaviours that can be performed during the cooking activity [14]. There are also diverse techniques that the user can apply in order to reduce the energy use, depending on the food prepared [15–17].

User-centred design methods can contribute to an understanding of how and why people use energy [18, 19], and this knowledge can inform the design of interventions to promote energy conservation. The design of behaviour interventions has been studied for many years across different disciplines [20]. The design of products and services can be used to motivate users to behave in a more sustainable way [21–23]. It is possible for designers to indicate a route they want users to take, via different methods and strategies. "Where users often make poor decisions, design can help counter this" [24]. Information and communication technologies (ICTs) can be used to increase the sustainability of products and services in many ways. Several examples can be found in the literature, from visualizations of resource consumption, and energy use feedback to persuasive applications [25, 26].

1.1 Evidence from Previous Study

As a previous study reported [27], people cook in diverse ways, using rather different procedures, resulting in diverse energy expenditure and time usage, even when cooking the same dish, using the same utensils and appliances. Participants rushed into the cooking tasks without much deliberation, consequently not following recommended preparation procedures and thus using more energy. Time issues and concerns about how long it takes to cook were recurrent aspects noted. Students generally boiled the kettle, pre-heated the hob, and used the bigger hob and high heat settings. Even though they wanted to cook quickly during the experiment, and to avoid extended preparation time, most of them used more water than needed, did not cover the pan, used more energy and eventually made the cooking process longer [27].

The interaction between participants and appliances during the cooking process presented a few moments of tension regarding the use of available time in relation to the task requirements [27]. The cooking activity could be divided in two main distinct phases. The first phase consists of the user preparing the utensils and ingredients to start cooking, and the second phase refers to when the user is cooking and waiting for the food to be ready. Participants' behaviours during these two phases and its relation to time indicate that both are distinct. The first phase includes activities like unpacking the food, selecting the pan and hob, pouring the water and setting everything ready to start the cooking process properly. The second phase constitutes, basically, stirring the food and watching it cook.

It was noted that there were temporal tensions during both phases of the cooking process. Temporal tensions are defined as the psychological construct arising from assessing the availability of temporal, mental, physical and social resources [28, 29]. The first phase is characterized by a hurrying feeling, when the time seemed to be short for the amount of preparation to be done. Some students performed different tasks at once, like pre-heating the hob whilst boiling the kettle, in an attempt to 'squeeze in' more actions "to fit in a time frame" [28]. The second phase denoted a waiting tension, when participants wanted to avoid the boredom of waiting by trying to make the cooking process quicker. The relationship between time and action is stretched, with participants anticipating outcomes that are about to happen [28] and trying to find distractions such as chatting or listening to music on their mobile phones. These two phases indicate a problematic situation where the availability of time in terms of the overall cooking goal could be better managed in order to avoid temporal tensions. Technology can be used to 'stretch time and slow things down' instead of only trying to make users to perform their activities more quickly [30].

Figure 1, below, displays the timeline for cooking noodles with the different steps undertaken during the cooking process. It was inspired by service design thinking [31], following practical guidance from the Service Design Blueprint technique [32] and contributed to the definitions of the proposed behaviour change intervention.

The preparation phase consists of a number of steps to start the cooking process according to the proposed 'ideal' method. A careful selection of steps should be made in order to achieve the best final results in terms of the quality of food, effort, time and energy use. This would address the problem of students rushing into the cooking process without much consideration (phase 1) and often being tempted to do something to alleviate the waiting boredom (phase 2).

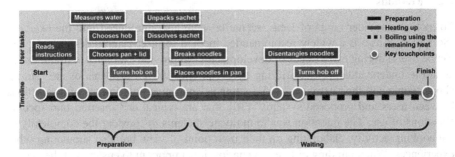

Fig. 1. Cooking timeline – preparation and waiting

The diagram above displays the preparation and waiting phases where a temporal tension might occur. Most participants failed to follow a procedure that could result in quicker preparation time and less energy use. They also seldom turned the hob off before the end of the cooking process in order to use the remaining heat stored in the metal plate. They wanted to avoid increasing the cooking time, indicating a temporal tension at the end of the process.

2   Scenario Analysis

In order to reduce temporal tensions during cooking, it is advised to incorporate the user's perspective into the development process. A user-centred design approach includes the understanding of context of use and specification of user requirements [33]. Following this approach, users were invited to generate new ideas that could contribute to the suitability and acceptance of such an intervention as described:

2.1   The Study

A sample of the target population was selected to participate in an idea generation session. A group of 35 students participated on this study (12 females and 23 males). They were all undergraduate students registered for a module on research methods. Participation was voluntary and not related to their attendance records or grades. They could work alone or in pairs and it was not mandatory to complete all questions.

Participants were made aware of the aims and objectives of this research during the briefing phase and with the findings of the previous study [27] via images and graphs from previous chapters of the first author's thesis [14]. They were also presented with the cooking timeline diagrams to understand the temporal tensions observed during cooking. Finally they were prompted to think about the concept of a cooking assistant, a mobile phone application that could help during the cooking activity giving instructions for the preparation process.

2.2   Methods

To motivate a wider range of ideas, scenarios were also introduced into the exercise. 'Scenarios of use' is a widely recommended method for user-centred design [34], and can be useful during early stages of developments "to provide examples of future use as an aid to understanding and clarifying user requirements" [33]. Scenarios are "stories about people and their activities" [35], acting as "narrative descriptions of interactions between users and proposed systems" [36], that are typical and inserted into specific situations of use. The intention was to motivate students to consider the complexity of the cooking activity, elaborating on their own point of view but also simulating other experiences. When building different scenarios, it is important to ensure that they cover different 'stories', as they "must have some 'point' that illustrates a design issue not raised previously by other scenarios" [36]. A scenario can be built considering 4 aspects of each situation [35]:

1. **Setting:** the state and the background of the episode
2. **Agents or Actors:** people involved in the episode

3. **Goals or Objectives:** the changes that the agents wish to achieve
4. **Actions or Events:** the plot, things that agents do and things that happen to them

Three different situations of cooking were presented to the students, who they asked to evaluate the introduction of an electronic cooking assistant into these scenarios. Then they were asked to contribute with ideas for aspects of the application that would motivate them to use it, follow the instructions and ultimately save energy for cooking. The proposed scenarios were:

A. **Cooking Something Quickly:** when the student is cooking his food as usual, when she just wants to have food, to 'fuel up' when rushing between lectures, and having the kitchen as a routine space just to get things done.
B. **Cooking as a Private Moment:** when the student is more relaxed and experimenting with food, trying to be more creative and possibly cooking something new, not particularly concerned about the time taken for cooking
C. **Cooking as a Social Experience:** when the student is cooking together with friends or flatmates, sharing the experience and the food, using the kitchen as a social space to enjoy the company, chat and eat (Table 1).

Table 1. Scenarios

Scenario	A Cooking something quickly	B Cooking as a private moment	C Cooking as a social experience
Setting	Kitchen as routine space	Kitchen as creative space	Kitchen as a social space
Agents	Student	Student	Friends
Goals	Have food	Relax, enjoy and create	Interact, enjoy, share the experience
Actions	Cook food as usual	Experiment with food, take time	Chat, listen to music, cook, taste

2.3 Procedure

After a briefing of the aims of the exercise, students were asked to discuss among themselves to elaborate creative solutions to the problems presented. One sheet of paper was handed to each student in order for them to complete a table with eight questions for each of the three scenarios. The questions were divided into two groups, corresponding to the two phases of distinct temporal tensions observed during the cooking process. The first phase, related to the 'preparation' phase, aimed to investigate the acceptance of the proposed mobile phone cooking assistant, and also to understand how to motivate students to take time to prepare the food with the correct process before rushing into the cooking itself. The second phase, namely "waiting", was designed to understand how to make people wait without feeling bored during the process, and also what could a system suggest the user could do in order to avoid this boredom. The questions used were:

1. In this scenario, do you think students will follow instructions from an app?
2. Why? (reason for answer)
3. What would encourage students to follow a preparation procedure?
4. How to motivate them to think before acting?
5. In this scenario, do you think students will wait and follow the instructions?
6. Why? (reason for answer)
7. What would encourage them to take their time, not rush and not feel bored waiting?
8. What could an app suggest them to do?

2.4   Data Analysis

The dataset from this study comprised of 30 sheets with responses to these 8 questions shown above, for each of the three scenarios. A broad range of responses came from each one of these questions, and to organize them in themes, the software NVivo was used. This facilitated the categorization of responses and allowed a further qualitative data analysis. The software also enabled the researcher to build patterns from responses and provided a clearer picture of the data, following recommendations from [37].

Preliminary analysis of the responses and familiarization with the data indicated that dozens themes were raised by the participants. Further examination of the data indicated that responses could be merged into a smaller number of categories. Participants mentioned frequently the need to obtain a 'value' from the experience, that it should be useful to them in some way. They also wanted to enhance the process, gain confidence, experiment with food, increase the quality, improve health and have more enjoyment during the task. Another category of responses indicated that participants wanted to use less effort and have fewer distractions when cooking, and that a cooking assistant should be easy to use.

It was observed that these themes were falling into categories that matched the ones from existing models for evaluation of technology acceptance and suitability. Since this study involved the evaluation of the acceptance of an electronic assistant, the Technology Acceptance Model (TAM) [38] and its developments [39–41] provided a suitable framework to help in grouping and analysing participants' responses. TAM postulates that *perceived usefulness* and *perceived ease of use* are the fundamental determinants of user acceptance. Other factors were added later as influences on these main constructs, such as social influences external conditions [41].

Responses to all the open ended questions were classified into these 4 categories: Perceived usefulness, Perceived ease of use, Social influence and External factors (Table 2).

The majority of the responses from this study, aggregating all 6 open ended questions, fell into the category of perceived usefulness of the technology (63 %). Previous studies also identified that perceived usefulness is indeed the best predictor of technology acceptance, since it correlates more strongly to usage than ease of use [38, 41]. Perceived ease of use was the second most frequent item (17 %), followed by external variables (11 %) and social influence processes (8 %).

Table 2. Scenarios results - overview

TAM × scenarios	A Cooking something quickly	B Cooking as a private moment	C Cooking as a social experience	Total	%
Perceived usefulness	107	102	61	270	63.38
Perceived ease of use	38	12	23	73	17.14
Social influence processes	1	2	32	35	8.22
External variables	21	16	11	48	11.27
Total	167	132	127	426	100.00

3   Results

The semantic analysis of themes gathered during this study allowed the definition of the most important requirements in each scenario, for the two main phases of the cooking process. This data indicated that any proposed intervention should be useful by adding value to the cooking process. This value is perceived as any improvement in an aspect of cooking, such as increasing the speed of the cooking process, reducing mental workload or improving the user experience for cooking. These requirements are shown in Table 3 below.

Data gathered during this session indicated the primary need was to consider the perceived usefulness of the application, and as a secondary consideration the proposed app needed to be perceived as easy to use in order to be adopted. Concepts of a richer user experience (UX) [42] were also suggested, including fun elements (games, quizzes, relaxing activities, social interactions) and improved visual appearance. Some external variables such as social factors can also influence the acceptance of technology, but to a lesser extent. In summary, participants required that the technology must fit the task they attempt to perform [43]. In line with previous studies involving the Technology Acceptance Model [7, 38] students need to recognize the application as being able to help them to accomplish the goal during the activity, preferably with added fun, otherwise it might not be perceived as useful, consequently failing to be really accepted.

3.1   The Proposed Intervention

Data from the studies conducted during this phase combined with the literature review indicated that participants need to perceive a benefit from using the application. Often people want to see the rewards from specific behaviours, as if asking 'what is in there for me?' [44]. The strategies developed here focus on the results of the scenario analysis and previous studies by providing benefits to the user including a shorter

Table 3. Scenarios and requirements

Scenario	A	B	C
First phase – preparation: How to make students use the app and follow instructions	**Make it useful** – Improve efficiency - Make the cooking process quicker, easier, and save energy – Improve quality, make healthier – Inform – benefits, how to be quicker, what can go wrong	**Make it useful** – Instigate gourmet / experiment /creativity / skills – Guarantee quality – Save money – Inform - instructions on complex steps, show benefits, what can go wrong, feedback	**Make it useful** – Improve quality and health – Inform about benefits and instructions on complex steps **Make it easy** – Easy to use – Allow manage food whilst with friends
	Make it easy – Easy to use – Quick to use	**Make it easy** – Improve visuals	**Improve social aspects** – Promote social interactions, engage friends to contribute – Impress friends with food
Second phase – waiting: User requirements – how to make students wait	**Make it useful** – Concentrate on food – Suggest how to improve speed, health and quality – Give external distractions – read, work, quiz, games, tips on energy, cooking, relax – Multitasking – prepare other parts of the dish, wash up, set table	**Make it useful** – Concentrate on food – suggest ingredients, how to improve speed, health, quality – Give external distractions – read, work, other tasks, tips on energy saving, waste use and better cooking – Multitask – other part of the dish, wash up, clear up, set table	**Make it useful** – Concentrate on food – How to improve speed, health, quality – Guide multitasking – inform how to prepare other dishes simultaneously – Enhance social aspects – share tasks with others, involve, give conversation topics, use online social networks

cooking time, a convenient process, and the possibility to have the final meal prepared according to their preferences, in a facilitated way. In order to design the application to be useful, reduce temporal tensions and promote energy saving, the strategy of applying persuasive technology was considered [45, 46]. From their examples of persuasive technologies as tools, it is possible to select strategies that could be embedded within an intervention intended to influence people's behaviours whilst cooking.

3.2   Structure of the Application

Continuing from Fig. 1, which presented the moments of temporal tension during cooking, Fig. 2, above, shows opportunities for a system to intervene during the cooking activity and to ultimately reduce these temporal tensions. Based on the Service Design Blueprint [32], this diagram includes the timeline, the physical evidences and inputs, the visible user actions, the 'checkpoints' and also the backstage actions that could be performed by the cooking application (bottom row of boxes). The roles of the user and a cooking agent are interrelated in order to produce an ideal process, aiming at energy saving, shorter cooking time, improved food quality, less effort and reduced temporal tensions.

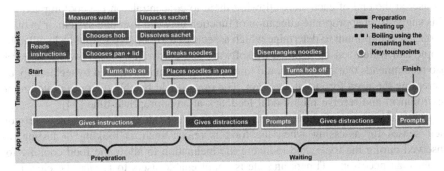

Fig. 2. Cooking timeline: user and app tasks

4 Discussion

Providing some sort of distraction during the waiting phase of cooking could be one of the strategies designed to reduce temporal tensions. Introducing one activity that provides cognitive absorption [47] during the second phase of the cooking process could work for this purpose, making time pass quickly during an engaging activity. It is argued that it is possible to develop interventions to foster *flow,* an ideal state when the challenges of the environment matches personal skills [48]. These interventions are generally used to make regular work settings a better source of flow giving more enjoyable interactions, with built-in goals, feedback, rules and challenges, without imposed demands or strict pacing. In a state of flow there is "a sense that one's skills are adequate to cope with the challenges at hand, in a goal-directed, rule-bound action system that provides clear clues as to how well one is performing. Concentration is so intense that there is no attention left over to think about anything irrelevant, or to worry about problems" [49]. Flow is much more likely to happen from a structured activity, and activities performed with flow can lead to a self-motivated dimension of behaviour [50]. Although flow theory is generally applied to playful activities, previous research found correlations between measurements of flow and use of office software such as spreadsheet and email tools [51] or internet browsing [52].

Oulasvirta and Tamminen [28] indicate the possibility of use of notifications as a form of reducing temporal tensions. Users could "delegate tasks to automatic devices that must somehow notify the user of important changes in the controlled task or process". The evidence that some students lost track of time during cooking, and the cognitive load associated with the task of calculating the duration of the cooking process (for even a simple cooking task) indicates that electronic timers with prompts can improve the time management for the activity. "By creating a system that does not demand a continual awareness of time progression, opportunities for engaging in activities that reduce the time pressure may be increased" [53]. ICT interfaces can provide a better support for allocation of attention, via context-triggered audible or tactile alerts intervening at the right time and leaving the users to dedicate their cognitive resources to the cooking activity itself. This aid could be provided through an electronic timer with prompts programmed for the specific meal being cooked to alert the user at the end of each step, allowing them to concentrate on the cooking actions. This suggests an appropriate allocation of function between user and system or in other words, "It is important to determine which aspects of a job or task should be handled by people and which can be handled by software and hardware" [33]. Previous research also recommends that systems should minimize the attention required by technology by decreasing the need for visual attention. The user should be able to concentrate on the environment and receive multimodal feedback at an appropriate time [54].

Other advantages of using a timer are that participants would not need to rely on their senses for assessing when the food is ready, such as looking or tasting, as observed during the trials, and reducing the inclination to allow the food cooking for longer than necessary. Timers and alerts could enable users to reduce the electricity usage by informing them when to switch the heat source off and use the remaining heat retained in the hob.

5   Conclusion

This paper addresses the topic of time management during cooking activities, aligned with a theoretical background on time perceptions and temporal tensions. This knowledge indicated the media and the content of an intervention to tackle wasteful behaviours. These propositions were presented to a group of students who analysed it according to specific scenarios. Their contributions confirmed the findings from previous studies that an application can contribute to make the cooking process more efficient (reducing time to prepare, minimizing effort involved and providing better results) and improve the user experience. The app could help users concentrate on the food preparation in order to follow a recommended procedure for efficiency and energy saving. At the same time, an app could provide a variety of distractions during the second phase of the cooking to minimize boredom, such as tips for better cooking, multitasking, quizzes, games and relaxation activities.

The qualitative data analysis from the requirements study showed that individuals are likely to be cautious in adopting a cooking assistant app because they do not want to spend additional time preparing the food, complicate the process, or compromise the quality of food. However, if the application has a value, or is perceived as being useful and easy to use, then it is more likely to be accepted. This information contributed to the process of specifying the design of a persuasive electronic intervention, for example via a mobile phone application, to change their behaviours for cooking.

The main hypothesis formulated here is that providing a way to reduce temporal tensions during cooking can improve the user experience and promote energy saving. It was demonstrated that ICT can provide the tools needed to manipulate time perceptions and therefore bring about changes in the specific behaviours that result in unnecessary energy usage. The developed application should be evaluated to understand its effectiveness in changing behaviours and achieving acceptance among the target population.

References

1. Department for Energy and Climate Change: UK energy in brief (2010). http://www.uea.ac.uk/~e680/energy/pdf_files/energy_in_brief/190-uk-energy-in-brief-2010.pdf
2. Attari, S.Z., Dekay, M.L., Davidson, C.I., Bruine De Bruin, W.: Public perceptions of energy consumption and savings. In: Proceedings of The National Academy of Sciences, vol. 107, pp. 16054–16059 (2010)
3. Geller, H., Harrington, P., Rosenfeld, A.H., Tanishima, S., Unander, F.: Polices for increasing energy efficiency: thirty years of experience in OECD countries. Energy Policy **34**, 556–573 (2006)
4. Crosbie, T., Baker, K.: Energy-efficiency interventions in housing: learning from the inhabitants. Build. Res. Inf. **38**, 70–79 (2010)
5. Gill, Z., Tierney, M.J., Pegg, I.M., Allan, N.: Low-energy dwellings: the contribution of behaviours to actual performance. Build. Res. Inf. **38**, 491–508 (2010)
6. Firth, S., Lomas, K., Wright, A., Wall, R.: Identifying trends in the use of domestic appliances from household electricity consumption measurements. Energy Build. **40**, 926–936 (2008)
7. Verhallen, T.M.M., Raaij, W.F.V.: Household behavior and the use of natural gas for home heating. J. Consum. Res. **8**, 253–257 (1981)
8. Berkholz, P., Stamminger, R., Wnuk, G., Owens, J., Bernarde, S.: Manual dishwashing habits: an empirical analysis of UK consumers. Int. J. Consum. Stud. **34**, 235–242 (2010)
9. Fuss, N., Bornkessel, S., Mattern, T., Stamminger, R.: Are resource savings in manual dish-washing possible? Consumers applying best practice tips. Int. J. Consum. Stud. **35**, 194–200 (2011)
10. Elizondo, G.M., Lofthouse, V., Bhamra, T.: An exploration of dishwashing habits in anglo and hispanic communities through the use of cultural probes. In: International Consumer Sciences Research Conference (ICSRC), Bonn, Germany, 18–20 July 2011
11. Stickdorn, M., Schneider, J.: This is Service Design Thinking. BIS Publishers, Amsterdam (2010)
12. Tang, T., Bhamra, T.: Putting consumers first in design for sustainable behaviour: a case study of reducing environmental impacts of cold appliance use. Int. J. Sustain. Eng. **5**(4), 288–303 (2012)
13. Elias, E.W.A., Dekoninck, E.A., Culley, S.J.: Assessing user behaviour for changes in the design of energy using domestic products. In: IEEE International Symposium on Electronics and the Environment, pp. 1–6, 19–22 May 2008
14. Oliveira, L.: Designing and evaluating a behaviour change intervention that introduces modification of time perceptions as a solution to promote sustainable behaviours. Ph.D thesis, Lough-borough Design School, Loughborough University, UK (2013)
15. Das, T., Subramanian, R., Chakkaravarthi, A., Singh, V., Ali, S.Z., Bordoloi, P.K.: Energy conservation in domestic rice cooking. J. Food Eng. **75**, 156–166 (2006)

16. Oberascher, C., Stamminger, R., Pakula, C.: Energy efficiency in daily food preparation. Int. J. Consum. Stud. **35**, 201–211 (2011)

17. Webster, J., Trevino, L.K., Ryan, L.: The dimensionality and correlates of flow in human-computer interactions. Comput. Hum. Behav. **9**, 411–426 (1993)

18. Kuniavsky, M.: Observing the User Experience: A Practitioner's Guide to User Research. Morgan Kaufmann, USA (2003)

19. Stamminger, R.: Modelling resource consumption for laundry and dish treatment in individual households for various consumer segments. Energy Effi. **4**, 559–569 (2011)

20. Fishbein, M., Ajzen, I.: Predicting and Changing Behavior. Taylor & Francis, London (2010)

21. Beale, R.: Slanty design. Commun. ACM **50**(1), 21–24 (2007)

22. Bhamra, T., Lilley, D., Tang, T.: Design for sustainable behaviour: using products to change consumer behaviour. Des. J. **14**, 427–445 (2011)

23. Jelsma, J., Knot, M.: Designing environmentally efficient services; a 'script' approach. J. Sustain. Prod. Des. **2**, 119–130 (2002)

24. Lockton, D., Harrison, D., Stanton, N.A.: The design with intent method: a design tool for influencing user behaviour. Appl. Ergon. **41**(3), 382–392 (2010)

25. Disalvo, C., Sengers, P., Brynjarsdóttir, H.: Mapping the landscape of sustainable HCI. In: Proceedings of the 28th International Conference on Human factors in Computing Systems, pp. 1975–1984, ACM Press, 10–15 April 2010

26. Goodman, E.: Three environmental discourses in human-computer interaction. In: Proceedings of the 27th International Conference Extended Abstracts on Human Factors in Computing Systems (CHI EA 2009), pp. 2535–2544. ACM Press, New York, NY, USA (2009)

27. Oliveira, L., Mitchell, V., Badni, K.: Cooking behaviours: a user observation study to under-stand energy use and motivate savings. Work J. Prev. Assess. Rehabil. **41**(1), 2122–2128 (2012)

28. Oulasvirta, A., Tamminen, S.: Temporal tensions in human-computer interaction. In: CHI 2004 Workshop on Temporal Aspects of Work (2004)

29. Oulasvirta, A., Tamminen, S., Roto, V., Kuorelahti, J.: Interaction in 4-second bursts: the fragmented nature of attentional resources in mobile HCI. In: Proceedings of SIGCHI Conference on Human Factors in Computing Systems (CHI 2005), pp. 919–928. ACM Press, New York (2005)

30. Hallnäs, L., Redström, J.: Slow technology-designing for reflection. Pers. Ubiq. Comput. **5**(3), 201–212 (2001)

31. Tang, T., Bhamra, T.: Understanding consumer behaviour to reduce environmental impacts through sustainable product design. In: Undisciplined! Design Research Society Conference, pp. 1–15 (2008)

32. Bitner, M.J., Ostrom, A.L., Morgan, F.N.: Service blueprinting: a practical technique for service innovation. California Manag. Rev. **50**, 66 (2008)

33. Maguire, M.: Methods to support human-centred design. Int. J. Hum. Comput. Stud. **55**(1), 587–634 (2001)

34. Bevan, N.: UsabilityNet methods for user centred design. In: Human-Computer Interaction: Theory and Practice (Part 1), vol. 1, pp. 434–438 (2003)

35. Carroll, J.M.: Five reasons for scenario-based design. Interact. Comput. **13**(1), 43–60 (2000)

36. Potts, C.: Using schematic scenarios to understand user needs. In: Proceedings of the 1st Conference on Designing Interactive Systems: Processes, Practices, Methods, and Techniques, pp. 247–256, ACM Press (1995)

37. Braun, V., Clarke, V.: Using thematic analysis in psychology. Qual. Res. Psych. **3**(2), 77–101 (2006)

38. Davis, F.D.: Perceived usefulness, perceived ease of use, and user acceptance of information technology. MIS Q. **13**(3), 319–340 (1989)
39. Venkatesh, V.: Determinants of perceived ease of use: integrating control, intrinsic motivation, and emotion into the technology acceptance model. Inform. Syst. Res. **11**(4), 342–365 (2000)
40. Venkatesh, V., Davis, F.D.: A theoretical extension of the technology acceptance model: four longitudinal field studies. Manag. Sci. **46**(2), 186–204 (2000)
41. Venkatesh, V., Bala, H.: Technology acceptance model 3 and a research agenda on interventions. Decis. Sci. **39**, 273–315 (2008)
42. Anderson, S.P.: Seductive Interaction Design: Creating Playful, Fun, and Effective User Experiences. New Riders, Berkeley (2011)
43. Goodhue, D.L., Thompson, R.L.: Task-technology fit and individual performance. MIS Q. **19**(2), 213–236 (1995)
44. Foster, D., Lawson, S., Wardman, J., Blythe, M., Linehan, C.: 'Watts in it for Me?': design implications for implementing effective energy interventions in organisations. In: Proceedings of the 2012 ACM Annual Conference on Human Factors in Computing Systems (CHI 2012), Austin, Texas, USA, pp. 2357–2366. Anonymous ACM, New York, USA (2012)
45. Fogg, B.J.: Persuasive Computer: Using Technology to Change What We Think and Do. Morgan Kaufman, San Francisco (2003)
46. Oinas-Kukkonen, H., Harjumaa, M.: Persuasive systems design: key issues, process model, and system features. Commun. Assoc. Inform. Syst. **24**(28), 485–500 (2009)
47. Agarwal, R., Karahanna, E.: Time flies when you're having fun: cognitive absorption and beliefs about information technology usage. MIS Q. **24**(4), 665–694 (2000)
48. Nakamura, J., Csikszentmihalyi, M.: The concept of flow. In: Snyder, C.R., Wright, E., Lopez, S. (eds.) Handbook of Positive Psychology, pp. 89–105. Oxford University Press, London (2002)
49. Csikszentmihalyi, M.: Flow: The Psychology of Happiness: The Classic Work on How to Achieve Happiness. Rider, London (2002)
50. Csikszentmihalyi, M.: Beyond Boredom and Anxiety. Jossey-Bass (Wiley), San Francisco (2000)
51. Wood, G., Newborough, M.: Influencing user behaviour with energy information display systems for intelligent homes. Int. J. Energy Res. **31**(1), 56–78 (2007)
52. Novak, T.P., Hoffman, D.L., Yung, Y.F.: Measuring the customer experience in online environments: a structural modeling approach. Mark. Sci. **19**(1), 22–42 (2000)
53. Martin, R., Holtzman, H.: Kairoscope: managing time perception and scheduling through social event coordination. In: Proceedings of the 2011 Annual Conference on Human Factors in Computing Systems, pp. 1969–1978, ACM Press (2011)
54. Rogers, Y., Sharp, H., Preece, J.: Interaction Design: Beyond Human Computer Interaction. Wiley, Chichester (2011)

A Feasibility Study of the Effect of Phone-Based Feedback of Other Commuters' Subjective Experiences on Driver Intentions to Change

Tracy Ross[1]($\boxtimes$), Andrea Burris[1], Luis Oliveira[1], Bronia Arnott[2],
and Vera Araujo-Soares[2]

[1] Loughborough University, Loughborough, UK
{t.ross,a.n.burris,l.oliveira}@lboro.ac.uk
[2] Newcastle University, Newcastle, UK
{bronia.arnott,vera.araujo-soares}@newcastle.ac.uk

Abstract. Encouraging people to make sustainable transport choices remains a global challenge and many interventions have been attempted. This study investigated the reflection on own/others' subjective experiences (SE) as an intervention using a smartphone application as the intervention tool. Participants were car drivers and used the app to automatically capture and reflect on their commute journeys and experiences. The experimental group were also able to reflect upon others' experiences across car, walk and cycle modes. Others' experiences were designed based on a previous self-report study. Results of the study showed that quantitative measures of intentions to change were not affected by the intervention but that qualitative data showed that the positive experience of the active transport modes did bring about reflection on behaviour and a potential influence on opinions and intentions which warrants further study.

Keywords: Behaviour change · Sustainable transport · Active travel · Own subjective experience · Others' subjective experience · Opinions · Outcome expectations · Intention to change · Reflection · Persuasion · Socio cognitive theory · HCI · Mobile

1 Introduction

A growing body of research investigates the use of self-tracking devices to influence behaviour in a range of activities. The application of technology can support the achievement of goals such as physical activity or increase self-understanding, which can lead to behaviour change [3]. With more wearable technologies being developed, there are more possibilities available for research based on persuasive strategies [7, 10]. Persuasive technology and methods can also be used to promote more sustainable travel behaviours [13].

Several studies have been conducted to test participants' responses to feedback received on personalised collected data on their own travel behaviours and choices [5].

© Springer International Publishing Switzerland 2015
A. Marcus (Ed.): DUXU 2015, Part I, LNCS 9186, pp. 548–558, 2015.
DOI: 10.1007/978-3-319-20886-2_51

The measures reported back to subjects often include reports, per mode, of quantifiable aspects such as cost, calories consumed or CO_2 produced [8].

A growing body of research is investigating the relation between subjectively experienced well-being and transport [4, 6]. There is some evidence that the way we feel can be influenced by the modes of transport we choose and our individual travel behaviours. Usually, people walking and cycling present higher levels of subjective wellbeing (SW) than car drivers and users of public transport [9, 11, 12]. Some of the explanations include individual beliefs that an active commute provides further benefits (outcome expectations) such as improved health from desirable physical exercise, harmony with environmental values, lower costs, less stress and feelings of autonomy [1].

Past studies have captured subjective wellbeing through post hoc recall and at a generic level, i.e. across all journeys of a specific type (e.g. walking). This study was part of a feasibility project which had an overall aim of investigating whether reflection on experiences captured *in situ*, immediately after each journey, could encourage a shift to more sustainable modes (or at least a change of opinion or behavioural intentions). This study in particular, focused on designing an interface to capture and present Subjective Experience (SE) which comprised subjective well-being and subjective outcome experiences and investigating how participants perceived that information alongside the more usual measures such as calorie expenditure and carbon dioxide footprint CO_2. The hypothesis was that, reflecting on the more positive experiences of active transport mode users, would cause a shift in car driver opinions or intentions to change.

2 Method

This feasibility study used a randomised controlled before and after design with 18 participants, 9 allocated to the control condition and 9 to the experimental condition. All participants used a smartphone application which logged their journeys automatically and allowed them to manually capture and review their Subjective Experience (SE) (comprised of subjective well-being as a 'smiley face' rating and subjective outcome experience as a free-text comment) on its completion (over a 2 week period in late autumn/early winter). Participants in the experimental condition received an additional behaviour change technique; feedback on other commuters' subjective experience. The participants first received a briefing on the use of the app and completed a pre- intervention questionnaire in which they indicated, using a 5-point Likert scale, their intention to change their mode of transport in the next month. They then used the app. for 2 weeks (with a contact email half way through to check everything was proceeding well). During the 2 week trial statistics were collected on the number of views of the test screens (i.e. 'Capture SE', 'Own SE', 'Others' SE' screens). The final assessment stage was a face-to-face meeting where participants began by completing a post- intervention questionnaire comprising of the same questions as in the briefing. They then completed an interview which was semi-structured, comprising of questions on their opinions and travel behaviours, their intentions to change in the future, and it also provided the opportunity to go through each screen of the app, participants were asked to indicate using a 7-point scale how easy to understand and informative they found each screen.

2.1   Smartphone Application Intervention

An existing smartphone application (app) was used as a basis for interface development in this study. The app was called CarbonDiem and was produced by TravelAi. This app was purposefully selected because it had the power to automatically detect transport mode, thus reducing participant burden. The app uses data from sensors on the phone, such as the accelerometer and GPS to achieve this. It is important to note that this app was originally developed as one element of a carbon measurement service for companies and not as an app for individual reflection. As this original intent was not communicated to the participants as part of this study, this may have influenced the participants' responses to these features, which should be taken into account when considering the results section. The app developers, in a spirit of openness, kindly allowed us to share feedback on their screens in this paper nevertheless. These screens accounted for the 'auto-detected behaviour' shown in Fig. 1.

The additional screens designed for the study were to (a) to capture and present one's own subjective experience ('self-reported' aspects shown in Fig. 1) and (b) to enable reflection of others' subjective experience ('researcher-created data' shown in Fig. 1).

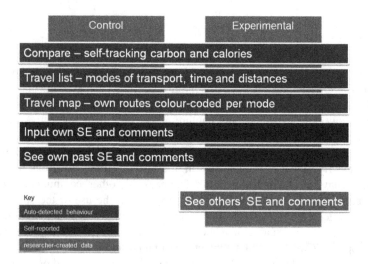

Fig. 1. Study design

2.2   Interface Design

The first four screens (Figs. 2 and 3) were part of the original app. The second three screens (Figs. 4 and 5) are those designed for this study. The titles used for the figures relate to the coded boxes in Fig. 1.

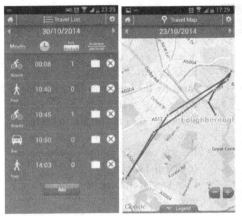

- Travel List with users' journeys each day. Includes mode, time, distance and purpose
- Travel Map of each journey (colour coded by mode)
- Modes available: Bicycle, Foot, Rail, Metro, Boat, Plane, Road (bus, car, motorbike, taxi)
- Data logged and available for the last 7 days.

Fig. 2. Travel list and travel map (original app screens)

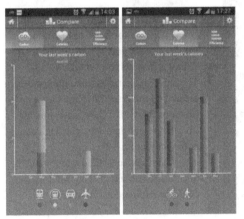

- Under the 'compare' icon users can see (i) 'Carbon', a graph of KG CO^2 per day per non-active mode (left hand screen), (ii). 'Calories', a graph of calories used per day per active mode (right hand screen) and (ii).'Efficiency', a graph of Km vs Kg of Co2, per day (not shown).
- All could be viewed by week or by month.

Fig. 3. Compare (original app screens)

2.3 Others' Subjective Experiences

Although 'Own SE' was obviously genuine, real-time information, the 'Others' SE' smiley faces and comments were created by the research team based on data collected in a previous study by the research team. The reason for this was that, although evidence shows that active mode users (walking, cycling), generally have higher reported subjective well-being (a component of this study's 'SE') by recall [9, 11, 12], this study could not take the risk of real 'other' travellers entering real-time data that countered this. This was because this study was part of a feasibility project to investigate whether other active transport users' higher SE can have an influence on car users. The others' active travel messages were skewed towards the positive and the others' car messages skewed towards the negative (70 % of the messages over the course of the study in each case) to give control over the experimental condition. There

- Capture own SE: comprised of 'subjective wellbeing' rating and 'subjective outcome expectation' comments (left hand screen)
- Input by the user manually, entering a rating (e.g. smiley face) and free text about how they felt on their most recent commute
- Display own SE ratings and comments (right hand screen).
- Data logged and available for the last 7 days

Fig. 4. Input/see own SE ratings and comments (study screens)

- Users saw others' SE by mode (changed twice per day to show past 12 hours), car, bike, walk only
- 2 quotes per each of 3 modes
- The smiley face ratings and quotes were created by the research team, based on a previous study i.e. they were not real-time travellers data (see further details below in section 2.3).
- This data was provided automatically once users submitted their SE data (but could be explored at any time)

Fig. 5. See others' SE ratings and comments (experimental only study screen)

was no literature to support these chosen percentages but given our aim to promote changes in opinions and intentions to change, and acknowledging that many car users may report positive experiences of car use we made this choice.

As stated, the precise content of the messages was designed based on messages produced in a previous diary study by the researchers, where 30 participants recorded SE in written form for the commute over a one week period, without restriction (all transport modes included in this study). The team gathered all these messages and using a behavioural change theory, Socio-Cognitive Theory (SCT) [2] categorised them into 3 main components of the SCT: self-efficacy, outcome expectations and socio-structural impediments and facilitators (e.g. weather). To minimise the risk that participants would not believe that the feedback from others was not collected at real time (i.e. were 'designed' by the team), the following measures were taken: (i) recruitment adverts stated that the study was for drivers, walkers and cyclists but that this phase was recruiting drivers only; (ii) the feedback of messages from others were sent around typical commute times; (iii) the messages were designed to be relevant to the area of the study (road names, etc.); (iv) the planned messages were regularly checked against the weather forecast to ensure a match.

2.4   Participants

All participants were drivers who commuted to Loughborough (population 59,000) on a minimum of 3 days per week, typically with single occupancy. As individuals they were physically able to walk or cycle (i.e. no mobility problems). The maximum commuting distance (including drop-offs such as at schools) was 10 miles (1 participant exceeded this by 1 mile).

Participants (n = 18) were randomly split in two groups (control/test condition). A briefing session was used to ensure successful download of the app and to explain to participants what they were required to do. All participants were told that the researchers were interested in gathering commuters' experiences. Information provided to the experimental group stated that the presence of others' SE was there for them to look at if they wished, in order that they were not primed to think this was a significant part (and purpose) of the study. After a briefing, the participants used the app for 2 weeks and then attended a session which comprised a questionnaire and a semi-structured interview. The participant demographics were:

- Control group: Age 22 to 48 years, mean 36 years (SD = 11.86); 1 male; 8 females; Commuting distance 1 to 11 miles, mean 3.76 (SD = 3.38).
- Experimental group: Age 27 to 56 years, mean 42 years (SD = 10.15); 1 male; 8 females; Commuting distance 1.5 to 9 miles, mean 4.56 (SD = 2.58).

3   Results

Data collected through the trial of the app, pre- and post- intervention questionnaires, semi-structured interviews and server stats (the latter only for the study screens; original app screen views could not be measured) were used within the analysis process. The semi-structured interviews were conducted individually with all 18 participants. Within the interviews various topics were explored including, intentions to change in the future; barriers to changing modes of transport, participants own subjective experiences (wellbeing and outcomes) and, for the experimental condition only, others' subjective experiences commuting to and from work. In addition it provided the opportunity to gain valuable feedback on the features of the intervention app and interaction with it. A thematic analysis was conducted on the qualitative data collected.

3.1   Interaction with the App (Study Screens Only)

During the 2 week trial of the app, the participants in the control condition submitted on average 19.67 comments and those in the experimental condition submitted on average 18.67 comments (for the 2 week study, 2 commutes per day, the maximum possible was 20). Table 1 gives an overview of the number of times the screens designed for this study were viewed by participants. The views of the 'Capture SE' screen are high because all other screens were accessed via this screen.

Table 1. Mean screen views of the study screens over the 2-week trial

	Screen		
	Capture SE	Own comments	Others' comments
Control	64.44	4.56	n/a
Experimental	71.11	3.78	22.44

3.2   Experiences Associated with Interacting with the App

By entering their own subjective experience ratings and comments, participants in both groups described that, as a result, they felt that they reflected on their own journeys more than usual, E8 (female, 27 years old) stated "It just kind of makes you think back about exactly what happened, how you felt while you were driving, how you felt while you were in the car." similarly C14 (female, 24 years old) stated "I sit there and try to think, what can I say today that doesn't involve talking about the traffic, which is the greatest influence on my journey enjoyment".

In the experimental condition participants indicated their interest and often enjoyment in reading other users' comments; many participants expressed a particular interest in the active commuters' comments as illustrated by E15 (female, 30 years old) who stated "It was interesting to see the comments... especially not just the car users, but cyclists because sometimes... cyclists might cycle a bit dangerously and cut you up, but it's also interesting to see their perspective". E11 (female, 37 years old) also expressed a similar view stating "Yeah, I did always read the ones on here. As a car driver, it makes you conscious of you know other people and their experiences and how things that you do can affect them." In addition to reflecting on their own commute, E11 also drew upon the prospect of changing modes of transport, stating "It's not a long walk for me, I have done it, I did used to cycle and obviously it ... it isn't stressful, it takes a bit more preparation in the morning."

The 'real-time' aspect of the app was positively perceived by participants E13 (female, 36) stated "I quite liked the different people's comments on how they got to work.

It was just quite interesting to see what other people were doing at the same time." Whilst, E2 (male, 46 years old) was interested in how other commuters were coping with real-time weather conditions, noting "I always had a flick, especially when the weather's been bad; see what other people have thought!"

Participants discussed their intention to change in the future, many expressed barriers to change to more active modes for their commute, reasons included perceiving their commute distance was too long for alternative modes, having children to drop-off en route and safety concerns in regards to cycling. Some expressed an intention to change when the weather was warmer (bearing in mind this study was conducted in the late autumn/early winter), E4 (female, 40 years old) stated "Probably in the summer because then I can walk with my daughter halfway, drop her off at school and then I can walk to work." Similarly C9 (female, 55 years old) stated "I would like to walk more rather than drive but it, again its weather dependent."

Participants rated their intention to change before and after the study using a 5-point scale (where weak intention = 1, and strong intention = 5), the mean scores before the intervention for the control and experimental conditions were 1.56 (SD = 0.73) and 2.11(SD = 1.05), and after 2 (SD = 1.12) and 2 (SD = 1) respectively. A Wilcoxon test showed no significant difference between the pre-intervention intention to change scores and post-intervention intention to change score, in either the control or experimental condition (control condition: Z = −1.13, p = 0.26; experimental condition: Z = −0.58, p = 0.56).

Other users' comments were accepted to be collected real time and directly from real people taking part in the study by a majority of participants in the experimental condition (6 out of 9). E12 (female, 48 years old) stated "No, no I just thought it was fun to do, I thought, oh all these people are having such a nice time, why am I so grumpy in the car!". Of the other 3, only 1 raised this prior to being told that they were not real-time and designed by the research team based on previous research, the other 2 only stated that they'd guessed this after being told.

3.3 Usability of Interface Design

The usability of the interface would obviously be a factor in the level of use of the system, so this was also explored. During the semi-structured interviews participants indicated on a 7-point Likert scale (where strongly disagree = 1 and strongly agree = 7) how informative and easy to use they found each screen of the app (Fig. 6).

Participants reported a majority of the screens were easy to use, as illustrated by Fig. 6. In particular the main 'intervention' screens - Capture SE, Others SE

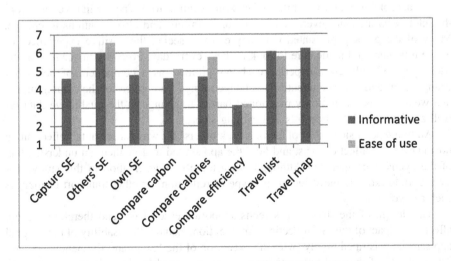

Fig. 6. Ratings of informativeness and ease of use for each screen

(experimental group only) and Own SE - were considered to be easy to use, scoring above 6 on average, as did the Travel Map screen.

The three screens identified as most informative were Others' SE (accessible to the experimental group), Travel List and Travel Map. Frequently participants expressed a lack of understanding of the compare efficiency screen which scored the lowest in both measures, participants expressed a lack of understanding of the word 'efficiency' in the context it is used within the app. However it is important to bear in mind that the app developers did not intend for this particular screen to be for reflection purposes when it was devised for the originally intended business use. It is also worth noting participants estimated level of views for the compare efficiency screen was also the lowest across both conditions.

The app icon was automatically displayed in the notification bar of the phone, showing information on users' carbon consumption in the last 7 days; a majority of participants accessed the app through this option, some also noted the ease of access played a role in prompting the completion of the SE ratings and comments after each commute as E8 (female, 27 years old) stated "It was quite easy to remember to do it because the symbol was always there."

All participants across both conditions were given the option to keep or uninstall the app after the trial. Out of the 18 participants, 9 participants chose to keep the app installed on their phone, 6 from the experimental group and 3 from the control group.

4   Discussion and Conclusions

The proposition being tested in this study was that reflecting on the more positive experiences of active transport mode users would cause a shift in car driver opinions, intentions or behaviours. The quantitative ratings of intention to change did not show a statistically significant difference before/after the study but we have to interpret this cautiously as we are not powered to detect differences. In general, the data collected reveals acceptability and feasibility of this intervention tool. The qualitative data from the interviews indicate several influences on opinions, and also intentions to change. Many of the participants stated that they enjoyed seeing the positive experiences of active travellers and made sure to look at these every day. From this it seems that the use of others' subjective experience shows promise as a component of behaviour change interventions. The intention to change ratings were given for the coming month and weather was a commonly mentioned barrier to change in the qualitative data (as well as distance, child drop-offs and cycling safety).

An unintended side-effect of feeding back others' SE was participants' reflection on how car drivers affect cyclists, and how the app started to give them an understanding of the cyclists' perspective. Although not a topic of investigation in this study, this aspect could indicate the value of this type of reflection for other transport challenges such as cyclist safety.

The design of the study app screens supported ease of use and therefore did not affect the impact of the 'SE reflection' intervention. Equally the usability of the original app screens was rated highly (with the exception of the 'Compare: Efficiency' screen). The usability of the study screens was further supported by the volume of 'Own SE' data collected which was close to the maximum of 20 (10 working days times 2 commutes). Others' SE was seen as more informative that 'Own SE' which probably explains why two thirds of the experimental group chose to keep the app after the trial (compared with one third of the control group).

In reflecting on the methodology, one of the most challenging aspects was to maintain believability of the others' real time collection of SE. The Method section explains how this was maximised and the results indicate that for the vast majority of participants the messages were perceived as real time.

In conclusion, as a first study into the use of reflection on others' SE as a behavioural intervention technique, this study shows that this approach has potential. Certainly, the participants' verbal reflection showed that it did make them contemplate more active/sustainable modes. Suggested further research includes: a study with larger numbers; a longer intervention period; the impact of repeating the study in more clement seasons; the combination with other behavioural change techniques shown to be effective in transport such as goal-setting and action-planning [14].

Acknowledgements. This study was carried out as part of the REFLECT project funded by the UK Engineering and Physical Sciences Research Council (EPSRC). The study was conducted by Loughborough University with significant support from Newcastle University. Thanks is also given to Jennifer Roberts of Sheffield University for her input. Loughborough University would also like to thank their collaborators TravelAi for providing the original app 'CarbonDiem' and their spirit of openness in allowing the sharing of results in this paper.

References

1. Anable, J., Gatersleben, B.: All work and no play? the role of instrumental and affective factors in work and leisure journeys by different travel modes. Transp. Res. Part A: Policy Pract. **39**, 163–181 (2005)
2. Bandura, A.: Social cognitive theory: an agentic perspective. Annu. Rev. Psychol. **52**, 1–26 (2001)
3. Fanning, J., Mullen, S.P., Mcauley, E.: Increasing physical activity with mobile devices: a meta-analysis. J. Med. Internet Res. **14**(6), e161 (2012)
4. de Vos, J., Schwanen, T., van Acker, V., Witlox, F.: Travel and subjective well-being: a focus on findings, methods and future research needs. Transp. Rev. **33**, 421–442 (2013)
5. Epstein, D.A., Cordeiro, F., Bales, E., Fogarty, J., Munson, S.A.: Taming data complexity in lifelogs: exploring visual cuts of personal informatics data. In: Proceedings of the 2014 Conference on Designing Interactive Systems, pp. 667–676. ACM (2014)
6. Ettema, D., Gärling, T., Eriksson, L., Friman, M., Olsson, L.E., Fujii, S.: Satisfaction with travel and subjective well-being: development and test of a measurement tool. Transp. Res. Part F Traffic Psychol. Behav. **14**, 167–175 (2011)
7. Fogg, B.J.: Persuasive Computer: Using Technology to Change What We Think and Do. Morgan Kaufman, San Francisco (2003)
8. Jariyasunant, J., Abou-Zeid, M., Carrel, A., Ekambaram, V., Gaker, D., Sengupta, R., Walker, J.L.: Quantified Traveler: Travel Feedback Meets the Cloud to Change Behavior. J. Intell. Transp. Syst. Technology Plann. Oper. **19**, 1–16 (2014)

9. Morris, E.A., Guerra, E.: Mood and mode: does how we travel affect how we feel? Transportation **42**, 1–19 (2014)
10. Oinas-Kukkonen, H.: A foundation for the study of behavior change support systems. Pers. Ubiquit. Comput. **17**, 1223–1235 (2013)
11. Olsson, L.E., Gärling, T., Ettema, D., Friman, M., Fujii, S.: Happiness and satisfaction with work commute. Soc. Indic. Res. **111**, 255–263 (2013)
12. Páez, A., Whalen, K.: Enjoyment of commute: a comparison of different transportation modes. Transp. Res. Part A Policy Pract. **44**, 537–549 (2010)
13. Prost, S., Schrammel, J., Röderer, K., Tscheligi, M.: Contextualise! personalise! persuade!: a mobile HCI framework for behaviour change support systems. In: Proceedings of the 15th international conference on Human-computer interaction with mobile devices and services, Munich, Germany. Anonymous ACM, New York, NY, USA, pp. 510–515 (2013)
14. Arnott, B., Rehakova, L., Sniehotta, F.F., Roberts, J.R., Araujo-Soares, V.: Efficacy of behavioural interventions for transport behaviour change: systematic review and meta-analysis. Int. J. Behav. Nutr. Phys. Act. **11**, 133 (2014)

Products with Biomimetic Shapes Convey Emotions More Effectively

Tyan-Yu Wu and Hon-Kai Chen[(✉)]

Chang Gung University, Taoyuan City, Taiwan
tnyuwu@mail.cgu.edu.tw, akai617@gmail.com

Abstract. Nowadays, a successful product should not only possess enhanced aesthetic quality and smart functionality, it should also satisfy consumers via the emotions they derive from using the product. Biomimetic designs are broadly used in product design to emphasize emotional interaction. Therefore, understanding the psychological effects of biomimetic products is becoming an important issue in the development of products with strong affective qualities. Adopting a cognitive-emotional approach, this study explored the emotions evoked in consumers by biomimetic products. This included an investigation of the following three hypotheses: (1) Consumers' emotions can be influenced by products with biomimetic features; (2) The emotions evoked in consumers by concrete biomimetic features (i.e., human contours, facial shapes and plant shapes) are greater than those evoked by less concrete features. The results indicated that consumers have different degrees of emotional responses to products exhibiting different levels of biomimicry. Furthermore, the results also showed that consumers had different degrees of emotional responses to different types of biomimetic products. Additional results are also discussed in the paper.

Keywords: Biomimicry · Product form · Product emotion

1 Introduction

1.1 Background

Biomimicry is defined as "the imitation of the models, systems, and elements of nature for the purpose of solving complex human problems" (http://en.wikipedia.org/wiki/Biomimetics). The term "biomimicry" comes from the Ancient Greek words "bios," meaning "life," and "mīmēsis," meaning "imitation." Biomimicry is commonly used in innovative technologies, having been applied in the development of various technologies to allow them to mimic the appearance, behavior or functional features of structures and materials found in nature (Janine, 1997). Nowadays, biomimicry is used in mechanical construction, morphology, materials science, green energy technology and other related fields (Kezhong and Zhihua, 2004). Environmental design specialists define biomimetic designs as biophilic, emphasizing the maintenance and restoration of natural elements in the built environment (Kellert et al. 2011). Biophilic designs have been reported to have a great impact on people's positive emotions and to increase people's well-being in daily life (Montana-Hoyos, 2010). Moreover, in the field of

© Springer International Publishing Switzerland 2015
A. Marcus (Ed.): DUXU 2015, Part I, LNCS 9186, pp. 559–566, 2015.
DOI: 10.1007/978-3-319-20886-2_52

product design, designers have been inspired by using natural shapes/forms or animal features in product designs, and their inclusion has led to the enhancement of emotional reactions among users when they subsequently use these products.

In the consumer market, the Italian kitchenware manufacturer Alessi has used natural elements such as plants, figures and natural contours as design elements to develop or shape its products. For example, the company's "magic bunny" toothpick holder and "Anna G." corkscrew wine opener were inspired, respectively, by rabbit shapes and human contours, as well as the movements of both species, which were utilized as metaphors in the kitchenware designs. Accordingly, we assume that products which incorporate biomimetic features as metaphors can enhance consumers' emotions. Along the same lines, it is speculated that products with strong product semantics can encourage users to interact with them more frequently and thus evoke their emotions more effectively. This is one of the hypotheses that were tested in this study.

1.2 Product Forms and Emotional Design

In a competitive consumer market, it is difficult for function-based products to effectively satisfy consumers' demands and inner desires (Petersen et al. 2004). At present, consumers often require a product to not only possess smart functionality and provide ergonomic satisfaction, but also to provoke an emotional response when used. Furthermore, Marzano (2000) and Desmet et al. (2001) have stated that, in the development of a new product, the emotional value of the product is an important factor in determining the product's ultimate success in the market. Moreover, Creusen and Snelders (2002) indicated that even the appearance of a product can cause pleasurable emotions among the consumers who observe it. On a related point, Norman (2007), a well-known cognitive psychologist, has claimed that there are three different levels of emotions: (1) sensory instinctive (i.e., "visceral") emotions; (2) behavior (i.e., "behavioral") emotions; and (3) intension reflection (i.e., "reflective") emotions. In this study, we have tended to focus on the first level of product emotions, visual instinctive emotions, in which users' emotions are basically derived from observing product appearances. Based on the results of prior research, we assumed that biomimetic designs have the potential to evoke consumers' emotional responses to a great degree.

1.3 Biomimetic Forms and Emotional Design

As mentioned above, biomimicry consists of a method for mimicking formations, colors and behaviors from natural life (Janine, 1997) in order to improve the quality of our own lives. In this context, a biomimetic product is herein defined as a "product that mimics the appearances, behaviors, functions or features of natural subjects including plants, animals or humans." In additions, "anthropomorphic" is an agent to natural entities, animals, and objects which provide human beings intent, motive, purpose or mood (Waytz et al. 2010). Both biomimicry and anthropomorphic concepts were utilized in this research.

Related research on robotic facial features has demonstrated that human preferences with regard to such features are affected by differences in the anthropomorphic degree of the features (Mori et al. 2012). Relatedly, the uncanny valley theory proposed that following an initial rise in the acceptability of such features as they approach a human-like appearance, their acceptability will then suddenly drop when the resemblance to humans becomes too close (Mori, 1970; Mori et al. 2012; Piwek et al. 2014). As for product aesthetics, the level of complexity in the appearances of products will result in a similar sort of uncanny valley in terms of reactions. The resulting graph of such responses is commonly referred to as the "inverted U-shape" (Berlyne, 1970). According to such results, we formulated two hypotheses: (1) consumers' emotions are influenced by products with biomimetic features; (2) the emotions of consumers evoked by concrete biomimetic features (i.e., features mimicking those of plants, human contours, and humanoid faces) are greater than those evoked by less concrete features.

2 Methods

2.1 Participants and Procedure

62 participants (31 males and 31 females ranging in age from 20 to 30 years old) participated in the test. In the experiment, the participants were asked to tick boxes in a questionnaire after observing stimuli which appeared in a random order.

2.2 Stimuli

Items of kitchenware were selected as the stimuli in the experiment because of their frequent usage in our daily lives and also due to their broad use of biomimetic designs. According to previous research results, the stimuli tested were confined to anthropomorphic features and plant features. More specifically, three types of biomimetic images incorporating, respectively, plant features, human contours, or human facial features were created and used in the experiment. Each type of stimulus contained four levels of biomimetic images, with the levels ranging from very concrete to least concrete. Physical models of a total of 12 stimuli were created, and each was photographed individually. Those photos were edited into 8 × 6 cm size images that were displayed in grey scale (Table 1).

2.3 Assessment

Mehrabian and Russell's (1974) emotional assessment (i.e., pleasure and arousal) paradigm was adopted to examine the participants' emotions because it has been used broadly in previous emotion-related research. A Likert scale consisting of nine response values per item was used.

Table 1. Stimuli incorporating plant features, human contours, or human facial features

Degree of concrete level	Type of Biomimicry		
	Plants	Human contours	Humanoid Faces
L1 Very abstract			
L2 Abstract			
L3 Concrete			
L4 Very concrete			

2.4   Experimental Design

In this study, there were three independent variables consisting of the plant, human contour, and humanoid facial features, while the emotional responses (i.e., pleasure and arousal) of the participants served as a dependent variable (see Table 2).

Table 2. Summary of variables

Variable	Type	Value
Biomimetic features	Independent	12 cases (4 shapes of plants, 4 shapes of figures, 4 shapes of humanoid faces)
Emotional responses	Dependent	Degree of valence (1–9 points) Degree of arousal (1–9 points)

3   Results

In this study, we examined the emotional responses of consumers resulting from different levels of biomimicry. More specifically, biomimetic forms including forms with plant, human contour, and humanoid facial features were tested in terms of the emotional responses they elicited.

The statistical results showed that the emotional scale (i.e., valence and arousal) adopted in this study demonstrated internal consistency and reliability with a Cronbach's alpha = 0.910. Furthermore, an ANOVA analysis was conducted to examine the effects of the biomimetic plant, human contour and human facial features in the forms ranging from the very concrete to least concrete forms. The results showed that there were significant differences between the effects elicited by the plant, human contour and human facial features for each level of concreteness ($F_{(11, 198.993)} = 61.750$, alpha = 0.05, $p < 0.001$).

3.1 Emotions Evoked by Biomimetic Forms with Different Levels of Concreteness

We examined the emotional effects (i.e., valence and arousal) of three types of bio-mimicry (i.e. plant, human contour and human facial features). As shown in Fig. 1, the results indicated that there were significant differences between the four levels of plant stimuli (Valence, $F_{(3, 39.208)} = 12.323$, $p < 0.001$; Arousal, $F_{(3, 21.575)} = 6.903$, $p < 0.001$).

Similarly, as shown in Fig. 2, the results indicated that there were significant differences between the four levels of human contour stimuli (Valence, $F_{(3, 67.726)} = 21.675$, $p < 0.001$; Arousal, $F_{(3, 50.048)} = 18.518$, $p < 0.001$). Specifically, the more concrete the form with human contours, the greater the level of emotion that was evoked.

Moreover, as shown in Fig. 3, the results indicated that there are significant differences between the four levels of humanoid facial stimuli (Valence, $F_{(3, 86.339)} = 26.831$, $p < 0.001$; Arousal, $F_{(3, 60.907)} = 19.552$, $p < 0.001$). Specifically, the more concrete the form with human facial features, the greater the level of emotion was evoked. However, the results also showed that the means values of emotion elicited displayed a slight drop after stimulus L3. This will be discussed in the next section.

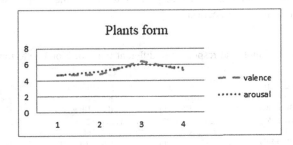

Fig. 1. The effects of stimuli with plant features on emotions

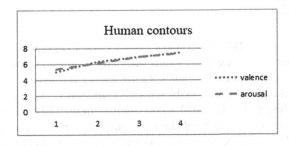

Fig. 2. The effects of stimuli with human contours on emotions

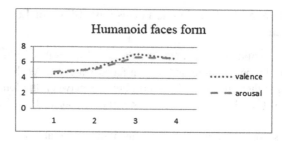

Fig. 3. The effects of stimuli with human facial features on emotions

3.2   Emotional Responses to Different Types of Biomimetic Forms

In this section, we further discuss the differences in participants' emotional responses to the different stimulus levels (i.e., L1, L2, L3, and L4). As shown in Table 3, the results indicated that there were no significant differences on the responses to the level 1, L2, level 3 stimuli in terms of both valence and arousal. Conversely, the results indicated that there was a significant difference on level 4 (Valence F $(2, 76.167) = 26.662$, $p < 0.001$; Arousal F $(2, 53.629) = 24.831$, $p < 0.001$). The results indicated that the participants' emotional responses followed the sequence of the responses to the human contour stimuli being greater than the responses to the human facial feature stimuli, which were in turn greater than the responses to the plant feature stimuli. This is discussed further in the next section.

Table 3. Emotional responses to different types of biomimetic forms

	L1	L2	L3	L4
Valence	$F(2,5.167) = 1.331$, $p = 0.267$ (PF = HF = HC)	$F(2,41.699) = 13.321$, $p < 0.001$ (HC > HF = PF)	$F(2,8.860) = 3.130$, $p = 0.46$ (PF = HF = HC)	$F(2,76.167) = 26.662$, $p < 0.001$ (HC > HF > PF)
Arousal	$F(2,7.597) = 2.058$, $p = 0.131$ (PF = HF = HC)	$F(2,23.070) = 6.879$, $p = 0.001$ (HC > HF = PF)	$F(2,11.812) = 4.342$, $p = 0.14$ (HC = HF > PF)	$F(2,53.629) = 24.831$, $p < 0.001$ (HC > HF > PF)

Note. PF: Plant forms, HF: Human facial forms, HC: Human contour forms;
L1: Least concrete, L2: less concrete, L3: concrete, L4: Most concrete;
(): Results from the multiple comparison tests ($\alpha = 0.05$)

4   Discussions

Mehrabian and Russell's (1974) emotional assessment paradigm was adopted to assess the participants' emotional responses in this study. We examined consumers' emotional responses to different types of biomimetic forms. For greater detail, we also examined consumers' emotional responses to biomimetic forms with different levels of con-creteness. Regarding to L1, L2 and L3, the results indicated that products with more concrete biomimetic forms exhibited stronger potential to evoke consumers' emotions then those with less concrete biomimetic forms (see Figs. 1, 2 and 3). However, we found that the mean values of the responses to both plant and humanoid facial forms appeared to drop slightly in response to the level 3 stimuli (Figs. 1 and 3), a finding which was in accordance with Berlyne's, (1970) inverted, U-shaped graph. Accordingly, this result further implied that the more concrete biomimetic forms are likely to have complex forms and to have a better chance to evoke emotions. In contrast to exhibiting an inverted U-shaped curve, the responses to the human contour stimuli (see Fig. 2) showed a positive linear relationship. It is possible that this was because even the level 4 stimulus was not concrete (real) enough in comparison to objects with a higher degree of human-likeness. It is suggested that this possibility be studied further in the future. In this case, it is believed that participants may prefer to observe more concrete forms and have greater emotional responses to such forms, but that the form should not appear to be too concrete (real), consistent with the Uncanny Valley theory of Mori (1970). It is believed that more concrete human-like forms will increase the degree of preference, before such form become too concrete. As shown in Table 3, the results indicated that the emotional responses to both the stimuli with human contours and the stimuli with human facial features were greater than the responses to the stimuli with plant features. This result implied that consumers' emotions are perhaps more strongly influenced by products with human features than by those with plant features. Current results were confirmed by the result of anthropomorphic robotic research from Cabibihan et al. (2006) and by Hekkert and Leder's (2008) study on products with human characteristics. In which, accordingly consumers had a preference towards a product with anthropomorphic features (Timpano and Shaw, 2013). In sum, it can be concluded from this research that products with biomimetic features, including plant features and human characteristics, should have a better chance to evoke consumers' emotions. The results also implied that more concrete forms have a greater chance to evoke emotions, at least until they reach a level of being too concrete (real). Overall, this research indicates that: (1) consumers showed different degrees of emotional responses to biomimetic forms with different levels of concreteness; (2) consumers showed different degrees of emotional responses to different types of biomimetic forms. Specifically, consumers showed greater emotional responses to products with anthropomorphic features. The results of this research can hopefully help designers to develop biomimetic products that elicit positive emotions.

References

Biomimicry. http://en.wikipedia.org/wiki/Biomimetics. Accessed 1 Feb 2015

Berlyne, D.E.: Novelty, complexity, and hedonic value. Percept. Psychophys. **8**(5), 279–286 (1970)

Cabibihan, J.J., Carrozza, M.C., Dario, P., Pattofatto, S., Jomâa, M., Benallal, A.: The uncanny valley and the search for human skin-like materials for a prosthetic fingertip. Paper presented at the 2006 6th IEEE-RAS International Conference on Humanoid Robots (2006)

Creusen, M., Snelders, D.: Product appearance and consumer pleasure. In: Green, W.S., Jordan, P.W. (eds.) Pleasure with Products: Beyond Usability, pp. 69–75. Taylor & Francis Group, New York (2002)

Desmet, P., Overbeeke, K., Tax, S.: Designing products with added emotional value: development and appllcation of an approach for research through design. Des. J. **4**(1), 32–47 (2001)

Hekkert, P., Leder, H.: Product aesthetics. In: Schifferstein, H.N.J., Hekkert, P. (eds.) Product Experience, pp. 259–285. Elsevier, Amsterdam (2008)

Janine, B.: Biomimicry: Innovation Inspired by Nature. Quill, New York (1997)

Kellert, S.R., Heerwagen, J., Mador, M.: Biophilic Design: The Theory, Science and Practice of Bringing Buildings to Life. Wiley, New York (2011)

Kezhong, C., Zhihua, Z.: Study on application of industrial design bionics. Art Des. **2**, 042 (2004)

Marzano, S.: Suffusing the organization with design consciousness. Des. Manag. J. (Former Series) **11**(1), 22–27 (2000)

Mehrabian, A., Russell, J.A.: A verbal measure of information rate for studies in environmental psychology. Environ. Behav. **6**, 233–252 (1974)

Montana-Hoyos, C.: BIO-ID4S: Biomimicry in Industrial Design for Sustainability. VDM Verlag, Verlag (2010)

Mori, M.: The uncanny valley. Energy **7**(4), 33–35 (1970)

Mori, M., MacDorman, K.F., Kageki, N.: The uncanny valley [from the field]. IEEE Robot. Autom. Mag. **19**(2), 98–100 (2012)

Norman, D.A.: Emotional Design: Why We Love (or Hate) Everyday Things. Basic books, New York (2007)

Petersen, M.G., Iversen, O.S., Krogh, P.G., Ludvigsen, M.: Aesthetic interaction: a pragmatist's aesthetics of interactive systems. Paper presented at the Proceedings of the 5th Conference on Designing Interactive Systems: Processes, Practices, Methods, And Techniques (2004)

Piwek, L., McKay, L.S., Pollick, F.E.: Empirical evaluation of the uncanny valley hypothesis fails to confirm the predicted effect of motion. Cognition **130**(3), 271–277 (2014). doi:10. 1016/j.cognition.2013.11.001

Timpano, K.R., Shaw, A.M.: Conferring humanness: the role of anthropomorphism in hoarding. Person. Individ. Differ. **54**(3), 383–388 (2013)

Waytz, A., Cacioppo, J., Epley, N.: Who sees human? the stability and importance of individual differences in anthropomorphism. Perspect. Psychol. Sci. **5**(3), 219–232 (2010)

Skeuomorphism and Flat Design: Evaluating Users' Emotion Experience in Car Navigation Interface Design

Lei Wu[1(✉)], Tian Lei[1], Juan Li[2], and Bin Li[3]

[1] Department of Industry Design,
Huazhong University of Science and Technology, Wuhan 430074,
People's Republic of China
{lei.wu,andrew.tianlei}@hust.edu.cn
[2] Department of Art and Design, Huaxia College,
Wuhan University of Technology, Wuhan 430070,
People's Republic of China
lijuan-xy@163.com
[3] School of Mechanical Science and Engineering,
Huazhong University of Science and Technology, Wuhan 430074,
People's Republic of China
libin999@mail.hust.edu.cn

Abstract. To study the difference of users' emotion experience between skeuomorphism and flat design, based on kansei engineering, cognitive psychology and human factors theory, we conducted a semantic differential (SD) experimental study in car navigation interface. The independent variables in this study was the visual representation method (VRM). The dependent variable were user experience rating (UER) and artificial texture rating (ATR). The main findings of this study are as follows: (1) we find that the users' emotion experience is mainly made up of stylization cognition factor (SCF), emotional cognitive factor (ECF) and the decorative cognitive factor (DCC); (2) The artificial texture rating (ATR) has a significant effect on user experience rating (UER). The research results can help designers to deeply understand the difference of user emotional impact between skeuomorphism and flat design, which could guide the designers better to design the car navigation interface.

Keywords: User experience · Emotion · Interface design · Skeuomorphism design · Flat design

1 Introduction

As we known, skeuomorphism design and flat design are both the two important design strategies in the produce-user interface design under the information society. Skeuomorphism is the design strategy of the product-user interface design that describes design elements functionally and originally transplanting from the real object. Mullay described that lots of computer interfaces have a skeuomorphism graphical user interface that emulates objects in the physical world [1]. Norman describes perceived affordances, where the user can tell what an object provides or does based on its appearance, which give rise to the skeuomorphism design [2].

However, flat design represents the minimalism design strategy that moves away from the realism of real object. Morson, S. argued that flat design removes all the elements that help target users to associate with what actually exists in the real world. The metaphors that we use to translate the virtual world to the physical world are being removed from the flat design. The visual cues we as designers created to reference real-world properties like light and shadows have been removed [3]. Gruman described that iPhone had wide usage of skeuomorphism metaphor in the IOS six. With the changes of IOS six to IOS seven, Apple had shifted from skeuomorphism design to the flat design. Flat design offers more clean lines and a lighter, bolder, and more colorful palette of colors to attract the users. The stripping away of the beauty visual design elements and real effects that makes lots of disorientation for target users. The question is how we could still provide those visual cues to users who live in a three-dimensional world but who are interacting within a two-dimensional interface design [4].

Design is the organization of visual information. Information organization in which the user more effectively cognitive received by the visual information of the interface. The object oriented ontological to suggest a re-definition of the concept of affordances in the interaction design. Thus we argue that the different appearance design as the discipline to deal with so much complex design problems. There have been lots of changes in enhancements of design elements in the produce-user interface design.

User experience is one of the significant reasons for the transition skeuomorphism design to flat design. However, there is lack of influencing factors study of the two different interface styles for emotional response experience of the users. In previous studies, Setlur studied two psychophysical studies using semantics as stimuli demonstrate that semantics decrease the time necessary to locate a file in a visual search task [5]. Dan discussed metaphor in the interaction design [6]. Hou research the use of regression to identify the potential relationship between icon style and user emotions [7]. Stevens discussed the role of skeuomorphism in the context of affording interaction in map symbol design [8]. Schneidermeier evaluate the usability of Windows 8 in comparison with Windows 7 with respect to effectiveness, efficiency and satisfaction [9]. Xenakis suggest a theoretical explanation that relates the underlying functionality of aesthetics, in particular of interaction aesthetics and of affordances in the design process [10]. Pucillo establishes a link between user experience research and affordance theory and postulates the concept of experience affordances [11]. However, little research has been focused on different user emotional impact between skeuomorphism and flat design in the car navigation interface design. Therefore, we started this design research. The theoretical framework of the study was shown in the Fig. 1.

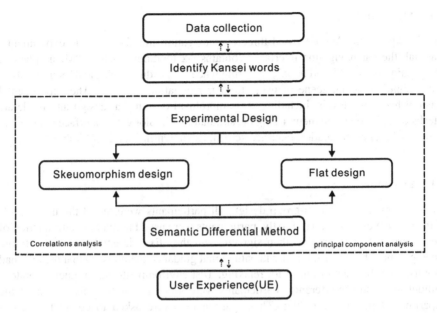

Fig. 1. The theoretical framework of this study

2 Research Method

2.1 Hypothesis

The hypothesis of this study is as follows:

H1: The consistency and differences user emotion experience between the skeuomorphism design and flat design.

H2: Main factors affecting the user emotion experience between the skeuomorphism design and flat design.

H3: Interaction between the Artificial Texture rating (ATR) and User Experience rating (UER) analysis.

In order to confirm this hypothesis, we designed a multiple-variable experiment study. The independent variables in this study were the three interface between skeuomorphism design and flat design in car navigation interface, which were the visual representation method (VRM). The dependent variable is the user experience rating (UER) and artificial texture rating (ATR).

2.2 Participants

A total of 45 undergraduates and graduate students of Huazhong University of Science and Technology were randomly selected to participate in this experiment, 23 male and 22 female, aged 20–27 (Mean = 23.67, $SD = 2.18$) which female of subjects accounted for 48.8 %, male subjects were 51.2 %.

2.3   Material

In this experiment, We designed three car navigation interfaces as the experimental material, the car navigation interfaces contains six modules: such as "Music player", "Navigation maps", "Road book", "Steering wheel", "Baidu search", and "Sina Weibo", it can simulate actual scene of using the car navigation interface. The experimental material had three levels, including skeuomorphism design, flat design and moderate interface design between them. Using the simulator technology, the interface is shown in a size of 7 inches navigation interface screen, as shown in Fig. 2 and Table 1.

2.4   Procedure

The experiment is a within-group design, all participants were tested the three levels of the experimental material. Firstly, participants were asked to read the introduction of the experiment requirements, then signatures in the "Experimental Consent". Before the experiment begin, combined with situational guidance methods, so that the user had 15 s listening to the soft music for relaxing. Test environments was a quiet laboratory without noise and interference. Participants were asked to careful observation on the experimental material for 30 s. Then, participants were asked to complete a questionnaire immediately after each test. After the experiment, a total of 135 questionnaires were collected.

We used the semantic differential method for measuring user emotion feelings. Nagamachi suggested that kansei engineering parametrically links the customer's emotional responses to the properties and characteristics of the product-user interface design [12]. Kansei engineering suggested that every artifact can be described in a certain vector space defined by semantic words. Therefore, we measured 15 pairs of

Material A   Material B   Material C

Fig. 2. The three level of the experimental material

Table 1. The comparison of the three level of the experimental material

Feature	Material A	Material B	Material C
Spatial depth	✓	✓	×
Shadow	✓	✓	×
High light	✓	×	×
Gradual change	✓	×	×
Texture	✓	×	×

Table 2. The kansei words and their corresponding semantic attributes of the experiment

Number	Question	Number	Question
Q1	Complex – Simple	Q9	Cool – Warm
Q2	Rough – Fine	Q10	Rational – Emotional
Q3	Traditional – Modern	Q11	Tough – Soft
Q4	Artless – Gorgeous	Q12	Boring – Interesting
Q5	Common – Unique	Q13	Old – Novel
Q6	Local – International	Q14	Elegant – Colorful
Q7	Artificial – Technology	Q15	Low-grade and High-grade
Q8	Thick – Light	Q16	Ugly – Beautiful

kansei adjectives (such as "Traditional – Modern", "Complex –Simple", and "Rational-Emotional," etc.). The questionnaire for the experiment included the 15 questions. The questionnaire were Printed on A4 paper, Single-sided printing. The evaluation of Kansei words was based on a 7-point Likert scale, where "7" indicated strong agreement, "1" indicated strong disagreement, and "4" was neutral, as shown in Table 2.

3   Results and Discussion

Using IBM-SPSS-Statistics 19 analysis and the results were as follows:

(1) The ANOVA analysis. The results showed that the lowest user experience rating and artificial texture rating is material A, the maximum user experience rating and artificial texture rating is material B, and material C is located in the middle level. Using the ANOVA analysis method, it has significant difference user experience rating between material A, B, C ($P < 0.05$), as shown in Fig. 3 and Table 3.

(2) Principal Component Analysis. We have 16 items of kansei words in the experiment study. The cronbach's alpha = 0.915, displays the scale of the project has high internal consistency. Mean ranges for each project is 3.65 ~ 4.62, the mean total scale of 75.8 (SD = 19.95). Kaiser-Meyer-Olkin Measure of the results of Sampling Adequacy (KMO) test = 0.883, Bartlett's Test of Sphericity result is $\chi^2 = 1585.8$ ($p < 0.001$), indicates that the information have higher degree of overlap between the variable sample data, which suitable for factor analysis.

In this study, we used principal component analysis (PCA) method. This method assumes that each variable is purely linear combination of the factors, the main statistics include the number of common factors, characteristic value of each factor, the contribution rate of each factor (i.e. the percentage of the variance of each factor provided total variance), the cumulative contribution rate, factor load, factor scores, etc. Then we used varimax rotation method for factor loading analysis, the variable with the highest load factor on each count to a minimum. Data analysis showed that each of the main factors for this experiment to explain the higher rate of the entire assessment model, in which the first three main factors explain the rate of the overall model more than 71.134 %, in line with the statistical requirements of this test. The three main

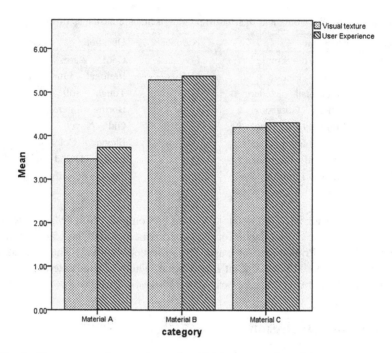

Fig. 3. The user experience rating and artificial texture rating of the three materials

Table 3. ANOVA analysis

User experience rating					
	Sum of squares	df	Mean square	F	Sig.
Between groups	62.637	2	31.319	21.871	.000
Within groups	189.022	132	1.432		
Total	251.659	134			

factors were extracted which could explain 32.709 %, 22.836 %, and 15.589 % of the total variance respectively after varimax rotation. It suggests that the users' emotion experience caused by visual representation method (VRM) can be totally explained 71.134 % by these three main factors.

The loadings of Q2, Q3, Q5, Q6, Q7, Q13, Q15 and Q16 on factor 1 were outstanding, which were 0.789, 0.768, 0.752, 0.746, 0.745, 0.742, 0.696 and 0.581 respectively. These facets mainly reflect the participants' stylization cognition factor in car navigation interface. So, it can be named stylization cognition factor (SCF). The loadings of Q9, Q10, Q11, and Q12 on factor 2 which were 0.879, 0.854, 0.783 and 0.711 respectively. These questions are closely correlated with users' emotional response, and accordingly factor 2 can be named emotional cognitive factor (ECF). The contributions of Q4, Q14, and Q5 to factor 3 were smaller, and their factor loadings were 0.827 and 0.706. These facets are closely related to the participants' decorative factor. So it can be called decorative cognitive factor (DCC). Thus, we find that the

Table 4. Total variance explained

Component	Initial eigenvalues			Rotation sums of squared loadings		
	Total	% of variance	Cumulative %	Total	% of variance	Cumulative %
1	7.261	45.381	45.381	5.233	32.709	32.709
2	2.472	15.449	60.830	3.654	22.836	55.544
3	1.649	10.304	71.134	2.494	15.589	71.134
4	.865	5.403	76.537			
5	.609	3.807	80.344			
6	.562	3.515	83.859			
7	.429	2.680	86.539			
8	.398	2.487	89.026			
9	.379	2.370	91.396			
10	.330	2.060	93.456			
11	.264	1.648	95.104			
12	.215	1.341	96.445			
13	.176	1.098	97.543			
14	.152	.951	98.494			
15	.125	.783	99.277			
16	.116	.723	100.000			

users' emotion experience is mainly made up of three mutually independent components which are stylization cognition factor (SCF), emotional cognitive factor (ECF) and the decorative cognitive factor (DCC), as shown in Table 4 and Fig. 4.

Extraction Method: Principal Component Analysis.

(3) The Correlation Analysis. The artificial texture rating (ATR) has a significant effects on user experience rating (UER). Using the scatterplot matrix analysis, we can

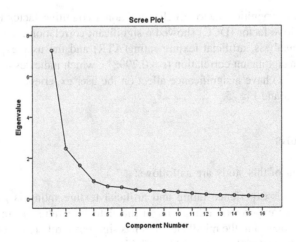

Fig. 4. The scree plot of the each main performance factors

Table 5. Correlation analysis

		Artificial texture rating	User experience rating
Artificial texture rating	Pearson correlation	1	.799**
	Sig. (2-tailed)		.000
	N	135	135
User experience rating	Pearson correlation	.799**	1
	Sig. (2-tailed)	.000	
	N	135	135

**. Correlation is significant at the 0.01 level (2-tailed).

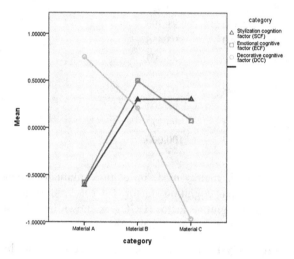

Fig. 5. The scatterplot matrix analysis of the main factors

see the stylization cognition factor (SCF), emotional cognitive factor (ECF) and the decorative cognitive factor (DCC) showed a significant correlation relationship. Using the correlation analysis, artificial texture rating(ATR) and the user experience rating (UER) showed a significant correlation (r = 0.799**), which indicates that the artificial texture rating(ATR) have a significance affect on the user experience rating (UER), as shown in Table 5 and Fig. 5.

4   Conclusions

The main finding of this study are as follows:

1. The lowest user experience rating and artificial texture rating is material A, the maximum user experience rating and artificial texture rating is material B, and material C is located in the middle level. It has significant difference user experience rating between material A, B and C (P<0.05).

2. The three main factors were extracted which could explain 32.709 %, 22.836 %, and 15.589 % of the total variance respectively after varimax rotation. It suggests that the users' emotion experience caused by visual representation method (VRM) can be totally explained 71.134 % by these three main factors. We find that the users' emotion experience is mainly made up of three mutually independent components which are stylization cognition factor (SCF), emotional cognitive factor (ECF) and the decorative cognitive factor (DCC). The stylization cognition factor (SCF), emotional cognitive factor (ECF) and the decorative cognitive factor (DCC) showed a significant correlation.

3. The artificial texture rating (ATR) has a significant effects $(r = 0.799**)$ on user experience rating (UER).

The research results can help designers to deeply understand the different user emotional impact between skeuomorphism design and flat design, which can better guide the designers to design the produce-user interface.

Acknowledgments. The research financial supports from the Fundamental Research Funds for the Central Universities HUST: (2014QN017) and (2013QN011).

References

1. Mullay: IBM real things. In: CHI 1998 Conference Summary on Human Factors in Computing Systems, pp. 13–14. ACM Press, New York (1998)
2. Norman, D.: Affordances and design. Unpublished Article (2004) http://www.jnd.org/dn.mss/affordances-and-design.html
3. Morson, S.: Learn Design for IOS Development, pp. 29–38. Apress, New York (2013)
4. Gruman, G.: iOS 7: The "Just What You Need" Book: What's New in iOS 7 for the iPhone® and iPad®. The Zango Group, San Francisco (2013)
5. Setlur, V., Albrecht-Buehler, C., Gooch, A., Rossoff, S., Gooch, B.: Semanticons Visual metaphors as file icons. Comput. Graphics Forum **24**(3), 647–656 (2005). Blackwell Publishing, Inc., Oxford
6. Saffer, D.: The role of metaphor in interaction design, pp. 3–7. Dissertation, Carnegie Mellon University (2005)
7. Hou, K.-C., Ho, C.-H.: A preliminary study on aesthetic of apps icon design. IASDR (2013)
8. Stevens, J.E., Robinson, A.C., MacEachren, A.M.: Designing map symbols for mobile devices: challenges, best practices, and the utilization of skeuomorphism. In: Proceedings of the 26th International Cartographic Conference, Dresden, Germany, pp. 25–30 (2013)
9. Schneidermeier, T., Hertlein, F., Wolff, C.: Changing paradigm – changing experience? In: Marcus, A. (ed.) DUXU 2014, Part I. LNCS, vol. 8517, pp. 371–382. Springer, Heidelberg (2014)
10. Xenakis, I., Arnellos, A.: The relation between interaction aesthetics and affordances. Des. Stud. **34**(1), 57–73 (2013)
11. Pucillo, F., Cascini, G.: A framework for user experience, needs and affordances. Des. Stud. **35**(2), 160–179 (2014)
12. Nagamachi, M.: Kansei/Affective engineering and history of kansei/affective engineering in the world. Kansei/Affective Engineering, Florida (2010)

Storytelling, Narrative and Fiction in DUXU5

Navigation in Interactive Visual Narrative for Children's Appbooks

Andréa Bellotti[✉], Pedro Biz, and Washington Dias Lessa

Escola Superior de Desenho Industrial ESDI UERJ, Rio de Janeiro, Brazil
{andrea.bellotti07,pedrotrg,washington.lessa}@gmail.com

Abstract. The paper analyses the role of navigation in children's appbooks interactive visual narrative. It is based on design categories for picture books analysis, proposed by Sophie Van der Linden [1], and on categories proposed by Janet Murray for interactive narrative analysis [2]. Linden explains how the structure of printed book articulates narrative, and Murray describes the aesthetic effects of digital narrative. User's active participation in the story unfolding, as also hypertext nonlinearity, extends children's appbooks design dimensions, inserting navigation as a relevant feature for the user experience. The navigation design has been analyzed in four appbooks, namely: *Jack and the Beanstalk, Monster's Socks, Petting Zoo* and *The Very Cranky Bear*.

Keywords: Children's appbooks · Navigation · Interactive visual narrative · Film languags

1 Introduction

Sophie van der Linden [1] proposes categories for the analysis of picture book design, considering that narrative is built textually and visually, through the relationship between text and image. Although picture books and children's appbooks are different artifacts, both convey children's literature. Therefore, it is appropriate for an investigation into the children's appbook to incorporate Linden's reflection.

The nature of interactive media, however, leads us to some transformations and reframing of graphic media categories. For example: (a) text can be animated; (b) if the film language is suggested in the printed book by means of successive images in a sequence of pages, thanks to video it gets an empirical presence in interactive media etc.

But we think that digital visual narrative analysis can be more effective if we use also the categories proposed by Janet Murray [2]: *immersion, transformation* and *agency*. The author highlights the importance of user-reader actions and how the aesthetic experience achieves a different intensity in the new media environment.

Features, such as hypertextuality and the use of game procedures, bring new possibilities to the narrative. In both hypertext and game, users move in a virtual space, where navigation becomes essential for reliable and fluid storytelling experiences.

Based on these theoretical references, and aiming to investigate the role of navigation in children's appbook interactive visual narrative, we selected four tablet

© Springer International Publishing Switzerland 2015
A. Marcus (Ed.): DUXU 2015, Part I, LNCS 9186, pp. 579–589, 2015.
DOI: 10.1007/978-3-319-20886-2_54

appbooks that show different characteristics and have been recognized for the quality of their realization (great impact in social media, prizes at book fairs and specialized conferences on children's ebooks). (1) *The Very Cranky Bear* [3], winner of *Parent's Choice Awards 2013* (Silver Honor Awards) is more traditional, close to its printed version; (2) *The Monster's Socks* [4], *Bologna Ragazzi Digital Award 2013* finalist for children's fiction, that has no printed version, incorporates some game features; (3) *Petting Zoo* [5], winner of *Parent's Choice Awards 2014* (Golden Awards), is a book of animated images without text; (4) the classic *Jack and the Beanstalk* [6], honor mention award in *Bologna Ragazzi Digital Award 2014*, presents a game structure. The analysis aim to contribute to the understanding of design issues present in the production of appbooks for children. It has an exploratory nature, in order to support researches to come.

2   Narratives

Considering that a literary piece results from the writer's work, the narrative "is the exposure of a text capable of evoking a world given as real or imagined through linked facts in time and determined space" [7]. In this context, the book design can bring comfortable reading and/or connotations due to typographic choices (e.g., a neutral font, or a "fancy" font etc.), but it may not modify the structure of the story. Picture books, however, call for a redefinition of traditional narrative. The participation of images on a *visual narrative* ranges from different degrees of visual emphasis to a totally visually structured storytelling. Although the term visual narrative could also be used for films or comics, we are dealing here with visual storytelling in books.

According to Sherline Pimenta [8], visual narrative is an essentially explicit way to narrate through images. The story displays a series of events connected by causality, temporality or order of occurrence; as narrative means the act of telling a story, or the story itself, or its order of presentation. Pimenta lists five characteristics of visual narratives, based on verbal narrative features: (1) the presence of a story is the most essential feature of the visual narrative; (2) the visual is constructed with the objective of communicating a story to the onlooker; (3) there is a presence of actors (participants), and an actor is a character in the story who performs an action; (4) the visual narrative has an 'universe' of its own, and the participants exist in this universe, that mimics the real or imagined world; (5) the visual narrative can be expressed on any medium, e.g. paper, stone, electronic device etc. [8].

Pimenta describes the visual narrative in digital media as an interactive visual narrative, characterized by three conditions: "(1) that it is essentially visual in nature; (2) has the narrative aspect to it; and (3) involves interaction from the viewer" [8]. The interactive visual narrative begins with the invention of virtual spaces and navigation systems to access them. The interaction can range from linear navigation to total immersion in the narrative mediated by characters and/or situations. The user-reader's interaction and choices are directly linked to the development of the story and to the perception of its movement.

To Murray one of the essential characteristics of digital environments is the simulated spatiality, in which users can move by their own. Rather than creating imaginary spaces from reading, or watching situations assembled from the clipping of scenes, like in the movies, the computer allows the users to transit through spaces with some control over their footsteps. In these terms, the navigation can be thought of as part of the narrative structure.

In this research, we focus on children's appbooks as interactive visual narrative, where the images match or exceed the text.

3 Categories Related to Structural Relations Between Text and Image According to Linden

Sophie van der Linden discusses the relations between text and image within the picture book in the chapter "Pages and book spaces" [1], from which we highlight the following structural features: types of diagramming; framing, field and extra-field; montage and junction.

3.1 Types of Diagramming

Dissociation. Dissociative diagramming is characterized by the alternation between text pages and image pages. In printed books the maximum separation between text and image is due to the book fold, which leads the reader to switch between viewing the image and reading the text. In the appbook, usually there is no such differentiation between pages. The most logical is the simple page display, but there are also cases in which the double-page spread can be also displayed as a flowable layout.

When the appbook reproduces the double-page spread, showing the fold mark and mimicking printed page flipping, the dissociative layout happens exactly as on printed books. However, beyond this kind of solution, an appbook with a dissociative layout, for instance, provides the possibility of enabling and disabling text by touching the screen, decreasing the reading rate and letting the users "read" the illustrations alone.

Association. Association diagramming combines at least one verbal statement to one visual statement on the same page. Text and images can be arranged in several ways on a single page or on a double-page spread. These different structures will have different implications, depending on the narrative intention. In the appbook, the associative diagramming can occur statically, as on a printed book; or it can happen through the fade-out feature (text color gradual darkening) of the image during screen transition.

Conjunction. Text and images are organized in an overall composition. It differs from associative diagramming because it presents several statements that show more contiguousness than continuity. Text and images are integrated, while in associative diagramming verbal and visual messages tend to be perceived separately.

3.2 Framing, Field and Extra-Field

The framing – from top to bottom (plongée), from bottom to top (contraplongée) or an oblique framing (that transmits a sense of instability), for instance – entails semantic effects to the storytelling. Besides that, the framing of a character (or any other element) tends to suggest an extra-field: framing in a picture book scene determine what is inside or outside of our field of vision. And the reader can infer the existence of another space beyond the frame boundaries.

These notions have arisen with the film, but can also be conveyed by the illustration. In the printed book these viewpoints are statically represented, and are developed page by page, whereas the appbook can actually simulate the camera movement.

3.3 Montage

The picture book can use the composition in double-page spread, referring to the film montage and making the page sequence more fluid. "If montage, in cinema, is the sequence of plans, in the picture book it is to organize the succession of double-page spreads" [1]. When transposed to an appbook, the double-page spread suffers adjustments: reductions, cuts, strains, reducing of the body font, etc. However, the camera motion feature may supply the function of the double-page spread in picture books, keeping the attention by means of a sequence plan.

3.4 Junction

"It is a sequence of articulated images connected by one or more links whether iconic, semantic, plastic, logical or only technical" [1]. The organization of narrative sequences has the function of joining, and these articulations may forecast fundamental changes in margins, vignettes and more. There is always an element that fulfills the role of making a transition.

4   Interactive Visual Media: Navigation and Orientation

Adapting Linden's categories to the digital media means considering how multimedia objects, animation and interactivity features influence the design relation between text and image. Although it is not a concern for Linden's research, it is our intent in this paper to discuss the navigation for the interactive visual media and its effects on narrative.

In hypermedia devices, navigation can be understood as a metaphor of the act of moving in space [9]. The printed page and the screen space are both two-dimensional planes. In the former, the sequence of different physical pages, bound by the book spine, establishes a physicality for the time dimension. In the latter, the narrative temporality is developed through the updating of a succession of images in the same visual plane.

According to Rosenfeld and Morville [10], we create navigation tools to avoid getting lost, either moving on land, on sea or in hypertext network. The authors summarize the utility of navigation tools on three points: "to define a path to follow, determine the position in space and find the way back" [10]. These three points are related to the notion of orientation: to know where you are, to know how to go ahead, and to know how to return to the beginning.

Tidwell [11] signs three "common-sense features" of navigation systems for web interfaces that we can use to understand digital narratives as well:

1. Good Signage: "Clear, unambiguous labels anticipate what you're looking for and tell you where to go; signs are where you expect them to be, and you're never left standing at a decision point without guidance".
2. Environmental clues: Culturally determined conventions integrated on interface, e.g., you would look for an "X" close button at the top right of a modal dialog. In real life could be a rock in a trail that signs the way back.
3. Maps: Gives a whole picture of space, summarizing everything you need to know to move without feeling lost, e.g. roadmap, sitemap, etc.

5   Immersion, Agency and Transformation

Involved with cyberliterature projects at MIT, Janet Murray [2] seeks to expand the notion of narrative under the influence of computer, presenting the possible experiences that stories can provide the reader. The author focuses on the fact that, in addition to the simulation of other media, the digital medium is developed as a hypertext tissue, in which the user involvement is crucial to the course of the narrative.

5.1   Immersion

Immersion is one of three aesthetic categories, which the author calls the *three narrative dimensions of pleasure*. "Immersion is a metaphorical term derived from the physical experience of being submerged in water." The expected sensation of "being surrounded by a completely other reality, as different as water is from air, that takes over all of our attention, our whole perceptual apparatus." In "a participatory medium, immersion implies learning to swim, to do the things that the new environment makes possible" [2]. Learning to swim is learning to interact in the digital environment. Murray points out that the challenge of narrative immersion is to avoid breaking the enchantment of the story. That keeps users delighted by both stimulating narrative plot and establishing engagement with the story.

5.2   Agency

Agency is the satisfaction of taking meaningful actions and the perceivable results of decisions and choices displayed on interface. The sense of agency responsiveness is fundamental in the project of navigation tools. When the controls do not work or do not match with the indicated directions, they awake in users the feeling of being lost. The sense of agency is related to the user autonomy. The highest autonomy level, described by Murray as intentional navigation, appears in a game when the player denies the story to explore the virtual territory just for fun.

Murray describes two configurations of the digital space with its own narrative power and agency intensity: "the solvable maze and tangled rhizome" [2]. The maze always leads to the exit, even if on their way find countless doors to open. The rhizome is a nonlinear undefined and intertwined path, with many entrances and exits. There is no correct starting and ending point, as the path is created by the user's moves.

5.3   Transformation

The third category, transformation, describes how the features of graphic interface offer users "countless ways of shape-shifting" [2]. The computer allows the storyteller to create stories with simultaneous realities, mosaics of multiple fragments and viewpoints, with not clearly determined closures. At the same time, it helps readers to be more than passive agents, allowing them to build their own ways on a narrative and making them feel as characters of the story.

6   Case Studies

6.1   The Very Cranky Bear

The Very Cranky Bear tells the story of three friends who, when getting shelter from the rain in a cave, find a very angry bear. The appbook was produced from the printed version, and maybe that's the reason why its narrative is fairly linear. The appbook design keeps almost the same configuration of the physical book. One configuration in particular, the film language, is leveraged in the digital environment. We identified two of Linden's categories related with film: (1) *Framing, field and extra field* (Fig. 1), performed by zoom and travelling effects simulated by framings and sequence of pages; (2) *Montage* (Fig. 2), in which camera zoom is activated by the user *agency* making the image sequence more fluid.

Fig. 1. Camera zoom (framing, field and extra-field)

Forest, rain and animals sounds are other features that emphasize film language, also suggesting that there is something beyond what is framed. They awaken in the reader the will to know what happens in this space that is not framed. Therefore, these film features work as an *environmental clue* for the navigation.

The camera view style inserts the reader in the story as a passive observer, who moves along the scenes. The navigation controls (Fig. 2) determine the pace and the

Fig. 2. Camera moving sequence (montage) and navigation controls

direction (forwards or backwards) of the narrative. In these conditions agency doesn't contribute very much to its development, as the autonomy of the user is restricted to few actions.

This appbook uses printed book language and uses, at the same time, multimedia to perform *immersion* through navigation. Although the appbook keeps diagramming static layout, the space environment is constructed with film shots, animated transitions and sound effects, substituting page flipping and double spread page.

6.2 Monster's Socks

The book tells the story of a monster called *Monster*, who is looking for its socks. On its way, as it talks to other characters it can figure out where they are. This appbook displays two navigation modes: the linear regular course of the story through navigation controls; and hyperlinked thumbnails scenes, jumping directly to specific scenes (Fig. 3).

Fig. 3. Thumbnails navigation (top), navigation controls (bottom), Yellow circle text activator (centered bottom) (Color figure online).

The arrow shaped buttons controls are placed in the lower corners, as in all other appbooks. But they work differently, acting as video game controls, in which users must keep the button pressed for moving the monster around the scene. This design stimulates handhold style of the joystick, keeping both hands always close to the buttons. When the monster crosses the entire scene, the buttons perform a new function, changing the scene.

The storytelling is directly related to the act of walking in space. The text turns visible only when Monster passes over yellow circles on the floor. The alternation between image and text changes the meaning of reading. When two paragraphs are alternated at the same scene, their meaning changes, making the story go on. Navigation leads to a change from dissociative to associative diagramming, unfolding the narrative. The user agency corresponds to the Monster movements, standing for printed book's text and flipping pages.

6.3 Petting Zoo

The sense of going to the zoo is provided by the only text within the appbook, which is the title "Petting Zoo". Besides a series of pets' illustrations, there is no scenario representing a zoo. The narrative is not a sequence of related events, but a sequence of depicted animals. Despite the book structure in linear sequence of scenes, each scene could be understood as an independent narrative, and when put together they display the Zoo ride. The animated transitions establish the sense of contiguity between the scenes (Fig. 4). They can be understood from the perspective of Linden's *junction*. Bellotti and Lessa describe the animated transition as "a fun metamorphosis of an animal into another, (...) a *junction* that becomes animated by using the features offered by the digital medium" [12].

Fig. 4. Scene transition

The user-reader's *immersion* happens by what Murray calls transformation, i.e. an imaginary part of the narrative not represented in the application. The more users imagine being inside the story, the more clearly they can interact in the space.

Another feature that enhance the feeling of *immersion* is the well-defined interaction model input, in contrast with the singular animated outputs for the interactive pets. The gesture inputs follow the same logic throughout the application: users swipe vertically and horizontally to "play" with the animals; to change a scene they must touch the lower right corner of the screen to go forwards, and the lower left corner to go backwards. There is an alternation between gestures repetition and the variety of animations, linking uniform conventions and surprising responses.

The narrative can be understood with the help of two navigation features. The first and most important is the linear displacement through the scenes, triggered by the navigation controls (arrow shaped buttons). The second, that is the summary (Fig. 5), features a mosaic of hyperlinks, allowing direct access to any scene. The orientation of the reader is provided by environmental clues, by animated transition between illustrations in response to the inputs gestures and by the background color shifting. The lack of scenario weakens the notion of a given place in time and space, encouraging the imaginary construction of the story. In a book where there is no text, the navigation features provide the means that take users for a zoo ride.

Fig. 5. Summary screen

Fig. 6. Navigation features (left to right image): a. navigation controls (bottom); b. blinking spot (on Jack's shirt); c. conversation ballons.

6.4   Jack and the Beanstalk

Based on a classic tale, this appbook presents a maze-like narrative, characterized by its multiple endings and by a sense of always going in search of the exit. The final location of the game – safely returning home – is always the same, but the actions and decisions taken along the giant's castle determine the conditions in which the character ends the game. Differently from the traditional tale, in this application the narrative plot changes as it is performed by the user *agency*.

Of the four appbooks, this one presents the greater *agency* and, at the same time, more navigation features. The arrow shaped buttons on the bottom of the screen go forwards and backwards on the scenes, changing their color as soon as all tasks are accomplished (Fig. 6a). Jack's movements are controlled by input gestures, according to the context of the scene. While he is climbing the beanstalk, the user swipes left or right to avoid obstacles on the way; or Jack walks along the castle halls when the user drags him with the finger.

As the inputs depend on the scene, the orientation is given both by signage and by environmental clues. The former correspond to conversation balloons (Fig. 6b) indicating what Jack needs to do; the latter to the scenario depicted as a cartoon, providing affordance (e.g. the end of the corridor has stairs indicating another level up). In addition there is another kind of signage – that appears as a blinking spot (Fig. 6c) – if users can't find out how to perform the task.

The summary (Fig. 7) is designed as a location map, so users can identify the chapters and all the tasks that must be completed for Jack's happy end. The appbook also provides a map giving access to all parts, regardless the order of reading.

Fig. 7. Summary screen

7   Considerations

In the four appbooks the main navigation controls are displayed as arrow shaped buttons placed on the bottom of the screen. The buttons are always visible, differently of textual ebooks, in which the navigation controls are hidden (flip gesture). At the same time, the controls of each appbook respond differently to inputs, according to design decisions, as could be specially seen on *Monster's Socks*.

As a trend, the navigation structure changes from the page flipping metaphor to animated transitions and hipertext jumps. Even in an appboks close to the printed book, like *The Very Cranky Bear,* motion graphics marks scene transitions, reinforcing its film style.

On three of the appbooks the summary is composed of hyperlinked objects, despite their different designs due to the logic of each narrative. The summary of *Jack and the Beanstalk* is a map, showing the path of the maze-like world. On the contrary, on *Petting Zoo* the summary screen gathers all the pets as they appear in the scenes.

These books exemplify combinations of categories from different means, aiming to promote the development of interactive visual narrative and the user involvement with the story. Their analysis enabled us to understand how the compatibility of the traditional structure of the book, film language and new technological resources fit together to create the interactive visual narrative, guiding users in the story, through scenes, images and texts.

This approach to children's appbooks, with the help of design and digital storytelling categories, shows that the designer of the interactive visual narrative must control both the story and the media features. As Janet Murray points out this "kind storyteller" ought to be half bard and half hacker.

References

1. Linden, S.: Para Ler o Livro Ilustrado. Cosac Naify, São Paulo (2011)
2. Murray, J.H.: Hamlet on the Holodeck. MIT Press, Cambridge (1997)
3. We Are Wheelbarrow: The Very Cranky Bear (version 1.7) [mobile application software]. http://itunes.apple.com.br. Accessed 2012
4. Hughes, M.: Monster's Socks (version 1.03) [mobile application software]. http://itunes.apple.com.br. Accessed 2012
5. Fox & Sheep: Petting Zoo (version 1.3) [mobile application software]. http://itunes.apple.com.br. Accessed 2012
6. Nosy Crow: Jack and the Beanstalk (version 1.0.1) [mobile application software]. http://itunes.apple.com.br. Accessed 2014
7. Teixeira, D.J., Nunes, J., Gonçalvez, B.: A narrativa visual interativa no livro digital infantil: um estudo a partir do book app treasure kai and the lost gold shark island. In: 5o Congresso Internacional CBL do Livro Digital, São Paulo (2014). http://www.congressodolivrodigital.com.br/site2014/trabalhos-cientificos
8. Pimenta, S., Poovaiah, R.: On defining visual narratives. IDC Des. Res. J. 3, 25–46 (2010). http://www.idc.iitb.ac.in/resources/dt-aug-2010/On%20Defining%20Visual%20Narratives.pdf
9. Santaella, L.: Navegar no ciberespaço: o perfil do leitor imersivo. Paullus, São Paulo (2004)
10. Rosenfeld, L., Morville, P.: Information architecture for the World Wide Web. O'Reilly, Beijing (1998)
11. Tidwell, J.: Designing Interfaces. O'reilly, Sebastopol (2011)
12. Lima, A.B. de S., Lessa, W.D.: O e-book infantil e as relações texto-imagem-interação. In: Anais do 11 Congresso Brasileiro de Pesquisa e Desenvolvimento em Design, Gramado (2014)

Human-Robot Interaction Ethics in Sci-Fi Movies: Ethics Are Not 'There', We Are the Ethics!

Myriam El Mesbahi[✉]

Laboratoire Ingénierie des Systèmes Informatiques (LISI), Computer Science Department, Faculty of Sciences Semlalia, Cadi Ayyad University (UCA), Boulevard Prince My Abdellah, 2390 Marrakech, Morocco
m.elmesbahi@edu.uca.ma

Abstract. Human-Robot interaction is a field seeing massive growth, and as robots gain more and more capabilities they will play an increasingly prominent part in our everyday lives. But, as robotic development continues to grow, one subfield of robotics research is lagging behind other areas: roboethics or ensuring that robot behavior adheres to certain moral standards. This paper explores robot ethics through the lens of some popular sci-fi movies involving robots as characters in their storyline. Different ethical issues related to human-robot interaction are cast and discussed. To overcome those issues, a survey was conducted to detect everyone's duty. Its results and implications are presented and may be of benefit to HRI researchers.

Keywords: Human-Robot interaction · Science-Fiction movies · Ethics

1 Introduction

Ensuring Human-Robot Interaction (HRI) is one of the greatest technological success stories of the present time. Robots are becoming more and more important in our daily lives. In fact, robots are rapidly cropping up into human beings environments, interacting with people in increasingly intrusive ways. They are appearing everywhere: in entertainment, healthcare, search and rescue, and many other venues where interaction is possible. In each of these cases, there is no question that robotic technology is making life easier, safer, or more convenient for human beings. Despite these benefits, concerns remain about what happens when robotic technology fails, resulting in economic loss, property damage, injury, or loss of life. Still, linked to the risk of errors, it may be unclear who is responsible for any harmful results. While literature sufficiently addresses the rapid and remarkable technological advances, the ethical implications of these interactions have been largely ignored. HRI is in need of practical guidance toward understanding ethical challenges. Science-Fiction movies have already predicted some applications of HRI, raising thereby questions about all the challenges they may create for ethics.

© Springer International Publishing Switzerland 2015
A. Marcus (Ed.): DUXU 2015, Part I, LNCS 9186, pp. 590–598, 2015.
DOI: 10.1007/978-3-319-20886-2_55

Over the past decades, numerous sci-fi movies dealt with HRI. HRI interrelations with sci-fi films have yet to be explored in details. In this paper, I survey some of the remarkable movies of film industry dealing with HRI, and comment on their ethical implications. The aim of this paper is to (1) outline the main ethical issues raised by HRI in Sci-Fi movies, (2) identify the major ethical implications for which designers, programmers, and end users must now be prepared, and (3) identify the possible precautionary ways that could be engineered to maximize robots benefits and minimize their harms. The remainder of the paper is organized as follows. Next section reviews some of the related work dealing with roboethics reported in the literature. Section 3 presents a formal investigation of the ethical issues reported by sci-fi movies. Section 4 describes my survey method and gives information about the obtained results. The last section summarizes the contributions, provides the conclusions, and indicates an outlook by which the research proposed in this paper can be extended.

2   Related Work and Motivation

Roboethics extends the field of computer ethics beyond concern for what people do with their computers to questions about what the robots do by themselves. In the robot ethics literature, Isaac Asimov's [1] laws of robotics have so dominated discussion about the ethics of HRI as to eclipse the day-to-day ethical challenges facing HRI research. To these three laws initially formulated in 1942, he added the zeroth law, in 1983. And, given the speed with which robotics technology advances, ethical challenges will continue to multiply. Later on, Ingram et al. [2] proposed a general code of ethics. To date, a number of roboethics initiatives have taken place at international and national levels. While a majority of the initiatives share the common goal of promoting discussions within the field, many of the initiatives have been limited to expert groups, or by national and disciplinary boundaries. However, robotics is the study of a pervasive technology that crosses national and disciplinary boundaries, and robotic products affect not only the experts but also lay users of the technology. Hence, roboethics discussions need to cross these boundaries. We can find inklings of ethics in HRI literature [3]; yet, most of this work is focused on a single theme and does not present a holistic picture in terms of human expectations.

Thereby, I propose to focus the effort more narrowly by emphasizing the unique ethical challenges of robots drawn from sci-fi. Sci-Fi movies have always been a medium for speculation about the future of technology and presented the robot long before it was possible to build one. These movies have brought forth ethical concerns amongst the public and designers, challenging the boundaries of currently existing policies. In order to conduct a deeper analysis of the impact of sci-fi movies on how humans perceive robots, I developed a questionnaire. Figure 1 shows that portrayal of robots in sci-fi movies affects human perceptions about HRI and its ethical issues.

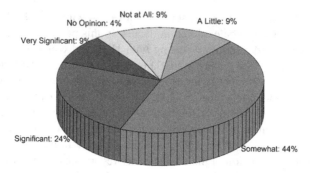

Fig. 1. Sci-Fi movies influence on humans' attitude towards robots

3   Roboethics in Sci-Fi Movies

Sci-Fi movies dealing with HRI raise serious ethical questions right now. Those movies also anticipate important and foresighted moral issues related to HRI. This study of sci-fi movies and their conception of ethics is valuable in the display of the ways people interact with robots in fiction. Thereby, it seems logical to be concerned about the possibility that what is now fiction from Asimov, Schreier, Spielberg, and others, will become lugubrious reality someday. Table 1 shows a list of movies which is meant to be illustrative of the distinctive ethical challenges arising in HRI research as seen in sci-fi. In terms of scope, I have taken into consideration – from the point of view of the ethical issues connected to robotics – a temporal range of more than three decades, in whose frame I could reasonably locate and infer certain foreseeable developments in the field. The selected movies emphasize the cultural differences between European,

Table 1. Sci-Fi Movies dealing with HRI by time period

Time period	Western movies	Eastern movies	European movies
70 s – 80 s	Westworld Blade Runner Terminator D.A.R.Y.L Chopping Mall Short Circuit 2	Castle in the Sky Death Ray on Coral Island	Le Roi et l'Oiseau
90 s - 2000	The Matrix Trilogy	Robotrix	Nemesis
After year 2000	I, Robot Astro Boy Robot & Frank RoboCop	Metropolis Casshern Hinokio Vexille Time of Eve Enthiran Robotropolis Mantera War Zone	Pinocchio 3000 Glenn 3948 Eva

Eastern, and Western movies. This survey provides the space to discuss ethical issues related to HRI that arise from sci-fi movies in different cultures: European, Eastern, and Western. HRI researchers can learn a lot from sci-fi movies, so that they can anticipate moral and ethical issues that may take place in near future. This section explores some of the ethical concerns that emerge from examining this body of work.

3.1 HRI Ethical Issues in Sci-Fi Movies

In this section, I present a detailed taxonomy of the most significant ethical issues related to HRI, which burst out from sci-fi movies. In the taxonomy herein, the specific ethical issues related solely to robotics are carefully evaluated. It is based on the application areas of robots, and on the specificity inherent to the HRI of these applications. This survey of HRI ethics in sci-fi movies is not overly biased towards Western and European movies, but also spots some of the Eastern films which are numerous. The latter reflect their unique cultural heritage, which is quite different from the well known Western and European cultures.

Movies often capture emerging scientific advances or even, to some extent, function as a source of enlightenment and inspiration to scientific discovery. Sci-Fi movies stand out in their predictive effort to grasp human interaction with future technology. They present technology as a double edged sword with both risks and benefits. Typically, the storylines in sci-fi movies reveal important ethical issues regarding:

- Moral agency: robots are either used in a good way or misused. Sci-Fi movies also depict robots' ability to make moral decisions, act with reference to right and wrong, and be held responsible for their actions;
- Consciousness: robots are having a human-like consciousness. Sci-Fi movies present robots as sentient machines, self-aware, having feelings and emotions;
- Identity: sci-fi movies offer a unique insight into humans and robots identities. They generally present people as robots addicted, aiming to find parts of their identities, recall aspects of their past, and get sense of who they really are;
- Relations: humans develop cognitive and affective bonds toward robots; resulting in the humanization of the human–robot relationship. In sci-fi movies, people tend to attribute personalities, emotions, goals, and intentions to robots;
- Privacy and surveillance: sci-fi movies tackle the effects of robots on privacy invasion, and direct surveillance. They usually present robots as invaders, having no decency, or courtesy norms.

Sci-Fi movies and the depiction of ethical issues in HRI have, of necessity, been closely intertwined. Cross-cultural sci-fi movies and HRI ethics remain largely unexplored. Yet, Table 1 European movies emphasize deontological ideas with regard to robots (judging a robot based on its actions' adherence to a set of rules), whereas Western movies discuss utilitarian ethics (judging a robot based on the maximization of its utility such as giving pleasure, or ensuring economic well-being), and finally Eastern movies represent robots as an additional partner in the global interaction of things. In the latter, robots are always seen as beneficial and friendly to humanity.

3.2   HRI Ethical Implications in Sci-Fi Movies

As already discussed, the aforementioned movies tackle ethical concerns. Thus, they generate ethical implications in HRI, emerging some fascinating moral questions: At what point should we consider a robot to be a full collaborator, thus affording it some rights and responsibilities, and if that point is reached, will we need to emancipate others? Can and should robots be punished for misbehavior, and, if so, how? Is it ethical for one robot to damage or destroy another member of its group? If not, how can we ensure that such behaviors do not occur? Under what circumstances can robots be put in positions of authority, with human beings required to obey them? If a robot malfunctions and harms someone, who is responsible: the robot's owner, its manufacturer, or the robot itself? Is it ethically wrong for robots to prey upon our emotional sensitivities - should they be required to remind us, explicitly or implicitly, that they are only machines? How safe do robots need to be before they're deployed in society at large? What does it mean to behave ethically? Should robots be able to refuse an order from a human, and what ethical standards should they be held to? Would an emotional component be beneficial to a robot? [3–5].

To give an answer to those questions, it is important to know how people perceive robots and what ethical standards they expect from them. Indeed, according to sci-fi movies, there is a variety of settings in which ethical questions about the selection of robot morphology and behaviors arise; particularly regarding manifestations of gender, race, and ethnicity. Another issue tackled in those movies - concerning diversity of platforms - is that many mechanistic robots conform to grey, boxy, masculine prototype. They also present robots as machines with a low amount of ethical concerns. However, survey participants do not share the same vision. As seen in Fig. 2, more than half of the participants (54 %) perceive robots as human-like machines. Moreover, 74 % of the

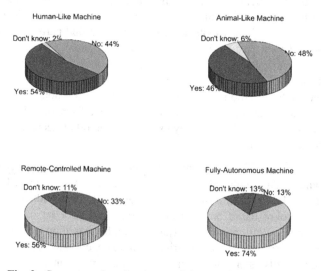

Fig. 2.   Survey results related to participants perception of robots

participants consider robots as fully-autonomous rather than remote-controlled machines. This surely implies that humans discern robots as self ethical decision makers, and peers endowed with higher ethical standards as shown in Fig. 3.

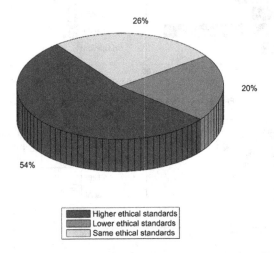

Fig. 3. Ethical standards wanted to be present during HRI

4   Ethical Issues: Who Is Responsible?

There are currently no international treaties, agreements or conventions governing the use of robots; which raises serious ethical questions. This survey provides a place to start looking for ethical similarities and differences between Western, Eastern, and European views of HRI. It is by no means exhaustive. Note, in particular, that I deliberately debate, for the purpose of this discussion, scenarios popular in science fiction. Looking at sci-fi movies provides a unique perspective on future interactions between human beings and robots.

4.1   The Survey

As part of this work, I conducted a survey to gauge the views of people on ethics in HRI. The survey instrument was prototyped and refined prior to release on the Internet to ensure that it was unambiguous, understandable, and easy to use. The first section of the survey gathered demographic information such as age, gender, occupation, education, geographic information, level of spirituality, attitudes toward technology, robots, and so on. The main section of the survey then probed a number of ethical issues traced by sci-fi movies. The last section assessed some of the background knowledge of the respondents. 55 candidates from different fields answered the survey, expressing their acceptance or rejection of robots seen in Table 1 movies. Specifically, the goal was to establish opinion on the use of robots and their ethical implications

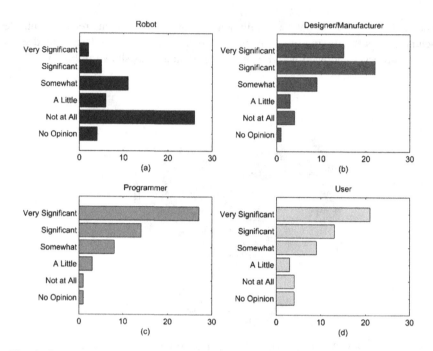

Fig. 4. Survey participants' perception of who is in charge of ethical issues during HRI

spanning the general public, robotics researchers, and policymakers to ascertain the current point of view maintained by these various groups on this subject. The survey serves as a benchmark for future opinion and also provides insights into what people are concerned about now.

In order to get an idea about who will be held responsible if an ethical issue appears during HRI, I defined the four following categories, based on the main actors taking part in the HRI research field.

- The ethics of how robots treat humans: in this case, it is robots who are the ethical subjects. Then, the question to ask is: what are the several ways to construe the ethical relationships between robots and humans?
- The ethics of people who design robots: in this case, it is robots designers and/or manufacturers who are the ethical subjects. Then, the question to ask is: how to design robots that could be truly ethical agents?
- The ethics of systems built into robots: in this case, it is robots programmers who are the ethical subjects. Then, the question to ask is: how to program robots to act ethically?
- The ethics of people who interact with robots: in this case, it is robots users who are the ethical subjects. Then, the question to ask is: how humans might act ethically through, or with, robots regardless of their communities (e.g., doctors, police professionals, and ordinary citizens)?

Figure 4 shows indeed participants' perception of who is to blame and take for responsible when any ethics related problem occurs during a HRI. Among the 55 participants to the survey, 26 (47 %) think that robots are not responsible for their misbehaviors and 6 of them (nearly 11 %) believe that robots have a little amount of responsibilities in regards to ethical issues raised by HRI. Whereas, almost all participants agreed that the first person to blame is the programmer, then the designer and/or the manufacturer, and finally the user. In fact, 27 (49 %) and 14 (25 %) participants sustain that it is respectively very significant/significant to hold programmers responsible for ethical issues. Afterwards, according to participants, designers and/or manufacturers are those to be hold accountable for ethical problems during HRI. More than half of them support this idea, with 22 (40 %) finding it significant and 15 (27 %) perceiving it as very significant. Finally, participants think that users should also be reprimanded if there is a lack of ethics during a HRI; with 21 (38 %) of them seeing it as very significant and 13 (24 %) finding it significant.

4.2 Recommendations and Precautionary Measures

Based on the aforementioned ethical problems tackled by sci-fi movies, the perception of robots by humans, and their perception of the people to be held responsible; it is necessary to guarantee some conditions and establish some precautions in HRI. From the individual researcher's point of view, she/he has to make it possible to adhere and implement the ethical code. Thus, some important steps must be taken such as:

- Decision-making capacity: empowering robots by a certain amount of freedom to identify situations and choose alternatives based on the values and preferences defined and accepted;
- Individual scientists' honesty and integrity: integrating ethical values into programming, software engineering, and design;
- Transparency of processes: making information available for public consumption;
- Continuous re-evaluation: improving educational system at all levels to prepare future generations ahead of time, and pursuing the state of development in robotics research field and its implications;
- Religious involvement: establishing adequate pro-active answers to the aforementioned ethical issues, by the religious scholars;
- Ethics assessment: expanding the ethics field of study to cater fully HRI and roboethics.

To sum up, I think that in order to fully understand the consequences of the deployment of robots in humans' life, a systematic ethical evaluation needs to be conducted to guide users, robots developers, and robots manufacturers and/or designers regarding the intended future use of robots. For sure, this study needs to be conducted prior to their deployment, not as an afterthought.

5   Conclusion and Future Work

This paper identified the most evident, urgent, and sensitive ethical issues discussed by sci-fi movies, leaving a place for a deeper analysis and further studies. These issues are but the tip of the iceberg regarding the ethical quandaries surrounding the use of robots in everyday life. It is my contention, nonetheless, that if robots will take a place in our daily life, it is people's duty to ensure they are as safe as possible. Robots are and will remain in the foreseeable future dependent on human ethical scrutiny as well as on the moral and legal responsibility of humans. As in every field of science and technology, sensitive areas open up, and it is the specific responsibility of the scientists who work in this field to face these new ethical issues.

I truly believe that ethical and moral decisions should be made by humans, not their creations. In fact, ethics should be understood as making a constructive contribution to work in HRI field of research. It is HRI researchers' duty to avoid as much as possible situations in which ethical problems are noticed or may occur. Thereby, since one of the crucial goals in HRI is to aim for broad user acceptance of robots, it is in the interest of HRI researchers to take ownership of HRI ethics issues, and to make attention to those issues a routine aspect of their everyday work. A culture of ethical awareness and refinement within the HRI community, taking into account the difference in genders, races, and cultures, will surely advantage the cause of HRI research. Actually, robo-ethics is not the ethics of robots, nor any artificial ethics, as shown in sci-fi movies. Ethics are not 'there', we are the ethics!

References

1. Asimov, I.: Runaround. Astounding Science Fiction, March 1942. Reprinted in I, Robot (1950)
2. Ingram, B., Jones, D., Lewis, A., Richards, M., Rich, C., Schachterle, L.: A code of ethics for robotics engineers. In: Proceedings of the 5th ACM/IEEE International Conference on Human-Robot Interaction (HRI) (2010)
3. Anya, O., Tawfik, H., Nagar, A., Westaby, C.: An ethics-informed approach to the development of social robotics. From Critique to Action: The Practical Ethics of the Organizational World 231(253), 23 (2011)
4. Calo, M.R.: Robots and privacy. In: Lin, P., Bekey, G., Abney, K. (eds.) Robot Ethics: The Ethical and Social Implications of Robotics. MIT Press, Cambridge (2012)
5. Nourbakhsh, I.R.: Robot Futures. MIT Press, Cambridge (2013)
6. Wallach, W., Allen, C.: Moral Machines: Teaching Robots Right from Wrong. Oxford University Press, Oxford (2009)

Design Perspectives to the Design of Interfaces Connected and Convergent for T-Commerce Applications

Marcelo Falco[✉] and Rachel Zuanon

Sense Design Lab, Ph.D. and Master's Design Program,
Anhembi Morumbi University,
São Paulo, Brazil
mfalco@gmail.com, rzuanon@anhembi.br,
rachel.z@zuannon.com.br

Abstract. Interactive digital television is at early stage as regards the interface design, especially in business transactions (t-commerce). Current attempts to transpose the problem related to linearity of narrative and temporal flows and audiovisual content obstruction by the interactive layer, although pointing out design perspectives - in addition to the structural and visual web patterns - are still insufficient as regards the design of interfaces connected and converged for t-commerce applications. This article considers these problems arise from the structural basis that support television scripts and streamings. In this sense, this article proposes the hybridization between the linear model, inherited from analogue condition, and nonlinear model, intrinsic to digital media, as a methodological strategy aiming to strength the creation of interactive audiovisual content connected and convergent for this context.

Keywords: Interface design · iDTV · T-Commerce · Second screen · Connectivity · Convergence

1 Introduction

Interactive Digital Television (iDTV) and Internet represent the possibility of access to a digital world of information and services. Consisting of a computerized system and operated via remote control, "television is one of the means of dissemination of information and mass entertainment, especially in Brazil where it is present in 90 % of households" [1]. However, iDTV is at early stage as regards the interface design, especially in business transactions (t-commerce) [2, 3]. The challenges of research and development in iDTV are broad and not fully investigated [4, 5]. Interactivity possibilities for iDTV not only represent dialogic perspectives between the television viewer

© Springer International Publishing Switzerland 2015
A. Marcus (Ed.): DUXU 2015, Part I, LNCS 9186, pp. 599–608, 2015.
DOI: 10.1007/978-3-319-20886-2_56

and television – taking them to the active condition of teleinteractor[1] - but also announce paradigm shifts on the television audiovisual language - regarding its pre-production, production and post-production stages [6].

Unlike traditional narratives for analog television that have limitations [7, 8] as the viewing flexibility and access to audiovisual content - imposed by a context governed by linearity - interactive digital television enables the expansion of this content and their narratives between different languages and platforms, in narrative and nonlinear temporal flows and, thereby, configure convergent and transmedia contexts. This context restates the relevance of rethinking how interfaces are dialoguing with the teleinteractors, once this communication sets up "a change in how we view our relationship with the media" [9] in a convergence relation.

In the scope of interface design of many applications for iDTV, and more specifically for t-commerce (business transactions in iDTV and object of this research), design perspectives, in addition to the structural and visual web patterns assimilated by e-commerce applications (electronic trading on the Internet) [10], are beginning to be outlined. The attempt of transposing the problem related to the linearity of the narrative and temporal flows can be identified in the contributions made by interactive videos for iDTV, in which the video and the use of elements of audiovisual language articulated to the interaction elements stand out, for example the case of Heineken Brewery [11] (Fig. 1). In the above-mentioned case, the teleinteractor views three options for the end of the video [A], for a period of time predetermined by the TV station [B]. The option chosen will be displayed at the iDTV interface [C]. In case the choice is not made by teleinteractor, one of the options is played randomly.

Fig. 1. Heineken advertising interactive video for iDTV [11]. (A) Options of favorite end. (B) Time for the teleinteractor to choose. (C) Scene of the selected video.

---

[1] Television viewer refers to the individual that only "watches" television, that is, receives information, but does not establish a dialogic relationship with the contents. On the other hand, the interactor condition is related to interactive digital media, which enable the exchange of information between the individual and the medium, as well as the possibility of this individual to transform content available according to their preferences. In this sense, the "teleinteractor" combines the features of television viewer and interactor and can be defined as one that, in addition to watching television, also interacts with the contents.

Another example is the interactive advertising of Kraft Foods [12], in which the teleinteractor can modify three times the video, through the selection of elements displayed in the show interface in the course of the narrative. These references, though opening perspectives for a nonlinear interaction with audiovisual content, do not impact the linear structure, on which the TV station's show schedule is drawn up, as they do not change the current duration set up for commercial advertising during the breaks of television broadcasts. In this regard, the choice of teleinteractor can be performed only at this period of time, otherwise it is automatically directed to one of the ends. These applications, from Heineken and Kraft Foods, consider the analog television business models, in this case understood by the commercial break and direct merchandising [1, 13], and are still employed by digital television.

In addition to this context, the problem of audiovisual content obstruction by the interactive layer also appear as one of the challenges in the interface design for t-commerce applications, and has found design paths dedicated to preserving the language of audiovisual media in the Second Screen or TV Connected applications [14] by connecting interactive digital television interface to the mobile device interfaces, such as tablets and smartphones.

Such connectivity is currently being used as a way to separate the layers of audiovisual content and interactivity by focusing the main video exhibition in the iDTV interface and transferring the interactive information content for mobile devices interfaces. For instance, in the iDTV applications of NantMobile [15] (Fig. 2) and KlugTV [16, 17], in which the teleinteractor places their iPhone or iPad in front of the TV, so that the embedded application recognizes the commercial interface and displays complementary content to television narrative on the first screen of the mobile device interface [18]. This condition causes the teleinteractor to purchase products, access further information, among other interactions, in concurrent action to the exhibition of the audiovisual content related to the show broadcasted on iDTV.

Fig. 2. iDTV interface of NantMobile that displays an additional content on iPhone or iPad [15].

These examples use as reference business transactions for mobile devices, they are called m-commerce. Despite the interaction with tablet or smartphone interface as a design solution aimed to curb the obstruction and/or interruption of television content generated by visual overlay of interactivity layer, the connectivity does not leverage the convergence among the media by limiting the interaction with the content available only on mobile devices, without providing the construction of dialogical links with the content displayed on the TV interface [19, 20].

In this sense, the hypothesis presented in this article assumes that the design problems within the interfaces of iDTV applications, especially the t-commerce applications, arise in the structural basis that support the design of television scripts and streamings. Thus, it is proposed the linear models, inherited from the analog condition, and nonlinear models, intrinsic to digital media, are hybridized in order to enhance the creation of interactive audiovisual content connected and convergent for t-commerce applications, once the individual application of these models is insufficient for this purpose. It is noteworthy that the main results of this research come from the application of this methodological approach as an object of study developed by students of Digital Design Bachelor's Degree and Undergraduate Research of Universidade Anhembi Morumbi, involved in the design of prototype applications for iDTV connected and convergent with Second Screen.

2   Linear TV Scripts and Streamings

Television works with the matrix of audiovisual language common on movies and videos, but it has developed genres and formats that are specific to it [2], such as news shows, documentaries, soap operas, series, sports shows, music shows, talk shows, interviews, among others [9]. Its schedule is conceived through television scripts and streamings, which are linear for analog television, both as regards its narrative and temporal structure.

The script is how content sequence and their respective durations are controlled. The linear script models are primarily structured in two columns, one dedicated to describing the scenes, the other aimed at sound specifications. The descriptive content covered in the script is fundamental and very important for the production and editing of audiovisual content, because there are elements and details of its production and post-production [21].

The television streaming uses the script as premise and, in this context, it follows the same linearity, foreseeing opening sequences, the amount and the stipulated time[2] of tv show itself and commercial breaks in a show, as shown below in the television streaming developed by the authors for a 30 min show prototype (Fig. 3).

In this sense, the TV station offers a range of audiovisual products that are interesting to the viewer in exchange for part of their time dedicated to viewing products, services or brands displayed on the TV [23]. In addition to the commercial breaks, TV stations start to mention or show products in a seemingly casual way, through the so-called

---

[2] Each show part should not last less than ten minutes, as well as the commercial break that should last more than two minutes and thirty seconds [22].

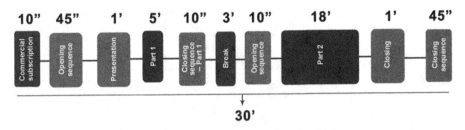

Fig. 3. Television streaming for a 30 min show

merchandising [24], thus, it is possible to shop these products presented in sales channels through the phone or the internet [25].

First used in the movies, nowadays merchandising is in every TV show [14]. It is often related to a promotional campaign and with the goal of highlighting the product in relation to others and to the environment in which it is inserted [26]. There are direct and indirect merchandising. In the direct merchandising, the product is displayed in the background and is related to show content, which can also be interpreted as a subliminal message[3], since most of the time, there is no intention to sell that particular product, but it is intended to stablish their image in the viewer's subconscious. On the other hand, the indirect merchandising is used when the advertisement is displayed during a television show, but not directly related to its content. In this case, the show host advertises or invites a third party to show it [1]. Sales or teleshopping channels are shows intended to the marketing and sale of products [27] and resemble the indirect merchandising because there is a host to demonstrate the product to the viewer.

These models of business transactions, which were developed in the context of a linear structure of analogue television, establish a one-way communication with the viewer, as regards the technological potential of the TV. However, with the arrival of iDTV, this technological potential is extended to the condition of interactive digital media, able to provide to commercial transactions new features aimed at establishing a two-way dialogue between television content and the teleinteractor.

3   Nonlinear TV Scripts and Streamings

Digital environments transform themselves. Textual, pictorial and sound elements become plastic and able to suffer changes and metamorphoses [3]. As regards the development of a digital project, five plans should be considered (Fig. 4): Strategy, Scope, Structure, Scheme and Surface. They constitute the conceptual frame to address the user experience and their tools involved in this construction.

---

[3] Subliminal messages, as they are not perceived by the human conscious, but cannot be ignored [28]. There is criticism of its use once "the ultimate goal of the subliminal message is to manipulate people's minds. The inclusions, words, icons and ideas cannot be perceived by the consumer at a normal level of consciousness, so there is no option to accept or reject the message, as the advertising without stimuli."

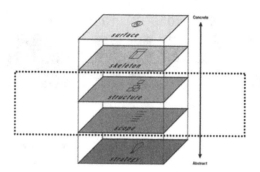

Fig. 4. Structure plans for interface design [29]

Nonlinear TV scripts and streamings are directly related to Scope and Structure plans. Scope refers to the definition of content and its functional specifications, explained earlier in the strategic plan. Structure Plan is responsible for defining how the content is organized and structured for browsing and interaction in the digital world [29].

The process of transposing linearity, intrinsic to analogue television, to nonlinearity of the narrative flows, enabled by interactive digital media, consider the idea of rhizome by allowing open and complex paths and segments, full of deviations, and composed of segment and escape lines [30]. Rhizomes are visual schemes that associate specific symbols, graphs[4], to the digital project.

The complexity of a diagram, such as a map or a metaphorical medium, which aims to show the path from one point to another, from one level of understanding to another [31], is directly linked to its interactive capability. The more options to choose, more elaborate becomes the corresponding map [6]. Similarly to the map[5] developed by the authors for a prototype of iDTV application (Fig. 4).

This direct association between the Scope and Structure plans respectively to the television script and streaming, by breaking the paradigms of linearity, provides other perspectives to the design development of business transactions on television, in which the autonomy of the parties regarding the whole, sets a perception of interconnectivity able to transpose the traditional hierarchy model and information centralization [32].

In this regard, commercial transactions on TV are seem as the condition of t-commerce applications and abandon the zero interactivity level, consisting of linear narratives from the beginning to the end; transact through the linear interactivity using the remote control to zap channels and select menu items; and assume the Linguistics, Creation and Continuous Command interactivities, which provide the teleinteractor with filling out forms, writing messages and the manipulation of sound and/or visual elements [35].

However, despite all the potential design of digital interactive media and, therefore, subject to allocation to T-commerce applications, in this context, it continues the replication of transactional web models (e-commerce) that contribute to the distortion of

---

[4] The graphs are made up of figures and graphic objects, such as circles, squares or any image that can be connected by relationships (connections), represented by lines and curves [33].

[5] The maps provide a visual representation of the streaming among the different interfaces presented to the user [34].

television audiovisual language. This problem motivates the hypothesis proposed in this article that consists of the hybridization between the linear model, inherited from analogue condition, and nonlinear model, intrinsic to digital media, as a methodological strategy able to enhance the creation of interactive transactional audiovisual content, that are connected and convergent.

4   Hybrid TV Scripts and Streamings

The convergence of services and applications is a process that involves and uses several platforms and devices to receive contents, services, games, television shows, integration with mobile devices, among others [23]. The convergence among television and other digital devices, however, stablish a dialogue, which is not restricted to technology relationship [36], but it is extended to the content of their narratives, through the connectivity between their scripts, leading to the setting of interactive media streamings in order to broaden the teleinteractor experience.

Current proposals of integration between the audiovisual narratives and interactive content add to the model used in the construction of linear scripts, third and fourth columns aiming to describe the interaction and to present the interface storyboards, respectively [1]. However, such proposals are limited as to show graphical representation that preserves the linearity of narrative and temporal flows used in the scripts from the analog television as well as on the range of connective possibilities that rhizomatic network, represented by diagrams, can provide to the design development of interactive television applications.

The proposal of transposing the limitations of the script models and linear television streaming, inherited from analogue condition, and proposing a methodological strategy for the nonlinear television scripts and streamings within the iDTV uses as reference the diagram and taxonomy to organize levels or layers, from general to specific. Each level of encapsulation indicates a level of abstraction and it is responsible for answering what it is and how the application and interactions work, representing connections as an area of a complex system [33]. For example, there is the hybridization, proposed by the authors, between the linear television streaming and the nonlinear diagram for the development of a T-commerce application (Fig. 5). In this context, hybridity constitutes a moment of revelation, a moment of freedom from which a new way is born [37] (Fig. 6).

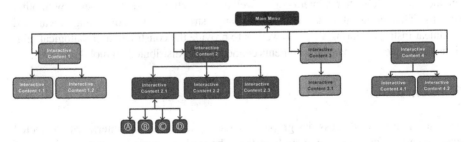

Fig. 5. Map for a T-commerce application for iDTV

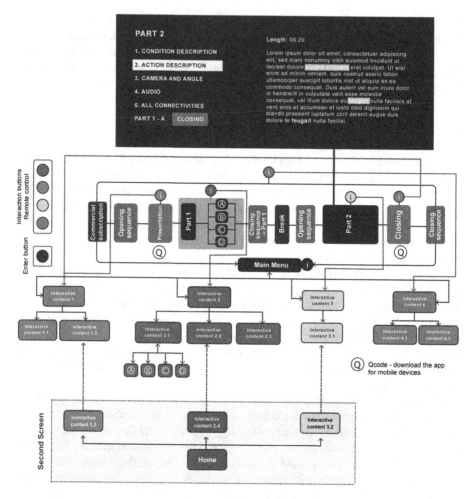

Fig. 6. TV Hybrid Script and Streaming of a t-commerce application

Intrinsically, each part has a script aiming to describe and detail - in addition to the scene environment, characters' actions, plans and camera movements and audio - the relationship and connection between audiovisual content and application interfaces, flow and interactions available to teleinteractor, as well as connectivity and convergence with other screens. This proposal enhances the television streaming, by combining linear and nonlinear instances during show, as well as to provide the construction of dialogical relations between content parts and contents connected and distributed on mobile devices.

5   Conclusion

This article aims to discuss design perspectives to the design of interfaces connected and converged for t-commerce applications. The study identified the main problems of the development in the linearity of the narrative and temporal flows originated from the television analog condition; and in the absence of dialogical relationships between audiovisual content and interactivity layer, both in scope of the current applications for iDTV, and also in those that employ the use of the second screen. In this context, there is the hypothesis of a hybrid narrative script and flow as design path able to associate the contributions from the linear and nonlinear models, focusing on semantic connectivity and not only technological, between audiovisual narratives and interactive content.

Future developments of this research still consider the extension of the hybridization concept between linear and nonlinear processes to production and post-production stages. It is expected, therefore, the drafting of a method for the development of interactive audiovisual content in the iDTV that would encourage the alignment between the productive processes carried out within the TV stations, audiovisual content producers and interactive content designers. Consequently, it is expected to motivate the development of t-commerce applications capable to transform the relationship between television and its audience, putting the viewer definitely in the active position of teleinteractor, but without mischaracterizing the language of the audiovisual media.

References

1. Chaudhry, A.: A Publicidade em Novos Meios e as Perspectivas para TV Digital no Brasil. In: Squirra, S., Becker, V. (eds.) TVDigital.br - Conceitos e estudos sobre o ISDB-TB. Ateliê Editorial, São Paulo (2009)
2. Cannito, N.: A televisão na era digital: interatividade, convergência e novos modelos de negócio. Summus, São Paulo (2010)
3. Murray, J.: Hamlet no Holodeck: o futuro da narrativa no ciberespaço. Unesp, São Paulo, Itau Cultural (2003)
4. Marcondes Filho, C.: Televisão: a vida pelo vídeo. Moderna, São Paulo (1988)
5. Moran, T.: The command language grammars: a representation for the user interface of interactive computer systems. Int. J. Man-Mach. Stud. **15**, 3–50 (1981). Academic Press
6. Leão, L.: O Labirinto da Hipermídia: Arquitetura e navegação no ciberespaço. Iluminuras, São Paulo (1999)
7. Mcluhan, M.: Os meios de comunicação como extensões do homem. Cultrix, São Paulo (2002)
8. Munari, B.: Design e comunicação visual. Martins Fontes, São Paulo (2001)
9. Jenkins, H.: Cultura da Convergência. Editora Aleph, São Paulo (2009)
10. Schlittler, J.P.: TV digital Interativa: Convergência das mídias e interfaces do usuário. Blucher, São Paulo (2011)
11. Heineken Legendary Football. https://www.youtube.com/watch?v=dRLZhxMZcbk
12. Ad News. http://www.youtube.com/watch?v=o4hpXgfdoEM
13. Kotler, P., Keller, K.L.: Administração e marketing. Pearson Prentice Hall, São Paulo (2006)
14. Gawlinski, M.: Interactive Television Production. Focal Press, Oxford (2003)
15. Idtv. http://idtv.me/img/shop.jpg
16. Klugtv. https://www.youtube.com/watch?v=GBdkrsm4-a4#t=58
17. Klugtv traz o conceito de second screen para a programação de TV. http://www. telaviva.com.br/26/06/2012/klugtv-traz-o-conceito-de-second-screen-para-a-programacao-de-tv/tl/285537/news.aspx

18. Carneiro, R.G.: Publicidade na TV Digital: Um mercado em transformação. Aleph, São Paulo (2012)
19. Johnson, S.: Cultura da Interface: Como o computador transforma nossa maneira de cri-ar e comunicar. Jorge Zahar Editor, Rio de Janeiro (2001)
20. Cooper, A., Reimann, R., Cronin, D.: About Face 3: The Essentials of Interaction De-sign. Wiley Publishing Inc., Indianapolis (2007)
21. Ramos, J.: Televisão, publicidade e cultura de massa. Vozes, Petrópolis (1995)
22. Ministério das comunicações. http://www.mc.gov.br/o-ministerio/273-lex/portarias/25399-portaria-n-354-de-11-de-julho-de-2012
23. Patriota, K.: Sob demanda, convergente e interativa: a customização da publicidade na televisão digital. In: Squirra, S., Fechine, Y. (eds.) Televisão Digital: Desafios para comunicação. Editora Sulina, Porto Alegre (2009)
24. Pinho, J.B.: Comunicação em Marketing. Papirus, Campinas (2001)
25. Monteiro, B.: A Centralidade da peça-piloto no processo de desenvolvimento de roupas de malha: um estudo de caso. Tese de Doutorado em Engenharia de Produção, COPPE/UFRJ (2004)
26. Blessa, R.: Merchandising no Ponto de venda. São Paulo, Atlas (2001)
27. de Souza, J.A.: Gêneros e formatos na televisão brasileira. Summus, São Paulo (2004)
28. Machado, D., Magron, M., Silva, S.: Mensagem Subliminar: um mergulho no inconsciente humano. Intercon, Salvador (2002)
29. Garrett, J.J.: The Elements of User Experience. AIGA–American Institute of Graphic Arts, New York (2003)
30. Deleuze, G., Guattari, F.: Mil platôs - capitalismo e esquizofrenia, vol. 1/Tradução de Aurélio Guerra Neto e Célia Pinto Costa, 1 ed. Ed. 34, Rio de Janeiro (1995)
31. Wurman, R.: Ansiedade da Informação 2: Um guia para quem comunica e dá instruções. Editora de Cultura, São Paulo (2005)
32. Ferrari, P.: Hipertexto, hipermídia: as novas ferramentas da comunicação digital. Contexto, São Paulo (2007)
33. Vassão, C.A.: Metadesign: ferramentas, estratégias e ética para a complexidade. Blucher, São Paulo (2010)
34. Chak, A.: Como criar sites persuasivos. Pearson Education do Brasil, São Paulo (2004)
35. Santaella, L.: Linguagem líquidas na era da mobilidade. Paulus, São Paulo (2007)
36. Lamardo, R., Santos Silva, C.E.: A publicidade e os desafios da convergência. In: Encontro ESPM de comunicação e marketing (2005)
37. Mcluhan, M.: Os meios de comunicação como extensões dos homens. Cultrix, São Paulo (1979)

How to Evaluate Use Scenarios and Stories

Ioanna Michailidou$^{(\boxtimes)}$, Charlotte Haid, and Udo Lindemann

Institute of Product Development, Technische Universität München,
Munich, Germany
{michailidou, lindemann}@pe.mw.tum.de,
charlotte.haid@tum.de

Abstract. Scenario-based methods, like the scenario-, storytelling- and story boarding-techniques, are broadly used in the context of user experience design. Practitioners cannot yet fully appreciate the benefits of scenario-based methods, because of the uncertainty that is often linked with the corresponding decision-making processes. This work aims at introducing a methodological proceeding for supporting the evaluation of use scenarios and stories, consisting of three modules. A checklist supports the initial assessment of scenarios by their creator, a questionnaire helps to identify if the content of scenarios represents the intended user experience, while a comparison-based method enables the association of possible media to visualize a scenario in the most appropriate way. Those findings ground on a literature study and exemplary application of the support. Increasing traceability of scenarios through a systematical assessment and a selection support would encourage usage of scenario-based methods and increase their acceptance.

Keywords: Scenario · Storytelling · DUXU methods and tools

1 Introduction

User experience design (UXD) aims at fulfilling users' needs and motives via product usage [1]. To achieve this goal, user experience (UX) designers collaborate closely with experts from various fields and invite users to participate in all stages of the design process from analysis of users' needs and context of usage to [co-]creation and evaluation of concepts [2]. However, user-centered design brings, along with its benefits, challenges for practitioners [3]. Communicating, visualizing and documenting results and "soft" UX aspects, in an understandable for various stakeholders - including end-users-way, is one of them. Furthermore, applying demanding methods that require special equipment and handling of large amounts of data could cause frustration to practitioners under cost and time pressure.

Scenario-based methods, i.e. methods and techniques making use of scenarios, offer a pragmatic methodological approach to deal with these issues. Scenarios or use scenarios are "explicit descriptions of hypothetical events concerning a product during a certain phase of its life cycle" [4]. Stories go beyond descriptions of a situation, because they have a plot, which enables the storyteller to reflect the interpretation on a certain subject [5]. User experience stories, in particular, portray "a specific, aimed interaction of a character with a system in physical and emotional context, focusing on

© Springer International Publishing Switzerland 2015
A. Marcus (Ed.): DUXU 2015, Part I, LNCS 9186, pp. 609–620, 2015.
DOI: 10.1007/978-3-319-20886-2_57

characters' needs motives and goals" [6]. Because of their characteristics, scenario-based methods are very useful in not only software, interaction and product design, but in UXD, as well [7–9]: Making use of natural language and thus being understandable for all stakeholders, without requiring special equipment, they have great advantages compared to other methods. Moreover, they are concrete and ground ideas in specific context, but meanwhile flexible and easily revised. However, there is a lack of clear guidance and a tendency to improvised and fragmental use of scenario-based methods.

After introducing the objectives and research methodology of this work, we present in Sect. 2 the three modules of the scenario evaluation methodology: a scenario assessment checklist, a questionnaire for assessing the UX-related content of scenarios and a proceeding for choosing appropriate scenario presentation media. We further describe how we applied each module within a student project. In Sect. 3, we discuss contradictory aspects in scenario assessment, before wrapping up the paper with the most important conclusions. In the whole paper, we use the simplified term "scenario" to describe the result of application of various scenario-based methods, like the scenario and storytelling techniques.

1.1   Objectives

This paper aims at introducing a methodological proceeding for evaluation of use scenarios and stories. A central barrier concerning usage of scenario-based methods, despite their benefits in the context of UXD, is uncertainty in the selection process and resulting lack of acceptance of scenarios. UX designers usually create more than one possible scenarios to express their ideas. But how to choose the variant which is most preferable to possible users and is also accepted by the design team? This work proposes systematical evaluation of alternative scenarios as a way to enable UX designers to decide for the scenario that best fulfils their goals and thus decrease their uncertainty. Meanwhile, making such decisions traceable would increase acceptance of scenarios from other stakeholders.

The main findings of this work are the new methodological proceeding and the literature-based collection of evaluation criteria. Those two core elements intend to (1) enable UX designers assess their scenarios; (2) enable other stakeholders (e.g. members of design team, potential users) give productive feedback; (3) create a comprehensible reasoning behind the choice of scenarios and thus increase their traceability and acceptance.

1.2   Research Methodology

Our study bases on literature review and application of methods in a student project. We reviewed literature on scenario-based methods (e.g. [7, 8]) to extract criteria for "good" scenarios and on evaluation methods (e.g. [9, 10]) to select appropriate approaches. The proposed proceeding was applied within the frame of a student project, in which scenario-based methods have been used for designing a novel device for tracking frequently lost items. This exemplary application provides examples of scenarios and insights in the practical application of the suggested support. In this section, we present the three modules of the support and give for each a short example from the initial method application within the student project.

2 Results: A Three-Module Scenario Evaluation Support

We introduce a methodological proceeding for evaluating scenarios. In short, the proceeding consists of following modules: (1) Support for initial assessment of scenarios from their creator via a checklist; (2) Support for assessment of scenario content via a questionnaire; (3) Support for assessment of scenario presentation via a comparison-based method.

2.1 Support for Initial Scenario Assessment

The checklist consists of criteria for "good" scenarios that can be used as heuristics by scenario creators or other members of the design team in the process of creating or assessing scenarios. Criteria concern content, expression, structure, audience-orientation and effect of scenarios. Scenario creators can go through the criteria and corresponding key questions depicted in Table 1 to understand the meaning of each criterion better and receive guidance to create or judge scenarios.

Table 1. Checklist for initial scenario assessment (based on [6–8, 11])

CONTENT	
Honesty	*Does the scenario base on real data?*
	Does the content of the scenario portray user research accurately, without distorting the real data?
Authenticity	*Does the scenario reflect the feeling of the original events and the way in which the participants themselves might express it?*
Richness in action detail	*Does the scenario describe the way things happened thoroughly?*
	Does the scenario provide more value than just a quote?
Relevance for UX issue(-s)	*Does the scenario identify a point-of-pain/a market gap/a new approach/a trend that is relevant for the UX issue?*
	Does the scenario help in explaining something about the UX in a way that gets beyond facts?
Representativeness	*Are the characters and situations representative?*
Preciseness	*Is the content of the scenario specific and tangible?*
	Is the point of the scenario explicit enough for the audience to comprehend without further explanations or adjustments?
EXPRESSION	
Clarity	*Does the scenario have a clear focus/a clear point?*
Simplicity	*Does the scenario use just enough details to help the audience recognize its focus and authenticity, and no more?*
	(...or does it involve many technical details/irrelevant information that might confuse the audience?)

	information that might confuse the audience?)
Accurateness	Is the message of the scenario direct?
	(…or does it describe "a story about the story"?)
Richness in contextual detail	Does the scenario provide enough contextual detail to help the audience relate to it?
	Does the scenario bring data to life by grounding it in a specific physical and emotional context?
Authenticity	Does the scenario use the characters' language?
Vividness	Does the scenario use active descriptions?
STRUCTURE	
Coverage	Does the scenario address all of the facts, even inconvenient details?
Coherence and plausibility	Do the facts and explanations delivered in the scenario make sense?
	Is the scenario believable?
Uniqueness	Is the explanation/solution delivered in the scenario convincing?
	(…or does it seem like there are many other explanations/ solutions that would work equally well?)
Fittingness	Do the presented facts fit well in the scenario?
	(…or have they been forced into place?)
Length	Is the scenario as long as it needs to be, but no longer?
	Are the contents provided efficiently?
AUDIENCE-ORIENTATION	
Resolution	Does the scenario provide an ending that suits the purpose of the story?
	Is the audience able to complete the "journey" in their minds?
	Is the audience able to relate and incorporate the contents of the scenario into their lives and design task?
Interactivity	Does the scenario evoke discussion and support participation?
	Is the scenario open-ended, so that it can be interpreted by the audience?
Suitability	Is the scenario told in a right way and right time for the right audience?
	Is it told from a perspective appropriate to the audience?
Understandability/ Introduction	Does the audience know enough about the context of the scenario?
	If not, does the scenario provide essential background information?
EFFECT	
Reproducibility	Is the scenario memorable?
	Can others retell the scenario?
Identification/ Immersion	Can the audience identify to/empathize with the characters of the scenario?
	Are the receivers interested in the result of the scenario?
Inspiration	Does the scenario inspire new ideas?
	Does it evoke reflection about design issues?

The criteria for good scenarios were used in two phases of the student project: before creating scenarios to inspire creators and after the first drafts were created to assess them. Goal of the student project was the development of a novel device to track frequently lost items in domestic environment, called "the SOS box". After having defined the development goals and the target user groups, the process for creating user experience stories [12] was applied. Three user experience stories with many variations were created - one for each of the personas "Grandmother Schmidtbauer", "Mr. Grünthal" and "Anna Meerwald". According to the UX story creation process, the stories were firstly structured in fragments, aka "substories" or "interaction scenarios", and then formulated in narration format. In the creation process, the criteria helped the practitioners, who had no previous experience in applying scenario-based methods, win a better orientation and understanding of the goals of scenario-based methods. The criteria were used as heuristics while textually formulating the substories and the list was iteratively extended throughout the development process. Two of the authors worked on the creation of substories and an initial creation of the three UX stories. Then, the substories were given to three independent authors that were asked to formulate the substories as narrations (in text format). Two researchers worked on assessing the scenarios according to the criteria, until the – many - variations were limited to one story per persona.

2.2   Support for Assessment of Scenario UX-Related Content

Scenarios should ideally describe a positive user experience. Based on the assumption that positive experiences emerge through product usage when interaction fulfills psychological needs and motives of users [1], scenarios describing the intended interaction should contribute to need fulfilment. When creating a scenario, UX designers should emphasize on the psychological needs and motives of potential users addressed by the new product. The process to create a UX story stresses this prioritization in its initial steps [12]. The question is *if the audience of the story can receive the emphasis on the selected needs* through the content of the scenario. To explore this, potential users are invited to assess the scenarios. Due to their characteristics, such specific nature and integration in context, scenarios provide a great basis for user testing. In a setting similar to pluralistic walkthroughs [13], UX designers walk the participants through scenarios that describe the future experience. Users are then asked to assess if the experience described in the scenario addresses the needs described in items of a questionnaire. We recommend using UXNQ [14] or ECHO and preferably a pre-selected and adapted set of items, so that the questions are relevant and the total questionnaire length not too long. The participants' responses will reflect which needs were met by the contents of the scenarios. The scenario, in which the questionnaire results match better to designers' goals, is the one to be preferred.

In the student project, two psychological needs from the needs collection of Sheldon et al. [15] were defined as overall development goals: autonomy and pleasure-stimulation. Using the "SOS box" should ideally enable users feel autonomous when they search for an object and are able to find it without having to ask for help and meanwhile have fun and enjoy the process of searching and finding. Because the "SOS box" addresses three user groups, we defined an additional, third need, for each of these groups. Elderly with physical restrictions, represented from the persona "*Mr. Grünthal*", have an intense need for security, i.e. want to feel free from threads and uncertainties. Fit elderly living alone, represented by the persona "*Grandmother Schmidtbauer*", often have the wish to feel connected with family or friends, so the need for relatedness is highly relevant. The "SOS box" was meant to be an inclusive design product. Young, busy "lifestylers", represented by "*Anna Meerwald*", are the third user group in consideration. To attract these users, the need for money-luxury should be addressed by the product. To evaluate if the user experience stories created for each user group address the three predefined needs, we conducted a questionnaire-based evaluation. Three items for each need were selected from the UXNQ [14] questionnaire. The participants had to assess in a five-point scale, if they agree with the statements, according to the contents of the user experience stories. Personas were used as archetypes for user groups: we invited participants corresponding to the user groups for each of the three stories to answer the questionnaire, after having read the story corresponding to their group. To encourage user participation further, we interviewed one participant per user group and discussed their opinions and ideas (Table 2).

Table 2. Extract from the questionnaire: Items regarding the need "autonomy"

AUTONOMY: not being restricted by external factors, being self-determined, acting according to own will, being independent						
By using the system, …						
	(Agreement)					
(Item)	Strongly agree	Agree	Neutral	Disagree	Strongly disagree	(No reply)
…I was free in my decisions	○	○	○	○	○	○
…I could act independently	○	○	○	○	○	○
…I could act without needing help or advice from others	○	○	○	○	○	○

2.3   Support for Assessment of Scenario Presentation Form

There are many possibilities to visualize scenarios, varying from textual descriptions to storyboards and even animated films. The third module of the method should help scenario creators decide for the best format depending on their scope and audience via a comparison-based method. To achieve this, two preliminary questions need to be clarified by the scenario creators: who is the audience/receiver of the scenario and what are the conditions of the presentation? Those two factors are crucial for the right choice of medium. There are many possible receivers of scenarios, like colleagues, managers, experts, even end-users. Each group has different expectations and background knowledge – therefore has to be addressed appropriately. Depending on the conditions of the presentation, there are further constraints: Is there a possibility to use digital media, or does the presentation have to be "on paper"? Is it possible to present the scenario and give explanations afterwards, or does the scenario have to stand for itself, for instance in a report or in an online questionnaire? Furthermore, the current phase of the development process influences the choice of medium. In early development phases, it is not possible to present visualizations of the new concepts, since ideas might not be implemented yet, while in late development phases it is great to show visualizations.

Table 3. Preliminary selection criteria for scenario presentation media

Medium	Development phase			Presentation format			
	Analysis	Conceptualization	Implementation	Digital	Paper-based	Live	Offline
Oral narration	+	O	O	+	–	+	–
Textual description	+	O	O	+	+	–	+
Text and pictures/ figures	+	+	+	+	+	+	+
Storyboard	O	+	+	+	+	+	+
Film	O	O	+	+	–	O	+

+ :	appropriate
O :	applicable
– :	not applicable

In the student project, we had the first user experience stories at the end of the conceptualization phase and wanted to address two different audiences to collect feedback: fellow designers and prospective users. First, we identified the particularities of the two different situations. In the case of presentation to fellow designers, scenario-creators deal with an audience with good knowledge of the product; the presentation aims at communicating UX-related issues and inspire discussions; there is the possibility of a live presentation. In the second case, the audience has no prior knowledge concerning the product, but is familiar with the context of usage and the points-of-pain. There was no possibility for a live presentation in all cases, since we wanted to reach as many participants as possible. Given that two of the three user groups involved elderly and possibly non-technology-affine users, paper-based presentations were preferable. According to the preliminary selection criteria depicted in Table 3, text with pictures and storyboards could be appropriate for both cases.

To decide which medium is preferable for the presentation to fellow designers, we compared both media (text + pictures and storyboard) under the aspect: "which format inspires new ideas and evoke reflection about UX-related design issues?", since this was the primer aim of the presentation. We created the same user experience story in two different formats and observed the reactions of the design team. Since the design team was familiar to the characters of the story already from the analysis phase, the textual descriptions did not provide any additional value compared to a storyboard, which was therefore selected as most appropriate medium in that case.

For making a decision in the case of the presentation to prospective users the focus lied on understandability, so we compared both media under the aspect: "which format communicates the idea most clearly?". Again, we created two visualizations for each user experience story and invited two persons matching each user group to assess them. We first gave the storyboards and asked the persons describe what they see. Then, we gave them the textual description with additional pictures to read. It turned out that in all cases, the persons could comprehend the contents of the storyboard correctly. Still, all participants assessed the contextual details provided in the textual descriptions as meaningful. Therefore, the textual description was preferred in this case.

3   Discussion

3.1   Criteria for "Good" Scenarios

The first module of the method (Checklist for initial scenario assessment) consists of literature-based criteria for good scenarios. Using the checklist in an exemplary application, we could identify contradictions and criteria that are worth further reflection.

Representativeness vs. Unexpectedness. Scenarios that represent familiar characters and situations enable the audience to identify with them easily. To facilitate identification, empathy and immersion is a desirable property of scenarios. Elements that surprise or contradict common beliefs can be the hardest to communicate, especially when they demonstrate a negative aspect. On the other hand, an unexpected twist in the plot or ending of the story - described as "key event" in [6] - may make it more interesting and memorable. If presented in a way that enables the audience understand why an unexpected element appears, a scenario can provide early anecdotal evidence for new user needs that may suggest new design directions. Such scenarios are of great value for UX designers.

Richness in Contextual Detail vs. Interactivity. A great benefit of scenarios is that they ground data in a specific context and thus help the audience create a better systemic understanding. In the field of user experience, understanding the emotional context is crucial. Understanding characters, their needs, motives and goals, their feelings and perceptions, will enable a deeper understanding of qualitative requirements and attributes of the intended user experience. Following the process to create a user experience story [12] can contribute in considering all relevant for emotional context aspects. On the other hand, scenarios cannot include all details: they should leave space for interpretation from the audience's side [7]. Being open-ended and easily revised [8], they can be adjusted according to the audience's reactions.

"Rosy" vs. Realistic Scenarios. During the process of evaluating scenarios, we often had the question whether a scenario should be formulated consistently positive and only represent positive actions and situations. On the other hand, it is more realistic that problems occur, for example, that the operation of a product feature does not work properly. Since negative formulations through a negative shadow on the product, we concluded that it is probably better to mention but not in association with the product. A scenario might mention problems, but ones that can be solved by the product or are not caused by it. Scenarios represent the concept of a new product and should of course be appealing and refer to users' needs. Moreover, although they may contain futuristic scenes, scenarios should generally be realistic and not represent scenes that exceed the imagination of the audience.

Suitability. As discussed in Sect. 2.3, not all media are appropriate for every audience. The same suitability issue is relevant for the content of scenarios. For instance, technical aspects are important for designers but irrelevant and probably distracting for end-users. We recommend creating slightly different versions for different audiences, like users, business stakeholders, managers, or colleagues.

Reproducibility. In positive scenario examples, we observed the effect of reproducibility. Every time a scenario inspired others to use it in their work, it was retold and reused. Including a clear and memorable message in the scenario can enhance this effect. Retelling a story is, in our opinion, definitely a measure of success.

3.2   Insights from Exemplary Application of the Support

The suggested support was applied in a student project with the goal to create a novel device for tracking frequently lost items in domestic environments. Three main user groups were defined in the analysis phase, with three personas and three relevant psychological needs representing them. In the analysis phase, development goals were explored within the design team with the help of oral narrations. At that stage, there was still no need to eliminate ideas or assess the narrations. Still, it was decided to proceed with the UX story creation process for each user group separately, because the experience of each user group had a different focus. In the conceptualization phase, the necessary inputs for creating a UX story, i.e. story elements, plot line and substories were defined for each user group. The design team members had no experience in story creation, so the checklist gave them a first orientation about what is important. Three independent authors iteratively created five to six substories each according to the criteria. This proceeding was very interesting, because each author brought a different perspective. So even though some variants were eliminated, insights remain. Still, the creative process quickly resulted into an amount of substories that was difficult to manage! The decision for the "best" UX story was met according to the feedback of fellow designers and end-users. To assess which story addresses the needs of potential end-users most effectively, three versions of a story were given to representative users, who evaluated via a questionnaire how they would feel like if they were the characters of the story. A textual description with explanatory pictures and a questionnaire were given to them. The story creators have decided that the format of text and pictures was the most appropriate in this case, according to a systematic comparison of possible media. Further interviews and think-aloud sessions with the end-users were conducted only in small scale, but are definitely recommended, because they provide a deeper understanding of prospective users' needs and interpretations. Possible UX stories were also discussed within the design team. For those presentations, storyboards were chosen as most appropriate media. A lesson learned from this procedure was that stories that are compared have to be presented in the same way and have the same detail level: we observed the effect that stories that were more detailed were more likable.

The evaluation of stories resulted into one UX story per persona. We believe that the systematic methodological approach gave to the design team the confidence, that the final UX stories communicate the intended experience adequately and that the communicated experience represent the most attractive UX concept. The proceeding (Fig. 1) is traceable and gives a basis for argumentation. Like UXD processes, the process of creating a scenario should be iterative and with continuous user involvement.

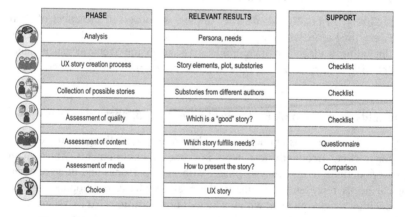

Fig. 1. Overview of application of the support for evaluation of UX stories in the student project "SOS box".

4 Conclusions

Although there is broad agreement on benefits of using scenario-based methods in UXD, their application is often blocked in design practice. A major reason for that is the uncertainty of designers and the lack of acceptance of scenarios because there is no support in the decision processes that take place throughout scenario creation. To our current knowledge there are no existing approaches addressing these issues systematically. This paper introduces a methodological proceeding to answer two important questions: Which scenario presents the best UX concept? Which scenario presents the UX concept best? A literature review on evaluation methods resulted in identification of appropriate approaches to compare and assess scenarios. We propose a new methodological proceeding consisting of three modules and identify criteria of good scenarios. Furthermore, we provide best practices for application of those methods. A limitation of the current study is that the findings base on an exemplary application of the support within the frame of a specific project. Future work focuses on applying the proceeding in further projects and identifying necessary refinements. Increasing traceability of scenarios through a systematical support is expected to encourage use of and rise acceptance of scenarios.

References

1. Hassenzahl, M.: Experience design: technology for all the right reasons. Synth. Lect. Hum.-Centered Inform. **3**(1), 1–95 (2010)
2. Roto, V., Law, E., Vermeeren, A., Hoonhout, J. (eds.): User Experience Whitepaper (2011). http://www.allaboutux.org/files/UX-WhitePaper.pdf
3. Goodman-Deane, J., Langdon, P., Clarkson, J.: Key influences on the user-centred design process. J. Eng. Des. **21**(2–3), 345–373 (2010)
4. Anggreeni, I., van der Voort, M.C.: Supporting scenario-based product design: the first proposal for a scenario generation support tool. In: Proceedings of the 19th CIRP Design Conference–Competitive Design. Cranfield University Press (2009)
5. Feldman, M.S., Sköldberg, K., Brown, R.N., Horner, D.: Making sense of stories: a rhetorical approach to narrative analysis. J. Public Adm. Res. Theor. **14**(2), 147–170 (2004)
6. Michailidou, I., von Saucken, C., Lindemann, U.: Extending the product specification with emotional aspects: introducing user experience stories. In: Proceedings of the International Conference on Engineering Design - ICED 2013, Seoul, Korea (2013)
7. Brooks, K., Quesenbery, W.: Storytelling for User Experience. O'Reilly Media, Inc., Sebastopol (2011)
8. Carroll, J.M.: Five reasons for scenario-based design. Interact. Comput. **13**(1), 43–60 (2000)
9. Lindemann, U.: Methodische Entwicklung technischer Produkte: Methoden flexibel und situationsgerecht anwenden, p. 70, 73, 85, 309. Springer, Heidelberg (2009)
10. Pahl, G., Beitz, W., Feldhusen, J., Grote, K.-H.: Konstruktionslehre. Grundlagen erfolgreicher Produktentwicklung. Methoden und Anwendung, 7. Auflage, Springer, Berlin (2007)
11. Thier, K.: Storytelling: eine narrative Managementmethode. Springer, Heidelberg (2006)

12. Michailidou, I., von Saucken, C., Lindemann, U.: How to create a user experience story. In: Marcus, A. (ed.) DUXU/HCII 2013, Part I. LNCS, vol. 8012, pp. 554–563. Springer, Heidelberg (2013)
13. Bias, R.G.: The pluralistic usability walkthrough: Coordinated empathies. In: Nielsen, J., Mack, R.L. (eds.) Usability Inspection Methods, pp. 65–78. Wiley, New York (1994)
14. Koerber, M., Eichinger, A., Bengler, K., Olaverri-Monreal, C.: User experience evaluation in an automotive context. In: Intelligent Vehicles Symposium (IV), 2013 IEEE, pp. 13–18. IEEE (2013)
15. Sheldon, K.M., Elliot, A.J., Kim, Y., Kasser, T.: What is satisfying about satisfying events? testing 10 candidate psychological needs. J. Pers. Soc. Psychol. **80**(2), 325–339 (2001)

Interactive Digital Storytelling and HCI Techniques Applied for Edutainment in Interactive Health Projects: Analysis of Two USC's Labyrinth Projects

Jorge I. Mora Fernández[1,2](✉)

[1] Prometheus Ph.D. Research Program, SENESCYT,
Group R&D&i SINAPSIS & Group R+D+C CICNETART, DIUC,
School of Medicine & School of Philosophy, Letters and Education Sciences,
University of Cuenca, Cuenca, Ecuador
multiculturalvideos@gmail.com
[2] Researcher Collaborator at the Labyrinth Project, Funded at USC,
Los Angeles, USA

Abstract. The interactive narratives for developing interactive & educational documentaries have served for developing interactive installations & products in galleries, exhibitions, museums, universities, webs & videogames. During the last years, these previous experiences of applying interactive narrative techniques in digital historical or educational products have served to developed interactive narratives applied to health education, treatment or recovery. Two of the projects developed by the USC's Labyrinth Project, directed by Marsha Kinder, are examples of the application of experiences in other narrative genres to health edutainment. This paper analyzes the interactive narrative elements integrated on the interfaces of the projects: *A Tale of Two MAO Genes* & *Interacting with Autism*. This analysis develops a model that describes the interactive immersive narrative elements integrated on their interfaces. It serves to identify the interactive narrative elements that create immersion in edutainment health projects so they can be applied on new narratives about recovering from addiction.

Keywords: HCI analysis · Edutainment · Health · Interactive Digital Storytelling · Immersion · Agency · Narrative paradox · Narrative closure · Narrative intelligibility · Transmedia · Hipermedia · Interactive documentary · Interface design

1 Introduction

Human Computer Interface, HCI, design & Interactive digital storytelling, IDS, techniques have been applied to the production of interaction design for edutainment interactive media projects since the beginning of the existence of the digital medium, as Janet Murray describes it [1]. However, is only during the last years that those immersive IDS & HCI techniques have been applied for communicating about health. The processes of developing edutainment through the creation of interactive database

© Springer International Publishing Switzerland 2015
A. Marcus (Ed.): DUXU 2015, Part I, LNCS 9186, pp. 621–633, 2015.
DOI: 10.1007/978-3-319-20886-2_58

narratives, first for fictional, artistic & historical contents, & lately for health contents, have been experienced by the USC's Labyrinth Project, a research initiative on interactive narrative & digital scholarship. Thus, after a scientific visit & an interview with its director, Marsha Kinder; about how to apply her IDS & HCI design experiences in the interactive narrative media project focus on recovering from addiction, that the Group I+D+C CICNETART is designing, it was clear the need to deeply analyze the interaction designs applied on the following Labyrinth's health projects. This research served to collect the HCI, Human Computer Interface, affordances ([1], p. 409) that develop immersion & agency of the users in two health projects: *A Tale of Two MAO Genes: Exploring the Biology & Culture of Aggression & Anxiety* [2], Fig. 1, & *Interacting with Autism, a video based resource* [3], Fig. 2.

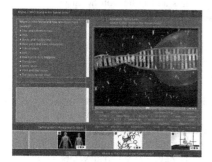

Fig. 1. Interactive DVD: A tale of two MAO genes: exploring the biology & culture of aggression & anxiety by Marsha Kinder.

Fig. 2. Interacting with Autism by Marsha Kinder, director of Labyrinth's Project.

The fist project is "an interactive science education project on a DVD that contains six hours of compelling multimedia material designed for diverse audiences – from K-12 to Graduate School, from science majors to the general public. It focuses on Dr. Jean Chen Shih's thirty years of pioneering molecular research on a crucial pair of brain enzymes, known as the MAO A & MAO B genes (monamine oxidase) that help control aggression & anxiety." [2]. *Interacting with Autism* combines scientific & personal documentaries with animation on a video-based website, "...that presents the most reliable evidence-based information currently available on Autism Spectrum Disorder (ASD). This website is designed primarily for those on the autism spectrum & their families, as well as educators & healthcare workers, to help them make informed choices about what approaches might be most effective for any specific individual diagnosed with autism. We are especially interested in reaching families from ethnic communities & economic groups who are usually under-served & whose children typically do not receive early diagnosis. For that reason, the website is bilingual— accessible both in English & Spanish." [3]. These interactive health projects are analyze through an original & detailed model of analysis to study the integration of IDS [4] techniques, Interactive Digital Storytelling, within the HCI & the interaction design. With all, the conclusions of the interaction design analysis serve to be applied on the

HCI & IDS designs of a health project about recovery from addiction, at the Group I+D +C CICNETART, www.cicnetart.org.

2 HCI & IDS Descriptions and Techniques to Include on the Analysis

Firstly, the goals, hypothesis & the concepts of the HCI & IDS study are described in order to develop an accurate model of analysis of the narrative interaction design integrated on the HCI. To include on the model & analyze the different interactive narratives & aesthetic elements, used by the mentioned projects of the Labyrinth group, is necessary to clarify some important practical & conceptual descriptions involved in the interactive narratives & interaction designs. Some of the most important to observe are: digital media affordances, immersion, agency & types of interaction, emergent narrative, hypermedia interface, hypermedia narrative cinema, narrative paradox, author-audience distance (AAD), narrative intelligibility, narrative closure.

2.1 Goals and Hypothesis

The goals of this research are to study how the interaction design & the narrative techniques were integrated successfully[1] to obtain the necessary interactor immersion & agency on the health edutainment contents. The model focuses on identifying the narrative & expressive techniques used on edutainment & on the interaction design that present, between others, good narrative intelligibility & closure [5]. The goal is looking for the pertinent interactive narrative concepts that serve to design effective interactive communications for health edutainment & behavioral change. In words of Ben Shaul ([6], p. 84) "...the complimentary lures that reinforce rather than dismantle the inter-actor's engagement when transitioning back & forth from cognitively constructing the hyper-narrative in her mind to behaviorally intervening in order to change its course". In brief, the final objective is to determine how the agency & immersion are obtained on interactive health edutainment projects through the "behaviorally intervention", with the HCI, "to change the course" of information organization, while keeping narrative intelligibility & closure.

The hypothesis of the research is that through the analysis of the HCI design on successful health projects is possible to describe how the four affordances of digital media ([1], p. 51): encyclopedic, spatial, procedural & participatory, are developed & integrated to obtain effective immersion & agency on new health edutainment projects. An effective HCI design allows the user to identify with the interactive narratives presented & transparently participate with: the values, the characters' situations, the actions, the spaces & the times narrated. Interactive health documentaries can present close ADD, good narrative intelligibility & closure as well as satisfactory immersion & agency.

---

[1] Here success is understood as the effective narrative communication between a user and a HCI system ([5], pp. 13, 22), through close ADD, narrative intelligibility and closure.

2.2   Immersion, Agency, Hypermedia Interface, Hypermedia Narrative Cinema and System Goal

According with Mateas and Murray ([7], p. 21): "Immersion is the feeling of being present in another place & engaged in the action therein. Immersion is related to Coleridge's "willing suspension of disbelief" when a participant is immersed in an experience, they are willing to accept the internal logic of the experience, even though this logic deviates from the logic of the real world." Integrating the previous concept with the types of interaction, Mora ([8], pp. 191, 509) describes immersion as: "...the identification & responsibility that the user feels about the development of the narrative actions & the processes that the character lives when he can mediate through the interface with the narrative forms & structures, thanks to the different types of interaction (selective, transformative & constructive) that the hypermedia expressions offer." In relationship with the concept of agency, Murray, J. ([7], p. 10): "Agency is the term I use to distinguish the pleasure of interactivity, which arises from the two properties of the procedural & the participatory. When the world responds expressively & coherently to our engagement with it, then we experience agency." "...agency can be intensify through the dramatic effect."

For the interface the synthetic definition of Moreno, I. ([9], p. 114) is: "the mix of hardware & software through the ones the reader-author communicates with the hypermedia program". It is complemented by the more extensive description of Mora, ([8], pp. 222, 511): "The interface is configured by a set of interactive expressions that serve to attract the spectator's attention, his receptive & participatory position in the communicative moment, & to invite him in becoming a reader-author through the different type of interactions with the narrative forms." "It is the physical & functional connection between the hypermedia system & the perceptional & communicative human systems." Another important concept is the hypermedia or interactive multimedia. Moreno I. ([9], p. 27) describes it as: "Hypermedia describes all the spectrum of interactive media from telecommunications, high-definition TV, videogame & the multimedia." The hypermedia interface concept is integrated by Mora ([8] p. 222) on the following description: "the organized set of interactive & multi-sensorial expressions organized under the representations that are allowed by the information technologies." Moreover, since the analyzed projects can be considered hypermedia narrative cinema, on this research the words of Ben Saul ([6], p. 7) are used to describe this concept: "a variety of hypotheses & actual works whose common denominator is their focus upon a computer-mediated interaction between users or "interactors" & moving audio-visual texts that strives, through the use cinematic strategies, to offer the interactor an option to change at predetermined points the course of action by shifting to other predetermined options". On that sense, the model of analysis integrates what are the types of narrative structures that are presented through the HCI from the health projects. This serves to observe how the hyper-narrative is balanced with the system goal. The hypermedia narrative structure [8] is materialized in the multimedia expressions that are articulated on the HCI design. The relationships between the hyper-narratives to the system goal of immersive-interactive media are considered from Bruni, L.E. ([5], p. 13) perspective as: "...experiences... ...are also related to the success of narrative communication between a user system & a system, which determines the degree to which the goals of that system have been accomplished. We see thereby a close relation between (1) the various aspects of narrative communication, (2) the interaction between user & the system, & (3) the achievements of the goals of the system."

2.3   HCI's Interactions, Types of Interactivity and Productive Interactivity

The concept of interaction used here is the one describes by Mora ([8], p. 171, 510): "To act interdependently or reciprocally in response to action coming from an interface, person, agent, force, function or object interdependently or reciprocally. It is specially applied to the communicative multi-sensorial dialog between human-machine or human/s-machine/s-human/s through the use of the hypermedia interface." It is also complemented with Murray's description of ([1], p. 426): "In digital media, human actions & computer responses are shaped into discrete interactions, which, if well formed, elicit the experience of agency in the interactor. Digital environments can also represent complex systems of interaction in simulations". In that sense, the complexity is formed thanks to the different types of interactivity that digital media projects can offer. The concept of interactivity used here is also the one described by Murray ([1], p. 426): "A design term that is... ...Composed of three separate entities: the procedural & participatory affordances of the digital medium, & the associated aesthetic pleasure of agency that results when the interactor is appropriately scripted to perform actions that the computer code can respond to appropriately." The types of interactivity that the interactor can developed within the HCI are referred by Mora and Moreno's concepts ([8], pp. 173–174) & summarized here: "...Three types of participation selective, transformative & constructive... ...Selective: the user interacts only selecting the options that the program offers... ...Transformative: the user no only can select the options proposed by the author, he can also transform them... Constructive: The system allows the user to select, transform even to build new proposals or recombination of possibilities that were not previewed by the original author. In that sense it allows to interact to create emergent narratives." Another important concept to be included in the model of analysis, due to its relationship with the constructive type of interaction with the system, is productive interactivity. Hurup Bevensee ([10], p. 62) describes it as: "To participate in the process of modifying narrative material through writing, navigating & interacting with objects embodied in an open world computer game, resulting in dramatic elements to the "next" player." Ryan [11] complements the description of productive interactivity as: "[participating] in the writing of text by contributing permanent documents to a database or a collective literary project".

2.4   Concepts Related with the "Narrative Paradox": ADD, Narrative Intelligibility and Narrative Closure

All these described concepts are included on the HCI model of analysis so it can be observed & study how the "narrative paradox" is resolved on the interaction design of the health projects. The "narrative paradox" is considered through Bruni, L.E. ([5],

p. 14) perspective: "With the advent of new media & its possibilities for interactivity in the generation & reception of narrative structures, the issue of "narrative paradox" arises, in which the relationship between authorship & interactivity is seen as being inversely proportional i.e.: the problem of having free-roaming interactive world & an author-controlled narrative at the same time... ...The paradox arises in all its implications with the "empowering" possibilities of digital media & presupposes an ideal of "emancipating" the audience from the "tyranny" of the author."

There are some other concepts that are necessary to describe & to observe to understand how the projects try to resolve the "narrative paradox", one of them is the ADD. According to Bruni ([5], pp. 14–15): "The Author-Audience Distance (ADD) is a function of "narrative intelligibility"... ...Eco introduces the concept of "aberrant decoding" in order to explain how messages can be interpreted differently... ...We refer here to this interpretation gap as the ADD which thereby illustrates the continuum that goes from complete aberrant decoding to perfect reception of the preferred decoding, depending on how defective is the sharing of the coding & system between author & audience."

Another important concept related with the "narrative paradox" & to the ADD is the narrative intelligibility. Bruni and Baceviciute ([5], p. 18) describe it on his study as "...the process in which the audience receives or generate meaning in a way that is close to what is intended, desired or expected by the author... ... i.e. the fidelity of the transmission, or how close the AAD is... ...this distance then depends on the alignment between the author's intended meaning & the one comprehended by the user." Another important concept is the narrative closure described by Bruni and Baceviciute ([6] p. 18) as: "...the process where the audience may construct its own meaning out of what is being mediated, independent on whether that meaning corresponds or gets close to what is intended by the author..."

In order to include a clear understanding & provide this research with a narrative intelligibility & closure the concept of emergent narratives is taken from Jenkins [12] definitions described on Bevensee and Schoenay-Fog words ([10], p. 61) as: "... narrative material through a rich environment & intelligent characters, with which the user is able to associate, interpret, & ultimately construct his/her own understanding of the story." This description is complemented with Truesdale et al. ([13], p. 65) perspective on emergent narratives (EN): "...the conceptual approach is to place an interactor within an interactive environment from which the narrative dynamically alters based on individual actions of both the interactor & any involved agents."

3   Model of Analysis

The following model of analysis, see Table 1, is designed focused on analyzing the IDS elements presented on the HCI & how the combinations of those elements on the interface serve to the activation & the existence of the practical concepts such as: immersion, agency, types of interaction, productive interactivity, emergent narrative, hypermedia narrative cinema, narrative paradox, author-audience distance, AAD, narrative intelligibility & narrative closure. This model of analysis of the interactive communicative & narrative dynamics is applied to the analysis of the selected Health

Labyrinths Projects: *A Tale of Two MAO Genes & Interacting with Autism*. The model goal is to analyze how the interface design generates immersion & agency through the different combination of interactive narrative elements & techniques. The first versions of the model where effectively used in doctoral & postdoctoral researches at the Visual Arts Department, UCSD, University of California San Diego, & the Interactive Media Division, at USC, University of Southern California, to analyze hypermedia HCI in interactive design & digital storytelling projects.

Table 1. Model of analysis of the interactive design, aesthetic, narrative elements & concepts, applied on HCI of IDS projects. (Source: Self-design).

1. Project Name & description of the interfaces & the conjunction of hypermedia expressions
1.1. Identifiable denomination of the hypermedia interface.
2. General characteristics of the interface & detailed description of the multimedia characteristics of the expressions that can allow interaction with any of the narrative elements. 2.1. Software. 2.2. Types of image or perceptive representations. 2.3. Hardware. 2.4. Typographic, Iconic & Symbolic descriptions
3. Features of the characters represented on the interface & general description of the potential interactions with the characters. 3.1. Character or avatar of 1st, 2d or 3rd Person. 3.2. Physical characteristics. 3.3. Sociological characteristics. 3.4. Psychological characteristics
4. Characteristics of the actions represented on the interface & general description of the potential interactions with the actions. 4.1. Type of structure. 4.2. Secondary theme or subplot. 4.3. Changing hierarchy
5. Characteristics of the spaces represented on the interface & general description of the potential interactions with the spaces. 5.1. Natural, constructed, mimetic-natural or mimetic-infographic. 5.2. Senses implied in the spatial perception. 5.3. Implicit space &/or explicit. 5.4. 2D/3D or 4D space. 5.5. Perspective 5.6. Focus or defocus. 5.7. Illumination & color temperature. 5.8. Props. 5.9. Space protagonist &/or hyperspace. 5.10. Absent space or suggested space, 5.11. Selection space with representation: coincident or different, & 5.12. Hyperspace
6. Characteristics of the time represented in the interface & general description of the potential interactions with the time. 6.1. Order. 6.2. Duration. 6.3. Frequency. 6.4. Temporal localization. & 6.5. Iteration
7. Aspects of the interactive narrative elements: characters, actions, spaces & times that have a type of interaction available: selective, transformative or constructive, which allow productive interactivity with emergent narratives
8. Values or spiritual principles, & unscrupulous values, available to be activated through the interaction with the narrative elements
9. Description how the immersion is achieved
10. Description how the agency is achieved
11. Description how the hypermedia narrative cinema structure & the relationship with the system is achieved
12. Description of how the "narrative paradox" is resolved integrating the ADD, with the narrative intelligibility & the narrative closure

The main focus of this model is to observe, describe & identify the elements & concepts that converge during the interaction with the HCI, which implement the described narrative concepts & combined them on a way that creates a better agency & immersion. Thus, some technological-aesthetic-narrative interfacial algorithms, or combinations, are found so they can be integrated in designing future health projects.

4 Discussion: Application of the HCI & IDS Model of Analysis, and the HCI & IDS Common Denominators

After applying the detailed model in both projects, *A Tale of Two MAO Genes & Interacting with Autism*, the common denominators on the HCI & IDS design are found. In relationship with the design of software both projects have a combination of iconic & symbolic intermediation with attractive typographic design, dynamic, push, sound & iteration on their HCI. The type of images or perceptive representations used on both projects are cine-mimetic & infographic audiovisual images. The hardware used on both projects allows mouse & touch pad intermediation. The typography used is bigger than 14 letters size, with cold colors for physical health descriptions, & warm colors for the psychological descriptions. Both projects use clear icons, & attractive symbols with complementary letters for developing pushing interactions.

The narrative characters presented on both health projects are real people presented from a 2^d & 3rd person perspectives to keep the objectivity. The protagonists are choral or collective, people involved in genetic research or within the autism context; thus, the themes become the main characters. Its multicultural approach includes people from all type of educational & economical levels. The narrative actions are structure on circular, basted & parallel encyclopedic narratives, with a main theme & several subplots that enrich & reinforce the main one, going deeper on the information provided. It presents a changing narrative with relationships between main & secondary actions. The narrative spaces presented on both health projects are natural, mimetic-natural, or mimetic-infographic when is necessary to describe spaces microscopically or psychologically. These are represented on 2D & 3D. The presented spaces give priority to the people, within medium shots & frontal positions, talking heads. The HCI sizes are computer based, 1440×852 & 1680×1050. The senses implied in the spatial perception are: view, ear & touch. The props used are clinical & scientific tools, on one project, & educational & therapeutic toys, on the other. The narrative times have the orders of flashback, flash-forward, meta-retrospective or meta-prospective related with the different secondary narratives, on the *MAO A&B project*, & meta-retrospective & meta-prospective during the secondary narratives on *Interacting with Autism*. They are pure diegesis, open. The temporal localization on the first project is changing, letting us to observe the research beginnings until its present & potential future, & on *Interacting with Autism* is the present, both let time iterations. In terms of the values, they have in common the following ones: honesty, hope, faith, courage, integrity, good-will, humility, fraternal love, justice, perseverance, service, responsibility, self-acceptance, patience, spiritual awakening. In the case of *A Tale of Two MAO Genes* presents also some unscrupulous values: animal brutality, greediness, and lack of integrity with nature.

On both projects the immersion effect on the interactive narrative is achieved not as on a spatial sense but on an intellectual, emotional & moral levels. The interface design presents the contents with enough textual questions, images & videos; representing several scientific & ethical subplots that invite the user to develop "the suspension of disbelief" & immerse in the well-documented multimedia & multi-perspective information. The multi-narrative access, the circular structure & the changing hierarchy provides the participant with enough interactions to satisfy his/her intellectual questions & to see the benefits, limits & difficulties of researching about genetics. The fact o being able to do transformative interaction to go deeper on the understanding of the concepts related with genetic research provides the sensation of navigating freely through the database. On *Interacting With Autism*, its theme, the real dramatic & hopeful personal stories provide the proper emotional immersion for the user to feel the responsibility to continue interacting within the encyclopedic, or database narrative, generating his/her own narrative structure experience, through selective & transformative interactions. Immersion is also helped through the constructive, or productive interaction, where an extra video or multimedia info about a theme related with autism can be requested or provided. The cine-mimetic documentaries serve to generate emotional agency through dramatic identification with real characters, in real situations, that invites the user to go deeper on a subject or change according with his/her mood or interest.

The *Two MAO Genes* project obtains agency thanks to the generous offer of cine-mimetic & infographic documentaries, text & info-graphic descriptions, its great procedural properties thanks to meaningful documents, & its participatory properties of letting navigate, trough a simple but functional interactive design, a huge database of genetic researches. Thus, interactors feel the freedom of navigating & building coherence according with their own psychological & emotional perspectives. The treatment of the narrative time, with openness, lets the users to review different historical moments of the genetic research &, in parallel, the scientific evolution & health applications, generating a dramatic identification with the subject. The fact of the participant being able, through the info-graphic clips, of traveling inside the human body, to understand processes that determine the emotional & mental human states, generates also dramatic identifications. On *Interactive with Autism* the effect of agency is built up based on the navigation & interaction with the plots & subplots of its open structures. Thanks to its interaction design, which provides easy access through menus, a basted narrative with parallel lines can be accessed & the structure is built on a great database of videos. The autism world responds with coherence since the great offer of subplots & characters, organized on the submenus of understanding, treating & living with autism, provide a detailed description of each video of the subplots, allowing the user to search & review the experiences he relates with.

The narrative structure of *A Tale of Two Mao Genes* is circular, since the subplots or subthemes can bee navigated circularly through arrows, & accessed to deeper or more general levels, in any moment, through square buttons. This is a simply way of presenting a database narrative full of scientific details & concepts, specially since the system goal is to educate to a huge variety of audiences [2] "from K-12, to Graduate school, from science major's to general public". The edutainment goal of a complex theme as genetics, the tale of how the MAO genes were discover, & their consequences on the biology & culture of aggression & anxiety, is achieved through an hypermedia HCI that allows multilevel access. These various aspects of narrative communication, the transformative structure interaction, & the selective interaction, of managing the level of content detail that the user wants to navigate on the system, are aspect that guaranties the achievement of the system of "edutainming" several audiences. Observing the hypermedia structure presented on the interface of *Interacting With Autism* it can be concluded that the simple use of well design icons & symbols, & the text clear descriptions in the submenus & the video menus, allows a transparent participation thanks to provide a clear narrative communication between the user & the system. The types of interaction: selective, transformative & constructive, which the user can develop, are clear for the user since he can select between video themes related with understanding, treating & living with autism. The shortness of the videos, as average around 4 min, & as maximum around 15 min, provides a dynamic experience from a complex subject. The system goal is achieved through providing a multilevel structure to an encyclopedic video source of the daily situation & the state-of-the-art research in autism.

The "narrative paradox" of *A Tale of Two MAO Genes* is resolved integrating a close ADD, with the narrative intelligibility & the narrative closure. The complex dynamics of procedural & participatory affordances allow the "all ages", attractive & functional interaction design, to access the encyclopedic multimedia contents. This makes the author-audience distance very close & receptive. Although the scientific coding between author & audience can be far, the system is presented on an immersive hypermedia HCI that allows the gap to be navigated on a simple & educative way, breaking the user's fear of the unknown. The narrative intelligibility is also diverse & with an attractive design, with infographic & audiovisual colorful designs, since the authors are very conscience that are presenting complex contents. This allows the user to comprehended better small clear pieces of information. The narrative closure is let to the user choice of interacting with the system, & of how deep on the database narrative he wants to go to complete his education. The circular & multi-access structures give the user the agency to generate his own narrative closure, his right structure & organization of the multimedia contents. However, there is not allowed any emergent narrative, this can make an interactive edutainment project boring after exploring it several times. In *Interacting with Autism* the narrative paradox is resolved very efficiently. The brief presentation & the video summaries, presenting the subthemes: understanding, treating & living with autism, helps to break a long initial ADD, for a complex theme as autism, in a short period of time. Through the professional & family video descriptions of the solutions, situations & difficulties of autism, complemented with the interaction of autistic children & adults, the user can have a clear overview & direct contact with autism, which otherwise would require a lot of time to understand, because a lot of the technicalities of the autism spectrum. This creates a "preferred decoding" & narrative intelligibility, since the language used by the real characters is common language explaining complex processes, rather than using technical languages. These facts, & the cine-mimetic-infographic videos presenting how an autistic person can perceive overwhelming multi-sensorial inputs on his daily living, help a lot to approach the coding distance between the authors & the audiences. That way the author intention of approaching the world of autism to the general audiences is obtained. Thus, the narrative closure is achieved thanks to this open narrative structure, where the interactor may construct its own experience.

5   Summary of the Discussion and Conclusions to Apply on Future HCI & IDS Projects of Edutainment in Recovery from Addiction

In summary, health edutainment HCI & IDS projects need to count with an interaction design that presents flow & transparent navigation through all the encyclopedic & database contents. Interactive webs full of short documentaries with interactive secondary narrative experiences around a main theme, like recovery from addiction, are good options for content organization. Transparent push interfaces with attractive combinations of icons, text & attractive symbols are needed to generate an initial immersion & agency within the users. There are some important problems to avoid on hypermedia narrative cinema, as described by Ben Saul ([6], p. 30): "...the major hyper-narrative split-attention stumbling blocks: non restriction of narrative threads, incoherent transitions between different narrative threads & non resolution of multi-threaded narratives." In this sense, the analyzed Labyrinth projects present effective circular, basted & parallel lines narratives that generate immersion on the main plots, genetics & autism, making complex themes attractive. The use of a variety of cases of recovery from addiction, perspectives, & techniques seems desirable for the future health project. It is also crucial on the interaction design to include all the types of interactions: selective, transformative & constructive, & productive interaction, to choose the content navigation, to transform the narrative structure & to nurture with meaningful new contents & comments the IDS. With all these techniques will be possible to create meaningful relationships, between the immersive sensorial, psychological or emotional moments & the interactive aesthetic, narrative, & values elements expressed through the HCI, on the health edutainment project about recovery from addiction.

The interaction design needs to implement as much as possible the properties of encyclopedic, special, procedural & participatory. As Murray ([1], pp. 53, 410) underlines: "In approaching interaction design as a cultural practice our aim is always to make an object that is satisfying in itself & that advances the digital medium by refining or creating the conventions that best exploit these four affordances." That is why for the health edutainment interactive narrative project about recovery from addiction we are looking into:

1. Creating encyclopedic information with optimized procedural processes, where the users can easily & fast access different multicultural experiences & techniques of recovering from addiction, archival of the history of recovering from addiction, documents & news about them, as well as to the possibility of uploading extra information.

2. Presenting several spatial & participatory options where the users can interact with the processes of recovering from addiction, on different intellectual & emotional levels, through real & virtual physical, mental & spiritual spaces. In this way, it will be procured the identification with the multidimensional & multicultural narratives, through the variety of characters & the types of interaction with them. This will activate the identification with the memories & the human imaginary of the past, present & future of the users with the people represented on the health project, & of

the participants if they have experienced similar personal, familiar or friendship situations.

Finally, the health edutainment interactive narrative project will try to serve as a digital media creation for informing about the history, current free possibilities to recover from addiction, & its current medical researches. Some embedded interactive narratives & documentaries will also serve to conduct new research, using neurocinema techniques, to determine what recovery techniques are more efficient & interactive for activating the human brain. This last research is being negotiated to be conducted at the Laboratory of Neuroscience ResearchGroup R&D&i Sinapsis, UCuenca, the Arthur C. Clarke Center for Human Imagination, directed by Sheldon Brown, at UCSD, and in collaboration with Pia Tikka, neurocinema artist & researcher at the Aalto University, in Finland.

Acknowledgements. This work was supported by the Prometheus Project, SENESCYT, Secretary of Higher Education, Science, Technology & Innovation of the Republic of Ecuador, by the DIUC, Direction of Research of the University of Cuenca, through the Research Group CICNETART R+D+C, "the Research Group SINAPSIS R&D&i, & the Schools of Medicine" & of Philosophy, Letters & Education Sciences, Careers of Social & Digital Communication & Cinema. It counts with the Collaboration of the Labyrinth's Project, lead by Marsha Kinder Ph.D. & funded at University of Southern California.

References

1. Murray, J.: Inventing the Medium. Principles of Interaction, Design as a Cultural Practice. The MIT Press, Cambridge (2012)
2. Kinder, M., Shih, J.C., Kang, K.H.A., Comella, R.: A tale of two MAO genes: exploring the biology & culture of aggression & anxiety. The Labyrinth Project, University of Southern California, USC, Los Angeles (2010)
3. Harris, M., Kinder, M., Mahoy, S.: Interacting with Autism, a video based resource. USC School of Cinematic Arts, USC, Los Angeles (2013). http://interactingwithautism.com/. Accessed 1 Jun 2014
4. Knoller, N.: The expressive space of IDS-as-art. In: Oyarzun, D., Peinado, F., Young, R., Elizalde, A., Méndez, G. (eds.) ICIDS 2012. LNCS, vol. 7648, pp. 30–41. Springer, Heidelberg (2012)
5. Bruni, E., Baceviciute, S.: Narrative intelligibility and closure in interactive systems. In: Koenitz, H., Sezen, T.I., Ferri, G., Haahr, M., Sezen, D., Catak, G. (eds.) ICIDS 2013. LNCS, vol. 8230, pp. 13–24. Springer, Heidelberg (2013)
6. Ben Shaul, N.: Hyper-Narrative Interactive Cinema: Problems and Solutions. Editions Rodopi B.V. Amsterdam, New York (2008)
7. Mateas, M., Murray, J.: A preliminary poetics for interactive drama and games, and from game-story to cyberdrama. In: Wardrip-Fruin, N., Harrigan, P. (eds.) First Person: New Media as Story, Performance and Game, pp. 2–33. The MIT Press, Cambridge (2004)
8. Mora Fernández, J.: La interfaz hipermedia: el paradigma de la comunicación interactiva. Modelos para implementar la inmersión juvenil en multimedia interactivos culturales. (Videojuegos, cine, realidad aumentada, museos y web). SGAE, Fundación Autor, Ediciones Autor, Colección Datautor, Madrid (2009)

9. Moreno Sánchez, I.: Musas y Nuevas Tecnologías: El relato hipermedia. Paidós Comunicación, Barcelona (2002)

10. Bevensee, S.H., Schoenau-Fog, H.: Conceptualizing productive interactivity in emergent narratives. In: Koenitz, H., Sezen, T.I., Ferri, G., Haahr, M., Sezen, D., Çatak, G. (eds.) ICIDS 2013. LNCS, vol. 8230, pp. 61–64. Springer, Heidelberg (2013)

11. Ryan, M.L.: Narrative as Virtual Reality. The John Hopkins University Press, Maryland (2001)

12. Jenkins, H.: Convergence Culture. New York University Press, New York (2007)

13. Truesdale, J., Louchart, S., Hastie, H., Aylett, R.: Suitability of modelling context for use within emergent narrative. In: Koenitz, H., Sezen, T.I., Ferri, G., Haahr, M., Sezen, D., Çatak, G. (eds.) ICIDS 2013. LNCS, vol. 8230, pp. 65–70. Springer, Heidelberg (2013)

A Toolkit for SE for Sustainability - A Design Fiction

Birgit Penzenstadler[✉]

Department of Computer Engineering and Computer Science,
California State University Long Beach, Long Beach, CA, USA
birgit.penzenstadler@csulb.edu

Abstract. This paper explores the what-ifs for a possible future scenario describing how to develop software systems for sustainability in different application domains in a generic software development setting. The design fiction we narrate is the following: Valery, a software developer at the fictitious software development company GreenCode, works on CodeFairy, an educational game targeted at attracting girls to computer science, and uses the software engineering toolkit GreenYaCode as development environment.

This toolkit helps to translate domain-dependent, high-level sustainability goals into software-specific constraints - i.e. it helps design sustainability into the software system. This is achieved by an extensive knowledge base that allows making recommendations to the software developer, and by best practices from open sources software development and user experience best practices.

Keywords: Education · Information design · Knowledge visualization · Design fiction · Future trends · Storytelling · Sustainability

1 Software Engineering for Sustainability

Sustainability from the point of view of software systems has two major aspects: The software system as technical implementation independent of its purpose, and the software system as means of interaction between users and application context. To define what sustainability for any kind of system, exact scoping needs to be performed by answering the questions of what to sustain, for whom, over which time frame, and at what cost [15]. Once that is established, we can apply systems thinking [16] and follow sustainability principles, e.g. [3], while honoring the axioms defined by Heinberg [7], to improve the sustainability of the given system. This encompasses the individual, social, economic, environmental, and technical sustainability aspects of a system [10]. For a software system, there are two scopes that may be chosen for an analysis, domain-dependent and domain-independent.

Scope (1): Domain-Dependent Sustainability. The software system in its application context, under consideration of the purpose of the software system. This scoping includes an analysis of the economic, social, and environmental dimensions of sustainability on a higher level. This part of the analysis

© Springer International Publishing Switzerland 2015
A. Marcus (Ed.): DUXU 2015, Part I, LNCS 9186, pp. 634–643, 2015.
DOI: 10.1007/978-3-319-20886-2_59

is largely within the responsibility of business analysts and domain experts. Following the code of ethics [1], it is our responsibility to support in translating the arising demands into system-related requirements. This is what we call domain-dependent sustainability: The Sustainability of a Software System and its Surrounding Application Context, is characterized by the domain experts. This scoping is domain-dependent and we call it domain-dependent sustainability, software engineers can translate those requirements into constraints for the software system.

Scope (2): Domain-Independent Sustainability. The artifacts and implementation of a software system, without any consideration of the purpose of the software system. This scoping focuses on the technical characteristics of the system and its operational environment. All domain-relevant information has already been refined into domain-independent constraints for a technical solution by business analysts. This is the responsibility of the software engineers. This is what we call domain-independent sustainability: The Sustainability of a Software System is its capacity to endure, i.e. its energy efficiency, its maintainability over a long period of time, and its adherence to standards and laws. This scoping is independent of the application domain of the software system; therefore we call this domain-independent sustainability.

In order to develop software systems that implement sustainability goals, we need the discipline of software engineering to embrace sustainability as major objective for systems development. **Software Engineering for Sustainability** (SE4S) denotes the concept of applying software engineering techniques to facilitate the refinement of higher level sustainability concerns as defined in the domain into lower level, technical requirements for the design and implementation of the system. This means the translation and refinement from domain-dependent to domain-independent sustainability.

In this paper, we present a design fiction of how SE4S can be supported in a toolkit. In more detail, the story line follows software developer Valery through her workday and points out open questions and research challenges by describing which inputs have to be made to implement the GreenYaCode toolkit system. We illustrate its usage with the support that it makes when Valery goes through the individual steps taken during software development.

2   Background

This section provides background information on design fiction, on free open source software development, and on the Software Engineering for Sustainability (SE4S) research project.

2.1   Design Fiction

Research is often inspired by visions of the future, for example the Vision 2050 [17]. These visions can take on various narrative forms, and can fall anywhere along the spectrum from utopian to dystopian [2]. Even though we recognize the importance of such visions to help us shape research questions and inspire rich design spaces to be explored, the opportunity to discuss them is rarely given in a research context [12].

2.2 Free Open Source Software Development and Open Innovation

Open-source software development has been a large part of the creation of the World Wide Web as we know it, with Tim Berners-Lee contributing his HTML code development as the original platform upon which the internet is now built [4]. Free and open sources software (FOSS) are software products available with its source code under an open-source license to study, change, and improve its design. Examples of some popular open-source software products are Mozilla Firefox, Google Chromium, Android, LibreOffice and the Apache OpenOffice Suite. FOSS is said to reduce costs, avoid lock-in, ease use, and provide open security [13].

2.3 SE4S Research Project

The Software Engineering for Sustainability (SE4S) research project has developed a number of contributions with regard to how software engineers can include sustainability as major objective into software systems development [11]. Specifically requirements engineers have the means to establish designing for sustainability early on during the development process [10], and quality engineers help carry it through the rest of the development process [8]. This paper proposes the vision of a toolkit to support these concepts in practice, so that every software developer can easily apply them in their daily work.

3 Vision of the Toolkit and its Application

It is the year 2020 and Valery has been working as software engineer at Green-Code for 5 years after graduating from California State University Long Beach with a Master's degree in Computer Science. She had been eager to find a software development company that would allow her to work on projects where she can foster environmental and social sustainability. When GreenCode emerged as an academic spin-off from the GreenIT lab at UC Irvine, she got in touch with their team and found an alike mindset of motivated software engineers who wanted to take their share of responsibility to make software systems that would improve the status quo in social responsibility and environmental protection.

They mainly work on projects in two domains: scientific software to facilitate research in their local environment, the ocean and the mountains, and educational software to improve the access to knowledge for children of all ages. In that latter domain, Valery has been assigned to the CodeFairy project, an educational game targeted at attracting girls to computer science.

Before GreenCode became an academic spin-off, the team had developed the SE4S toolkit GreenYaCode, a software development environment that helps to translate domain-dependent, high-level sustainability goals into domain-independent, software-specific constraints — i.e. it helps design sustainability into the software system. GreenCode is a web-based SE4S guide that provides easy access to the reference models and related examples in form of a knowledge database, see the wireframe in Fig. 2. This knowledge base can be extended over time with further examples from case studies and with recommender systems that actively guide the user, i.e., the requirements engineer. This is the most flexible way of accommodating the pace of change in popular programming languages and therefore provides the greatest possible outreach to the software development community. The toolkit ties together efforts in software engineering for sustainability, free open source software development, recommender systems, usability best practices, open innovation, and user engagement.

SE4S starts with requirements engineering and determining the stakeholders for the system, which is the basis for being able to elicit requirements. In more detail, there are four elicitation and analysis steps that are preempted by guiding questions [10]. For CodeFairy, Valery develops a number of artifacts that document the information needed to start the actual design process. She composes a business case, stakeholder model, goal model, system vision, domain model, usage model, and non-functional requirements, all by using the guidance provided by GreenYaCode to make sure the sustainability goals issued by the stakeholders for CodeFairy are incorporated into the design process. These artifacts form the basis that allows to decide on the implementation platform and to start the design of CodeFairy. In the following, we will walk through those steps and their application for CodeFairy (Fig. 1).

3.1   Scope System and Derive System Vision

Fig. 1. CodeFairy

Clear scoping lies the foundation for successful systems development. The scoping allows for deriving a system vision, a conception of what is to be developed commonly agreed upon by all stakeholders. Valery opens the GreenYaCode start page and the quick start guide provides the guiding question for the first step: *Does the system under consideration have an explicit purpose towards environmental or social sustainability? If yes, this can be analyzed in depth. If no, it can be considered whether such an aspect is desirable and feasible to add.*

For CodeFairy, the purpose is to engage girls from the age of twelve to learn coding in a playful way. Inspired by "The Hour of Code"[1] and "Alice"[2], CodeFairy provides means to understand concepts in computer science and mathematics, and shows how they are applied when making software. It promotes social sustainability in terms of education and gender equality in STEM. On this basis, Valery develops a system vision using an integrated diagramming tool that helps her define the system boundary, operational context and the most central user features of CodeFairy.

---

[1] http://code.org/.
[2] www.alice.org.

3.2   Analyse Sustainability of Context

The second guiding question posed by GreenYaCode is: *Does the system under consideration have an impact on the environment?* We need to analyze what are the direct (first order), indirect (second order), and systemic as well as potential rebound effects (third order) [9].

GreenYaCode provides an analysis checklist of influencing factors for each of those orders of effect. Most obvious are the first order effects. First order effects are the resources that the system itself (the application on different devices and the database) consume. For software, that is predominantly the energy that a software consumes, which can be influenced by good design strategies and energy-efficient code. For the hardware part of a system, measures include following green IT principles. The second order effects are the resources the system triggers in its application domain. That means, the developer has to look at how the software system interacts with its operational environment. Which processes are triggered, for example which machines are used or what do users do because of having this software system in place? The third order effects remain to be observed in the long run but can be predicted using future scenario techniques and extrapolation. In simple terms, imagine what could happen if the user base of this system increases dramatically and many people use the system over many years in high intensity. How could that affect overall resource consumption and how could that change behavior?

For CodeFairy, the first order effects are the energy that the software uses and the usage of laptops or desktop machines to run the software. Second order effects are increased computer literacy and software engineering knowledge (education is part of individual sustainability), increased social skills in collaboration with other girls on teams (social sustainability) but also increased hardware usage in classroom and therefore e-waste (environmental impact). Third order effects might be increased rates of female students in computer science if outreach is successful (potential individual, social, and economic benefits) but also further environmental impact due to increased energy usage and e-waste production. However, as CodeFairy would not be the reason for ordering new hardware, but rather sharing common resources (laptops or computers that are used in class anyways), this environmental impact is comparatively small.

3.3   Find Sustainability Stakeholders

The third guiding question is: *Is there an explicit stakeholder for sustainability?* In case there is an explicit stakeholder who advocates for environmental sustainability, there is already a significant representative who issues objectives, constraints and considerations to support that quality in the system under consideration. In case there is no such advocate, it can be decided to establish such a role. Otherwise, at the very least, a domain expert should be established as a representative for sustainability for providing information on applying environmental standards, legislation, and regulations.

To find sustainability stakeholders, GreenYaCode provides a reference list of stakeholders who might have an interest in sustainability concerns. The reference list is ordered by sustainability aspect and describes for each stakeholder role that is common in software development, what their interest w.r.t. in a specific sustainability aspect is, for example a user is interested in their own individual sustainability, and a network administrator is mainly interested in the technical sustainability of the system they have to maintain. Furthermore, the list references dedicated sustainability stakeholders, for example legal representatives for environmental regulations.

For CodeFairy, the usual software development stakeholders have to be considered. In addition, Valery might engage a sustainability consultant to, for example, add a case study system with environmental objectives, so the students can learn how software systems can support and help to protect the environment.

3.4   Elicit Sustainability Objectives, Goals and Constraints

The fourth guiding question is: *What are the sustainability goals and constraints for the system?* Independent of whether the system has an explicit purpose for supporting environmental sustainability or not, there certainly are a number of objectives that pertain to the different dimensions of sustainability that may be chosen to apply. For example, a social network might not have an explicit

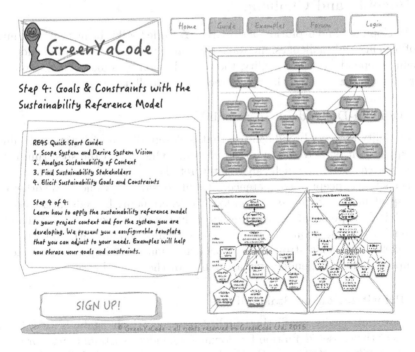

Fig. 2. Wireframe of the reference model screen of the toolkit

environmental purpose, but it certainly has objectives supporting social sustainability. Furthermore, any system will at least have some constraints with respect to the environment, as stated in Q2.

To elicit sustainability objectives, goals and constraints, GreenYaCode provides the sustainability reference model. Examples for instances are depicted in the wireframe on the right side in Fig. 2. It shows an example that distinguishes three levels of abstraction: The business goals (*What benefits is this system going to bring?*), the usage goals (*What can the user do with the system?*), and the system goals (*How will the system provide that?*). Each of those should be analyzed for the five sustainability aspects.

For CodeFairy, a central business objective is to increase the education of girls in software engineering and thereby reach out early on to get them excited about STEM fields. A usage goal derived from this business objective is to have them interact with the system in a playful way so the intrinsical motivation remains high. A system goal deducted from that usage goal is that the user interface must be simple and intuitive enough so the target age group is addressed adequately. This way, Valery can develop a goal model that brings together the interests of the different stakeholders (who are the issuers of these objectives), that includes the different aspects of sustainability, and that uses continuous, integrated software engineering techniques for requirements that can be traced back to their originators.

4 Benefits and Challenges

The development and evolution of the GreenYaCode toolkit brings with it a number of benefits and challenges, inter alia the transition from domain-dependent to domain-independent sustainability, the prioritization by stakeholders, economic return on investment, and the acceptance of the toolkit.

4.1 Domain-Dependent Sustainability

Sustainability is a very broad concept that is closely tied in with personal values. Consequently, it is used in very different forms. One end of the spectrum is the *capacity to endure* [14], which can be interpreted as "survival of the fittest", and that leads to a concept of competence without considering values. The other end of the spectrum is *life flourishing forever* [5], where flourish needs interpretation that will include personal values. Consequently, domain-dependent sustainability is strongly dependent on the project context and tied in with the values of the stakeholders. This strong interdependence makes it impossible to clearly decompose domain-dependent sustainability for the general case.

4.2 Prioritization by Stakeholders

There are potentially conflicting quality criteria, which again is tied to the specifics of the chosen definition for domain-dependent sustainability; for example sustainability and privacy: On one hand the absolute availability of information would make sustainability easier in many domains, and that is in conflict with privacy. For example, if companies had to provide all information on how "green" (environmentally sustainable) they really are with consumption of any type of resources, their processes, and their waste production. On the other hand, privacy can be understood as part of the individual sustainability of a person, for example security breaches in online banking. Consequently the occurrence of the conflict again depends on the definition of the domain-dependent sustainability and which values that definition is based on. Finally, how it is prioritized again depends on the importance that these stakeholders assign to it.

4.3   Economic Return on Investment

For the economic perspective, (1) Valery can get credit for her company by contributing back into the knowledge base of GreenYaCode and (2) she can provide added value for her company by using GreenYaCode to demonstrate how sustainability is designed into the system. This is because the toolkit provides the traceability to prove the integration of sustainability throughout the development process and into the final product.

The first point, the contribution back into the knowledge base, is a central principle in any open collaboration. For solving sustainability issues, sharing our knowledge and building up the databases that provide examples for best practices, is vital to success as there are so many different factors that have to be taken into account. A specific economic benefit of contributing back to the knowledge base will depend on the implementation of the tool. One way to imagine a win-win situation is to offer free use of the tool if the results that they were used for are contributed back to the knowledge base. In case of confidentiality issues, the contributions could be made more abstract or names and numbers could be modified and sources anonymized.

The second point, providing added value to the company by demonstrating that sustainability was designed into the system, is relevant for marketing. As sustainability has received an increased awareness by companies in all application areas and business domains, it is likely that sustainability standards will develop that require the use of certain reference models to ensure compliance with such standards. In an ideal world, the GreenYaCode toolkit could become one of the toolkits to ensure this compliance.

4.4   Tool Acceptance

To facilitate their application in practice for any proposed concept (including SE4S), it is necessary to provide adequate tooling to disseminate them. However, establishing new reference tools within a development company always faces challenges of acceptance. It is easier to stick to established tools and avoid learning curves for new tools, unless the benefits early on significantly outweigh the initial effort.

There are several open source development environments, for example Eclipse, that may welcome plug-ins that access GreenYaCode and use its reference models for providing additional guidance within their programming environments. The availability of such plug-ins is likely to increase application of SE4S in practice because the integration reduces the user effort for looking up yet another reference. Contributing to free open source software is an incentive to improve your coding skills and get familiar with large projects [6]. Therefore, students with interest in sustainability should be encouraged to engage in such activities.

5   Conclusion and Future Work

As this is design fiction, we cannot present an evaluation of the concepts presented in this paper. However, the fiction is based on elements that have resulted from previous research and now have to be integrated into an encompassing guidance for software engineering for sustainability. The contribution of this paper is to provide a research roadmap for software engineers who aim at making our profession a part of the way of our society towards sustainability and to outline questions and challenges that have to be solved along that way.

Future work includes:

- The iterative implementation of the proposed tool vision in increments with a growing list of features and capabilities.
- The qualitative evaluation of applicability and usability in feasibility studies in collaboration with software development companies in different contexts.
- The long-term evaluation of benefits for systems' development in terms of the impact on the different dimensions of sustainability and the return on investment.

Acknowledgements. This work is partially sponsored by the Deutsche Forschungsgemeinschaft under the EnviroSiSE project (grant number PE 2044/1-1). We would like to thank Ankita Raturi for feedback on an earlier version of this paper.

References

1. ACM, Inc. Acm code of ethics (1999). http://www.acm.org/about/se-code
2. Baumer, E.P.S., Ahn, J., Bie, M., Bonsignore, B., Borutecene, A., Buruk, O.T., Clegg, T., Druin, A., Echtler, F., Gruen, D., Guha, M.L., Hordatt, C., Kruger, A., Maidenbaum, S., Muller, M., Norooz, L., Norton, J., Ozcan, O., Patterson, D., Riener, A., Ross, S., Rust, K., Schoening, J., Silberman, S., Tomlinson, B., Yip, J.: CHI 2039: speculative research visions. In: Proceedings of alt.CHI of the ACM CHI Conference on Human Factors in Computing Systems (2014)
3. Becker, C., Chitchyan, R., Duboc, L., Easterbrook, S., Penzenstadler, B., Seyff, N., Venters, C.: Sustainability design and software: the karlskrona manifesto. In: Proceedings of the International Conference on Software Engineering (2015)
4. Berners-Lee, T.: Tim Berners-Lee on the Web at 25: The Past, Present and Future. Wired, UK (2014)
5. Ehrenfeld, J.R.: The roots of sustainability. MIT Sloan Manag. Rev. **46**(2), 23–25 (2005)

6. Fish, S.: How to start contributing to or using Open Source Software (2014). http://teachingopensource.org/index.php/How_to_start_contributing_to_or_using_Open_Source_Software

7. Heinberg, R., Lerch, D.: What is sustainability? The post carbon reader: managing the 21st century's sustainability crises (2010)

8. Lago, P., Kocak, S.A., Crnkovic, I., Penzenstadler, B.: Framing sustainability as a software quality property. Commun. ACM (2015, Accepted for publication)

9. Meadows, D.: Leverage points – places to intervene in a system (1999). http://www.donellameadows.org/wp-content/userfiles/Leverage_Points.pdf

10. Penzenstadler, B.: Infusing green: requirements engineering for green in and through software systems. In: 3rd International Workshop on Requirements Engineering for Sustainable Systems (2014)

11. Penzenstadler, B., Raturi, A., Richardson, D., Tomlinson, B.: Safety, security, now sustainability: the non-functional requirement of the 21st century. IEEE Softw. Spec. Issue Green Softw. **31**(3), 40–47 (2014)

12. Penzenstadler, B., Tomlinson, B., Baumer, E., Pufal, M., Raturi, A., Richardson, D., Cakici, B., Chitchyan, R., Da Costa, G., Dombrowski, L., Edwardsson, M.P., Eriksson, E., Franch, X., Hayes, G.R., Herzog, C., Lohmann, W., Mahaux, M., Mavin, A., Mazmanian, M., Nayebaziz, S., Norton, J., Pargman, D., Patterson, D.J., Pierson, J.-M., Roher, K., Six Silberman, M., Simonson, K., Torrance, A.W., van der Hoek, A.: ICT4S 2029: What will be the Systems Supporting Sustainability in 15 Years? In: 2nd International Conference on ICT for Sustainability (ICT4S 2014), Stockholm, Sweden, August 2014

13. Stewart, W.: Free Open Source Software Main Page (2014). http://www.freeopensourcesoftware.org

14. SustainAbility. Sustainability: Can our society endure? (2014). http://www.sustainability.com/sustainability

15. Tainter, J.A.: Social complexity and sustainability. J. Ecol. Complex. **3**, 91–103 (2006)

16. Waddington, C.H.: Tools for Thought. Basic Books Inc., New York (1977)

17. World Business Council for Sustainable Development. Vision 2050: A New Agenda for Business (2010). http://www.wbcsd.org/WEB/PROJECTS/BZROLE/VISION2050-FULLREPORT_FINAL.PDF

Delphi Method to Explore Future Scenario Possibilities on Technology and HCI

Adriano Bernardo Renzi[✉] and Sydney Fernandes de Freitas

Escola Superior de Desenho Industrial – UERJ, Rio de Janeiro, Brazil
adrianorenzi@gmail.com, sydneyfreitas@terra.com.br

Abstract. Based on the pattern shown in the nose of innovation graphic of Bill Buxton, this paper investigates future developments and construct a future scenario regarding technology, interaction and expectations of affordances in the next 5 to 10 years. The research is based in the Delphi method to help construct scenarios of possibilities as it helps identify expectations of incremental and drastic innovations. The method brings together specialists on user experience, usability, information architecture, technology and network, with experience and points of view from five different cities around the world.

Keywords: Management of DUXU processes · Science-fiction and future trends · Usability methods and tools

1 Nose of Innovation

Bill Buxton [1], principal researcher at Microsoft Research and professor at Technical University of Eindhoven and Toronto University, shows a graphical representation of the "nose of innovation" with a length of 20 years, from concepting and first testings to product's uprising advancements and increment innovations.

First concepts and research regarding touch screen interaction can be traced back to the 60's and early 70's, where documentation from IBM labs in collaboration with the University of Illinois shows PLATO IV with a touch sensitive plasma screen connected to a local network. And during the same period, Xerox's PARC laboratory starts to work on the project ALTO6. Many years later, as the touch screen technology reaches the uprising direction in the nose of innovation graphic, the popularization of touch screen artifacts, such as smartphones and tablets, are more and more in our day-to-day lives and do much more than just call someone. Although it has been many years of research and tests, when reaching the uprising part of the innovation nose, the increment innovations appear faster (Fig. 1).

Previous research [10] with users who have never interacted before with touch screen devices showed that their perception of gestural interaction affordances were based on (1) direct short-clicks, (2) clicks-and-drag and (3) page flips. All users' choices to click on and gestural interaction exploration, as well as response expectations, were related to their cultural conventions of internet interaction models, hyperlinks on websites, computer software icons and mouse actions. Their mental models, based on previous

© Springer International Publishing Switzerland 2015
A. Marcus (Ed.): DUXU 2015, Part I, LNCS 9186, pp. 644–653, 2015.
DOI: 10.1007/978-3-319-20886-2_60

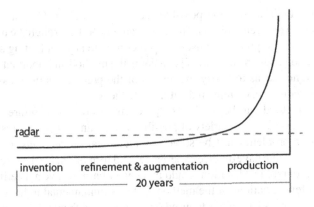

radar

| invention | refinement & augmentation | production |

20 years

Fig. 1. Nose of innovation (source: Business Week 2008)

experiences with internet and desktop computers, influenced their perception of functionalities and affordances while performing the proposed tasks with a touch screen device.

During the testing sessions users unconsciously reached for similarities of previous experiences, personal interaction references and learning concepts from reference groups [11]. The results observed indicate users' references based on commonly used devices, their related interactions and possibly online advertisings about touch screen features, mostly depicting direct short-clicks, click-and-drag gesture, image expansion-contraction and page flipping. These references seems to influence not only users' perception of affordances, but also their expectations of technology use and its benefits.

The uprising of the nose of innovation and new research for new products can bring many possibilities of incremental and radical innovations. The interactions that people are experiencing now are building the basis of mental model, affordances and expectations for the innovations of the near future. This article presents a research based on the Delphi Method with the objective of understanding the possibilities of technology development and human-computer interactions in the next five to ten years to help create a future scenario. Ten specialists in technology and interaction agreed to participate in this research.

2 The Delphi Method

Theodore J. Gordon and Jerome C. Glenn [8] in their book "Futures Research Methodology" (2009) point the origin of the method on the 60's, at the research laboratory RAND, in Santa Monica, California. The focused mostly on military issues regarding technology development, as well as, potential political scenarios. RAND researchers explored possibilities in a primitive quantitative simulation model with computers that had not enough capacity to record the amount of data.

The method objectives to surface most possible scenarios of a specific topic based on specialists knowledge. Gordon and Glenn [8] and Justo [3] describe the proceedings as a reunion of specialists from different areas of expertise to concentrate their analysis on a specific topic, share opinions, present comments and discuss issues until reaching a consensus and build a common possible scenario. Lindeman [4] points that it is a method to combine different opinions from separated experts, through the use of a series of questions in order to produce consensus and eliminate any conflicting situation that a meeting in person could result. Pill [7] considers the method an important tool in cases where there are no means to verify the results of the predictions or in cases to detect breaks and innovations in certain areas of knowledge.

The Delphi method can be used to help construct present or future scenarios on specifics subjects, surfacing a variety of possibilities. It can bring better results in situations (1) where a problem can't be solved by analytical proceedings, (2) the invited specialists to participate have diverse experiences and formation, (3) the size of the group (or specialists geographical location) could make very hard to have a meeting in person.

There are a few variations of the method, but it is fundamental to have a controlled debate with participants specialists focused on the proposed theme. It is more interesting when the participants work in different areas in order to present different points of view. As for example, if the topic of discussion would be the terrorism scenario in the next 5 years, could be interesting to have specialists of border security, airport security and explosives as well as specialists of international relations, cultural and religion researchers discussing and exchanging ideas regarding the possible scenarios. Gordon and Glenn [8] put the Delphi method in three kinds of situational judgement:

1. prediction of future developments, as for example "scenario of the smartphones development in the next 10 years";
2. prediction of possibilities of an event in the future and related recommendations, as for instance "the possibility of establishing an exact date when man will land on Mars";
3. ways to achieve or avert future situations, "the political scenario and water supply in 15 years from now"

The three types of questionnaire proposed by Gordon and Glenn [8] can ask for a variety of specialists as participants: from experts on the subject, specialists that are in contact with technology research and state of the art regarding the subject, specialists related to ethics, moral, cultural, social from determined area to specialists on scenarios' probabilities.

Since the major objective of this research is to map the scenario of the technology and interactions in the next 5 to 10 years in order to understand better the expectations, mental models and affordances, the elaboration of the questionnaire focused primary on "prediction of future developments". The direction choice influenced directly the choice of questions as well as the types of specialists to invite.

The key to success reside in the experts invited, since the results of the method depends directly on the specialists knowledge regarding the subject and cooperation between all involved in the method. It is essential to include people that can contribute significantly to the research. The search for potential participants can start and be directed through university or research facilities' recommendations, known authors with publications on the specific subject or researchers' chain of contacts. For the application of the method, we used all three directions to choose and invite specialists, plus the direct contact through international conferences. After as few months of search, 27 specialists throughout the world were invited to participate in the method. Ten specialists agreed to be part of the research: one from Los Angeles, one from Amsterdam, one from São Paulo, one from Lisbon, six from Rio de Janeiro.

In order to reach the objectives of the method the experts selected for invitation had to be specialists in areas related to state of the art of technology and human-technology interaction research. The filtering procedure tried to group experts from different experience positions that could bring different points of view. The invitees had to work in at least 3 of the related areas:

1. prospecting – the specialist is involved in acquisition of information and research associated with products/systems not yet available in the market for consuming or purchase.
2. research – the specialists is involved in products/systems testing. Or the specialist has to conduct/participate of users experience research and mental model mapping. Or he/she has been involved in academic research related to technology, HCI, UX and usability.
3. project planning – the specialist frequently participates in strategic and conceptual projects creation, either being physical products, systems or services. Or he/she acts in systems (or services) architecture planning.
4. development/programing – the specialist participates directly in mechanical, graphic or programming development of products or systems.
5. propagation of knowledge/articulation of information – write scientific articles, foment propagation of products/systems or knowledge, or writes to channels with opinion influence regarding technology.

The filtering helped to bring together representatives of all 5 areas in order to have a diversity of activities among the selected specialists and obtain opinions from different points of view. The relation between participants and the 5 areas are:

- specialist 1 (prospecting-research-project planning);
- specialist 2 (prospecting-research-project planning-propagation of knowledge);
- specialist 3 (research-project planning-propagation of knowledge);
- specialist 4 (prospecting-research-propagation of knowledge);
- specialist 5 (prospecting-project planning-development);
- specialist 6 (project planning-development-propagation of knowledge);
- specialist 7 (prospecting-research-project planning-propagation of knowledge);
- specialist 8 (prospecting-research-project planning-propagation of knowledge),
- specialist 9 (prospecting-research-project planning-development-propagation of knowledge);
- specialist 10 (research-project planning-propagation of knowledge).

3   Proceedings

The central point of the method [3] is to reach a consensus among the specialists on a specific theme in order to create a scenario. It is important that each participant's identity is anonymous during the method proceedings to keep the opinions completely formal and impersonal. Knowing the identity of an worldwide admired specialist could be intimidating and could interfere on the elaboration of opinions.

For this research, all exchange of information and display of specialists opinions occur by e-mail, having me as central point of connection. The use of e-mail facilitated the reach of the method throughout 5 cities from 3 different countries. Video conferences could bring schedule disagreements and identity disclosure. All names were substituted by code letters to preserve the identity of the specialists.

Since the experts are from three different countries, all questions were elaborated in english and portuguese. All collected answers and opinions were translated to both languages, so there wouldn't be the risk of misinterpretation from the participants. If an invited expert had a different native language (that wouldn't be portuguese nor english), the participant could specify a preference between the two options or a third option could be included with the help of a translator.

After the invitation acceptance and selection of participants, the proceedings have four phases. Although there can be different ways to approach it, depending on the developing of the method and the participants, Gordon and Justos follow similar directions:

1. Formulation of a questionnaire strategically planned [7] to bring opinions regarding the theme, but from a variety of approaches. The questions have to be clear and objective to the participants, to avoid any chance of misinterpretation. The questionnaire is sent separately to each expert in the chosen language. The questionnaire for this research was elaborated with 6 questions, as follows:
   - How do you see the development and evolution of mobile devices (such as smartphones, Ipods, tablets, Ipads, Iphones) in 5 years and 10 years?
   - How do you think touch screen interaction will develop and evolve in the next 5 years? And in the next 10 years?
   - What will happen to social network in 5 years and 10 years?
   - What kind of products of digital interaction will be available for purchase in 5 years? And in 10 years?
   - How the use of 3D interaction will evolve in 5 years? And in 10 years? What will be the possibilities?
   - Which new media will be available to read books, newspapers, magazines etc. in 5 years and 10 years?
2. The second phase starts only after all specialists have submitted their answers. All collected responses were translated to both languages and complied in a single document. Each expert's name was substituted by a code letter to keep identity anonymous. The answers are organized by questions, so all experts could access information easier. The document with all compiled answers was once more sent by e-mail to each participant. This time each specialist reads the opinions of everyone and can comment, agree, add new information or disagree with any part of it. The dynamics of this phase is shown in the example:

   respondent A: "In 10 years, I think these devices will already surpass the input of data limitations (through voice or gestural interaction) e battery life, and will substitute almost totally the use of computers by common people".

comment respondent G: "I agree: the phone, with extension devices such as rings and watches and pens that are smart will constitute most computer use."

If there are two or more disparate opinions, a longer exchange of e-mails may be necessary to clarify the points of view, base arguments, and clear any doubts.

3. The third phase puts together all answers and all comments for a second round of analysis between the experts. It is expected to have any arguments focused to a central objective at this point. If necessary, certain subjects can be investigated into a deeper level of information and detail.

4. The fourth phase is to collect all answers, comments, additions and opinions from the previous phases for comparison and analysis of content. A final document if prepared describing the scenario. For this research, the scenario was presented in 6 parts, each one focused in one specific question of the initial questionnaire. The final scenario was sent to every participant and, as a final round, all specialists could add comments to the final scenario.

4   Results: Future Scenario Possibilities

The construction of the scenario is based on collected opinions, advancements and innovations proposed and agreed by the totality of the experts or at least the majority of the participants. The suggestions that were exposed by a few and had not been contradicted, were also included in the scenario, but considered as a lesser possibility.

– About the development and evolution of mobile devices in 5 years and 10 years:

In the next 5 years, the day-to-day use of PCs will go down drastically. Most of its purchase and use will remain only for professional and specific activities. The use of smartphones and tablets will be more and more common in our lives, based on its easiness for common day-to-day tasks. Comparatively, it is already harder for someone to sit at one's desk, turn on a desktop computer just to check e-mail, browse some latest news, research on the web or update one's social network. Considering a generation that first met digital technology through smartphones and tablets, the use of PCs becomes more and more irrelevant and distant. The specialists point a tendency for a more precise and easier touch screen interaction, in lighter, more flexible devices. Mobile artifacts will be more and more used to solve personal chores, like bill payments, products registration and tickets purchase. The big amount of input data will bring advances in capturing data through gestural, voice and optical interaction. The battery technology will not grow as fast as the interaction and apps advancements and will not fulfill user's necessities for day-to-day tasks. Higher concern regarding exponential generation of technological trash.

In 10 years, interaction will transcend tablet and smartphone devices and will be integrated to the environment around us (refrigerators, walls, tables, wearables) or projected on surfaces. Tablets and smartphones, completely common and with banal use will leave the center of attention. Tendency of devices being more simple and unified, leaving behind the physical existence as we know today. Brain-interface interaction begins.

People more and more dependent of apps to perform daily tasks. Higher interaction between apps and more precise data about users. New questions surface regarding privacy and open exhibition of personal life in social and political degree. Advancements of one-to-one advertisement as a reflex.

New social inquiries are brought up with the fast technological integration in our lives: what happens to one's data after he/she dies?

– About touch screen interaction development and evolution in the next 5–10 years

Faster and faster, everything will be touch screen. Advancements regarding better precision and interaction with flexible surfaces. Kids that today easily interact using touch and try to amplify this touch experience with various objects that do not have the touch screen feature, like physical books and magazines, will receive the new advancements in touch interaction as a natural development for them, leaving buttons, mouses and trackers for the old guys. Advancements in precision and use of gestural, ocular and voice interaction. Conductive make up and nails with sensors. New possibilities with smart glasses.

In 10 years, it is expected that technology quickly becomes more precise and spread to our day-to-day objects. Touch screen will get closer and closer to intuitive touch. Input sensors and touch interaction in everything around us. Almost all surfaces will have potential to become touch screen: refrigerators, wind shields, walls, tables, mugs, clothes, nails, steering wheels, disposable cups, flexible pelicle to apply on skin. Gestural and ocular interactions evolve to new dimensions. Possible advancements in brain-computer interactions. The use of thought as a new interaction dimension.

– About the social network in 5 years and 10 years

In five years the social network will be even more blended to our daily life. Companies and services will be more integrated to social network actions or they won't make any sense. Exchanged experiences will be more automatic. Sense of immediacy will increase, leading expectations to acquire information closer and closer to real time. Use of sensors in public spaces will actively participate in this real time information. Use of social network will be more present as a tool to donation campaigns, petitions, denunciation, propagation of alerts, opportunities and political campaigns. Higher impact in democracy and social movements. Attention and preoccupation to truthfulness of news and information.

Surge of new easier simpler social networks, focused on specific niches of personal and professional interests. Gradual increase of awareness regarding privacy and personal information on the web. Big data starts to encumber data management and filtering gets more active.

In 10 years, technology will be more blended to social network, as well as with public environment. New metaphores and words will arise with these interaction changes. Necessity of new means of interaction in order to make up for the quantity of information around us. Social network becomes an important media for public political decisions. New notions of credibility, power and democracy.

Regarding privacy, there are two predicted paths among the specialists: (1) growth of privacy awareness and perception of possibility of harmful effects due to personal expose on the web; (2) growth of ultra expose of efemeral and personal information on the web. Extreme expose on niche network.

Automatic identification and people profile exposure through wearable artifacts and public environments, linking common affinities, friends and relations.

- About products of digital interaction available for purchase in 5–10 years

In 5 years, technology will start to disappear from sight and be more integrated to objects and accessories around us. Wearables will be more and more common (glasses, watches, key holders, bracelets, shoes, hats and coats). The processing will be on the server's side and the portable artifacts will serve as data inputs and outputs.

Beginning of interaction with home objects and appliances. Smartphones and tablets will be completely assimilated by population and more integrated with objects and places, creating a network of information around us. All activated by sensors. Our smartphone will connect with our TV, which will connect with our pen and credit card and our car. Desktops for personal use will be extinct. In some countries, the digital interaction will be tested and used in health, logistic and production areas. 3D print can have an important role in personalized shopping experience, eradicating the necessity of products storage. Instead, with 3D printing, products can be produced by demand.

In 10 years, all objects and artifacts will be imbued with digital interaction. Smart glasses and wearable accessories will be commonly used among people. The computer ubiquity will have reached its maturity and smart/electronic homes (houses, building, offices) will be an important tool for this evolution, saving time, resources and energy. The paradigm of product purchase will gradually be substituted by the idea of product use (rental), as well as the notion of acquiring being substituted by the notion of usage. Walls around us will be touch screen displays, creating the possibility of total customization of environments. Everything that can be digitally interactive, will be. EEG advancements on brain-computer interface and the start of molecular computer. Beyond hand gestures, possibility of body sign language to interact and control devices.

- About the use of 3D interaction development in 5–10 years

In 5 years, 3D interaction will evolve especially through games. Movement input will be more sophisticated and precise, but it will still be directed to one person at a time. Technology such as Microsoft Kinect (combined with Omni treadmill) or leap motion are already capable to detect whole body movements or just hands with great precision. Initiatives like Oculus Rift will advance technologically, will be lighter, smaller and more accessible. With the gamification of several of our services (psychology and storytelling) we will see this technology spreading to other areas, such as education and shopping business. The augmented reality should be more and more integrated to our everyday lives.

3D interaction will be common use and greatly used to access data where 2 billion videos will added daily by almost everybody throughout the world. Also, television 3D will advance into augmented reality projection as well as gestural interaction. The "fake" 3D system, with the use of parallax effect, will present a better aesthetic 3D feeling and less discomfort, but with the cost of higher processing devices. Holography, for now, will not be a common everyday thing.

In 10 years, the main focus seems to be holographic interfaces, but the opinions of the specialists divide in two: (1) surge of holographic interactions with possible link to production in 3D printing, with software that allow molding to create sculptures, mechanical parts and even clothing; (2) interaction 3D gets closer to holography, mas still needs a few more years to reach such interaction. Indication of human-computer interaction based on three-dimensional thinking. Knowledge and communication will be allocated in 3D virtual environments, which will be explored with the 3D projection advancements. Specialists suggests the access with the help of glasses with movement sensors to let user's interactions using avatars in virtual ambiences.

– About new media available to read books, newspapers, magazines in 5–10 years

In 5 years, there will be a fusion or at least an oncoming between tablets and e-book readers, combining the advantages from the e-ink displays with the LED displays. Both artifacts will become more flexible and lighter. Objects from our everyday life will also be a support for reading: walls, tables, wind shields, mirrors and watches. There will be a reduction in physical book production as a reflex of the growth in the e-books market. Newspapers, magazines and printed books will decrease exponentially. Implementation of 4D media, with sound, maybe touch and smell.

In the Brazilian scenario, audio books can advance and get popular finally, maybe as a result of the increase of traffic jams or overload of information, which could direct people to a behavior even more passive to access information. The international scenario, where audio books have been already popular for some time, the expectations reside mainly on the fusion e-ink and led in reading artifacts and lightness and flexibility of displays for reading, as well as wearable.

In 10 years, the newspapers and magazines will not be published as we know today. They will be in formats more and more dynamics and interactive that will break the paradigm of the idea of a closed/finished story. Maybe this bring the abandon of printed books, taking the physical book to a vintage object, like vinyl records are today. Due to the quantity of information available, smart artifacts will only scratch the surface of the massiveness of information that will offer personalized data for each person. On the other hand, people may demand more of the "old and slow journalism", where stories has its own time to reach the bottom of the subject and show a variety of options that build trust and accountability.

The notions and significances of what is "reading" start to change to knowledge access. E-glasses or e-lens will be means to access augmented reality and reading material. Going out on a trip around the (physical) world without notations, reference points, comments, diagrams, maps will sound like absurd. The real world with augmented reality, will be the big book of experiences. When we get to a square in a city, we will know that 10 min before other tourists have been there and left comments, some of them interesting enough that we may want to try too. Possibility of the first marriage between a human and a data base. Possibility of implant texts and images directly into our brains.

5   Conclusion

The method brought up a variety of future possible scenarios of technology and interactions, but although the specialists came from different parts of the world and with a variety of points of view, it was interesting to see many similar ideas and expectations for the future. The expert's view of the future shows the natural uprising line of the nose of innovation graphic of Buxton with a numerous incremental innovations around touch screen interaction, and its outgrowth to a more precise and more natural gestural interaction. As the incremental innovations are released on the market for consumption, there is an increasing absorption of the technology in our lives, evolving more and more to a ubiquity connection to information and knowledge.

Future drastic innovations are brewing (and being tested) today and are represented by the beginning thin line of the nose of innovation graphic. These expectations appear in the results of the Delphi method as not so certain possibilities, mentioned by just a few. But never the less, mighty possibilities, as for example the use of 3D interaction to mold objects for 3D printing already being tested at a university in Rio de Janeiro, as well as, the use of nails and make up for intecation, as presented as the paper "FX e-makeup for muscle based interaction", presented by Katia Vega et al. [10] at HCII 2014. Following the nose of innovation theory, in 2030 these possibilities could be common place in our day to day life.

Although the method can't bring certainties, it surely can bring out major and lesser possibilities of a future scenario, based on the experience, mental models and expectations of the experts involved in the technique.

References

1. Busxton, B.: The long nose of innovation. Business Week, New York, NY (2008)
2. Dalkey, N., Brown, B., Cochran, S.W.: The Delphi method III: use of self ratings to improve group estimates. Technol. Forecast. Soc. Change **1**, 283–291 (1970)
3. Justo, C.: A técnica Delphi de formação de consensos. Observatório Português dos Sistemas de Saúde (2005)
4. Lindeman, C.A.: Delphi survey of priorities in clinical nursing. Nurs. Res. **24**(6), 434–441 (1975)
5. Morin, R.: Espace de conception et modele d'interation multi-tactile gestuel – un ennvironnement de developpment pour enrichir le modele. Thèse de doctorat, Univertisé de Toulouse. Toulouse (2011)
6. Thomson, W.A., Ponder, L.D.: Use of Delphi methodology to generate a survey instrument to identify priorities for state allied health associations. J. Allied Health Behav. Sci. **2**, 383–399 (1979)
7. Pill, J.: The Dephi method: substance, context, a critique and na annotated bibliography. Socio-Econ. Plan. Sci. **5**, 57–71 (1971)
8. Glenn, J.C., Gordon, T.J.: Futures research Methodology, version 3.0. Millenium Project, Washington, D.C. (2009)
9. Renzi, A.B., Freitas, S.: Affordances and gestural interaction on multi-touch interface systems: building new mental models. In: HCII 2014, Crete, Greece
10. Vega, K., Arrieta, A., Esteves, F.: FX e-makeup for muscle based interaction. In: HCII 2014, Crete, Greece

Incorporating Fictionality into the Real World with Transmedia Storytelling

Mizuki Sakamoto and Tatsuo Nakajima[(⊠)]

Department of Computer Science and Engineering, Waseda University, Tokyo, Japan
{mizuki,tatsuo}@dcl.cs.waseda.ac.jp

Abstract. Ubiquitous computing technologies now offer attractive possibilities to embed fictionality in the real world. This opens a new arena to navigate human behavior. Virtual forms representing fictionality and incorporated into our daily artifacts and media will become an infrastructure for navigating human behavior through the incorporated fictionality. In this paper, we describe two topics towards the realization of such a goal. The first topic presents that transmedia storytelling is a promising technique to incorporate fictionality into the real world. The second topic shows that the value-based analysis framework is a promising tool to analyze a sense of reality on the fictionality embedded into the real world and the reality is essential to make human behavior navigation successful. We present two case studies to demonstrate the effectiveness of our approach.

Keywords: Fictionality · Transmedia storytelling · Human behavior navigation · Value-based analysis framework · Reality · Ideology · Metapore

1 Introduction

Navigating human behavior is essential to solve various serious social problems. For example, achieving social sustainability cannot be solved only by technologies, and it is essential that people alter their attitude and behavior [16]. Information technologies are effective to navigate human behavior towards better lifestyle [19]. Ubiquitous computing technologies enable us to incorporate fictionality into the real world through virtual forms that draw computer generated dynamic visual information [21]. Specifically, a concept named procedural rhetoric make the persuasiveness of the visual information more powerful [2]. Transmedia storytelling [3, 14] is a useful tool to incorporate the fictionality in the real world though a network of virtual forms embedded in the real world, where transmedia storytelling allows the fictional stories to be fragmented into several different media distributed in the real world. Virtual forms are considered as a desirable infrastructure to incorporate fictionality represented as transmedia storytelling into the real world [19].

In video games, players enjoy the fictional world through the real world interaction [7]. Game studies scholars introduce a term called *magic circle* [5] where a player plays a game inside a *magic circle* that is not recognized in the real world. However, incorporating fictional worlds in the real world needs to be indistinct between inside and outside of the *magic circle*. *Virtual forms* will be interfaces between the real world and

© Springer International Publishing Switzerland 2015
A. Marcus (Ed.): DUXU 2015, Part I, LNCS 9186, pp. 654–665, 2015.
DOI: 10.1007/978-3-319-20886-2_61

fictional world and we believe that transmedia storytelling is a promising way to design the interface.

Fictional stories may contain ideological messages that make us aware of the important social issues while we are living in the daily life [22]. Specifically, Japanese popular culture such as games and animations offers tremendous examples including ideological messages to increase the tension in the drama [20]. When a character or an item appeared in the fictional stories is presented on *virtual forms*, the character or good can be used as a leitmotif of the stories to remind these ideological messages and they make navigating human behavior more effective [19].

In order to incorporate fictionality into the real world for navigating human behavior, a feeling of reality is essential because a people lose a sense of the immersion if they do not feel the reality on visual images that *virtual forms* draw on. However, there is currently no good methodology to discuss how to assess a sense of reality on the fictionality represented as transmedia storytelling. The *value-based analysis framework* is a promising tool to discuss how visual image represented on *virtual forms* offer a sense of reality. Ubiquitous computing technologies allow us to embed *virtual forms* into our daily artifacts surrounding us [15]. For example, augmented reality technologies by using micro projectors easily add a virtual layer on our real world. The framework allows us to design more effective *virtual forms* and how to embed them in our daily artifacts in our surrounding environment.

In this paper, we show two case studies that incorporate fictionality in the real world through transmedia storytelling. The case studies make the boundary between a real word and a fictional world blurred. The first case study is to explicitly use social media to incorporate fictionality in the real world. When observing several fictional events occurred in the fictional world through social media in the real world, the reality of the fictional event is increased. The second case study is to blur the boundary between a fictional world and a real world by mixing the scene and event in a real world into a fictional world. In particular, by using real scenes of the real world in a fictional world, people feel that they are staying in a fictional world even if they visit to the real world. After introducing the overview of the case studies, we analyze them with the *value-based analysis framework*, and show that the framework is a promising tool to assess a sense of reality on the fictionality incorporated into the real world.

The remaining sections are structured as follows. Section 2 presents how ideological messages are incorporated into fictional stories. In Sect. 3, we show that a virtual character used in fictional stories can be used as a leitmotif to remind the ideological message. This is very important to present fictional stories on virtual forms and navigate people's attitude and behavior to solve serious social issues. The Sect. 4 introduces the *value-based analysis framework* and Sect. 5 discusses how a sense of reality is increased when incorporating fictionality in the real world. In Sect. 6, we show two case studies and analyze their reality with the *value-based analysis framework*. Section 7 summarizes the paper.

2   Fictional Stories and Ideological Value

The story already plays an important role in product advertisements because it increases the appeal of the target product [8]. Using fictionality to incorporate stories makes our experiences richer because the stories can translate the meaning of the visual representation on virtual forms more easily. Fictional stories are particularly useful tools for enhancing our daily experiences for increasing our buying impulse. Fictional stories can represent stories that do not exist in the real world or stories from the future. The stories can flexibly offer us a broad range of information using nonexistent artifacts such as magic. It is easy to embed ideological messages in these stories and make it possible to teach about various social issues. Additionally, the stories are useful to encourage a user to alter his/her undesirable behavior and attitude because their positivity can be used to increase people's self-efficacy.

Many Japanese fictional animation and game stories like *Yu-Gi-Oh!* animation story [28] typically contain serious ideological messages that are important and that make our daily life more desirable. We believe that this observation is very important to use the fictional stories as a tool to incorporate the ideological value to the real world. In particular, the ideological messages can be used to alter a user's attitude and behavior [18, 19]. However, only incorporating the ideological messages does not alter a user's attitude and behavior. Also, a user's intrinsic motivation should be developed towards his/her behavior and attitude changes.

3   Virtual Characters as the Leitmotif of Ideological Message

Currently, virtual characters are widely used in our daily life. For example, famous *Disney* characters such as *Mickey Mouse* and *Donald Duck* provoke empathetic feelings easily, anytime and anywhere, and *Hello Kitty* and *Pokémon* are now found all over the world [1]. In animations and games, each virtual character has its own personality and story, which can be used as a medium to convey special information and messages to people. If people are familiar with the fictional story behind an animation or a game, then the story's characters will easily recall the leitmotif of the story without requiring much additional information beyond just an action or an interaction with the story's characters. Specifically, many Japanese animated and game stories contain serious ideological messages that are important and that make our daily life more desirable. We believe that this observation is very important when considering how to use virtual characters in various future real world information services. Currently, our daily life is becoming increasingly complex, and we need to manage significant information every day. In our modern society, there are many real social problems that need to be solved urgently, but it is hard to convey important ideological messages to people without presenting a large amount of additional information to them. For example, education is a traditional heavy-weighted method to teach the importance of ideological messages, which takes a long time to learn.

In the contemporary Japanese society, several posters for public service announcements have adopted the idea to use virtual characters from recent popular animation stories. For example, *K-ON!* has been used for promoting a national survey in Japan [29]. In the story of *K-ON!*, high school girls try to realize their dreams with cooperative efforts among them. This becomes a persuasive message conveying the idea that everyone's participation is important for the national survey. NFGD that promotes guide dogs' training has created two posters using popular characters from *Puella Magi Madoka Magica* [26]. The girl that has been used in one of the posters is rebellious, but very considerate to her friends. The girl used in the other poster is very close to her friend and keeps thinking and caring of her friend even when they are far from each other. Many young girls admire these two girls, nowadays. If people want to imitate these magic girls, then the posters contain the implicit, strong persuasive message that becoming a puppy walker is one of the ways to become like them. The example shows the effectiveness of using virtual characters that have their background stories to attract people. It is good evidence that virtual characters could be used to convey ideological messages that might play significant role in changing people's current attitude. In Japan, the majority of young people have been enjoying animation and game stories for a long time and they know the popular animation and game characters and their stories very well. This we believe is a good prerequisite for using virtual characters to enhance emotional feelings and success-fully convey ideological messages through the characters' stories.

4   Value-Based Analysis Framework for Increasing a User's Intrinsic Motivation

Figure 1 shows our basic approach to using the six values proposed in [15, 18] to increase people's intrinsic motivation. These values were extracted from experiences with building several smart artifacts incorporating *virtual forms*. The values are a useful design tool to design products and services. After presenting a brief overview of the framework, we show how the values can be used to incorporate fictionality in the real world.

The first value is the *informative value*. This value offers sufficient information to the user and helps him/her to make a better decision. A typical example is an augmented reality service that superimposes useful information on a video. The service provides the user with detailed information about his/her daily environment such as shopping information and route information.

The second value is the *empathetic value*. This value is achieved and enhanced by adding some similarity with a user. It is usual that a person has strong empathy on another person when they have some similarity between them. As described in [13], a user can feel a close relationship with even a product which has some similarities with the users.

The third value is the *economic value*. This value provides the user with a sense of ownership. In particular, physical tangibility is important for increasing the sense of ownership of an object. For example, people like to possess expensive jewelry or artwork. The rarity is a key to increase the sense of ownership, and collecting rare objects also increases the social status of the user. The sense of ownership of an object is very important for allowing a user to create his/her own original "empathetic story" with the object; this story describes the user's feelings and attachment to the object and how the user's daily life has changed once he/she possessed the object.

The fourth value is the *aesthetic value*. Aesthetics is an important concept to make daily objects more attractive. Aesthetics is a branch of philosophy addressing the nature

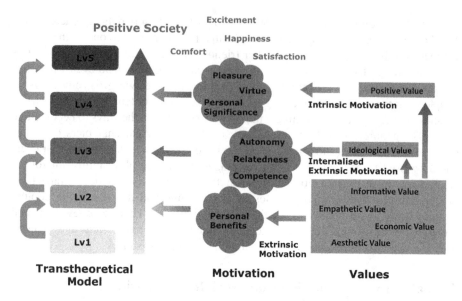

Fig. 1. Enhanced value-based analysis framework

of art, beauty, and taste, particularly the creation and appreciation of beauty. For example, Japanese traditional folk crafts represent aesthetic values, which are always very important for increasing our quality of life.

The fifth value is the *positive value*. The positive value increases their happiness, excitement, satisfaction and comfort, and stimulates their positive emotion through pleasure, personal significance and virtue [4]. This *positive value* also increases people' feelings of competence that increases human intrinsic motivation to change their attitudes and behaviours; it also helps them maintain their changes.

The final and sixth value is the *ideological value*. This value reminds a user of important ideological concepts, such as friendship, justice and so on. This value is not explicitly presented to a user, but special stories carrying important ideological messages are used to implicitly explain the importance of these concepts. If a user knows the stories, then the characters appearing in the stories can be used as metaphors to demonstrate the ideological value.

The *empathetic*, *economic*, and *aesthetic values* offer people extrinsic incentives, and the *informative value* provides reasons to change attitude or tips and tactics for making better decisions. Our framework is based on the *transtheoretical model* [12], which is a psychological model for changing people's attitudes. These four values are used as tools in the model to change the user's current behavior by reminding him/her of the importance of changing his/her behavior and encouraging this change at an early stage. The *ideological value*, however, makes people's dreams and expectations explicit and teaches the user how to change his/her attitude to realize his/her dream. The *positive value* increases people's self-efficacy to realize their dreams. These values are used to increase the intrinsic motivation of the user to change his/her attitude in the latter stage of the *transtheoretical model*.

The combination of extrinsic motivation, *ideological values* and *positive values* strongly enhances the intrinsic motivation and changes people's way of thinking. At first, the four values are used to increase the user' extrinsic motivation, but after the user understands the ideological messages, which are represented as the ideological value in the stories, the *positive value* convinces him/her to achieve the ideological message in the real world through the association of the real world and the virtual world in the fictional story. In this step, the *positive value* changes the extrinsic motivation of the four values into intrinsic motivation. For example, playing against a favorite virtual character becomes the player's extrinsic motivation. However, after gaining an understanding of the background story of the character, the empathy for the character can drive intrinsic motivation because the user now knows how the character tries to realize the ideological message in the fictional story.

As described in Sect. 3, a virtual character can be used as a leitmotif of a fictional story. The value based analysis framework suggests that virtual characters or items can be considered as a leitmotif of a fictional story offering the ideological messages. The empathetic and aesthetic values are especially useful to attract people. Usually, people remember virtual characters or items that offer *empathetic* or *aesthetic value* well. Therefore, if these virtual characters or items appear in the real world, people also remember their stories. If the stories contain strong ideological messages, the characters remind these ideological messages in the real world as well. This effect is called the *priming effect* that is an implicit memory effect in which exposure to a stimulus influences a response to a later stimulus. If the rare items in the fictional stories appear in the real world, this is also used as the priming effect.

When the framework is used to increase a feeling regarding the reality of a fictional story, we need to consider how the value is investigated in the fictional story. Then, we discuss how the value in the story is consistent with the value in the real world. For example, the *empathetic value* is increased by the use of an attractive virtual character from a fictional story. If the character is shown in the real world through the use of an augmented reality technology, the *empathetic value* is also increased in the real world. When the same aesthetic scene is shown in both the fictional and the real world, the *aesthetic value* increases the belief in the reality of the fictional world. The *economic value* is increased when the item appearing in a fictional story appears also in the real world, and many people think that they would like to own the item in the real world. A mission in a fictional story can be achieved by contributing funds in the real world. The *informative value* increases if some information related to a fictional story is shown in the real world and the information cannot be distinguished from the factual information. The fictional story may be fragmented into several media and they are distributed in the real world when transmedia storytelling is used. Some of the information appears on the Web, and the user is not aware that it is a fake Web site that presents a fictional story not a real story. The *positive value* and *ideological value* increase the reality if the primary message of the fictional story is related to a serious social problem in the real world. For example, if the message is related to social sustainability in a fictional world, the mission to achieve sustainability in the real world is also encouraged [22].

5 Achieving Reality When Incorporating Fictional Stories

It is a very important issue to consider how to obtain and keep the reality in the real world [17, 22]. Even if fictional stories are incorporated, the *virtual forms* should convey their realities to users. In particular, if a fictional story is embedded in the real world, the reality in the story shown on the *virtual forms* is essential. For example, a person, who has frequently watched animation movies, does something in the real world, feels that adding popular virtual characters from the animation into the real world makes it more enjoyable and exciting. The desire to follow these characters becomes also an incentive for him or her to alter his or her behavior. A negative feedback may be used to stop immoral play, but altering a user's attitude in general is not easy [11]. The most important insight is that there is a possibility to use a virtual character as a metaphor that recalls the story of the character in the player's mind while gaming, and in this way the story may convey the leitmotif containing ideological concepts like the importance of friendship, honesty, justice, thoughtfulness and so on as described in Sect. 3. In the real world, characters and key items in the animation story are incorporated, but the animation story may not explicitly shown during his or her actions. The person needs to recall himself/herself the story during his/her play. More tight integration of the daily behavior and the animation story offers a possibility to design new transmedia storytelling. The movement of a virtual character from the fictional world to the real world offers a tight integration between a fictional story and a game. This approach makes a stronger association between a story in the fictional world and the real world through a virtual character than the current approach, and the boundary between the two worlds becomes more blurred. This approach would have the power to alter the people's attitude and behavior.

Past experiments show that the reality of the characters, such as facial expressions, movement and behavior, is essential to increase the enjoyment of our daily activities [18, 21]. Reality is an important criterion to evaluate a design. In our case, the virtual character's behavior should be consistent with the character's behavior in the animation story and this is important to feel the reality in the game. For example, items that are not used by the character in the animation should not be used in the real world as well, and the movement of the virtual character in the real world should be consistent with its typical movement in the animation. The number of items owned by the character should be consistent with the real game situation as well. Too realistic expressions, however, may cause the *uncanny valley* problem [10] if we can perceive that the achieved reality is not completely realistic.

One of the most important design issues is that the *virtual form* should be natural like traditional real materials. However, the *virtual form* may exaggerate the effect in the real world, which might make the *virtual form* even more exciting and attractive to the user than the original one. A feeling of the reality is important so that a user continues to enjoy the fictionality embedded into the real world for a long time. It is, however, hard to say and define, when and how a user feels the reality on an expression presented in a *virtual form*. It is not just enough to make the *virtual form* as close as possible to the realistic expression because a user may not feel the reality or may not be satisfied or attracted by extremely realistic expression. A user sometimes feels the reality to unrealistic, exaggerated expressions or to expressions that include reality elements partially. It is an important issue to investigate the question of how a user feels the reality in a next step of our research.

There are also a couple of issues to be considered in terms of the reality. The first important issue is that there should be a proper reason why the items and characters exist in our world for increasing the reality of a user's experience. There should be a plausible reason why a virtual character is appeared in the real world. The second important issue is that the behavior of the items and characters should be consistent with their behavior in the fictional world. In particular, if a user is familiar with the fictional story, this issue is very important [22]. There is also an alternative way to increase the reality of the fictional world by adding the interaction in the real world [19]. If there is an interaction between a user and a fictional story, he or she can create more engagement on the story. This is a reason why we usually have more engagement on gaming than watching animations. Users feel the reality of the fictional story because their intervention has strong influence on the story. If the reality is lost, a user's experience is just like watching a story that is unrelated to the user's daily life. Then, the relationship with the real world is also lost, and the user's engagement is also decreased.

6 Fictional Stories in the Real World

Alternative Reality Games (ARG) [9, 23] are a promising approach for conveying messages to users using multiple channels. Fictional stories are embedded into a game that is played in the real world and that uses multiple channels. The channels offered in the game are used to exploit the game's fictional story. For example, in *Perplex City* [27] trading cards are used to introduce the characters and the story. Web sites, emails, phone calls, and SMS messages are then cooperatively used to solve riddles in the mystery story. Because the media is tightly integrated with our daily activities, we feel that the fictional story is realistic. For example, social media such as *Twitter* and *Facebook* have become very popular. Thus, fictional stories that are embedded in social media increase the feeling that the stories are occurring in the real world. The form to represent a story affects the way an ideological message is conveyed to a user. The transmedia storytelling divides a story across multiple media so that it is possible to choose the most suitable form to attract a user and to convey a message to him/her.

Theme parks with entertainment attractions, rides, and other events in a location are designed to be enjoyed by a large number of people. A theme park is more elaborate than a simple city park or playground and usually provides attractions that are meant to target particular age groups, although some are aimed towards all ages. A theme park is a typical way to integrate fictional stories into our activities in the real world. *Disneyland* is a typical and the most famous theme park. Many *Disney* characters appear in Disneyland. Each attraction at the park is constructed based on a *Disney* story. Because the stories are very popular with most people, we feel that the character exists in the real world when we are at *Disneyland*, and we feel that we can meet the *Disney* characters and enjoy being with them during our visit [6].

For discussing the possibility of the approach to enhance daily artifacts through transmedia storytelling, we show some existing examples, and analyze them by using the value-based analysis framework.

In this subsection, we present two case studies that use fictional stories in the real world. The first case study is a promotion for *Meiji fruit gummi candy*. We can communicate with one of the characters in the story, and the story changes according to that communication. Thus, we feel that the story is nonfictional. The case study shows a possibility to incorporate a story through social media like Facebook. The second case study is a recent trend for young people called *Seichi Junrei*. A user of a fictional story visits the place that the story is based on and expands the story by himself/herself. This ability increases his/her desire to join the story. The case study shows how a user can be involved in a story and offers some hints to enhance our current approach.

The promotion movie for *Meiji fruits gummi candy* is *Megumi and Taiyo Tweet Love Story* [25]. In the story, a heroine *Megumi* eats a grape gummi candy when she needs to think deeply. When using a fictional story, it is not easy to know how the audience feels the reality of the story through only its video movie. *Tweet Love Story* uses the social media service, *Twitter*, to make us feel the reality of the story. The audience can talk with the story's hero *Taiyo* via *Twitter*. *Taiyo* replies to our advices on how to get closer to *Megumi*. *Megumi* and *Taiyo* also talk with each other on *Twitter* so that everyone can see their conversation. The audience's advices have a strong impact on the conversation between *Megumi* and *Taiyo*; since, the story changes its ending according to our advices to *Taiyo*, which makes us feel the story nonfictional in our real world.

Taiyo works at a vineyard, and there are scenes showing healthy and delicious grapes. These scenes give information showing the product's excellent quality. Finally, the story uses a character designer whose characters are currently very popular in many media. Thus, the audience easily feels empathy for the characters even though the story and its characters are original.

The case study shows that the communication with virtual characters in a fictional story increases the user's belief in the reality of the story. In particular, the recent trend in social media makes it easy to realize such communication because the communication can be automatically generated by computers. For example, it is possible to realize this approach on *Facebook*. A *Facebook* page owned by a virtual character is a promising tool to allow interaction between us and the virtual character. If we become a friend with the virtual character on *Facebook*, we can communicate with it everyday, and thus feel that the communication is realistic. Therefore, we believe that the character exists in the real world.

In this case study, the most important issue is how people feel *Taiyo* and *Megumi* as people who live in the real world. The case study adopts real-time communication between *Taiyo* and *Megumi* in social media. If we feel strong empathy with *Megumi*, we also have interests in the gummi candy that *Megumi* likes. Also, the story presents that the gummi candy is healthy with the information that the grape is a healthy food as the *informative value*. The *value-based analysis framework* makes it possible to propose a proper direction to improve the story. For example, if fair trade is used to sell the product, the fact can be used to exploit the *ideological value*. Also, if eating a gummi candy is a cheap way to maintain our health, the fact can be used to exploit the *economic value*. If the story emphasizes that eating gummi candy leads to more healthy society it can be used as the *positive value*.

The second case study, *Seichi Junrei* is a typical geek culture activity in Japan, particularly related to Japanese animation, manga (comic) and games, in which people visit famous locations from animation, manga and games. *"Seichi"* means *"Holy Land"*, *"Junrei"* means *"Pilgrimage"*. Anime fans arrive at a specific location and take pictures with the same screen/angle as it appears in the animation and upload them to their blogs. The most important aspect of *Seichi Junrei* is that something is brought from the fictional story to the real world. The fans create new stories using these pictures and the virtual characters from the fictional stories and share them within their community. This phenomenon is a very interesting example of harmonizing the real world and the fictional world. We believe that interactive pervasive games or social information services based on fictional stories are promising tools for increasing the reality of the fictional world, and the tools enhance the *Seichi Junrei* phenomena by realizing a tighter integration between the fictional and the real world. The experiences described in this paper will offer useful insights to help design tools that will realize new types of transmedia storytelling.

Recent animated movies use many scenes from the real world to increase the reality of fictional movies. A user of *Seichi Junrei* tries to find the scene that appears in the movie in the real world and takes a photo of the scene. The user enjoys finding these scenes and visiting the location of the scenes. Then, he/she takes a photo, similar to a scavenger hunt. The photos are usually uploaded to the Web, and many other people enjoy looking at the photos.

In Japan, especially, animated movies have recently been used to promote the local districts that are used in the stories. Some districts plan to attract people who like the story by offering extra original new stories to those who visit the districts. This strategy suggests that there is possibility to promote the districts with fictional stories. If real products that are famous in a district appear in the stories, then it will increase the feeling that the stories are realistic especially if the stories' audience is familiar with the products. If the stories are attractive, they will also promote the products to people who do not live in the district.

In this case study, the *positive value* and the *economic value* are the most important key factors. If the item with the strong *aesthetic* or *economic value* appearing in the fictional story becomes tangible in the real world, the reality of the fictional story is increased. The *empathetic value* is also essential for people to have strong empathy with the story. The *informative value* is also important to exploit the story in the real world. In particular, mysterious facts in the story are very effective to immerse the story in the real world. The *value-based analysis framework* makes it possible to propose some improvements on the story. If the story contains strong ideological messages as the *ideological value* and it offers the proper *positive value*, the approach offers enough power to encourage people to act in social movement.

7　Conclusion and Future Direction

This paper presented how fictional stories can be embedded into the real world without losing a sense of reality. We described two case studies and show that the value-based analysis framework is a good tool to assess how fictionality is incorporated in the real world without losing the reality.

In the next step, we are interested to design future services by using *virtual forms* and incorporating fictionality through the *virtual forms*. Our past experiences with persuasive ambient mirrors [11] and playful AR based training systems [24] are useful to design these new services.

References

1. Allison, A.: Millennial Monsters: Japanese Toys and the Global Imagination. University of California Press, Berkeley (2006)
2. Bogost, I.: Persuasive Game: The Expressive Power of Video Games. MIT Press, Cambridge (2007)
3. Dena, C.: Transmedia practice: theorising the practice of expressing a fictional world across distinct media and environments. Dissertation Thesis, University Sydney (2009)
4. Desmet, P.M.A., Pohlmeyer, A.E.: Positive design: an introduction to design for subjective well-being. Int. J. Des. 7(3), 5–19 (2013)
5. Huizinga, J.: Homo Ludens: A Study of the Play-Element in Culture. The Beacon Press, Boston (1955)
6. The Imagineers: Walt Disney Imagineering. Disney Book Group (2010)
7. Juul, J.: Half-Real: Video Games between Rea Rules ad Fictional Worlds. MIT Press, Cambridge (2005)
8. Mattila, A.S.: The role of narratives in the advertising of experiential services. J. Serv. Res. 3(August), 35–45 (2000)
9. McGonigal, J.: Reality is Broken: Why Games Make us Better and How they Can Change the World. Penguin Press, New York (2011)
10. Mori, M.: On the uncanny valley. Energy 7(4), 33–35 (1970). Translated by Karl F. MacDorman and Takashi Minato, Elsevier
11. Nakajima, T., Lehdonvirta, V.: Designing motivation in persuasive ambient mirrors. Pers. Ubiquit. Comput. 17(1), 107–126 (2013)
12. Prochaska, O., Velicer, W.F.: The transtheoretical model of health behavior change. Am. J. Health Promotion 12(1), 38–48 (1997)
13. Ruth, M., Schoormans, J.P.L., Schifferstein, H.N.J.: Product attachment: design strategies to stimulate the emotional bonding with products. In: Schifferstein, H.N.J., Hekkert, P. (eds.) Product Experience. Elsevier, Amsterdam (2007)
14. Ruppel, M.N.: Visualizing transmedia network: links, paths and peripheries. Dissertation Thesis, University of Maryland (2012)
15. Sakamoto, M., Nakajima, T., Alexandrova, T.: Enhancing values through virtuality for intelligent artifacts that influence human attitude and behavior. In: Sakamoto, M., Nakajima, T., Alexandrova, T. (eds.) Multimedia Tools Applications. Springer, New York (2014). doi: 10.1007/s11042-014-2250-5

16. Sakamoto, M., Nakajima, T.: Micro-crowdfunding: achieving a sustainable society through economic and social incentives in micro-level crowdfunding. In: Proceedings of International Conference on Mobile and Ubiquitous Multimedia (2013)
17. Sakamoto, M., Nakajima, T., Akioka, S.: Designing enhanced daily digital artifacts based on the analysis of product promotions using fictional animation stories. In: Yoshida, T., Kou, G., Skowron, A., Cao, J., Hacid, H., Zhong, N. (eds.) AMT 2013. LNCS, vol. 8210, pp. 266–277. Springer, Heidelberg (2013)
18. Sakamoto, M., Alexandrova, T., Nakajima, T.: Augmenting remote trading card play with virtual characters used in animation and game stories – towards persuasive and ambient transmedia storytelling. In: Proceedings of the Sixth International Conference on Advances in Computer-Human Interactions (2013)
19. Sakamoto, M., Nakajima, T., Akioka, S.: A methodology for Gamifying smart cities: navigating human behavior and attitude. In: Streitz, N., Markopoulos, P. (eds.) DAPI 2014. LNCS, vol. 8530, pp. 593–604. Springer, Heidelberg (2014)
20. Sakamoto, M., Nakajima, T.: The GamiMedia model: gamifying content culture. In: Rau, P. (ed.) CCD 2014. LNCS, vol. 8528, pp. 786–797. Springer, Heidelberg (2014)
21. Sakamoto, M., Alexandrova, T., Nakajima, T.: Introducing virtuality to enhance game-related physical artifacts. Int. J. Smart Home 8(2), 137–152 (2014)
22. Sakamoto, M., Nakajima, T.: Gamifying intelligent daily environments through introducing fictionality. Int. J. Hybrid Technol. 7(4), 259–276 (2014)
23. Szulborski, D.: This is Not a Game: A Guide to Alternate Reality Gaming. Lulu.Com, Morrisville (2005)
24. Yamabe, T., Nakaima, T.: Playful training with augmented reality games: case studies towards reality-oriented system design. Multimed. Tools Appl. 62(1), 259–286 (2013)
25. Meiji Megumi and Taiyo. http://www.meiji.co.jp/sweets/candy_gum/fruits_gummi/part1/. Accessed 28 Sept 2012
26. NFGD: Guide Dogs Help Spread the Original Poster. http://www.nkoku.jp/pos. Accessed 12 Oct 2012
27. Perplex City. http://perplexcitywiki.com/wiki/Main_Page. Accessed 28 Sept 2012
28. Yu-Gi-Oh! Trading Card Game. http://www.yugioh-card.com/en/. Accessed 28 Sept 2012
29. Kyoto Prefecture and Ministry of Internal Affairs: National Survey Promotion Video. http://www.youtube.com/watch?v=IdAkKZKEfGU. Accessed 28 Sept 2012

Author Index

Printed in the United States
By Bookmasters